Cultural Diversity in the United States

Cultural Diversity in the United States

A Critical Reader

Edited by

IDA SUSSER
and
THOMAS C. PATTERSON

Copyright © Blackwell Publishers Ltd 2001

First published 2001

2 4 6 8 10 9 7 5 3 1

Blackwell Publishers Inc.
350 Main Street
Malden, Massachusetts 02148
USA

Blackwell Publishers Ltd
108 Cowley Road
Oxford OX4 1JF
UK

Library of Congress Cataloging-in-Publication Data
Cultural diversity in the United States: a critical reader / edited by Ida Susser and Thomas
  C. Patterson.
      p.   cm.
    Includes bibliographical references and index.
    ISBN 0-631-22212-X (alk. paper) – ISBN 0-631-22213-8 (pb.: alk. paper)
    1. Pluralism (Social sciences) – United States.   2. Multiculturalism – United States.
  3. Anthropology – United States.   4. United States – Social conditions.   5. United
  States – Ethnic relations.   6. United States – Race relations.   I. Susser, Ida.
  II. Patterson, Thomas Carl.
  E184.A1 C847 2000
  305.8'0973 – dc21

                                                                                00-060813

British Library Cataloguing in Publication Data
A CIP catalogue record for this book is available from the British Library.

Typeset in 10½ on 12 pt Sabon
by Best-set Typesetter Ltd., Hong Kong
Printed in Great Britain by TJ International, Padstow, Cornwall

This book is printed on acid-free paper.

Contents

Foreword

American anthropology has as its cornerstone the in-depth study of the human and cultural diversity of the United States of America. From chronicling Native American cultures in the 19th century, to collecting data on the effects of nutrition and the environment on immigrants in the United States at the turn of the 20th century, to studying the cultures of the rural South and Appalachia in the 1920s and 1930s, to examining urban black culture and race relations in cities all over the United States from the 1960s to the 1990s, anthropology has built up a body of research and ethnographic data on issues of cultural diversity that span a century in this country. At the beginning of a new century and of a new millennium anthropologists once again are focusing on cultural diversity and pluralism and will hopefully frame the discussion, or even debate in some circles, about the value of this diversity and what it brings to this unique social experiment we call a democracy here in the United States.

As President of the American Anthropological Association from 1995 to 1997, I urged my colleagues to reclaim their legacy as the premier discipline to document, and share with a wider public what we know about race, cultural pluralism, and how those diverse experiences and perspectives continue to shape and redefine, often in contested ways, the landscape of America. I am pleased to write the Foreword for a book that does just that.

This volume reflects our organization and disciplinary commitment to the four fields of anthropology: cultural, biological, linguistic anthropology, and archaeology; and its two dimensions of research and application of research. For the past decade, research in the fields of social science, business and education has been very clear that valuing cultural diversity is good for the United States. The corporate world says it is good for business and for the bottom line. Having an educated workforce that reflects the diversity of the demographics of the country provides these companies with the ability to tap more mini-markets domestically. But equally important is the fact that most corporations need people who are effective in an increasingly global market as well.

In education, especially higher education, it is becoming clear just how much students benefit from being exposed to a culturally diverse environment. They develop better critical thinking skills, they get better grades, they tend to form more cross-group and cross-gender friendships, and once they graduate they are more likely to be engaged in civic activity and more likely to vote.

A better understanding of cultural diversity and structural inequality can also help each citizen see and understand how our differences matter, and how they do not, or should not. For example, institutionalized racism in the United States still affects all people of color, but the peculiar and unique history of black/white racism must be understood within the context of the institution of slavery and its aftermath; a condition experienced by no other ethnic group or immigrant group in the United States. Native Americans had still another kind of unique experience which decimated their numbers and nearly made some tribes extinct. It is the deep understanding of these different group experiences, as well as the connections among people based on race, gender, and class that gives anthropology its "edge" in the cultural diversity arena.

Anthropology also has the responsibility to problematize the sanitizing effect of the umbrella term "cultural diversity." While it is convenient to use the term to be inclusive, it should not mask the fact that many of our nation's political leaders are moving away from an agenda of social justice that was begun earlier in the 20th century, and want to pretend today that we are all living together in a society where there are only superficial differences separating us. Relationships are a lot more complex and layered than that analysis.

This volume on cultural diversity situates the issues historically, biologically, linguistically, as well as contemporarily. Like good anthropology, the chapters focus on the individual and how their various identities are shaped and molded by their environments, as well as how they in turn influence and help shape their environments. The writings on "race," ethnicity, class, gender, and age provide important windows through which the reader can understand cultural and biological diversity in the United States.

The American Anthropological Association's long-range and strategic planning documents echo the sentiments of many anthropologists, who want anthropology to be a field of study and research that also has practical applications for the diverse world in which we live. This volume is an example of how what we have done in documenting human biodiversity in the 19th and 20th centuries is still very relevant and much needed for the 21st century.

Yolanda T. Moses
President, American Anthropological Association
1995–97

Preface

This volume represents a long-term cooperative and evolving project on the part of many committed people and several organizations within the American Anthropological Association (AAA), as well as the Association itself, as part of an ongoing effort to address concretely through anthropological scholarship the wide range of public issues, concerned with inequality, race, immigration, health and education, confronting U.S. society as it enters the new millennium.

In 1995, Ida Susser (then-president of the Society for the Anthropology of North America, or SANA), together with Helán Page (then-president of the Association of Black Anthropologists), Steve Arvizu (then-president of the Association of Latino/Latina Anthropologists), and Michael Winkelman (chair of the External Relations Committee of the AAA) presented a proposal to the AAA Executive Assembly to edit an AAA volume on diversity in the United States. James Peacock, president of the AAA, appointed an editorial board made up of Yolanda Moses (then president-elect of the AAA), Louise Lamphere (later president-elect of the AAA), Michael Winkelman, and Carol Mukhapody, with Steve Arvizu presiding over the group and Ida Susser as coordinating editor. Patsy Evans as minority representative on the AAA staff assisted with the project. This editorial board selected topics and solicited initial contributions. As the chapters were submitted, Ida Susser, Tom Patterson, Louise Lamphere, June Nash, Michael Winkelman, Carol Mukhapody, and Maria Vesperi assisted in editing many of the contributions.

Eventually, Ida Susser and Tom Patterson worked to finalize the list of contributors, build a coherent theme, edit the completed chapters, and carry the project to publication.

Among the many people who have assisted us with this project, we would like to thank Bill Davis, Julie Philpot and Susan Skomol of the American Anthropological Association. We would also like to thank, especially, Joan Vincent for a thorough and critical review, Emily Martin for her support and energy at crucial junctures, and Jane Huber, our editor at Blackwell Publishers, for her persistence, patience, and hard work in helping us through the publication process.

Ida Susser

Acknowledgments

Portions of the following essays appear in this book. We thank all holders of the copyrights for the journals and books in which the essays originally appeared for permission to reprint them here.

"Do We All Reek of the Commodity?: Consumption and the Erasure of Poverty in Lesbian/Gay Studies" by Jeff Maskovsky to be published in *Anthropology Comes Out: Lesbians, Gays, Cultures*. Eds. Ellen Lewin and William Leap.

"The Construction of Poverty and Homelessness in U.S. Cities" by Ida Susser in *Annual Reviews of Anthropology* 1996.

"Conclusions" by Lee Baker in *From Savage to Negro*, Berkeley, University of California Press, 1998.

"The Peopling of the Americas: Anglo Stereotypes and Native American Realities" by C. Loring Brace and A. Russell Nelson to be published in *General Anthropology*.

Notes on Contributors

Steven F. Arvizu is president of Oxnard College, Oxnard, California. He has conducted extensive research in the anthropology of education with a focus on cross-cultural leadership and empowerment, and is past-president of the Association of Latino/Latina Anthropologists. He co-authored *Cross-Cultural Literacy: Ethnographies of Communications in Multiethnic Classrooms* and recently published *Putting Something Back: Comparative Histories of Chicano Activists*.

Lee D. Baker is associate professor of Cultural Anthropology at Duke University and the author of *From Savage to Negro: Anthropology and the Construction of Race, 1896–1954*.

Thomas Biolsi is professor of Anthropology at Portland State University in Oregon. He has done most of his research on Rosebud Reservation, South Dakota. His most recent book is *"Deadliest Enemies": Law and the Making of Race Relations on and off Rosebud Reservation*.

A. Lynn Bolles is professor of Women's Studies, affiliate professor in Anthropology, Afro-American Studies and Comparative Literature at the University of Maryland, College Park and author of *We Paid Our Dues: Women Trade Union Leaders of the Caribbean*.

C. Loring Brace is a biological anthropologist who is interested in the evidence demonstrating the relationships between living human populations and their probable ancestors back in the Pleistocene era. His principal focus has been on elucidating the processes by which archaic human form has become transformed into that visible in the world today. He is professor of Anthropology in the Department of Anthropology and curator of Biological Anthropology in the Museum of Anthropology at the University of Michigan.

Karen Brodkin is professor of Anthropology and Women's Studies at the University of California, Los Angeles. She is author of *Sisters and Wives, Caring by the Hour, How Jews Became White Folks and What that Says about Race* *in America*, co-editor of *My Troubles are Going to have Trouble with Me*, as well as many scholarly articles. Her work deals with race, gender and grass-roots activism in the United States.

Douglas Foley, professor of Anthropology and of Education at the University of Texas in Austin, specializes in U.S. race/ethnic relations and anthropology of education. His recent publications include *Learning Capitalist Culture*, *The Heartland Chronicles*, and *Crossing the Color Line: Reflections of a White Anthropologist*.

Judith Goode is professor of Anthropology and Urban Studies at Temple University. For several decades she has been engaged in research into the ethnography of race, ethnicity and class in Philadelphia and the United States. She served as past-president of the Society for Urban Anthropology and the Society for the Anthropology of North America and has published five books and many articles.

Alan H. Goodman is professor of Biological Anthropology in the School of Natural Sciences, Hampshire College. He is also the co-director of Hampshire College's U.S. Southwest and Mexico Program and an associate director of the New York African Burial Ground Project, and was previously the dean of the school. His research and teaching focuses on the interaction between political–economic processes and human biologies, such as how ideas of "race" and items such as Coca-cola ultimately may have consequences for humans "under the skin."

Kenneth J. Guest has conducted extensive research on religious beliefs and practices in the People's Republic of China and among Chinese immigrants in New York City. A graduate of Columbia University's East Asian Studies Program, he lived and worked in Hong Kong and mainland China for two years and since 1994 has been studying the intersection of religion, immigrant incorporation and transnational migration among Chinese in New York. Currently a Pew Religion and Immigration Fellow at the Social Science Research Council, he teaches at Hunter College and is completing his doctorate in the Anthropology Program of the City University of New York.

Peter Kwong is a professor in the Department of Urban Affairs and Planning and director of the Asian American Studies Program at Hunter College in the City University of New York. His research focuses on the intersection of labor, immigration, and race. He is also a community activist, journalist, and producer of video documentaries. He is the author of *Chinatown, New York: Labor and Politics, 1930–1950*, *The New Chinatown*, *Forbidden Workers: Illegal Chinese Immigrants and American Labor* and co-author of *Chinese Americans: The Immigrant Experience*.

Louise Lamphere is University Regents Professor of Anthropology at the University of Albuquerque, New Mexico, and president of the American Anthropological Association from 1999 to 2001. She has carried out extensive fieldwork in the northeastern and southwestern U.S., with a specific focus on women, immigration, work and family. She co-edited *Woman, Culture and Society*, an important early collection of feminist anthropology. She has also written *From Working Daughters to Working Mothers: Immigrant Women in a New England Community*, co-authored *Sunbelt Working Mothers: Reconciling Factory and Family*, edited *Structuring Diversity: Ethnographic Perspectives on the New Immigration*, and co-edited *Situated Lives: Gender and Culture in Everyday Life*.

Jeff Maskovsky is an assistant professor at Montclair State University in New Jersey. He has been carrying out ethnographic research on poor people's political participation and the politics of health care and HIV/Aids in Philadelphia, and is currently engaged in a collaborative study of the effects of state policies on civic participation in three poor neighborhoods in the city. His forthcoming volume (with Judith Goode) is entitled *New Poverty Studies: The Ethnography of Power, Politics and Impoverishment in the United States*.

Ruben G. Mendoza is currently an associate professor and founding director of the Institute of Archaeology, Center for Social and Behavioral Sciences, California State University Monterey Bay, Seaside. In addition to his role as a founding or planning faculty member of CSU Monterey Bay, Dr. Mendoza initiated the Alta California Mission Research Project and the Museum Education Project programs at Old Mission San Juan Bautista, California. These conjoined programs have worked to address scientific concerns with the archaeology and history of the Hispanic colonial mission of San Juan Bautista on the one hand, and museum education and service learning on the other. Recent publications address Hispanic colonial and Native American archaeology, ancient Mesoamerica and Africa, early California, and multimedia applications in anthropology.

Sally Engle Merry is professor of Anthropology at Wellesley College. Her areas of research are the anthropology of law, race/class/gender, and colonialism. She is the author or editor of four books, including *Urban Danger: Life in a Neighborhood of Strangers*, *Getting Justice and Getting Even: Legal Consciousness among Working Class Americans*, and *Colonizing Hawai'i: The Cultural Power of Law*. She is currently working on the international movement against violence against women as a new form of global legality.

Yolanda T. Moses is currently president of the American Association of Higher Education. She is past-president of City College of the City University of New York as well as of the American Anthropological Association (1995–7). She has published widely on issues of race, education, and the significance of anthropology to public policy.

Kirby Moss, a post-doctoral scholar in the Department of Anthropology at the University of North Carolina specializes in U.S. race/ethnic relations and public anthropology. His ethnography of poor whites entitled *The Color of Class: Deconstructing the Paradox of Poor White Privilege* is forthcoming.

Cheryl Mwaria is associate professor of Anthropology at Hofstra University where she is currently the director of Africana Studies. As a medical anthropologist she has conducted research in the United States, Africa and the Caribbean. She has written on childbirth and childrearing, biomedical ethics, women's health and race relations. She recently co-edited *African Visions: Literary Images, Political Change, and Social Struggle in Contemporary Africa*.

June Nash has carried out field work in an industrial community in the U.S. northeast and with migrant workers in New York City. She has also worked with Mayas in Chiapas Mexico, and miners in Bolivia. Her publications include *In the Eyes of the Ancestors: Belief and Behavior in a Mayan Community, From Tank Town to High Tech: The Clash between Industrial and Community Cycles*, and *We Eat the Mines and the Mines Eat Us: Dependency and Exploitation in Bolivian Tin Mining Communities*. Her growing attention to issues of globalization over the past two decades is expressed in her forthcoming book *Mayan Visions: The Quest for Autonomy in an Era of Globalization*.

A. Russell Nelson is currently an assistant research scientist at the University of Michigan Museum of Anthropology, serving as a consultant for Native American groups in the southwest, and pursuing forensic work in Wyoming. His research focuses principally on skeletal morphological indicators of population relationships between past and recent Native American populations and their resemblances to various Asian groups.

Thomas C. Patterson is professor and chair of Anthropology, University of California at Riverside. He has written widely on the social history of U.S. anthropology. His recent books include *Change and Development in the Twentieth Century* and *Inventing Western Civilization*.

Curtis C. Roseman is a professor in the Geography Department at the University of Southern California and the co-editor of *EthniCity: Geographic Perspectives on Ethnic Change in Modern Cities*. His research interests center around the migration of ethnic groups and the changing distribution of urban and ethnic populations especially within the United States.

Elizabeth M. Scott is an independent consultant (Zooarch Research) and an adjunct research associate with the Illinois State Museum. Her research interests include subsistence and social inequality, feminist and historical materialist approaches to the study of complex societies, and the archaeology of the colonial and post-colonial New World. She is the editor of *Those of Little Note: Gender, Race and Class in Historical Archaeology*.

Merrill Singer is the chief of research at the Hispanic Health Council, Hartford, Connecticut, and assistant clinical professor, Department of Community Medicine, University of Connecticut Health Center, as well as a research affiliate, Department of Psychology, Yale University. He is an applied medical anthropologist who specializes in health and poverty, the political economy of health, substance abuse, and HIV/AIDS. He has published widely in the health social science literature, including co-authoring *Critical Medical Anthropology* and *Medical Anthropology and the World System* and has edited books on HIV/AIDS, and African American religion.

Ida Susser is professor of Anthropology at Hunter College and the Graduate Center of the City University of New York. She has conducted research in New York City with a particular interest in changing patterns of inequality, social movements, poverty, and gender, and was the founding president of the Society for the Anthropology of North America. She has also carried out fieldwork in Puerto Rico and Southern Africa, focussing on environmental movements and community mobilization for the care and prevention of HIV/AIDS. She is the author of *Norman Street: Poverty and Politics in an Urban Neighborhood*, co-author of *Medical Anthropology and the World System*, and co-editor of *AIDs in Africa and the Caribbean* as well as many scholarly articles.

Bonnie Urciuoli, professor of Anthropology at Hamilton College, is a linguistic anthropologist. She has studied Spanish–English bilingualism and race/class issues in New York City, and has written *Exposing Prejudice: Puerto Rican Experiences of Language, Race, and Class*. She is currently examining the construction of "multiculturalism" in college discourses, and the discourse on "communication skills" in the United States.

Maria D. Vesperi is associate professor of Anthropology at New College, an all-honors college of the Florida State University System. A former editorial writer and columnist, she is also a trustee of the Poynter Institute for Media Studies, a school for working journalists. She is past-president of the Society for the Anthropology of North America and the author of *City of Green Benches: Growing Old in a New Downtown*, and co-editor of *The Culture of Long-Term Care: Nursing Home Ethnography*.

J. Diego Vigil is a professor of Anthropology and Chicano Studies at the University of California. With a focus on Mexican Americans and other ethnic minorities, he has conducted research on ethnohistory, education, culture change and acculturation, and adolescent youth issues, especially street gangs. This work has resulted in several books, including *Barrio Gangs* and *From Indians to Chicanos: The Dynamics of Mexican American Culture*, and many articles.

Michael Winkelman is a senior lecturer in the Department of Anthropology, Arizona State University, where he took a central role as an action anthropologist to implement a "cultural diversity" requirement in the General Studies Curriculum. He is the author of college textbooks on ethnic relations in the United States and ethnic sensitivity in social work. He has served as the director of the Ethnographic Field School in Ensenada, Baja California, Mexico since 1988.

Part I

Introduction

1

Cultural Diversity in the United States

Ida Susser

In an effort to contribute towards constructive social change, this volume offers an anthropological analysis that reexamines the social and political history of the United States, and attempts to provide a grounded historical context for concepts such as cultural pluralism, multiculturalism, and cultural diversity. Chapters here demonstrate the heterogeneity present in the United States from the first settlers and examine the changing definitions of race and ethnicity in the construction of a nation. We aim to confront national stereotypes and critically review commonly accepted images with respect to nation and identity. The collected work represents an effort to address public discourse and public policy concerning race, class, nation, and gender in the United States in order to inform ongoing dialogue and debate from an anthropological perspective.

American anthropologists have more legitimacy intervening in the workings of their own nation/state than in advocating change in societies where they are not citizens and are often members of a privileged elite. This makes it incumbent upon U.S. researchers to elaborate their findings in terms of the implications for people in this society. Indeed, as global interrelations intensify, studying U.S. society, power, and inequality will have major ramifications for our understanding of events and experiences for people in many other national contexts. Thus, this volume represents a concerted effort to use the tools of anthropological analysis to illuminate contested issues such as race, gender, class, and ethnicity in the United States and to provide a framework for the understanding of inequality.

Anthropologists have begun to reexamine the representations of nationalism, ethnicity, imperialism, and race in the United States in our own discipline, including who is cited and remembered and who ignored and forgotten (Vincent 1990; di Leonardo 1998; Harrison 1995, 1998; Gailey 1998; Brodkin 1998; Baker and Patterson 1994). Benefiting from such revisionist history, this book examines the creation both in the imagination and in the establishment of state power of what we tend to view unproblematically as the United States.

The historical processes which connect the United States to world capitalism have long been transparent to historians and anthropologists (e.g. Hobsbawm 1994; Williams 1966; Wolf 1982; Hall 1991; Nash 1981; Leeds 1994; Mintz

1985). However, their work concerning the turbulent interconnections of trade and colonialism has not been fully incorporated into our understandings of the generation of inequality and difference, in terms of race, nationality, religion, household, and gender in the United States today. The concept of the United States itself has a history of shifting frontiers and contested boundaries. Borders between the United States, Canada, and Mexico, created historically through the competition of colonial powers, have been intermittently porous in response to shifts in the need for labor, political contingencies, and unequal development. The global connections of advanced capitalism and such corresponding government policies as the North American Free Trade Agreement are more recent ways in which we have to reconsider the changing boundaries of the United States and the space that we describe (Fernandez-Kelly 1998; Gledhill 1998; Gutmann 1998; Smith 1998).

As we are all aware, the United States was founded on a history of conquest, colonial exploitation, patriarchal assumptions, labor migration, and slavery. From the initial formation of the thirteen states divisions emerged with respect to religion, language, and cultural practice. Patterns of landownership, slavery and class, definitions of democracy, and the expectations of civil society differed by state and region and certainly differed dramatically from the United States of today (Schudson 1999). Unifying myths and practices have been constructed along with the imposition of federal and state control. From the first, the nation depended on the recreation of identity, possibly based on participation in, and powerfully recreated by, memories of the American Revolution. Nevertheless, as played out in blood and suffering in the Civil War, inequality was always intertwined with socially constructed differences of color and also justified by constraints and discrimination with respect to gender, immigration, and indigenous peoples (see Chapters 2, 8, and 25, this volume; Kessler-Harris 1982; Brodkin 1998). This book examines the long-term processes and struggles which revolved around civil rights, access to employment and national institutions. As several chapters demonstrate, government policies, with respect to documentation, immigration quotas, quarantine, legal definitions of indentured servitude, the land rights of indigenous peoples, and slavery were important determinants of differentiation. Such historical processes limited who was officially granted full national rights and set the stage for continuing patterns of inequality as well as the emergence of social movements and identity politics.

Within contemporary identity groups of the 1980s and 1990s we find a mix of nationalism, feminism, religious community, and revolutionary fervor. But, as many have noted, history is frequently oversimplified when viewed only as the politics of identity. The complex interweaving of race, gender, immigration, class, and political opportunity needs to be addressed, as well as the significance of agency in a society in which both continuity and change are endemic.

Throughout the history of the United States, populations have struggled with inequality and its concomitant and changing definitions of difference. At times groups have crossed ethnic and nationality lines to combat class inequalities. Other groups have constructed communal identities which have served as a base from which to struggle against inequities related to class but fueled also by racial or religious discrimination. Although many of the craft unions of the late 19th century were based on the exclusion of new immigrant workers, a few earlier worker organizations formed in the 1860s included black as well as white workers. In the early 1900s, in the frequently described cauldron of the Lower East Side of New York City, and the working-class mill towns of New England, the formation of unions among Jewish, Italian, and Irish populations was based upon, but reached beyond, ethnic and religious identity. At the same time, many worker organizations enforced black/white and gender distinctions which mirrored those of their employers (Gutman 1976; Montgomery 1979; Brodkin 1998).

Analyses in this volume explore the formation of social movements and the construction of political identities as they changed in relation to state policies and shifts in social relations over time.

The social construction of gender and the position of women in U.S. society has been contested since the creation of the United States as a nation. Women with many different ethnic and racial identities have fought for equal employment opportunities, reproductive freedom, freedom of sexual orientation, and against sexual harassment and battering (Bookman and Morgen 1987; Sacks and Remy 1984; Mullings 1997; Gailey 1998). Historically, women have also worked for their voices to be heard in the public discourse with respect to inequality. In the 1920s and 1930s educated women worked to build community centers and training programs for working-class women of all groups. Undeniably, the category "woman" is fractured by class and the social construction of race. Thus, African American women have battled jointly with African American men for equal employment opportunities and separately from men for a Black feminist public voice (Mullings 1997; Collins 1990). In this volume we examine the issue of women's place and gender within the context of the creation of the state and shifting patterns of inequality.

Communal identities are constructed and remade in the battle for recognition of humanity. Cultural studies has elucidated connections between popular culture and the creation of communal identities of resistance (Hall 1991; Williams 1982). Musical narratives contained in Rap music, opposition to school rules, and even failure at work and at school have been interpreted as signifying modes of resistance in advanced capitalism (Willis 1977; Bourgois 1995; Hebdige 1979; see also Chapter 20, this volume).

Nevertheless, postmodernism has taught us to be wary of defining the world only in terms of narratives of power or its opposition in resistance. Robin Kelly argues that narrow emphasis on the glaring inequities of class and race risks ignoring the creativity and agency inherent in the art, dance, and social vitality of the urban poor of the United States. In fact, a focus on misery, poverty, and crisis alone contributes to the objectification of a population (Somers 1997; Kelley 1997; Hebdige 1979). Such critiques direct researchers to a more open-ended approach to the analysis of class, difference, and inequality which includes human emotions, manners and representations, and enjoyment as well as misery (see Chapters 18 and 20, this volume; Lock and Scheper-Hughes 1990; Stoler 1991; Roseberry 1997). We cannot, however, neglect an analysis of the commodification of pleasure, such as the sale of cigarettes through the targeting of minorities and young women, nor the structuring of the state with its policies which may either reinforce or reduce patterns of inequality (Baer et al. 1997). To be sure, family, race, religion, gender, and sexuality are all powerful symbolic categories, which generate human warmth, happiness, caring, and communal solidarity. They are, as well, building blocks for the maintenance of inequality and our analyses will fail if they do not integrate these two crucial perspectives. Nor should it be forgotten that inequality can be measured at times in the silencing and invisibility of whole populations, such as happened with the working poor and homeless in the United States of the 1990s (Susser 1996).

A crucial limitation of postmodern analysis arises around the concept of "hybridity." While attempting to address the reality of the changing identities available to an individual, this concept negates the possibility of a unified long-term political identity leading to agency and political change (Harris 1993; Nash 1997; Lilla 1998). In other words, if individuals are viewed as chameleon products of their historical situations, there is no place in the analytic framework from which to understand how a group of people might build a critique of the society in which they find themselves. For example, Nelson Mandela, who clearly represents what many might understand as a hybrid personality, held a consistent and lifelong set of beliefs which involved a critique of class and race oppression and was crucial in the transformation of the South African state. Born to Xhosa chiefly status but trained as a lawyer in a South African law school in British constitutional law, Mandela risked capital punishment and death in prison, in the cause of the poor black population of South Africa. The concept of hybridity emphasizes Mandela's conflicting western and traditional identities, elite versus commoner status, to the detriment of a recognition of the possibility of his long-term political commitment to constitutional freedom and equality for all people.

Similarly, the concept of "discourse" generates a diffuse and unidentifiable context of power just as "public culture" implies an amorphous undifferentiated arena which has no place for the significance of collective action or human agency in the search for equality and human rights. While we build on the insights of cultural analysis, a constant tension and contradiction arises between exposing the roots of terminology and unexamined beliefs, and addressing the real sources of power and inequality in the United States as represented in the ever-merging major corporations, powerful, wealthy lobbies, and associated government executives (Roseberry 1997).

For these reasons, this volume presents several perspectives, many voices and contrasting foci of study. Since much of the public debate concerning education, health, and other dimensions of inequality in the United States centers on questions of biological and cultural difference, we draw here on the broad and interconnected range of anthropological knowledge. We examine controversial concepts such as race and gender from the perspective of the fossil record, genetics, patterns of health and disease, as well as archaeological evidence and linguistic variation. Chapters consider the social construction of race in the history of physical and medical anthropology. They note the research in these fields that shows the lack of foundation in skeletal and genetic data for race as defined in the United States. As Loring Brace and Russell Nelson show, even the term

"Native Americans" has no clear meaning in the fossil record. There were several migrations to North America and the physical characteristics of the different populations that journeyed across the Bering Strait were strikingly varied. Since in their definitions of their topics anthropologists contributed to the image of Native Americans as a separate "race" and exotic "others," it is crucial that we redress this misrepresentation in our current reviews of U.S. anthropology.

Although professional anthropologists have studied the United States only since the late 19th century, most anthropologists concentrated first on Native Americans and later on the experiences of isolated ethnic groups, most recently defined as "others." Yet there was also research conducted against the grain, concerned with the destructive policies of the Bureau of Indian Affairs (Lesser 1933; Mooney 1896) and confronting ethnic, class, and racial stereotypes (for review and discussion of some of these works, see Lewis 1998). W. E. B. Du Bois conducted a neighborhood ethnography among African Americans in Philadelphia – hardly an exotic and mysterious group. Pioneering work addressing factory employment, class, and ethnicity was conducted by W. L. Warner during the Great Depression. At the same time, U.S. scholars such as Franz Boas, Ruth Benedict, Ruth Landes, Gene Weltfish, Alexander Lesser, and Allison Davis intervened in public debate concerning inequality, race, and gender.

In the postwar period of the 1950s, much of the anthropological research both by American and British scholars in urban third world settings, itself a product of the independence movements and reevaluations precipitated by World War II, laid the groundwork for conducting ethnographic work in complex societies and for discounting the "exotic" in the definitions of appropriate populations and theoretical formulations (Steward 1956; Wolf 1956; Wilson 1941; Gluckman 1955; Cohen 1969; Peattie 1970; Watson 1958; Magubane 1979; Vincent 1982).

Later, the political turmoil of the 1960s precipitated a reevaluation of anthropological scholarship. This was signaled by the publication of such works as *Reinventing Anthropology* (Hymes 1969) and Vine Deloria's (1969) *Custer Died for Your Sins*, and the appearance of such new journals as *Critique of Anthropology*. The political demands of this period for civil rights, women's rights and Native American reparations led the way for research concerning power, culture, and social movements within the United States.

Researchers, many of whom tried to act as advocates for oppressed peoples, became aware of the contradictory role of anthropologists as the "handmaidens of imperialism" (Gough 1968; Caulfield 1969; Asad 1973). They were obliged to recognize that the discipline's excessive focus on colonial populations was itself a product of global inequality. Either the discipline itself was moribund or, alternatively and more constructively, the method and theory of anthropology might serve to illuminate the experience of global inequality, class, and nation in the centers of the capitalist "north"/"west" (as we might designate the industrialized world of the 1970s).

In addressing the centers of global capital, researchers had to confront a longstanding perception in anthropology that research "at home" in the United States (unless it were among Native Americans or small communities such as the Amish), does not challenge scholars to negotiate cultural difference and to come to reevaluate ethnocentric and atheoretical approaches to society. Such a view is based on a particularly geocentric, static, and idealized hegemonic definition of culture as well as on a distancing and hierarchical vision of a mysterious, unchanging, and exotic "other." In this volume, theoretical arguments and ethnographic cases challenge this perception. As a long lineage of "invisible" anthropologists have demonstrated since the 19th century, U.S. research has been equally or more substantively and theoretically challenging as research conducted elsewhere (Vincent 1990).

In recognizing that anthropology cannot depend on any exclusive claim to foreign lands or strange behavior and, thus, in confronting the vacuousness of the concept of the exotic "other," the anthropology of the United States has generated self-conscious and far-reaching theoretical controversy.

In terms of cultural challenges which may illuminate ethnocentrism, crossing class boundaries can lead to cultural dissonance as challenging and illuminating as crossing national or ethnic boundaries. Indeed, current literature attests that crossing national or ethnic boundaries in search of difference does not necessarily lead to an understanding of silenced and subordinated populations. Writers such as Gayatri Spivak argue that previously colonized subaltern populations have been deprived of a voice in the analysis of their own societies. In fact, the assumptions of an approach which insists on the identity and mystery of the "other" reduces our vision of humans to impenetrable individuals lacking the ability to understand experiences beyond our own. As critical research in Africa and later subaltern studies in India have taught us, only if we consider frameworks of colonialism and class in the hierarchy of relations between researcher and the populations studied can we begin to penetrate this silence.

Clearly, traversing national boundaries in search of cultural contrast while remaining in the restricted environment of what nowadays is recognized as a global elite may be less illuminating than studying people, advantaged and disadvantaged, within the same nation (Appadurai 1990). In fact, contemporary global elites are not defined or limited by region. In advanced capitalist society in both "first" and "third" world cities, local poverty can be found side by side with mobile international wealth. Similarly, older distinctions of industrial versus non-industrial nations no longer have the same salience (Castells 1996). Countries emerging from half a century of communist rule may be more similar to one another in their cultural constructions than they are to their neighboring capitalist states. For these reasons, it is no longer reasonable, if it ever was, to view culture in any holistic sense in terms of area and language without considering class, political relations within global capitalism and other forms of inequality.

Thus, in contemporary societies in many parts of the world, the wealthy and the poor are separated less by geography than by divisions of education, employment, information, and capital (Castells 1996). While populations are shifting in response to changing global economies, many migrants remain in similar relations of inequality as they search for new entrées for educational opportunities, employment, and political representation. Anthropological approaches have begun to take account of these transformations of society and culture in studies of immigration, transnationalism, and diaspora. This book provides the groundwork for examining the impact of such changing global relations in the centers of capital.

In crossing boundaries, the anthropology of the United States must offer an approach that builds on, but also enriches, the understanding of other disciplines. Such ethnographic research is concerned with the construction of culture within historical and political processes. In this volume, we first dissect American culture. We trace the historical creation of national identity, citizenship, gender divisions, sexual orientation, race, and the changing nature of class consciousness. We examine hegemonic constructions of whiteness, considering the invisibility of the white poor and the scapegoating of the racially defined poor. We examine biologically defined issues of health, aging, and gender and demonstrate the inseparability of such apparently/inherently biological considerations from the social construction of categories and groups in the United States. We present this research in an effort to reopen questions of equity and human rights as we enter the third millennium.

To conceptualize events in contemporary America requires consideration of the shift from modern industrialization to what some call the information society, flexible accumulation, or, simply, advanced capitalism. The partial welfare state, created in the United States in the first half of this century has been under concentrated assault in recent decades. A detailed understanding of the processes of change in global and national political economies is central to concomitant shifts in our concepts of family, gender, leisure, and even knowledge and how we seek it. As the chapters here demonstrate, these changes have led already to redefinitions of race, citizenship, and diversity. They underlie changing policies concerning immigration and have to be taken into account in registering the experiences of new immigrant populations and the entitlements they are or are not permitted to access. These processes of change have been documented in their impact on urban space and the increasing racial and class segregation of U.S. neighborhoods, schools, and public spaces (Smith 1996; Marcuse 1996). As I note later in this volume, in Chapter 14, on urban poverty, over the past twenty years American ethnographers have begun to produce an overall analysis of the shaping of people's lives within the changing patterns of industrialization and deindustrialization (e.g. Susser 1982; Vesperi 1986; Zavella 1987; Lamphere 1987; Sacks 1988; Pappas 1989; Nash 1989; Bourgois 1995; Stack 1996; Sharff 1997; Sanjek 1998).

Following Thomas Patterson's historical introduction to the political economy of diversity in the United States, Part II of this volume considers the untenability of race as a biological category through Alan Goodman's discussion of the problem of racial interpretation of skeletal remains and an analysis of the fossil record in the Americas by Loring Brace and Russell Nelson. Cheryl Mwaria disentangles the genetic variation of disease from popular categories of race, and Merrill Singer documents medical anthropological approaches to diversity and delineates the connection between patterns of disease and social inequality.

Part III begins with Lee Baker's examination of the social construction of race in the United States and of ongoing conflicts over the interpretation of constitutional rights. Sally Merry develops a processual analysis of immigration, citizenship, and the legal creation of "racialized identities." Thomas Patterson's discussion of the archaeological record of the Americas brings with it a history of imperial states, gender inequality, and patterns of cultural resistance. The findings of historical archaeology with respect to the confinement of women to the domestic sphere, emerging class divisions, and the undocumented lives of slaves in settler society are highlighted by Elizabeth Scott.

In Part IV, focusing on contemporary conflicts, Thomas Biolsi explores the contested issues of land rights and sovereignty for Native Americans. Bonnie Urciuoli examines the social context of language variation among African Americans, Spanish–English bilingual populations and Native Americans. Drawing on ethnographic research among documented and undocumented Latino food store workers, June Nash delineates the relationship between the new immigration and resurgent labor struggles. Inequality and representations of diversity in U.S. cities are the concerns of my essay. Kenneth Guest and Peter Kwong revisit theories of ethnic enclaves using New York's Chinatown to illuminate class divisions within culturally defined populations. Chapters by Lynn Bolles, Michael Winkelman and Maria Vesperi analyze issues of family structure, psychocultural models and aging with respect to the experience of inequality, diversity and the dynamic creation of culture in U.S. society. In the last chapter of Part IV, Jeff Maskovsky analyzes the intersections between sexual minorities, queer theory and the significance of class in the U.S.

In Part V, two chapters challenge predominant theoretical perspectives on diversity in the United States, integrating current analyses of class, race, and cultural identity. Douglas Foley and Kirby Moss show how postmodernism and cultural studies ("post-Marxism") underlie and illuminate recent ethnographic research. Karen Brodkin investigates the underpinnings of the dualistic breakdown of race in the United States, as well as the ways in which Western social theory confronted or incorporated racial stereotypes.

Steven Arvizu introduces Part VI with a discussion of how an anthropological understanding of diversity can be integrated into the educational curriculum. Diego Vigil and Curtis Roseman outline a method for teaching students to recognize the significance of place and migration within varying conceptions of ethnicity. Ruben Mendoza analyzes the social values that underlie the shaping of museum exhibits and develops methods or teaching students to critically analyze such presentations. Judith Goode discusses the history of immigration, the significance of class divisions, and the changing constructions of nationality and ethnicity in the United States, countering essentialist notions common among students. Many chapters provide annotated bibliographies, recommendations of specific approaches, readings and films, as a way to introduce textured and politically controversial analysis in the classroom. In her Afterword, Louise Lamphere suggests ways in which this volume moves us toward a processual analysis of the United States and the contemporary politics of culture.

The population of the United States faces changes already in motion. As the structure of employment becomes less secure and public assistance is no longer assured, as corporate for-profit health care determines life chances, education is increasingly privatized, investment in public needs decreases, and ideas of legitimate dependency are reconsidered, we run the risk of constructing hostile identity politics and categorizing population groups such as immigrants or the underclass as the source of the nation's problems (Jones and Susser 1993; and Chapters 6, 13, 14, and 15, this volume). However we understand the transformation of the country, in terms of flexible accumulation or informational technology, it is evident that the particular configurations of family policy, education, health care and employment that are currently emerging differ in significant ways from those currently being reconstructed among European nations or other centers of global capital, such as Japan or Hong Kong. In some western European nations, such as France and Sweden, increased wealth is being translated into broader social services, day care and educational opportunities for most of the population, accompanied by new forms of hostility to immigrants. In the United States and in Great Britain we have witnessed a reduction of social supports and increasing inequality for the population in general, also accompanied in many situations by increasing hostility to new immigrants, and in the United States, specifically, racism. Only when the origins of inequality and the roots of diversity and common ground are clearly exposed can people in the United States begin to work together to construct a more humane social policy.

REFERENCES CITED

Appadurai, A.
    1990   Disjuncture and Difference in the Global Cultural Economy. *Public Culture*
        2(2):1–24.
Asad, T., ed.
    1973   *Anthropology and the Colonial Encounter.* London: Ithaca Press.
Baer, H., M. Singer, and I. Susser, eds.
    1997   *Medical Anthropology in the World System.* Westport, CT: Bergin and Garvey.
Baker, L., and T. Patterson, eds.
    1994   Race, Racism and the History of U.S. Anthropology. *Transforming Anthro-
        pology* 5(1–2).
Bookman, A., and S. Morgen
    1987   *Women and the Politics of Empowerment.* Philadelphia: Temple University
        Press.
Bourgois, P.
    1995   *In Search of Respect: Selling Crack in El Barrio.* Cambridge, UK: Cambridge
        University Press.
Brodkin, K.
    1998   *How Jews Became White Folks and What That Says about Race in America.*
        New Brunswick, NJ: Rutgers University Press.
Castells, M.
    1996   *The Rise of the Network Society.* Malden, MA: Blackwell.
Caulfield, M.
    1969   Culture and Imperialism: Proposing a New Dialectic. In Hymes, pp. 182–
        213.
Cohen, A.
    1969   *Custom and Politics in an Urban Community.* Manchester, UK: Manchester
        University Press.

Collins, P. H.
  1990   *Black Feminist Thought.* New York: Routledge.
Deloria, V.
  1969   *Custer Died for Your Sins: An Indian Manifesto.* New York: Macmillan.
di Leonardo, M.
  1998   *Exotics at Home.* Chicago: University of Chicago Press.
Fernandez-Kelly, P.
  1998   Discussion: Globalization, Restructuring, and Women's Poverty. Invited
         Session of Society for the Anthropology of North America at American Anthropo-
         logical Association, Philadelphia.
Gailey, C.
  1998   Feminist Methodologies. In *Handbook of Anthropological Methods.* Russell
         Bernard, ed. Washington, DC: American Anthropological Association.
Gledhill, J.
  1998   The Mexican Contribution to Restructuring U.S. Capitalism. *Critique of
         Anthropology* 18(3):279–296.
Gluckman, M.
  1955   *Custom and Conflict in Africa.* Oxford: Basil Blackwell.
Gough, K.
  1968   New Proposals for Anthropologists. *Current Anthropology* 9:403–407.
Gutman, H.
  1976   *Work, Culture and Society in Industrializing America.* New York: Vintage
         Books.
Gutmann, M.
  1998   For Whom the Taco Bell Tolls. *Critique of Anthropology* 18(3):297–316.
Hall, S.
  1991   The Local and the Global: Globalization and Ethnicity. In *Culture, Globali-
         sation, and the World System: Contemporary Conditions for the Representation of
         Identity.* A. D. King, ed. Pp. 119–39. London: Macmillan.
Harris, L.
  1993   Postmodernism and Utopia, an Unholy Alliance. In *Racism, the City and the
         State.* M. Cross and M. Keith, eds. Pp. 31–44. London: Routledge.
Harrison, F.
  1995   The Persistent Power of "Race" in the Cultural and Political Economy of
         Racism. *Annual Review of Anthropology* 24:47–74.
  1998   Introduction: Expanding the Discourse on "Race." *American Anthropologist*
         100(3):609–631.
Hebdige, D.
  1979   *Subcultures: The Meaning of Style.* London: Routledge.
Hobsbawm, E.
  1994   *The Age of Extremes: A History of the World, 1914–1991.* New York: Vintage
         Books.
Hymes, D., ed.
  1969   *Reinventing Anthropology.* New York: Vintage Books.
Jones, D., and I. Susser, eds.
  1993   The Widening Gap Between Rich and Poor. *Critique of Anthropology* 13(3).
Kelley, R.
  1997   *Yo' Mama's Disfunktional!* Boston: Beacon Press.
Kessler-Harris, A.
  1982   *Out to Work.* New York: Oxford University Press.

Lamphere, L.
1987 *From Working Daughters to Working Mothers.* Ithaca, NY: Cornell University Press.
Lesser, A.
1933 The Pawnee Ghost Dance Hand Game: A Study of Cultural Change. *Columbia University Contributions to Anthropology*, 16. New York: Columbia University Press.
Leeds, A.
1994 *Cities, Classes and the Social Order.* Roger Sanjek, ed. Ithaca, NY: Cornell University Press.
Lewis, H.
1998 The Misrepresentation of Anthropology and Its Consequences. *American Anthropologist* 100(3):716–732.
Lilla, M.
1998 The Politics of Jacques Derrida. *New York Review of Books*, June.
Lock, M., and N. Scheper-Hughes
1990 A Critical-Interpretive Approach in Medical Anthropology: Rituals and Routines of Discipline and Dissent. In *Medical Anthropology: Contemporary Theory and Method.* Thomas M. Johnson and Carolyn Sargent, eds. Pp. 47–72. Westport, CT: Praeger.
Magubane, B.
1979 *Political Economy of Race and Class in South Africa.* New York: Monthly Review Press.
Marcuse, P.
1996 Space and Race in the Post-Fordist City: The Outcast Ghetto and Advanced Homelessness in the United States Today. In *Urban Poverty and the Underclass: A Reader.* E. Mingione, ed. Pp. 176–217. Cambridge, MA: Blackwell.
Mintz, S.
1985 *Sweetness and Power: The Place of Sugar in Modern History.* New York: Viking Penguin.
Montgomery, D.
1979 *Workers Control in America.* New York: Cambridge University Press.
Mooney, J.
1896 The Ghost-Dance Religion and the Sioux Outbreak of 1890. *Fourteenth Annual Report of the Bureau of Ethnology, 1892–'93.* Pp. 653–1136. Washington, DC.
Mullings, L.
1997 *On Our Own Terms: Race, Class and Gender in the Lives of African American Women.* New York: Routledge.
Nash, J.
1981 Ethnographic Aspects of the World Capitalist System. *Annual Review of Anthropology* 10:393–423.
1989 *From Tank Town to High Tech.* Albany: SUNY Press.
1997 When Isms Become Wasms: Structural Functionalism, Marxism, Feminism and Postmodernism. *Critique of Anthropology* 17(1):11–32.
Pappas, G.
1989 *The Magic City.* Ithaca, NY: Cornell University Press.
Peattie, Lisa
1970 *The View from the Barrio.* Ann Arbor: University of Michigan Press.

Roseberry, W.
 1997   Marx and Anthropology. *Annual Review of Anthropology* 26:25–47.
Sacks, K.
 1988   *Caring by the Hour: Women, Work, and Organizing at Duke Medical Center.*
    Urbana: University of Illinois Press.
Sacks, K., and D. Remy
 1984   *My Troubles Are Going to Have Trouble with Me: Everyday Trials
    and Tribulations of Women Workers.* New Brunswick, NJ: Rutgers University
    Press.
Sanjek, R.
 1998   *The Future of Us All: Race and Neighborhood Politics in New York City.*
    Ithaca, NY: Cornell University Press.
Schudson, M.
 1999   *The Good Citizen: A History of American Civic Life.* Cambridge, MA:
    Harvard University Press.
Sharff, J.
 1997   *King Kong on 4th Street.* Boulder, CO: Westview Press.
Smith, N.
 1996   *The New Urban Frontier: Gentrification and the Revanchist City.* New York:
    Routledge.
 1998   Injuries of Scale. Interlocutor presentation at the Annual Meeting of the
    American Anthropological Association, Philadelphia, December.
Somers, M.
 1997   Deconstructing and Reconstructing Class Formation Theory: Narrativity,
    Relational Analysis, and Social Theory. In *Reworking Class.* J. Hall, ed. Pp. 73–105.
    Ithaca, NY: Cornell University Press.
Spivak, Gayatri
 1995   Can the Subaltern Speak? In *The Post-Colonial Studies Reader.* Bill Ashcroft,
    G. Griffiths, and H. Tiffin, eds. Pp. 24–29. London: Routledge.
Stack, C.
 1996   *Call to Home: African Americans Reclaim the Rural South.* New York: Basic
    Books.
Steward, J.
 1956   *The People of Puerto Rico: A Study in Social Anthropology.* Urbana:
    University of Illinois Press.
Stoler, A.
 1991   Carnal Knowledge and Imperial Power: Gender, Race and Morality in
    Colonial Asia. In *Gender at the Crossroads.* M. di Leonardo, ed. Pp. 51–101.
    Berkeley: University of California Press.
Susser, I.
 1982   *Norman Street: Poverty and Politics in an Urban Neighborhood.* New York:
    Oxford University Press.
 1996   The Social Construction of Poverty and Homelessness in U.S. Cities. *Annual
    Review of Anthropology* 25:411–435.
Vesperi, M.
 1986   *City of Green Benches.* Ithaca, NY: Cornell University Press.
Vincent, J.
 1982   *Teso in Transformation: The Political Economy of Peasant and Class in
    Eastern Africa.* Berkeley: University of California Press.
 1990   *Anthropology and Politics: Visions, Traditions, and Trends.* Tucson:
    University of Arizona Press.

Watson, W.
  1958   *Tribal Cohesion in a Cash Economy.* Manchester, UK: Manchester University
    Press.
Williams, E.
  1966   *Capitalism and Slavery.* New York: Capricorn Books.
Williams, R.
  1982   *The Sociology of Culture.* New York: Schocken Books.
Willis, P.
  1977   *Learning to Labor: How Working Class Kids Get Working Class Jobs.* New
    York: Columbia University Press.
Wilson, G.
  1941   *An Essay on the Economics of Detribalization in Northern Rhodesia.*
    Livingstone, Northern Rhodesia: Rhodes Livingstone Institute.
Wolf, E.
  1956   Aspects of Group Relations in Complex Societies. *American Anthropologist*
    58:1065–1078.
  1982   *Europe and the People without History.* Berkeley: University of California
    Press.
Zavella, P.
  1987   *Women's Work and Chicano Families.* Ithaca, NY: Cornell University Press.

2

Class and Historical Process in the United States

Thomas C. Patterson

Class, racial, ethnic, and gender diversity in the United States is intimately related to the historical development of capitalism. After land seizures and a number of unsuccessful attempts to use Native Americans for labor, the British colonists turned to indentured servants and then to African slaves. In response to a series of rebellions by bond servants and slaves over oppressive work conditions in the late 17th century, plantation owners in Virginia forced the enactment of legislation that racialized the workforce and separated bond servant from slave. By 1700, interracial marriages, which were not unusual in the 1670s and 1680s, had been banned in one colony after another. White racial identity was accentuated as the supply of African slaves increased, and poor whites came to form a buffer between the landowners and the slaves who constituted the most oppressed layer of the workforce (Goldfield 1997:39–45).

By 1700, the number of slaves in the North American colonies was greatest in South Carolina, where the plantation owners were shifting from rice to cotton. African slaves grew cotton, the raw material that was spun and woven into cloth by the urban proletariat appearing in Manchester and other factory cities in England. As Marx (1963 [1847]:111) noted:

> Direct slavery is just as much the pivot of bourgeois industry as machinery, credits, etc. Without slavery you have no cotton; without cotton you have no modern industry. It is slavery that gave the colonies their value; it is the colonies that created world trade, and it is world trade that is the pre-condition of large-scale industry.

In the colony, the landowners spent large sums of money to police slaves, to maintain separate Indian territories, to keep the supply of land limited, and to foment black–Indian hatred in order to prevent escaped slaves from seeking asylum in cimarron communities established in remote mountains and swamps (Willis 1963). Racial identity was often a mutable category on the colonial frontiers, where individuals were black under some circumstances and Indian in others (e.g. Hart 1998). In other words, from their inception, racial categories were both ambiguous and arbitrary.

The weight of the taxes levied by the Crown on the colonies fell disproportionately on the lower classes. As a result, the artisans, laborers, mechanics,
seamen, and indentured servants of the northern cities were among the first to
protest the exactions of the colonial governments and to challenge the legitimacy of their authority. In contrast to large segments of the wealthy classes, the
urban workers and the poor resisted the exactions of the Crown and agitated
for change, and they were often ruthlessly suppressed as a result. For example,
when "a motley rabble of saucy boys, Negroes and mulattoes, Irish teagues and
outlandish Jack Tars" voiced their complaints in 1770, they were massacred.
John Adams, who would later become president of the United States, defended
the British soldiers who fired the shots partly because he disapproved of the
conduct of the patriotic rabble (quoted by Blackburn 1988:105 n. 31). By virtue
of the central role they played in the Revolution, the urban workers and the
poor were able to make the struggle more democratic; however, they were too
few in number and too disorganized to play a leading role in the events that
ensued (Goldfield 1997:60; Nash 1979:201–247).

Nonetheless, the protests of the working poor led to boycotts of British products that eventually spread to the women of the wealthier classes. Consequently,
on the eve of the Revolution, many women were substituting goods of their own
making for the imported products they had once purchased. During the war,
patriotic women ran farms and businesses while their husbands were away; they
also joined urban protests, organized petitions, and helped soldiers and widows.
After the war, however, they too were unable to translate their activities
into new forms of political participation (Formisano 1974). As Paula Baker
(1994:88) has noted:

> Women's style of [political] participation and their relationship to authority were
> not yet greatly different from those of many men. Until the 1820s – and in some
> states even later – property restrictions on suffrage disenfranchised many men.

However, the egalitarian rhetoric of the Revolution laid the foundations for
new forms of participation in the public sphere and of political mobilization
by women during the Early Republic. These ranged from teaching school to
advocating prison reforms and temperance (Kerber 1980; Norton 1980). With
the rise of mass political parties in the 1830s and the elimination of property
requirements for suffrage by one state after another, women realized that they
were denied political rights and excluded from participating in political parties
because of their sex.

While women were missing from political debate at the Constitutional Convention, they were clearly on the mind of the Founding Fathers. The Federal-
ists who believed that the U.S. economy should be balanced between industry
and agriculture also felt that women should be employed in factories so that
their male kin could continue to pursue farming as a livelihood. From the early
1800s onwards, thousands of young women toiled for low wages in the northern textile and shoe factories; in the 1830s, they also organized some of the first
labor unions in the country and struck for higher wages (Baxandall and Gordon
1995:21–22, 68–70; Foner 1947:109–110).

The Founding Fathers limited popular democracy in the wake of the Revolutionary War to merchants, landholders, and plantation owners who wished to secure property rights for themselves. The war veterans who had gained victory in the first anti-colonial struggle were encouraged to settle in the Indian country west of the Allegheny and Appalachian mountains, where they could claim property, retain their independence, and escape wage labor. They came into increasing contact with Native American communities from Georgia and the Carolinas to Pennsylvania, Ohio, and Michigan. In addition, legislation promising free education, tax relief, and monetary credits for children was introduced in Virginia in 1784 to promote white–Indian intermarriage. However, as the demand for land increased along the frontier, the Indian policies of the federal government shifted after 1830 from a civilizing and educational mission backed by coercion to the removal of all indigenous peoples from their natal homelands to territories located west of the Mississippi River in the Louisiana Purchase (Sheehan 1973:175–178, 243–280).

Slavery had a profound shaping effect on political debate before and during the Revolution. During the rebellion, the calls of the Sons of Liberty for life, liberty, and the pursuit of happiness (property) were also heard by the slave populations in Virginia and the Carolinas. On the eve of the war, the white colonists feared a slave uprising. Their fears were further fueled when the royal governor of Virginia issued a proclamation in November 1775 offering lifelong freedom to any slave who could escape, reach British lines, and would bear arms against the Americans. The plantation owners responded by threatening dire consequences for those slaves who fled. Most of the escaped slaves fought for the British; some fought for the Americans; others took refuge with Indian tribes in the mountains and beyond. Perhaps 20 percent of the American slaves gained their freedom during the war. However, given the political climate after the war, many of them relocated to Nova Scotia (Nash 1986:271–275).

Slavery continued to shape political discussion after the war. At the Constitutional Convention in 1787, the central issue was the three-fifth compromise which allowed the Southern states to count 60 percent of the slave population in the census. This gave the plantation owners congressional representation that far exceeded their numbers. In the 19th century, the issue of slavery resurfaced and was debated by the regional elites and their political agents every time new states petitioned for admission to the Union. In 1850, Frederick Douglass remarked that blacks, more than 90 percent of whom were in the South, were discriminated against both legally and in the public mind because their skin color was linked with "the degradation of slavery and servitude" (quoted by Goldfield 1997:92).

The modern factory system expanded rapidly in the northern and eastern United States after 1820 to meet the demands of an ever-growing number of residents for the commodities they produced. This meant that U.S. society articulated three distinct modes of production: slavery, pre-capitalist commodity production, and wage-labor capitalism with corresponding class relations and dominant ideologies. The South was dominated by slavery but also exhibited pre-capitalist commodity production. In this circumstance, slaves were exploited by the slaveholding elite but not by the non-slaveowning white farmers; as a result, the slaveholders often promoted a highly egalitarian worldview that cemented a cross-class alliance with non-slaveowning white farmers. The wage-labor capitalism dominant in the North underpinned class structures, the visible expression of exploitation, in the industrializing cities as well as further distinctions between white elites and wage workers in the cities and petty commodity producers in the countryside; the dominant ideology of the region stressed free labor as opposed to either wage-labor or self-employment. As the country expanded westward, the petty-commodity production of the initial (self-employed) settlers was soon engulfed by wage-labor capitalism in the northern territories and states and by slavery in the South (Ashworth 1995).

The articulation of different modes of production formed the backdrop for immigrants arriving in the United States before the Civil War. The U.S. population doubled from 10 to 20 million between 1820 and 1840 because of immigration from different parts of Europe. However, the expansion of industrial capitalism in the North during the 1830s did not translate automatically into more jobs for either native or immigrant workers, because the industrialists began to rely increasingly on machines that expanded productivity. For the workers, the greater reliance on machines resulted in unemployment, lower wages, and demands for 10- rather than 12- or 16-hour workdays (Foner 1947:50–54).

This was the context in which many Irish immigrants arrived; they were mostly Gaelic-speaking peasants who had been dispossessed from their lands by English lords. What began as a trickle of Irish immigrants in the late 18th century became a steady flow by 1820 and a torrent by the mid-1840s. Altogether more than 3 million Irish men, women, and children arrived between the late 1780s and 1855. The discrimination they felt at the hands of the Anglo-Saxon ruling class carried over to the United States, where they were discriminated against by a native-born Anglo-Saxon elite and by unemployed native-born workers in the North (Horsman 1981:27–33; Quinn 1945:551; 1958:27). They confronted the Naturalization Act of 1790 which placed a 5- to 19-year residency requirement for citizenship, and the government recorded them in a separate category in the decadal censuses of the era. The Irish immigrants worked as unskilled laborers and servants who lived in urban slums. They dug canals, mined coal, and toiled at various tasks that were deemed too dangerous for expensive slaves to undertake. The "wild Irish," "white niggers" occupied the lowest rung of a waged-labor force stratified by ethnicity and race. By virtue of their tenuous grip on whiteness, Irish workers occasionally competed with and displaced free blacks from unskilled jobs in the northern and western cities (Roediger 1991:138–145).

Anti-Irish sentiments, the war with Mexico looming on the horizon, and the arrival of Chinese immigrants in the 1840s led many politicians to adopt polygenic views on race. That is, the various races and nationalities could be arranged hierarchically with white Anglo-Saxons at the top and other groups – Chinese, American Indians, Irish, and blacks – occupying lower positions on the scale. The concepts of racial hierarchies, buffer races, and the inferiority of racial hybrids and their relation to regional class structures were codified at this time in Europe and the United States (Patterson and Spencer 1994). Similar constructions were forged to account for the consolidation of patriarchal social relations and to explain the places of white working, middle-class, and elite women in 19th-century U.S. society (Grossberg 1983; Scott 1970; Smith-Rosenberg 1971; Smith-Rosenberg and Rosenberg 1973).

There were multiple critiques of the class structures in antebellum America. Southern intellectuals, like John Calhoun, pointed out that the freedom of northern wage workers was little more than the freedom to sell their labor power for a fraction of its value or to starve. The labor movement frequently evoked the image of "wage slavery" to point to similarities between the conditions of slaves in the South and poorly paid wage workers in the North. Striking women at a textile factory in Lowell called themselves the "white slaves" of New England in the 1830s because of their long workdays and impoverished circumstances. Abolitionists, like William Lloyd Garrison, opposed slavery in the South at the same time they promoted "... the acceptance of the free labor market and the capitalist order of the North" (Foner 1980:76; Friedman 1982).

The antislavery movement was particularly appealing to women. As Stephanie Coontz (1988:237) has pointed out, it

> influenced women's consciousness by starting them thinking about the sexual degradation and exploitation of female slaves. A number of women saw parallels in their marriage relations fairly early in the movement's history, especially when Southerners defended slavery as analogous to a husband's power over his wife.

Frederick Douglass, Sojourner Truth, and other black leaders also saw connections between the circumstances of free women and slaves and were early proponents of women's rights and racial and sexual equality. However, the women's suffrage movement, at least the Stanton-Anthony wing, severed its alliance with the black civil rights movement after the Civil War, because the constitutional amendments enacted after the war which emancipated the slaves granted voting rights to freedmen but not to freedwomen or white women. In a word, the Fourteenth Amendment pitted the civil and political rights of women against those of freedmen (Coontz 1988:249 n. 80).

Federal legislation following in the wake of the North's victory also dissolved slavery and institutionalized capitalist social relations in the South; however, these laws did not specify how the workforce would be organized and disciplined. Such decisions were left to the various state legislatures in the South. The black Codes – a series of state laws first enacted in Mississippi in 1865 and then elsewhere by the end of the decade – limited the economic options of the black workforce outside of plantation work (Foner 1988:198–200). By 1877, the Southern planter class, which quickly regained control of the state apparatuses, had also established new structures of capital accumulation based on debt peonage. Black sharecroppers and tenant farmers, and white ones in the up-country, had become steadily more indebted to landlords by the eve of World War I (Angelo 1995). The black Codes, which largely excluded freedmen and freedwomen from the emerging industrial workforce in the increasingly capitalist South, formed a backdrop for reconstructing the gender ideologies in the white population. These stressed chivalry, honor, and manliness, and the role of men as protectors of white women and children. At the same time, they saw white women, especially those working in factories, as more independent and less helpless than their mothers and aunts had been portrayed earlier (Bederman 1995; Whites 1995:199–224).

The Compromise of 1877, which effectively blocked blacks from industrial jobs in the North, also established the foundations for political parties that crossed class lines. The Republicans consisted of Northern industrialists, merchants, and yeoman farmers, wealthy agrarian capitalists in the West, and poor whites in the up-country of the South. The Democrats enlisted workers and marginal farmers in the North and West and the planter elite in the South. As a result, ruling class fractions in both parties were able to wage class war against marginalized workers and farmers in the regions where they were dominant and to forge alliances with the oppressed classes of the other regions. In addition, they promoted nativist, anti-immigration policies in the North and racist ones in the South and the West (Bensel 1990:366–415).

More than 23 million immigrants, mostly from southern and eastern Europe, settled in the United States between 1880 and the eve of World War I. The Italian, Jewish, Russian, Greek, and Slavic immigrants who arrived during that period constituted more than a tenth of the country's population. They sought work in the industrial cities of the Northeast and Great Lakes states, where they were joined by native-born immigrants from rural areas. Together they constituted a large reserve army of labor that kept wages low and joined a labor force that was stratified in complex ways by ethnicity and gender. As Karen Brodkin has noted, they constituted 42 percent of workers in mining and manufacturing industries in 1880 and 58 percent of the workers in 1910. "In contrast, a staggering 44 percent of all native-born white male workers in 1910 worked in farming, lumbering and livestock raising far from the industrial centers" (Brodkin 1998:12).

The armories built in the working-class neighborhoods where the immigrants lived bear witness to how the state and the ruling class viewed them: savages and barbarians, potentially unruly mobs, whose members had a penchant for violence, immorality, and crime, whose craniometry hinted at mental inferiority, and whose ancestors lacked the refinements of civilization and perhaps even the capacity to acquire them. The immigrants constituted new buffer races that separated Protestants from northern Europe from Indians, Blacks, and Asians (Haller 1971; Patterson and Spencer 1994; Pick 1989).

Calls for further territorial expansion were heard after the Indian wars of the 1870s and 1880s were quelled and the rebellious tribes were resettled on reservations that were divided into 160-acre plots allotted to Indian men by the Dawes Act of 1887. The imperialists rooted their arguments for the penetration and control of foreign markets in the language of Manifest Destiny, Social Darwinism, and scientific racism (Westin 1972). With their encouragement, the United States annexed Western Samoa in 1890, attempted to acquire Hawaii in 1893, and gained Puerto Rico, the Philippines, and Cuba, for all intents and purposes, during the Spanish-American War of 1898. It incorporated the residents of these newly acquired territories in complex ways into the racial hierarchies of the day; for example, in order to circumvent laws restricting immigration from Asia, Filipinos were distinguished from Asians and acquired their own category in the decadal censuses after 1900 (Hing 1993; Sayler 1995).

The outbreak of World War I in 1914 stemmed the flow of immigrants from Europe, creating labor shortages in the industrial cities of the North and the Midwest. Between 1916 and 1929, more than 1.5 million African Americans left the South in search of better lives. This flow was renewed at the beginning of World War II when A. Philip Randolph, long-time head of the Brotherhood of Sleeping Car Porters, forced President Franklin Roosevelt to issue Executive Order 8802 which banned discrimination in defense industries and government. This edict integrated the war industries, and more than a million African American men and women moved out of the South in its wake and found work in defense plants across the country. Later, Randolph would force President Harry S. Truman to issue another executive order integrating the armed services. These added fuel to the black civil rights movement of the 1950s, culminating in the federal legislation of the 1960s which established racial equality in law but not in fact.

The black civil rights struggle also energized and inspired leaders of a number of loosely organized movements with overlapping agendas in the late 1960s and 1970s. As Victor Wallis (1998:37) remarked, the

> initial antiracist and antiwar constituencies were reinforced by demands for women's liberation, for the rights of other oppressed national or ethnic minorities, for an end to all forms of discrimination (including by sexual orientation, age, and disability), and for sweeping curbs on environmental degradation.

These movements succeeded in getting their agendas into the arena of public debate. Their efforts have resulted in legislative victories, such as the establishment of the Environmental Protection Agency or the Occupational Health and Safety Agency, although many of their victories were subsequently gutted or watered down through the carefully organized and orchestrated actions of corporate and conservative opponents. The movements also gained a foothold in college and university curricula through the formation of women's, black, Native American, Puerto Rican, Chicano, gay or environmental studies programs, for example, during a period when there was steadily diminishing support for higher education in the United States.

The United States now has the largest immigrant population in the world. Ten million immigrants entered legally after 1969; another 3 million used provisions of the Immigration Reform and Control Act of 1986 to legalize their status; and several millions more who entered illegally or overstayed their visas have successfully disappeared. Whereas 95 percent of the immigrants at the beginning of the 20th century came from Europe, more than 75 percent of the legal arrivals today are from Latin America and Asia. The new immigrants are an internally diverse group: well-educated Koreans and Chinese, impoverished second-wave Cambodian and Hmong families, and working-class men and women from the Caribbean, Mexico, and Central America. Nearly 70 percent of the new immigrants have settled in a few metropolitan areas – New York, Los Angeles, Miami, or the San Francisco-Oakland-San Jose triangle, 20 percent of whose populations are now foreign-born (Rumbaud 1991).

The arrival of enormous numbers of Latin American and Asian immigrants beginning in the 1970s coincided with the reorganization of the U.S. class structure and with the appearance of new groups of previously disconnected individuals who sensed that they had something in common. The immigrants were acutely aware that women, American Indians, Chicanos, Puerto Ricans, and gays and lesbians, to name only a few, were demanding recognition of rights and claims based on their identities. The politics of many of these movements celebrated differences and demanded equal recognition and rights because of them. Their goal was to ensure the survival of community. In some instances, the new immigrants followed their lead and adopted similar tactics.

Opponents of the goals of these movements rooted their claims in another strand of liberal thought that privileged the rights of the individual and demanded that differences be ignored (Taylor 1992). This view was embodied in the U.S. Supreme Court's 1974 Bakke decision. The judges held that the admissions policies of a medical school that set aside a certain number of places for members of groups that were historically underrepresented in the profession, discriminated against a white male who was denied admission even though he had higher test scores than some minority-group members accepted into the program. The new forms of social consciousness constructed in the 1970s and 1980s were also buttressed by economic circumstances. They were sustained by massive immigration and the changing complexion of the large cities coupled with deindustrialization, growing unemployment, the flight of capital to states with permissive work laws and large reserve armies of labor, and the upward redistribution of wealth.

The debates that ensued underwrote the culture wars that have raged in the United States for the past 25 years (Hunter 1991). Multiculturalism, antiracism, antisexism, women's studies, and political correctness have a lot to do with the inequalities that exist between communities, with power relations, and with the social and cultural hierarchies that have crystallized in the United States. These, in turn, provide the background against which the essays in this volume were written.

Acknowledgments

I want to thank Wendy Ashmore, Karen Brodkin, and Ida Susser for their constructive comments on and criticisms of an earlier draft.

REFERENCES CITED

Angelo, Larian
 1995 Wage Labour Deferred: The Reconstruction of Unfree Labour in the U.S. South. *Journal of Peasant Studies* 22(4):581–644.

Ashworth, John
  1995   *Slavery, Capitalism and Politics in the Antebellum Republic*, vol. 1. *Commerce and Compromise, 1820–1850*. Cambridge, UK: Cambridge University Press.
Baker, Paula
  1994   The Domestication of Politics: Women and American Political Society, 1780–1920. In *Unequal Sisters: A Multicultural Reader in U.S. Women's History*. Vicki L. Ruiz and Ellen C. DuBois, eds. Pp. 85–110. London: Routledge.
Baxandall, Rosalyn, and Linda Gordon, eds.
  1995   *America's Working Women: A Documentary History, 1600 to the Present*. New York: W. W. Norton.
Bederman, Gail
  1995   *Manliness and Civilization: A Cultural History of Gender and Race in the United States, 1880–1917*. Chicago: University of Chicago Press.
Bensel, Richard F.
  1990   *Yankee Leviathan: The Origins of Central State Authority in America, 1859–1877*. Cambridge, UK: Cambridge University Press.
Blackburn, Robin
  1988   *The Overthrow of Colonial Slavery, 1776–1848*. London: Verso.
Brodkin [Sacks], Karen
  1994   How Did Jews Become White Folks? In *Race*. Steven Gregory and Roger Sanjek, eds. Pp. 103–130. New Brunswick, NJ: Rutgers University Press.
  1998   Global Capitalism: What's Race Got to Do with It? Keynote Address, Annual Meeting of the American Ethnological Society Distinguished Lecture. May 8, 1998, Toronto.
Coontz, Stephanie
  1988   *The Social Origins of Private Life: A History of American Families 1600–1900*. London: Verso.
Epperson, Terrence
  1991   "To Fix a Perpetual Brand": The Social Construction of Race in Virginia, 1675–1750. Ph.D. thesis, Department of Anthropology, Temple University.
Foner, Eric
  1980   *Politics and Ideology in the Age of the Civil War*. New York: Oxford University Press.
  1988   *Reconstruction, 1863–1877: America's Unfinished Revolution*. New York: Harper and Row.
Foner, Philip S.
  1947   *History of the Labor Movement in the United States*, vol. 1. *From Colonial Times to the Founding of the American Federation of Labor*. New York: International Publishers.
Formisano, Ronald P.
  1974   Deferential-Participant Politics: The Early Republic's Political Culture. *American Political Science Review* 68(3):473–487.
Friedman, Lawrence J.
  1982   *Gregarious Saints: Self and Community in American Abolitionism, 1830–1870*. Cambridge, UK: Cambridge University Press.
Goldfield, Michael
  1997   *The Color of Politics: Race and the Mainsprings of American Politics*. New York: New Press.
Grossberg, Michael
  1983   Who Gets the Child? Custody, Guardianship, and the Rise of a Judicial Patriarchy in Nineteenth-Century America. *Feminist Studies* 9(2):235–260.

Haller, John S.
  1971 *Outcasts from Evolution: Scientific Attitudes on Racial Inferiority,*
    1859–1900. Urbana: University of Illinois Press.
Hart, William B.
  1998 Black "Go-Betweens" and the Mutability of "Race," Status, and Identity on
    New York's Pre-Revolutionary Frontier. In *Contact Points: American Frontiers*
    from the Mohawk Valley to the Mississippi, 1750–1830. Andrew R. L. Clayton
    and Fredrika J. Teute, eds. Pp. 88–113. Chapel Hill: University of North Carolina
    Press.
Hing, Bill Ong
  1993 *Making and Remaking Asian America through Immigration Policy,*
    1850–1990. Stanford: Stanford University Press.
Horsman, Reginald
  1981 *Race and Manifest Destiny: The Origins of American Racial Anglo-Saxonism.*
    Cambridge, MA: Harvard University Press.
Hunter, James D.
  1991 *Culture Wars: The Struggle to Define America.* New York: Basic Books.
Kerber, Linda K.
  1980 *Women of the Republic: Intellect and Ideology in Revolutionary America.*
    Chapel Hill: University of North Carolina Press.
Marx, Karl
  1963 [1847] *The Poverty of Philosophy.* New York: International Publishers.
Nash, Gary
  1979 *The Urban Crucible: The Northern Seaports and the Origins of the American*
    Revolution. Cambridge, MA: Harvard University Press.
  1986 *Race, Class, and Politics: Essays on American Colonial and Revolutionary*
    Society. Urbana: University of Illinois Press.
Norton, Mary B.
  1980 *Liberty's Daughters: The Revolutionary Experience of American Women,*
    1750–1800. Ithaca, NY: Cornell University Press.
Patterson, Thomas C.
  1994 *The Theory and Practice of Archaeology.* Englewood Cliffs, NJ: Prentice Hall.
Patterson, Thomas C., and Frank Spencer
  1994 Racial Hierarchies and Buffer Races. *Transforming Anthropology*
    5(1–2):20–27.
Pick, Daniel
  1989 *Faces of Degeneration: A European Disorder, c. 1848–c. 1918.* Cambridge,
    UK: Cambridge University Press.
Quinn, David B.
  1945 Sir Thomas Smith (1513–1577) and the Beginnings of English
    Colonial Theory. *Proceedings of the American Philosophical Society* 89(4):543–
    560.
  1958 Ireland and Sixteenth Century European Expansion. *Historical Studies*
    1:20–32.
Roediger, David R.
  1991 *The Wages of Whiteness: Race and the Making of the American Working*
    Class. London: Verso.
Rumbaud, Rubén G.
  1991 Passages to America: Perspectives on the New Immigration. In *America at*
    Century's End. Alan Wolfe, ed. Pp. 208–244. Berkeley: University of California
    Press.

Sayler, Lucy E.
  1995   *Laws Harsh as Tigers: Chinese Immigrants and the Shaping of Modern Immigration Law*. Chapel Hill: University of North Carolina Press.
Scott, Anne F.
  1970   *The Southern Lady: From Pedestal to Politics, 1830–1930*. Chicago: University of Chicago Press.
Sheehan, Bernard W.
  1973   *Seeds of Extinction: Jeffersonian Philanthropy and the American Indian*. New York: W. W. Norton.
Smith-Rosenberg, Carroll
  1971   Beauty, the Beast and the Militant Woman: A Case Study in Sex Roles and Social Stress in Jacksonian America. *American Quarterly* 23(4):562–584.
Smith-Rosenberg, Carroll, and Charles Rosenberg
  1973   The Female Animal: Medical and Biological Views of Woman and her Role in Nineteenth-Century America. *Journal of American History* 60(2):332–356.
Taylor, Charles
  1992   *Multiculturalism and "The Politics of Recognition."* Princeton, NJ: Princeton University Press.
Wallis, Victor
  1998   Keeping the Faith: The U.S. Left 1968–1998. *Monthly Review* 50(4):31–46.
Westin, Ruben F.
  1972   *Racism in U.S. Imperialism: The Influence of Racial Assumptions on American Foreign Policy, 1893–1945*. Columbia: University of South Carolina Press.
Whites, Lee Ann
  1995   *The Civil War as a Crisis in Gender: Atlanta, Georgia, 1860–1890*. Athens: University of Georgia Press.
Willis, William
  1963   Divide and Rule: Red, White, and Black in the Southeast. *Journal of Negro History* 48(3):157–176.

Part II

The Biology of Difference?

3

Biological Diversity and Cultural Diversity: From Race to Radical Bioculturalism

Alan H. Goodman

On July 28, 1996, college students Will Thomas and Dave Deacy were late for the Columbia Cup hydroplane race. To save time they stepped down and walked along a shallow bank of the Columbia River. Will Thomas stopped to pick up what first appeared to be a smooth rock in the river. The smooth rock turned out to be a human skull. Because they wanted to see all of the race, they quickly hid the skull. Will Thomas later admitted: "There were a couple of kids fartin' around and I thought they would find it" (*Tricity Herald*, July 27, 1997).

After the race Thomas and Deacy retrieved the skull and turned it over to a police officer. A return to the location where the skull was discovered led to the finding of most of the rest of the skeleton, now called Kennewick Man, so named for the Richland County, Washington, town in which "he" was found. To determine more about the individual, perhaps a murder victim, the police called in Floyd Johnson, the Benton County coroner. Because all that remained were bones and teeth, Johnson soon rang up James Chatters, an independently employed anthropologist: "Hey, buddy, I got a skull for you to look at," Johnson said.

In addition to determining that the skeleton was likely to have been a male, about 40–50 years old, Chatters noted what he took to be "Caucasoid traits" such as a dolichocephalic (narrow) skull and narrow face. He thought that the individual might have been a European settler (1997:9). While he interpreted the tooth shapes as indicating Asian ancestry, Chatters writes of the craniofacial morphology: "Many of these characteristics are **definitive** of modern day Caucasoid peoples, while others . . . are typical of either race" (1997:9, emphasis added). The idea that Kennewick Man was a recent settler was definitively rejected by the discovery of the tip of an ancient spear point embedded in his hip bone and a radiocarbon date of 9,300 years before the present for one of his finger bones. If Kennewick Man is a settler, then he is a much older one than previously assumed.

It is broadly agreed by anthropologists that most or all Native Americans (or American Indians) came from northern Asia, geographically, genetically, and culturally (I use Native American and American Indian interchangeably to refer to the first peoples of the Americas). Thus, the presence of what Chatters referred to as "Caucasoid features" in a skull of great antiquity has generated considerable excitement. He suggested (1997:10) that Kennewick Man's scientific study might "alter conventional views of how, when, and by whom the Americas were peopled." The headline of a widely circulated article by Boyce Rensberger of the *Washington Post* declared: "Skeletons Suggest Caucasoid Early American" (April 15, 1997). The subheading of Douglas Preston's feature article in the *New Yorker* asks: "And why is the government withholding Kennewick Man, who might turn out to be the most significant archaeological find of the decade?" (June 16, 1977:70). In numerous articles in neo-Nazi publications such as the large-circulation, anti-Semitic *Spotlight*, Louis Beam, an "Ambassador at Large" for the Aryan Nation, uses the interpretation of Kennewick Man as a Caucasoid as proof that North America is a white homeland (Mozzochi 1998).

Intersecting with the interpretation of Kennewick Man as a "Caucasian" is compliance with the Native American Graves Protection and Repatriation Act of 1990 (NAGPRA; Public Law 101–601). NAGPRA gives Native Americans a role in the disposition of remains found on federal lands, as Kennewick Man was, and deemed to be ancestral to them. Assuming he is their ancestor, five Northwest tribes, led by the Confederated Tribes of the Umatilla Indian Reservation, filed a "claim" for the skeleton. Countering this claim, a group of eight anthropologists and archaeologists asked for further study of the remains because they may not be directly linked to these Native Americans or to any contemporary Native Americans. The scientists were joined in their claim by the Asatru Folk Assembly, a group that mixes pagan religion with neo-Nazi leadership. The Asatru think that Kennewick Man is their ancient one.

The story of Kennewick Man raises important issues that I hope to address in this chapter. Are racialized descriptions of biology useful in this and other contexts? How do we determine if Kennewick Man is biologically ancestral to the Umatillas, another Native American group, or any group of Native Americans? More generally, what is the connection between biological ancestry (writ in genes!) and cultural ancestry? How does biological variability relate to cultural diversity, and how should the relationship be theorized?

At first one might think that human biology might have nothing to do with cultural diversity. After all, for almost a century, or since the time of Franz Boas, it has been a main axiom of anthropology not to conflate race with behavior and culture (Boas 1940). But, as the story of Kennewick Man illustrates, biology has not been disentangled from culture. Laws and commonly held beliefs often privilege biology (unchanging blood and genes) over lived experience. Social hierarchies are still often made to seem natural and permanent as if imbued with a sense of nature. And biological diversity is still often and inappropriately reduced to the old idea of racial types, and subsequently used to explain culture, behavior, and socioeconomic positions.

In this introductory essay I begin by briefly reviewing the rise and demise of the idea that race describes and explains human diversity. From this review two key points emerge: (1) race is an idea and, as such, it is inconsistent with the facts of human biological diversity (in fact, race is a shamefully obsolete and potentially harmful way to think about human diversity); and (2) race and racism are sociopolitical realities (and as sociopolitical realities, they have biological consequences). Said somewhat differently, the main points of this chapter are that race is obviously real and deeply significant as a social category. When Boas advocated separating race from culture and behavior, he did not know how to think of biology free of racism. I advocate the reverse. Because race and racism are sociopolitical realities, they affect individual biologies. Understanding this presents a new and radical biocultural agenda. The continuance of "race" and ethnic differences in health calls for explication of the biology of inequality and racism.

The Invention and Reification of Race

The idea of biological race embodies the following central beliefs: (1) that the human species is divisible into a small and discrete number of categories; (2) that these categories are fixed and old; (3) that an individual's biology and behavior are in large part explainable by which race the individual is a member of; and (4) that races are hierarchically arranged (Hannaford 1996; Smedley 1999). When it is stated in this fashion, one can show when and where racial thinking began and see which, if any, of its central characteristics have been challenged in subsequent years.

Hannaford (1996) maintains that the idea of race coalesced in Europe after 1492, the year Columbus "rediscovered" the Americas and the Jews were expelled from Spain, and before the first enslaved African landed in the Caribbean and North America. Before this time concepts of "us" and "other" were common. But this sense of difference was not systematically related to biology. The "Other" might be feared, reviled, or an object of desire; but they were not thought to be different and less worthy based on biological theorizing. By the 1600s the word "race" (or a version of it in another language) was found in most European language dictionaries.

The Platonic notion of ideal types and the Christian concept of a great chain of being are deep concepts about the world that paved the way for the idea of race. The Platonic notion of ideal types holds that the physical and material world is derived from a real world of pure ideals. This "world of ideals" is explicitly stable; evolution does not exist, except in the potential for devolution from the ideal. The method of science/philosophy is not experimental and empirical, but aims to discover or imagine the ideal types through thinking about them. An inanimate object such as a chair, although a human construction, is to be evaluated insofar as it maintains more or less closely the characteristics of the ideal type of chair. In a similar way, animals and plants are evaluated in relation to how they resemble the ideal type of each respective animal and plant. Humans could also be evaluated in relationship to their ideal types. For

Plato, there were ideal male and female types, and ideal soldiers, servants, and aristocrats.

In the idea of a great chain of being in early Christianity, all "God's creatures" are considered to occupy a rung on the great chain (Lovejoy 1936). The higher the rung, the closer to God; the lower, the further from God. As is made clear in illustrations in books well into the 20th century, white Europeans occupied the top rungs, while others were further down the chain, typically placed between Europeans and primate species. Each race had a fixed and unchanging place relative to God.

Platonic idealism, of course, is flawed because it rests on the assumption that there are ideal types "out there" that are unchanging and with preordained functions, and places in life to match these functions. It was thoroughly incapable of seeing how these types are socially constructed. This lack of reflectiveness is all the more obvious in the more explicit ranking of races embedded in the great chain of being.

The above notwithstanding, before 1492 there was no obvious public or scientific concern with thinking that human differences were innate, fixed, or racial (Hannaford 1996; Smedley 1999). This changed when Europeans began to explore different parts of the world in the name of God and in search of gold and glory. Then, the idea of race became useful as a means of justifying European capitalist expansion. At this point the study of human variation becomes an important endeavor and with it was born a theory of racialism, the belief that humans are and always have been divided into a fixed number of discrete human races (types). The goals of this science of racialism were to describe these types and demonstrate how they are manifest in behavioral and biological characteristics. The science starts with efforts at classification and explanation by Buffon (1749) and Linnaeus, in the tenth edition of his *Systema Naturae* (1758), and extends through to works by the early French, German, and English natural historians, who tinkered with these classification schemes and began to consider why variation existed. For Linnaeus, race explained customs, systems of government, and psychological characteristics.

From this point race was widely used by scientists and politicians, and became a popularly recognized idea, so much so that it was taken to be reality. It filtered into languages and etched itself on the minds of 18th- to 20th-century Europeans (Hannaford 1996; Smedley 1999; Stepan 1982; Todorov 1993). The processes by which a folk idea such as race becomes a scientific one and is then made-to-seem real is surely variable. However, it is clear that ideas that are useful to the ruling class (with control of legislation, access to and control over information, etc.) tend over time to be accepted as certain, natural, and real.

The concept of race remains a typological and non-evolutionary concept. Surprisingly, then, many continue to use race despite the fact that the notion of fixed, ideal types should logically have been replaced well over 100 years ago with the advent of Darwinism and the dominance of evolutionary theory in biology and anthropology. The concept survives, where it obviously does not fit either fact or theory, because: (1) it became reified by constant use, (2) it became conflated with human variation, and (3) it was and is politically useful.

Anthropology and Race

Boas being the main exception, up until World War II anthropology was the study of race. How intimate and how close is the association between anthropology and racialism can be seen in Tylor's definition of anthropology as the study of "man and the races of man" (Tylor 1946 [1881] in Smedley 1993:2). Furthermore J. Deniker's (1904) textbook in Charles Scribner's "Contemporary Science Series" is titled *The Races of Man: An Outline of Anthropology and Ethnography*. What comes before the colon, "the races of man" is aligned with what comes after the colon, "an outline of anthropology and ethnography." Here, all that we think of as involved in the study of anthropology – comparative and evolutionary approaches to biological variation as well as human custom, religion, myth, political institutions, and language – is subsumed under a study of different types of humans, called races. Deniker starts with a section on "distinctive morphological characteristics of human races" and then moves seamlessly on to physiological characteristics, ethnic characters, linguistic characters, material life, and psychic life. The association of racialism and anthropology is absolute.

In physical anthropology the sway of racialism and biological determinism remained for a very long time. Earnest Albert Hooton, founding father of American physical anthropology and, as a professor at Harvard, the advisor to the first generation of physical anthropologists, decried the obvious racism of the great chain of being. At the same time he continued to use race as a taxonomic tool and he continued to make generalizations based on differences among races, including that "we are fairly safe to assume that the Australian is far less intelligent than is the Englishman" (Hooton 1946:158).

What is evident in the writing of Hooton and other major figures in physical anthropology around the middle of this century was their lack of comfort with typology and their problems in fitting the data to typological notions. Few saw beyond typology, however, or saw how they were constrained by the reification of race (Blakey 1987; Brace 1982). One who did and became an outsider in his own discipline, Ashley Montagu, called race man's most dangerous myth, and the phlogiston of his time (Montagu 1962, 1963, 1964).

Although race began to leave the anthropological and scientific lexicon after World War II (Lieberman et al. 1989), a perusal of the literature makes clear that the idea of race never disappeared (Goodman and Armelagos 1996). The recent popularity of *The Bell Curve* (Herrnstein and Murray 1994) and the pop-racial sociobiology of Phillippe Rushton (1995) provides a clear reminder.

The Demise of Race

The decline in popularity of the concept of race is commonly held to be due to changing politics, including the entrance of women and Jewish scholars into anthropology after World War II (Barkan 1992). This opening up of anthropology may certainly be important, but it should not overshadow the fact that there are profound and fundamental scientific reasons that speak against race. As Begley (1995) declared in *Newsweek*, when it comes to a critique of race, "science got here first."

As Montagu made clear over half a century ago, race is not a reality; it is not a thing. Race is a biological concept; it is a way of constructing and thinking about human variability. We tend to think of it as a reality, because it has become reified by its constant use and the lack of questioning of its underlying reality.

Definitions of race are varied and protean. For example, some classifications are based on geographic origin (with some assumed biological concordance), others are based on clusters of traits, and others still are based on bureaucratic and social definitions (again, with an assumption of a biological basis). There is no agreed definition (Brace 1982). Furthermore, all efforts at a scientific (widely accepted, reliable) definition have failed. Brace captured the assumptive and protean nature of race when he comments on racialist research:

> The connection between the biology discussed and the races named at the end is never clearly spelled out, and in fact the attentive reader cannot discover, from the information presented, just how the racial classification was constructed – other than the fact that this just seems to be the way anthropologists have always done things.   (Brace 1982:21)

With differences in definition it is not surprising that there is also no agreement on the names and numbers of races. Thus, in forensic anthropology this powerful act of naming is left in the hands of bureaucrats and politicians with minimal knowledge of human variation. The inability to define race, the inability to agree on how many races there are, and the inability to agree upon what biological criteria make a race, show that this concept is slippery at best, making for problematic politics and biology. The following six points summarize why race is not a useful shorthand for human variation.

(1) *Race is not an evolutionary concept.*   Humans change through time and space. Race, however, cannot account for these changes. This is one of the problems faced by those who want to racialize Kennewick Man. Human biologies change over decades because of population mixing and other evolutionary forces. However, these changes cannot be accounted for by a static and typological concept.

(2) *Most traits are continuously varying and clinally distributed.*   Traits change in a multitude of increments from one individual or group to another. If groups are defined on the basis of biological trait frequencies, then there are typically no clear borders between where one group begins and another ends. Say, for example, we decide to use height to define groups. If we determined that there were to be two groups, then where would one make the division between tall and short people? It could be at 70 inches, 71 inches, or 200 cm. The "cutoff" point is arbitrary and a matter of convenience. Those near the

cutoff on either side are more like each other than they are like others in their group. Similarly, it is impossible to fix boundaries between races. There are no natural gaps. The division point is arbitrary and up to the whim of the classifier. Worse, this classification of a continuous trait into discrete units diminishes the true nature of human variation.

(3) *Most trait pairs are nonconcordant.* That is, traits tend to vary in different ways. The significance of this fact is that knowing the distribution of one trait can rarely explain or predict the distribution of a second. For example, knowing skin color provides no insight into height or any other anthropometric attribute. Why should it? These traits are under different selective pressures. They are not packaged together. This is why race is said to be "only skin deep."

(4) *Within-group variation is much greater than between-group variation.* There is so much variation within any purported race, about 94 percent of total genetic diversity (Lewontin 1972; Nei and Roychoudhury 1982), that extrapolation from the group to the individual is essentially meaningless. This fact suggests that two individuals of the same purported race are only marginally more genetically alike than any two individuals chosen at random. Because of nonconcordance and within-group variation, the concept has little explanatory power. If we know race, we know little more. Race tells us little about the processes governing human variation and it has trivial predictive value for knowing something about individuals.

(5) *The classification is not stable across space and time.* Division points are arbitrary and up to the whim of the classifier. Thus, an individual who might be classified as "European" or "white" at one time and place is classified as "mixed," "Hindu," "quadroon," "octoroon," "colored," "mulatto," "mestizo," or "black" at another time and place (Lee 1993). Jews were considered to be a separate race (or even many racial types) before World War II, and then they became white after the war (Sacks 1994). Similar "whitening" happened for the Irish and Southern Europeans. Fish (1995) writes of how his wife and daughter "change race" when they fly from the United States to Brazil. Their biologies do not change, but the cultural classification system does. Changing racial classification is fine and appropriate for a social construct. However, because sciences such as medicine are based on repeatability, changing classifications are disastrous for a scientific construct.

(6) The unexamined movement from social definition of race to biology leads to conflation of biology and lived experience. This clouds whether observed racial types are due to lived experience, genes, or a tangled gene–environment combination. Furthermore, when genes come into play, the assumption is that a racial analysis might substitute for a more detailed individual genetic analysis.

Thomas Patterson (Chapter 9, this volume) writes that diversity "is socially and culturally constructed." Thus, the salient categories of diversity – and the meanings of these categories – are produced, and vary, over time and cultural space. Race is such a category. We tend to think of race as deep and primordial. Race seems self-evident. But the deepness of this thought that race is universal, inherent, and real, only shows the power of a racial worldview (Smedley 1999).

What I have tried to do above is to "problematize" not the classification itself, but the implied biological basis of the classification. This implied biological basis of race has led to racialism and racism. Thus, it is useful to decouple race as a biological term from social groupings. This should clarify the biology of oppression and racism. African American babies die at a rate twice that of European American babies (David and Collins 1991, 1997), not because of race (read biology), but because of institutional and other forms of racism. Over a century ago Darwin said: "if the misery of our poor be caused not by the laws of nature, but by our institutions, great is our sin."

From Race to Radical Bioculturalism

Although race is a biological myth, biology and race are still important. They are just different, and they connect in different ways. In this section I provide examples of how race as biology fails as a scientific device and suggest ways in which it might be replaced.

Race and human evolution

Archaeologists and prehistorians have a tendency to think about populations and cultures of the past as interacting like billiard balls. They are discrete: when one ball is in motion it either collides with another ball or it misses altogether. If it hits another ball then it either deflects off, or it moves the hit ball. Sometimes the hit ball is displaced and goes somewhere else, possibly into a pocket, extinct forever. The key point is that the billiard balls do not change their essence. The "8 ball" does not become a 7.9 or 8.1.

The current debate over human origins, between the supporters of the multiregional model (in situ evolution and population continuity; Wolpoff and Caspari 1997) and the out-of-Africa model replacement (Stringer and McKie 1996), is an example of this. The billiard ball of a population that came out of Africa either hit all the others and knocked them into the pockets (replacement), or it missed (continuity). No middle group is left for intermingling and partial replacement. In presenting some of the questions that Kennewick Man might help us answer, Chatters (1998) presupposes replacement and asks how and by whom Kennewick and his clan were replaced. The white billiard ball (Kennewick Man's alleged group) was knocked off the table by one of a darker hue.

It might be useful to think of ancient peoples as nearly always being in motion. Affiliations were constantly shifting and the borders between one group and another were generally fuzzy. The political scientist Eqbal Ahmad (Hampshire College) has often pointed out that ethnic hybridity and multiculturalism are the rules; the past was a multicultural and multiethnic place. If true, biology should reflect this, and, indeed, it does. Genetic change was (and is) not dramatic (or racial) but slow and continuous. One group bumped into another and they exchanged partners, and the process continued into the next valley and valleys beyond.

The conceptual lens through which the peopling of the Americas is viewed leads to a vision of populations (and their genes) as race-like billiard balls. To the contrary, archaeological evidence indicates that the Americas have long been a place of extensive trade networks and contacts. Groups were in constant interaction, sometimes hostile, frequently utilitarian, often friendly. Biological analyses need to take this into account.

The billiard ball model developed as part of the 19th-century worldview in which miscegenation, or race crossing, was a great fear. The builders of the Egyptian pyramids were assumed to be whites, but the modern-day Egyptians were Other. The only way left open to get from ancient to contemporary Egypt was through population replacement. The same worldview considered contemporary Native Americans as non-white and the builders of the Mesoamerican and Mayan pyramids as a mystery group. Both of these racist scenarios were overturned by evidence of cultural and genetic continuities. The change is that the white billiard ball never was there to begin with. Now, Chatters's interpretation of Kennewick Man (1998), interestingly, represents an attempt to reinsert the white billiard ball. But the crude billiard ball model remains in nearly all analyses.

I am willing to bet that the peopling of the Americas was more complex than has been realized. The many families and bands that likely wandered across the Bering Strait without doubt carried genetic residues of individuals who resided across the Pacific. After all, the idea of race was not yet invented and these ancient peoples probably did not share fears of miscegenation with their 19th-century chroniclers. Groups and individuals could certainly have entered the Americas from further to the south. Why not? The point is that thinking in terms of race oversimplified the peopling of the Americas. And the same thinking is not going to let us see the complexities of past human interactions in North, Central, and South America.

Forensic anthropology

One of the fundamental goals of skeletal biology and its daughter field of forensic anthropology is accuracy with regard to the demographic characterization of individuals and groups. Parts of this characterization include the assignment of race or ancestry.

While forensic anthropologists lament that due to migration and intermixture it is more difficult to assign race now than in the past, with few possible exceptions such as Sauer (1992, 1993), the reality of races seems never to have been seriously questioned. In most cities in the United States the dichotomy of white and black is no longer as obvious as it once seemed. Asians, Native Americans, and various Hispanic groups make less certain the work of assigning race to a skeleton. The American "melting pot" makes the job of assigning race harder (St. Hoyme and Iscan 1989). Harder, yes, yet the underlying validity of the paradigm of human races is nearly unquestioned.

Forensic research articles on the determination of race are relatively uniform. Race is known from some form of documentation (such as a researcher's observations or death registration) and multivariate techniques are used to discriminate among two or more racial groups (Thompson 1982). Forensic reports typically involve completing a series of measurements and observations and then estimating race based on fit to a formula.

Perhaps the most widely used method of racial assessment, and one of the few methods to be independently evaluated, is Giles and Elliot's (1962) discriminant function for separating white, black and Native Americans based on cranial measurements. Like most techniques, this method is very good at identification of race on the test sample. This is an obvious and somewhat circular truth because it is upon the test sample that the best formulae to distinguish groups are constructed. However, when formulae are tested in other contexts the rate of correct identification is seriously reduced if the groups are not part of the same population. The Giles and Elliot (1962) formulae have been tested at least four times on individuals of known Native American ancestry. In three of the four cases the percentage of correct identifications is actually less than chance. As I have said before, this is not even good enough for government work (Goodman 1997).

The problem of applying racial formulae to determining the race of bones in different places is well known in forensic anthropology (Brues 1992; Sauer 1992). However, the reason for the problem and its implications has not been widely acknowledged. It is the forensic anthropologist's goal to provide "bureaucratic race," that which is officially recognized (St. Hoyme and Iscan 1989). However, bureaucratic races change and they may have little to do with biology (Lee 1993). Finally, biologies change too. Native Americans from Maine are not biologically homogeneous with those from Minnesota. The inability to use a formula derived in one place for skulls in another tells us that we are not dealing with the same population.

Fortunately, race is not an essential concept for forensic anthropology. The rhetoric of racial types could easily be changed to that of continental ancestry without affecting law enforcement efforts. More importantly, the applied goal of forensic anthropology is to describe as well as possible how individuals looked, and other aspects of their biologies. To think one has done this by plugging data into an equation and degrading the information to an estimate of racial affinity is misleading. Perhaps we can do better by going back to description – to the description of facial and postcranial architecture and other keys to individual identification. After all, the forensic puzzle is not the identification of race, it is the identification of an individual.

Race and biomedical research

Racial differences in health and disease are hot topics. In the last few years the National Institutes of Health inaugurated a new "Research Center on the Psychobiology of Ethnicity" to study how different groups respond to medications (Holden 1991), and a journal titled *Ethnicity and Disease* was launched to foster the study and the spread of information on aspects of the intersection of human variation and disease (Cooper 1991). Concerned with the use of race and ethnicity in medical research, the Centers for Disease

Control and Prevention (CDC) convened an expert workshop on the "use of race and ethnicity in public health surveillance" (MMWR 1993). Is race a useful way to think about human biological variation in studies of morbidity, mortality, and health care?

At least two fundamental problems repeatedly arise when assuming that the measured race differences in disease rates are biological and can be generalized to a racial propensity or predisposition. First, the environment is rarely controlled for. Second, the results once assumed to be genetic are reduced to the equating of genetic with pan-racial. Thus, one is often faced with a double leap of scientific faith: that a disease is genetic in etiology and that genetic equates with a racial-genetic predisposition.

A paper entitled "Transitional Diabetes and Gallstones in Amerindian Peoples: Genes or Environment?" (Weiss 1991) illustrates this problem. By the title ". . . Genes or Environment?" the author makes clear that he purports to test whether high rates of disease are the result of genes or environment. Of course, the dichotomy of genes or environment is a false one, and the author is surely using this for pedagogical purposes. Yet, aside from this point of simplification, how balanced is the analysis? One paragraph is devoted to environmental etiology and ends with the sentence: "Many potential confounding factors make these results difficult to interpret" (Weiss 1991:111). Having dismissed environmental etiology, the author proceeds to discuss at length and in very optimistic tones preliminary research that shows weak correlations between genetic markers and diabetes rates, not questioning at all the correlative nature of the research. The notion that diseases such as diabetes, gallstones, and obesity are prevalent in Native Americans because of a genetic predisposition is reified further by the development of the term "New World Syndrome" (Weiss et al. 1984).

Research on race and anemia provides a further example of the public health implication of assuming that group differences are due to biological race. In the 1970s Garn and colleagues presented data on the distribution of hemoglobin levels in blacks and whites in the United States. They reported an approximate 1.0 g/dl mean difference (blacks less than whites; Garn, Smith, and Clark 1974; Garn, Ryan, et al. 1975; Garn 1976). Following this work, the suggestion was made to institute separate cutoffs for anemia for blacks and whites.

Robert Jackson (1990, 1992, 1993) has reexamined some of these same data and has introduced new data. He controls for obvious environmental factors such as iron intake, and eliminates from analysis low hemoglobin values that may be related to genetic anemias. In doing this he finds that the mean hemoglobin difference between blacks and whites is reduced to the 0.2–0.3 g/dl range.

Despite these data very knowledgeable researchers such as Pan and Habicht (1991) continue to call for separate hemoglobin cutoffs for classification of anemia in blacks and whites. However, if the black cutoff is reduced just 0.5 g/dl, from 12.0 g/dl to 11.5 g/dl, half the difference proposed by Garn et al. (1974), the prevalence of anemia in nonpregnant, nonlactating black women (18–44 years) is estimated to be reduced "on paper" from 20 to 10 percent (Pan and Habicht 1991).

Yet still, separate cutoffs are supported despite the fact that the purported "race" difference in iron metabolism has no known genetic basis, especially not one that suggests that blacks are uniformly more efficient than whites in their metabolism of iron, or that they somehow do just as well on 0.5 g/dl less hemoglobin. Nor has it been proven that the difference is pan-racial. This issue, of course, is more than a theoretical one: separate cutoffs lead to profound health implications when one considers some of the functional consequences (in learning, work, and immunological capacity) of low hemoglobin values in ranges near anemia cutoff values (Scrimshaw 1991).

The report from the CDC workshop on race in medical research highlights the fact that the lack of clarity over whether race differences are reflective of genetic or nongenetic factors is a serious constraint to public health (MMWR 1993). Among its conclusions are that "because most associations between disease and race have no biological basis, race – as a biological concept – is not useful in public health surveillance" (1993:12).

Further, racial categories are too broad to be meaningful, there is no clear definition of race, the Office of Management and Budget (OMB) Directive 15 (which delineates the racial categories for federal agencies) has no scientific basis, distinctions between race and ethnicity are unclear, concepts of race change over time, and their meanings differ among individuals. The CDC report goes further still in its conclusion that emphasis on race in public health reinforces racist stereotyping and diverts attention from underlying socioeconomic factors (MMWR 1993:12–13). Somewhat conversely, it may be useful to maintain race as a social construct and as a means to monitor the health consequences of racism.

I agree with the CDC finding that this untheorized use of race is extremely problematic (see also Dressler 1993; Hahn et al. 1992; Hahn 1992). The implications of the undertheorizing are that differences are assumed to be due to genetics, and this approach reinforces a form of victim blaming. Yet the 2.4-fold higher relative risk of infant mortality of black babies over white babies in the United States cannot be explained by genetic predisposition (David and Collins 1991). How this difference might be related to different experiences of whites and blacks has recently been shown by David and Collins (1997). They find that babies born in Illinois to African-born women have birth weights that are closer to the babies of U.S.-born white women than to babies of U.S.-born black women.

This study shows how the experience of race is more important than the genetics of race. The CDC report suggests that racism, in both its material and ideological components, is more real than race. Racism and socioeconomic factors undoubtedly have more of an effect on health and biological welfare than race as biology. Unfortunately, the mixed messages of what race differences in morbidity and mortality signify continues to confuse the public, and many researchers. Perhaps the only way to clarify the message is to change the language.

Conclusions

Boas called for the separation of biology from culture because it was clear to him that biology could not account for differences in cultural position and achievement. I agree. But biology and culture still are intertwined in interesting and important ways. How we see an individual is based in part on biological cues, and the consequence of seeing and thinking about difference may be biological. That is, ideas about racial difference have consequences under the skin – they affect stress levels, birth weights, infant mortality rates, and more.

In a sense, by thinking of race as a sociopolitical concept or a social formation, we are turning it upside down. It is in this way, however, that we might reintegrate anthropology and move toward what could be called **radical bioculturalism** (Goodman and Leatherman 1998).

Acknowledgments

Parts of this chapter have been adopted from previous publications on race (Goodman 1995, 1998). A wide circle of colleagues have contributed to the ideas expressed in this paper. I am particularly in debt to George Armelagos (Emory), Lee Baker (Columbia), Michael Blakey (Howard), John Marks (University of North Carolina, Charlotte), Debra Martin (Hampshire College), and the late Ashley Montagu.

REFERENCES CITED

Barkan, E.
   1992   *The Retreat of Scientific Racism.* New York: Cambridge University Press.
Begley, Sharon
   1995   Three Is Not Enough. *Newsweek*, February 13:67–69.
Blakey, Michael
   1987   Skull Doctors: Intrinsic Social and Political Bias in the History of American Physical Anthropology. *Critique of Anthropology* 7(2):7–35.
Boas, Franz
   1940   *Race, Language and Culture.* New York: The Free Press.
Brace, C. Loring
   1982   The Roots of the Race Concept in American Physical Anthropology. In *A History of American Physical Anthropology, 1930–1980.* Frank Spenser, ed. Pp. 11–29. New York: Academic Press.
Brues, Alice
   1992   Forensic Diagnosis of Race – General Race vs. Specific Populations. *Social Science and Medicine* 34(2):125–128.
Chatters, J.
   1997   Encounter with an Ancestor. *Anthropology Newsletter*, January: 9–10.
   1998   Human Biological History, not Race. *Anthropology Newsletter*, February: 19, 21.
Cooper, R.
   1991   Celebrate Diversity – Or Should We? *Ethnicity and Disease* 1(1):3–7.
David, R. J., and J. W. Collins
   1991   Bad Outcomes in black Babies: Race or Racism? *Ethnicity and Disease* 1:236–244.
   1997   Differing Birth Weight among Infants of U.S.-Born Blacks, African-Born Blacks, and U.S.-Born Whites. *New England Journal of Medicine* 337:1209–1214.

Deniker, J.
  1904   *The Races of Man: An Outline of Anthropology and Ethnography*. New York: Charles Scribner's.
Dressler, W.
  1993   Health in the African American Community: Accounting for Health Inequalities. *Medical Anthropology Quarterly* 7(4):325–345.
Fish, Jefferson
  1995   Mixed Blood. *Psychology Today*, November/December: 56–61, 76, 80.
Garn, S. M.
  1976   Problems in the Nutritional Assessment of Black Individuals. *American Journal of Public Health* 66:262–267.
Garn, S. M., N. J. Smith, and D. C. Clark
  1974   Race Differences in Hemoglobin Levels. *Ecology of Food and Nutrition* 3:299–301.
Garn, S. M., A. S. Ryan, G. M. Owen, et al.
  1975   Income Matched Black–White Differences in Hemoglobin Levels after Correction for Low Transferrin Saturations. *American Journal of Clinical Nutrition* 28:563–568.
Giles, E., and O. Elliot
  1962   Race Identification from Cranial Measurements. *Journal of Forensic Sciences* 7:217–257.
Goodman, A. H.
  1995   The Problematics of "Race" in Contemporary Biological Anthropology. In *Biological Anthropology: The State of the Science*. N. T. Boaz and L. D. Wolfe, eds. Pp. 215–239. Bend, OR: International Institute for Human Evolutionary Research.
  1997   Bred in the Bone? *The Sciences*, March/April: 20–25.
  1998   Archaeology and Human Biological Variation. *Conference on New England Archaeology Newsletter* 17:1–8.
Goodman, A., and G. J. Armelagos
  1996   Race, Racism and the New Physical Anthropology. In *Race and Other Misadventures: Essays in Honor of Ashley Montagu in his Ninetieth Year*. Larry T. Reynolds and Leonard Lieberman, eds. Pp. 174–186. Dix Hills, NY: General Hall.
Goodman, A. H., and T. L. Leatherman
  1998   Transversing the Chasm between Biology and Culture. In *Building a New Biocultural Synthesis: Political-Economic Perspectives on Human Biology*. Alan H. Goodman and Thomas L. Leatherman, eds. Pp. 3–42. Ann Arbor: University of Michigan Press.
Hahn, R.
  1992   The State of Federal Health Statistics on Racial and Ethnic Groups. *Journal of the American Medical Association* 267(2):268–271.
Hahn, R., J. Mulinare, and S. Teutsch
  1992   Inconsistencies in Coding Race and Ethnicity between Birth and Death in U.S. Infants. *Journal of the American Medical Association* 267(2):259–263.
Hannaford, I.
  1996   *Race: The History of an Idea in the West*. Baltimore: Johns Hopkins University Press.
Herrnstein, Richard, and Charles Murray
  1994   *The Bell Curve: Intelligence and Class Structure in American Life*. New York: Free Press.
Holden, C.
  1991   New Center to Study Therapies and Ethnicity. *Science* 251:748.

Hooton, E.
1946   *Up from the Apes*. New York: Macmillan.
Jackson, R, T.
1990   Separate Hemoglobin Standards for Blacks and Whites: A Critical Review of the Case for Separate and Unequal Hemoglobin Standards. *Medical Hypotheses* 32:181–189.
1992   Hemoglobin Comparisons between African American and European American Males with Hemoglobin Values in the Normal Range. *Journal of Human Biology* 4:313–318.
1993   Hemoglobin Comparisons in a Sample of European and African American Children. *Ecology of Food and Nutrition* 29:139–146.
Lee, S. M.
1993   Racial Classifications in the U.S. Census: 1890–1990. *Ethnicity and Racial Studies* 16(1):75–94.
Lewontin, R. C.
1972   The Apportionment of Human Diversity. *Evolutionary Biology* 6: 381–398.
Lieberman, L., B. W. Stevenson, and L. T. Reynolds
1989   Race and Anthropology: A Core Concept without Consensus. *Anthropology and Education Quarterly* 20(2):67–73.
Lovejoy, A. O.
1936   *The Great Chain of Being*. Cambridge, MA: Harvard University Press.
Montagu, A.
1962   The Concept of Race. *American Anthropologist* 64:919–928.
1963   *Race, Science and Humanity*. New York: Van Nostrand.
1964   *Man's Most Dangerous Myth: The Fallacy of Race*. New York: Meridian Books.
Morbidity and Mortality Weekly Report (MMWR)
1993   Use of Race and Ethnicity in Public Health Surveillance, 42 (No. RR-10). Center for Disease Control and Prevention, Atlanta.
Mozzochi, J.
1998   Race and Relics. *The Dignity Report* 5:4–7.
Muir, D.
1993   Race: The Mythic Roots of Racism. *Sociological Inquiry* 63(3):339–350.
Nei, M., and A. K. Roychoudhury
1982   Genetic Relationship and Evolution of Human Races. *Evolutionary Biology* 14:1–59.
Pan, W. H., and J. P. Habicht
1991   The Non-Iron-Deficiency-Related Differences in Hemoglobin Concentration Distribution between Blacks and Whites and between Men and Women. *American Journal of Epidemiology* 134:1410–1416.
Rushton, J. P.
1995   *Race, Evolution and Behavior*. New Brunswick, NJ: Transaction Books.
Sacks, Karen
1994   How Did Jews Become White Folks? In *Race*. S. Gregory and R. Sanjek, eds. Pp. 78–101. New Brunswick, NJ: Rutgers University Press.
Sauer, N.
1992   Forensic Anthropology and the Concept of Race: If Races Don't Exist, Why Are Forensic Anthropologists so Good at Identifying Them? *Social Science and Medicine* 34:107–111.

1993 Applied Anthropology and the Concept of Race: A Legacy of Linnaeus. In *Race, Ethnicity and Applied Bioanthropology*. C. C. Gordon, ed. NAPA Bulletin 13:79–84. Washington, DC: American Anthropological Association.

Scrimshaw, N.
1991 Iron Deficiency. *Scientific American*, October: 46–52.

Shanklin, E.
1994 *Anthropology and Race*. Belmont, CA: Wadsworth.

Smedley, A.
1999 *Race in North America: Origin and Evolution of a Worldview*. 2nd edition. Boulder, CO: Westview Press.

Stepan, N.
1982 *The Idea of Race in Science: Great Britain, 1800–1960*. New York: Macmillan.

St. Hoyme, L. E., and M. Y. Iscan
1989 Determination of Sex and Race: Accuracy and Assumptions. In *Reconstruction of Life from the Skeleton*. M. Y. Iscan and K. A. R. Kennedy, eds. Pp. 53–93. New York: Liss.

Stringer, C., and R. McKie
1996 *African Exodus*. New York: Henry Holt.

Thompson, D. D.
1982 Forensic Anthropology. In *A History of American Physical Anthropology, 1930–1980*. F. Spenser, ed. Pp. 357–369. New York: Academic Press.

Todorov, T.
1993 *On Human Diversity*. Cambridge, MA: Harvard University Press.

Weiss, K.
1991 Transitional Diabetes and Gallstones in Amerindian Peoples: Genes or Environment? In *Disease in Populations in Transition*. A. C. Swedlund and G. J. Armelagos, eds. Pp. 105–123. Hadley, MA: Bergin and Garvey.

Weiss, K., R. Ferrell, and C. L. Hanis
1984 A New World Syndrome of Metabolic Diseases with a Genetic and Evolutionary Basis. *Yearbook of Physical Anthropology* 27:153–178.

Wolpoff, M., and R. Caspari
1997 *Race and Human Evolution*. New York: Simon and Schuster.

ANNOTATED BIBLIOGRAPHY

Blakey, M. (1987) Skull Doctors: Intrinsic Social and Political Bias in the History of American Physical Anthropology. *Critique of Anthropology* 7(2):7–35. [Excellent treatment of the work and correspondences of Ales Hrdlicka, one of the founding fathers of physical anthropology, especially in relationship to race and naturalism.]

Goodman, A. H. (1997) Bred in the Bone? *The Sciences*, March/April: 20–25. [On how race is used in forensic and medical research. Goodman maintains that the same illogic that plagues studies of race and intelligence is also seen in these areas of research. He maintains that the use of race in less publicized areas causes just as much harm as its use in more politicized arenas.]

Gould, S. J. (1996) *The Mismeasure of Man*. 2nd edition. New York: W. W. Norton. [Gould presents a now classic treatment of the history of research into race differences in behavior and intelligence. He provides a detailed treatment of early research on cranial size, shape, and capacity, and race, criminality, and the history of development of the IQ test. The second edition also addresses *The Bell Curve*, Herrnstein and Murray, 1994.]

Hannaford, I. (1996) *Race: The History of an Idea in the West*. Baltimore: Johns Hopkins University Press. [A thorough history of the development of race as a political idea. Hannaford tracks the political idea from "pre-race" (before 1492) through to the present. He contrasts race with other civic ideals.]

Hoberman, J. (1997) *Darwin's Athletes*. Boston: Houghton Mifflin. [On race and athletic performance. Although Hoberman never gives up the idea of race as biologically useful, he does show how changes in the performance of black athletes has dramatically shifted ideas about race. In the 19th century whites were generally thought to be superior in all attributes – moral, intellectual, and physical. Now the dominant discourse is of an evolutionary trade-off between morality and intelligence and physical ability.]

Marks, J. (1995) *Human Biodiversity*. Chicago: Aldine. [This is a highly readable textbook on human variation and also a history of how human variation has been studied in physical anthropology.]

Montagu, A. (1964) *Man's Most Dangerous Myth: The Fallacy of Race*. New York: Meridian Books. [A classic treatment on why race is not a valid biological concept.]

Reynolds L. T., and L. Lieberman, eds. (1996) *Race and Other Misadventures: Essays in Honor of Ashley Montagu in his Ninetieth Year*. Dix Hills, NY: General Hall. [Excellent series of articles on the history and misuses of race in physical anthropology and beyond.]

Smedley, A. (1999) *Race in North America: Origin and Evolution of a Worldview*. Boulder, CO: Westview Press. [Similar to Hannaford, this book provides a very useful history of race. Smedley focuses more on how race became a reified worldview and she also focuses more on anthropology and the academy.]

Stringer, C., and R. McKie (1996) *African Exodus*. New York: Henry Holt. [On race in human evolutionary research. Stringer and McKie suggest that because of recent evolution, weare all Africans under the skin.]

Tucker, W. (1994) *The Science and Politics of Racial Research*. Chicago: University of Illinois Press. [An excellent history of the misuse of race in psychology.]

4

The Peoplings of the Americas: Anglo Stereotypes and Native American Realities

C. Loring Brace and A. Russell Nelson

Stereotypes

The intent of NAGPRA, the Native American Graves Protection and Repatriation Act, was that those who are legitimately tied by descent to the remains of people and their productions, intentionally or inadvertently removed from American soil and now located in various repositories such as museums and private collections, should be entitled to the return of what was rightfully theirs. As a general principle, this seems only fair and above-board, but there are some curious twists to what is often promoted as simple justice, and one of these is a legacy of Anglo-Saxon ethnocentrism that has come back to haunt us in a most misunderstood and unrecognized fashion. In spite of their knowledge and good intentions, all too many professional anthropologists have unwittingly accepted the simplistic stereotype of this tradition.

This is how it goes. All Anglos know that they are the descendants of immigrant ancestors. Yes, we know that most mainstream Americans are not descendants of English emigrants and that there is something just a bit odd in referring to those whose Old World antecedents were French, German, or Italian – or Greek, Russian, Syrian, Armenian, or whatever – as "Anglos," yet English is the accepted language of the country, and the cultural baggage that came along with the circumstances that produced that phenomenon has made us all Anglos willy-nilly – well, except for those whose ancestors unwillingly came from Africa. And then there's East Asia. When forced to look at it from a somewhat broader perspective, the Anglos have to admit that they are a most heterogeneous lot.

Whatever their ultimate origins, Americans of immigrant ancestry realize that they are all newcomers to a continent that had been inhabited, end-to-end, by predecessors who were not related to them. Consequently, it is generally conceded that all the remnants of prior human existence in the New World, whether those be artifacts or the bones of the people themselves, ipso facto belonged to those predecessors. The feeling has generally arisen, then, that the living descendants of the original Americans have the right to claim ownership of those remnants if they should choose to do so.

Many are now making that choice, but, ironically, by that very act they are demonstrating the extent to which they have accepted Anglo-American stereotypes. While it is true that Anglos now accept the "logic" of the claim that all prehistoric remains in the western hemisphere were those of the First Americans, and therefore the living representatives of those people have legitimate rights of ownership, there is a horrendous stereotype involved in that assumption. This is the implicit belief that all of those "First Americans" represented a single invariant entity. When the living descendants of the indigenous Americans make blanket claims of ownership to whatever has come out of the ground, this is a sign that they have bought the same stereotype.

Until the advent of post-Columbian immigrants, however, the original human inhabitants of the hemisphere had no sense of common identity. Those who lived on the other side of the mountain – or river, or lake – were not thought of as just manifestations of the same thing, who happened to live elsewhere. They were thought of as being competitors at best, although more often they were considered to be enemies. In any case, they were the "other." It wasn't until Europeans put them all into the status of their own collective "other" that they ever achieved any kind of perception of a common heritage. In 1772 Don Antonio Ulloa first articulated a version of the often-quoted European generalization: "An Indian is an Indian, if you've seen one, you've seen them all" (discussed in Prichard 1851:290). It was from this that the feeling arose that whatever emerged from the soil was part of a common heritage that was the equal birthright of all surviving Native Americans.

The time has come to test those contradictory assumptions. Is the immigrant assumption true that "if you've seen one, you've seen them all"? Or is the original Native American assumption true that all were different and unrelated? There is an ancillary question that also needs to be tested. This relates to the long-term suspicion that the original inhabitants of the western hemisphere were not only more closely related to the living peoples of East Asia than to anybody else in the world, but may themselves, in fact, have been immigrants from eastern Asia in the not-too-remote past.

Even this latter question, however, had been thought of in simplistic fashion because of the stereotypic perception of East Asians as "Mongoloids," again a version of the "seen one . . . seen all" kind of oversimplification. When we stop and think about it, we realize that "Caucasoids" from Northwest Europe and the Middle East are not all exactly the same thing – think, for example, of the contrast in appearance between Prince Philip on the one hand and Osama bin Laden on the other. A little bit of actual investigation can show that the Mongols from Ulan Baator north of the Gobi Desert and the Ainu from Hokkaido at the northeast end of the Japanese archipelago are really quite different from each other, and that the Manchu and the Han Chinese differ as much from them as they do from each other.

What about the Native Americans? Do they display a comparable extent of difference from each other? And if differences can be identified, can these be linked to the differences evident in the several parts of eastern Asia? When an actual effort is made to test the inhabitants of the various regions involved, the answer to most of these questions is a clear-cut yes.

Morphometric Comparisons

To assess the quantitative similarities and differences between the inhabitants of the areas under consideration, we have assembled a body of data consisting of some two dozen craniofacial measurements made on each of a selection of 859 individual skulls from eastern Asia and adjacent Oceania, and from 758 skulls spanning the western hemisphere from Alaska to Newfoundland and from Baffin Bay to Tierra del Fuego. We could have used a far larger number of samples and individuals (we have several thousand individuals from the New World and even more from East Asia), but what we chose here was a series of samples that most clearly depicts the distinctions displayed in both parts of the world. The raw measurements were converted into C-scores as pioneered by W. W. Howells (1986). These were used to generate Euclidean distance figures that were then converted into dendrograms where the distance between the twigs is proportionate to the magnitude of those Euclidean distance figures. The details of this multivariate procedure are spelled out in Brace et al. (1989). The branching diagrams, or dendrograms, exhibit in treelike fashion the closeness or distance between any given group and the others.

Asia and Oceania

We have used ten samples to stand for the peoples of eastern Asia and immediately adjacent Oceania. These are displayed in Figure 1. Twigs that branch off close to each other, as the Ainu and Polynesians, indicate that the people represented are morphologically very similar to each other. Both closely resemble the Jomon, the pre-agricultural inhabitants of the entire Japanese archipelago. The argument has been advanced that the Jomon are the ancestors of the Ainu, the surviving aborigines of Hokkaido, the northernmost of the Japanese islands, and also, via migration south and eastwards, the ancestors of the Polynesians – the inhabitants of "Remote Oceania" (Brace et al. 1989). That little cluster of Jomon, Ainu, and Polynesians is itself as different from the form represented by anyone else in Asia as it is possible to be and still be considered of Asian origin. Interestingly enough, the Mongols are as atypical of the appearance of anyone else on the Asian continent as any of the samples available. This has been demonstrated repeatedly in previous analyses (Brace and Hunt 1990; Pietrusewski et al. 1992), and it can serve as the basis for the generalization that the term "Mongoloid" is misleadingly inappropriate to use in referring to the physical characteristics that typify people of mainland Asian origin.

Our Chinese sample is of what would be called "Han Chinese" ranging from Shanghai, Shandong, Hebei, and Henan to Sichuan. These are obviously related to the Yayoi rice farmers who invaded southwestern Japan starting in 300 B.C.E. Not surprisingly, they tie with the Chinese Neolithic samples from Huang He (Yellow River) sites ranging from Xian in Shaanxi, central China, to Shandong in the east. The close link to Micronesia is somewhat more unexpected. Our

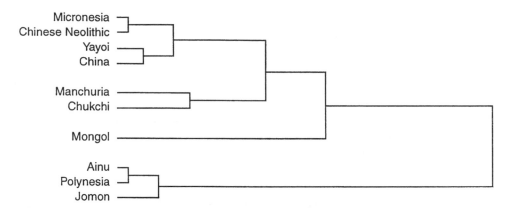

Figure 1 A Euclidean Distance dendrogram generated from the C-scores of the ten Asian and Pacific populations used. The samples are identified by name. The Yayoi sample represents the first rice agriculturalists in Japan; the Ainu are the living aborigines of Hokkaido, the northernmost of the Japanese islands; and the Jomon are the pre-agricultural – that is, pre-Yayoi – inhabitants of the entire Japanese archipelago.

Micronesian samples come from five of the Caroline Islands, largely in the western part of the archipelago.

The Western Hemisphere

In Figure 2, we have used nine samples to stand for the diversity represented in the New World. Only two of these come from South America. In part this is because we have had access to far fewer representatives of the southern hemisphere. We actually do have samples from Bolivia and Brazil, but since these tie tightly with our larger Peruvian sample, we have chosen the latter to stand for the bulk of the continent. As can be seen, it clusters closely with Mexico and with an assortment of samples from the southern United States, ranging from Alabama through Arkansas, Arizona, and southern California at Malibu on the coast just west of Los Angeles. The tie between the southern portions of what is now the United States with Meso- and South America is ancient, as is indicated by the linkages of the Kentucky and Tennessee Archaic with that southern cluster, and also by the fact that individual Paleoindian specimens such as Spirit Cave and Wizard Beach from Nevada and Buhl from Idaho also are closer to that southern grouping than to any other when they are tested by discriminant analysis (Nelson 1998). Our southern cluster, then, has to represent the configuration established by the first inhabitants of the western hemisphere.

As can easily be seen from Figure 2, the other inhabitants of the hemisphere are clearly distinct from the descendants of the initial population. The tie between the Inuit and the Aleuts is not unexpected, and the sharing of features between the Aleuts and the Athabascans has been previously discussed (Ousley 1995). As our only representatives of the Northwest Coast, we put in the Haida for reasons that will become apparent when we discuss Figure 3. Perhaps the

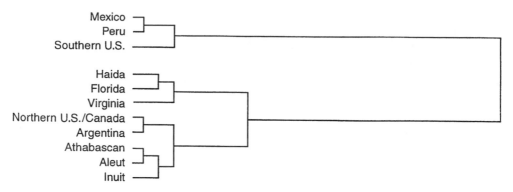

Figure 2 A Euclidean Distance dendrogram generated from C-scores for 11 groups of New World samples.

biggest surprise in Figure 2, however, is the tie between what we have identified as the Northern United States–Canada group and what we have called "Argentina." That latter actually includes a sampling of individuals from Patagonia and Tierra del Fuego at the southern end of South America. In our individual tests, we have been able to show that they clearly are the same people. The Northern United States–Canada group includes an east–west spectrum of Blackfoot, Minnesota, Michigan, Ontario, Iroquois, and Massachusetts samples, and, at its eastern extent, a north–south range that runs from the Newfoundland Archaic to Maryland and Virginia. Our small sample of Florida Archaic from the Windover site also fits in this spectrum, although we did not use it to construct the cluster depicted here. Whatever else it shows, Figure 2 clearly demonstrates that there is no one essence that one could call "Indian" in the New World.

An Asian-American perspective

Now if we combine the samples used to make up our Asian picture in Figure 1 with those used to make our New World picture in Figure 2, and use them to make a single composite dendrogram as in Figure 3, just look at what we find. Mesoamerica, South America and the southern United States still cling together to stand for what has to represent the descendants of the first humans to enter the western hemisphere. They have no obvious ties to any Asian groups. This could be because they have been separated from their Asian sources for the longest period of time, but it could also be because we do not have an adequate sampling of the northern inhabitants of the Far East.

The Jomon connection

In Figure 3, the Mongols still remain remote from the rest of mainland East Asia, but the Yayoi jump over and tie with them. This may tell us something about the composition of the population on the Korean peninsula from which

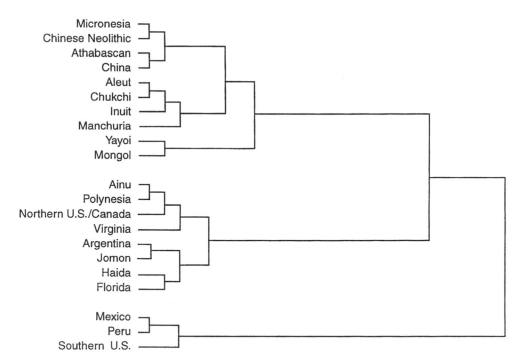

Figure 3 A Euclidean Distance dendrogram generated from the C-scores that are produced when all the samples used in Figures 1 and 2 are combined in a single Asian-American analysis.

the Yayoi farmers were derived before they crossed the Korea Strait to colonize southwestern Japan in ±300 B.C.E. One of the more surprising things shown in Figure 3, however, is the tie between the prehistoric people of Japan plus the modern Ainu not only with the people of Remote Oceania but also with the populations all the way across the U.S.–Canada border and from the Northwest Coast right down to the tip of South America. Although we do not show it in the dendrogram represented here, we have done other runs with a lot of other groups thrown at each other, and one set that fits in is from the San Francisco Bay area and adjacent parts of northern California. These tie nicely to the Haida in the north and the miscellaneous specimens we have called Argentina in Figure 3. The two specimens we have from Baja California also fit into this group.

It is our guess that what we can see in the recent inhabitants of the areas represented are the descendants of the terminal- and immediately Post-Pleistocene marine-resource-utilizing people who spread from Early Jomon Japan starting maybe as much as 12,000 years ago. Since their adaptation was geared to the sophisticated exploitation of the products of the sea, there was relatively little direct competition with the preceding hunters of the New World who had initially made use of the available megafauna as their subsistence base. There would have been virtually no opposition to a spread along the west coast of the entire hemisphere right down to its southern end by a canoe-using seafood-exploiting people, and the entire western shore of the continent could have been traversed and intermittently occupied in leisurely fashion in only a few millennia or so.

At the same time, the region of swamps, streams, and lakes left by the melting glaciers across the continent from west to east but north of the game-supporting plains would also have been prime territory for a water-resource-exploiting people even if what was being exploited was of a freshwater rather than a marine nature. As was true for the people spreading down the west coast fringe, those spreading east across the previously glaciated parts of North America would not have been in direct competition with their hunting and gathering predecessors who pursued their subsistence activities largely in the main continental regions to the south. At the moment, there is no other way to explain why it is that the Native American sample we have from Virginia ties just as closely to Jomon Japan as do the Haida. This does not show in the simplified picture presented in Figures 2 and 3, but it is clearly evident when we run our Virginia sample as a separate twig. In any case, as is shown in Figure 3, our combined northern U.S.–Canadian sample ties nicely in with the descendants of the Jomon – the Ainu of Hokkaido and the Polynesians of Remote Oceania – and at only a slight remove from the Haida, the Argentine sample, and the Jomon themselves.

The maritime Arctic and the Manchurian connection

The other marine-resource-utilizing people in the picture are the Inuit and their relatives. In some of our efforts at testing various samples, we can show a tendency to tie with the Jomon-derived cluster, and it is just possible that they represent an offshoot that had subsequently focused on utilizing what was available further north of what could be handled by Pleistocene and immediately post-Pleistocene levels of technological sophistication. Not unexpectedly, the Aleut tie with the Chukchi right across the Bering Strait, and these two then are linked with the Inuit. This grouping in turn clusters with the Manchu from Heilongjiang Province in the northeast of China. One would have to guess that the skin boat technology, sea-mammal-hunting and ice-fishing capabilities that allowed the Inuit to exploit the arctic regions of the New World from Alaska to Greenland were a late derivative of the marine resource focus of the northeast Asian coast after the end of the Pleistocene.

The Chinese–Athabascan connection

The Chinese remain tied with the Chinese Neolithic and Micronesia, but the other major surprise visible in Figure 3 is that the Athabascans are drawn tightly into that Chinese cluster. We can change the appearance of affinities by changing the nature of the samples used, but in this case, no matter how we rearrange things, the Chinese–Athabascan tie remains. Here it would seem that biological anthropology has provided a measure of support for what the brilliant linguist, Edward Sapir, had proposed to investigate before the outbreak of war in the

Far East in the late 1930s and the collapse of his own health put a stop to things before they could even be initiated (Darnell 1990). The irony in this instance is that Sapir had no use for biological anthropology as a part of anthropology per se (Darnell 1998).

The Athabascans can be regarded as the last Asian group to have made a separate incursion into the western hemisphere. If the first group made a go of it by exploiting the concentration of Late Pleistocene four-footed game animals, and the Jomon-derived group focused on the marine resources of the west coast and the lake and stream area left by the departed glaciers to the north, the Athabascan incursions may have been made possible by a focus on the extraction of nourishment from plant food resources in a manner quite unknown to earlier populations. It was such a Mesolithic kind of development that paved the way for the control of plants which generated the rise of agriculture in the temperate parts of eastern Asia maybe 9,000 years ago. While agriculture as such was not possible in the more boreal parts of Asia, the techniques of pounding, shredding, soaking, leaching, and cooking of all manner of plant material made it possible to survive in areas where the quantities of fish and game were not in themselves sufficient.

The extraordinary ingenuity of those northern exploiters of plant resources was documented in admirable fashion by that giant of American anthropology, Franz Boas. Often chided for having devoted nearly 300 pages of his *Ethnology of the Kwakiutl* to a presumably frivolous collection of "Recipes" (Boas 1921), that remarkable work documents as nothing else does how an essentially Mesolithic way of life was able to extract sustenance from the most "unobvious resources" (Hayden 1981:525). Although the Kwakiutl, as coastal dwellers, focused heavily on the products of the sea, Boas demonstrates how a sophisticated concentration on the "unobvious" parts of the plant world could enable a people to survive without coming into direct competition with fishing or hunting cultures. Of course, people with a focus on plants also fished and hunted, the fisherfolk also hunted and collected plant foods, and the hunters fished and collected as well.

It may have been such a concentration on the plant world that enabled the fourth and last component of the pre-European inhabitants of the New world, the Athabascan-speaking peoples, to have found a niche not preempted by the earlier entrants into the western hemisphere. Athabascan groups ranged from the Yukon drainage of Alaska and Northwest Canada inland from the coast, and they had gotten south as far as Arizona and northern Mexico by just under a thousand years ago. Their craniofacial configuration allies them more closely to the living Chinese than to any other population in either hemisphere.

Craniofacial pattern: antiquity and stability

The final question that needs mention concerns whether any of these four morphological patterns could have emerged by transformation from any of the others within the time span involved in the spread from Asia into the western hemisphere. Although this cannot be definitive at the present time, the answer is almost certainly no. For one thing, the 15,000 years or so of residence in the New World from the Arctic to the equator has not resulted in any systematic differentiation of human skin color corresponding to differences in latitude. Natural selection certainly produced the latitude-associated differences in skin color evident in the long-term regional inhabitants of the Old World. Evidently, however, a residence in a given area of vastly longer than 15,000 years was required.

Is it possible, however, that the adaptively unimportant aspects of cheek-bone formation or cranial contour could change from one of the observed configurations to another in that period of time? Although we cannot give a definitive answer, we can note that discriminant function tests show that the Jomon craniofacial pattern was clearly present at Minatogawa in Okinawa 18,000 years ago and at the Upper Cave of Zhoukoudian, just west of Beijing in China, 28,000 years ago (Brace and Tracer 1992). That pattern is preserved essentially unchanged today in northern Japan, the Northwest Coast of North America, across the Northern Plains of the United States and Canada to the east coast, and at the southern tip of South America. To give us some perspective from another part of the world, in Europe it can be shown that the Cro-Magnon configuration continues in the people who still inhabit the northwestern fringes such as the British Isles and Norway. At the same time, the post-Pleistocene craniofacial configuration that runs from France across through central and eastern Europe is clearly a different and unrelated pattern. The same kind of discriminant function test shows that an essentially African craniofacial pattern was present at Qafza in Israel over 90,000 years ago (Brace 1996). Evidently, and despite major changes in size and robustness, the kinds of craniofacial patterns for which our measurements provide documentation tend to remain stable for long periods of time.

Conclusions

Whatever else the material assembled here may indicate, the one firm conclusion to emerge is the demonstration that the "Native" inhabitants of the western hemisphere were not all minor variants of the same thing. The long-standing Anglo stereotype, that to have seen one Indian is to have seen all, is simply not true. The descendants of the first entrants into the New World – presumably the Late Pleistocene megafauna hunters – remain morphologically distinct from all the other known groups of people in both the Americas and in Asia.

The second craniofacial pattern to invade the western hemisphere was basically indistinguishable from the inhabitants of Jomon Japan dating from the end of the Pleistocene and surviving in Asia as the Ainu of the northernmost of the Japanese islands. The marine resource adaptation allowed Jomon-derived people to spread across the Bering Strait after the end of the Pleistocene and down the west coasts of North and then of South America. The historic inhabitants of Patagonia and Tierra del Fuego still retain the craniofacial configuration of their Jomon ancestors. A branch of this movement exploited the lake and river country left where the Pleistocene glaciers had melted. This branch colonized the entire stretch along the U.S.–Canadian border and down the eastern coast of the continent from Newfoundland to Florida. Another Jomon-derived movement in Asia proceeded directly south via the Ryukyus, Taiwan, and the Philippines starting in the Middle Jomon approximately 4,000 years ago. With the addition of the coconut and taro, these people spread into the Remote Pacific as Polynesians.

The third craniofacial pattern, the Inuit-Aleut configuration, spread widely across the arctic of the New World from Alaska to Greenland and down as far as Labrador. This was made possible by a specialization for northern use of the maritime resource utilization approach. It is not possible at present to say whether it represents a derivative from the earlier Jomon tradition, or whether it had separate origins. The Manchu of northeastern China and the Chukchi of northeastern Siberia are the representatives of this group on the Asian mainland, and may give a hint as to the location of their ultimate origins.

The fourth and final craniofacial pattern to enter the New World is that found among the Athabascan people inland in the Yukon drainage areas of Alaska and Northwest Canada and extending down the western edge of the continent just inland of the shore people and getting as far as Arizona and northern Mexico. These were able to exploit areas more sparsely utilized by the earlier entrants into the continent only because of the sophisticated plant-food-processing techniques developed by their post-Pleistocene Mesolithic predecessors north of the areas where Asian agriculture had its independent origins. The Athabascan craniofacial pattern still remains more similar to that now characteristic of China than to any other in either hemisphere.

Evidently, the distinctions between the various Asian-derived original inhabitants of the western hemisphere date back to before their initial movement into the New World. The craniometric data suggest that there were four such distinct groups, a conclusion that, although somewhat different in details, fits nicely with the general picture presented by analysis of mtDNA haplotype lineages (Wallace and Torroni 1992). Although it seems apparent that those distinctions had to have arisen in Asia at some time back in the Pleistocene, at the moment there is no way to make an accurate determination as to just when that might have been.

REFERENCES CITED

Boas, Franz
    1921   Ethnology of the Kwakiutl Based on Data Collected by George Hunt, Chapter 4. Thirty-fifth Annual Report of the Bureau of American Ethnology, pp. 305–601. Washington, DC: Government Printing Office.
Brace, C. Loring
    1996   Cro-Magnon and Qafzeh – Vive la Différence. *Dental Anthropology Newsletter* 10(3):2–9.
Brace, C. Loring, Mary L. Brace, and William R. Leonard
    1989   Reflections on the Face of Japan: A Multivariate Craniofacial and Odontometric Perspective. *American Journal of Physical Anthropology* 78(1):93–113.

Brace, C. Loring, and Kevin D. Hunt
  1990   A Non-Racial Craniofacial Perspective on Human Variation: A(ustralia) to Z(uni). *American Journal of Physical Anthropology* 82(3):341–360.
Brace, C. Loring, and David P. Tracer
  1992   Craniofacial Continuity and Change: A Comparison of Late Pleistocene and Recent Europe and Asia. In *The Evolution and Dispersal of Modern Humans in Asia.* Takeru Akazawa, Kenichi Aoki and Tasuku Kimura, eds. Pp. 439–471. Tokyo: Hokusen-Sha.
Darnell, Regna
  1990   *Edward Sapir: Linguist, Anthropologist, Humanist.* Berkeley: University of California Press.
  1998   Camelot at Yale: The Construction and Dismantling of the Sapirian Synthesis, 1931–1939. *American Anthropologist* 100(2):361–372.
Hayden, Brian
  1981   Research and Development in the Stone Age: Technological Transitions Among Hunter-Gatherers. *Current Anthropology* 22(5):519–548.
Howells, William W.
  1986   Physical Anthropology of the Prehistoric Japanese. In *Windows on the Japanese Past: Studies in Archaeology and Prehistory.* Richard J. Pearson, Gina L. Barnes, and Karl L. Hutterer, eds. Pp. 85–99. Ann Arbor: Center for Japanese Studies, University of Michigan.
Nelson, A. Russell
  1998   A Craniofacial Perspective on North American Indian Population Affinity and Relations. Ph.D. dissertation, Department of Anthropology, University of Michigan, Ann Arbor.
Ousley, Stephen D.
  1995   Relationship between Eskimos, Amerindians, and Aleuts: Old Data, New Perspectives. *Human Biology* 67(3):427–458.
Pietrusewsky, Michael, Li Yongyi, Shao Xiangqing and Nguyen Quang Nguyen
  1992   Modern and Near Modern Populations of Asia and the Pacific: A Multivariate Craniometric Interpretation. In *The Evolution and Dispersal of Modern Humans in Asia.* Takeru Akazawa, Kenichi Aoki and Tasuku Kimura, eds. Pp. 531–558. Tokyo: Hokusen-Sha.
Prichard, James Cowles
  1851   *Researches into the Physical History of Mankind.* 4th edition, vol. 5. *History of the Oceanic and American Nations.* London: Houlston and Sons.
Wallace, Douglas C., and Antonio Torroni
  1992   American Indian Prehistory as Written in the Mitochondrial DNA: A Review. *Human Biology* 64(3):403–416.

5

Diversity in the Context of Health and Illness

Cheryl Mwaria

Nowhere can issues of biocultural diversity and change be addressed as clearly in the curriculum as they can be in medical anthropology, for there is a long-held axiom in the subdiscipline that concepts of health and disease are intrinsic to every culture and are, therefore, variable. Medical anthropology is concerned with the myriad factors contributing to disease, that is, the etiology of disease, and the varied ways in which human populations respond behaviorally to disease (clinical manifestations) and illness (the sufferer's experience). These responses, taken together, form a society's medical system (the beliefs and practices directed toward the alleviation of disease and illness and the promotion of health). It is not only the assumptions concerning health and disease that are culturally based but the very language we use and the questions we raise that are culturally driven as well. The United States as a genetically and culturally diverse society provides a fertile background for examining empirical evidence pertaining to genetic, environmental, ethical, and access issues relating to health and disease. This chapter discusses the ways in which medical anthropology as a fundamental component of the curriculum can be used to examine diversity with respect to these issues and challenge some previously held curricular assumptions along the way.

Medical anthropology is one of the newest subdisciplines in anthropology, but it has clearly experienced spectacular growth, particularly over the last two decades. Prior to 1960, as David Landy (1977:5) has asserted, "not a single book in anthropology has been devoted to the topic as a theoretical concern": that is, with the exception of Rivers' (1927) theoretical classic, *Medicine, Magic, and Religion*. Today, in addition to Alland's (1970) pioneering and considerably influential *Adaptation in Cultural Evolution: An Approach to Medical Anthropology*, and Landy's own classic anthology, *Culture, Disease, and Healing: Studies in Medical Anthropology* (1977), there have been a growing number of textbooks in the genre including: Foster and Anderson's *Medical Anthropology* (1978); Wood's (1979) *Human Sickness and Health: A Biocultural View*; McElroy and Townsend's (1979, 1989) *Medical Anthropology in Ecological Perspective*; Moore et al.'s *The Biocultural Basis of Health: Expanding Views of Medical Anthropology*; Helman's (1994) *Culture, Health and Illness: An*

Introduction for Health Professionals; Anderson's (1996) *Magic, Science, and Health: The Aims and Achievements of Medical Anthropology*; and most recently Baer, Singer, and Susser's (1997) *Medical Anthropology and the World System: A Critical Perspective*.

Taken together, the theoretical perspectives of these texts vary, with an emphasis perhaps on an ecological paradigm, that is, the examination of health and disease in an environmental context and with it, the concept of adaptation. According to McElroy and Townsend (1989:5): "Medical ecology is concerned with one basic question. . . . How do these people survive in this particular environment? How do they cope with disease? And how do they solve problems that affect their health?" There have been, however, alternative perspectives including a cognitive or "meaning-centered" paradigm and a critical paradigm. Singer (1996:497), as a proponent of the latter perspective, argues that medical ecological approaches can be faulted for failing to appreciate the fact that "it is not merely the idea of nature – the way [external reality] is conceived and related to by humans – but also the very physical shape of nature, including the course of human biology, that has been deeply influenced by an evolutionary history of hierarchical social structures – that is to say, by the changing political economy of human society."

Critical medical anthropology raises, therefore, a different set of questions (Baer et al. 1997:230): "Whose social realities and interests (e.g. which social class, gender, or ethnic group) do particular cultural conceptions express, and under what set of historic conditions do they arise?" Such questions are vital to an understanding of patterns of health, disease, and illness as they appear in the varied populations comprising the United States, if for no other reason than that the persistent practice of the medicalization of difference in public policy has had a very real effect on patterns of health, disease and illness in the country. This is not to say that critical medical anthropology can ignore biology; it cannot and does not. For example, a critical medical anthropology perspective can elucidate the relationship between biology and social structure with relation to resource allocation, for two emergent and pivotal health problems confronting our species in the new millennium: the return of infectious disease with increasing virulence; and providing a safe food supply. The reemergence of increasingly virulent infectious disease is to a large extent the product of the misuse of antibiotics and a poor understanding of evolutionary principles. It is also the consequence of the destruction of forest environments, thereby bringing humans into contact with new pathogens (Garrett 1994; Ewald 1994). The threat to our food supply is the result of contamination due to factory farming methods here, and the importation of food from countries forced to use contaminated water sources.

Each of these problems is a product of human decision making, but given the global interconnectedness of all societies, decisions made in one country may well affect people in another. We must expand explanations of disease patterns to incorporate both fundamental principles of evolution and the very real role that differentials of power and perspective play with respect to these patterns. Acknowledging such linkages must be the starting point for curricular change.

The Significance of Genetic Issues versus the Insignificance of Race

In order to understand the complex interplay between political, cultural, and biological factors as they affect health and the spread of disease in diverse populations of the United States, we must first confront the paradox concerning the concept of race. It is simply this: though the use of the term is linguistically pervasive in our society, the scientific and popular definitions are clearly at odds. Moreover, upon a more detailed analysis, there is no consensus on the definition of the term. This has resulted in the abandonment of the use of the term in many contemporary textbooks, or at best the assertion that because of a lack of consensus, the term itself is invalid. At best such an approach is both confusing and misleading. At worst, it leaves students with the inevitable ridiculous conclusion that there are no biological differences between human populations. Students should first be presented with some theoretical insights focusing on an explanation of the mechanisms governing biological variation. These include at least a rudimentary understanding of evolution with respect to the following concepts: genes, proteins, gene pools, gene frequencies, and continuous versus discontinuous variation. There are two formidable obstacles to such a discourse.

First, anthropology, like the vast majority of academic disciplines, in the face of a growing amount of both theoretical and empirical evidence, has become increasingly fragmented. As Mukhopadhyay and Moses (1997:525–526) have asserted: "we think it is time to consider relinking the cultural and the biological, but within a radically different paradigm. This paradigm would situate human biodiversity within a sociocultural framework, in effect reuniting culture and biology by embedding biology in society and culture." The end result of this fragmentation has been that specialists in the various subdisciplines are increasingly unfamiliar with developments or, at times, lack even a basic grasp of concepts outside their own areas of specialization. This, in and of itself, has often led to a conflation of terms and consequent misunderstandings. The concept of race typifies this.

Second, students, faced with a rapidly increasing body of knowledge to master, often resist requirements that they feel are beyond the scope of their interests. Thus learning basic genetic concepts is often viewed as irrelevant.

Once students grasp these basic genetic concepts they can comprehend the biological concept of race defined by Brues (1977:1) as "a division of a species that differs from other divisions by the frequency with which certain hereditary traits appear among its members." As such it has two charact eristics: (1) it is a group of populations that share some biological characteristics; and (2) these populations differ from other populations according to these characteristics, or more specifically according to the gene frequencies governing these characteristics. Armed with these insights, one can understand the problems of applying the biological concept of race to our species *Homo sapiens sapiens*.

What then are the problems with applying the biological concept of race to our species? They can be summarized as follows. There has never been a consensus on the number of "races." This is a by-product of the arbitrary choice of phenotypic (observable) characteristics used to delineate human populations. Moreover, those characteristics that have been chosen, skin color, hair type, hair color, the shape of the nose, eye, or head are continuously variable traits and therefore do not allow for the division of the species into discrete units. Indeed similarities in these characteristics do not necessarily denote common ancestry. In order to be useful, such traits would also need to correspond. That is, the classification would have to work for a number of independent traits. Therefore, classification developed from one trait would also have to show the same pattern in other traits. This is clearly not the case. Finally, racial classification is regarded as discrete. It represents a form of typological thinking and therefore ignores variation within groups. In other words, it ignores Mendel's work on independent assortment. It is for these reasons that physical anthropologists and indeed most biologists do not find the large-scale categories known as "races" useful when employed to differentiate between human populations. This does not mean, however, that human populations cannot be compared on the basis of gene frequencies. Nor does it mean that it is never useful to do so. Such comparisons, and indeed any explanation of human biological variation, are better analyzed by focusing on micro evolutionary forces using individuals or local populations as the unit of analysis. This is particularly true when comparing rates of disease between various populations in the United States. In so doing one does not have to "throw the baby out with the bath water" by arguing that human variation either does not exist or is solely the product of social forces. We are, as biological beings, still subject to evolutionary forces. Nevertheless, with humans culture overtakes biology as the critical arena of variation.

Cultural differences, too, continue to be confused with biological diversity in group labeling. Linguistic ability and social behavior are often used to categorize people into groups. For instance, in the United States, the term "Latino" (formerly, Hispanic) is used to lump together peoples as diverse as recent immigrants from South America and those U.S. citizens who are descendants of Native Americans and colonists of the Southwest, California, and Central America. While the overall category may serve political purposes, it obscures cultural diversity and population ancestry alike. Students should be informed about basic anthropological insights into group formation: that is, that people form groups on the basis of perceived shared interests. While such interests are often based on responses to exclusion from power by elite groups, there is nothing essential about them. Indeed, they are subject to historical change as are gene frequencies in biological populations. Such labels are also used carelessly, not only by the lay public, but by the U.S. government in collecting vital statistics, particularly with respect to data on disease incidence. Consider the following example. When collecting infant mortality statistics, race or ethnicity of infants of "mixed" parentage are recorded according to the following rules: (1) if one parent is white, the fetus or infant is assigned to the other parent's race; (2) when neither parent is white, the fetus or infant is assigned to the father's race (*Monthly Vital Statistics*, supplement 1989, cited in Molnar 1998:31–32). This is clearly a reflection of the historical practice of restricting elite status by assigning such children to the politically disadvantaged group. In so doing it suggests that physical and behavioral traits come only from that group. The term "race" was replaced by "ethnic group" in the 1990 census, but this self-classification, while potentially useful for political purposes, reveals almost nothing about the range of biological variation. Recognizing "race" as a social construct, we should be concerned, not with "racial" differences with respect to incidence of disease, but with (1) biological responses to the environment; (2) behavior directing gene flow between generations; (3) population size or isolation as factors influencing variation between generations and among populations; and (4) issues of access both to quality health care and "healthy" environments.

Given these considerations, we must acknowledge that there are a number of both congenital abnormalities and genetic diseases that occur more frequently in some populations than in others. A closer look at three of them, Tay-Sachs disease, cystic fibrosis (CF), and sickle cell anemia (SCD, or sickle cell disease), demonstrates the enormous variability down to the level of the individual's nuclear DNA polymorphisms that can be found in populations in the United States. More importantly, these diseases illustrate the ways in which comparisons of populations must take into account not only genetics, but anthropological explanations of population structures and gene flow.

If we look at rates of Tay-Sachs among the Ashkenazic Jewish populations in the United States, we see that it occurs once in every 2,500 births as compared to 1 in 500,000 non-Ashkenazic births (Ludman et al. 1986). This means that one in 25 persons in the Jewish population are carriers, but show no signs of the disease. Tay-Sachs disease causes an interruption of the regulatory process maintaining a balance of gangliosides in cell cytoplasm. The interruption leads to an accumulation of excess gangliosides in the neuronal cells, causing the brain to become swollen and distended. Infants with the condition have severely impaired brain function and fail to develop normal neurological responses, resulting in loss of muscle control followed by paralysis, and loss of hearing and sight by the end of the first year. The victims of Tay-Sachs disease lack hexominidase A (Hex A) because of their inheritance of the recessive allele producing this enzyme, and are therefore unable to metabolize ganglioside molecules normally. While the genetic and physiological properties of the disease are well known, the question of why this disease has persisted at such high frequencies remains and requires an anthropological explanation. Initially, the most promising hypothesis explaining the persistence of the disease was related to the size and relative isolation of the ancestral Ashkenzic Jewish population. The ancestral population was small, numbering between 1,000 and 5,000 people who migrated from the Middle East about 1,000 years ago. Such a numerically small population, accompanied by generations of endogamy, which was a religious prescription, and isolation, socially reinforced by patterns of discrimination, would allow for an extreme form of genetic drift known as the Founders Effect. There is, however, an even more promising hypothesis, given the discovery of two abnormal Hex A alleles: selection favoring the heterozygote. Its proponents (Chakravarti and Chakraborty 1978) opine that the crowded ghetto environments, in which Ashkenazic Jews were forced to live in Eastern Europe, fostered endemic typhoid and tuberculosis at high levels. These diseases acting as selective forces may have favored carriers of the Hex A deficient allele, who had lower mortality rates, survived longer, and had higher fertility rates offsetting the loss of Tay-Sachs infants. High rates of endogamy and relatively high fertility rates continued to characterize migrants from the Eastern European populations who settled in the United States until recently. If present patterns of exogamy and lowered fertility continue or grow, we would expect to see a lower rate of Tay-Sachs in the United States.

Cystic fibrosis (CF), inherited as an autosomal recessive, is the most common lethal genetic disease in European-derived populations in the United States. The disease prevalence ranges from 1 in 500 to 1 in 3,800 births in those of European ancestry as compared to the extremely low 1 in 17,000 for those of African descent and an even lower 1 in 90,000 births among Asians in Hawaii.[1] Weiss (1993) gives an overall rate of carrier frequency for those of European descent in the States of 1 in 20. Cystic fibrosis is a disease of the exocrine glands and as such produces secretions of thick viscous substances that damage the lungs and pancreas. Patients suffer respiratory and digestive problems which before 1950 generally resulted in death in infancy. Today, survival rates have improved in the United States, but generally hover around 24 years. Genetic research has improved understanding of the physiology of the disease and led to the identification of 24 different mutations, but just as with Tay-Sachs, the persistence of high frequencies of the recessive alleles in certain populations raises questions as to why such frequencies are maintained. This is particularly intriguing given that homozygous recessives died before the age of reproduction until quite recently, and those that survive now have very low fertility rates. As Francis Collins (1992:774), director of the Human Genome Project, suggests: "there may have been some heterozygote selection or a very strong founder effect for this population." According to some researchers (see Meindl, 1987), just such a selective force can be seen in the correlation of CF with tuberculosis. Tuberculosis (TB, or "consumption") appeared with epidemic force in England just as the Industrial Revolution emerged and with it the concentration of Northern Europeans in urban centers. Poverty, inadequate nutrition, and crowded, squalid, unventilated housing combined to facilitate the spread of tuberculosis, the "white plague," and with it CF, on to the Continent. Given massive immigration from Europe to the United States, by the late 19th century it was a major cause of death on both sides of the Atlantic. Anything providing resistance to TB would allow its carriers to live longer and result in a higher rate of reproduction. Carriers of the CF allele in this type of environment would have such an advantage in that the viscous secretions produced in the heterozygote contain mucopolysaccharides that facilitate the rapid repair of cellular tissue damage caused by TB.

For my last example of the linkage between sociocultural factors and the persistence of polymorphisms in the United States, let us turn our attention to sickle cell disease (SCD). This is acquired through the inheritance of homozygous recessive alleles that produce only hemoglobin molecules with the valine substitution in the beta chain. This relatively simple change in amino acid sequencing results in the deformation in shape of hemoglobin cells when oxygen is taken up in the surrounding tissues. People who inherit SS hemoglobin may survive without clinical symptoms, depending on the rate of oxygen consumption, for long periods. An increased demand for oxygen, however, such as is caused by strenuous exercise, may lead to a crisis involving the distortion and reduction of cells, increased free hemoglobin, anemia, and many other problems resulting in high mortality rates. In the United States, the frequency of the Hb gene in the African American population, numbering 33 million, averages about 5 percent. Of these, about 10 percent are carriers, that is, heterozygotes (AS genotypes) whose clinical symptoms, though serious, have much lower mortality rates.

Medical anthropologists and biologists agree that it is difficult to demonstrate natural selection in humans. Indeed, there is little direct evidence of superior fitness of heterozygotes for any polymorphisms and it is difficult to test hypotheses of phenotype fitness in specific environments such as the relative immunity of human heterozygote carriers to a particular disease (Molnar 1998:144). There is, however, more complete evidence for disease selection by human hemoglobin variants in malarial environments. Two classic studies pertaining to sickle cell disease provide such evidence. In the 1940s Linus Pauling (Pauling et al. 1949) demonstrated the molecular differences of hemoglobin of people with sickle cell disease whose variants are transmitted between generations according to Mendelian laws. Since then hundreds of hemoglobin variants have been detected. A decade later, Frank Livingstone (1958) demonstrated that malaria became endemic in sub-Saharan Africa about 2 thousand years ago when Bantu peoples, having acquired iron hoe technology, established horticultural villages in tropical rain forest habitats, thereby facilitating the spread of malaria-bearing mosquitoes. The disease malaria is caused by several species of *Plasmodium*, each causing a different type of the disease. Humans are hosts to four species of *Plasmodium*, including the one causing the deadly malaria falciparum, transmitted through the bite of the *Anopheles* mosquito. The *Anopheles gambiae* mosquito is best adapted to the conditions created through human habitation in tropical rain forests, open sunlit garden plots, village clearings, and stagnant water. Under these conditions, any degree of immunity conferred by genotype would enhance survival and reproduction. Studies show that red blood cells containing certain types of abnormal hemoglobin, those that are more fragile with a shorter life span and lower energy level, are less able to support malarial parasite growth. Such is the case with people who have sickle cell trait (SCT), that is, those who are heterozygous for the gene. They have longer life spans, higher live birth rates and lower parasite counts than those with normal hemoglobin in the areas where malaria falciparum is endemic (Molnar 1998:158). The distribution of the S allele and malaria seems to support this argument. The S allele is found with appreciable frequencies in Africa, the Mediterranean, Saudi Arabia, India, and the Americas, with the greatest frequencies in central Africa, northeast India, Arabia, and Greece (Erhardt 1973; Livingstone 1985; Molnar 1998; and Schroeder and Munger 1990). Thus the hypothesis that the concordant distributions of gene and disease are the result of natural selection has been supported by evidence for differential fitness of the AS heterozygote in malarial environments as well as the distribution of the S allele and malaria (Molnar 1998:158).

Thus far our discussion of sickle cell trait has been from the perspective of medical ecology. If we are truly to understand the impact of the frequency of this trait among African Americans living in the United States we must take our discussion to another level, as would be required from the perspective of critical medical anthropology. Edelstein (1986) has argued that in the heterozygote (AS), red blood cells function normally under most circumstances, rarely sickling. However, in the United States, where about 10 percent of African Americans are carriers, there has been considerable confusion over the relative health risks faced by heterozygous (AS) individuals versus homozygous (AA) normals, resulting in loss of jobs in lucrative and prestigious fields. Sickle cell trait carriers were believed to be at high risk when exercising heavily, working at high altitudes; flying planes was considered beyond their capabilities. As Molnar (1998) points out: "Throughout the 1970s the Navy tested recruits and nearly all officers coming on duty for sickle cell trait. Army personnel were also screened but only those applying for airborne duties were examined." Major commercial airlines also joined this confusion by grounding or even firing personnel with SCT (Bowman 1977). Such misunderstanding has been grounds for rejection of African Americans with SCT from the Air Force, and was the cause of at least one forced resignation from the Air Force Academy in Colorado Springs (see Duster 1990). By 1981 the ban on cadets with SCT was ended but several major corporations have continued to test prospective employees (see Kevles 1995).

Though this issue has faded from public attention, groundless fears over blood transfusions and the confusion of SCT with SCD persist. Furthermore, there remains confusion over just who can acquire SCT, even within the medical community itself: the *Journal of the American Medical Association* reported an inquiry as to whether there were any documented cases of SCT or SCD in persons of European extraction. Though the answer was affirmative (Powars 1994), its emphasis on phenotypic traits associated with race was somewhat misleading, giving the impression that sickle cell was an African gene. Given persistent patterns of racial/ethnic discrimination in the United States, it is imperative that students be cognizant of the ways in which discrimination affects perception of epidemiological patterns as well as disease patterns themselves.

Environmental Issues Related to Health in the United States

Historically, ethnic diversity in the United States derived from two sources: the diverse indigenous populations of Native Americans; and the diverse populations of immigrants, both voluntary and involuntary. Though there has been a significant amount of gene flow between these diverse populations, effectively removing any genetic isolation, patterns of socially constructed isolation and inequality of access to health resources have led to dramatic differences in disease patterns and rates of morbidity and mortality at varying points in time. Far too often explanations of these epidemiological patterns have been laid solely at the feet of "cultural behaviors and beliefs." As Ann Millard (1992:4) has opined: "the characterization of culture as 'cultural beliefs' implies that it is a collection of unarticulated elements of no particular significance that results in the blind following of tradition." Though medical anthropology has sometimes unwittingly contributed to this misconception, more recent analyses have focused on inequities of power and the "medicalization" of difference bringing new insights to the relationship between environment and health.

The very establishment and growth of the United States was accompanied by the dislocation and destruction of myriad indigenous peoples who had successfully managed local ecosystems for long-term sustained use. In addition, these societies were, in general, characterized by internal social equality which allowed for the satisfaction of human needs without elevating production and consumption beyond local subsistence demands. This pattern is in marked contrast to that of industrialized capitalist and "postrevolutionary" communist states alike. As anthropologist John Bodley (1990:4–5) has noted, the notion of "progress" has ushered in an "explosion" of population growth and consumption of resources "unparalleled in scope" and "catastrophic [in the] nature of the transformations that it has initiated." Any critical examination of environmental issues related to health in the United States must focus on investigations of inequalities of race, gender, and class that have accompanied this transformation.

Prior to the arrival of Europeans and Africans in the Americas, Native Americans had developed a substantial and effective pharmacopeia as well as varied therapies for the treatment of diseases and ailments that challenged them. They also employed the age-old techniques of flight and quarantine under some circumstances, though not all. These weapons, however, proved to be ineffective when culture contact introduced, either deliberately or inadvertently, new pathogens for which they had no immunities, and thereby radically altered the environment. Biologist Paul Ewald's (1994) seminal work on the evolution of virulence suggests that human behavior appears to influence whether pathogens evolve into benign or harmful forms, in that "it often determines the route and timing of transmission" (Ewald 1993:86). This seems to have been the case with respect to the introduction of Old World pathogens into the New World. As historian James Merrell (1989:237) stated: "Old World pathogens served as the shock troops of the European invasion, softening up the enemy before battalions of busy farmers waded ashore." These "virgin soil" epidemics were so devastating that they killed their hosts before the newly arrived, uninvited guests had even left their vessels, as in 1616 when a ship-borne plague killed Indians living in New England's coastal villages. The Indians "died in heapes, as they lay in their houses." Many Europeans saw the "hand of God" at work, presaging the devastation that was to come to indigenous populations at their hands. Disease alone was not responsible for the devastation of indigenous populations; the social and economic disruption brought about through patterns of warfare and persistent racism and discrimination all took their toll. According to Kraut (1994:17–18): "Survivors often merged with remnants of other tribes, further diluting tribal rituals and lines of authority. Every merger required a process of assimilation not unlike that which characterizes patterns of international migration."

Nor was it only Native Americans who faced the ravages of disease as a result of the environmental changes wrought by immigration. African slaves and European immigrants themselves all suffered from the effects of New World pathogens and brought with them new pathogens from the Old World. In the case of the slaves, ship-borne disease sometimes killed as many as 25 percent of the passengers before arrival in the Americas. Those that survived faced the cruelty and degradation of slavery and its extraordinary rates of infant mortality, which was twice that of whites in 1850, the same ratio that characterized Washington D.C. some 130 years later. As Jacqueline Jones (1985:35–36) has noted, "fewer than two out of three black children survived to the age of ten in the years between 1850 and 1860; the life expectancy at birth for males and females was only 32.6 and 33.6 years respectively." Actual rates of morbidity and mortality among the slaves are difficult to come by, but there is no shortage of "medical" treatises associating blackness itself with illness. This "medicalization" of difference can be seen in the leading medical literature of the time. Sander Gilman (1985:138) noted that as late as 1851 the *American Journal of Insanity* published an article, based on the inaccurate census of 1840, that declared:

> It is obvious, however . . . that there is an awful prevalence of idiocy and insanity among free blacks over free whites, and especially over slaves. Who would believe, without the fact in black and white, before his eyes, that every fourteenth colored person in the State of Maine is an idiot or a lunatic?

That same year (1851) saw the publication of Samuel Cartwright's article in the *New Orleans Medical and Surgical Journal* which not only equated blackness with madness, but also described a number of psychopathological diseases purported to appear only among blacks, the most notable being "drapetomania" – a disease causing slaves to run away – and "dysaesthesia" – better known as "rascality" or resistance to work.

As for early European immigrants to the United States, they, like the slaves, often experienced horrific mortality rates on board ship, and as they were clustered into crowded, unsanitary urban ghettos or compelled to work under extremely hazardous conditions. Allen Kraut (1994:2) in his insightful book documenting the immigrant experience, *Silent Travelers*, speaks of the "double helix of health and fear" characterizing the intersection of American public health policy and immigration, arguing:

> Just as continual replenishment of the American population through immigration has shaped the politics, economics, and culture of American society, ethnic pluralism has defined American medical culture and its approach to public health. Medicine has been an important instrument employed by native-born Americans to assimilate immigrants into American society in a manner that would most effectively preserve the established order's cultural preferences and priorities. Immigrants have engaged in a love/hate relationship with America's public health priorities, at times resisting them as an unwelcome

intrusion in their lives and at other times embracing them as a path to upward mobility.

Nor were their experiences uniform. When disease suspected to have been brought by immigrants broke out, public health officials, bolstered by the native-born populace, sometimes quarantined entire ethnic communities regardless of any given individual's exposure to the disease. Such was the case in San Francisco at the beginning of the 20th century when bubonic plague struck a Chinese immigrant, Chick Gin. Chinese immigrants lacked the protection of citizenship as a result of immigration policy, and so the entire community experienced the full force of racist and nativistic policies which literally sealed off their community in quarantine. Their experience, however, is in sharp contrast to that of the Irish, and the defiant Mary Mallone, who as "Typhoid Mary" remained clinically free of symptoms, but spread typhus to at least 53 known individuals, some even after she had been warned of her infectious state. The Irish were fairly well established politically by 1906, the time of the first outbreak traced to Mary, and she was able to gain enough sympathy and support to be released from custody with assurances that she "knew how to take care of herself." Unfortunately, the defiant Mary continued in her trade as cook, infecting at least 20 more people. Despite this she continued to be viewed as an innocent victim.

The United States saw substantial and significant shifts in its economic base as it moved from an agrarian society to an industrialized giant, followed by a retreat from manufacturing. Each of these periods was accompanied by massive shifts in labor organization and environmental changes that have had a significant impact on rates of disease and injury in diverse segments of the population. Consider the following: farm labor is today the most hazardous and lowest paid type of work. Skin cancers, resulting from overexposure to the sun, are prevalent. Even more hazardous and lethal are the effects of exposure to chemical pesticides (there are currently some 45,000 sold in the States), including leukemia, lymph node cancer, multiple myeloma (bone cancer), brain cancer, birth defects, spontaneous abortion, sterility, amenorrhea, liver and kidney dysfunction, nervous system disorders, anxiety, depression, and immunological abnormalities, that frequently accompany farm work. As a result, most jobs in this sector have been left to immigrant and migrant laborers. Over 90 percent of them are Latinos from various parts of Central America, and the rest are Mexican Americans, Native Americans, African Americans, and Southeast Asians. Migrant laborers often fail to seek medical help when it is needed because of fear of job loss, lack of knowledge about their rights as workers, lack of access to medical care, fear of deportation, and lack of fluency in English. This was poignantly illustrated by the death of 5-year-old Sandra Navarrete who died of complications from chicken pox and whose undocumented immigrant parents did not seek medical help until it was too late because they didn't know where to go, had little money, and did not speak English. The media seemed to think their failure was due to something intrinsic in Mexican culture that prevented them from seeking aid.[2]

Other environmental changes affecting health can be seen with the embrace of the "car culture" that typifies the United States. The turning away from mass transportation in favor of gas-guzzling cars has greatly added to pollution and an increase in respiratory diseases, among others. Road accidents are a leading cause of death and injury as well, though at disparate rates with respect to race, class, and gender. Adolescent and young adult males seem to be the predominant victims, perhaps because of greater indulgence in risk-taking behaviors.

In general, poor people in the United States, particularly members of ethnic minorities, are relegated to areas where industrial pollution is the greatest, or, conversely, find their neighborhoods selected as areas where it is permissible to pollute. They suffer higher morbidity and mortality rates as a result (witness, for example, the markedly increased rates of asthma, particularly among minority children, and sarcoidosis among African American adults; see Baer et al. 1997:55–57). Rundown housing and poor sanitation take their toll on children and adults alike. According to *The World Health Report 1997*, housing poverty, that is, homes lacking safe shelter, piped water, and adequate sanitation and drainage, contributes significantly to ill health. In the United States during the 1980s, the number of shelter beds available for the homeless in cities of over 100,000 inhabitants nearly tripled. Studies in developed countries show that people spend more than 90 percent of their time indoors, making the dwelling place a critical meeting between people and their environment (World Health Organization 1997:12). Clearly the chronically poor, most of whom are women and children, are those suffering the highest rates of homelessness. Far from being the result of cultural beliefs and practices, or the genetic makeup of a group, as is sometimes argued, the poor, who in the United States largely consist of ethnic minorities, suffer higher rates of morbidity and mortality because of their poverty.

Environmental and occupational issues as related to health have become a growing concern in the United States. Experiences at Love Canal, Three Mile Island, and the industrial pollution of our rivers and lakes have raised awareness of the fact that these are not local issues, but rather reflect social, political, and medical policy issues as well. There is a role here for medical anthropologists, as Susser (1988:195) argues:

> Occupational and environmental health issues represent the intersection of two major areas of anthropological concern: work and health. Struggles surrounding work and health provide channels for the illumination of class, state, and power relations in complex society. Focusing on such situations allows the anthropologist to move away from the study of discrete geographic communities or categorical groups in society to the study of interacting forces that determine the degree of hazard to which workers and their communities are subjected.

Access to Health Care

Yet another area in which medical anthropology has played a key role is in examining the relationship between diversity and access to health care. The United States remains the only industrialized country that does not provide guaranteed access to health services for all of its citizens. Spiraling health costs and inadequate services have combined to make access to health care a major problem for most Americans. As we have seen, political and social policies with respect to patterns of immigration, housing, and the organization of labor in the United States have resulted in considerable inequities along race, class, and gender lines, and these in turn have had a significant impact on health. Medical anthropologist Leo Chavez and sociologists Estevan Flores and Marta Lopez-Garcia (1992:22) verify these conditions in their study "Undocumented Latin American Immigrants and U.S. Health Services: An Approach to the Political Economy of Utilization." In it they argue:

> Immigrants may bring with them cultural differences, but if structural obstacles to health are lowered, for example, by acquiring private medical insurance, then even undocumented immigrants are likely to seek health care. This emphasizes the need to separate out culture-specific concepts of disease, illness, and disability from other factors that affect health seeking behavior. This does not mean that culture-specific health knowledge is unimportant, only that it cannot be blamed, a priori, for the inadequate health care many undocumented immigrants receive.

The same can be said for other diverse populations in the United States. For example, women and children are disproportionately the victims of domestic violence, yet still suffer from inadequate protection and shelter. Consequently, fear often prevents them from seeking medical assistance, even in the face of battery. Medical anthropologist Linda Whiteford, writing from the perspective of the political economy of medical anthropology, while remaining conversant with critical medical anthropology, has shown how women can be denied access to health care via the law. In an examination of the impact of the 1987 Florida statute that expanded child abuse to include drug dependent newborns, resulting in the incarceration of their mothers, Whiteford (1996:252) argues that the law has a clearly sexist, racist, and classist orientation whose effect is to isolate poor women, particularly those dependent on public facilities, from other women and to reify second-class citizen status. Since its inception in Florida where incarcerated women were denied access to prenatal care and addiction treatment, four additional states including Colorado, California, Illinois, and Kentucky have charged women with giving drugs to their newborns.

Our final example of issues related to access to health care comes from the work of medical anthropologist Leith Mullings, whose 1989 study of the health status of African Americans finds this population's health status "significantly improved," as is reflected in the dramatic increase in life expectancy, a decrease in the absolute prevalence of disease, and the shift from infectious to chronic disease as the principal cause of death. However, she argues: "if one compares the health of African-Americans to that of Euro-Americans, the relative disadvantages in terms of mortality and morbidity have, for many diseases, remained the same, or in some cases increased." An explanation of the persistence of racial disparities in disease requires, in Mullings' (1989:172) opinion, "distinguishing analytically the influence of socioeconomic factors from genetic differences, and elucidating the interaction of the socioeconomic structure with both cultural traits and genetic differences." In the case of African Americans, improvement in health status came about through the use of strategies to change their status as well as by confronting the exclusionary attributes of health institutions in this country. As Mullings (1989) opines, "there is a complex interaction between culture/lifestyle 'choices' and the structure of differential distribution of jobs, rewards, and resources," including access to health care.

Bioethics and Medical Anthropology: The Role of Diversity in Ethics

The field of bioethics, as a subdiscipline of moral philosophy, has grown with the development of medical technology. Bioethics came into the spotlight in the United States only in the 1970s with new treatment techniques, such as dialysis and heart transplant surgery, which called for the selection of patients. By the 1980s, passive euthanasia, the ethical treatment of newborns, and mandatory screening of people for the HIV virus were all being debated. For the most part, anthropologists steered clear of these debates, leaving them to the philosophers, theologians, lawyers, and physicians whose opinions dominated the popular and professional literature. Nor was there much public debate on resource allocation or the implications of ethical decisions for disparate and diverse segments of society. In part, this was a reflection of the conceptual foundation of bioethics, whose origins in law and philosophy place emphasis on individual rights and autonomy. As Jessica Muller (1994:450) states: "Grounded in these traditions, bioethics emphasizes logic, codified rules and techniques, and rigorous, precise, objective thinking." As such, there seemed little room for an anthropological perspective with its traditional emphasis on the concept of cultural relativity, a concept deemed better suited to the examination of non-Western moral values. Lieban (1990:221), acknowledging the limited influence of anthropology in bioethical debates, notes that there has been a "tendency, consistent with relativistic methodology perhaps, to view the ethical aspects of health care in other cultures as cultural givens and to neglect ways in which they may relate to moral questions and ambiguities." This situation is rapidly changing, however, as anthropologists increasingly turn their attention to ethical debates in medical care. Jessica Muller (1994) and Patricia Marshall (1992), in separate issues of *Medical Anthropology Quarterly*, have each drawn attention to the contributions of anthropologists to bioethical theory and decision making. While much of this work has focused on issues outside of the United States (Kaufert and O'Neil 1990, on informed consent in Canada; Lock and Honde 1990, on reaching consensus on death in Japan; and Scheper-Hughes 1987, on child survival in Brazil, to name but a few), a growing number of anthropologists have turned their attention to bioethical issues in the context of cultural pluralism in the United States (Hahn 1982, 1987; Iris and Segal 1989; Levin 1986; Scheper-Hughes and Lock 1986, 1987; Levin et al. 1991; Marshall et al. 1991; and Mwaria 1997).

Muller (1994) outlines "four overlapping dimensions of an anthropological approach to bioethics." In her words: "They pertain to the contextual nature of bioethical dilemmas, the cultural embeddedness of moral systems, the multicultural character of many bioethical dilemmas, and the challenge of examining the field of bioethics as a cultural phenomenon" (Muller 1994:453). Nevertheless, she cautions, "just as it may be dangerous to assume that all moral conduct in health care settings can be explained by recourse to a set of four principles, so it is equally dangerous to assume that there is only one anthropological approach to bioethics" (1994:453).

Clearly medical anthropologists will play a growing role in the discourse on bioethical theory. Marshall (1992) points to the following areas for future research: truth telling and disclosure of information; informed consent; death and dying; critical care; and selection of organ transplant recipients. Each of these issues and, I would add, the current debate on physician-assisted suicide, or active euthanasia, is of concern in the United States. In order for medical anthropologists to play a meaningful role in these debates, they must adopt a critical perspective by incorporating issues of diversity, power inequities, and the distribution of resources by the state into their analyses.

Conclusion

Medical anthropology has a great deal to contribute to the discourse on the relationship between diversity, ethnic pluralism, and health issues in the United States. To do so we must remain faithful to our holistic approach to the study of *Homo sapiens sapiens* by incorporating data from each of our subdisciplines, and expanding our theoretical perspectives beyond local concepts of belief systems and ecological adaptations to raise new questions pertaining to the ever-changing relationships between diverse populations, ethnic pluralism, and resource allocation in relation to the health issues confronting us in the 21st century.

NOTES

1 The following discussion is based largely on Stephen Molnar's (1998) detailed and comprehensive work, *Human Variation: Races, Types, and Ethnic Groups*.
2 For a detailed comparison of the experiences of Chick Gin and Typhoid Mary at the hands of the health authorities, politicians, and the public, see Allen Kraut (1994:78–104).

REFERENCES CITED

Alland, Alexander
    1970 *Adaptation in Cultural Evolution: An Approach to Medical Anthropology.* New York: Columbia University Press.
Anderson, Robert
    1996 *Magic, Science, and Health: The Aims and Achievements of Medical Anthropology.* Fort Worth, TX: Harcourt Brace College.

Baer, Hans, Merrill Singer, and Ida Susser
  1997 *Medical Anthropology and the World System: A Critical Perspective.* Westport, CT: Bergin and Garvey.
Bodley, John
  1990 *Victims of Progress.* Mountain View, CA: Mayfield.
Bowman, J. E.
  1977 Genetic Screening Programs and Public Policy. *Phylon* 38:117–142.
Brues, Alice M.
  1977 *People and Races.* New York: Macmillan.
Cartwright, Samuel A.
  1831 Report on the Diseases and Physical Peculiarities of the Negro Race. *New Orleans Medical and Surgical Journal* 7:691–713.
Chakravarti, A., and R. Chakraborty
  1978 Elevated Frequency of Tay-Sachs Disease among Ashkenazic Jews Unlikely by Genetic Drift Alone. *American Journal of Human Genetics* 30:256–261.
Chavez, Leo R., Estevan T. Flores, and Marta Lopez-Garcia
  1992 Undocumented Latin American Immigrants and U.S. Health Services: An Approach to a Political Economy of Utilization. *Medical Anthropology Quarterly* 6(1):6–26.
Collins, Francis S.
  1992 Cystic Fibrosis: Molecular Biology and Therapeutic Implications. *Science* 256:774–779.
Duster, T.
  1990 *Backdoor to Eugenics.* New York: Routledge.
Edelstein, S. J.
  1986 *The Sickled Cell: From Myths to Molecules.* Cambridge, MA: Harvard University Press.
Erhardt, C. L.
  1973 Worldwide Distribution of Sickle Cell Disease: A Consideration of Available Data. In *Sickle Cell Disease: Diagnosis, Management, Education and Research.* H. Abramson, J. F. Bertles, and D. L. Withers, eds. St. Louis, MO: Mosby.
Ewald, Paul
  1994 *Evolution of Infectious Disease.* Oxford: Oxford University Press.
Foster, George M., and Barbara G. Anderson
  1978 *Medical Anthropology.* New York: John Wiley.
Garrett, Laurie
  1994 *The Coming Plague: Newly Emerging Diseases in a World out of Balance.* New York: Farrar, Straus, and Giroux.
Gilman, Sander
  1985 *Difference and Pathology: Stereotypes of Sexuality, Race and Madness.* Ithaca, NY: Cornell University Press.
Gould, Stephen Jay
  1981 *The Mismeasure of Man.* New York: W. W. Norton.
Hahn, Robert
  1982 Culture and Informed Consent: An Anthropological Perspective Making Health Care Decisions: The Ethical and Legal Implications of Informed Consent in Patient–Practitioner Relationship. President's Commission for Making Ethical Decisions in Medicine. Washington, DC: Government Printing Office.
  1987 Perinatal Ethics in Anthropological Perspectives. In *Ethical Issues at the Outset of Life.* William B. Weil and Martin Benjamin, eds. Pp. 213–238. Boston: Blackwell Scientific.

Helman, Cecil
　1994　*Culture, Health and Illness: An Introduction for Health Professionals*. Oxford: Butterworth Heinemann.
Iris, Madelaine, and Susan R. Segal
　1989　Strategies for Service Provision: The Use of Legal Intervention. In *A System Approach to Case Work of Elder Abuse: Practice and Policy*. R. Filenson and S. Ingman, eds. Pp. 104–116. New York: Vintage Books.
Jones, Jacqueline
　1986　*Labor of Love, Labor of Sorrow*. New York: Vintage Books.
Kaufert, Joseph, and John O'Neil
　1990　Biomedical Rituals and Informed Consent: Native Canadians and the Negotiation of Clinical Trust. In *Social Science Perspectives on Medical Ethics*. George Weisz, ed. Pp. 41–64. Philadelphia: University of Pennsylvania Press.
Kevles, Daniel J.
　1995　*In the Name of Eugenics*. Cambridge, MA: Harvard University Press.
Kraut, Allen
　1994　*Silent Travelers: Germs, Genes and the "Immigrant Menace."* New York: Basic Books.
Landy, David, ed.
　1977　*Culture, Disease, and Healing: Studies in Medical Anthropology*. New York: Macmillan.
Levin, Betty Wolder
　1986　Caring Choices: Decision Making about Treatment for Catastrophically Ill Newborns. Ph.D. dissertation, Columbia University, New York.
Levin, Betty Wolder, John Driscoll, and Alan R. Fleischman
　1991　Treatment Choices for Infants in the NICU at Risk for AIDS. *Journal of the American Medical Association* 265(22):2976–2981.
Lieban, Richard
　1977　The Field of Medical Anthropology. In Landy. Pp. 11–31. New York: Macmillan.
　1990　Medical Anthropology and the Comparative Study of Medical Ethics. In *Social Science Perspectives on Medical Ethics*. George Weisz, ed. Pp. 221–240. Philadelphia: University of Pennsylvania Press.
Livingstone, F. B.
　1958　Anthropological Implications of Sickle Cell Gene Distribution in West Africa. *American Anthropologist* 60:533–562.
　1985　*Frequencies of Hemoglobin Variants*. New York: Oxford University Press.
Lock, Margaret, and Christian Honde
　1990　Reaching Consensus about Death: Heart Transplants and Cultural Identity in Japan. In *Social Science Perspectives on Medical Ethics*. George Weisz, ed. Pp. 99–120. Philadelphia: University of Pennsylvania Press.
Ludman, M. D., G. A. Grabowski, J. D. Goldberg, and R. J. Desnick
　1986　Heterozygote Detection and Prenatal Diagnosis for Tay-Sachs and Type 1 Gaucher Diseases. In *Genetic Disease: Screening and Management*. T. P. Carter, and A. M. Wiley, eds. Pp. 19–48. New York: Alan R. Liss.
Marshall, Patricia
　1992　Anthropology and Bioethics. *Medical Anthropology Quarterly* 6(1):49–64.
Marshall, Patricia, David C. Thomas, and J. Paul O'Keefe
　1991　Disclosing HIV Status: Ethical Issues Explored. *Journal of the American Dental Association* 122:11–15.

McElroy, Ann, and Patricia Townsend
  1979 *Medical Anthropology in Ecological Perspective.* Boulder, CO: Westview Press.
  1989 *Medical Anthropology in Ecological Perspective*, 2nd edition. Boulder, CO: Westview Press.
  1996 *Medical Anthropology in Ecological Perspective*, 3rd edition. Boulder, CO: Westview Press.
Meindl, R. S.
  1987 Hypothesis: A Selective Advantage for Cystic Fibrosis. *American Journal of Physical Anthropology* 74:39–45.
Merrell, James H.
  1989 *The Indians' New World, Catawbas and Their Neighbors from European Contact through the Era of Removal.* Chapel Hill: University of North Carolina Press.
Millard, Ann V.
  1992 The Anthropological Analysis of Health. *Medical Anthropology Quarterly* 6(1):3–55.
Molnar, Stephen
  1998 *Human Variation: Races, Types, and Ethnic Groups.* Upper Saddle River, NJ: Prentice Hall.
Moore, Lorna G., Peter Van Arsdale, Joanne F. Glienberg, and Robert A. Aldrich
  1980 *The Biocultural Basis of Health: Expanding Views of Medical Anthropology.* Prospect Heights, IL: Waveland Press.
Mukhopadhyay, Carol, and Yolanda Moses
  1997 Reestablishing "Race" in Anthropological Discourse. *American Anthropologist* 99(3):517–533.
Muller, Jessica H.
  1994 Anthropology, Bioethics, and Medicine: A Provocative Trilogy. *Medical Anthropology Quarterly* 8(4):448–467.
Mullings, Leith
  1989 Inequality and African-American Health Status: Policies and Prospects. In *Race: Twentieth Century Dilemmas – Twenty First Century Prognoses.* W. Van Horne, ed. Pp. 154–182. Madison: University of Wisconsin Institute on Race and Ethnicity.
Mwaria, Cheryl
  1997 Physician-Assisted Suicide: An Anthropological Perspective. *Fordham Urban Law Journal* 24(4):859–868.
Nesse, Randolph M., and George C. Williams
  1996 *Why We Get Sick.* New York: Vintage Books.
Pauling, L., H. A. Itano, S. J. Singer, and I. C. Wells
  1949 Sickle Cell Anemia, a Molecular Disease. *Science* 110:543–548.
Powars, D. R.
  1994 Sickle Cell Disease in Non-Black Persons. *Journal of the American Medical Association* 271(23):1885.
Rivers, W. H. R.
  1927 *Medicine, Magic and Religion.* London: Kegan, Paul, Trench, Trubner.
Scheper-Hughes, Nancy
  1987 *Child Survival: Anthropological Perspectives on the Treatment and Maltreatment of Children.* Dordrecht: D. Reidel.
Scheper-Hughes, Nancy, and Margaret Lock
  1986 Speaking Truth to Illness: Metaphors, Reification, and a Pedagogy for Patients. *Medical Anthropology Quarterly* 17(5):137–140.

1987   The Mindful Body: A Prolegomenon to Future Work in Medical Anthropology. *Medical Anthropology Quarterly* 1:6–41.
Schroeder, W. A., and E. S. Munger
1990   Sickle Cell Anemia, Genetic Variations, and the Slave Trade to the United States. *Journal of African History* 31:163–180.
Singer, M.
1996   Farewell to Adaptationism: Unnatural Selection and the Politics of Biology. *Medical Anthropology Quarterly* 10(4):496–515.
Susser, Ida
1988   Introduction: Directions in Research on Health and Industry (Special Issue on Work). *Medical Anthropology Quarterly* 2(3):195–199.
Weiss, K. M.
1993   *Genetic Variation and Human Disease: Principles and Evolutionary Approaches*. Cambridge, UK: Cambridge University Press.
Whiteford, Linda
1996   Political Economy, Gender, and the Social Production of Health and Illness. In *Gender and Health: An International Perspective*. C. Sargent, and C. Brettell, eds. Pp. 242–259. Upper Saddle River, NJ: Prentice Hall.
Wood, Corrine Shear
1979   *Human Sickness and Health: A Biocultural View*. Palo Alto, CA: Mayfield.
World Health Organization
1997   *Conquering Suffering, Enriching Humanity: The World Health Report 1997*. Geneva: WHO.

6

Health, Disease, and Social Inequality

Merrill Singer

Diversity, Inequality, and the Coming of Age of Medical Anthropology

The entire history of medical anthropology can be read as a conflicted encounter with the issues of diversity and inequality. Using medical anthropology's historic encounter with diversity and inequality as a contextualizing frame, this chapter examines the contemporary AIDS epidemic as a case study for classroom discussion of medical anthropology. Since the beginning of the epidemic over 200 anthropologists have worked in AIDS research, program development and implementation, advocacy, and policy development; the global AIDS crisis has been both a significant challenge to medical anthropology and an important influence on current developments within the discipline. The epidemic illustrates the critical importance of diversity and inequality. The final section identifies resources and relevant publications.

Racism in the manger: the prehistory of medical anthropology

One of the first professional organizations in anthropology was initiated by an individual whose interests included both medicine and anthropology. In 1862 James Hunt, a physician who specialized in speech pathology, especially stuttering, launched the Anthropological Society of London. The perspectives that Hunt brought into the emergent field of anthropology included the belief that people of African origin constituted a separate species from Europeans and that they were not suited to civilization. Such racist sentiments were not unusual in Hunt's day, and, directly or indirectly, many early anthropologists contributed to the construction of an ideology of superior and inferior peoples and cultures that rationalized social inequality.

To the degree that Hunt's pernicious views had some lasting impact on medical anthropology, it may have been through his nephew, W. H. R. Rivers, who is generally recognized as a founder of medical anthropology; one of the prizes awarded by the Society for Medical Anthropology bears his name. In 1898 Rivers, fellow physician C. G. Seligman, and anthropologist Alfred Haddon initiated the Cambridge Torres Straits expedition, one of the earliest anthropological field research projects. Using data collected during the expedition, Rivers refuted popular beliefs and argued that the ethnomedical practices of non-Western societies "are not a medley of disconnected and meaningless customs" (Rivers 1924:51). Rather, he argued, they constitute internally coherent structures of cultural beliefs about the causes of disease. However, Rivers also maintained that non-Western ethnomedical traditions and Western biomedicine constitute completely separate domains (Wellin 1977).

In sharply separating the dominant healing system of Western societies from the ethnomedical practices of non-Western peoples, Rivers was stepping into the shadowy footprints laid down by his uncle James Hunt. Both of these early anthropologists, the one concerned with human biology and the other with human culture, separated the world into two disconnected parts: the West and the rest. Additionally, a legacy of Rivers' approach has been the tendency to believe that indigenous medical systems can only be studied and understood in terms of magical and religious beliefs. As pointed out by Foster and Anderson (1978:6), "this stereotype, uncritically accepted by a majority of anthropologists during the last half century, has severely limited us in our understanding of non-Western medical systems." This approach also limited medical anthropology's understanding of biomedicine, because it was not seen as being "susceptible to the same sort of cultural analysis to which [anthropologists] readily subject[ed] other medical systems" (Gaines and Hahn 1985:4).

In sum, racialist thinking was introduced early into anthropological studies of healing systems. While this perspective would falter during the post–World War II era under the growing weight of cultural relativist ethnographic studies, it tended to be replaced by a micro-level focus that, however much an advance in medical anthropology's handling of diversity in some regards, failed to fully confront and eliminate earlier tendencies within the field.

The social functions of biomedical ideology: emergent medical anthropology in context

The work of Erwin Ackerknecht (1971), a physician with an abiding interest in indigenous healing, provides a link between the early collection of information about health practices and what would become medical anthropology after World War II. Ackerknecht readily acknowledged that the primary explanatory model he brought to his studies of indigenous medical beliefs and practices derived from Boasian historical particularism and British functionalism. He sought to show that indigenous medical practices are integral and integrated components of their respective cultural systems and hence cannot be understood except in relation to the larger culture pattern which they reflect and of which they are a functionally interrelated part. While they might sometimes be effective in healing illness, the largest contribution of primitive medical practices, he argued, is in helping to shore up and maintain their encompassing cultural system. However, Ackerknecht, like Rivers, was largely blind to the ways his work ethnocentrically imposed biomedical categories and concepts onto the beliefs and practices of non-Western peoples, as well as to the cultural nature and social structural role of biomedicine.

After World War II there was a marked increase in the number of anthropologists concerned with health issues, and a growing range of opportunities for employment in this arena. Anthropologists associated with international development programs accepted "uncritically the superiority of modern medicine and modern health care delivery" and sought to make them attractive and available to indigenous peoples (Foster 1980:848). Failing to see the highly political nature of international health aid, many of them felt that the real problem facing anthropologists in international public health lay in surmounting cultural resistance to Western medical practices (Marriott 1955).

The postwar period also witnessed a movement of anthropologists into clinical settings in the West in the roles of teacher, researcher, administrator, and in some cases clinician. The impact of this development has been telling, because in the clinical setting anthropologists have had to adopt and to rationalize the acceptance of subservient, support roles relative to physicians. Consequently, clinically based anthropologists have stressed the importance of compliance. While these sentiments are understandable given the distribution of power and decision-making authority in medical settings, it would appear, as Hunter (1985:1302) concludes, that to a large degree anthropologists working in hospitals, clinics, and medical schools have been "co-opted by the medical establishment."

Notable in this regard, is Polgar's (1962:179) observation, in contrasting medical anthropology's role with that of anthropologists working in colonial settings, that "it is certainly easier to share the value of improving health . . . than to aid the operations of a colonial administration." That there might be an underlying or even direct relationship between the two roles, in that both may structure inequality along class, racial, gender, and ethnic lines, is not always appreciated (O'Neill 1989), and, when it is appreciated, medical anthropologists have been cautioned not to get "overwhelmed with the association between colonialism and Western medicine" (Kundstadter 1978:400). Sometimes, however, the association is overwhelming. Packard (1989:689), for example, notes that in South Africa prior to the fall of the apartheid government, "white medical authorities had considerable influence on the development of popular thinking among whites about the status of Africans in South African society and in the development and persistence of . . . stereotypes" that legitimated oppressive policies against the African majority. Packard supports this argument with findings from an assessment of South African medical journals, conference reports, commission testimonies, and other medical records showing that tuberculosis and other diseases were construed in medical discourse as proof of the physiological susceptibility of Africans to life in white cities, supporting thereby the oppressive structure of apartheid segregation.

Inherently, the biomedical model tends to lend itself to this type of use because it narrowly locates the causes of ill health in the actions and organs of sufferers.

A sick individual is regarded as a set of physical symptoms, rather than as a person who belongs to a social class in a particular society. This process turns our attention away from the political roots of disease, and conceals these roots by providing us with an alternative explanation. By and large, says this explanation, people are responsible for their own health. If they get sick it is a chance occurrence, no-one is to blame. . . . If people get cholera, it is because they do not use "safe, chlorinated water." If children are malnourished, their parents do not feed them properly, and they have more children than they can look after properly. Illness is seen as nature's revenge on people who live unhygienically and do not observe rules of cleanliness.   (de Beer 1986:70)

The potential for biomedical co-optation of medical anthropology – that is, for the quiet incorporation of key "Western ideological medical assumptions . . . [that are] intrinsic both to structures of domination within Western contexts and to the controlling articulation of the West with non-Western peoples" – is rooted in the role medical anthropologists often play in the clinical setting and in the limited examination of biomedicine as a socioeconomic system that has characterized much work done within the subdiscipline (Kapferer 1988:429).

The encounter unveiled: contemporary debates in the field

The general acceptance of medical anthropology during the 1970s and early 1980s helped to gloss over underlying problems in the ideology and roles of medical anthropology, the problems described in the title of this chapter as "the burdens of oppression." Within a few years of medical anthropology's formal arrival, however, its perspectives, approaches, and activities became the subject of internal critiques and heated debates. In no small way, medical anthropology's handling of social inequality – and in the eyes of some, its unintended hegemonic support of inequality – have been central to these disputations.

The dominant, if tacit, theoretical perspective within the field at the time was an approach called medical ecology. Rooted in both cultural ecology and evolutionary theory, this approach embraces adaptation, defined as behavioral or biological changes at either the individual or group level that support survival in a given environment, as the core concept in the field. From this perspective, health is seen as a measure of environmental adaptation. In other words, a central premise of medical ecology is that a social group's level of health reflects the nature and quality of the relationships "within the group, with neighboring groups, and with the plants and animals [as well as nonbiotic features] of the habitat" (McElroy and Townsend 1996:12). Beliefs and behaviors that improve health or protect societal members from disease or injury are adaptive.

Understanding human biology and behavior as an interactive set of adaptations to ecological and social challenges makes a lot of sense to many medical anthropologists. Yet others began to question this approach. Good (1994:45), for example, questioned the utility of treating disease as a natural object and medical systems as utilitarian social responses to intrusive natural conditions. Lost in such understanding, he maintained, was full appreciation of the human cultural/symbolic construction of the world that people inhabit. In other words, humans can only experience the external material world through their cultural frames, and thus diseases, as they are known, consciously and somatically by sufferers and healers alike, are containers packed with cultural content. Even science or biomedicine do not offer culture-free accounts of the physical world.

Critical medical anthropologists, while agreeing with much in interpretative medical anthropology's critique of the ecological model, asked questions about the origin of dominant cultural constructions, including: whose social realities and interests (e.g. which social class, gender, race, or ethnic group) do particular cultural conceptions express, and under what set of historic conditions do they arise? Further, they pointed out that the medical ecological model did not squarely address the fact that "it is not merely the idea of nature – the way [external reality] is conceived and related to by humans – but also the very physical shape of nature, including of course human biology, that has been deeply influenced by an evolutionary history of hierarchical social structures – that is to say, by the changing political economy of human society" (Singer 1996a:497).

The problem inherent in narrowly conceptualizing the health aspects of the human/environmental relationship in terms of adaptation can be illustrated with the case of the indigenous people of Tasmania, an island that lies just off the southeastern tip of Australia. Tasmania was successfully inhabited by Aboriginal people for over 30 thousand years prior to the arrival of Europeans at the end of the 18th century; nonetheless, medical ecologists cite the Tasmanians as a case of *maladaptation* that led to the dying out of these people by 1876.

> In about 12,000 years of isolation from the mainland, the Tasmanians *devolved*, losing the ability to make many tools, to make fire, and to construct rafts or catamarans that would have allowed them to fish and travel. The division of labor between men and women was inefficient, endangering women. Their political ecology emphasized raiding, capture of women, and competitiveness between tribal bands. During the cold season they went hungry, and their clothing and housing were inadequate. . . . [In sum] their way of life was far from ideal, and the society quickly collapsed after Europeans arrived. (McElroy and Townsend 1996:112, emphasis in original)

The impression given by this account is that the arrival of European settlers on Tasmania in the late 18th century played but a small part in the disappearance of a society that was poorly adapted to its environment. A closer examination of the historic political economic events surrounding the nature and impact of European arrival suggest a different conclusion. Within 30 years of the landing of the British on Tasmania, the indigenous population, which had been stable at around 4,000–5,000 prior to contact, dropped to a mere 111. This shocking level of depopulation, which was occurring not just in Tasmania but throughout Britain's Third World colonies, led the British House of Commons to constitute a 15-member Select Committee on Aborigines, which published its findings in 1837. The committee concluded that the lands of indigenous people "had been usurped; their property seized; their character debased; . . . European vices and diseases have been introduced" (quoted in Bodley 1975:25). Douglas Oliver (1961:161), an anthropologist with extensive experience in Oceania, reports the exact nature of these "European vices," noting that the aboriginal peoples of Australia and Tasmania

> were the victims of playfulness: the sport-loving British pioneers occasionally relieved the boredom of isolation by hunting "abos" in lieu of other game. More frequently, however, these hunts were serious undertakings: now and then aborigines would be brash enough to kill or steal livestock pastured on their horde territories, and that called for systematic drives of extermination by the white owners. Aboriginal men, women, and children would be rounded up and shot; to slay a pregnant woman was, logically, doubly commendable. Sometimes the same objective was accomplished by leaving poisoned food. . . . The tragedy was played to its finish in Tasmania, where all [indigenous people] were wiped out . . . by 1876. . . . One efficient colonial administrator even declared an open season against the Tasmanians, culminating in the infamous "black Drive" [an open season on the hunting of Tasmanians] of 1830.

Quite simply, the "disappearance" of the Tasmanians was not a consequence of maladaptation to their environment. They were victims of the wave of genocidal extermination that characterized the colonial era. Adding insult to grave injury, the 7,000 Tasmanians who identify themselves as aborigines today have, in the words of an aboriginal rights leader, "had to fight the stigma that we didn't exist" (quoted in Quammen 1996:396).

Ironically, the ultimate lesson of the Tasmanian case is that a people's will to survive even against enormous social and political odds may be the real measure of importance in assessing the meaning of health at the population level. Also, the Tasmanian case starkly reveals that the higher rates of morbidity and mortality commonly found among the poor and the oppressed reflect patterns of social inequality and unequal access to health-conferring resources rather than failed adaptation to natural environments. One goal of the critical medical anthropologists is to explain how socially meaningful realities, including beliefs about health and illness, are created and maintained by a group of people in response to a given set of social relations and conditions. They are also concerned with developing a comprehension of how socially structured relations, like those among social classes, genders, or ethnic groups, place subordinated social strata in harm's way. In short, they attempt to understand the ways political-economic forces, cultural practices, and biological factors combine to produce both people's ideas about disease (and risk) and associated behaviors. They are interested as well in the actual manifestation and distribution of disease and other indicators of poor health.

Consequently, critical medical anthropologists are concerned with the historic pathways through which particular health beliefs and practices emerge (for example, the frequent U.S. emphasis on individual responsibility for getting sick because of so-called lifestyle "choices") and through which specific diseases come to be recognized, labeled, and imbued with social meanings (for example, the 19th-century biomedical identification of hysteria as a disease of women that was caused by the uterus and cured through a hysterectomy). In their view, the act of "discovering" a disease is a social act that entails far more than the objective accumulation of medical knowledge about the natural world and the pathogenic microorganisms or malignant tissues to be found there. It involves the creative process of coming to "see" an underlying similarity in the always varied signs and symptoms presented by diverse patients. While the identification of a new disease or the diagnosis of a particular disease in a specific patient, in retrospect, generally is described as one of discovering a reality that exists in the natural world, in actuality it is one of social construction. So too are the meanings culturally linked to the disease in question (for example, the painful stigma attached to some diseases). Critical medical anthropologists argue that the biomedical model came into existence and rose to prominence because of the structure of social relations in society that its practices help to reinforce.

Debates among medical anthropologists since the mid-1980s, focusing on issues of diversity and inequality, fueled efforts to reconstruct medical anthropology as something more than a handmaiden of biomedicine.

Engaging Diversity in Medical Anthropology: The Case of AIDS

AIDS, because of its distribution, the ways in which societies have responded to it, and the fact that it remains a pressing health issue in the contemporary world, offers an important window on the social and cultural construction of health and disease within the context of diversity. While anthropologists were slow to become involved in research and intervention initiatives pertaining to AIDS, more than 200 anthropologists are currently engaged in these initiatives. As a result, "it is safe to assert that no topic in the entire field of anthropology commands more attention and more scholarly involvement at the present time" (Bolton and Orozco 1994:vi). This has produced an extensive anthropological literature documented in *The AIDS Bibliography* (Bolton and Orozco 1994), in M.A. theses and doctoral dissertations, in ethnographies (e.g. Sobo 1999; Green and Sobo 2000), in edited collections (e.g. Farmer et al. 1996; Feldman 1990, 1994; Herdt and Lindenbaum 1992; Marshall et al. 1999; Sobo 1999; Singer 1998; Van Vugt 1994), in reviews (e.g. Farmer 1997), and in sections on AIDS in anthropological textbooks (e.g. Baer et al. 1997). Cultural diversity and social inequality have been central topics in much of this work.

AIDS, nationality, and ethnicity

Epidemics, and the social ways in which people respond to them, provide a window on the nature of human societies. Briggs' (1961:77) description of 19th-century cholera as "a disease of society in the most profound sense" applies as well to many other epidemics, including the contemporary global AIDS pandemic. One "lesson" from past epidemics is the frequent pattern of "victimizing and stigmatizing of helpless members of minority groups and the indifference of public officials callous to human suffering" (Fee and Fox 1992:2). This suggests that epidemics are shaped as much by social as they are by biological factors. The AIDS epidemic is no different.

Among the range of social factors that shape the direction, extent, and character of an epidemic, *the structure of social relations that grow out of the system of economic production* have particular importance. This realization draws our attention to the role of political-economic relationships in understanding epidemics, including AIDS. Bateson and Goldsby (1988:2) assert that AIDS has spread "along the fault lines of . . . society and become a metaphor for understanding . . . society." By referring to AIDS as a metaphor for society, they draw attention to the ways in which the AIDS crisis exposes the nature and consequences of social inequality within and between nations and groups in the contemporary world, and the impact of these relations on health. Indeed, it is not inappropriate to say that AIDS has revealed itself as a disease of society – not merely a social disease, but a disease of stratified and oppressive social relations that exist locally within communities, nationally within the social systems of individual countries, and internationally within the global system of nations. Throughout its known history, AIDS "has repeatedly demonstrated its ability to cross all borders: social, cultural, economic, political" (Mann et al. 1992:3), but often this has not brought people closer together to appreciate their common plight and their shared needs as human beings. Rather, the epidemic commonly has led to increased conflict and social contestation, usually along preexisting lines of tension. AIDS very likely has become the most political affliction visited upon the human species in modern times. This disease reminds us just how political are all facets of health, illness, treatment, and health-related discourse. This point is illustrated below in the discussion of three faces of AIDS: AIDS in Haitians, AIDS in the inner city, and AIDS in women.

The issue of origin: AIDS in Haiti

As the second New World colonial creation to successfully overthrow European political dominance and the world's first independent black republic, Haiti has long held a special place in Euro-centered global politics and political discourse. This place was defined early in Haitian history. Following on the heels of the American Revolution, and certainly inspired by the American victory over British colonialism, a general slave rebellion was launched in Saint-Domingue in 1791. A little over a decade later, rebellious forces under Jean-Jacques Dessalines proclaimed independence from France and adopted the indigenous Indian name of Haiti for their new nation. Fearful of the lessons of a triumphant slave rebellion, the West condemned Haiti to the status of an international pariah state, a position that was sustained through the projection onto the former colony of an image of dangerous and bizarre Otherness. In the Western imagination, Haiti was constructed as "another world far from what they know as ordinary" (Barry et al. 1984:337). Thus voodoo, the indigenously formed syncretic religious system of Haiti, became synonymous in the West with evil, the epitome of so-called "black magic," zombiism, strange trances, unearthly feats, and unbridled animalistic sexuality.

With the appearance of AIDS, this distorted portrayal was generalized, and Haitians were represented as dangerously infectious and life-threatening by their very nature. By 1982, only a year after the identification of the first AIDS cases, Haitians were labeled as a "risk group" by the U.S. Centers for Disease Control. As a consequence, it was not long before being a Haitian meant being "perceived as an AIDS 'carrier'" and "the fact that AIDS was found among heterosexuals in Haiti . . . [was read as] evidence that Haiti was the source of the disease" (Gilman 1987:102). The U.S. press carried stories quoting Dr. Bruce Chabner of the National Cancer Institute, who reported: "we suspect that this [disease] may be an epidemic Haitian virus" (quoted in Farmer 1992:2). The politico-ideological context for these developments lay in the well-established constructed images of Haiti.

The link with voodoo was asserted or suggested in both medical and social science texts. Voodoo practices were considered a cause of the syndrome by two MIT physicians (Moses and Moses 1983). Other "bizarre" or "weird" features alleged to be characteristic of Haiti also were implicated.

> Some U.S. researchers proposed that AIDS began with an outbreak of African swine fever in Haitian pigs, and the swine virus had been passed to humans. Others suggested that a Haitian homosexual may have contracted the swine virus from eating undercooked pork, and then passed it on to homosexual partners from the United States during acts of prostitution. . . . Others proposed that Haitians may have contracted the virus from monkeys as part of bizarre sexual practices in Haitian brothels. (Sabatier 1988:45)

"Even cannibalism, the most popular nineteenth-century smear, was resuscitated during discussions of Haiti's role in the AIDS pandemic" (Farmer 1990:438). In the dark light cast by such linkages, in 1990 the U.S. Food and Drug Administration banned Haitians in the U.S. from donating blood.

All along, Haitian physicians studying the disease had produced evidence to support an alternative, more mundane, although no less politically significant explanation of the high prevalence of AIDS among Haitians. They found that most early cases could be traced to a red-light prostitution district in Port-au-Prince, and that none of the stored blood samples drawn from Haitian adults during the 1977–79 outbreak of dengue fever carried antibodies to HIV. These data were consistent with the hypothesis that HIV was not indigenous to the country but rather had been introduced into Haiti in the late 1970s or early 1980s either by tourists or returning Haitians coming from the United States or Europe (Pape et al. 1986). It is well known that many foreigners came to Haiti during the 1970s tourist boom seeking sex. Not surprisingly, admitting to exchanging sex for desperately needed tourist dollars was quite frequent among early Haitian AIDS patients.

Driven by poverty that was itself the product of Haitian subordination to external economies and internal stratification, prostitution became a means of survival for some rural migrants to Haiti's crowded capital. In short, the politics of AIDS among Haitians and other Caribbean peoples are the politics of political-economic domination and, as a result, "the map of HIV in the New World reflects to an important degree the geography of U.S. neocolonialism" (Farmer 1992:261). But this set of political relations was successfully submerged in more exotic accounts of Haitian AIDS, images that exuded racism while they mystified hegemony. The mundane and age-old tale of political-economic domination leading to sexual domination that is a good piece of the real story of Haitian AIDS, remained hidden behind newfangled renditions of the master's fear of the rebellious subordinate. And, in various guises, this is a significant part of the history and politics of AIDS everywhere, from the preoccupation with "discovering" the African origins of the epidemic to the effort to construct AIDS as a disease peculiar to the bodies of gay men and people of color, a disease of the distant and diminished Other.

Ironically, Haitians have their own theory of how AIDS, or *sida* as it is known in Creole, came to their island and how it spread to large numbers of individuals living throughout Haiti, especially among those in urban areas from the poor and working classes. This theory, while no less a cultural creation than other popular ideas about AIDS, nonetheless reflects a clearer understanding of the global system than is commonly found among North Americans and is an example of the fact that those at the bottom often have a somewhat better, less mystified, understanding of the actual nature and structure of oppression than those higher up the ladder of social power.

AIDS and the inner-city health crisis

When it comes to issues of health and well-being, it is reasonable to describe the United States as constituting (at least) two separate if intertwined societies: people of the inner city and everyone else. While poverty is by no means confined to the inner city, and neither are all oppressed ethnic minorities or people of color, the intersection of urban poverty and socially devalued ethnicity (especially being African American and Latino, and in some parts of the country Native American and Asian as well) has proven to be a particularly unhealthy combination. One consequence has been the rampant spread of AIDS in many U.S. inner-city areas. Almost half of people in America who have been diagnosed as having AIDS are African Americans and Latinos from impoverished urban neighborhoods.

In retrospect, it is clear that AIDS was a profoundly unexpected disease, "a startling discontinuity with the past" (Fee and Fox 1992:1). As McCombie (1990:10) suggests, global public health efforts that predate the beginning of the AIDS epidemic, such as the smallpox eradication program, "reinforced the notion that mortality from infectious disease was a thing of the past." Consequently, whatever the actual health needs of the heterogeneous U.S. population, the primary concerns of the health care system were the so-called Western diseases – that is, chronic health problems, such as cancer, of a developed nation with an aging population. However, it is evident that low-income, marginalized areas of U.S. cities have been rocked by an explosive chain reaction of interconnected health crises. Examination of these phenomena suggests that standard epidemiological terms like "epidemic," endemic," and "pandemic" do not adequately label the contemporary inner-city health scene, which is characterized by a set of closely interrelated endemic (long-enduring) and epidemic (rapidly spreading) conditions, all of which are strongly influenced by a broader set of political-economic and social factors, including high rates of unemployment, poverty, homelessness and residential overcrowding, substandard nutrition, environmental toxins and related environmental health risks, infrastructural deterioration and loss of quality housing stock, forced geographic mobility, family breakup and disruption of social support networks, youth gang and drug-related violence, and health care inequality. As a result, as McCord and Freeman (1990) have observed, men in Bangladesh have a higher probability of survival after age 35 than men in Harlem. More generally, "the death rate in blacks is higher than that in whites, and for many causes of death mortality differentials are increasing rather than decreasing" (Navarro 1990:1238). However, these differences cannot be understood only in terms of racial inequalities, there are significant class factors involved as well. The vast majority of urban-dwelling African Americans, as well as Latinos, "are members of the low paid, poorly educated working class that have higher morbidity and mortality rates than high-earning, better educated people" (Navarro 1990: 1240). Indeed, these mortality differentials are directly tied to the widening wealth and income differentials between the upper and lower classes of U.S. society.

Rather than treating AIDS in isolation as a new epidemic, I have suggested the term *syndemic* to refer to the synergistic or intertwined and mutually enhancing health and social problems facing the urban poor (Singer 1994). Studies show that urban minority populations suffer from disproportionately high rates of preventable infant mortality and low birthweight, diabetes, hypertension, cirrhosis, tuberculosis, substance abuse, human immunodeficiency disease, and sexually transmitted diseases (Council on Scientific Affairs 1991; Secretary's Task Force on black and Minority Health 1985; Turner et al. 1989). The differences are striking, and infant mortality, often used as a general reflection of the health of a population, provides a disturbing example.

> African American children are twice as likely to be born prematurely, die during the first year of life, suffer low birthweight, have mothers who receive late or no prenatal care, be born to a teenage or unmarried parent, be unemployed as teenagers, have unemployed parents, and live in substandard housing. Furthermore, African American children are three times more likely than whites to be poor, have their mothers die in childbirth, live in a female-headed family, be in foster care, and be placed in an educable mentally-retarded class. (Hope 1992:153)

Consequently, household income is the single best indicator of an infant's vulnerability, with poor families having infant mortality rates that are one and a half to three times higher than wealthier families (Nersesian 1988:374).

Class disparities in mortality rates are not limited to infancy; substantial differences also have been found among older children. For example, children from inner-city poor families are more likely to die from respiratory diseases or in fires, than children from wealthier suburban families. Inadequately heated and ventilated apartments also contribute to death at an early age for poor urban children. Hunger and poor nutrition are additional factors. Studies in Hartford, Connecticut, have shown a significant link exists between hunger, malnutrition, and inner-city poverty, especially among ethnic minorities (Damio and Cohen 1990; Pérez-Escamilla et al. 1996). Federal cuts in food assistance programs have contributed to significant drops in the number of children receiving free and reduced-price school lunches, producing growing reports of hunger and malnutrition from pediatricians in cities around the country (Physician Task Force on Hunger in America 1985).

Cardiovascular disease commonly has been portrayed as primarily a consequence of either genetic predisposition or "lifestyle choice," including such factors as personal eating or exercise habits. Research by David Barker and his colleagues shows that the lower the birthweight of a newborn, or the body-weight of a one-year-old infant, the greater the level of risk for developing heart disease or stroke in adulthood. Low-birthweight babies, they report, have higher blood pressure and higher concentrations of the clotting factors fibrinogen and factor VII as well as low-density-lipoprotein (LDL) cholesterol than adults, factors that are associated with susceptibility to cardiovascular disease. Numerous attempts have been made to explain excessive levels of premature morbidity and mortality from cardiovascular diseases, especially heart diseases, stroke, and hypertension. Some explain this pattern in terms of racial-genetic predisposition; however, research by Barker and others reveals the likely relationship of these diseases to the larger syndemic health crisis and thus to poverty and social inequality (Dressler 1991).

Smoking and tobacco use are significant causes of cardiovascular and other diseases. Ethnic minority populations suffer from higher rates of smoking-caused disease and death than do whites (Rivo et al. 1989). Tobacco use has been found to be an important factor in low birthweight, indicating the multiple consequences of tobacco promotion for minority communities. Beyond the immediate health effects of smoking, Nichter and Cartwright (1981:237) argue that for poor families in particular smoking is damaging in three additional ways:

> First, smoking leads to and exacerbates chronic illness, which in turn reduces adults' ability to provide for their children. Smoking also daily diverts scarce household resources which might be used more productively. And third, children living with smokers are exposed to smoke inhalation [i.e. passive smoking] and have more respiratory disease.

Alcohol-related problems have been found to be especially common among Latino and African American men. Studies in the Bay Area and Hartford have found that, compared to a national sample of men, Puerto Rican men were much more likely to report health problems associated with drinking, to have a friend or spouse complain about their drinking, or to have alcohol-related problems with the police (Singer et al. 1992). Similarly, studies of inner-city African Americans have found they experience higher than average rates of physiological complications, such as esophageal cancer and cirrhosis mortality, related to long-term heavy alcohol consumption (Marlin et al. 1980). While both Latino and African American cultures include strong proscriptions on alcohol consumption (in certain contexts, for certain social subgroups, or in relationship to particular religious belief systems), inner-city areas are populated by people who embrace a range of values and social practices related to drinking (Gaines 1985). Although abstinence is notably high among particular social groupings in the inner city, drinking-related problems are comparatively high for both African Americans and Latinos.

The association between drug use and deteriorated inner-city areas has been discussed in the social science literature since the 1920s. A summary of recent epidemiological studies indicates that, while there is a decline in current illicit drug use nationally, "minorities, particularly blacks and Hispanics, are more likely to reside in central city areas and may therefore be more at risk for drug abuse and ultimately more at risk for the negative social and health consequences associated with drug abuse" than the general U.S. population (Kopstein and Roth 1990:1–2). Among adults over 35 years of age, African American men are the population subgroup most likely to report illicit drug use at least once in their lives, in the past year, and in the past month. Some 37 percent of African American men in this age group report lifetime use, compared to 25 percent of white men. An examination of individual drug prevalence patterns also confirms the high level of risk among ethnic minority groups. Data from the National Institute on Drug Abuse's national drug abuse warning network for monitoring the medical consequences of drug abuse (DAWN) as reported by participating hospital emergency rooms and medical examiner offices, show African American patients were the most likely group to mention use of an illicit drug in conjunction with their emergency room visit. The data suggest that, directly and indirectly, drug abuse disproportionately affects inner-city ethnic minority populations. Importantly, despite this fact, Kopstein and Roth (1990:51) note that "blacks presenting with a drug abuse problem at the emergency rooms in the DAWN system were more likely than whites to be treated and released. Whites, on the other hand were more likely to be admitted to the hospital."

Both African Americans and Latinos have been found to be overrepresented among the large number of injection drug users (IDUs) in U.S. urban areas (Friedman et al. 1990). David Musto, whose book *The American Disease* (1987) is a classic in the drug field (even though drug use, or even injection drug use, are clearly international and not peculiarly North American problems), has assembled data to suggest a steady rise in the number of IDUs from the 1970s on. By 1987, aggregated data from state alcohol and drug agencies indicate that there were about 1.5 million IDUs in the United States. Friedman, Sotheran, et al. (1987), using New York State Division of Substance Abuse Services admissions data, estimate that the ethnic composition of injection drug users in New York City is 38% African American, 38% Latino, and 23% white, while the city as a whole is 52% white, 24% African American, and 20% Latino.

These data suggest that under conditions of discrimination, poverty, deprivation, homelessness, unemployment, and frustrated expectations, mood-altering drugs found an open market in inner-city areas (Susser 1996). This response to oppressive conditions was facilitated by the ready availability of drugs in ghetto and barrio neighborhoods, a consequence of Mafia targeting of these areas for drug distribution. As Waldorf (1973:23) observes: "Heroin is seemingly everywhere in black and Puerto Rican ghettos and young people are aware of it from an early age." Drugs offer insulation from the outside world allowing users to

> feel that their harsh and hostile environment cannot penetrate their lives. They escape from their problems, other people, and feel better. (Waldorf 1973: 89)

The transmission of AIDS, of course, has been closely linked to drug injection; approximately 35 percent of AIDS cases reported to the Centers for Disease Control and Prevention (CDC) (1997a) are among injection drug users. The ethnic and gender breakdown of new injection drug use–related AIDS cases reported in 1995 was: 20% female, 13% men who have sex with men, 50% African American, and 24% Latino (Centers for Disease Control and Prevention 1996). Among women, 51% of all U.S. AIDS cases are African American, and another 20% are Latina (Centers for Disease Control and Prevention 1990). Among children, over 75% of AIDS cases are among ethnic minorities. The incidence of heterosexually acquired AIDS is almost 10 times greater for African Americans and 4 times greater for Latinos than for whites (Aral and Holmes 1989). Similarly, "[a] disproportionate share of the burden of adolescent AIDS cases is borne by minority youth" (Miller et al. 1990:160). Importantly, the median survival time of individuals diagnosed with AIDS varies by ethnicity. In Connecticut, prior to the introduction of new AIDS treatments, the median survival in months was 11.2 for whites compared to 7.7 for African Americans and 10.2 for Latinos (Connecticut Department of Health Services 1990), reflecting the broader differences in the general health and access to health services of these populations. Since the introduction of increasingly effective combination therapies with antiviral agents, there has been a drop in the number of estimated AIDS deaths (for example, by 13% between 1995 and 1996). However, the decline for non-Latino whites between 1995 and 1996 was 21% compared to 2% for African Americans and 10% for Latinos (Centers for Disease Control and Prevention 1997b).

Men who have sex with men (MSM) make up the largest proportion (44 percent) of persons who have been diagnosed with AIDS (Centers for Disease Control and Prevention 1997b). Rates of HIV/AIDS are especially high among ethnic minority MSM and account for 31 percent of the reported cases among MSM. Minority MSM suffer from what Friedman, Jose, et al. (1998) refer to as "multiple subordination," and are often cut off from support structures for people with HIV/AIDS that have developed in the predominantly middle-class, gay-identified community.

There has been a dramatic rise in the incidence of syphilis in the United States, "attributable to a very steep rise in infection among black men and women" since the mid-1980s (Aral and Holmes 1989:63). By 1991, 85 percent of primary and secondary syphilis cases recorded were among African Americans (Hahn et al. 1989). In part, this sharp increase has been linked to sex for drugs or money exchanges associated with cocaine use. Blood test data show that low income, urban residence, and lack of education are all associated with positive blood results for syphilis. The rate of incidence for gonorrhea infection, pelvic inflammatory infection, herpes simplex virus type 2, hepatitis B, and cervical cancer with a suspected STD etiology is 2.3 times greater among African Americans than whites (Hahn et al. 1989; Aral and Holmes 1989; Centers for Disease Control and Prevention 1992).

As this epidemiological overview suggests, the diseases and conditions that make up the inner-city syndemic are closely intertwined. Poverty contributes to poor nutrition and susceptibility to infection. Poor nutrition, chronic stress, and prior disease produce a compromised immune system, increasing susceptibility to new infection. A range of socioeconomic problems and stressors increase the likelihood of substance abuse and exposure to HIV. Substance abuse contributes to increased risk for exposure to an STD, which can, in turn, be a co-factor in HIV infection (Ho 1996). HIV further damages the immune system, increasing susceptibility to a host of other diseases. In this way, HIV increases susceptibility to tuberculosis; however, there is growing evidence that the tuberculosis bacterium, in turn, can activate latent HIV. Locating and reconceptualizing AIDS within the broader syndemic that plagues the inner-city poor, helps to demystify the rapid spread of the disease in marginalized populations. In this context, AIDS itself emerges as an opportunistic disease, a disease of compromised health and social conditions, a disease of poverty. For this reason, it is important to examine the social origins of disease and ill health, as well as the immediate causes (e.g. particular pathogens) of specific health problems. In the case of AIDS, conceptually isolating this disease from its wider health environment has resulted in the epidemiological construction of "risk groups" and "risk behaviors" which, rather than unhealthy living and working conditions, discrimination, racism, and homophobia, and the ways in which these conditions foster the spread of the Human Immunodeficiency Virus, have become the primary focus of public health efforts.

Women and AIDS

Early in the epidemic it was assumed that AIDS was a disease of men, in particular, gay men. The die was cast as the first reported cases of what later would be called AIDS were documented in the public health literature. All of the patients were gay men from New York and California. Within two months of the first report on AIDS, however, similar symptoms began showing up among female (and male) injection drug users in New York, and also among their children. Soon a matching set of symptoms was reported among women in other states as well. Despite these early cases, AIDS in women, and the gender-specific manifestations of the disease were not recognized for a number of years. AIDS came to be defined in terms of its particular symptomatic expression among men. Consequently, many women in the United States and elsewhere died of AIDS but were never counted in the upwardly spiraling AIDS statistics.

The initial standard definition of AIDS was the combined state of exhibiting antibodies (created by the body's immune system to fight off the disease) to the

Human Immunodeficiency Virus (HIV) and the presence of one or more specified degenerative or neoplastic diseases (indicating that the immune system was failing in its mission to protect the body from the invading pathogen). However, there were many individuals who expressed clinical symptoms and laboratory abnormalities that suggested infection with HIV but did not meet the CDC criteria for AIDS. Most notable in this regard were opportunistic HIV-related conditions common among or peculiar to women. Various conditions, including pelvic inflammatory disease and yeast infection, as well as cervical cancer are more frequent, more severe, and less responsive to treatment among HIV seropositive women, suggesting a diminished immune system capacity. However, these conditions were not officially defined or treated as manifestations of AIDS.

As a result of social pressure – pressure from AIDS activists and women more than from the biomedical world – the official definition of AIDS was changed in January 1993. Now, diseases like invasive cervical cancer in women who were seropositive (i.e. infected with HIV) were included as opportunistic conditions and counts of remaining T-cells (because T-cells, an important component of the immune system, are targeted by HIV) became part of the definition of having AIDS. As a result, during the first 3-month period after the redefinition, the number of women diagnosed with AIDS increased by over 200 percent compared to the same period a year before.

One of the early signs that HIV could and would spread among women was the high rate of heterosexual transmission that was occurring among non-drug-using women in Africa in the early 1980s. But recognition of the implications of the spread of HIV in Africa did not happen for at least two reasons. First and foremost, there is the issue of racism. The initial cases in Africa of what later was labeled AIDS were documented by physicians working in Kinshasa toward the end of 1981. AIDS research in Africa has focused on "sexual promiscuity" (that is, sexual relations with multiple partners), which often is attributed to moral weakness. Sexual behavior among people of African origin frequently has been explained in terms of exotic cultural norms without consideration of the powerful social and economic constraints underlying this "high-risk" behavior (Romero-Daza and Himmelgreen 1998). Additionally, focus on stigmatized AIDS "risk groups" (e.g. prostitutes) downplayed social structural features of the African epidemic. These emphases increased the isolation of women who became infected with the virus, especially those in monogamous relationships who got HIV from their primary partners. The second reason is that, since the beginning of the AIDS pandemic, there has been an almost unconscious invoking of "otherness" (that is, thinking of AIDS as a disease that only strikes other people, people different from us) and an intense stigmatization of those who have become infected. Consequently, the heterosexual transmission of AIDS in Africa was not treated as relevant to the United States.

As the epidemic developed and the number of AIDS cases among women in America mounted, it became clear that women experience the negative impacts of AIDS in three different ways. First, they must endure their own risk of infection and the physiological and emotional consequences of the disease as it progresses to incapacitation and possible death. Second, they face the risk of transmitting the virus to their offspring, and the subsequent guilt and grief associated with disease and death in children. Third, as the traditional caregivers in many societies, women are usually responsible for nursing infected family members. While women in less developed areas of the world more commonly experience this threefold burden, it is increasingly a reality for the many inner-city women in industrialized nations who face the burden of the AIDS syndemic.

There is general agreement that AIDS has had a significant impact on the lives of women, but an accurate count of the numbers of women infected by HIV is difficult to achieve for several reasons. Women in the less developed areas of the world are believed to be at higher risk of HIV infection because of problems related to undiagnosed sexually transmitted diseases (STDs) and to childbirth complications (Ulin 1992). However real this biological susceptibility may be, the underlying causes for women's increased risk of HIV infection and AIDS are the power inequalities women face in relation to men and to societal institutions. For example, women's disadvantageous economic status, coupled with limited employment opportunities, often forces them into sexual relations with multiple partners from which they derive material support for their own survival and that of their children (Romero-Daza 1994). Furthermore, women's need for economic support and fear of physical violence limit their power to demand the use of condoms by their partners, which increases their risk of becoming infected (Weeks et al. 1995).

In the United States, the changing nature of the epidemic in recent years has demonstrated increasing risk of infection among women, regardless of their participation in drug use or of their sexual practices. AIDS is now the number-one killer of women between the ages of 25 and 44. Proportionate increases in reported AIDS cases between 1992 and 1993 were significantly higher among women than men. Moreover, while the estimated number of deaths among persons with AIDS declined by 15 percent for men between 1994 and 1996, for women there was a 3 percent increase (Centers for Disease Control and Prevention 1997a).

Understanding the processes by which women become infected with HIV requires recognition of the multiplicity of factors that shape their potential exposure to the virus and that limit their options for prevention. Women's primary risk of infection in the United States remains injection drug use. Studies suggest that women injectors may be at greater risk than their male counterparts through higher injection rates (Weeks et al. 1991) and more frequent use of previously-used needles (Barnard 1993), in part because when they share needles with men, women tend to inject after the men. Nevertheless, unprotected sexual contact with infected male partners accounts for an increasing percentage of cases (Centers for Disease Control and Prevention 1995). In 1992, for the first time ever, female cases attributed to heterosexual transmission exceeded those attributed to injection drug use alone. Currently, heterosexual transmission is the second most common route of HIV infection for women in the United States (Stoneburner et al. 1990).

It is well recognized that women in poverty are far more likely to have sex partners who inject drugs, have high rates of STDs and HIV, and face discrimination in access to health care and other services (Nyamathi et al. 1993). Combined with addiction, poverty decreases viable economic options for women, and increases their need to exchange sex for money or drugs to support themselves and their families. Moreover, women's economic dependence on men, gender expectations which force them into submissive roles, and the psychological pressure on women to deny risk with primary partners as a means of affirming trust in their relationships and personal self-worth, influence some women, particularly those in poorer economic circumstances, to limit AIDS preventive measures (Kane 1990). At issue are the specific ways in which power is exercised by women and men in decision making about sexual behaviors, how gender relations and roles mediate behavior changes particularly related to sexual activity or drug use with male partners, and how poverty affects each of these factors.

Women of color in the United States face the greatest risk of HIV infection, including infection through heterosexual transmission. Studies of AIDS knowledge, perceived HIV risk, and risky practices have shown high knowledge levels among African American women, despite lower perceived risk, and high rates of risky sexual activity, especially when accompanied by cocaine/crack use (Flaskerud and Nyamathi 1989). This pattern of high risk coupled with limited perception of risk is especially common among Latina women who are linguistically and socially isolated from the surrounding non-Latino community (Singer et al. 1998). Other factors such as poor self-esteem, attitudes about condom use or sexual assertiveness, and beliefs regarding male/female relationships potentially increase the risk, or impede the prevention, of HIV transmission specifically among African American and Latina women. At the same time, some cultural beliefs and attitudes offer promise for encouraging risk reduction. For example, the idealized role of Latino men as protectors of their family's well-being could be used as an incentive for the use of condoms to protect a pregnant woman from becoming infected and transmitting the virus to her unborn child. Clearly, multiple factors, including many that are the direct result of social inequality, interact to create multiple levels and sources of HIV risk for women in the United States, particularly for women of color. Among these women, sociocultural and biological vulnerability interact synergistically to put them regularly in harm's way.

RESOURCES

In medical anthropology, there have been some efforts to develop educational tools for classroom use, such as *Teaching Medical Anthropology* (Todd and Ruffini 1979) developed by the Society for Medical Anthropology; the *Training Manual in Medical Anthropology* (Hill 1991) produced by the American Anthropological Association; or the educational video *Anthropologists at Work: Making a Difference* (which features several medical anthropologists talking about their work and includes an accompanying handbook designed to answer student questions about the video) produced by the National Association for the Practice of Anthropology; However, on the whole the production of teaching aids other than textbooks remains an under-developed area. The issues of diversity and inequality in U.S. society have rarely been primary topics, although they have been addressed in articles appearing in the primary journals of the field: *Medical Anthropology*, *Medical Anthropology Quarterly*, *Social Science and Medicine*, *Culture, Medicine and Psychiatry*, and *Human Organization*. In *Medical Anthropology and the World System* (1995) Hans Baer et al. address issues of diversity, inequality, and health. Other help-ful resources are the web page of the Society for Medical Anthropology: <http://www.people.memphis.edu/~sma> and the Society for Medical Anthro-pology's monthly column in the *Anthropology Newsletter*.

On the specific topic of AIDS and diversity, other resources are available: *The AIDS Bibliography* (Bolton and Orozco 1994), *The Anthropology of AIDS: Syllabi and Other Teaching Resources* (Bolton and Kempler 1992), and the newsletter of the AIDS and Anthropology Research Group. Special issues devoted to sets of articles on AIDS have appeared in a number of anthropology journals, including *Medical Anthropology Quarterly* (4[1], 1990), *Practicing Anthropology* (15[4], 1993), *Medical Anthropology* (10[2], 1989; 14[2–4], 1990; 18[1], 1997), and *Culture, Medicine, and Psychiatry* (17[4], 1993). Also of interest are special issues of non-medical anthropological journals, including one entitled "Hispanics and AIDS" in the *Hispanic Journal of Behavioral Sci-ences* (12[4], 1990), a set of articles on African Americans and AIDS in *Trans-forming Anthropology* (4[1–2], 1993), and a special issue of the *Journal of Sex Research* (28[2], 1991) entitled "Anthropology, AIDS, and Sex."

REFERENCES CITED

Ackerknecht, Erwin
    1971   *Medicine and Ethnology: Selected Essays*. Baltimore: Johns Hopkins Univer-
        sity Press.
Aral, S., and K. Holmes
    1989   Sexually Transmitted Diseases in the AIDS Era. *Scientific American*
        264(2):62–69.
Baer, Hans, Merrill Singer, and Ida Susser
    1997   *Medical Anthropology and the World System*. Westport, CT: Bergin and
        Garvey.
Barnard, M.
    1993   Needle Sharing in Context: Patterns of Sharing Among Men and Women
        Injectors and HIV Risks. *Addiction* 88:837–840.
Barry, T., B. Wood, and D. Preusch
    1984   *The Other Side of Paradise*. New York: Grove Press.
Bateson, Mary Catherine, and Richard Goldsby
    1988   *Thinking AIDS: The Social Response to the Biological Threat*. Reading, MA:
        Addison-Wesley.
Bodley, John
    1975   *Victims of Progress*. Menlo Park, CA: Benjamin/Cummings.

Bolton, Ralph, and Erika Kempler
1992 *The Anthropology of AIDS: Syllabi and Other Teaching Resources.* Washington, DC: American Anthropological Association.

Bolton, Ralph, and Gail Orozco
1994 *The AIDS Bibliography: Studies in Anthropology and Related Fields.* Arlington, VA: American Anthropological Association.

Briggs, A.
1961 Cholera and Society in the Nineteenth Century, Past and Present. *Journal of Historical Studies* 19:76–96.

Centers for Disease Control and Prevention
1990 HIV/AIDS Surveillance: U.S. AIDS Cases Reported Through July 1990.
1992 Summary of Notifiable Diseases, United States, 1991. *Morbidity and Mortality Weekly Report* (MMWR) 40(53).
1995 Update: AIDS Among Women – United States, 1994. *Morbidity and Mortality Weekly Report* 44:81–84.
1996 AIDS Associated with Injecting-Drug Use – United States, 1995. *Morbidity and Mortality Weekly Review* 45(19):392–398.
1997a *HIV/AIDS Surveillance Report* 9(1):1–16.
1997b Update: Trends in AIDS Incidence, Deaths, and Prevalence – United States, 1996. *Morbidity and Mortality Weekly Review* 46(8):165–173.

Connecticut Department of Health Services
1990 *AIDS in Connecticut: Annual Surveillance Report*, December 31.

Council on Scientific Affairs
1991 Hispanic Health in the United States. *Journal of the American Medical Association* 265(20):248–252.

Damio, Grace, and L. Cohen
1990 *Policy Report of the Hartford Community Hunger Identification Project.* Hartford, CT: Hispanic Health Council.

de Beer, Cedric
1986 *The South African Disease.* Trenton, NJ: African World Press.

Dressler, William
1991 Social Class, Skin Color, and Arterial Blood Pressure in Two Societies. *Ethnicity and Disease* 1(1):60–77.

Farmer, Paul
1990 The Exotic and the Mundane: Human Immunodeficiency Virus in the Caribbean. *Human Nature* 1(4):415–445.
1992 *AIDS and Accusation.* Berkeley: University of California Press.
1997 AIDS and Anthropologists: Ten Years Later. *Medical Anthropology Quarterly* 11(4):516–525.

Farmer, Paul, Margaret Connors, and Janie Simmons, eds.
1996 *Women, Poverty and AIDS.* Monroe, ME: Common Courage Press.

Fee, Elizabeth, and Donald Fox
1992 Introduction: The Contemporary Historiography of AIDS. In *AIDS: The Making of a Chronic Disease*. E. Fee, and D. Fox, eds. Pp. 1–19. Berkeley: University of California Press.

Feldman, Douglas, ed.
1990 *Culture and AIDS.* New York: Praeger.
1994 *Global AIDS Policy.* Westport, CT: Bergin and Garvey.

Flaskerud, J. H., and A. M. Nyamathi
1989 Black and Latina Women's AIDS Related Knowledge, Attitudes, and Practices. *Research in Nursing and Health* 12:339–346.

Foster, George
  1980 Anthropological Research Perspectives on Health Problems in Developing
    Countries. *Social Science and Medicine* 18:847–854.
Foster, George, and Barbara Anderson
  1978 *Medical Anthropology.* New York: John Wiley.
Friedman, Samuel, Benny Jose, Bruce Stepherson, Alan Neaigus, Majorie Goldstein,
    Pat Mota, Richard Curtis, and Gilbert Ildefonso
  1998 Multiple Racial/Ethnic Subordination and HIV among Drug Injectors. In
    Singer, ed., pp. 105–127.
Friedman, Samuel, A. Sotheran, B. Abdul-Quader, Benny Primm, Don Des
    Jarlais, A. Kleinman, C. Mauge, Doug Goldsmith, W. El-Sadr, and R.
    Maslansky
  1987 The AIDS Epidemic among Blacks and Hispanics. *Milbank Memorial Fund
    Quarterly* 65(2):455–499.
Friedman, Samuel, Meryl Sufian, and Don Des Jarlais
  1990 The AIDS Epidemic among Latino Intravenous Drug Users. In *Drugs in
    Hispanic Communities.* Ronald Glick, and Joan Moore, eds. Pp. 45–54. New
    Brunswick, NJ: Rutgers University Press.
Gaines, Atwood
  1985 Alcohol: Cultural Conceptions and Social Behavior among Urban Blacks.
    In *The American Experience with Alcohol: Contrasting Cultural Perspectives.*
    L. Bennett, and G. Ames, eds. Pp. 171–197. New York: Plenum Press.
Gaines, Atwood, and Robert Hahn
  1985 Among the Physicians: Encounter, Exchange and Transformation. In *Physi-
    cians of Western Medicine.* Robert Hahn, and Atwood Gaines, eds. Pp. 3–22.
    Dordrecht: D. Reidel.
Gilman, Sander
  1987 AIDS and Syphilis: The Iconography of Disease. In *AIDS: Cultural
    Analysis, Cultural Activism.* Douglas Crimp, ed. Pp. 87–108. Cambridge, MA: MIT
    Press.
Good, Byron
  1994 *Medicine, Rationality, and Experience.* Cambridge, UK: Cambridge University
    Press.
Green, Gill, and Elisa Sobo
  2000 *The Endangered Self: Managing the Social Risks of HIV.* London:
    Routledge.
Hahn, Robert, L. Magder, S. Aral, R. Johnson, and S. Larsen
  1989 Race and the Prevalence of Syphilis Seroactivity in the United States Popula-
    tion: A National Sero-Epidemologic Study. *American Journal of Public Health*
    79(4):467–470.
Herdt, Gil, and Shirley Lindenbaum, eds.
  1992 *The Time of AIDS.* Newbury Park, CA: Sage.
Hill, Carole, ed.
  1991 *Training Manual in Medical Anthropology.* Washington, DC: American
    Anthropological Association.
Ho, John
  1996 The Influence of Coinfections on HIV Transmission and Disease Progression.
    The AIDS Reader 6(4):114–116, 137.
Hope, K.
  1992 Child Survival and Health Care among Low-Income African American
    Families in the United States. *Health Transition Review,* 2(2):151–164.

Hunter, S.
1985 Historical Perspectives on the Development of Health Systems Modeling in Medical Anthropology. *Social Science and Medicine* 21:1297–1305.

Kane, Stephanie
1990 AIDS, Addiction, and Condom Use: Sources of Sexual Risk for Heterosexual Women. *Journal of Sex Research* 27:427–444.

Kapferer, Bruce
1988 Gramsci's Body and a Critical Medical Anthropology. *Medical Anthropology Quarterly* 3:426–432.

Kopstein, A., and P. Roth
1990 *Drug Use among Ethnic Minorities*. Rockville, MD: National Institute on Drug Abuse.

Kundstadter, Peter
1978 The Comparative Study of Medical Systems in Society. In *Culture and Healing in Asian Societies: Anthropological, Psychiatric and Public Health Studies*. Arthur Kleinman, Peter Kundstadter, E. Russel Alexander, and J. Gate, eds. Pp. 393–406. Cambridge, MA: Schenkman.

Mann, Jonathan, Daniel Tarantola, and Thomas Netter
1992 *AIDS in the World*. Cambridge, MA: Harvard University Press.

Marlin, J., C. Kaelber, C. Sorenson, C. Dadovrian, and N. Munch
1980 *Trends of Cirrhosis of Liver Mortality. U.S. Alcohol Reference Manual*. Rockville, MD: National Institute on Alcohol Abuse and Alcoholism.

Marriott, McKim
1955 Western Medicine in a Village of Northern India. In *Health, Culture and Community*. Benjamin Paul, ed. Pp. 239–268. New York: Russell Sage Foundation.

Marshall, Patricia L., Merrill Singer, and Michael Clatts, eds.
1999 *Integrating Cultural, Observational, and Epidemiological Approaches in the Prevention of Drug Abuse and HIV/AIDS*. Bethesda, MD: National Institute on Drug Abuse.

Maxwell, Bruce, and Michael Jacobson
1989 *Marketing Disease to Hispanics*. Washington, DC: Center for Science in the Public Interest.

McCombie, Susan
1990 AIDS in Cultural, Historic, and Epidemiologic Context. In *Culture and AIDS*. Doug Feldman, ed. Pp. 9–28. New York: Praeger.

McCord, C., and H. Freeman
1990 Excess Mortality in Harlem. *New England Journal of Medicine* 322: 173–175.

McElroy, Ann, and Barbara Townsend
1996 *Medical Anthropology in Ecological Perspective*. 3rd edition. Boulder, CO: Westview Press.

Miller, Heather, Charles Turner, and Lincoln Moses
1990 *The Second Decade*. Washington, DC: National Academy Press.

Moses, Peter, and John Moses
1983 Haiti and the Acquired Immune Deficiency Syndrome. *Annals of Internal Medicine* 99(4):565.

Musto, David
1987 *The American Disease: Origins of Narcotic Control*. Oxford: Oxford University Press.

Navarro, Vicente
  1990   Race or Class Versus Race and Class: Mortality Differentials in the United
      States. *The Lancet* 336:1238–1240.
Nersesian, W.
  1988   Infant Mortality in Socially Vulnerable Populations. *Annual Review of Public
      Health* 9:361–377.
Nichter, Mark, and Elizabeth Cartwright
  1981   Saving the Children for the Tobacco Industry. *Medical Anthropology*
      5:236–256.
Nyamathi, A., C. Bennett, B. Leake, C. Lewis, and J. Flaskerud
  1993   AIDS-Related Knowledge, Perceptions, and Behaviors among Impoverished
      Minority Women. *American Journal of Public Health* 83:65–71.
Oliver, Douglas
  1961   *The Pacific Islands*. Garden City, NY: Anchor Books.
O'Neill, John
  1989   The Cultural and Political Context of Patient Dissatisfaction in Cross-
      Cultural Clinical Encounters. *Medical Anthropology Quarterly* 3:325–
      344.
Packard, R.
  1989   The "Health Reserve" and the "Dress Native": Discourses on Black Health
      and the Language of Legitimation in South Africa. *American Ethnologist*
      16(4):686–703.
Pape, J., B. Liataud, F. Thomas, J.-R. Mathurin, M.-M. Saint-Amand, M. Boncy, V. Pean,
      R.-I. Verdier, M.-M. Deschamps, and Z. Johnson
  1986   Risk Factors Associated with AIDS in Haiti. *American Journal of Medical
      Sciences* 29(1):4–7.
Pérez-Escamilla, Raphael, David Himmelgreen, and Ann Ferris
  1996   *The Food and Nutrition Situation of Inner-City Latino Preschoolers in Hart-
      ford: A Preliminary Needs Assessment*. Hartford, CT: University of Connecticut and
      the Hispanic Health Council.
Physician Task Force on Hunger in America
  1985   *Hunger in America: The Growing Epidemic*. Boston: Harvard University
      School of Public Health.
Polgar, Steven
  1962   Health and Human Behavior: Areas of Interest Common to the Social and
      Medical Sciences. *Current Anthropology* 3:159–205.
Quammen, David
  1996   *The Song of the Dodo*. New York: Touchstone.
Rivers, W. H. R.
  1924   *Medicine, Magic and Religion*. New York: Harcourt Brace.
Rivo, M., V. Kofie, E. Schwartz, M. Levy, and R. Tuckson
  1989   Comparisons of Black and White Smoking-Attributable Mortality, Morbidity,
      and Economic Costs in the District of Columbia. *Journal of the National Medical
      Association* 81:1125–1130.
Romero-Daza, Nancy
  1994   Migrant Labor, Multiple Sexual Partners, and Sexually Transmitted Diseases:
      The Makings of an Epidemic in Rural Lesotho. Ph.D. dissertation, State University
      of New York at Buffalo, Buffalo, NY.
Romero-Daza, Nancy, and David Himmelgreen
  1998   More than Money for Your Labor: Migration and the Political Economy of
      AIDS in Lesotho. In Singer, ed., pp. 185–204.

Sabatier, Renee
  1988   *Blaming Others: Prejudice, Race and Worldwide AIDS.* Washington, DC: Panos Institute.
Secretary's Task Force on Black and Minority Health
  1985   *Crosscutting Issues in Minority Health,* vol. 2. Washington, DC: U.S. Department of Health and Human Services.
Singer, Merrill
  1994   AIDS and the Health Crisis of the Urban Poor: The Conceptualizing of the SAVA Syndemic. *Free Inquiry in Creative Sociology* 24(2):99–110.
  1996   Farewell to Adaptationalism: Unnatural Selection and the Politics of Biology. *Medical Anthropology Quarterly* 10(4):496–515.
Singer, Merrill, ed.
  1998   *The Political Economy of AIDS.* Amityville, NY: Baywood.
Singer, Merrill, Dai Hanteng, Margaret Weeks, and Dorca Malave
  1998   AIDS Risk Perception among Women Drug Users in Hartford, CT. *Women and Health* 27(1/2):67–85.
Singer, Merrill, Freddie Valentin, Hans Baer, and Z. Jia
  1992   Why Does Juan García Have a Drinking Problem? The Perspective of Critical Medical Anthropology. *Medical Anthropology* 51(1):89–95.
Sobo, E. J.
  1995   *Choosing Unsafe Sex: AIDS-Risk, Denial and Disadvantaged Women.* Philadelphia: University of Pennsylvania Press.
Sobo, E. J., ed.
  1999   Special Issue: *Cultural Models and HIV/AIDS. Anthropology and Medicine* 6(1):5–163.
Stein, Z.
  1990   AIDS and HIV in Southern Africa. In *Action on AIDS in Southern Africa.* Z. Stein, and A. Zwi, eds. Pp. 5–7. New York: CHISA.
Stoneburner, R., M. Chaisson, I. Weisfuse, and P. Thomas
  1990   The Epidemic of AIDS and HIV-I Infection among Heterosexuals in New York City. *AIDS* 4:99–106.
Susser, Ida
  1996   The Construction of Poverty and Homelessness in U.S. Cities. *Annual Review of Anthropology* 25:411–435.
Todd, Harry, and Julio Ruffini
  1979   *Teaching Medical Anthropology.* Washington, DC: Society for Medical Anthropology.
Turner, Charles, Heather Miller, and Lincoln Moses
  1989   *AIDS: Sexual Behavior and Intravenous Drug Use.* Washington, DC: National Academy Press.
Ulin, P. R.
  1992   African Women and AIDS: Negotiating Behavioral Change. *Social Science and Medicine* 34:63–73.
Van Vugt, Johannes, ed.
  1994   *AIDS Prevention and Services.* Westport, CT: Bergin and Garvey.
Waldorf, Dan
  1973   *Careers in Dope.* Englewood Cliffs, NJ: Prentice Hall.
Weeks, Margaret, Merrill Singer, Jean Schensul, Z. Jia, and Maryland Grier
  1991   *Project COPE: Preventing AIDS among Injection Drug Users and Their Sex Partners: Descriptive Data Report.* Hartford, CT: Institute for Community Research.

Weeks, Margaret, S. S. Williams, Jean Schensul, Merrill Singer, and Maryland Grier
    1995   AIDS Prevention for African American and Latina Women: Building Cultural
    and Gender Appropriate Intervention. *AIDS Prevention and Education* 7:251–264.
Wellin, Edward
    1977   Theoretical Orientations in Medical Anthropology: Continuity and Change
    Over the Past Half-Century. In *Culture, Disease, and Healing*. David Landy, ed.
    Pp. 47–58. New York: Macmillan.

Part III

Historical Development of Contemporary Diversity

7

The Color-Blind Bind

Lee D. Baker

Anthropologists who study North Americans are forced to grapple with the cultural politics of race – a set of contradictory issues that bedevils even the most sophisticated ethnographer. Whether one is interested in mavens of internet startups in Silicon Valley or mothers of teenagers in Hope Valley, the politics of race, racism, and racial formation shape North American worldviews in indelible ways. In recent years, there has been a tendency for people in the United States to discount specific racial categories by emphasizing, instead, the nation's multiculturalism.

Anthropologists have tended to follow this trend too. Resisting the use of spurious categories that essentialize difference, anthropologists have challenged ideas about bounded cultures and have continued to denounce categories of race. Although many anthropologists engage in these efforts as part of a larger commitment toward antiracism, there are often unintended consequences to these actions because the efforts tend to blur the specificity of social history and political interests of particular racial groups. Like politics generally and American racial politics in particular, ideas, initiatives, and even ethnographies can become appropriated and co-opted by people who articulate different political projects. Denouncing categories of race and challenging bounded cultures are important efforts; however, anthropologists should be aware of some of the unintended consequences, or ways in which efforts to engage one set of academic issues can actually help articulate a political agenda inimical to the original goal of producing antiracist scholarship.

In this chapter I outline how members of various institutions and interest groups deploy ideas about a color-blind society in ways that erode the hard-fought victories of the Civil Rights movement. I sketch this outline in an effort to explore some of the unintended consequences that arise when anthropologists argue that North Americans should eliminate distinctions based upon race. One of these consequences that I explore more fully is the way in which this prohibition can curb the ability to identify institutional racism that has a disparate impact upon our institutions, neighborhoods, and electoral districts.[1] I also explore how these efforts provide resources for people who call for a color-blind society that eliminates affirmative action and majority-minority electoral districts while abandoning school desegregation. This would in turn shift the cause of disparate socioeconomic indicators from racism to culture, from social structures to individual behavior.

Faye V. Harrison (1995), in "The Persistent Power of 'Race,'" has forcefully argued that anthropologists have moved away from using racial categories in an effort to avoid the articulation of social categories that essentialize culture. As a proxy for this overall movement, consider the way the American Anthropological Association (AAA) advised the White House Office of Management and Budget (OMB) to eliminate the use of racial categories on the year 2000 census. As reported in the *Anthropology Newsletter* (October 1997), the AAA Executive Committee passed a motion that was forwarded to the OMB, which turned on the fact that "biological-sounding terms [such as race] add nothing to the precision, rigor, or actual basis of information being collected to characterize the identities of the American population."

Although the motion was motivated by antiracist politics and supported by rock-solid science, the AAA perhaps should have advised the OMB to simply pivot the subject position of those ominous boxes from how people identify culturally (which is complex, hybrid, and often situationally contingent) to how people are identified racially. While this reifies racial categories, it can be done in an explicit effort to ameliorate historically rooted racism that manifests itself in racial disparities that range from low birthweight babies to per capita school expenditures. Ultimately, the census is about identification, not identity.

Regardless of the contradictory political implications, the movement away from using racial categories to identify people is rooted in a tradition of antiracism, begun almost a century ago. Anthropologists have always been in the forefront of challenging ideas about race and, for successive generations, anthropologists have challenged the meaning of the actual concept of race (Lieberman et al. 1989). There is a rich and important history with regard to how generations of anthropologists have moved to a "no-race" position. While it perhaps began with Boas' earliest critiques, it took on practical political significance during World War II. During the war, U.S. anthropologists played important roles in asserting notions of racial equality in the international arena. Ruth Benedict and Gene Weltfish, for example, wrote a pamphlet entitled *The Races of Mankind* (1943) to educate military personnel about the lack of racial differences. Congress, however, denounced the publication as subversive and recalled it after its initial distribution (Mintz 1981:151). In the wake of the Jewish Holocaust, M. F. Ashley Montagu chaired the first of two committees of "Experts on Race Problems" for the United Nations Educational, Scientific, and Cultural Organization (UNESCO). The initial committee of scholars issued a *Statement by Experts on Race Problems*, published in 1951. It was a clear and striking declaration, from the foremost authorities, that there was no scientific basis to make racial distinctions. The group of UNESCO scientists recommended that "it would be better when speaking of human races to drop the term 'race' altogether and speak of ethnic groups" (Montagu 1951:13). Besides Montagu, other contributors included some of the country's leading scholars in race relations, like E. Franklin Frazier, Gunnar Myrdal, and Otto Klineberg. Claude Lévi-Strauss and Theodosius Dobzhansky were also contributing authors (Montagu 1951:118–119).

During the early 1960s, politically engaged anthropologists began to team up with population geneticists to claim "the employment of the term 'race' [is] inapplicable to most human populations as we find them today" (Montagu 1962:919). The assertion of racial equality couched in ideas of population genetics became a dominant discourse in anthropology. It is perhaps best typified by Sherwood Washburn's presidential address to the American Anthropological Association on November 16, 1962. Washburn followed Montagu's position that new studies on population genetics challenged the very idea of racial distinctions. Washburn concluded by stating:

> All kinds of human performance – whether social, athletic, intellectual – are built on genetic and environmental elements. The level of the kinds of performance can be increased by improving the environmental situation so that every genetic constitution may be developed to its full capacity. Any kind of social discrimination against groups of people, whether these are races, castes, or classes, reduces the achievements of our species, of mankind. (Washburn 1963:530)

Although many anthropologists were articulating a strong position with regard to racial equality, Washburn warned that some anthropologists still regard races as biological types. He suggested that "this kind of anthropology is still alive, amazingly, and in full force in some countries; relics of it are still alive in our teaching today" (1963:522). This was a subtle way to admonish people like Carleton Coon who still employed racial taxonomies positioned in something like the great chain of being (Haraway 1989:204). Although population geneticists began to question the biological basis for racial classification, and cultural anthropologists began to focus on "ethnic groups," the social and historical significance of racial categories was sorely undertheorized.

This movement within anthropology away from race as an analytical and conceptual category led many anthropologists to use ethnicity as the chief organizing principle for exploring human diversity (Harrison 1995:48; Baker 1995:187; Goodman 1995:216; Lieberman and Jackson 1995; Smedley 1993:6). The use of ethnicity as a surrogate for race tended to euphemize, blur, and even deny how racial categories emerge and persist. More importantly, by ignoring race and racism as integral aspects of the U.S. experience, it allowed conservatives and well-meaning liberals to help advance a romantic ideal of a color-blind society – which turns a blind eye to white supremacy.

The United States is not a color-blind society because black babies are almost three times as likely as white babies to be born with no prenatal care and twice as likely to die during their first year. Black college graduates are as likely to face unemployment as young white people who never attended college, and virtually half of all black children are living in poverty. Of course I could trot out disparities in wages, prison sentencing, unemployment, and many other social indices, or I could reflect upon the O. J. trial, the Million Man March, or the campaign finance scandal to demonstrate that the United States is simply not a color-blind society. While many anthropologists are tackling, effectively, critical issues involving race, they unfortunately do not have the same impact on public discourse or on the construction of race as their predecessors a hundred or even fifty years ago (Goode 1996; Susser 1992; Gregory 1998; Page 1997; Brodkin 1998; Williams et al. 1997).

At the dawn of the new millennium, the most salient types of social science concerning race are produced by think tanks advancing ideas that black people are deficient culturally or biologically, by sociologists advancing ideas about the declining significance of race and the increasing significance of class, and by well-meaning scholars advancing a multiculturalism that does not interrogate class or social categories of race. If we can draw any inferences from the last century and a half of anthropology to help understand why these approaches are popular, we can see that during periods of racial realignment particular approaches to the understanding of race come to the fore to shape public opinion, public policy, and laws, which often justify or quicken the realignment.

In the 1850s, the first "American School" of anthropologists defended the enslavement of African Americans before the Civil War, and in the 1890s, the first generation of professional anthropologists defended Jim Crow and ideas of racial inferiority. In the 1920s and 1930s, the eugenics movement dominated discussions of race when nativism and the threat of eastern European immigrants dominated the political landscape. It was not until a racial realignment during World War II that Boas' and his students' more progressive ideas of race and culture began to dominate in the United States. Even then, it was the idea that there was no basis to claims of racial inferiority, and not its companion thesis about cultural relativity (Baker 1998). During the turbulent 1960s, anthropologists with more radical ideas about the insignificance of biological categories helped to emphasize the structural and environmental explanations of racial inequality that shaped Great Society programs and the war on poverty. Since the mid-1980s, the United States has been undergoing another racial realignment in the way people view and experience different racial categories. This period is dominated economically by rapid deindustrialization and equally rapid growth in service, information, and technological production. Culturally, it is dominated by fears of downsizing, immigration, affirmative action, crime, and the "underclass."

Images and Realities

All people of color have been engaged in an incipient class formation process as a consequence of the Civil Rights movement, affirmative action programs, and rising numbers of college graduates (Brooks 1992:34–66). This process began precisely at the point when the U.S. economy moved from an industrial and manufacturing base to being an economy motored by finance, information, and service (Harvey 1989). As the economy became increasingly deindustrialized, cities lost hundreds of thousands of manufacturing jobs and billions of dollars in federal funds. These trends were augmented by a general pattern of uneven development that has systematically decimated many inner cities and led to an increase in violent crime, infant mortality rates, high school dropouts, and drug trafficking (Kennedy et al. 1990). The combination of decomposing inner cities and the loss of high-paying union, manufacturing, and industrial jobs drove an invisible wedge between the more mobile clerical and professional people of color and the structurally underemployed, underpaid, and unemployed in the inner cities (Edsall and Edsall 1992:27–28; Wilson 1978).

Within the African American community specifically, there has been a structural rift developing, accompanied by the construction of two competing images perpetuated primarily in the media. The first image – a positive one – is primarily formed on prime-time television sitcoms such as *The Cosby Show* and through genuinely positive media personalities such as Oprah Winfrey or local newscasters. In addition to television, there are a myriad elected and appointed African American public officials ensconced within popular culture, contributing to the idea that "Blacks have made it." This image is reified by an even larger number of upwardly mobile African Americans who are part of the so-called professional middle class (Brooks 1992:34–66).

The second image of African Americans – a negative one – is framed by crime and ideas of "the underclass." This image is produced at the movie theater, on the nightly news, and by pundits and politicians who view "illegitimacy" and crime in terms of an individual's lack of family values (Gingrich and Armey 1994:37–39, 70–71). This image of the "underclass" is almost always couched in the criminal activity of people of color (Williams 1994:348). As a *Time Magazine* cover story put it: "The universe of the underclass is often a junk heap of rotting housing, broken furniture, crummy food, alcohol and drugs" (quoted in Franklin 1991:98). To round out this image, one merely needs to envision the black male gang member contemplating his next carjacking on a dimly lit street corner covered with graffiti and littered with garbage, 40-ounce beer bottles, and crack vials. And, of course, listening to rap music lyrics pounding "Fuck tha Police!"

These two opposing images, successful assimilated minority and "gangster/welfare mother," serve to bifurcate prejudice along class lines, which allows individuals to circumvent specific allegations of individual racial discrimination.[2] This circumvention occurs because the construct of race that is imposed upon poor blacks is often juxtaposed with the construct used for and by the amorphous "black middle class." If one begins to isolate racial inequalities within the criminal justice, welfare, and education systems along racial lines, one need only look to the burgeoning black middle class to conclude that individuals relegated to the so-called "underclass" can make it or pull themselves up by their bootstraps.[3] Nevertheless, the appearance of more people of color in the professions and universities, coupled with growing numbers of unemployed or underemployed whites, due to the shrinking manufacturing and defense industries, creates an illusion that unqualified blacks and Hispanics are stealing contracts, jobs, and admission spots from more qualified whites.

Racism and racial discrimination are no longer demarcated by a rigid color line policed by people and signs exclaiming "No Coloreds Allowed" or "Whites Only." Racism now is manifested in the far more subtle forms of not being invited to play golf, and punitive immigration policies for Mexico, Cuba, and Haiti. Home financing, jobs, and child poverty are all linked to class, but these are products of the institutional racism that still plagues the United States in ways that cannot be tied to disparate treatment of individuals. Also, institutionalized racism still abounds in our public schools. In the District of

Columbia, for example, the public schools rank as some of the worst in the country, but across the Potomac River in Fairfax, Virginia, they are ranked as some of the best.

Since the most debilitating racism today is not blatant discrimination against individuals, there must be some institutional vehicle in place to identify systemic racism. Without the ability to identify the admittedly flat-footed, but still very salient, social categories of race, we lose the ability to identify racial disparities – the hallmark of institutionalized racism.

One of the best ways to identify racism and sexism at the beginning of the 21st century is to track disparate impact. For example, the Supreme Court found in *Griggs v. Duke Power Co.* (1971) that "practices that are fair in form" can be "discriminatory in operation" (p. 850). Most of the formal cases addressing disparate impact are class action employment suits litigated under Title VII of the 1964 Civil Rights Act. The ability to document racial disparities has been an effective legal tool to stem racism in employment practices, housing projects, and electoral districts. Away from the strict scrutiny of the courtroom, identifying disparate impact becomes an even more persuasive tool to bolster public opinion and formulate public policy.

One may question, could we not track disparate impact with ethnicity? While specific ethnicities are racialized in predictable patterns, ethnicity is a far more plastic and contingent grouping that ultimately turns on identity and beliefs about culture. This distinction between race and ethnicity is thrown into vivid relief when I walk out my back door and stroll down 125th Street – affectionately known as the "Heart of Harlem."

The everyday lives of Puerto Ricans, Dominicans, Haitians, Nigerians, and African Americans commingle and converge in this community in a way that has transposed historic segregation into a form of congregation that exhibits the rich tapestry of the African diaspora. Although many New Yorkers integrate ethnicity into their identities, the tourists who gaze at the exotic residents of Harlem from the double-decker tour buses simply see the masses of dark bodies through a prism of race and class. Like taking a tour of a dangerous safari park, tourists can view the black and dangerous underclass from a safe distance, under the protection of a seasoned tour guide.

Black people, regardless of ethnicity, are more often denied home mortgages, incarcerated, placed in special education, and brutalized by police than the other racialized peoples. When New York City police officers beat and sodomized Abner Louima, and cut down Amadou Diallo in a hail of gunfire, they did not see hard-working ethnic immigrants seeking the American Dream; they operated from a racialized worldview that often eclipses the Constitution and somehow justifies frenzied racial violence that has filled the blood-stained pages of U.S. history.

One could also ask, what happens to that amorphous category of "Hispanic," if social constructs of race are used to identify people? The fact that Latinos are often identified as an ethnic group lends credence to explanations that the abysmal Latino high-school completion rates are the result of culture as opposed to racial discrimination. For example, William Julius Wilson (1996:98) has explained that "Mexicans come to the United States with a clear conception of a traditional family unit that features men as breadwinners," and he goes on to explain that if young women become pregnant, "pressure is applied by the kin of both parents to [quit high school, get a job and] enter into marriage."

Thus, following Wilson's approach and others, culture and not racial discrimination, typified by the English-only movement and California's Proposition 186, forms the basic explanation of Latinos' disparate social indices. Shifting the focus from race to ethnicity allows proponents of a so-called color-blind society to ignore racism and explain disparate impacts in terms of culture, behavior, and lack of merit.

Color-Blind Congress?

In 1985 Ronald Reagan reconstituted the U.S. Civil Rights Commission by appointing Clarence Pendleton, Jr., as Chair. Pendleton made the number-one priority of the Commission the investigation of "reverse discrimination." Pendleton reassured Reagan that the Commission was "working on a color blind society that has opportunities for all and guarantees success for none" (Omi and Winant 1986:1). The revamping of the Civil Rights Commission was a benchmark in the erosion of the progress made by people of color during the Civil Rights movement.

One strategy Republicans used during the 1980s to eliminate race-based preferential hiring, promotion, college admissions, and contract procurement was to appropriate the rhetoric of the Civil Rights movement. After all, it was the Rev. Dr. Martin Luther King, Jr., who had a dream that his children would be judged solely on the "content of their character." From Reagan's Civil Rights Commission in the 1980s to the proposed California Civil Rights Initiative in the 1990s, neoconservatives have rearticulated the notion of racial equality by conflating it with "traditional" American and family values (e.g. Gingrich and Armey 1994). Simultaneously, less conservative interests failed to confront structured racial inequality. While conservatives have been dismantling affirmative action programs, liberals have been consumed with promoting notions of multiculturalism and furthering ethnic diversity.

The changing politics of race are not limited to assaults by Republicans; the Democrats have also used the palatable idea of a color-blind society to further their agenda. By itself, affirmative action is a political wedge; however, taken with the challenges of minority-majority congressional districts, it is a political double-edged sword that has eviscerated the Democratic Party along racial lines, adding another dimension to the changing politics of race. If Republicans' vociferous challenges of affirmative action programs are put alongside their tacit consent to minority-majority voting districts, the true partisan nature of efforts to dismantle affirmative action becomes clear.

Republicans have illustrated the perils of affirmative action with regard to school admissions, contracting, and employment, but they have been conspicuously silent about the so-called perils of minority-majority congressional districts drawn after the 1990 decennial census. The explicit creation of minority-majority districts helped to nearly double the African American representation in Congress, arguably one of the nation's best affirmative action programs. While the Republican leadership wants to achieve a color-blind society by dismantling affirmative action programs, generally they do not want to dismantle the structure of color-conscious congressional districts that Supreme Court Justice Sandra Day O'Connor declared "bears an uncomfortable resemblance to political apartheid."

There are two reasons why Republicans did not link the debates about affirmative action and racial redistricting and did not incorporate the so-called perils of "racial gerrymandering" into their arguments for a color-blind society. First, the same political and legislative thicket that gave rise to the largest African American delegation to Congress in 1992, also contributed to the rise of a Republican majority in Congress and, specifically, its stronghold in the South. David Lublin, a political scientist at the University of South Carolina, provides a conservative calculation that between six and nine House seats shifted from Democrat to Republican control after 1990 as a direct result of the creation of safe minority districts in the South (Lublin 1994). In 1995, Georgia's racially polarized congressional delegation exemplified these dynamics: of its 11-member delegation, the 8 Republicans were white and the 3 Democrats were black.

The second reason why members of the Grand Old Party did not address the "quotas" used for redistricting mirrors the reasons why they attacked so-called quotas with regard to affirmative action. The formation of minority-majority congressional districts formed a wedge issue within the Democratic Party. The Party was forced to grapple with the harsh reality that minority-majority districts in the South increase minority representation but decrease Southern Democrats' overall representation in Congress.

In most of the redistricting cases, the plaintiffs who challenged the constitutionality of minority-majority districts were activists within the Democratic Party. These plaintiffs were motivated by the fact that racial redistricting reduces the number of Democrats in their state's delegation to Washington. They successfully posed legal arguments that drawing congressional districts by "computerized hunting for concentrations of blacks" creates "bizarre and tortured" districts that violate the Equal Protection clause. As in the affirmative action debate, blacks were pitted against whites within an already fractured Democratic Party. On the last day of the Supreme Court's 1994–95 term, the Court ruled (5–4) that using race as a predominant factor for drawing congressional districts was unconstitutional (*Miller v. Johnson*, 94–631).

A Color-Blind Court!

The Court's most activist decisions during its 1994–95 term concerned how the government can use racial classifications to achieve racial equality; however, it also struck down congressional term limits and allowed a veterans group to deny a gay, lesbian, and bisexual group a spot in its St. Patrick's Day parade. With three disjointed opinions delivered in June 1995, affirmative action, court-ordered school desegregation, and minority-majority congressional districts were all hobbled by narrow 5–4 majorities.

The Court's conservative majority, consisting of the Chief Justice William H. Rehnquist, Antonin Scalia, Clarence Thomas, and often Sandra Day O'Connor and Anthony Kennedy, practiced a form of judicial activism that ostensibly insured that the Constitution remained color-blind. On the surface it sounded ideal; however, the effect of this bloc's interpretation of the Fourteenth Amendment proved Constitutional scholar Derrick Bell's axiom that "racial patterns adapt in ways that maintain white dominance" (Bell 1992:12).

In 1896 the Supreme Court ruled on *Plessy v. Ferguson*, a watershed case that made Jim Crow segregation the law of the land, ushering in a new era of race relations for the 20th century. During the Supreme Court's 1994–95 term, its justices delivered similar watershed decisions, ushering in a new era of race relations for the 21st century.

The *New York Times* headlined "Farewell to the Old Order in the Court" and explained how "the birth struggle of a new era is not a pretty sight. It is messy, it is unstable, it is riveting" (Greenhouse 1995:E1). Many newspapers and magazines noted the sweeping changes the Court made during its 1994–95 term, specifically with regard to racial issues. The *Washington Post* perfunctorily concluded: "The Supreme Court redistricting decision is likely to change the politics of race" and The *Atlanta Constitution* headlined "Blacks Fear Return to 'Dark Days of the 19th Century' " and declared that the Court "pulled the rug out from under gains they have made from courthouse to Congress in the last 30 years" (Christiansen 1995:A1). The *New York Times's* depiction of a "new era" in race relations is particularly cogent because it captured how social and political transformations, combined with the actions of the Court and Congress, are contributing to a racial realignment. On the House floor, Representative Major Owens (NY) summed up the legislative branch's role in this new era:

> When you combine an assault on affirmative action with a Republican Contract With America, you create a kind of scorched earth approach to the reordering of our society. Government by an elite minority, for the benefit of the elite minority, becomes the driving philosophy . . . now they want to spread, use that power to spread a racist, anti-immigrant brew throughout the minds of America, to poison the minds of the American voters.   (104 Cong. 1 Sess. H2380)

The Supreme Court's role in ushering in the terms and conditions of racial categories for the 21st century is illustrated by its 1994–95 term. In *Adarand Constructors v. Peña* (No. 93–1841) the Court ruled that federal affirmative action programs, specifically a minority preference provision in a federal highway contracting program, must be held to the same strict scrutiny standard as state and local programs. Writing for the Court, O'Connor declared that her decision to vacate the judgment of the Court of Appeals was "derive[d] from the basic principle that the Fifth and Fourteenth Amendments to the Constitution protect *persons*, not *groups*."[4] Justice Clarence Thomas wrote a concurring opinion, and he declared that "as far as the Constitution is concerned, it is irrelevant whether a government's racial classifications are drawn by those who wish to oppress a race or by those who have a sincere desire to help those thought to be disadvantaged." He concluded: "In my mind, government sponsored racial discrimination based on benign prejudice is just as noxious as discrimination inspired by malicious prejudice. In each instance, it is racial discrimination, plain and simple."[5] Justice Stevens, in his dissent, blasted the Court's majority:

> There is no moral or constitutional equivalence between a policy that is designed to perpetuate a caste system and one that seeks to eradicate racial subordination. Invidious discrimination is an engine of oppression, subjugating a disfavored group to enhance or maintain the power of the majority. Remedial race-based preferences reflect the opposite impulse: a desire to foster equality in society.[6]

While the *Adarand* decision did not eliminate all federal affirmative action programs, it indicated that the government is not allowed to develop programs to ameliorate past discrimination. In another Court action, it let a Circuit Court decision stand that invalidated the University of Maryland scholarship program for outstanding African American scholars.

With the same division, the Court ruled in *Missouri v. Jenkins* (No. 93–1823) that a federal district court in Missouri had improperly ordered the state to pay for a desegregation plan for Kansas City's schools. This case related directly to *Brown v. Board of Education*. After *Brown*, the Kansas City Missouri School District (KCMSD) never dismantled its Jim Crow schools, and twenty years later, 39 of KCMSD's 77 schools had student bodies that were more than 90 percent black and a full 80 percent of black schoolchildren in the district attended these schools. In 1984, a full thirty years after *Brown* the District Court found that KCMSD had failed to reform its segregated public schools. The District Court concluded that both the state and the school district "defaulted in their obligation to uphold the Constitution."[7] However, by the time it finally ordered desegregation there were few white students left in the inner-city district to integrate the schools. With uneven development and many middle-class whites and blacks moving to the suburbs, the court devised an interdistrict desegregation plan to increase the "desegregative attractiveness" of the district by reversing "white flight" to the suburbs. The court-ordered plan amounted to the creation of an entire magnet school district. The Supreme Court ruled in 1995, 41 years after *Brown*, however, that the District Court had exceeded its authority.

Justice Thomas exploited the problematic nature of the social science research used to win *Brown* to write a persuasive concurring opinion that forcefully articulated the Court's color-blind thesis. Thomas demonstrated that

> the [lower] court has read our cases to support the theory that black students suffer an unspecified psychological harm from segregation that retards their mental and educational development. This approach not only relies upon questionable social science research rather than constitutional principle, but it also rests on an assumption of black inferiority.[8]

By criticizing the research done some 60 years earlier, Thomas advanced conservative ideals of black self-help. Thomas framed this important opinion by stating: "It never ceases to amaze me that the courts are so willing to assume that anything that is predominantly black must be inferior. . . . The mere fact that a school is black does not mean that it is the product of a constitutional violation."[9]

The District Court that oversaw the desegregation order of the Kansas City schools cited *Brown* for its rationale that a racial imbalance in the school system was a constitutional violation that harmed African American children. Justice Thomas found this citation inimical to the principles of the Constitution and directly challenged what amounts to a sacred American text. Thomas assumed that the District Court's position "appears to rest upon the idea that any school that is black is inferior, and that blacks cannot succeed without the benefit of the company of whites." He substantiated this assumption by claiming:

> The District Court's willingness to adopt such stereotypes stemmed from a misreading of our earliest school desegregation case. In *Brown v. Board of Education* the Court noted several psychological and sociological studies purporting to show that *de jure* segregation harmed black students by generating "a feeling of inferiority" in them. Seizing upon this passage in *Brown*, . . . the District Court suggested that this inequality continues in full force even after the end of *de jure* segregation.[10]

While Thomas was quick to point out that "under this theory, segregation injures blacks because blacks, when left on their own, cannot achieve," he failed to explain that this theoretical perspective is over 60 years old, or to consider the decades of research since that time which document the denial of resources to poor students in predominantly black schools. Thomas simply explained: "to my way of thinking, that conclusion [in *Brown*] is the result of a jurisprudence based upon a theory of black inferiority."[11] By only using the term "black," Thomas skillfully blurred the line between race and class. He simply collapsed the concepts of race and class into a commonsense understanding about "black inferiority."

The Court did not stop at affirmative action and school segregation, it ruled to invalidate congressional districts that were drawn to include a majority of racial minorities in its boundaries. In *Miller v. Johnson* (94–631) the Court invalidated Georgia's 11th congressional district, which was created to produce a third majority-black district. Using the same color-blind principle as O'Connor in *Adarand*, Justice Kennedy explained that

> the Equal Protection Clause of the Fourteenth Amendment provides that no State shall deny to any person within its jurisdiction the equal protection of the laws. Its central mandate is racial neutrality in governmental decision making. Though application of this imperative raises difficult questions, the basic principle is straightforward: Racial and ethnic distinctions of any sort are inherently suspect and thus call for the most exacting judicial examination. . . . This rule obtains with equal force regardless of the race of those burdened or benefited by a particular classification.[12]

The principle of a color-blind Constitution that the conservative bloc of the Supreme Court used to challenge District Court desegregation orders, minority-majority voting districts, and federal affirmative action mirrors the editorial position of several leading magazines that have grappled with the science and politics of race.

What Difference Does Difference Make?

The cover story of the February 13, 1995, issue of *Newsweek* was entitled "What Color Is Black? Science, Politics and Racial Identity." In a provocative set of articles, the writers and editors of *Newsweek* looked at race as a "notoriously slippery concept that eludes any serious attempt at definition" (Morganthau 1995:63). While the authors mentioned that *The Bell Curve* revived an old controversy about racial inequality, they correctly concluded that "the bottom line, to most scientists working in these fields, is that race is a mere 'social construct' – a gamey mixture of prejudice, superstition and myth" (Morganthau 1995:63). Although the editors and article authors identified race as a social construct, they only detailed how biological ideas of race are not appropriate categories. They did not adequately illustrate how the social category of race still dictates people's lives. In one article, an author suggested that racial categories will eventually not matter, by explaining that "what we call people matters a lot less than how we treat them" (Cose 1995:70). With articles that discussed the joys and tragedies of biracial families, the end of affirmative action, and a summary of scientists denouncing race as a biological category, the unmistakable editorial position was that racial categories are not particularly useful, and the United States, as a whole, should become more color-blind or race-neutral.

The authors of this collection of articles turned to biological anthropologists to support this editorial position. Sharon Begley, in "Three Is Not Enough: Surprising New Lessons from the Controversial Science of Race," quoted anthropologist C. Loring Brace who stated: "There is no organizing principle by which you could put 5 billion people into so few categories in a way that would tell you anything important about humankind's diversity" (Begley 1995:67). Begley also cited Alan H. Goodman, who is a biological anthropologist and critical race theorist. Begley first explained how

> the notion of race is under withering attack for political and cultural reasons. But scientists got there first. Their doubts about the conventional racial categories – black, white, Asian – have nothing to do with a sappy "we are all the same" ideology. Just the reverse. "Human variation is very, very real," says Goodman. "But race, as a way of organizing [what we know about that variation], is incredibly simplified and bastardized."

Newsweek concluded this article by stating that race does not matter and the best way to understand the meaning and origin of humankind's diversity is to use "a greater number of smaller groupings, like ethnicities" (Begley 1995:69).

At one level the editors of *Newsweek* and *Discover* (which ran a similar cover story with an identical editorial position in its November 1994 issue) must be commended for tackling these issues head-on and in a particularly sophisticated manner. In many respects, the public discourse is catching up with what anthropologists have been writing since the 1940s. *Newsweek* even credits M. F. Ashley Montagu with pioneering the concept that assuming biological differences have anything to with racial categories is, as the title of his book suggests, *Man's Most Dangerous Myth* (1952 [1942]).

In another respect, however, the editors of these magazines are selectively appropriating particular aspects of the anthropological discourse on race to bolster the popular ideal of a color-blind meritocratic society. This particular line of thought is difficult to criticize, yet it has emerged as the rationale for the conservative bloc of the Supreme Court.

During the 1990s, certain anthropologists began advancing critical race theories within the field (Harrison 1995; Gregory and Sanjek 1994). However, these anthropologists are rarely featured in *Newsweek* or on *Nightline*. What is fascinating to me is the fact that the news media appropriate or skillfully subvert progressive biological anthropologists' arguments about the inanity of biological concepts of race to advance a vulgar color-blind thesis. Critical cultural anthropologists are rarely called upon to explain that while biological categories of race are meaningless, social categories of race are very real, meaningful, and still dictate life chances and opportunities. Whether it is the discourse on multiculturalism and cultural studies, or the declining significance of race and the "underclass," anthropological ideas loom large, but critical anthropologists are woefully absent from the process of shaping how these public debates impact lives and effect change.

Truth or Consequences

Anthropologists who study North America have a responsibility to understand the political context within which their research and teaching is situated. The cultural politics of race can be volatile and contradictory. At the extreme, the tectonic aspects of racial formation can ignite a campus or an entire neighborhood into a blaze of violence, or they can spin an individual out of control into a spree of homicides. Generally, though, the dynamics of racial formation are measured out at a glacial pace, inscribing and describing white privilege and supremacy while demarcating access to resources and mapping boundaries of achievement. Anthropologists can and should draw upon their unique set of skills to help students, journalists, activists, and even administrators sort through the contradictions that arise from capitalist democracies which articulate racial inequality.

At the beginning of this chapter I highlighted the fact that anthropologists who advocated the abolition of racial categories perhaps, unwittingly, bolstered political agendas inimical to the goals of antiracist scholarship. On the other hand, by not abolishing the use of racial categories, one supports vacuous, spurious, and admittedly essentialized categories that shore up folks on the soul patrol who police authenticity and employ sophisticated surveillance techniques that probe any threat to racial solidarity.

Whereas I advocate speaking truth to power, I illustrated how power can easily subvert the scholarship produced to unseat it. When it comes to better understanding the dynamics of racial formation processes in North America, it is incumbent upon anthropologists to be aware that their own writing, research, and teaching become part of the contradictory processes that at once challenge and articulate the cultural politics of race, racism, and democracy.

NOTES

1 *Griggs v. Duke Power Co.* (1971), *New York City Transit Authority v. Beazer* (1979), *Rogers v. Lodge* (1982), *Arlington Heights v. Metropolitan Housing Development Corp* (1977).

2 Many people structure their racist attitudes and prejudice along class lines. Since they don't feel any animosity towards middle-class people of color they feel that they are exempt from allegations of racism. This dynamic is clearly demonstrated in *Race: How Blacks and Whites Think and Feel about the American Obsession* by Studs Terkel (1992). There is rising animosity, though, among the so-called middle-class white Americans who perceive their jobs are being taken away by "preference" programs and affirmative action. Yet the allegation of racism is still circumvented because people couch animosity in ideas of meritocracy. The affirmative action debate is where these animosities get expressed. These issues were at the center of partisan debates that shaped the presidential campaigns during the 1996 elections. Speaking as a presidential candidate, Robert Dole questioned on ABC's *This Week* with David Brinkley: "Why did 62 percent of white males vote Republican in 1994? I think it's because of things like this [affirmative action programs], where sometimes the best qualified person does not get the job because he or she may be of one color" (see 104 Cong. 1 Sess. S2154).

3 Political scientists, sociologists, and legal scholars have all demonstrated that institutional racism often persists within various work and market places, legislative bodies, and court rooms, despite efforts to manage or institute ethnic diversity (Edsall and Edsall 1992; Guinier 1994; Terkel 1992; Winant 1994). The other line of reasoning is, of course, Herrnstein and Murray's in their *Bell Curve* (1994), that the few blacks who are very bright have made and will make it and the others are simply shackled by their own cognitive inability. Both lines of thought eschew structural racism as a cause of racial inequality.

4 *Adarand Constructors v. Peña* No. 93–1841 (1995), Opinion:25, emphasis original.

5 *Adarand Constructors v. Peña*, Concur:2–3.

6 *Adarand Constructors v. Peña*, Dissent:2.

7 *Missouri v. Jenkins* No. 93–1823 (1995), Dissent:3.

8 *Missouri v. Jenkins*, Concur:2.

9 *Missouri v. Jenkins*, Concur:1–2.

10 *Missouri v. Jenkins*, Concur:6.

11 *Missouri v. Jenkins*, Concur:10.

12 *Miller v. Johnson* No. 94–631 (1995), Opinion:1, citations omitted.

REFERENCES CITED

Baker, Lee D.
    1995 Racism in Professional Settings: Forms of Address as Clues to Power Relations. *Journal of Applied Behavioral Science* 31(2):186–202.
    1998 *From Savage to Negro: Anthropology and the Construction of Race, 1896–1954*. Berkeley: University of California Press.
Begley, Sharon
    1995 Three Is Not Enough. *Newsweek*, February 13:67–69.

Bell, Derrick A.
    1992   *Faces at the Bottom of the Well: The Permanence of Racism*. New York: Basic
        Books.
Benedict, Ruth, and Gene Weltfish
    1943   *The Races of Mankind*. New York: Public Affairs Committee.
Brodkin, Karen
    1998   *How Jews Became White Folks and What That Says About Race in America*.
        New Brunswick, NJ: Rutgers University Press.
Brooks, Roy L.
    1992   *Rethinking the American Race Problem*. Berkeley: University of California
        Press.
Christensen, Mike
    1995   Blacks Fear Return to "Dark Days of the 19th Century." *Atlanta Journal/
        Constitution*, June 30:A1.
Cose, Ellis
    1995   One Drop of Bloody History. *Newsweek*, February 13:70–72.
Edsall, Thomas B., and Mary D. Edsall
    1992   *Chain Reaction: The Impact of Race, Rights, and Taxes on American Politics*.
        New York: W. W. Norton.
Franklin, Raymond S.
    1991   *Shadows of Race and Class*. Minneapolis: University of Minnesota Press.
Gingrich, Newt, and Dick Armey
    1994   *Contract with America: The Bold Plan to Change the Nation*. New York:
        Random House.
Goode, Judith
    1996   On Sustainable Development in the Megacity. *Current Anthropology*
        37(1):131–132.
Goodman, Alan H.
    1995   The Problematics of "Race" in Contemporary Biological Anthropology. In
        Biological Anthropology: The State of the Science. N. T. Boaz, and L. D. Wolfe,
        eds. Pp. 215–239. Bend, OR: International Institute for Human Evolutionary
        Research.
Greenhouse, Linda
    1995   Farewell to the Old Order in the Court: The Right Goes Activist and the Center
        Is Void. *New York Times*, July 2: E1, E4.
Gregory, Steven
    1998   *Black Corona: Race and the Politics of Place in an Urban Community*.
        Princeton, NJ: Princeton University Press.
Gregory, Steven, and Roger Sanjek
    1994   *Race*. New Brunswick, NJ: Rutgers University Press.
Guinier, Lani
    1994   *The Tyranny of the Majority: Fundamental Fairness and Representative
        Democracy*. New York: Free Press.
Haraway, Donna J.
    1989   *Primate Visions: Gender, Race, and Nature in the World of Modern Science*.
        New York: Routledge.
Harrison, Faye V.
    1995   The Persistent Power of "Race" in the Cultural and Political Economy of
        Racism. *Annual Review of Anthropology* 24:47–74.
Harvey, David
    1989   *The Condition of Postmodernity: An Enquiry into the Origins of Cultural
        Change*. London: Blackwell.

Herrnstein, Richard, and Charles Murray
  1994   *The Bell Curve: Intelligence and Class Structure in American Life*. New York:
    Free Press.
Kennedy, M., M. Gastón, and C. Tilly
  1990   Capital Investment or Community Development. In *Fire in the Hearth: The
    Radical Politics of Place in America*. Mike Davis, ed. Pp. 97–136. London: Verso.
Lieberman, Leonard, and Fatimah C. Jackson
  1995   Race and Three Models of Human Origin. *American Anthropologist* 97:
    231–242.
Lieberman, Leonard, Larry T. Reynolds, and Blaine W. Stevenson
  1989   Race and Anthropology: A Core Concept without Consensus. *Anthropology
    and Education Quarterly* 20(2):67–73.
Lublin, David I.
  1994   Gerrymander for Justice? Racial Redistricting and Black and Latino
    Representation. Ph.D. dissertation, Harvard University, Cambridge, MA.
Mintz, Sidney
  1981   Ruth Benedict. In *Totems and Teachers: Perspectives on the History of Anthro-
    pology*. Sydel Silverman, ed. Pp. 141–170. New York: Columbia University Press.
Montagu, Ashley M. F.
  1951   *Statement on Race: An Extended Discussion in Plain Language of the
    UNESCO Statement by Experts on Race*. New York: Henry Schuman.
  1952[1942]   *Man's Most Dangerous Myth: The Fallacy of Race*. New York: Harper
    Brothers.
  1962   The Concept of Race. *American Anthropologist* 64:919–928.
Morganthau, Tom
  1995   What Color Is Black? *Newsweek*, February 13:63–65.
Omi, Michael, and Howard Winant
  1986   *Racial Formation in the United States*. New York: Routledge.
Page, Helán E.
  1997   Black Male Imagery and Media Containment of African American Men.
    American Anthropologist 99:99–111.
Smedley, Audrey
  1993   *Race in North America: Origin and Evolution of a Worldview*. Boulder, CO:
    Westview Press.
Susser, Ida
  1992   Sex, Drugs and Videotape: The Prevention of Aids in a New York City Shelter
    for Homeless Men. *Medical Anthropology* 14(24):307–322.
Terkel, Studs
  1992   *How Blacks and Whites Think and Feel about the American Obsession*. New
    York: New Press.
Washburn, Sherwood
  1963   The Study of Race. *American Anthropologist* 65:521–531.
Williams, Brett
  1994   Babies and Banks: The "Reproductive Underclass" and the Raced, Gendered
    Masking of Debt. In *Race*. Steven Gregory, and Roger Sanjek, eds. Pp. 348–365.
    New Brunswick, NJ: Rutgers University Press.
Williams, Brett, Tonya Ramos, and Jaqueline Brown
  1997   *Rapid Ethnographic Assessment, Park Users and Neighbors, Civil
    War Defenses of Washington and Anacostia Park, District of Columbia, for Park
    Management Plans*. Washington, DC: Juárez and Associates for National Park
    Service.

Wilson, William J.
  1978 *The Declining Significance of Race*. Chicago: University of Chicago Press.
  1996 *When Work Disappears: The World of the New Urban Poor*. New York: Alfred A. Knopf.
Winant, Howard
  1994 *Racial Conditions: Politics, Theory, Comparisons*. Minneapolis: University of Minnesota Press.

8

Racialized Identities and the Law

Sally Engle Merry

Anthropologists generally agree that everyday racial categories are historical phenomena which develop over time. However, when the everyday cultural categories of race become encoded in law, they acquire new legitimacy and force. They can have painful consequences for racially designated groups. Laws governing immigration, naturalization, citizenship, political participation, and sexual interaction have enormous consequences for the lives of excluded groups. Administrative practices of counting and dividing up the population reinforce racial categories. Laws rarely create racial categories: most often they rigidify existing social distinctions and impose consequences upon individuals based on these distinctions.

Racialized identities are formed by etching sharp lines through the ambiguities of social personhood. Social identities do not remain fixed but are constantly being refashioned as populations blend and change. Law is one of the most important institutions through which racial identities are maintained. Laws sometimes use "race" to specify who can enter a country, who can participate in its political institutions, who can have sex with whom, and who can live in which neighborhood. Laws define boundaries to social interaction by establishing principles of separation ranging from miscegenation to separate railroad waiting rooms. Governmental processes that mark, count, classify, and label render racial identities visible and produce knowledge of a population using that criterion. The lines and edges drawn in social fields characterized by ambiguities are boundaries that surround identities and circumscribe social interaction.

Focusing on the processes by which law creates racial identities is a valuable way to understand diversity in the United States. Instead of seeing race as created by discrete "cultures," this approach examines processes of exclusion which produce such "cultures." The analytical framework shifts from understanding any particular racial or ethnic category to understanding how and why ethnic and racial categories are formed. Beginning from the social processes which circumscribe races, we can highlight how laws create and rcify racial categories.

A focus on law also reveals the cultural power of a concept of rights to dismantle racial categories. Law is radically antiracist in its concept of rights and equality before the law. Rights attach to all individuals regardless of their social positions. The proponents of critical race theory, while arguing that racial divisions in the United States are profound and fundamental to the social order, rather than expressions of class inequalities, nevertheless hold out hope that rights can provide a way to achieve social justice. While law was fundamental to the creation of racial distinctions in the 19th and early 20th centuries, such landmark decisions as *Brown v. Board of Education* (1954) challenge racial inequalities and undermine race thinking. The tendency to attach law to alleged "races" has significantly diminished since the 1960s. There were indications of a return to racial thinking in the 1980s and 1990s, however, in demands to restrict immigration to whites, the appearance of books on the differing intellectual abilities of racial groups, and new intellectual and political defenses of racial, ethnic, and gender inequalities (Smith 1997:4–5).

Ironically, one contemporary effort to redress past racial injuries itself relies on a classification of persons on the basis of race. It is this feature of affirmative action which gives it its power and at the same time renders it subject to critique. The legal classification of race was fundamental to the creation of the inequalities and exclusions that the present system is seeking to redress. Used now to counter inequality, it seems illegitimate and incompatible with the dominant postwar movement to eliminate race as a category of legal personhood. While few would contest the ongoing significance of racialized identities in private life, many question whether racial classifications should be recognized in public law and institutions. Many worry that affirmative action will bring back a legal categorization of race. Some advocate a "color-blind" system, arguing that past wrongs cannot be undone by creating new racial categorizations.

This position ignores the extent and historical depth of the legal categorization of race and its enduring legacy (see Baker, Chapter 7, this volume). Using these categories may be necessary to redress historical injuries. Some argue that it is only when legal categories of race are used to allocate benefits rather than to administer disqualifications that they are contested. There has, of course, been a long history of protest against the use of legal categories for exclusion, beginning with the movement for the abolition of slavery (Williams 1992; Glazer 1997; Crenshaw et al. 1996; Ancheta 1998; Lawrence and Matsuda 1997; Skrentny 1996).

The creation of legal identities does not simply determine social life. The law in books is not the same as the law in action. People do not always behave in the way the laws require. Although laws have often defined racial identities, they have an impact only if they are implemented by courts, immigration officials, police, prosecutors, and attorneys. Their impact depends also on support within the everyday legal consciousness of the members of a society.

This chapter shows how the law takes existing social conceptions of racial difference and converts them into principles of inclusion and exclusion backed by the authority, legitimacy, and sanctioning power of the state. The categories themselves are rigidified and naturalized. Laws have often used racial characteristics to define who is and is not a desirable citizen of the United States. The first half of the chapter shows the changing understandings of race in the United States and the contradictory roles that law has played in developing and changing these understandings. The second half is a case study of the social and legal structures of race in Hilo, Hawaii, during the 19th and early 20th centuries; it reveals the intimate linkage between legal regulations and social practices in the construction of race. The chapter then returns to the issues affirmative action raises about the value and significance of entitlement programs based on race.

Creating Racial Identities through Legal Regulations

Citizenship and naturalization

The fundamental question of who could be a citizen arose at the founding of the United States. Citizenship was understood to confer certain rights to self-governance and protection from the state. Because the new American republic was imagined to be self-governing, the founders were anxious to limit those who would acquire the rights to citizenship and to participation in the political sphere to people loyal to the country and capable of self-government (Fuchs 1990:16–17). They used race and gender restrictions to effectively limit citizenship and participation to white males until the 20th century. Although the United States adopted the policy that any native-born person was a citizen, an incorporative strategy not followed by all nations, the question of who was allowed to participate fully in governance or who was eligible for naturalization provided fertile ground for creating legal identities based on "race."

The question of naturalization raised profound worries about who would be given the power to govern U.S. society. Originally, debates centered on how long a person had lived in the country, assuming that with protracted residence a person would learn loyalty and enough about political institutions to participate responsibly. All were expected to wait five years for naturalization. By the 1830s, almost all states allowed people of all religions to become citizens (Fuchs 1990:14). But at the founding moment of the country, there was already an exclusion based on race. Naturalized citizenship was granted to "white" immigrants only, a restriction in force until 1952. No people of color could participate politically except in those states that allowed free native-born blacks to participate (Fuchs 1990:16). Indeed, liberalism, as a political philosophy, was originally imagined as a form of governance exercised by those with the reason and capacity to do so and implicitly always excluded those considered incapable of governing, whether because of weak character, alien loyalties, or incapacities based on racial or gender identities (Mehta 1997). Current research explores the complexity of the category of citizenship itself and the extent to which it has always been circumscribed by race, ethnicity, gender, and even religion; partial and differential citizenship are ways of conceptualizing this variability (Smith 1997).

Slavery, of course, was the most fundamental denial of citizenship. As a legal category, American slavery was created as a racialized status, but its legal foundations predate the creation of the United States. While the first Africans arrived in Virginia in 1619, slavery as a distinctive legal institution was not fully established until 1661. At this time, a distinction was drawn between free wage labor, indentured service for a time period, and slavery, a status with no limitation on the period of service and one which increasingly became hereditary, the distinctive key to this status. Only Africans were made slaves while whites served as indentured labor. By the end of the 17th century, there was racial slavery in all the English colonies even though it was not an institution familiar to the English (Jordan 1974:26, 33–36, 54). From the late 17th century onward, the African captives brought to the colonies were categorized as slaves according to the regulations of the new institution, which was defined fundamentally by skin color.

Even free African Americans were denied full citizenship by law. In the early 19th century, states in both the North and the South passed laws disenfranchising free blacks. In the South they were barred from military service and prohibited from testifying against whites in court. They were denied other rights of citizens such as protection from search without a warrant, jury trials for less than capital crimes, and carrying arms. Laws prevented them from marrying whites. The 1857 Dred Scott decision promoted the theory that African Americans could not be citizens because they were black. However, the Civil Rights Act of 1866 and the subsequent Fourteenth Amendment asserted that any person born or naturalized in the United States was a citizen and that no state should restrict these rights or deny any person the equal protection of the law (Fuchs 1990:92–95).

However, state and local laws and public opinion virtually eviscerated these laws. By the early 20th century, a series of state and local laws, called Jim Crow laws, segregated a wide range of public facilities: churches, schools, housing, jobs, public transportation, hospitals, prisons, and even cemeteries, on the basis of race (Woodward 1966:7). It was this body of law that formed the object of the Civil Rights movement and was gradually eliminated by 1965. The landmark Civil Rights Act of 1964 and the Voting Rights Act of 1965 prohibited local officials from using devices such as literacy tests to prevent any citizens from registering to vote (Fuchs 1990:171–173). While African Americans still face extensive racist practices, the laws defining citizenship by physical features have been dismantled.

Until the mid-20th century, the right to become a naturalized citizen was reserved to whites. The law restricting naturalization to "whites" remained in force from 1790 to 1952. During that period, a series of laws and court decisions determined who was "white" and who was not. In 1855, a Chinese immigrant who applied for citizenship was denied because he was not "white." In 1922, the U.S. Supreme Court denied citizenship to a culturally Americanized Japanese immigrant, saying that he could not be a naturalized citizen because he was not a Caucasian even though he spoke English, his children attended an American school, and he belonged to an American church. A court decision in 1921 affirmed that Koreans, even if they had performed military service for the United States, were Mongolians and ineligible for citizenship. Although a 1910 court decision held that Asian Indians were whites and therefore eligible for naturalization, a 1923 Supreme Court decision determined that they were not white since whites were only the peoples of northern or western Europe and although Asian Indians might be Caucasian, the founding fathers had used the term "white." A 1934 Supreme Court decision determined that the 1790 Naturalization Law excluded Chinese, Japanese, Hindus, American Indians, and Filipinos from becoming naturalized citizens. While Filipinos could enter the country as "American nationals" when the Philippines were a U.S. colony, they were not granted citizenship and were excluded from land ownership. However, Filipinos could not be excluded in the 1924 Immigration Act because of their colonial status, so the United States decided to move toward independence for the Philippines. In 1946, at the time of Philippines independence, Filipinos were allowed to become naturalized citizens (Takaki 1989:113, 207–208, 272, 299–300, 315, 325, 331, 362).

Decisions restricting naturalization had larger consequences for non-white immigrants. The Immigration Act of 1924 denied immigration quotas to people ineligible for naturalization. Non-white aliens were subject to anti-miscegenation laws and denied ownership of land under the California Alien Land Law of 1913, which excluded those not eligible for naturalization from owning land. The law made it illegal to own "real property" for "aliens ineligible for citizenship" and restricted leases to three years. Japanese farmers were forced to list their property as owned by their American-born children or a corporation. In 1920, a law prohibited aliens ineligible for citizenship from leasing such land, acquiring such land under the names of native-born minors, or having stock in any corporation owning real property. A 1923 amendment to this law made it illegal for them to "acquire, possess, enjoy, use, cultivate, occupy, and transfer real property" (Takaki 1989:205). Similar laws were enacted in Washington, Arizona, Oregon, Idaho, Nebraska, Texas, Kansas, Louisiana, Montana, New Mexico, Minnesota, and Missouri (Takaki 1989:206–207). Whether or not these laws were fully enforced, they redefined the position of first-generation immigrants as permanent aliens in the language of nationality-based racial identities. As Japanese and other non-white immigrant farmers struggled to place ownership of their lands in the names of infant children or friendly whites, their sense of exclusion was enhanced. The decision to intern the Japanese and Japanese-American population in California during World War II, often leaving their lands open for seizure by others, represented a further extension of this policy of racially limiting property rights. Thus, once the identity of citizens was allocated on a racial basis, it provided the opportunity for other racially discriminatory forms of legislation.

Immigration restrictions

The first century of existence of the United States was marked by a sense of unlimited resources and a shortage of people. Immigration proceeded largely unchecked until the middle of the 19th century, when opposition to Chinese immigrants began to develop. By 1870 demands for Chinese exclusion were heard, based on concern by white workers that they would undersell their labor, and on images of the Chinese as sly and sneaky. As the frontier closed, frustrated white immigrants in the West turned on the Chinese. In 1882, Chinese laborers were excluded, and, in 1888, "all persons of the Chinese race," indicating a clear biological basis to the exclusion, although class-based exemptions were made for Chinese officials, teachers, students, tourists, and merchants. The law was renewed in 1892 and extended indefinitely in 1902 (Takaki 1989:111–112).

Japanese immigrants were excluded in the 1908 Gentlemen's Agreement in which Japan agreed not to permit emigration of laborers to the United States. Women who immigrated as picture brides and other family members continued to come until that loophole was closed in 1921 (Takaki 1989:204, 208). Theodore Roosevelt's 1907 executive order prohibited the migration of Japanese and Koreans from Hawaii to the mainland. The Alien Land Act of 1913 barred Koreans, and others prohibited from naturalization, from owning land in California (Takaki 1989:272).

In 1924, Congress passed a restrictive immigration law pegged to concepts of race. This system favored the racial groups considered desirable by the men who promoted and enacted the law: those from northern and western Europe, rather than those considered less desirable, from eastern and southern Europe. Although Canadians and Latin Americans were still free to enter without quota restrictions, immigration from most other countries was limited to a quota of 2 percent of the number of foreign-born residents from them in 1890. After 1927, a total quota of 150,000 was parceled out in proportion to the distribution of national origins in the white population in the United States in 1920. The law also prohibited the entry of individuals who were already "aliens ineligible for citizenship," a racialized category that included immigrants from Japan and other Asian countries (Higham 1955:324).

The impact of the 1924 laws was felt strongly among populations now excluded. For example, first-generation Japanese immigrants felt they had no future in America, except through their children, and were doomed to be foreigners forever (Takaki 1989:212). The 1924 exclusion represented a triumph of concepts of biological difference over cultural difference and a despair over the possibilities of assimilating American Indians and African Americans.

However, by the mid-20th century, the practice of legal exclusions based on race began to change, largely because of political engagement by members of excluded groups. Amendments to the Immigration and Nationality Act of 1952 made in 1965 changed immigration policy from the national origins concept to one of equal quotas from all countries with an emphasis on family reunification. These laws reduced the sharp inequities by assigning quotas of 20,000 to each country with a total of 170,000 in the Eastern Hemisphere while continuing to admit immediate relatives of U.S. citizens without numerical restriction. Visas were allocated in large part to relatives of citizens or residents. This was a major shift away from the system based on race and place of birth established in 1924 (Fuchs 1990:233, 278).

The anomalous status of American Indians

Native American peoples were defined as domestic dependent nations rather than citizens in a series of Supreme Court decisions in the 1820s. In the late

19th century, they could become citizens only if they were acculturated and chose to do so. In the early 20th century, they finally became citizens, but with diminished rights. There have long been fundamental contradictions in American Indian law between the rights of man doctrines, stated first in the Declaration of Independence, and the categorization of Native Americans as "merciless Indian savages" of our frontiers who are denied the rights of man (Smith 1997:459–463). In his important opinions defining the relations between Native Americans, states, and the federal government, Chief Justice John Marshall defined the natives as having some rights, but not rights to complete sovereignty or to dispose of their lands at will. He referred to them as "fierce savages" in whose hands the country would remain an undeveloped "wilderness" (Mertz 1995 [1988]:372). In a trilogy of cases decided in 1822, 1831, and 1832, Marshall declared a European "right to take possession [of North America] notwithstanding the occupancy of the natives, who were heathens" and thus did not have private property protections, and that the lands were effectively "vacant" (Biolsi 1995:12; Churchill 1996:41). Marshall defined Indian nations not as foreign nations but as "domestic, dependent nations" (Churchill 1996:41). In his 1831 decision, Marshall wrote that they were a people "in a state of pupilage; their relation to the United States resemble[s] that of a ward to his guardian" (Hoxie 1984:214). The Marshall doctrine of domestic dependent nations gradually developed through Supreme Court decisions into the doctrine that native nations had subordinate sovereignty under the "plenary" power of the United States for governance and jurisdiction (Churchill 1996:42).

These decisions created an ambiguous status for American Indians. They were neither members of sovereign nations nor citizens of the United States. In the 1866 Civil Rights Act, ex-slaves were made citizens but not unassimilated Native Americans, since "Indians [were] not taxed." The Fourteenth Amendment which made all persons born or naturalized in the United States citizens and guaranteed due process and equal protection of the laws, eliminated the exclusion of "Indians not taxed," but the framers of the law still wanted to claim sovereignty over the tribes and to deny that they and women were members of the American political community. In 1884, the Supreme Court decided that the Indian was not a citizen even when he had "severed his tribal relation" (Biolsi 1995).

The Dawes Act of 1887 divided up reservation land into individual allotments inalienable for 25 years and gave Indians rights to land and to citizenship if they were "ready." All allottees were to receive all the legal rights and privileges of U.S. citizens, thus making citizenship available to those who chose to assimilate into the Anglo-American culture. Yet, many Indians were not interested in becoming citizens. The U.S. government maintained a trust authority over Indian lands and in a series of decisions in the early 20th century held that these lands were not taxable by state or county governments, part of a paternalistic policy in which Native Americans were not treated as civic equals. Moreover, court decisions affirmed that even citizen Indians were regarded as Indians by race and subject to the jurisdiction of Congress within reservations (Hoxie 1984:70, 211, 218; Churchill 1996; Smith 1997:461–462).

Debates continued into the early 20th century about whether Indian citizens were to be treated like all other citizens or whether they should receive special federal protections, particularly with regard to their lands and alcohol consumption. Thus, their citizenship was defined partially on the basis of their "racial" identity. There was a progressive infantilization of African Americans and Indians in the early 1900s as both groups were reconceptualized as incapable of self-government. Virtually every state with a significant Indian population had voting regulations that limited Indian participation in elections. In 1924, when all Indians were granted citizenship, it was a citizenship restricted by notions of guardianship (Hoxie 1984:106, 220–223, 232–236).

Thus there is a central and enduring tension between defining Indian people as members of sovereign nations who are legally different and defining them as wards, legally the same as other U.S. citizens if still "savage," "uncivilized," or "primitive" and requiring paternalistic restrictions on citizenship rights (Biolsi 1995).

Legal regulations of social interaction

Laws preventing sexual relations and marriages among races were established in the late 17th century, soon after English settlers began to think of themselves in terms of color. At first, they imagined themselves as English and free in opposition to other nations with different political systems; then as Christians in opposition to heathen Indians; and finally in the late 1600s as white in opposition to black. They began to outlaw miscegenation as this race consciousness developed. By 1700 two northern and all plantation colonies prohibited miscegenation. The anti-miscegenation laws, which grew increasingly strict and were concerned with prohibiting contact even between mulattoes and whites, culminated in the one-drop rule for defining mulattoes in 1915. Penalties were also increasingly harsh. By 1940, all seventeen states in the South except West Virginia had outlawed mixed marriages, and most defined a Negro as a person with one-eighth or more Negro blood (Jordan 1974:44, 71; Williamson 1980:11, 97, 108).

Like blacks, Chinese were viewed as threats to white racial purity. Similar laws restricting consensual sexual intercourse were passed by dominant whites. Although these restrictions clearly failed to prevent sexual relations among whites and Chinese just as they had for African Americans and European Americans, they did define these relations as illegal and undesirable. Most states had miscegenation laws in the 19th century. In 1880 California prohibited marriage of a white person to a "Negro, mulatto, or Mongolian." After a successful 1933 challenge from a Filipino wishing to marry a white woman who claimed he was Malay rather than Mongolian, the state legislature amended the law to include "Malay race" in the restricted category. Twelve other states prohibited marriages between whites and Filipinos. Arizona, Nevada, North Carolina, and Oregon had statutes forbidding sexual relations between Indians and whites in the early 20th century (Takaki 1989:101–102, 330; Hoxie 1984:235).

State laws also restricted the ability to testify in court on the basis of race. In 1854, the California Supreme Court lumped Chinese with Indians, Negroes, or mulattoes, as people who could not testify in court against a white. The Chinese took their struggle against this treatment to the courts time and again. The 1870 Civil Rights Act, for protection of blacks, included protections for Chinese as well, freeing them from special taxes and granting them equal rights to give evidence in court (Takaki 1989:103, 113–114, 272; Hoxie 1984).

State laws also separated individuals of different races. In 1859, California established segregated schools for blacks, Indians, and Chinese. By the 1890s, Indians were also being educated largely in separate schools, and the Jim Crow laws had established separate schools as well as a wide range of other separate facilities for African Americans.

It is clear that legally based racial distinctions have significant consequences in creating different social positions on the basis of an alleged "racial" identity. Eliminating these laws has not eliminated the social inequalities they produced. However, the removal of these laws does undermine the legitimacy of these systems of classification and exclusion and diminishes their validity.

Creating "Race" in Hawaii

This case study of the construction of racial identities in 19th- and early 20th-century Hawaii illustrates the way processes of legal regulation contribute to the creation of "race." It describes the creation of categories of indigenous Hawaiians, imported workers for the sugar plantations, and the self-construction of a white racial identity by the economically dominant white population. Laws constructing racial identities underscored economic and political inequality in this very diverse population. These distinctions drew on the ideologies and legal arrangements of the mainland as well. In Hawaii, they created a world in which everyone had a distinct racial identity despite widespread intermarriage and cultural sharing of foods, arts, values, and language. The population spoke a patois which incorporated English, Hawaiian, Filipino, Japanese, and Chinese words and grammatical structures (Merry 2000).

The harbor town of Hilo, along with other urban areas of Hawaii, is now a field of interconnected, complex identities. Despite the cross-hatching of ancestry, community members are imagined and counted as a series of distinct, bounded populations. According to the 1990 Census, South Hilo was 34% Japanese, 26% white, 19% Hawaiian, 12% Filipino, 3% Chinese, 1% Korean, 1% other Asian or Pacific Islander, 0.5% black, and 0.5% Native American. These self-reported figures imply that the categories of ethnic identity are unambiguous. In practice, most of the population is extensively intermarried, so that ethnicity is a matter of some choice among possible alternatives and is heavily influenced by lifestyle, social class, and self-perception. For example, the Japanese American community is predominant in government and educational activities and largely middle-class. The white population consists of two groups, those descended from Portuguese sugar workers, who consider themselves Portuguese rather than *haole* (whites), and whites from the mainland or elite long-term whites who are called *haole*.

Cross-cutting these ethnic divisions is the important distinction of local or outsider, marked largely by accent and dialect. Locals speak pidgin, an inflected version of English that immediately marks its speaker as someone who belongs on the island and separates him or her from newcomers. At the same time, speaking "standard" English is essential to upward social mobility and professional status. Those who speak only pidgin face obstacles in job advancement, particularly in the tourist industry. Older plantation workers were taught that this was a second-rate language and are often very apologetic about their "bad" English. Many professionals who grew up in Hawaii are able to speak both pidgin and standard English and switch easily between them.

An examination of the historical processes of identity formation in Hilo and elsewhere in Hawaii provides insight into how identities emerged from the tumultuous changes that occurred after 1800: Christian missionization in the early 19th century, the burgeoning sugar plantation economy in the late 19th century, and the land trusts and other benefits established by the United States in the early 20th century to compensate Native Hawaiians for lands it appropriated. The local situation was shaped by global discourses about plantation labor, the threats of Chinese immigrants, and the need to compensate indigenous peoples in expanding Euro-American settler states.

Early 19th-century Hawaii was dominated by trading relationships between the chiefly elite of Hawaiian society, the *ali'i*, and a band of mostly New England adventurers and merchants, who settled in the port towns of Honolulu, Lahaina, and Hilo to provision the ships of the China trade and to service the ships of the Pacific whale fishery. Congregational and other Calvinist missionaries who arrived from New England in 1820 and sought to convert the "heathen" native peoples antagonized the merchant community. Disputes erupted between them about whether commerce or Christianity was the more effective route to civilization. By 1850, the Native Hawaiian population was plummeting because of introduced diseases, economic displacement, and out-migration; changes in the Kingdom's legal structure also allowed aliens to purchase land for the first time. By 1876, the booming sugar plantation economy demanded a larger labor supply than the dwindling Hawaiian community could provide, and a racialized labor system became entrenched. Asian and European immigrants worked for a small number of American and British supervisors and plantation managers. Consequently, there was an extraordinarily heterogeneous community by the time U.S. imperialists annexed Hawaii in 1898 (Merry 2000).

The Native Hawaiians were not incorporated into this system. Their identities were forged in their earlier encounter with missionaries, where the key opposition was between the heathen and the saved. The missionaries sought to incorporate those Hawaiians who partook of a Christian life as church members and to suspend or excommunicate those who failed to abide by their principles. Unlike many other parts of the colonial world, incorporation and assimilation dominated relations between foreign and indigenous populations in 19th-century Hawaii. In marked contrast to the dual legal systems prevalent in many British colonial states, the assumption in Hawaii (under the influence of politically powerful missionaries) was that Native Hawaiians who changed their cultural practices and loyalties could be accepted into at least the legal and political systems of white society.

The lot of the plantation laborers was vastly different. As the need for labor became acute, planters imported a succession of foreign workers from China, Japan, Portugal, Puerto Rico, Korea, the Philippines, and more recently the Pacific Islands and Mexico. The laborers came under a contract labor law that imposed criminal penalties on those who failed to work. Legally they were bound laborers.

Plantations, with their distinctive forms of discipline and order, increasingly dominated Hilo while the labor they imported changed its social composition dramatically. The low pay, grim working and living conditions, brutal treatment by overseers and quasi-slave contract labor system drove each group of immigrants out of the plantations as soon as possible. Planters constantly sought new sources of labor. During the 1860s, Hawaiians did much of the arduous work of hoeing, cutting, and hauling cane; however, by the 1870s, the practice of importing foreign laborers under three-year contracts was widespread (Beechert 1985). Despite complaints in the U.S. press that this was a quasi-slave system, it was not abolished until formal annexation to the United States made it illegal. Chinese labor was imported from 1852 until public protest against Chinese immigrants induced the government to restrict the flow in 1886 and to exclude them in 1893 unless they were willing to work as contract laborers and to leave when their contracts expired (Sullivan 1923:511; George 1948:27). Anxious for a white population whom they imagined would make better citizens than the Chinese, planters brought workers and their families from Portugal, Madeira, and the Azores between 1877 and 1913 (Lydon 1975:52). Between 1885 and 1907, they imported mostly Japanese workers. The white managers defined each group of immigrants in terms of racialized labor capacities and subjected them to an extensive apparatus of control because of their alleged need for authority.

Legal regulations determined citizenship, immigration, and labor. During the period of the Hawaiian Kingdom, anyone who swore an oath of allegiance could become a citizen. As whites gained power in the Kingdom during the 1880s, they restricted voting rights on the basis of property and race and excluded Asian immigrants. The white-dominated government, which took power in 1893 after the queen was ousted by representatives of the United States, imposed even greater race and property restrictions on citizenship and political participation (Coffman 1998). As on the mainland, Asians could not become naturalized citizens.

The differential preference for various groups of laborers led to different legal patterns of immigration. Portuguese workers were allowed to come as families; Chinese and Filipino workers came as single men. Although Japanese workers usually came as single men, they were subsequently allowed to import wives from Japan. The consequences of the different immigration policies were enormous for a community's ability to create its own institutions and to produce an assimilated second generation which, after Hawaii's annexation to the United States in 1898, was automatically endowed with citizenship.

Differential treatment of laborers on the plantations contributed significantly to the creation of essentialized, bounded identities. The strict allocation of jobs and housing on the basis of "nationality" reinforced social boundaries, while differential pay rates exacerbated hostilities. In the early 20th century, all social life was conceived through these categories, including baseball teams and schools. Early union movements followed these lines as well, although by the 1920s cross-national unions gradually emerged and became more effective (Merry 2000).

Forms of counting, measuring, and producing knowledge about the population reinforced racial categorization. While census categories changed over time, race remained a fundamental concept. Court records similarly encoded identities, reflecting an assumption that these identities represented knowledge essential for the judgment of criminal cases. After World War II, efforts to count and measure continued, although the difficulty of sorting and labeling had become more obvious. Nevertheless, the shift to a self-report strategy in the census and in police and court records retains the notion of a fixed identity but transfers the locus of announcement to the individual him- or herself.

These processes were influenced by the transfer of global categories of identity. The Christian mission in Hawaii was deeply shaped by the experiences of other missionary endeavors in its approaches and forms of understanding. Missionaries frequently moved and communicated with each other through publications such as the *Missionary Herald*. The sugar plantation was also a transnational institution whose forms of labor management and social ordering were developed through shared discourses across national and colonial boundaries (Curtin 1990). The contract labor system and its underlying legislation was a global institution, circulated along with ideas about distinctive racialized labor capacities. Finally, conceptions of indigenous peoples transplanted from mainland North America shaped evolving policies toward Native Hawaiians.

Forms of racialized identities

Two rather different sets of identities were developed in large part by the white elites: one described the Native Hawaiians, the other the imported Asian laborers. When the missionaries arrived in the 1820s, the dominant discourse was one of savagery and heathenism and the need to minister to souls on these dark shores. As the Hawaiians resisted the enormous cultural and moral changes envisioned by the mission, the missionaries began to search for "natural" flaws in their character or intellect – for example, their inability to think abstractly – to account for their failure (Andrews 1836). By the middle of the 19th century, as *haoles* attempted to make Native Hawaiians into a plantation labor force, this discourse was replaced by one of childlike indolence and laziness. The frustrating efforts to transform marriage and sexual practices added a recurring complaint about licentiousness, heard loudly in missionary reports from the field.

For example, Titus Coan (1882:249), a missionary who had lived in Hilo for almost fifty years, described the Hawaiians as a primitive race, claiming that "our native converts were as children, and up to this day many of them need milk rather than strong meat." He thought the Hawaiians were "naturally indolent" and "lack economy" even though they worked hard when necessary. "We teach them industry, economy, frugality, and generosity," he wrote, "but their progress in these virtues is slow. They are like children needing wise parents or guardians" (Coan 1882:254–255). The character of this "infant race" is amorous and subject to bad influences from foreigners and from some laws which encourage licentiousness and others which, while wholesome, are unenforced (1882:256). They are followers rather than leaders. They are inclined to be untruthful, speaking lies as soon as they are born, but this trait also is rooted in their racialized nature. "This is a severe charge, but it is a trait probably in all savage races" (1882:256). Coan concludes that their piety is imperfect: "Their easy and susceptible natures, their impulsive and fickle traits, need great care and faithful watching" (1882:257).

Elite whites such as Coan produced a Hawaiian identity which allowed them to define themselves as adults, even fathers, in relation to feminized children, while diminishing the agentic capacity of the Hawaiians. Writing in a missionary newspaper in 1844, Robert Wyllie praised Hawaiian seamen as docile and competent. Another described Native Hawaiians as "children of the Pacific . . . [with] an aesthetic love of the beautiful beyond what is found in the most highly-cultivated circles" (Chambers 1864:255). He thought these brave, kind, and beautiful people would soon disappear because of infanticide: "The mothers are idle, they dislike the trouble of bringing up families, and they desire above all things to preserve their charms, which the nursing of children diminishes."

While the Hawaiians were romanticized and economically marginalized, the Asian immigrant groups were viewed as a threat by *haole* elites, undesirable as citizens. Morally repugnant habits such as gambling, thievery, and opium smoking attached to essentialized biological identities. These practices were seen as threatening to the fragile moral capacity of the Native Hawaiians. As the planters demanded more labor, they confronted Hawaiian and other local resistance by bringing in new immigrant groups. During the 1860s and 1870s, the Chinese were particularly subject to public attack.

The debates about Chinese workers began in the 1850s. While planters claimed they were good laborers, long-term residents, including many Native Hawaiians and the Honolulu press, complained they were troublesome and prone to violent crimes and resistant to planter control. The anti-Chinese movement was fed by Native Hawaiian fears that their shrinking numbers would be engulfed by the newcomers, by the missionaries who believed they had a bad influence on the Native Hawaiians, and by the anti-Chinese movement in California which was increasingly the most important area for Hawaii's contact and trade in the post–gold rush era (Lydon 1975:23–29).

After an incident in 1881, an editorial in the Honolulu *Advertiser*, drawing on a global discourse, observed that Europeans the world over had learned "to distrust him [the Chinese] as treacherous, and ready to shed human blood and take human life in revenge for the slightest provocation" (quoted in Lydon 1975:50). Henry M. Whitney, the paper's editor, waged an extensive anti-Chinese editorial campaign in the late 1860s and 1870s complaining that the Chinese (in the essentialized singular) was a pagan with no regard for life so that all who dealt with the coolie felt insecure. Whitney thundered in his newspaper that Chinese brought disease, smoked opium, and had a demoralizing effect on "the Hawaiian" in the essentialized singular (Lydon 1975:31).

The absence of Chinese women exacerbated the criminal image of the immigrant men. Between 1853 and 1890, only 5–10 percent of the Chinese population were women. In the mid-1870s, the *Advertiser* portrayed Chinese men as sexual predators and argued that their promiscuity caused sterility in Hawaiian women. Indeed, Chinese competition for Hawaiian women may have fueled Hawaiian resistance to more Chinese immigration. An 1880 bill passed by the Legislature but not signed by King Kalakaua (probably in response to planter pressure) restricted the immigration of "Asiatic" men by specifying that for each five male immigrants there should be three females (Lydon 1975:43, 62).

By 1877, there was considerable pressure to stop Chinese immigration altogether because of the perceived threats to public health and safety. By 1886, Chinese immigration had virtually ended. Walter Murray Gibson, the prime minister, was able to engineer this cessation only by offering the planters a new source of labor: Japan (Beechert 1985:88–89). At the same time, an 1890 law allowed Chinese workers to come to Hawaii as long as they did only agricultural labor and stayed no more than five years. Declared unconstitutional in 1892, the law became a constitutional amendment in 1892 (Beechert 1985:92–93). By the 1880s, an anti-Japanese movement was already being fueled by a similar movement on the mainland (Takaki 1989; Okihiro 1991).

After the elimination of the contract labor system, the planters attempted to institute a passbook system for workers and to use an old vagrancy statute to compel workers to work on public works as prisoners (Okihiro 1991:36). Because annexation increased the possibilities of Japanese migration to the mainland, the anti-Japanese movement in the United States resulted in a 1907 executive order keeping Japanese, among others, from the mainland and produced the 1908 Gentlemen's Agreement, by which Japan agreed to restrict emigration. As a result, the flow of labor from Japan was cut off except for the parents, wives, and children of Japanese residents. An increase in picture brides produced a shift in gender ratios from a virtually all-male population in 1890 to near parity in 1920 (Okihiro 1991:38, 58). When the Japanese workers engineered a strike in 1909, they were seen as an alien threat, even as they began to make claims in non-racialized American terms to equal pay for equal work (Okihiro 1991). The first unionization attempts followed racial lines, but Japanese, Filipino, and other categories of workers formed alliances by the 1920s even though the planters endeavored to keep each ethnicity separate in order to impede the labor movement (Beechert 1985).

Economically and politically powerful whites pressed for restrictions on the rights of Asians to become naturalized citizens in the 1880s and 1890s (Fuchs 1961; Coffman 1998). Because American laws denied naturalization to Asian immigrants, nearly 60 percent of Hawaii's population at the time of annexation was disenfranchised (Okihiro 1991:13). Although the Native Hawaiians were a numerical minority at the time of annexation, this exclusion allowed them to continue to exercise significant political power. As the children of the Asian immigrants became voters in the 1930s and 1940s, Native Hawaiians began to lose political power and economic position, and now rank at the bottom of the social hierarchy in income, educational attainment, health, and longevity. They have become a largely poor, urban population (Blaisdell and Mokuau 1994). In the last two decades a powerful movement to reclaim Hawaiian language and culture and to assert sovereignty has swept Hawaiian communities, paralleling similar movements among colonized indigenous peoples in New Zealand, Canada, Australia, and the mainland United States (Trask 1993; Hasager and Friedman 1994; Merry 1997).

An intriguing document produced by Lorrin Thurston, a leading business-man and central figure in the 1893 coup, argued the benefits of annexing Hawaii to the United States. He tries to sell the benefits of annexation to an increas-ingly racially nativist and balky American public fearful of the multi-hued population of the islands. He describes the Native Hawaiians, "only 33,000 in number" as "a conservative, peaceful and generous people" and reminds readers that they are not Africans but Polynesians, brown rather than black (Thurston n.d.:27). There is, he said, no color line between whites and native Hawaiians in marriage or in political, social, or religious affairs. He describes the Por-tuguese, the only significant element of the workforce which is white, as con-structive members of society, emphasizing that they commit a smaller proportion of criminal offenses than any other nationality in the country and are "a hard-working industrious, home-creating and home-loving people who would be of advantage to any developing country. They constitute the best laboring element in Hawaii" (Thurston n.d.:28).

Thurston portrayed the Chinese and Japanese as "an undesirable population from a political standpoint, because they do not understand American princi-ples of government" (n.d.:28). In flagrant disregard of actual population move-ments, he asserts that these groups neither want to stay permanently in Hawaii nor to migrate to the United States. The remaining inhabitants, Thurston con-tinues, are Americans, English, and Germans:

> strong, virile men who have impressed their form of government upon the much larger population living there, and have acquired the ownership of more than three-fourths of all the property in the country. If they were able to do this against the hostility and in the face of an unfavorable monarchy, why is there any reason to believe that they will be any less strong under the fostering influence of the republican Government of the United States?   (n.d.:29)

Celebrating these changes as the victory of masculinized white racial supremacy, Thurston draws on the developing transnational consciousness of white racial supremacy, always male, linked to the high colonialism of Europe and the United States. For imperialist thinkers, the image of Hawaii governed by a class of 4,000 Americans and other Anglo-Saxons ruling 145,000 people of different racial/ethnic heritage seemed perfectly reasonable, legitimated by racialized and gendered conceptions of identity. Citizenship laws underscored and reinforced these conceptions, enacting them in the realm of legal definitions of identity (Maurer 1997).

Indeed, from annexation to 1946, a small, interrelated group of *haole* busi-nessmen exerted enormous political and economic power over a numerous and heterogeneous non-propertied class (Okihiro 1991:13). White power was described as paternal, male, mature, and physically marked by stature. In a retrospective newspaper article written in 1940, Carl Carlsmith, one of the leading attorneys of Hilo, expresses this ideology of racialism:

> To be a plantation manager in the 1890s was to possess not only wealth but social and political position and a right to guide the destinies and affairs of people in the district. Judges, sheriffs and all other officers were appointed by the government residing at Honolulu. A new appointment was not usually made till approved by the managers. New enterprises were not likely to succeed unless they met with the managerial sanction. At Waiakea was C. C. Kennedy and at Wainaku was John A. Scott. Both had grown old in the sugar industry and both were charitable and kindly even if strict in the conduct of all local affairs.
>
> Beyond Waiakea there was Goodale at Onomea, Deakon at Pepeekeo, Moir at Honomu, George Ross at Hakalau, McLellan at Laupahoehoe, Walker at Ookala, Albert Horner at Kukalau, Lidgate at Paauallo, Moore at Paahau, John Watt at Honokaa and Forbes at Kukuihaele. *These were all men of great dignity, tall of stature and important because of the responsibilities given into their keeping.* (*Hilo Tribune Herald*, December 30, 1940:37; my emphasis)

Their height was more symbolic than physical. Carlsmith translated power and authority into tallness, masculinity, and whiteness, just as in the earlier descriptions of Native Hawaiians, subordination and powerlessness were translated into soft eyes and feminine acquiescence.

Thus, cultural conceptions of racial identity legitimated the passage and implementation of laws restricting groups designated by race. Ideas of white racial supremacy promoted the control and exclusion of various categories of non-white labor, the exclusion of non-whites (except for Native Hawaiians) from naturalized citizenship after annexation, and the retention of significant political and economic power by a small white elite. The reliance on an exclusively male labor force of Chinese workers exacerbated the tendency of Chinese immigrants to rely on opium and prostitutes for consolation, actions which legitimated anti-Chinese feeling in the minds of the non-Chinese residents of Hawaii and California.

In the early 20th century Native Hawaiians were legally defined in racial terms in order to provide a benefit to compensate them for the takeover of the Hawaiian Kingdom and its Crown lands (Kauanui 1998:86). In 1920, the U.S. Congress allocated parcels of land to the Native Hawaiian people to serve as a homeland. The Hawaiian Homelands were to be awarded as homesteads and ranches to Native Hawaiians with a blood quantum of 50 percent or higher. Racial classification became the basis for property rights, while Hawaiian land became a criterion of a Native Hawaiian racial classification. Despite the promise of this scheme, large numbers of Native Hawaiians linger for years on waiting lists and substantial portions of Homelands property have been leased to plantations and for government and commercial uses such as airports and shopping malls. As the proportion of the population of Native Hawaiians with the requisite blood quantum falls, the number eligible for this benefit also drops.

The divisive effects of the blood quantum system are a major concern for contemporary Hawaiian sovereignty activists (Trask 1993; Hasager and

Friedman 1994). The allocation of a benefit on the basis of blood quantum rather than self-identification violates contemporary understandings of Hawaiian identity. It draws a legal line separating groups which feel the same. Other benefits to Native Hawaiians, such as attendance at the Kamehameha Schools or participation in a plebiscite on the future of Native Hawaiian Sovereignty held in 1996, are open to all who self-identify as Native Hawaiian. Here the legal definition of a benefit on the basis of "race" serves to create social boundaries within an ethnic group.

Conclusions

The first part of this chapter described the history of legal creations of racial categories in the United States. The second part showed how regulations about immigration, citizenship, and entitlements grew out of existing racial conceptions and contributed to reinforcing and legitimating them in Hawaii. Regulations about citizenship, immigration, and sexual interaction enshrine identities and attach important privileges and restrictions to them. These examples show how race is not a "natural" phenomenon nor an expression of cultural differences but a product of economic, social, and legal processes. Laws which attach benefits and exclusions based on "race" make racial identities consequential and formalize everyday social practices using the sanctioning power and legitimacy of the state. Laws do cultural work, naturalizing identities and practices of exclusion and separation.

The contemporary strategy of offering particular entitlements for different races continues to reinforce identities based on race. Yet these programs, such as affirmative action or the Hawaiian Homelands, are to some extent focused on repairing the damages of previous legalizations of race. A race-blind system has the advantage of moving beyond the legalization of race, but it fails to provide redress for the history of distinction and exclusion embedded in previous racial categories. The idea of differentiated types of persons marked by skin color, eye shape, and hair texture is a product of several centuries of legal regulation in the United States. Variations in physical characteristics were used to create boundaries which were then strenuously policed and reinforced. Despite the fact that some individuals crossed these boundaries, or "passed," the boundary itself was resolutely asserted and maintained by energetic state action as well as by private but publicly tolerated forms of violence such as lynching. As critical race theorists argue, racial distinction is now fundamental to the social organization of the United States, so that claiming to be "race-blind" simply fails to acknowledge its enduring power in structuring social life.

Legal strategies have been essential to achieving racial justice in the United States. Most racially discriminatory legal regulations are a feature of the past. Despite their formative importance in constituting the United States and its categories of "race," the vast majority of racially discriminatory laws have been eliminated in recent years. This analysis of the significance of legal definitions of racial categorizations provides reasons to contest any new efforts to create exclusionary or discriminatory racial identities through law but also recognizes that the approach adopted by affirmative action builds on a long legacy of using similar laws to exclude rather than to confer remedial benefits.

Acknowledgments

The research described in this chapter was supported by the National Science Foundation, the National Endowment for the Humanities, and the Canadian Institute for Advanced Research.

REFERENCES CITED

Ancheta, Angelo
  1998 *Race, Rights, and the Asian American Experience*. New Brunswick, NJ: Rutgers University Press.
Andrews, Lorrin
  1836 Unthinking Character of the People. *Missionary Herald*, October, vol. 32: 390–1.
Beechert, Edward D.
  1985 *Working in Hawaii: A Labor History*. Honolulu: University of Hawaii Press.
  1993 Patterns of Resistance and the Social Relations of Production in Hawaii. In *Plantation Workers: Resistance and Accommodation*. Brij V. Lal, Doug Munro, and Edward D. Beechert, eds. Pp. 45–69. Honolulu: University of Hawaii Press.
Biolsi, Thomas
  1995 Bringing the Law Back In: Legal Rights and the Regulation of Indian–White Relations on Rosebud Reservation. *Current Anthropology* 36:545–571.
Blaisdell, Kekuni, and Noreen Mokuau
  1994 Kanaka Maoli: Indigenous Hawaiians. In Hasager and Friedman, pp. 49–68.
Chambers
  1864 A Doomed People. *Eclectic Magazine*, February, 64:250–256.
Churchill, Ward
  1996 *From a Native Son*. Boston, MA: South End Press.
Coan, Titus
  1882 *Life in Hawaii: An Autobiographic Sketch of Mission Life and Labors (1835–1881)*. New York: Anson D. F. Randolph.
Coffman, Thomas
  1998 *Nation Within: The Story of America's Annexation of the Nation of Hawaii*. Kane'ohoe, HI: Epicenter.
Crenshaw, Kimberle, Neil Gotanda, Gary Peller, and Kendall Thomas
  1996 *Critical Race Theory: The Key Writings that Formed the Movement*. New York: New Press.
Curtin, Philip D.
  1990 *The Rise and Fall of the Plantation Complex: Essays in Atlantic History*. Cambridge, UK: Cambridge University Press.
Fuchs, Lawrence H.
  1961 *Hawaii Pono: An Ethnic and Political History*. Honolulu: Bess Press.
  1990 *The American Kaleidoscope*. Hanover, CT: Wesleyan University Press.
George, Milton
  1948 *The Development of Hilo, Hawaii TH, or a Slice Through Time at a Place Called Hilo*. Ann Arbor: Edwards Letter Shop.

Glazer, Nathan
    1997   *We Are All Multiculturalists Now.* Cambridge, MA: Harvard University Press.
Hasager, Ulla, and Jonathan Friedman, eds.
    1994   Hawaii: Return to Nationhood. International Work Group for Indigenous
    Affairs, Document No. 75. Copenhagen.
Higham, John
    1955   *Strangers in the Land: Patterns of American Nativism, 1860–1925.* New York:
    Atheneum.
Hoxie, Frederick E.
    1984   *A Final Promise: The Campaign to Assimilate the Indians, 1880–1920.*
    Cambridge, UK: Cambridge University Press.
Jordan, Winthrop
    1974   *The White Man's Burden: The Historical Origins of Racism in the United
    States.* New York: Oxford University Press.
Kauanui, J. Kehaulani
    1998   Rehabilitating the Native: Defining "Hawaiian" (Citizens) in the Hawaiian
    Homes Commission Act. Qualifying essay, University of California at Santa Cruz.
Lawrence, Charles R., III, and Mari Matsuda
    1997   *We Won't Go Back: Making the Case for Affirmative Action.* New York:
    Houghton Mifflin.
Lydon, Edward C.
    1975   *The Anti-Chinese Movement in the Hawaiian Kingdom, 1852–1886.* San
    Francisco: R. and E. Research Associates.
Maurer, Bill
    1997   *Recharting the Caribbean: Land, Law, and Citizenship in the British Virgin
    Islands.* Ann Arbor: University of Michigan Press.
Mehta, Uday S.
    1997   Liberal Strategies of Exclusion. In *Tensions of Empire: Colonial Cultures in a
    Bourgeois World.* Frederick Cooper and Ann L. Stoler, eds. Pp. 59–87. Berkeley:
    University of California Press.
Merry, Sally Engle
    1997   Legal Vernacularization and Transnational Culture: The Ka Ho'okolokolonui
    Kanaka Maoli, Hawaii 1993. In *Human Rights, Culture and Context: Anthropo-
    logical Perspectives.* Richard Wilson, ed. Pp. 28–48. London: Pluto Press.
    2000   *Colonizing Hawaii: The Cultural Power of Law.* Princeton, NJ: Princeton
    University Press.
Mertz, Elizabeth
    1995 [1988]   The Uses of History: Language, Ideology, and Law in the United States
    and South Africa. In *The Law and Society Reader.* Richard Abel, ed. Pp. 361–382.
    New York: New York University Press.
Okihiro, Gary
    1991   *Cane Fires.* Philadelphia: Temple University Press.
Skrentny, David
    1996   *The Ironies of Affirmative Action.* Chicago: University of Chicago Press.
Smith, Rogers M.
    1997   *Civic Ideals: Conflicting Visions of Citizenship in U.S. History.* New Haven,
    CT: Yale University Press.
Sullivan, Louis R.
    1923   The Labor Crisis in Hawaii. *Asia Magazine* 23:511–534.
Takaki, Ronald
    1989   *Strangers from a Different Shore: A History of Asian Americans.* Boston, MA:
    Little, Brown.

Thurston, Lorrin A.
   n.d.   A Handbook on the Annexation of Hawaii [ca. 1897]. Pamphlet. Archives of
      the American Antiquarian Society, Worcester, MA.
Trask, Haunani-Kay
   1993   *From a Native Daughter: Colonialism and Sovereignty in Hawaii.* Monroe,
      ME: Common Courage Press.
Williams, Patricia
   1992   *The Alchemy of Race and Rights.* Cambridge, MA: Harvard University Press.
Williamson, Joel
   1980   *New People: Miscegenation and Mulattoes in the United States.* New York:
      Free Press.
Wilson, William J.
   1973   *Power, Racism, and Privilege.* New York: Free Press.
Woodward, C. Vann
   1966   *The Strange Career of Jim Crow.* New York: Oxford University Press.
Wyllie, Robert
   1844   Native Seamen. *The Friend*, p. 79. Newspaper published in Honolulu, Hawaii
      State Archives.

9

Diversity and Archaeology

Thomas C. Patterson

Class, ethnicity, race, and gender are not natural categories; they are socially and culturally constructed. It is important to realize this in light of renewed claims since the 1980s that human diversity and the exploitative, repressive, and oppressive relations manifested in class, ethnic, gender, and racial hierarchies are rooted in biology or in the kind of deep historical past explored by archaeologists. Since archaeological data do not support such claims, it is imperative that we contest this terrain. Otherwise, we ignore the significance of George Orwell's (1983[1949]:32) observation that "Who controls the past ... controls the future; who controls the present controls the past," as well as the import of George Santayana's (1953[1905–1906]:82, 409) dictum that, since history tends to repeat itself, "those who cannot remember the past are condemned to repeat it."

That such diversity is constructed means that the categories of ethnicity, gender, and race are produced in the complex interplay of various historically constituted and contingent forces, relations, and practices that are both structural and cultural. It also means that the categories themselves were forged and reproduced by the peoples whose activities bolster and sustain those relations and practices rather than by the anthropologists who study them. It further implies that while some societies are cross-cut by gender, ethnic, and racial divisions, others may not exhibit such diversity. In other words, there are and certainly were societies where race and ethnicity were not meaningful categories or did not bear the same load they have had in the United States in the late 20th century, and there are and were societies where gender reflected a technical division of labor rather than difference. Class and state formation constitute an important circumstance in which social and cultural diversity – based on gender, ethnic, or racial distinctions – has been constructed, reproduced, and contested (Comaroff 1987; Gailey 1987; Patterson and Spencer 1994). State-based societies – that is, civilizations – always involve exploitation, repression, and oppression, on the one hand, and the formation of complex social hierarchies, on the other (Patterson 1997).

For more than a century, archaeologists have had a largely undertheorized understanding of the significance of class and state formation. It is bound up with the importance they attribute to the scribes and writing systems found in civilized societies, with the distinction they draw between history and prehistory, and with those processes that led to formation of capitalist states in the West during the 17th and 18th centuries. In this scheme, civilized societies are state-based. Since the texts recorded by scribes and bureaucrats have survived, civilized societies are also historic societies. In contrast, there are also prehistoric societies – peoples without history – that are kin-organized and do not leave written records. A few prehistoric civilizations are also known – for example, the tributary states forged by the Aztecs and the Incas a century or so before the native inhabitants of the Americas were slowly drawn into the political economy of the West after 1500 as a result of imperial expansion, colonial settlement, and the transatlantic slave trade (Patterson 1995:54–66, 106–119; Trigger 1984, 1986).

In practice, archaeologists concerned with civilizations have begun to recognize that ethnicity, class structures, and gender systems play different roles in organizing diversity in state-based societies. Archaeologists concerned with kin- organized societies have begun to recognize that gender systems underwrite diversity in tribal societies. However, only the historical archaeologists – who are concerned mainly with European settler colonies and secondarily with those peoples who were subjugated, enslaved, or otherwise affected by overseas colonial expansion and settlement as well as by the rise of capitalism – have claimed that race (a category based on hereditary differences in physical appearance) had a role in structuring diversity in the societies they study. This implies that diversity based on racial differences became meaningful only during the past two or three centuries in the West and, furthermore, that it is intimately linked with imperialist expansion, colonialism, and the growth of capitalism. Archaeologists, like other social scientists, are beginning to realize that class, gender, race, and ethnicity intersect, and that the interplay of these systems rooted both in economic class relations and in differences that are socially and culturally constituted can create, reinforce, and reproduce complex social hierarchies and structures of power.

That the categories of gender, ethnicity, and race are socially and culturally constituted does not mean that they lack material expression or that they do not leave traces or footprints in the archaeological record. As archaeologists became aware of the issues of class-based and socially constituted diversity, those who accepted the challenge they raised, and investigated them, built on wider currents of social thought combined with the traditional methodological toolkit of the discipline.[1] As you know, archaeologists work with artifacts – objects that were made, modified, or moved by people – and with their spatial relationships, especially those which indicate that the artifacts are contemporary and date to the same era (Childe 1956; Patterson 1994:3–4). Since the kind of diversity with which we are concerned here is socially constructed, the issues for archaeologists in this instance are epistemological and methodological: that is, how to interrogate the archaeological record so that questions about diversity can be raised in ways that permit them to be answered given the constraints imposed by the nature of archaeological evidence. An important constraint is that there is nothing necessarily intrinsic in an object, which indicates that it was produced or used exclusively by the members of a particular gender, racial, or ethnic group. In order to explore the material expressions of diversity and the conditions in which they occur, it is essential to examine the archaeological record from multiple points of view (Paynter et al. 1994:310–314).

Let us now review briefly a few instances drawn from various parts of the world in which archaeologists have successfully interrogated the archaeological record to reveal gender, ethnic, and racial distinctions, in particular past societies. Furthermore, let us also consider the configurations (or bunches) of evidence and lines of argument that led archaeologists to draw certain inferences about the remains they studied. Efforts such as these provide models for investigating diversity in the archaeological record of the United States.

Ethnicity

Archaeologists have relied mainly on stylistic differences to identify tribal or ethnic diversity in the archaeological record. They believed that style was connected with other aspects of the cultures and societies they studied; more specifically, stylized objects – like the shirts worn by some ancient people or the decorated pottery vessels they drank from – conveyed information about group membership and marked boundaries between the members of different social groups (Brumfiel 1987, 1989; Brumfiel et al. 1994; Wobst 1977). These are the kinds of objects recovered in archaeological excavations that provide additional information about their temporal and spatial distributions. Inquiries correlating style with culture or ethnicity were launched in Europe by Gustav Kossinna (1911) and subsequently elaborated by V. Gordon Childe (1929), both of whom portrayed the landscape of Europe as a mosaic of cultures that were continually shifting in time and space. In this mosaic, there was greater variation between the different groupings that made up this landscape than among the archaeological assemblages that constituted one of the groupings.

Dorothy Menzel (1959), for example, recognized that there were four regionally distinct styles of pottery decoration on the south coast of Peru during the 15th century that both preceded and were contemporary with the Inca occupation of the area. She viewed these differences as the material traces or manifestations of ethnic groups that were enveloped and incorporated into the Inca imperial state during the 1470s. Further differences in architecture, settlement patterns, and grave lots – that coincided with the spatial distribution of the four pottery styles – led her to infer that there were

> marked differences in social and political organization among the south coast valleys at the time they were conquered by the Inca. Chincha had a powerful centralized government, while Pisco was probably divided. Ica had a centralized organization of some kind. ... Acarí seems to have had no central authority and no point where there was a concentration of prestige. (Menzel 1959:140)

While historical information supports her conclusion in this instance, other investigations revealed that the kind of stylistic diversity Menzel described appeared in coastal Peru toward the end of the first millennium B.C.E., and that it coincided in time with the appearance of other features in the archaeological record – the construction of fortified hilltop retreats, weapons such as stone-headed maces, burials containing headless individuals or persons entombed with trophy heads, individuals with wounds or dart points embedded in vital areas – which suggest widespread raiding, and the increased prominence of "war leaders" as well as class and state formation (Patterson 1991:26–41; Schaedel 1985). This, however, is not revealed in the written record.

The Intersection of Class Structures and Ethnicity

Class structures in tributary states or civilizations reflect the fact of exploitation and the distribution of goods as well as the position of different groups in the whole social division of labor. This position is defined by the control each group has over its means of production and labor and by its relation to other classes (de Ste. Croix 1984:100). In class-stratified societies, the members of the ruling classes extort goods or labor from the direct producers; they use the power of the state apparatus, which they control, to ensure that the direct producers provide the goods or labor they demand. Archaeologists have used diverse kinds of evidence to demonstrate the existence of class distinctions – for example, contemporary differences in interment practices, variations in the quantity and kinds of grave goods associated with the different types of interment, as well as differences in stature and overall health (Haviland 1967; McCarthy and Graff 1980; Menzel 1976; Paynter and McGuire 1991).

In precapitalist civilizations, class structures typically cross-cut other classifications of people – for example, the estate structures of Han China and feudal Europe and ethnic groups that were forged in the Andes, sometimes by peoples who occupied the same place in the system of production and sometimes by the imperial state itself. Complex social hierarchies appear when different forms of social classification intersect and cross-cut. As the existing categories are reconstituted and new ones emerge, their relations with each other and with emergent groupings must be continually renegotiated. In such conditions, the various ethnic groups occupy different positions in the power structure (e.g. Brumfiel 1994). In the Inca imperial state, other ethnic groups were subordinated in complex ways to the Incas, whose members had privileges and entitlements that were denied to the members of the other collectivities.

In the Andes, the Inca imperial state had some capacity to impose its specifications on the textiles and pottery produced by the artisans of the various ethnic groups whose labor time it appropriated for a portion of each year (Costin 1986; D'Altroy 1992:182–185; D'Altroy and Bishop 1990; Rowe 1979). These standards were the traditional pottery and weaving styles in the Inca homelands, and they were alien elsewhere in the Andes. As a result, these locally produced imitations of Inca vessel shapes or decorations tended to appear rather abruptly in areas on the margins of the expanding state, and their initial appearance in the archaeological record coincided largely with the incorporation of the local ethnic groups into the empire. In other words, the Incas, who stood at the apex of the hierarchy of ethnic groups, imposed some of its standards on other Andean peoples through the agency of the state it controlled.

In another set of studies, Menzel (1960; 1976:221–246) focused her attention on variations between the assemblages constituting one of the cultural groupings on the south coast of Peru during the time of Inca rule. Here she examined configurations of evidence that revealed differences in the distribution and use of certain classes of artifacts. Such differences often occur in the kinds and ranges of grave goods placed in the tombs of individuals with different social ranks. For example, ruling-class individuals frequently have more grave goods, more diverse kinds of goods, and certain goods that are used only by members of that social class.

These differences shed light on the interplay of ethnicity and class in the Ica Valley on the south coast. Local leaders who supported the Inca state and benefited from their association with it lived in an elite residential center and used Inca-style pottery vessels, copies of Inca-style vessels, or fancy pots that combined local and Inca decorative features. In contrast, the peasants lived in villages outside the elite center, used pottery manufactured in a style with local antecedents, looted tombs for antiques that were manufactured and used before the Incas subordinated the valley communities, and used these heirlooms as sources of artistic inspiration. When Inca control collapsed in the early 1530s, the peasants reasserted the dominance of the local artistic tradition, purging the art style and, more importantly, their leaders of all traces of Inca influence. Thus, Menzel's work provides us with a window on the relations of distribution and consumption that characterized the class structure of Ica, and on the reconstitution of the Inca ruling class; it also allows us to pose questions and draw conclusions about forms of peasant resistance and rebellion as well as about the invention and maintenance of artistic traditions during periods of outside rule and the reorganization of ruling class structures (Patterson 1991:105–106).

Peru is by no means the only region where archaeologists have discerned class differences in the archaeological record. Maya specialist Edward Schortman (1980:31) remarked in the context of analyzing the first-millennium C.E. settlement patterns around Quirigua that

> we must understand that the traits used to distinguish Quirigua from its valley neighbors, and also used to define the "Maya area" in general, are most probably associated with elite level activities.

His statement leads one to understand that we may have more information about the beliefs and practices of the Maya ruling class than we do about those of the peasants who grew the foods they ate and artisans who made the objects they used – that is, the individuals who lived in huts that dotted the countryside surrounding the core areas of the great civic centers, like Tikal. It implies that the distinctive features of Classic Maya civilization refract the activities of a ruling class whose members resided in different city states. Other scholars of Mesoamerican history – for example, Michael Coe (1992:69) or Linda Schele and David Freidel (1990) – have made statements about the class structure of Maya society that sustain this view.

Gender Systems

Gender differences refer to the ways in which sexual differences that are per‐
ceived to be natural are constructed in a particular society. These constructions
have two levels. The first is concerned with what the members of a particular
society consider to be natural: biology, occupation, age, sexual preference, and
possession of female essence are only a few of the criteria mentioned in the
ethnographic and historical literature. The second level is concerned with the
significance the members of those particular societies attach to the sexual dif‐
ferences they selected to constitute men, women, and possibly other genders
(Gailey 1988). Several collections of essays, published since 1990, document
the existence of gendered divisions of labor in past societies and explore the
ways in which gender systems have underwritten diversity and cross-cut other
systems of classification in both state-based and kin-organized societies (e.g.
Claassen 1992, 1994; Claassen and Joyce 1997; Gero and Conkey 1991; Nelson
1997).

Gender distinctions and systems have been recognized through differences in
the kinds of grave goods associated with male and female skeletons from the
same population and through changes in the frequencies of the objects associ‐
ated with their production activities (Brumfiel 1991, 1996a, 1996b). Elizabeth
Brumfiel compared data from pre-Aztec and Aztec archaeological contexts in
the Valley of Mexico in order to explore the transformation of women's roles
in the system of production and of their identities as the communities to which
they belonged were incorporated into the Aztec state in the early 15th century.
She began with Sahagun's observations that weaving and cooking were women's
work and that a woman's status was linked to her skill as a weaver; she exam‐
ined changes in the frequencies of cooking pots and tortilla griddles, on the one
hand, and spindle whorls, on the other, to draw inferences. The Aztec state drew
labor away from the household. These data indicate changes in the relative
importance of women's productive activities as well as a reorganization of their
daily work schedules. In general, they probably worked longer hours than their
pre-Aztec counterparts did. While their ancestors cooked stews, they spent a
good deal of time preparing more labor-intensive tortillas and dry foods that
could be wrapped in them and consumed elsewhere. They also continued to
weave cloth, though perhaps less intensively than their ancestors did in pre-
Aztec times; however, this varied regionally.

> Within the Valley of Mexico, extra-domestic institutions [i.e. the market] light‐
> ened the work of women in meeting tribute assessments, but these institutions
> required a more mobile labor force, supported by more labor-intensive patterns of
> food preparation. Outside the Valley of Mexico, labor was more closely linked to
> the household. The burden of tribute cloth production fell squarely upon the
> female members of household units who retained less labor-intensive methods of
> food preparation.   (Brumfiel 1991:242–243)

Brumfiel (1996a) further argued that women resisted the exactions of the state,
but not in domains, like the production of tribute cloth, that could be closely

supervised. Examining the amount of time they spent decorating weaving implements led her to conclude that the women in these communities viewed weaving tribute cloth as a chore; however, weaving maguey cloth for use in the household, which required a different kind of spindle whorl, was a culturally significant activity that defined their status and prestige as women.

She also explored how the women in these subordinated communities reacted to the dominant ideology of the Aztec state, which stressed the power of men. Controlling women's labor and sexuality enhanced their wealth and provided opportunities for making alliances and rewarding allies. While the state's representations of women were either mutilated or androgynous, the ceramic figurines found in individual households were not. The frequencies of female figurines varied from one community to the next; they suggest that gender inequality had not suffused all levels of Aztec culture, and that it was probably more intense in those communities that participated in the market (Brumfiel 1996b).

In the Andes, Christine Hastorf (1991, 1993) showed another kind of change that occurred after communities were incorporated into the Inca state. The bone chemistry of dated skeletons from the central highlands showed that the diets of Wanka men and women changed differentially after the arrival of the Incas. The Wanka men began to consume more maize, probably in the form of beer provided by the state, than the women did.

Skeletal remains and their associated artifacts provided information about a division of labor based on gender and age in coastal Peru during the sixth millennium B.C.E. At Paloma, most of the adolescent and adult males exhibited growths in their middle ears – a condition caused by prolonged immersion in cold water. This suggests that they, rather than the female members of the community, swam, fished, and dove for the mollusks they consumed. The presence of weaving implements in the graves of women and older men suggests that the production of textiles was not gender-specific but related to age. This division of labor changed in the late third millennium B.C.E. as agriculture became more important in the region. In the fishing villages, both male and female skeletons exhibited the middle ear lesions, whereas only a small proportion of the men and none of the women residing in inland farming hamlets had them. In other words, the labor practices of men and women converged to some degree in economically specialized settlements that were linked together by exchanges of the goods they produced and perhaps by the matrimonial mobility of their members. Once agricultural production became the determinant economic activity in coastal Peru, the production–consumption units in some fishing villages were probably not nuclear families (Patterson 1991: 14–19).

Race

Only the historical archaeologists, who have traditionally been concerned with development of European settler colonies, have dealt with race as a culturally and socially constructed category that might under certain conditions leave footprints in the archaeological record. They use changes in the patterns of archaeological associations to explore race (Epperson 1991; Mullins 1993). During the 1970s, some of them began to examine the quarters of enslaved African Americans on antebellum plantations and creole communities in the South; this was followed by studies at sites that were used or inhabited by other "minorities that are both culturally and physically distinct from the white majority in the United States" (Singleton 1995:121; cf. Schuyler 1980).

By the late 1980s, several scholars had begun to reconceptualize historical archaeology as the archaeology of capitalism (Leone 1995; Orser 1988, 1990; Paynter 1988). From their perspective, the invention of race, the constitution of racial categories, and the construction of racial hierarchies, as well as the exploitation and oppression they imply, must be viewed as integral features of capitalist development and must be related to other aspects of its rise in the West, such as the consolidation of a new class and power relations.

For example, Dell Upton (1982) showed that the number of rooms in large farmhouses in the mid-Atlantic region began to decline in the 1660s, and that this decline coincided in time with (1) the appearance of a new pattern in which the master's house was separated from servants' quarters, and (2) the arrival of increasingly larger numbers of enslaved people from Africa. In this regard, a French Huguenot exile who traveled in the area in 1686–87 wrote that

> some people in this country are comfortably housed. Whatever their rank, and I know not why, they build only two rooms with some closets on the ground floor, and two rooms in the attic above; but they build several like this, according to their means. They build also a separate kitchen, a separate house for the Christian slaves, some for the negro slaves, and several to dry the tobacco, so that when you come to the home of a person of some means, you think you are entering a fairly large village. (Chinard 1934[1687]:119–120; quoted by Upton 1982:48)

This implies that the plantation settlement type only appeared after slavery came to form the foundation of the Virginia economy. It also coincided in time with the appearance of Chesapeake pipes, some of which bore complex motifs that had West African but no North American antecedents. This implies that at least some of the pipes found in plantation settlements after 1680 were decorated by enslaved individuals from West Africa or by their children (Deetz 1993:96–97).

Terrence Epperson (1992, 1998) draws an important conclusion from this evidence. He writes that the Huguenot exile's observations about plantations in the Chesapeake

> reflect [...] a transitional phase in the spatial ordering of Chesapeake plantations. The spatial separation between masters and laborers was obviously well-established by the late 1680s. However, the primary dichotomy within the labor force was still between "Christians" and "Negroes and other nonbelievers." Racism, or even race consciousness, cannot be posited as an *a priori* cause or motivation for the spatial segregation between masters and bound laborers or between "Christian" and "Negro" slaves. Indeed, the construction of racial difference is, in part, a *result* of processes of spatial segregation. (Epperson 1998:2)

It is useful to keep in mind that the first classifications of humanity based on skin color and other physical characteristics also appeared in the 1680s (Epperson 1994; Patterson and Spencer 1994:20).

The plantation settlement type developed through time. During the 18th century, the plantation settlement and its associated landscape also attempted "to control slaves and simultaneously to render them invisible" (Epperson 1990:32). As a result, plantations were also sites of class struggle characterized by unequal power relations and unequal access to force. The forms of oppression ranged from food rationing and physical punishment to less obvious ones, like the imposition of Euro-American names, and the forms of resistance they elicited from the enslaved community were equally as subtle.

Mark Leone and his associates have found caches of objects in several 18th-century townhouses in Annapolis, including the Carrollton House which was occupied by the wealthiest family in the Maryland colony (Leone 1995). While there was nothing particularly apparent about the use or meaning of the pins, buttons, coins, and pieces of bone and glass that constituted the caches, especially when they were considered in isolation from one another, scholars familiar with the African American and West African cultural traditions have identified them as diviners' bundles (Broadway 1997; Wilford 1996). The caches and their locations in the homes suggest that West African or African American slaves practiced divination in the basements, even as their owners lived out their own lives on the upper floors.

In another context, Leone and his associates have hypothesized that the African or African American presence in the Chesapeake was not confined to the archaeological records derived from dark basements but rather that they inscribed their existence in the landscape itself, such as formal Georgian-style gardens (Leone, personal communication). The William Paca Garden is Georgian in style; that is, it is composed of a series of terraces divided into squares or rectangles which are separated by a central stairway that descends from the house to a curvilinear pond on the lowest level that deviates from the right angles and straight lines that dominate the rest of the garden (Leone 1984:30). In their view, the pond, which was produced by Black laborers, represents the realization in the garden of the "man without hands" – a West African proverb that talks about the capacity of humans to dominate nature. In other words, they inscribed their culture in the dominating space.

Studies of African American households in Annapolis and in Western Massachusetts, which date to the late 19th century, raise another set of issues related to the purchase of commodities in the market and the creation of an American consumer culture. The enslaved communities on plantations were relatively self-sufficient and supplemented food and other rations through trapping, fishing, garden plots, and the production of use-values, some of which may have been sold or bartered in markets. This meant that their material culture differed from that of the plantation owners. However, in urban areas, like Annapolis and Greater Barrington, Massachusetts, African Americans, who participated in the capitalist wage economy, used their wages to purchase goods in the market – many of which were the same mass-produced items purchased by non-African Americans residing in the same town or city. For example, the distinctive feature of the material remains at the Maynard-Burgess House – a property occupied by two African American families in Annapolis from 1847 to 1980 – was that the first occupants relied heavily on fish and small game acquired outside the market, and that the later residents used dishes that were handed down rather than purchased (Mullins 1993). At the Du Bois House, few if any of the objects recovered were distinctive of an African American material culture or differed from what might be found in neighboring houses inhabited by Euro-Americans (Paynter et al. 1994). In other words, the residues of a highly varied African American material culture are perhaps more easily recognized on early-19th-century plantations than they are in Maryland or New England where the purchase and consumption of mass-produced commodities was a prominent feature of everyday life for African Americans, who were simultaneously marginalized and partially excluded from the very markets where those goods were available (Mullins 1996).

Discussion

The issue is not whether archaeologists are able to recognize the kinds of cultural diversity created by differences of ethnicity, gender, or race. Various archaeologists have recognized footprints of such diversity in the archaeological record, and it has formed part of their analyses for a number of years. The issue is rather whether archaeologists have, in fact, elected to use theoretical and methodological frameworks that allow them to recognize and explore this diversity and its implications. For those who have recognized it, the archaeological record is populated by men and women who belong to wider communities and different social classes; for those who have not, it is the product of faceless individuals, or potsherds and stone tools that seem to procreate without human intervention.

My goals in this chapter have been to show ways in which archaeologists have already addressed issues of cultural diversity, and to suggest directions that might be used to enrich our students' appreciation of the construction of such diversity in past societies as well as our own.

Acknowledgments

An abbreviated version of this paper was presented in the symposium "Cultural Diversity in the United States: Rewriting the Curriculum" organized by Maria Vesperi and sponsored by the Anthropology of North America for the annual meeting of the American Anthropological Association, November 19–23, 1997, Washington, DC. It has profited from discussions over the years with Wendy Ashmore, Elizabeth Brumfiel, Terrence Epperson, Christine Gailey, Mark Leone, Robert Paynter, Warren Perry, and Karen Spalding.

NOTES

1   Second-wave feminism fueled the early interest in women and gender systems in archaeology in the late 1970s and early 1980s (e.g. Conkey and Spector 1984; Peradotto and

Sullivan 1984; Pomeroy 1975). However, many of the younger women in anthropological archaeology do not link their interests in women and gender with feminism and resort to a kind of feminist empiricism – an "add women and stir" approach – in their research. They fear that they will be discriminated against in the labor market if they openly make that connection.

REFERENCES CITED

Broadway, Bill
  1997   Digging up Some Divining Inspiration. *Washington Post*, August 16:D7–D8.
Brumfiel, Elizabeth M.
  1987   Elite and Utilitarian Crafts in the Aztec State. In *Specialization, Exchange, and Complex Societies*. Elizabeth M. Brumfiel and Timothy K. Earle, eds. Pp. 102–118. Cambridge, UK: Cambridge University Press.
  1989   Consumption and Politics at Aztec Huexotla. *American Anthropologist* 89(3):676–686.
  1991   Weaving and Cooking: Women's Production in Aztec Mexico. In *Engendering Archaeology: Women and Prehistory*. Joan M. Gero and Margaret W. Conkey, eds. Pp. 223–251. Oxford: Basil Blackwell.
  1994   Ethnic Groups and Political Development in Ancient Mexico. In *Factional Competition and Political Development in the New World*. Elizabeth M. Brumfiel and John W. Fox, eds. Pp. 89–102. Cambridge, UK: Cambridge University Press.
  1996a   The Quality of Tribute Cloth: The Place of Evidence in Archaeological Argument. *American Antiquity* 61(3):453–462.
  1996b   Figurines and the Aztec State: Testing the Effectiveness of Ideological Domination. In *Gender and Archaeology*. Rita Wright, ed. Pp. 143–166. Philadelphia: University of Pennsylvania Press.
Brumfiel, Elizabeth M., Tamara Salcedo, and David K. Schafer
  1994   The Lip Plugs of Xaltocan: Function and Meaning in Aztec Archaeology. In *Economies and Polities in the Aztec Realm*. Mary C. Hodge and Michael E. Smith, eds. Pp. 113–132. Albany, NY: Institute of Mesoamerican Studies, State University of New York at Albany.
Childe, V. Gordon
  1929   *The Danube in Prehistory*. Oxford: Oxford University Press.
  1956   *Piecing Together the Past: The Interpretation of Archaeological Data*. London: Routledge and Kegan Paul.
Chinard, Gilbert, ed.
  1934[1687]   *A Huguenot Exile in Virginia; Or, Voyages of a Frenchman Exiled for his Religion, with a Description of Virginia and Maryland*. New York: Press of the Pioneers.
Claassen, Cheryl, ed.
  1992   *Exploring Gender through Archaeology: Selected Papers from the 1991 Boone Conference*. Madison: University of Wisconsin Press.
  1994   *Women in Archaeology*. Philadelphia: University of Pennsylvania Press.
Claassen, Cheryl, and Rosemary A. Joyce, eds.
  1997   *Women in Prehistory: North America and Mesoamerica*. Philadelphia: University of Pennsylvania Press.
Coe, Michael D.
  1992   *Breaking the Maya Code*. London: Thames and Hudson.

Comaroff, John L.
 1987 Of Totemism and Ethnicity: Consciousness, Practice, and Signs of Inequality. *Ethnos* 52(3):301–323.
Conkey, Margaret W., and Janet Spector
 1984 Archaeology and the Study of Gender. In *Advances in Archaeological Method and Theory*. Michael B. Schiffer, ed. Vol. 7, pp. 1–38. Orlando, FL: Academic Press.
Costin, Cathy
 1986 From Chiefdom to Empire State: Ceramic Economy among the Prehispanic Wanka of Highland Peru. Ph.D. dissertation in anthropology, University of California at Los Angeles. Ann Arbor, MI: University Microfilms.
D'Altroy, Terence N.
 1992 *Provincial Power in the Inka Empire*. Washington, DC: Smithsonian Institution Press.
D'Altroy, Terence N., and Ronald A. Bishop
 1990 The Provincial Organization of Inka Ceramic Production. *American Antiquity* 55(1):120–138.
Deetz, James
 1993 *Flowerdew Hundred: The Archaeology of Virginia Plantation, 1619–1864*. Charlottesville: University of Virginia Press.
de Ste. Croix, Geoffrey E. M.
 1984 Class in Marx's Conception of History, Ancient and Modern. *New Left Review* 146:94–111.
Epperson, Terrence W.
 1990 Race and the Disciplines of the Plantation. *Historical Archaeology* 24(4):29–36.
 1992 "To Fix a Perpetual Brand": The Social Construction of Race in Virginia, 1675–1750. Ph.D. dissertation in anthropology, Temple University, Philadelphia. Ann Arbor, MI: University Microfilms International.
 1994 The Politics of Empiricism and the Construction of Race as an Analytical Category. In *Race, Racism, and the History of U.S. Anthropology*. Lee D. Baker and Thomas C. Patterson, eds. *Transforming Anthropology* 5(1):15–19.
 1998 Critical Race Theory and the Archaeology of the African Diaspora. Paper presented at the Annual Meeting of the Society for Historical Archaeology, January 6–10. Atlanta, GA.
Gailey, Christine W.
 1987 *From Kinship to Kingship: Gender Hierarchy and State Formation in the Tongan Islands*. Austin: University of Texas Press.
 1988 Evolutionary Perspectives on Gender Hierarchy. In *Analyzing Gender: A Handbook of Social Science Research*. Beth B. Hess and Myra M. Ferree, eds. Pp. 32–67. Newbury Park, CA: Sage.
Gero, Joan M., and Margaret W. Conkey, eds.
 1991 *Engendering Archaeology: Women and Prehistory*. Oxford: Basil Blackwell.
Hastorf, Christine A.
 1991 Gender, Space, and Food in Prehistory. In *Engendering Archaeology: Women and Prehistory*. Joan M. Gero and Margaret W. Conkey, eds. Pp. 132–159. Oxford: Basil Blackwell.
 1993 *Agriculture and the Onset of Political Inequality before the Inka*. Cambridge, UK: Cambridge University Press.
Haviland, William A.
 1967 Stature at Tikal, Guatemala: Implications for Ancient Maya Demography and Social Organization. *American Antiquity* 32(3):316–325.

Kossinna, Gustav
1911 *Die Herkunft der Germanen.* Leipzig, GER: Kabitzsch.
Leone, Mark P.
1984 Interpreting Ideology in Historical Archaeology: The William Paca Garden in Annapolis, Maryland. In *Ideology, Power and Prehistory.* Daniel Miller and Christopher Tilley, eds. Pp. 25–36. Cambridge, UK: Cambridge University Press.
1995 A Historical Archaeology of Capitalism. *American Anthropologist* 97(2):251–268.
McCarthy, John P., and Stephen H. Graff
1980 Differential Mortality and Status: Implications for Archaeology. Paper presented at the Annual Meeting of the Society for American Archaeology, Philadelphia.
McDavid, Carol, and David W. Babson, eds.
1997 In the Realm of Politics: Prospects for Public Participation in African-American and Plantation Archaeology. *Historical Archaeology* 31(3).
Menzel, Dorothy
1959 The Inca Occupation of the South Coast of Peru. *Southwestern Journal of Anthropology* 15(2):125–142.
1960 Archaism and Revival on the South Coast of Peru. In *Man and Culture: Selected Papers of the Fifth International Congress of Anthropological and Ethnological Sciences.* Anthony F. C. Wallace, ed. Pp. 596–600. Philadelphia: University of Pennsylvania Press.
1976 *Pottery Style and Society in Ancient Peru: Art as a Mirror of History in the Ica Valley, 1350–1570.* Berkeley: University of California Press.
Mullins, Paul
1993 "A Bold and Gorgeous Front": The Contradictions of African America and Consumer Culture, 1880–1993. Paper presented at the School of American Research, Santa Fe.
1996 The Contradictions of Consumption: An Archaeology of African America and Consumer Culture, 1850–1930. Ph.D. dissertation in anthropology, University of Massachusetts, Amherst. Ann Arbor, MI: University Microfilms International, No. 9709634.
Nelson, Sarah M.
1997 *Gender in Archaeology.* Walnut Creek, CA: Altamira Press.
Orser, Charles E., Jr.
1988 The Archaeological Analysis of Plantation Society: Replacing Status and Caste with Economics and Power. *American Antiquity* 53(4):735–751.
1990 Archaeological Approaches to New World Plantation Slavery. In *Archaeological Method and Theory.* Michael B. Schiffer, ed. Vol. 2, pp. 111–154. Tucson: University of Arizona Press.
Orwell, George
1983[1949] *1984.* New York: Penguin Books.
Patterson, Thomas C.
1991 *The Inca Empire: The Formation and Disintegration of a Pre-Capitalist State.* Oxford: Berg.
1995 *Toward a Social History of Archaeology in the United States.* Fort Worth, TX: Harcourt Brace.
1997 *Inventing Western Civilization.* New York: Monthly Review Press.
Patterson, Thomas C., and Frank Spencer
1994 Racial Hierarchies and Buffer Races. In *Race, Racism, and the History of U.S. Anthropology.* Lee D. Baker and Thomas C. Patterson, eds. Transforming Anthropology 5(1–2):20–27.

Paynter, Robert
    1988   Steps to an Archaeology of Capitalism: Material Change and Class Analysis.
    In *The Recovery of Meaning: Historical Archaeology in the Eastern United States*.
    Mark P. Leone and Parker B. Potter, Jr., eds. Pp. 407–434. Washington, DC: Smith-
    sonian Institution Press.
Paynter, Robert, Susan Hautaniemi, and Nancy Muller
    1994   The Landscapes of the W. E. B. Du Bois Boyhood Homesite: An Agenda for
    an Archaeology of the Color Line. In *Race*. Steven Gregory and Roger Sanjek, eds.
    Pp. 285–318. New Brunswick, NJ: Rutgers University Press.
Paynter, Robert, and Randall H. McGuire
    1991   The Archaeology of Inequality: Material Culture, Domination, and Resistance.
    In *The Archaeology of Inequality*. Randall H. McGuire and Robert Paynter, eds.
    Pp. 1–27. London: Routledge.
Peradotto, John, and J. P. Sullivan
    1984   *Women in the Ancient World: The Arethusa Papers*. Albany: SUNY Press.
Pomeroy, Sarah B.
    1975   *Goddesses, Whores, Wives, and Slaves: Women in Classical Antiquity*. New
    York: Schocken Books.
Rowe, John H.
    1979   Standardization in Inca Tapestry Tunics. In *The Junius B. Bird Pre-Columbian
    Textile Conference*. Ann P. Rowe, Elizabeth P. Benson, and Anne-Louise Schaffer,
    eds. Pp. 239–264. Washington, DC: Textile Museum and Dumbarton Oaks.
Santayana, George
    1953[1905–1906]   *The Life of Reason or The Phases of Human Progress*,
    one-volume edition. New York: Charles Scribner's Sons.
Schaedel, Richard
    1985   The Transition from Chiefdom to State in Northern Peru. In *Development and
    Decline: The Evolution of Sociopolitical Organization*. Henri J. M. Claessen, Pieter
    van de Velde, and M. Estellie Smith, eds. Pp. 159–169. South Hadley, MA: Bergin
    and Garvey.
Schele, Linda, and David Freidel
    1990   *A Forest of Kings: The Untold Story of the Ancient Maya*. New York: William
    Morrow.
Schortman, Edward M.
    1980   Archaeological Investigations in the Lower Motagua Valley. *Expedition* 23(1):
    28–34.
Schuyler, Robert L., ed.
    1980   *Archaeological Perspectives on Ethnicity in America: Afro-American and
    Asian American Culture History*. Farmingdale, NY: Baywood.
Singleton, Theresa A.
    1995   The Archaeology of Slavery in North America. *Annual Review of Anthropol-
    ogy* 24:119–140.
Trigger, Bruce G.
    1984   Alternative Archaeologies: Nationalist, Colonialist, Imperialist. *Man* 19(3):
    355–370.
    1986   Prehistoric Archaeology and American Society. In *American Archaeology Past
    and Future: A Celebration of the Society for American Archaeology, 1935–1985*.
    David J. Meltzer, Don D. Fowler, and Jeremy A. Sabloff, eds. Pp. 187–216.
    Washington, DC: Smithsonian Institution Press.
Upton, Dell
    1982   The Origins of Chesapeake Architecture. In *Three Centuries of Maryland
    Architecture*, pp. 44–57. Annapolis: Maryland Historical Trust.

Wilford, John N.
  1996   Slave Artefacts under the Hearth. *New York Times*, August 27:C1, C7.
Wobst, Martin
  1977   Stylistic Behavior and Information Exchange. In *For the Director: Research Essays in Honor of James B. Griffin*. University of Michigan Museum of Anthropology Papers 61:317–342.

10

The Roots of U.S. Inequality

Elizabeth M. Scott

Most archaeological research on the period since European contact in the United States is in some way about cultural diversity. The United States began as colonies of immigrants, Native Americans, and enslaved Africans; research about such a past cannot help but be about cultural diversity. However, not all historical archaeologists have addressed this topic explicitly or critically. In this chapter, I try to highlight those who have done so, and thus do not attempt to cover all of the information about the U.S. past that historical archaeologists have uncovered. The chapter will relate, however, what archaeologists have discovered about the ways in which class, gender, race, and ethnicity were created by and reflected in material culture, and how these factors structured daily life in the past.

How Archaeologists Study Cultural Diversity in the U.S. Past

Archaeologists who study the post-European contact period in the United States have at their disposal a variety of data sources. These include not only archaeological materials (such as artifacts, architectural remains, and plant and animal remains), but also extant structures and architectural features, pictorial evidence (such as photographs, paintings, sketches, lithographs, and maps), oral histories, and written records (ranging from governmental to personal). No one data source used alone will reveal as much about past societies as several data sources used together, so archaeologists of the post-contact United States (traditionally called historical archaeologists) often draw on one or more sources in addition to the archaeology.

There have always been groups of people in the American past who are less visible in, or absent from, written and pictorial records, and for whom few oral histories remain. Archaeology allows those who were economically, politically, and socially marginalized by middle- and upper-class Euro-American men to be more visible. Even when written and oral history records exist, archaeological evidence provides information not often included in those records, such as the locations of various activities in a household or houselot and the resulting spatial divisions between men, women, and children in a household or neighborhood; interaction or lack of interaction between ethnic and racial groups and between classes; the ways in which people chose to spend their incomes and how social status was displayed for others to see; the foods people ate and how they disposed of their refuse, suggesting the variety of ways in which people conceived of cleanliness, odors, and sanitation. Sometimes, as well, the archaeological evidence contradicts that in the documents, and the reasons for this have to be explored.

Archaeologists infer economic ranking or "class" using a combination of sources. Census, tax, and church records often provide evidence of income and occupation for individual households and neighborhoods. The ceramic, metal, and glass vessels often recovered from historical archaeological sites may be dated and assigned a past monetary value through reference to manufacturers' records, probate inventories, and storekeepers' merchandise accounts. Other categories of artifacts, as varied as clothing, items of personal adornment, household furnishings, architecture, and cuts of meat, also may be understood to have been of high, medium, or low cost in the time period under study. The determination of whether a household or neighborhood was upper, middle, or lower class in a particular time period, then, depends on multiple lines of evidence, both material and documentary.

In a similar fashion, ethnicity, race, and gender may be associated with various kinds of material culture. Using these same kinds of records, plus oral histories and pictorial records, archaeologists get clues to the ways in which architecture, landscape, and material items were used by women and men in various ethnic and racial groups. Thus, even for a household with few written records, archaeologists often are able to reveal the economic position of the residents, perhaps the ethnic or racial group with which they affiliated themselves, and the genders of the residents, as well as an idea of the activities that were conducted in and around the house, all by comparison with other archaeological assemblages and broader written records containing dating and pricing information.

In these and other ways, archaeologists of the post-contact United States reveal how class, gender, race, and ethnicity have been culturally constructed and have material and spatial expression. However, archaeologists also go beyond this and reveal how these aspects structured life in past societies – dividing individuals here, combining them there – having explicit and implicit effects on daily life. Nearly all historical archaeologists discuss evidence for economic position or class for the sites they study, but a much smaller number combine this with an examination of race and ethnicity, and fewer still include questions about gender.

The Roots of Our Inequalities

One way of showing that the gender, racial, ethnic, and class inequalities in present-day U.S. society are not due to "biological" or "natural" differences is to show how they came to be, that is, that there are specific historical reasons for the social inequalities we see in the United States today. Historical archae-ology provides evidence of political, economic, and social factors at work at specific times in the past and of how these changed, or stayed the same, through time. It also provides a means to see domination and resistance by various groups in the past.

Although most historical archaeologists include archaeological and historical evidence for the socioeconomic position of the people who lived on the sites they study, a much smaller number of archaeologists have approached economic inequality in the U.S. past as a research topic per se. Among the most promi-nent of these has been Mark Leone (1978, 1984, 1988a, 1988b, 1995). His studies reveal how the spread of particular kinds of architecture, landscaping, and material objects was linked to the spread of capitalism and the accompa-nying shift in emphasis from the communal to the individual, from production for the household to production for others, and from lesser to greater social distinction based on wealth.

Leone has been most concerned with elucidating how inequalities among various groups of people came into being and were perpetuated. This involves analysis of the material evidence for social, economic, and political inequality (found in probate inventories and tax records, as well as the artifacts, buildings, and landscapes of the past) plus analysis of the ideology that served to hide or mask that inequality. Thus, he has shown how, in the Chesapeake region between 1730 and the 1770s, during which time there was ever greater inequal-ity of wealth, various kinds of material culture became more and more popular and widespread and served to enforce the idea of the autonomous individual: place settings of cutlery and dishes; dishes of varying sizes and shapes for different functions; clocks and watches; razors; and chamber pots (Leone 1988a). These items, and the changes in personal behavior that they required, reflected and reinforced a society in which people were wage-earners and were expected to be punctual about work; were concerned with individual appear-ance and cleanliness conforming to broader norms and expectations; and followed broader rules of dining etiquette. These were ways in which indi-vidual men and women learned to be autonomous selves, inculcating ideas of time, work, and discipline that were suited to a profit-oriented society based on capitalism.

At the same time, the wealthiest group in society, growing smaller and smaller, was trying to maintain its dominant position in the face of what it saw as the unreasonable and injurious colonial policies of Great Britain. Members of this group used clocks, telescopes, musical instruments, architecture, and landscape techniques to create "order" in nature, and believed this legitimized their right to create "order" among the less powerful in society (Leone 1988a, 1984). Elaborate gardens and cities were laid out using rules of perspective and optical illusion to guide the eye along particular lines of sight, resulting in reinforcement of the existing social order with the wealthy dominating a landscape. Architecturally, public and religious buildings changed with the Revolution from an emphasis on undifferentiated masses of people with a monarch or religious leader (seen in baroque architecture) to an emphasis on individual citizens or groups of citizens interacting (seen in panoptic architecture; Leone 1995).

Of course, inequalities in society were masked by a pre-Revolutionary ideology that emphasized equality of individual liberty (Leone 1988a). This was necessary in order for poorer people to join with the wealthy and defeat Britain; it was also the ideology that survived after the Revolution and enabled the wealthy to remain in control. For those fifty or so years preceding the Revolution, people came more and more to think of themselves as individuals and to believe that all individuals were capable of attaining wealth and prosperity, thus reproducing a society suited for capitalism.

Archaeology is able to show how this social order came into being, was perpetuated, and emerged stronger than ever after the Revolution, laying the groundwork for the move from merchant to industrial capitalism in the 19th century. Groups of people "bought into" the ideology of individual freedom and a society of equals, and thus followed rules of behavior and purchased material culture that perpetuated this notion. It may be seen, in hindsight, that the underlying contradiction of an ideology proclaiming equality and individual liberty in a slaveholding society would inevitably demand some form of resolution, seen years later in the Civil War.

Concomitant with Leone's studies is a critique of mainstream U.S. history and historical archaeology, revealing how their reconstructions of the past often legitimate present-day power relations without questioning or reflecting on them. Other scholars who have conducted studies along similar lines include Russell Handsman (1983, 1984, 1990), Charles Orser, Jr. (1996; see citations below), Paul Shackel (1992, 1993), Barbara Little (1988, 1992), and Robert Paynter (1988).

In addition to economic inequality, archaeologists also have examined racial inequality in the American past. This research has most often concerned African Americans in colonial, antebellum, and postbellum periods. Culturally-defined concepts of class and race are closely intertwined, and Charles Orser, Jr., has been perhaps the most prolific of archaeologists addressing both of them, most often for the postbellum period (1987, 1988a, 1988b, 1988c, 1989, 1991, 1992). Leland Ferguson has written extensively on African Americans in the colonial centuries (1991, 1992). Theresa Singleton is perhaps the best known of those who work with African American sites from the antebellum period (1985, 1988, 1996; Singleton and Bograd 1995). These and other archaeologists have found artifactual, architectural, and subsistence evidence that indicates not only continuity of African ways of doing, but also the changes that occurred because of slavery, tenancy, and freedom, revealing what became, literally, African American here in the United States; they also have revealed cultural constructions of race and their effects on social and economic mobility for African Americans.

For example, on two South Carolina plantations, the houses that slaves built for themselves in the 18th century had mud walls and were probably similar to houses found in many parts of Africa, with thatched roofs. The arrangement of the rooms (single, sequential rooms) as well as the exterior surrounding the house (yard, vegetable gardens, animal pens, etc.) also are similar to those in African houses and villages (Ferguson 1992; Singleton 1996). In the 19th century, the mud walls often were replaced with frame construction, but the placement of the rooms remained similar to that in the earlier houses. Even when slave quarters were laid out and built according to a plantation owner's directions, enslaved men, women, and children often used those spaces in African ways. Using local clay deposits, African women made ceramic vessels for cooking and consuming foods, beverages, and medicines; these suggest preparation of the "one-dish" meals common in Africa (usually a starch of some kind eaten with various condiments) and soups and stews (Fairbanks 1984; Ferguson 1991, 1992; Singleton 1996). The animal food bones from many slave sites support such an interpretation (e.g. Young 1997; Reitz 1987; McKee 1987; Crader 1989). Objects used in healing, religious, and other rituals have been found in and around slaves' houses, often with markings or other characteristics that have parallels in African societies (e.g. Brown and Cooper 1990; Wilkie 1996, 1997; Stine et al. 1996; Klingelhofer 1987; Russell 1997).

However, changes occurred as well in African American life, in the face of forced relocation in the New World and the economic, social, and political constraints of a society based first on slavery and later on racial hierarchies. Several studies have revealed how African Americans made the shift from slavery to tenancy in plantation settings (e.g. Orser 1988c, 1991; Epperson 1990; Babson 1990; Stine 1990). Other studies have shown how post-Emancipation African Americans in rural (Geismar 1982) and urban communities (e.g. Muller 1994; Cabak et al. 1995) and pre-Emancipation free (Martin et al. 1997) and enslaved (Heath 1997) African Americans participated in the broader consumer economy and constantly negotiated their status within a Euro-American-dominated society.

Although to a lesser degree than African Americans, other culturally defined racial and ethnic groups have been the focus of study by historical archaeologists. Material remains of clothing, jewelry, foods, ceramic dishes, houses, and outbuildings are combined with documentary evidence to reveal households or communities of people in various racial or ethnic groups. These include Asian Americans, primarily Chinese immigrants and their descendants (e.g. Wegars 1993; Akin 1992), as well as Native American groups (e.g. Birk and Johnson 1992; Trubowitz 1992; Perttula 1994; Grange 1997). Various European ethnic groups and their descendants have been studied; these include a predominance of research on British groups (e.g. Deetz 1977, 1988; Noel Hume 1983; Harrington 1989), as well as French (Heldman 1991; Birk 1991; Waselkov 1997), Spanish (Deagan 1983; Williams and Fournier-Garcia 1996), Swiss (Penner 1997), Italian (Wegars 1991), Basque (Fitzgerald et al. 1993), and Jewish (Heldman 1986; Halchin 1985; Scott 1996; Stewart-Abernathy and Ruff 1989) groups.

Historical archaeology, for the most part unconsciously, has tended to treat British colonial and Anglo-American sites as the "norm," from which sites of other racial and ethnic groups deviate. This is partly because British and Anglo-American sites are those from which the discipline of historical archaeology originated and which still make up the majority of sites studied by historical archaeologists. However, treating Anglo-American sites as "normal" also reflects the more widespread tendency in U.S. society to treat Anglo-American culture as "normal," the one from which all others deviate (as "subcultures"). Thus, most archaeological studies of non-Anglo groups carefully detail the material and documentary evidence that supports the affiliation of a particular racial or ethnic group with the past residents of a site. Many such studies also discuss how race or ethnicity affected the socioeconomic position and daily lives of the people who lived at the site, that is, how race or ethnicity combined with class to structure people's lives.

By contrast, archaeological studies of Anglo-American sites seldom emphasize the evidence that supports such a designation, nor do they explicitly discuss how being white and Anglo-American might have privileged the site residents in a variety of ways when compared with persons in other racial or ethnic groups. Hopefully, historical archaeologists will take this next step and consciously examine the role race and ethnicity played in the lives of Anglo-Americans, especially when combined with class. Cultural anthropologists have begun turning their attention to the problem of how "whiteness" is defined in present-day U.S. society (e.g. Hartigan 1997; Krause 1998); archaeology should be able to provide a necessary temporal perspective on the topic.

In addition to class, racial, and ethnic inequality, historical archaeologists recently have begun examining gender inequality. Not only have scholars made women more visible than they have been previously in reconstructions of the American past, but they are asking questions about men's roles as well, and how gender ideology affected both men's and women's lives in the past. Archaeologists often are able to distinguish the material remains of men's and women's activities and personal effects. By analyzing the locations of these activities vis-à-vis rooms, houses, yards, gardens, neighborhoods, or public buildings, archaeologists have shown how, in particular places and times, men and women occupied different (or similar) spaces in the physical and ideological landscape. Archaeologists have shown how one's position in society and the activities one carried out in daily life were structured not only by class and race or ethnicity, but by one's gender as well.

Many archaeological studies of gender inequality have concerned Euro-American women of various classes: for example, women in logging camp families (Brashler 1991); prostitutes and urban working-class women (Seifert 1991, 1994); middle-class prostitute reformers (De Cunzo 1995); middle-class domestic reformers (Spencer-Wood 1987, 1991); middle-class and poorer women in Western boom towns (Purser 1991); middle- and upper-class urban home-makers (Wall 1991, 1994); and wealthy, middling, and poorer women in Anglo-American households (Yentsch 1991a, 1991b; Gibb and King 1991).

Other archaeological studies have focused on the ways in which gender intersects with class, race, and ethnicity to structure men's and women's lives in past societies. Such studies have concerned Native American communities (Handsman 1990; Whelan 1991; Spector 1991, 1993; Bassett 1994; Jackson 1994;

James 1995), African American communities (Singleton and Bograd 1995; Muller 1994; Young and Cabak n.d.), multiethnic colonial and urban communities (Scott 1991a, l991b; McEwan 1991; Little 1997), religious communities (Kryder-Reid 1994; Savulis 1992), and predominantly male communities (Hardesty 1988, 1994; Starbuck 1994).

Everett Bassett's 1994 study provides a good example. He examined the ways in which gender, ethnicity, and class structured the lives of Apache men and women who were involved in the construction of Roosevelt Dam in Arizona in the early years of the 20th century. Using photographs, written documents, ethnographies, oral histories of Apache men and women who worked on the project, and the archaeological remains of their camps, he was able to show how this particular group of Apaches largely rejected the "civilizing" efforts of the U.S. government and missionaries and was able to maintain traditional Apache social organization and division of labor.

The remains of their dwellings, or wickiups, were clustered in a way that reflected the social organization. Wickiups were constructed and maintained by women, who also carried out most of the activities in and around them. Several individual wickiups, lived in by nuclear families, were found clustered together in what were settlements of an extended family or kin group; several of these extended family clusters also occurred together, reflecting a larger social group. Thus, the Apaches working on the Roosevelt Dam structured their camps and settlements as they wanted, at a time when the U.S. government and missionaries were imposing Euro-American forms of housing and use of space on Native Americans elsewhere. The Apache men at Roosevelt also practiced a form of labor sharing which defeated the capitalist ethic of individualism and entrepreneurial gain; men in related family groups would share work (literally working one another's shifts) so that the income was shared among the whole extended family.

A final area of inquiry in historical archaeology in recent years, and one that bears on the history of inequalities in U.S. society, concerns doing the archaeology of the Other versus the archaeology of one's own class/ethnic/racial/gender group. This has been explored most extensively in African American archaeology. Most historical archaeologists are Euro-American, and it is only very recently that their position as producers of academic knowledge about the African American past has been questioned, partly by some of those same Euro-American archaeologists (e.g. Leone 1995; Epperson 1990, 1996; Orser 1998), partly by new African American historical archaeologists in the profession, and partly by broader critiques of white Western scholarship put forth by scholars of color. In addition, the African American descendant community has become increasingly involved in archaeological and historical investigations of its past.

One recent example of such involvement is the African Burial Ground project in New York City. During the construction of a new office building to house the U.S. General Services Administration, hundreds of burials were encountered in an area shown on 18th-century maps to be the "Negroes Burying Ground," which was used from sometime before 1712 until 1794 (La Roche and Blakey

1997; Epperson 1996). More than 400 burials were removed before the combined efforts of concerned African Americans – political officeholders, artists, clergy, archaeologists, physical anthropologists, and ordinary citizens – stopped the excavations, forced a change in the archaeologists conducting the excavations, and redirected the research that would be conducted on the previously excavated remains. It took tremendous effort and perseverance on the part of those concerned African Americans to bring enough pressure to bear on the federal government so that the investigations and disposition of the remains reflected the spiritual, historical, and political concerns of the descendant community.

Criticism and consciousness raising by academics and non-academics has resulted in much reflection on the part of both Euro-American and African American archaeologists who study African Americans in the past (contributors to McDavid and Babson 1997; Blakey 1983; Leone 1995). Issues of dominance and resistance, inclusion and exclusion, and the relationship between Euro-American archaeologists and members of descendant communities are all brought to bear on the discussion. These same issues have been addressed concerning Native Americans and historical archaeologists by McDonald et al. (1991), Spector (1991, 1993), Handsman and Lamb Richmond (1995), and Rubertone (1996). Indeed, similar dialogues have occurred between archaeologists and Native American groups over the repatriation of previously excavated Native American remains as occurred between archaeologists and the African American descendant community over the African Burial Ground (Epperson 1996). The demands brought to archaeologists in both cases concerned respect for the dead and the role the descendant community would play in determining what would be done with the human remains and accompanying artifacts.

Concluding Thoughts

The particular social, political, and economic contexts must be kept in mind when considering the roles that class, ethnicity, race, and gender may have played in the past. It should be clear, for example, that not all women led similar lives, nor all African Americans, nor all upper-class individuals. Women in different classes and in different racial or ethnic groups had different gender roles and often subscribed to different gender ideologies. African Americans carried out their daily lives differently depending on whether they were men, women, or children; whether enslaved or free; if free, whether they were in upper, middle, or lower economic classes; whether they lived in rural areas or urban ones, North or South. Upper-class individuals in U.S. society have been overwhelmingly white and of Euro-American descent. However, within this group, men's roles and power differed from women's, usually resulting in a subordinate status for women. Yet in spite of these differences, there are also the similarities, things held in common by members of one class, one gender, one ethnic or racial group.

In capitalist societies, differential access to wealth and other resources is often said to be the primary structuring element in society. However, ethnic and racial factors are often used to deny or provide this access, as is gender; when all of these are combined, a very complex social hierarchy is in place. At particular times and places, one or more variables might become more important than the others. For example, when the British conquered and colonized the French colonies of North America around 1760, French settlers often maintained and even asserted their ethnic identity while living next door to the British colonists who were in economic and political control; they did so through the language they spoke, the clothes they wore, the foods they ate, and the way they built their houses (Heldman 1991; Scott 1996). A second example concerns the middle and elite classes of New York City who, in the midst of the profound economic changes and restructuring of labor that occurred between 1790 and 1840, began redefining gender roles and spaces; this can be seen in changes in household size and in an increasing elaboration of dinners and teas by women in these households (evident in the changes in ceramic dishes found there), along with an increasing separation of men's workplaces from the home (Wall 1994). Although in neither example is any one factor acting alone, ethnicity and gender can be seen to have been, at times, as important as economic class, perhaps more so, in structuring people's lives. This has been true over and over again in U.S. history; most people today can probably think of times when ethnic identities are emphasized or periods in their lifetimes when gender roles have been redefined.

Archaeologists try to tease apart these variables or factors, to see the evidence of each in the remains of clothing, dishes, jewelry, tools, foods, and structures, and in the spatial arrangement of rooms, houselots, formal gardens, plantations, camps, towns, and cities. This information not only helps make more visible groups which have been largely excluded from mainstream U.S. history and which might be largely excluded from U.S. society today, but also provides a means to celebrate the cultural diversity that has been present in U.S. society for more than 500 years (and well into the thousands of years when pre-contact Native American cultures are included). However, in piecing together the broken fragments and faded papers of our past, archaeologists also have found the roots of our inequalities – be they economic, racial, ethnic, gender, or other inequalities. To ignore that part of the story would be to err by omission. The evidence found by archaeologists can serve to foster pride in racial and ethnic heritages, in the accomplishments of women, and in the perseverance of working-class people. But it can also serve as a tangible reminder that there is a history to the divisions in present-day American society and that history need not repeat itself.

ANNOTATED BIBLIOGRAPHY

Cabak, Melanie A., Mark D. Groover, and Scott J. Wegars
    1995   Health Care and the Wayman A. M. E. Church. *Historical Archaeology* 29(2):55–76.
This article interprets excavations at the Wayman A. M. E. Church in Bloomington, Illinois, which recovered, unexpectedly, many medical artifacts. Limited historical and oral history data document a long history of African American churches providing health

care to counter the inequality African Americans often experienced in obtaining adequate medical care. The project is also noteworthy in that the African American congregation initiated the request for archaeological research and worked with the archaeologists from beginning to end.

Ferguson, Leland G.
  1992 *Uncommon Ground: Archaeology and Early African America, 1650–1800.* Washington, DC: Smithsonian Institution Press.
This book combines archaeological, architectural, ethnographic, photographic, oral history, and folklore data to interpret the lives of African Americans in colonial plantation societies in North America. Ferguson also discusses his own processes of discovery, how historical archaeologists generally have interpreted various aspects of African American life, and provides a critique of such interpretations by way of his own past mistakes. He also provides reflection on his own upbringing in the South and how he as a white male came to be studying African American sites.
If time does not permit reading the entire book, several of his main points are addressed in his chapter entitled "Struggling with Pots in South Carolina," pp. 28–39 in McGuire and Paynter's 1991 volume (see below).

McGuire, Randall H., and Robert Paynter, eds.
  1991 *The Archaeology of Inequality.* Oxford: Basil Blackwell.
This volume contains essays on racial, ethnic, gender, and economic inequalities and ranges from the 18th to the mid-20th centuries. The authors particularly address the ways in which material culture (artifacts, landscapes, and the built environment) creates and reflects domination and resistance by various groups in the American past.

Orser, Charles E., Jr., ed.
  1990 Historical Archaeology on Southern Plantations and Farms. *Historical Archaeology* 24(4):1–126.
This thematic issue of *Historical Archaeology* contains articles addressing race and racism on plantations, African American slave and tenant communities on plantations, and African American and Euro-American farms in the South. It also includes critiques and commentary by four archaeologists on these and other topics in African American archaeology.

Scott, Elizabeth M., ed.
  1994 *Those of Little Note: Gender, Race, and Class in Historical Archaeology.* Tucson: University of Arizona Press.
This volume contains eight case studies which examine the interrelatedness of gender, race, ethnicity, and class in structuring past U.S. society. They cover Native American and African American communities, all-male and predominantly male communities, and working women in urban communities, from the 18th century to the early 20th century.

Seifert, Donna J., ed.
  1991 Gender in Historical Archaeology. Theme issue. *Historical Archaeology* 25(4): 1–155.
This thematic issue of *Historical Archaeology* contains nine articles concerning archaeological and historical evidence for the role played by gender in structuring past U.S. society. The case studies span the country from east to west and from the 16th century through the mid-20th century.

Singleton, Theresa A., and Mark D. Bograd
  1995   The Archaeology of the African Diaspora in the Americas. *Guides to the Archaeological Literature of the Immigrant Experience in America*, No. 2. Tucson, AZ: Society for Historical Archaeology.
This includes a critical review essay organized around various topics that have been addressed by historical archaeologists in African American archaeology, as well as an exhaustive bibliography of the literature.

Spector, Janet D.
  1993   *What This Awl Means: Feminist Archaeology at a Wahpeton Dakota Village*. St. Paul: Minnesota Historical Society Press.
This is the first book-length treatment of historical archaeological site interpretation using a feminist perspective. It interprets a village of the Wahpeton Dakota in southeastern Minnesota, occupied in the early to mid-19th century, using written documents, paintings, archaeological remains, and oral histories. Particularly enlightening are Spector's discussions of the ways in which feminist theory and the involvement of the Dakota descendant community affected her research and interpretations, perhaps most vividly seen in the narrative she used to ground the whole book. She also includes a critique of the discipline's academic training and a reflexive discussion of involvement with Dakota peoples.
  If time does not allow reading the entire book, her main points and the narrative may be found in her chapter entitled "What This Awl Means: Toward a Feminist Archaeology," pp. 388–406 in *Engendering, Archaeology: Women and Prehistory*, edited by Joan M. Gero and Margaret W. Conkey (1991, Oxford: Basil Blackwell).

Acknowledgments

I want to thank Tom Patterson, Ida Susser, and Donald Heldman for their helpful comments and suggestions on earlier drafts of this chapter.

REFERENCES CITED

Akin, Marjorie Kleiger
  1992   The Noncurrency Functions of Chinese Wen in America. *Historical Archaeology* 26(2):58–65.
Babson, David W.
  1990   The Archaeology of Racism and Ethnicity on Southern Plantations. *Historical Archaeology* 24(4):20–28.
Bassett, Everett
  1994   "We Took Care of Each Other like Families Were Meant to": Gender, Social Organization, and Wage Labor among the Apache at Roosevelt. In *Those of Little Note: Gender, Race, and Class in Historical Archaeology*. Elizabeth M. Scott, ed. Pp. 55–79. Tucson: University of Arizona Press.
Birk, Douglas A.
  1991   French Presence in Minnesota: The View from Site Mo20 near Little Falls. In *French Colonial Archaeology: The Illinois Country and the Western Great Lakes*. John A. Walthall, ed. Pp. 237–266. Urbana: University of Illinois Press.
Birk, Douglas A., and Elden Johnson
  1992   The Mdewakanton Dakota and Initial French Contact. In *Calumet and Fleur-de-Lys: Archaeology of Indian and French Contact in the Midcontinent*. John

A. Walthall and Thomas E. Emerson, eds. Pp. 203–240. Washington, DC: Smithsonian Institution Press.

Blakey, Michael L.
  1983 Sociopolitical Bias and Ideological Production in Historical Archaeology. In *The Socio-Politics of Archaeology*. Joan M. Gero, D. M. Lacy, and Michael L. Blakey, eds. Pp. 5–16. Research Reports 23, Department of Anthropology, University of Massachusetts, Amherst.

Brashler, Janet
  1991 When Daddy Was a Shanty Boy: The Role of Gender in the Organization of the Logging Industry in Highland West Virginia. *Historical Archaeology* 25(4): 54–68.

Brown, Kenneth L., and Doreen C. Cooper
  1990 Structural Continuity in an African-American Slave and Tenant Community. *Historical Archaeology* 24(4):7–19.

Cabak, Melanie A., Mark D. Groover, and Scott J. Wegars
  1995 Health Care and the Wayman A. M. E. Church. *Historical Archaeology* 29(2):55–76.

Crader, Diana C.
  1989 Faunal Remains from Slave Quarter Sites at Monticello, Charlottesville, Virginia. *Archaeozoologia* 3:1–12.

Deagan, Kathleen A.
  1983 *Spanish St. Augustine: The Archaeology of a Colonial Creole Community.* New York: Academic Press.

De Cunzo, Lu Ann
  1995 Reform, Respite, Ritual: An Archaeology of Institutions: The Magdalen Society of Philadelphia, 1800–1850. *Historical Archaeology* 29(3):1–168.

Deetz, James F.
  1977 In *Small Things Forgotten: The Archaeology of Early American Life.* Garden City, NY: Anchor Press/Doubleday.
  1988 Material Culture and Worldview in Colonial Anglo-America. In *The Recovery of Meaning.* Mark P. Leone and Parker B. Potter, Jr., eds. Pp. 219–233. Washington, DC: Smithsonian Institution Press.

Epperson, Terrence W.
  1990 Race and the Disciplines of the Plantation. *Historical Archaeology* 24(4):29–36.
  1996 The Politics of "Race" and Cultural Identity at the African Burial Ground Excavations, New York City. World *Archaeological Bulletin* 7:108–117.

Fairbanks, Charles H.
  1984 The Plantation Archaeology of the Southeastern Coast. *Historical Archaeology* 18(1):1–14.
  1991 Struggling with Pots in Colonial South Carolina. In *The Archaeology of Inequality.* Randall H. McGuire and Robert Paynter, eds. Pp. 28–39. Oxford: Basil Blackwell.
  1992 Uncommon Ground: Archaeology and Early African America, 1650–1800. Washington, DC: Smithsonian Institution Press.

Ferguson, Leland G.
  1991 Struggling with Pots in Colonial South Carolina. In *The Archaeology of Inequality.* Randall H. McGuire and Robert Paynter, eds. Pp. 28–39. Oxford: Basil Blackwell.
  1992 *Uncommon Ground: Archaeology and Early African America, 1650–1800.* Washington, DC: Smithsonian Institution Press.

Fitzgerald, William R., Laurier Turgeon, Ruth Holmes Whitehead, and James W. Bradley
1993 Late Sixteenth-Century Basque Banded Copper Kettles. *Historical Archaeology* 27(1):44–57.

Geismar, Joan H.
1982 *The Archaeology of Social Disintegration in Skunk Hollow: A Nineteenth-Century Rural Black Community.* New York: Academic Press.

Gibb, James G., and Julia A. King
1991 Gender, Activity Areas, and Homelots in the 17th-Century Chesapeake Region. *Historical Archaeology* 25(4):109–131.

Grange, Roger T., Jr.
1997 The Pawnee and the Impact of Euro-American Cultures: Three Centuries of Contact and Change. *Journal of American Archaeology* 12:87–111.

Halchin, Jill Y.
1985 Excavations at Fort Michilimackinac, 1983–1985: House C of the Southeast Row House. Archaeological Completion Report Series, No. 11. Mackinac Island State Park Commission, Mackinac Island, Michigan.

Handsman, Russell G.
1983 Historical Archaeology and Capitalism, Subscriptions and Separations: The Production of Individualism. *North American Archaeologist* 4(1):63–79.
1984 Merchant Capital and the Historical Archaeology of Gender, Motherhoood, and Child Raising. Paper presented at the Annual Meeting of the Council for Northeast Historical Archaeology, SUNY Binghamton, New York, October.
1990 Corn and Culture, Pots and Politics: How to Listen to the Voices of Mohegan Women. Paper presented at the Society for Historical Archaeology Conference, Tucson, Arizona, January 11.

Handsman, Russell G., and Trudie Lamb Richmond
1995 Confronting Colonialism: The Mahican and Schaghticoke Peoples and Us. In *Making Alternative Histories: The Practice of Archaeology and History in Non-Western Settings.* Peter R. Schmidt and Thomas C. Patterson, eds. Pp. 87–117. Santa Fe, NM: SAR Press.

Hardesty, Donald L.
1988 The Archaeology of Mining and Miners: A View from the Silver State. Special Publications Series, No. 6. Tucson, AZ: Society for Historical Archaeology.
1994 Class, Gender Strategies, and Material Culture in the Mining West. In *Those of Little Note: Gender, Race, and Class in Historical Archaeology.* Elizabeth M. Scott, ed. Pp. 129–145. Tucson: University of Arizona Press.

Harrington, Faith
1989 The Emergent Elite in Early 18th Century Portsmouth Society: The Archaeology of the Joseph Sherburne Houselot. *Historical Archaeology* 23(1):2–18.

Hartigan, John, Jr.
1997 Establishing the Fact of Whiteness. *American Anthropologist* 99(3):495–505.

Heath, Barbara J.
1997 Slavery and Consumerism: A Case Study from Central Virginia. *African-American Archaeology* 19:1–8.

Heldman, Donald P.
1986 Michigan's First Jewish Settlers: A View from the Solomon-Levy House at Fort Michilimackinac, 1765–1781. *Journal of New World Archaeology* 6(4): 21–33.
1991 The French in Michigan and Beyond: An Archaeological View from Fort Michilimackinac toward the West. In *French Colonial Archaeology: The Illinois*

Country and the Western Great Lakes. John A. Walthall, ed. Pp. 201–217. Urbana: University of Illinois Press.

Jackson, Louise M.
 1994 Cloth, Clothing, and Related Paraphernalia: A Key to Gender Visibility in the Archaeological Record of Russian America. In *Those of Little Note: Gender, Race, and Class in Historical Archaeology.* Elizabeth M. Scott, ed. Pp. 27–53. Tucson: University of Arizona Press.

James, Steven R.
 1995 Change and Continuity in Western Pueblo Households during the Historic Period in the American Southwest. *World Archaeology* 28(3):429–456.

Klingelhofer, Eric
 1987 Aspects of Early Afro-American Material Culture: Artifacts from the Slave Quarters at Garrison Plantation, Maryland. *Historical Archaeology* 21(2):112–119.

Krause, Elizabeth L.
 1998 "The Bead of Raw Sweat in a Field of Dainty Perspirers": Nationalism, Whiteness, and the Olympic-Class Ordeal of Tonya Harding. *Transforming Anthropology* 7(1):33–52.

Kryder-Reid, Elizabeth
 1994 "With Manly Courage": Reading the Construction of Gender in a Nineteenth-Century Religious Community. In *Those of Little Note: Gender, Race, and Class in Historical Archaeology.* Elizabeth M. Scott, ed. Pp. 97–114. Tucson: University of Arizona Press.

La Roche, Cheryl J., and Michael L. Blakey
 1997 Seizing Intellectual Power: The Dialogue at the New York African Burial Ground. *Historical Archaeology* 31(3):84–106.

Leone, Mark P.
 1978 Archaeology as the Science of Technology: Mormon Town Plans and Fences. In *Historical Archaeology: A Guide to Substantive and Theoretical Contributions.* Robert L. Schuyler, ed. Pp. 191–200. Farmingdale, NY: Baywood.
 1984 Interpreting Ideology in Historical Archaeology: Using the Rules of Perspective in the William Paca Garden in Annapolis, Maryland. In *Ideology, Power, and Prehistory.* Daniel Miller and Christopher Tilley, eds. Pp. 25–35. Cambridge, UK: Cambridge University Press.
 1988a The Georgian Order as the Order of Merchant Capitalism in Annapolis, Maryland. In *The Recovery of Meaning.* Mark P. Leone and Parker B. Potter, Jr., eds. Pp. 235–261. Washington, DC: Smithsonian Institution Press.
 1988b The Relationship between Archaeological Data and the Record: 18th Century Gardens in Annapolis, Maryland. *Historical Archaeology* 22(1):29–35.
 1995 A Historical Archaeology of Capitalism. *American Anthropologist* 97(2):251–268.

Little, Barbara J.
 1988 Craft and Culture Change in the 18th-Century Chesapeake. In *The Recovery of Meaning.* Mark P. Leone and Parker B. Potter, Jr., eds. Pp. 263–292. Washington, DC: Smithsonian Institution Press.
 1992 Explicit and Implicit Meanings in Material Culture and Print Culture. *Historical Archaeology* 26(3):85–94.
 1994 "She Was . . . an Example to Her Sex": Possibilities for a Feminist Historical Archaeology. In *Historical Archaeology of the Chesapeake.* Paul A. Shackel and Barbara J. Little, eds. Pp. 189–204. Washington, DC: Smithsonian Institution Press.

1997 Expressing Ideology without a Voice, or Obfuscation and the Enlightenment. *International Journal of Historical Archaeology* 1(3):225–241.

Martin, Erika, Mia Parsons, and Paul Shackel
1997 Commemorating a Rural African-American Family at a National Battlefield Park. *International Journal of Historical Archaeology* 1(2):157–177.

McDavid, Carol, and David W. Babson, eds.
1997 In the Realm of Politics: Prospects for Public Participation in African-American and Plantation Archaeology. *Historical Archaeology* 31(3):1–152.

McDonald, J. Douglas, Larry J. Zimmerman, A. L. McDonald, William Tall Bull, and Ted Rising Sun
1991 The Northern Cheyenne Outbreak of 1879: Using Oral History and Archaeology as Tools of Resistance. In *The Archaeology of Inequality*. Randall H. McGuire and Robert Paynter, eds. Pp. 64–78. Oxford: Basil Blackwell.

McEwan, Bonnie G.
1991 The Archaeology of Women in the Spanish New World. *Historical Archaeology* 25(4):33–41.

McKee, Larry W.
1987 Delineating Ethnicity from the Garbage of Early Virginians: Faunal Remains from the Kingsmill Plantation Slave Quarter. *American Archaeology* 6(1): 31–39.

Muller, Nancy Ladd
1994 The House of the Black Burghardts: An Investigation of Race, Gender, and Class at the W. E. B. DuBois Boyhood Homesite. In *Those of Little Note: Gender, Race, and Class in Historical Archaeology*. Elizabeth M. Scott, ed. Pp. 81–94. Tucson: University of Arizona Press.

Noel Hume, Ivor
1983 *Martin's Hundred*. New York: Alfred A. Knopf.

Orser, Charles E., Jr.
1987 Plantation Status and Consumer Choice: A Materialist Framework for Historical Archaeology. In *Consumer Choice in Historical Archaeology*. Suzanne M. Spencer-Wood, ed. Pp. 121–137. New York: Plenum Press.
1988a Toward a Theory of Power for Historical Archaeology: Plantations and Space. In *The Recovery of Meaning*. Mark P. Leone and Parker B. Potter, Jr., eds. Pp. 313–343. Washington, DC: Smithsonian Institution Press.
1988b The Archaeological Analysis of Plantation Society: Replacing Status and Caste with Economics and Power. *American Antiquity* 53(4):735–751.
1988c *The Material Basis of the Postbellum Tenant Plantation: Historical Archaeology in the South Carolina Piedmont*. Athens: University of Georgia Press.
1989 On Plantations and Patterns. *Historical Archaeology* 23(2):28–40.
1991 The Continued Pattern of Dominance: Landlord and Tenant on the Postbellum Cotton Plantation. In *The Archaeology of Inequality*. Randall H. McGuire and Robert Paynter, eds. Pp. 40–54. Oxford: Basil Blackwell.
1992 Beneath the Material Surface of Things: Commodities, Artifacts, and Slave Plantations. *Historical Archaeology* 26(3):95–104.
1996 *A Historical Archaeology of the Modern World*. New York: Plenum Press.
1998 The Challenge of Race to U.S. Historical Archaeology. *American Anthropologist* 100(3):661–668.

Paynter, Robert
1988 Steps to an Archaeology of Capitalism: Material Change and Class Analysis. In *The Recovery of Meaning*. Mark P. Leone and Parker B. Potter, Jr., eds. Pp. 407–434. Washington, DC: Smithsonian Institution Press.

Penner, Bruce R.
  1997   Old World Traditions, New World Landscapes: Ethnicity and Archaeology of
         Swiss-Appenzellers in the Colonial South Carolina Backcountry. *International
         Journal of Historical Archaeology* 1(4):257–321.
Perttula, Timothy K.
  1994   French and Spanish Colonial Trade Policies and the Fur Trade among the
         Caddoan Indians of the Trans-Mississippi South. In *The Fur Trade Revisited*.
         Jennifer S. H. Brown, W. J. Eccles, and Donald P. Heldman, eds. Pp. 71–91. East
         Lansing: Michigan State University Press and Mackinac State Historic Parks.
Purser, Margaret
  1991   "Several Paradise Ladies Are Visiting in Town": Gender Strategies in the Early
         Industrial West. *Historical Archaeology* 25(4):6–16.
Reitz, Elizabeth J.
  1987   Vertebrate Fauna and Socioeconomic Status. In *Consumer Choice in Historical
         Archaeology*, Suzanne M. Spencer-Wood, ed. Pp. 101–119. New York: Plenum
         Press.
Rubertone, Patricia E.
  1996   Matters of Inclusion: Historical Archaeology and Native Americans. *World
         Archaeological Bulletin* 7:77–86.
Russell, Aaron E.
  1997   Material Culture and African-American Spirituality at the Hermitage.
         Historical Archaeology 31(2):63–80.
Savulis, Ellen-Rose
  1992   Alternative Visions and Landscapes: Archaeology of the Shaker Social Order
         and Built Environment. In *Text-Aided Archaeology*. Barbara J. Little, ed.
         Pp. 195–203. Boca Raton, FL: CRC Press.
Scott, Elizabeth M.
  1991a   Gender in Complex Colonial Society: The Material Goods of Everyday Life
         in a Late Eighteenth-Century Fur Trading Community. In *The Archaeology of
         Gender*. Dale Walde and Noreen C. Willows, eds. Pp. 490–495. Calgary, Alberta:
         Department of Archaeology, University of Calgary.
  1991b   A Feminist Approach to Historical Archaeology: Eighteenth-Century Fur
         Trade Society at Michilimackinac. *Historical Archaeology* 25(4):42–53.
  1996   Who Ate What? Archaeological Food Remains and Cultural Diversity. In *Case
         Studies in Environmental Archaeology*. Elizabeth J. Reitz, Lee A. Newsom, and
         Sylvia J. Scudder, eds. Pp. 339–356. New York: Plenum Press.
Seifert, Donna J.
  1991   Within Sight of the White House: The Archaeology of Working Women.
         Historical Archaeology 25(4):82–108.
  1994   Mrs. Starr's Profession. In *Those of Little Note: Gender, Race, and Class in
         Historical Archaeology*. Elizabeth M. Scott, ed. Pp. 149–173. Tucson: University of
         Arizona Press.
Shackel, Paul A.
  1992   Modern Discipline: Its Historical Context in the Colonial Chesapeake.
         Historical Archaeology 26(3):73–84.
  1993   *Personal Discipline and Material Culture: An Archaeology of Annapolis,
         Maryland, 1695–1870*. Knoxville: University of Tennessee Press.
Singleton, Theresa A.
  1985   *The Archaeology of Slavery and Plantation Life*. Orlando, FL: Academic
         Press.
  1988   An Archaeological Framework for Slavery and Emancipation, 1740–1880.

In *The Recovery of Meaning.* Mark P. Leone and Parker B. Potter, Jr., eds. Pp. 345–370. Washington, DC: Smithsonian Institution Press.

1996 The Archaeology of Slave Life. In *Images of the Recent Past: Readings in Historical Archaeology.* Charles E. Orser, Jr., ed. Pp. 141–165. Walnut Creek, CA: Altamira Press.

Singleton, Theresa A., and Mark D. Bograd
1995 The Archaeology of the African Diaspora in the Americas. *Guides to the Archaeological Literature of the Immigrant Experience in America,* No. 2. Tucson, AZ: Society for Historical Archaeology.

Spector, Janet D.
1991 What This Awl Means: Toward a Feminist Archaeology. In *Engendering Archaeology: Women and Prehistory.* Joan M. Gero and Margaret W. Conkey, eds. Pp. 388–406. Oxford: Basil Blackwell.

1993 *What This Awl Means: Feminist Archaeology at a Wahpeton Dakota Village.* St. Paul: Minnesota Historical Society Press.

Spector, Janet D., and Mary K. Whelan
1989 Incorporating Gender into Archaeology Courses. In *Gender and Anthropology: Critical Reviews for Research and Teaching.* Sandra Morgen, ed. Pp. 65–94. Washington, DC: American Anthropological Association.

Spencer-Wood, Suzanne M.
1987 A Survey of Domestic Reform Movement Sites in Boston and Cambridge, ca. 1865–1905. *Historical Archaeology* 21(2):7–36.

1991 Towards an Historical Archaeology of Materialistic Domestic Reform. In *The Archaeology of Inequality.* Randall H. McGuire and Robert Paynter, eds. Pp. 231–286. Oxford: Basil Blackwell.

Starbuck, David R.
1994 The Identification of Gender at Northern Military Sites of the Late Eighteenth Century. In *Those of Little Note: Gender, Race, and Class in Historical Archaeology.* Elizabeth M. Scott, ed. Pp. 115–128. Tucson: University of Arizona Press.

Stewart-Abernathy, Leslie C., and Barbara L. Ruff
1989 A Good Man in Israel: Zooarchaeology and Assimilation in Antebellum Washington, Arkansas. *Historical Archaeology* 23(2):96–112.

Stine, Linda France
1990 Social Inequality and Turn-of-the-Century Farmsteads: Issues of Class, Status, Ethnicity, and Race. *Historical Archaeology* 24(4):37–49.

Stine, Linda France, Melanie A. Cabak, and Mark D. Groover
1996 Blue Beads as African-American Cultural Symbols. *Historical Archaeology* 30(3):49–75.

Trubowitz, Neal L.
1992 Native Americans and French on the Central Wabash. In *Calumet and Fleur-de-Lys: Archaeology of Indian and French Contact in the Midcontinent.* John A. Walthall and Thomas E. Emerson, eds. Pp. 241–264. Washington, DC: Smithsonian Institution Press.

Wall, Diana diZerega
1991 Sacred Dinners and Secular Teas: Constructing Domesticity in Mid-19th-Century New York. *Historical Archaeology* 25(4):69–81.

1994 *The Archaeology of Gender: Separating the Spheres in Urban America.* New York: Plenum Press.

Waselkov, Gregory A.
1997 The Archaeology of French Colonial North America: French–English Edition.

Guides to Historical Archaeological Literature, No. 5. Tucson, AZ: Society for Historical Archaeology.

Wegars, Priscilla
  1991 Who's Been Workin' on the Railroad? An Examination of the Construction, Distribution, and Ethnic Origins of Domed Rock Ovens on Railroad-Related Sites. *Historical Archaeology* 25(1):37–65.
  1993 *Hidden Heritage: Historical Archaeology of the Overseas Chinese*. Amityville, NY: Baywood.

Whelan, Mary K.
  1991 Gender and Historical Archaeology: Eastern Dakota Patterns in the 19th Century. *Historical Archaeology* 25(4):17–32.

Wilkie, Laurie A.
  1996 Medicinal Teas and Patent Medicines: African-American Women's Consumer Choices and Ethnomedical Traditions at a Louisiana Plantation. *Southeastern Archaeology* 15(2):119–131.
  1997 Secret and Sacred: Contextualizing the Artifacts of African-American Magic and Religion. *Historical Archaeology* 31(4):81–106.

Williams, Jack S., and Patricia Fournier-Garcia
  1996 Beyond National Boundaries and Regional Perspectives: Contrasting Approaches to Spanish Colonial Archaeology in the Americas. *World Archaeological Bulletin* 7:63–76.

Yentsch, Anne
  1991a The Symbolic Division of Pottery: Sex-Related Attributes of English and Anglo-American Household Pots. In *The Archaeology of Inequality*. Randall H. McGuire and Robert Paynter, eds. Pp. 192–230. Oxford: Basil Blackwell.
  1991b Engendering Visible and Invisible Ceramic Artifacts, Especially Dairy Vessels. *Historical Archaeology* 25(4):132–155.

Young, Amy L.
  1997 Risk Management Strategies among African-American Slaves at Locust Grove Plantation. *International Journal of Historical Archaeology* 1(1):5–37.

Young, Amy L., and Melanie A. Cabak, eds.
  n.d. *Engendering African-American Archaeology*. (in press).

Part IV

Diversity: Where Are We Now?

11

Contemporary Native American Struggles

Thomas Biolsi

In February 1973 members of the American Indian Movement (AIM) seized the little town of Wounded Knee on the Pine Ridge Reservation, home of the Oglala Lakota, in South Dakota. As Vine Deloria, Jr., explains the event, urban Indian activists who had been schooled in social protest by watching the black movement, linked up with traditional Lakota people on the reservation "with roots in the tireless resistance of generations of unknown Indians who ... refused to melt into the homogeneity of American life and accept American citizenship" (Deloria 1985[1974]:20). Indeed, when the occupiers of Wounded Knee, now surrounded by military-equipped U.S. marshals and FBI agents and – because of that – watched closely by the media, declared the "Independent Oglala Nation," the concept of native *sovereignty* as the legal status of Indian people in the United States was thrust into the public consciousness.[1] While many non-Indians continued, and continue, to understand Indian issues as "domestic" matters concerning a "racial minority," Indian people who did not already assume it quickly came to recognize that "Wounded Knee II" was about indigenous *nationhood* and the struggle against *colonialism*. When the U.S. Justice Department brought criminal charges against the occupiers, the latter's attorneys argued that "the courts of the United States do not have the power and jurisdiction to judge the guilt or innocence of individuals who are citizens of other Nations for alleged crimes committed on the soil of other Nations" (*U.S. v. Consolidated Wounded Knee Cases* 1975:236).

This chapter will sketch the contemporary political and legal struggles of Native American people. There is no question that Indian people and their communities are positioned in *systems* of racial, and other forms of inequality: systems that include other "minority" peoples and, indeed, privileged whites. The social systematicity of oppression is a key paradigmatic principle of the anthropological approach to diversity that must never be lost sight of in our classrooms and in our scholarly questions and writing. The situation of Native American people has complex continuities with, and linkages to, the situations of other oppressed peoples in America.[2] However, it is also clear that in many ways the Native American struggle is not "the same fight."

Native people were never racialized or otherwise treated in the same ways as other minorities in the United States. From the beginning, in fact, indigenous peoples were treated under American law as autonomous nations with whom the United States entered into international relations. The treaties are the historical record of those relations. While the subsequent history of the legal treatment of Native Americans by the United States is a checkered one, Indian people still find much of value in the indigenous rights they can effectively claim under federal law in the United States. When viewed in comparison to the legal situation of other minorities, the native situation is quite noteworthy. No other group in the United States has claim to autonomous homelands – reservations – with the attendant authority of self-determination, to some extent free even from the U.S. Constitution. This unique legal situation is why much of the Native Struggle – although not all, as Wounded Knee, and the earlier Alcatraz occupation, make clear – takes place in the courts and the halls of Congress. Protecting and extending the federally recognized rights of Indian self-determination is vitally important, and it should come as no surprise that Indian peoples in the United States have come to find "strategic essentialism" a critical framework for empowerment.

What are the specificities of the Native American political struggle? This chapter will attempt to do something Indian people – and perhaps especially Vine Deloria, Jr. – have been asking anthropologists to do for a long time: to take seriously and *listen* to what Indian people themselves say their issues are. The aim is to give the reader a usable "road map" of contemporary Native American political issues.

Sovereignty

Sovereignty is now a household word among Indian people both on and off (where most Indian people live) the reservations.[3] The concept includes both the insistence that Indian "tribes" are, in fact, nations with inherent – *pre-constitutional* – rights to self-determination and autonomy, and the proposition that the primary source of oppression experienced by Indian people, and that must be struggled against, is not so much racism, precisely, as colonialism: the historic interference of the United States in the internal affairs of indigenous nations.

The Wounded Knee occupation, interestingly, had been an anti-colonial action against not just oppression by the United States, but also against the presence of the Oglala Sioux Tribal Council, which the occupiers saw as an alien organization inconsistent with both treaty law and Lakota tradition. The Oglala Sioux Tribal Council, like most tribal governments in the United States, had been organized in the 1930s under the provisions of the Indian Reorganization Act (IRA) in order to foster Indian self-government under a model of reform invented by non-Indian politicians and bureaucrats in Washington (see Biolsi 1992). From the perspective of indigenous sovereignty, however, the problem was that IRA tribal governments were based on a *delegation* of limited tribal autonomy from the United States – a "gift" of power from the colonizers to the colonized – rather than a recognition of the inherent independent-nation status which preexisted the formation of the United States and which was legally recognized by the United States in its execution of the treaties (see Deloria

1985[1974]; Deloria and Lytle 1983). Indeed, the designer of the IRA and Indian self-government, Commissioner of Indian Affairs John Collier, believed that the IRA was an exercise precisely in "indirect rule" (Biolsi 1992).

While AIM and Wounded Knee did not succeed in replacing the IRA tribal governments, a very remarkable thing did happen as a result of 1973: IRA tribal governments all over the United States got the message that Indian tribes are nations with inherent rights of sovereignty. This did not happen overnight, but because of organizations like the Institute for the Development of Indian Law (see for example Berkey 1976; Kickingbird et al. 1983) and the National Congress of American Indians, as well as the remarkably creative work of Indian attorneys such as Deloria, by the late 1970s and the early 1980s, tribal governments throughout the United States had begun to assert rights to sovereignty in unprecedented ways.

These rights claims are, in some ways, quite simple and straightforward, and amount merely to an insistence upon complete territorial jurisdiction within reservation boundaries without the intervening jurisdictions of other sovereigns. The potentially interfering sovereigns include both state governments and their subdivisions, and the United States itself. In *California v. Cabazon Band of Mission Indians* (1987) for example, a tribal government successfully resisted the attempt by the State of California to enforce state law over reservation gaming operations (in this case, bingo and poker). The Court found that California's legitimate concern to prevent the infiltration of organized crime into gaming operations within the state was preempted by the "compelling federal and tribal interests" (California: 1095) of "Indian sovereignty," "Indian self-government," and "tribal self-sufficiency and economic development" (California: 1092).

The tribal success in *California v. Cabazon* did not, however, end once and for all tribal struggles against the interference of state authority. In 1988 Congress enacted the Indian Gaming Regulatory Act, which limits tribal operations to those lawful within the state and requires tribes to enter into gaming compacts with state governments. Congress was able to require this of tribes because of the century-old Supreme Court assumption that Congress has "plenary power" over Indian affairs in the United States and may intervene in tribal self-government as it sees fit (in the "interests" of Indian people), without tribal agreement (on plenary power, see Deloria 1985[1974]; Wilkins 1997). State approval, in other words, is required by Congress for tribal gaming. Getting cooperation from the states is no easy matter for the tribes, especially where they seek to open gaming operations on off-reservation lands taken into tribal ownership for the purpose of opening casinos. It must be remembered, also, that states necessarily see tribes as competitors for the potential revenues available to governments from gaming. As of this writing, there is no mechanism by which tribes can force states to enter into compacts, and some tribes have even opened operations without state compacts, an act of sovereignty which they call "uncompacted" gaming, but which the states (who do not have authority to close down a tribal operation on Indian land) call "illegal" (National Gambling Impact Study Commission 1999:6.10).[4]

Protection from *federal* interference in tribal autonomy also remains central for tribal governments, although it is less often aggressively asserted by tribes and less successful because of the plenary power doctrine. Nevertheless, there have been some remarkable successes. Among the best-known cases is *Santa Clara Pueblo v. Martinez* (1978). Julia Martinez, a pueblo member, and her daughter who was not a member, sued the tribal government of Santa Clara Pueblo, New Mexico, for violation of their rights under federal law. Martinez had children by a non-pueblo member, and because of a tribal ordinance limiting enrollment to children of male pueblo members only, these children could not be enrolled as tribal members, even though they had grown up in the community and were culturally and socially pueblo members. Martinez and her daughter argued that the tribal ordinance violated their federal guarantee of equal protection of the law on the basis of sex (if Martinez had been a man, she would have been entitled to enroll her children) and ancestry (the daughter would have been eligible for enrollment had her father been Santa Clara). The Court was not convinced by these arguments, however, and held that the federal courts had no authority to interfere in the internal affairs of tribes, except for *habeas corpus* cases. *Santa Clara v. Martinez* underscored the pre-constitutional and extra-constitutional legal status of Indian tribes: tribal authority flows not from grants of power by the federal government, but from the inherent sovereignty that predated the Constitution and that is not constrained by the Constitution.

Closely connected to the applicability of the U.S. Constitution to Indian tribes is the issue of tribal authority over non-tribal members both on and off the reservation. In this area, tribes have had very mixed success in their struggle to exercise sovereignty. In an important early case, *Oliphant v. Suquamish Indian Tribe* (1978), a non-Indian, who had been arrested on Port Madison Reservation in Washington by the Suquamish Tribal Police and charged in tribal court with assaulting an officer and resisting arrest, asserted that the tribal government had no jurisdiction over him because he was a non-Indian. The case eventually went to the Supreme Court which reasoned that although Indian tribes may aboriginally have had the authority to exercise jurisdiction over foreigners among them, there are "inherent limitations on tribal powers that stem from their incorporation into the United States" (*Oliphant*: 210).

It is difficult to overestimate the degree to which this decision represented a blow to tribal government. Sovereignty in the modern world of states necessarily entails continuous and discrete territorial jurisdiction over a bounded area (on the evolution of the modern system of territorial states, see Ruggie 1998), and the effect of the *Oliphant* decision was to deny tribal governments the right even to issue a traffic ticket to a non-Indian. Tribal officials continue to be agitated over this holding, and to seek ways to circumvent it, including simply exercising tribal criminal law without any jurisdictional regard for the *race* of the perpetrator, leaving it for the defendant to challenge tribal jurisdiction under federal law if he or she so chooses. It is important to understand that this is a highly charged matter for many Indian people, and it is often pointed out that the attempt to deny basic territorial jurisdiction to tribes – something that is regularly assumed by all non-tribal governments, including towns and counties in the United States – is nothing less than *racist*.

Oliphant also opened the question of tribal criminal jurisdiction over non-member Indians. On most reservations in the United States, there are significant numbers of "foreign" Indians who are not enrolled in the tribe, but have married in or otherwise reside on the reservation. When the tribal government on the Salt River Reservation in Arizona charged a "non-member Indian" with illegally firing a weapon,[5] the non-member filed a petition for a writ of *habeas corpus* in United States District Court, claiming a violation of federal law. The argument in *Duro v. Reina* (1990) was that since *Oliphant* had denied tribes the right to exercise criminal jurisdiction over *non-Indians*, allowing tribes to exercise criminal jurisdiction over *non-member Indians* would amount to a denial of equal protection on the basis of race. The district court granted the writ, and when the case went to the Supreme Court, it agreed with the defendant that the situation of a non-member Indian regarding tribal jurisdiction was precisely parallel to that of the non-Indian examined in *Oliphant*. Tribes, the Court concluded in *Duro*, have "only the powers of *internal* self-governance," and have no more right to exercise criminal jurisdiction over a non-member Indian than they do over a non-Indian (*Duro v. Reina* 1990:708).

While this might seem like a success for the civil rights of Indian people, *Duro*, like *Olpihant*, was a blow for tribal self-government, both in principle, and practically, since tribes do regularly deal with substantial numbers of non-member Indians within their borders. As one of my Lakota informants from South Dakota puts it, limiting tribal jurisdiction to "tribal members" is tantamount to emasculating Indian tribes into "Boy Scout troops." Governments, after all, are not voluntary associations. Governments necessarily exercise *territorial* jurisdiction, and the tribes did not take *Duro* lying down. After concerted political lobbying from the tribes (see Biolsi 2001:ch. 5), Congress enacted a permanent "*Duro* fix" in 1991 which amended the Indian Civil Rights Act of 1968 to specify among the rights of tribes the right "to exercise criminal jurisdiction over all Indians" (104 Stat. 1892; 105 Stat. 646).

While *Oliphant* apparently settled the matter of criminal jurisdiction over non-Indians, tribes were prepared to fight on the question of civil/regulatory jurisdiction. There has been much litigation over the right of tribes to exercise such jurisdiction over non-Indians within their reservation borders. The Supreme Court's *Montana v. U.S.* (1981) decision insisted that "[i]t defies common sense" (*Montana*: 560) to assume that non-Indians who lawfully live within reservation boundaries – and there are many thousands of such people across the United States – come under tribal jurisdiction. Nevertheless, the Court did admit that, owing to its retained sovereignty, a tribe does possess civil and regulatory jurisdiction over the activities of non-Indians "who enter consensual relationships with the tribe or its members, through commercial dealing, contracts, leases, or other arrangements" (*Montana*: 565). A tribe also has authority over non-Indian activity that "threatens or has some direct effect on the political integrity, the economic security, or the health or welfare of the tribe" (*Montana*: 566). Precisely what these areas of tribal authority are has continued to be litigated since *Montana* (for example, *Brendale v. Yakima* [1989];

Strate v. A-1 Contractors [1997]; *Lewis v. Allen* [1998]), but it is clear that tribes have authority to

> tax the personal property owned by a non-Indian located on the reservation. A tribe also can tax the income received by a non-Indian company from its reservation business. A non-Indian who wishes to sell liquor or conduct a commercial transaction on the reservation must comply with tribal law. A tribe can regulate hunting and fishing by non-Indians on Indian land. A tribe also can enforce its health and building requirements and its clean air and water regulations on non-Indians within the reservation. Non-Indians who buy goods on the reservation can be charged a tribal sales tax. (Pevar 1992:155 [footnotes omitted]; see also Getches et al. 1993; Canby 1998)

Among the most noteworthy recent cases to question the authority of tribal courts to exercise civil jurisdiction over non-Indians is *Estate of Tasunke Witko, a.k.a. Crazy Horse v. Hornell Brewing Co.* (1996). This was a cultural appropriation case in which the descendants of the Oglala Lakota chief Crazy Horse sued the corporate producers of "The Original Crazy Horse Malt Liquor." The suit was brought in the Rosebud Sioux Tribal Court in South Dakota. The complaint charged that Hornell Brewing was illegally appropriating the commercial publicity value of the name Crazy Horse, property that under Lakota customary law remains part of the estate for seven generations. The suit sought an injunction against use of the name by the defendants, compensation under Lakota customary law (tobacco braids, blankets, and horses), and monetary damages in excess of 100 million dollars (Amended Complaint 1993). The defendant argued that it had not operated on Rosebud Reservation, nor engaged in any activity that might have brought it within the lawful jurisdiction of the tribal court. The tribal court did in fact dismiss the case on these grounds in 1994. The Rosebud Sioux Supreme Court, however, reversed this jurisdictional holding, pointing out that the *harm* to the plaintiffs had taken place on Rosebud Reservation, bringing the matter under the tribe's long-arm statute. The case was remanded to the tribal court for hearing on the merits (*Estate of Tasunke Witko, a.k.a. Crazy Horse v. Hornell Brewing Co.* 1996). While it looked like both new intellectual-property and new tribal-jurisdiction law was in the making, the defendants managed to convince the Eighth Circuit Court of Appeals that the tribe did not have jurisdiction. The court insisted that the activities in question had occurred "outside the confines of a reservation," and thus outside of tribal jurisdiction (*Hornell Brewing Company v. Rosebud Sioux Tribal Court* 1998:1091; see also Novello 1993; Singer 1996; Newton 1997).

The courts have not been the only place where tribes have pressed the matter of, and must remain vigilant regarding, indigenous sovereignty. Notwithstanding the indigenous sovereignty of tribes recognized by the courts, because of the doctrine of plenary power, Congress has the authority to diminish powers of tribal self-determination, or it may expand them as it did in the case of the *Duro*-fix mentioned above. In 1975, in the wake of militant activism and strong tribal lobbying, Congress enacted the Indian Self-Determination Act (88 Stat.

2203) which authorizes individual tribes to enter into "self-determination contracts" (known popularly as "638 contracts") with the federal government to assume the administrative supervision of, and budgets for, federal services delivered to their reservations, such as health care, child welfare, law enforcement, and so on. Tribes have used this procedure to greatly expand tribal government operations, and some tribes have assumed much expanded responsibility and funding for delivery of erstwhile federal services through self-governance compacts, authorized by Congress in 1991, which provide more administrative freedom to the tribes than do 638 contracts (Tribal Self-Governance Demonstration Project Act). In 1978, Congress passed the Indian Child Welfare Act, which delegated to tribal courts substantial jurisdiction over cases involving foster care placement or termination of parental rights with respect to children enrolled in tribes or eligible for enrollment, even when those children are not living on reservations. Congress' declared intention here was to help insure "the continued existence and integrity of Indian tribes" (Indian Child Welfare Act 3069).

Because of the increasing lobbying power of the tribes, Congress also takes tribal interests in their sovereignty and self-government into consideration in enacting "general" legislation. The Personal Responsibility and Work Opportunity Reconciliation Act ("Welfare Reform") of 1996, for example, provides for tribes, as well as states, to implement TANF (Temporary Assistance for Needy Families) programs with direct federal funding (see Division of Tribal Services 1998; National Congress of American Indians n.d.). As of this writing, 21 tribes have taken advantage of this provision and implemented tribal TANF programs independent of the states in which they are located (Division of Tribal Services 1999).

The executive branch has also sought to recognize and support tribal sovereignty, since, notably, the Nixon Administration. President Clinton issued a memorandum in 1994 which directed the executive departments to assume a "government-to-government" relationship with tribes "reflecting respect for the rights of self-government due the sovereign tribal governments" (Government-to-Government Relations with Native American Tribal Governments 1994). A 1998 executive order (Executive Order 13084) requires departments to put into place processes for consultation with tribal governments and to avoid promulgating regulations that might interfere with the rights of tribes to self-government.

On the other hand, there are interests in Congress at the present time that would undermine the progress tribes have made in the struggle for sovereignty. To some, tribal sovereignty represents "racial discrimination" because of the "special rights" Indians claim that distinguish them from other American citizens. The high-profile success of a handful of tribes in gaming operations has helped to make this perspective politically credible by stirring non-Indian resentment against tribal sovereignty. Among recently proposed legislation, the most potentially damaging to tribal sovereignty have been a provision to subject federal funding for tribal governments to "means testing" (see National Congress of American Indians 1997), and one to deny tribal governments the right of sovereign immunity (the freedom from suit that all governments claim to some extent; see Frank 1998; National Congress of American Indians 1998; Richardson 1998).

Rights Claims of Individual Indian People

Writing in the wake of Wounded Knee, Vine Deloria pointed out in 1974 that civil rights are "anathema" to Indian people (Deloria 1985[1974]:23). This is largely because the threats to indigenous sovereignty have often come in the form of civil rights discourse and the constitutional rights claims of non-Indians. We have already seen in the *Santa Clara Pueblo v. Martinez* case how tribes responded to the proposition of the federal courts "protecting" the "civil rights" of tribal members.[6] When Congress launched an attack on the legal status of tribes in the 1950s, seeking to *terminate* that status, the rhetoric was one of civil rights, of treating Indian people the same as all other American citizens. Anathema, indeed.

One of the perennial matters in the legal status of Native Americans has been the question of the fairness of racial differentiation under the law. Four years before *Regents of the University of California v. Bakke* (1978) challenged the affirmative action program of U.C. Berkeley, non-Indian employees of the Bureau of Indian Affairs (BIA) filed a class action suit against the BIA's "Indian preference" policy for hiring and promotion. The claim in *Morton v. Mancari* (1974) was that the policy, as a racial preference, violated both the provisions of the Equal Employment Opportunity Act (1972) and the due process clause of the Fifth Amendment of the Constitution (prohibiting the deprivation of property without due process). The Supreme Court held, however, that the policy was not a racial preference at all, but part of a federal policy of fostering Indian self-government, begun in the 1930s, by replacing non-Indian BIA personnel with tribal members: "The preference, as applied, is granted to Indians not as a discrete racial group, but rather, as members of quasi-sovereign tribal entities" (*Morton*: 554).

The larger lesson here is that, from an indigenous perspective, "special" legal treatment of Indian people is decidedly *not* to be understood as "affirmative action," as attempts at rectification of past racial discrimination (not that any Indian person would suggest that racism is not an ongoing fact of Indian life). Rather, the differential treatment of tribal members under the law flows from indigenous nationhood: the difference in legal status is parallel with *nationality*, not race, and is, thus, not fruitfully understood as "special" rights. Tribal representatives continually fight against the habit, of people unfamiliar with Indian affairs, of understanding those affairs in racial terms, drawn from the political struggles of other disempowered peoples in America.

For example, the Ninth Circuit Court of Appeals handed down an important decision that violates the indigenous understanding of "race" and tribal citizenship in *Dawavendewa v. Salt River Project* (1998). Harold Dawavendewa, a Hopi, claimed that he had been discriminated against on the basis of "national origin" – prohibited by Title VII of the 1964 Civil Rights Act – by a private employer operating on the Navajo Reservation and giving employment preference to enrolled Navajos. The appeals court was convinced by this argument.

Assimilating Indian preference policy into affirmative action theory in a way which made tribal governments cringe, the court insisted that Indian preference hiring is countenanced by federal law only "to compensate for the effects of past and present unjust treatment, not in order to authorize another form of discrimination against particular groups of Indians – tribal discrimination" (*Dawavendewa*: 1121–1122). From the point of view of the Navajo Nation and other tribes, however, what is at issue here is not "tribal discrimination," but the right of governments to regulate the employment of aliens within their borders. It is a basic matter of sovereignty.

It would not be correct to say, however, that individual rights claims have only been harmful in the struggles of Native American people. Far from it, and Vine Deloria himself has been a litigant in a key case. In 1992 Deloria, along with six other prominent Native Americans filed a petition with the Trademark Trial and Appeal Board of the U.S. Department of Commerce to revoke the Washington Redskins trademark (*Harjo et al. v. Pro-Football, Inc.,* 1998). The petitioners argued that the word *redskins* "was and is a pejorative, derogatory, denigrating, offensive, scandalous, contemptuous, disreputable, disparaging and racist designation for a Native American person" (*Harjo*: 5) and that the mark itself "disparages Native American persons, and brings them into contempt, ridicule, and disrepute" (*Harjo*: 6). On this basis the petitioners asked for the cancellation of the registrations. The Trademark Trial and Appeal Board granted the petition for cancellation. While this decision does not prevent Pro-Football, Inc., or anyone else, from using the trademark, it does deny the corporation exclusive use of the trademark, and thus puts at risk sizeable profits from the sales of Redskins paraphernalia. Among the teams still using racist images of Indians are the Cleveland Indians ("Chief Wahoo"), the Atlanta Braves (the "tomahawk chop"), and the University of Illinois at Urbana ("Chief Illiniwek"; see *Indian Country Today* 1998, 1999; see also Johnson and Eck 1995).

A critical case that involved the civil rights of individual Indian people concerned the right of members of the Native American Church (NAC) to practice their religion free from state interference. The NAC – also known as the "Peyote Church" or "Peyote Religion" – has as part of its sacrament the ingestion of peyote (see LaBarre 1964; Slotkin 1975; Stewart 1987; Aberle 1991). While the federal government initially attempted to prohibit NAC services on the reservations, since 1965 federal law has exempted the ceremonial use of peyote by Indians on reservations. Since many NAC members live off-reservation, however, the question remained regarding exemption from state drug laws. As of 1994, 28 states had enacted exemptions similar to that of the federal government, but 22, including Oregon, had not (American Indian Religious Freedom Act Amendments of 1994). In 1983 Alfred Smith, a Klamath Indian and member of the NAC, and Galen Black, a non-Indian member, were fired from their jobs with a private drug-rehabilitation agency in Oregon for ingestion of peyote. When they applied for state unemployment benefits, their applications were denied on the grounds that they had been fired for "misconduct," because they had ingested what is a controlled substance under Oregon criminal law. Both the Oregon Court of Appeals and the Oregon Supreme Court sided with Smith and Black, finding that the Oregon Employment Division had violated their First Amendment right to the free exercise of religion. The Supreme Court, however, balked at the proposition that "an individual's religious beliefs excuse him from compliance with an otherwise valid law prohibiting conduct that the State is free to regulate" (*Employment Division v. Smith* 1990:1600). Since Oregon's drug law is a "neutral, generally applicable regulatory law" (*Smith*: 1601) – that is, a general law passed without the intention of singling out any religion – it is perfectly consistent with constitutional protections of religious freedom, and NAC church members are not exempted from its enforcement.

As in the *Duro* case, however, tribal advocates were not prepared to accept the finding in *Smith*, and a national movement for the restoration of religious freedom for Native Americans was organized. As a result of this movement, Congress enacted the American Indian Religious Freedom Act Amendments of 1994, which exempted from any state or federal prohibition "the use, possession, or transportation of peyote by an Indian for bona fide traditional ceremonial purposes in connection with the practice of a traditional Indian religion" (for an excellent extended treatment of *Smith*, read against the background of indigenous sovereignty, see Wilkins 1997; see also Deloria 1992; Deloria and Wilkins 1999).

Conclusion

This survey has hardly exhausted the breadth of the political fronts that engage Indian people at the present time.[7] This brief sketch does, however, give the reader some sense of the political topography negotiated by Indian people and tribal governments. That topography is extremely complex, and rights-claims strategies never come with guarantees. It is obvious, for example, how civil rights can be "anathema" for Indian people, but how they can also be critically important. The rights of tribal sovereignty also come without guarantees. Because much federal Indian law, upon which the rights of tribes depend, is exceptional in the larger liberal legal universe of equality before the law, many questions regarding Indian sovereignty end up being litigated in the courts, and most Indian law cases are judicial close calls that can easily go either way, and can easily be reversed in a higher court. Furthermore, because of the plenary power doctrine, Congress has the legal authority to roll back tribal sovereignty. It is for these reasons that tribal governments and their advocates are continuously vigilant over Congress and the courts (see Biolsi 2001).

But the rights of sovereignty come without guarantees in another sense. In an increasingly worldwide market economy and globalized political regime ("flexible accumulation," for short), how reliable a protection can sovereignty be for human rights? The Native American claim to sovereignty is, after all, an insistence upon smaller and more autonomous nations, not upon larger frameworks of rights claims. A former president of the Rosebud Sioux Tribe was once told by the governor of South Dakota: "If you are a sovereign nation, then why don't you do something about the STDs on the reservation?" The governor's point is clear: in the overwhelming neoliberal ideology that prevails at present, being a nation entails being "responsible for yourself." Native American claims to sovereignty (inadvertently, and unfortunately) dovetail with the larger discourse of neoliberalism in desocializing human rights and human welfare: these become – ideologically – "local responsibilities" at precisely the same time as they are becoming part and parcel of global processes in reality (see Biolsi 2001:ch. 6). Furthermore, rights strategies based in sovereignty do not by any means come with guarantees for women's rights, or the rights of other "minorities" *within* tribal nations. What is absolutely clear is that the political topography is not stable, and how Native American people respond to the challenges will bear careful scrutiny by their allies, anthropologists included. Will sovereignty be sufficiently flexible, or will new frameworks of rights claims – perhaps involving unprecedented coalitions – be developed?

NOTES

1   In fact the sovereignty discourse had been articulately expressed the previous November (1972), when the "Trail of Broken Treaties Caravan" presented a list of 20 points to the federal government. Deeply rooted in the document was the proposition that Indian people in the United States were to be "governed by treaty relations" (Twenty Point Proposal of the Trail of Broken Treaties, in Pommersheim 1979:142. See Deloria 1985 ([1974]:48–53 for an analysis).
2   Important thinking about this matter has been done by George Pierre Castile (1992) and Gerald Sider (1993).
3   There are presently 554 federally recognized tribes in the United States. The 1990 census put the reservation Indian population at 437,431, with a total U.S. Indian population of 1,878,285. Measuring the Native American population is an extremely complex task because of the self-report method used by the census bureau versus the specific criteria (often involving demonstrable "blood quanta") required by tribes and the federal government for legal enrollment (see Snipp 1989:ch. 2; 1997; Thornton 1998a).
4   As of 1998, 260 tribal casinos and bingo halls were operating, which represents less than half of the 554 federally recognized tribes. In 1997 revenues from tribal gaming reached $6.7 billion. The twenty largest operations accounted for 50.5 percent of this figure (National Gambling Impact Study Commission 1999:6.2; see also Cornell et al. 1998).
5   The defendant had actually killed a tribal member, and had been charged under federal law, but the charges had been dismissed.
6   But see MacKinnon (1987) for the counterargument.
7   Among the more obvious issues omitted are fishing rights (Cohen 1986; Institute for Natural Progress 1992; Fixico 1998; Ulrich 1999), water rights (McCool 1994[1987]; Burton 1991; Guerrero 1992; Fixico 1998), environmental racism (Churchill and LaDuke 1992; Grinde and Johansen 1995), and repatriation and reburial (American Indian Culture and Research Journal 1992; Swidler et al. 1997; Thornton 1998b).

REFERENCES CITED

Published sources

Aberle, David F.
    1991   *The Peyote Religion among the Navajo*. Norman: University of Oklahoma Press.
American Indian Culture and Research Journal
    1992   Special Issue on Repatriation, vol. 16(2).

Berkey, Curtis
    1976   The Inherent Powers of Indian Government. *American Indian Journal of the Institute for the Development of Indian Law* 2(5):15–18.
Biolsi, Thomas
    1992   *Organizing the Lakota: The Political Economy of the New Deal on Pine Ridge and Rosebud Reservations.* Tucson: University of Arizona Press.
    2001   *"Deadliest Enemies": Law and the Making of Race Relations on and off Rosebud Reservation.* Berkeley: University of California Press.
Burton, Lloyd
    1991   *American Indian Water Rights and the Limits of Law.* Lawrence: University Press of Kansas.
Canby, William C.
    1998   *American Indian Law in a Nutshell.* 3rd edition. St. Paul, MN: West Group.
Castile, George Pierre
    1992   Indian Sign: Hegemony and Symbolism in Federal Indian Policy. In *State and Reservation: New Perspectives on Federal Indian Policy.* George Pierre Castile and Robert L. Bee, eds. Pp. 165–186. Tucson: University of Arizona Press.
Churchill, Ward, and Winona LaDuke
    1992   Native North America: The Political Economy of Radioactive Colonialism. In *The State of Native America: Genocide, Colonization, and Resistance.* M. Annette Jaimes, ed. Pp. 241–266. Boston: South End Press.
Cohen, Fay G.
    1986   *Treaties on Trial: The Continuing Controversy over Northwest Indian Fishing Rights.* Seattle: University of Washington Press.
Cornell, Stephen, Joseph Kalt, Matthew Krepps, and Jonathan Taylor
    1998   *American Indian Gaming Policy and Its Socio-Economic Effects. A Report to the National Gambling Impact Study Commission.* Cambridge, MA: Economics Resource Group.
Deloria, Vine, Jr.
    1985[1974]   *Behind the Trail of Broken Treaties: An Indian Declaration of Independence.* Austin: University of Texas Press.
    1992   Trouble in High Places: Erosion of American Indian Rights to Religious Freedom in the United States. In *The State of Native America: Genocide, Colonization, and Resistance.* M. Annette Jaimes, ed. Pp. 267–290. Boston: South End Press.
Deloria, Vine, Jr., and Clifford M. Lytle
    1983   *American Indians, American Justice.* Austin: University of Texas Press.
Deloria, Vine, Jr., and David E. Wilkins
    1999   *Tribes, Treaties, and Constitutional Tribulations.* Austin: University of Texas Press.
Division of Tribal Services (Office of Community Services, U.S. Department of Health and Human Services)
    1998   TANF Guidance.
    <http://www.acf.dhhs.gov/programs/dts/trbcht811.htm>
    1999   Tribal TANF Plans.
    <http://www.acf.dhhs.gov/programs/dts/part-a.htm>
Fixico, Donald L.
    1998   *The Invasion of Indian Country in the Twentieth Century: American Capitalism and Tribal Natural Resources.* Niwot: University Press of Colorado.
Frank, Billy, Jr.
    1998   "American Indian Equal Justice Act" is not Equal. *Indian Country Today* April 6–13: A5.

Getches, David H., Charles F. Wilkinson, and Robert A. Williams, Jr.
  1993   *Federal Indian Law: Cases and Materials.* 3rd edition. St. Paul, MN: West Publishing.
Grinde, Donald A., and Bruce E. Johansen
  1995   *Ecocide of Native America: Environmental Destruction of Indian Lands and Peoples.* Santa Fe, NM: Clear Light.
Guerrero, Marianna
  1992   American Indian Water Rights: The Blood of Life in Native North America. In *The State of Native America: Genocide, Colonization, and Resistance.* M. Annette Jaimes, ed. Pp. 189–216. Boston: South End Press.
Indian Country Today
  1998   "Redskins" Trademark Revoked. April 19–26: A1.
  1999   Chant, Chop Bad Medicine for All, and Coalition Attacks Sports Racism. November 15–22: B3.
Institute for Natural Progress
  1992   In Usual and Accustomed Places: Contemporary American Indian Fishing Rights Struggles. In *The State of Native America: Genocide, Colonization, and Resistance.* M. Annette Jaimes, ed. Pp. 217–239. Boston: South End Press.
Johnson, Kim Chandler, and John Terrence Eck
  1995   Eliminating Indian Stereotypes from American Society: Causes and Legal and Societal Solutions. *American Indian Law Review* 20(1):65–107.
Kickingbird, Kirke, Alexander Tallchief Skibine, and Lynn Kickingbird
  1983   *Indian Jurisdiction.* Washington, DC: Institute for the Development of Indian Law.
LaBarre, Weston
  1964   *The Peyote Cult.* Hamden, CT: Shoe String Press.
MacKinnon, Catharine
  1987   Whose Culture? A Case Not on Martinez v. Santa Clara Pueblo. In *Feminism Unmodified: Discourses on Life and Law.* Pp. 63–69. Cambridge, MA: Harvard University Press.
McCool, Daniel
  1994[1987]   *Command of the Waters: Iron Triangles, Federal Water Development, and Indian Water.* Tucson: University of Arizona Press.
National Congress of American Indians
  1997   "Means Testing" Federal Funding for Indian Tribal Governments. <http://www.ncai.org>.
  1998   Testimony on Tribal Government Sovereign Immunity. <http://www.ncai.org>.
  n.d.   Welfare Reform Page. <http://www.ncai.org>.
National Gambling Impact Study Commission
  1999   Final Report. <http://www.ngisc.gov/reports/finrpt.html>.
Newton, Nell J.
  1997   Memory and Misrepresentation: Representing Crazy Horse in Tribal Court. In *Borrowed Power: Essays on Cultural Appropriation.* Bruce Ziff and Pratima V. Rao, eds. Pp. 195–224. New Brunswick, NJ: Rutgers University Press.
Novello, Antonia C.
  1993   Crazy Horse Malt Liquor Beverage: The Public Outcry to Save the Image of a Native American Hero. *South Dakota Law Review* 38(1):14–21.

Pevar, Stephen L.
   1992   *The Rights of Indians and Tribes: The Basic ACLU Guide to Indian Tribal Rights*. 2nd edition. Carbondale: Southern Illinois University Press.
Pommersheim, Frank
   1979   *Broken Ground and Flowing Waters: An Introductory Text with Materials on Rosebud Sioux Tribal Government*. Rosebud, SD: Sinte Gleska College Press.
Richardson, Paul
   1998   Gorton Takes Second Swing to Curb Tribal Sovereignty. *Indian Country Today*, March 23–30: A1.
Ruggie, John G.
   1998   *Constructing the World Polity: Essays on International Institutionalization*. New York: Routledge.
Sider, Gerald
   1993   *Lumbee Indian Histories: Race, Ethnicity, and Indian Identity in the Southern United States*. Cambridge, UK: Cambridge University Press.
Singer, Joseph William
   1996   Publicity Rights and the Conflict of Laws: Tribe Court Jurisdiction in the Crazy Horse Case. *South Dakota Law Review* 41:1–44.
Slotkin, J. S.
   1975   *The Peyote Religion: A Study in Indian–White Relations*. New York: Octagon Books.
Snipp, C. Matthew
   1989   *American Indians: The First of This Land*. New York: Russell Sage Foundation.
   1997   Some Observations about Racial Boundaries and the Experiences of American Indians. *Ethnic and Racial Studies* 20(4):667–689.
Stewart, Omer C.
   1987   *Peyote Religion*. Norman: University of Oklahoma Press.
Swidler, Nina, Kurk E. Dongoske, and Roger Anyon, eds.
   1997   *Native Americans and Archaeologists: Stepping Stones to Common Ground*. Walnut Creek, CA: Altamira Press.
Thornton, Russell
   1998a The Demography of Colonialism and "Old" and "New" Native Americans. In *Studying Native America*. Russell Thornton, ed. Pp. 17–39. Madison: University of Wisconsin Press.
   1998b Who Owns Our Past? The Repatriation of Native American Human Remains and Cultural Objects. In *Studying Native America*. Russell Thornton, ed. Pp. 385–415. Madison: University of Wisconsin Press.
Ulrich, Roberta
   1999   *Empty Nets: Indians, Dams, and the Columbia River*. Corvallis: Oregon State University Press.
Wilkins, David E.
   1997   *American Indian Sovereignty and the U.S. Supreme Court: The Masking of Justice*. Austin: University of Texas Press.

Court cases and unpublished court records

Amended Complaint, *In the Matter of the Estate of Tasunke Witko, a.k.a. Crazy Horse v. Hornell Brewing Co. et al.*, Rosebud Sioux Tribal Court, 1993, Civ. No. 93–204.

Brendale v. Yakima, U.S. Supreme Court, 1989, 109 S.Ct. 2994.

California v. Cabazon Band of Mission Indians, U.S. Supreme Court, 1987, 480 U.S. 202.

Dawavendewa v. Salt River Project, U.S. Court of Appeals for the Ninth Circuit, 1998, 154 F.3d 1117.

Duro v. Reina, U.S. Supreme Court, 1990, 109 L.Ed.2d 693.

Employment Division v. Smith, U.S. Supreme Court, 1990, 110 S.Ct. 1595.

Estate of Tasunke Witko, a.k.a. Crazy Horse v. Hornell Brewing Co. et al., Rosebud Sioux Supreme Court, 1996, unpublished.

Harjo et al. v. Pro-Football, Inc., U.S. Department of Commerce, Patent and Trademark Office, Trademark Trial and Appeal Board, 1998, Paper No. 100, <http://www.uspto.gov/web/offices/com/sol/foia/ttab/2aissues/1999/1999.htm>.

Hornell Brewing Co. v. Rosebud Sioux Tribal Court, U.S. Court of Appeals for the Eighth Circuit, 1998, 133 F.3d 1087.

Lewis v. Allen, U.S. Court of Appeals for the Ninth Circuit, 1998, 94–35979, unpublished.

Montana v. U.S., U.S. Supreme Court, 1981, 450 U.S. 544.

Morton v. Mancari, U.S. Supreme Court, 1974, 417 U.S. 535.

Oliphant v. Suquamish Indian Tribe, U.S. Supreme Court, 1978, 435 U.S. 191.

Regents of the University of California v. Bakke, U.S. Supreme Court, 1978, 438 U.S. 265.

Santa Clara Pueblo v. Martinez, U.S. Supreme Court, 1978, 436 U.S. 49.

Strate v. A-1 Contractors, U.S. Supreme Court, 1997, 117 S.Ct. 1404.

U.S. v. Consolidated Wounded Knee Cases, U.S. Dist. Ct. for the Dist. of Nebraska and South Dakota, 1975, 389 Fed. Supplement 235–245.

Statutes and executive orders

American Indian Religious Freedom Act Amendments of 1994, 108 Stat. 3125.

Civil Rights Act, 1964, 78 Stat. 241.

Government-to-Government Relations with Native American Tribal Governments, Memorandum for the Heads of Executive Departments and Agencies, 1994, 25 U.S.C.A. 450.

Executive Order 13084, 1998, 25 U.A.C.A. 450.

Indian Child Welfare Act, 1978, 92 Stat. 3069.

Indian Civil Rights Act, 1968, 82 Stat. 77.

Indian Self-Determination Act, 1975, 88 Stat. 2203.

Personal Responsibility and Work Opportunity Reconciliation Act, 1996, PL 104–93.

Tribal Self-Governance Demonstration Project Act, 1991, 105 Stat. 1278.

12

The Complex Diversity of Language in the United States

Bonnie Urciuoli

What Does it Mean to Study Linguistic Diversity?

In the United States, people tend to imagine linguistic diversity as a mosaic or quilt. In this linguistic imaginary, each piece is labeled – "Southern," "Brooklynese," "Ebonics," "Bilingualism," and so on – and typified as collections of words and phrases used by certain kinds of people. The words and phrases are imagined as packages that stand out against the linguistic background, the middle-class English standard. This way of imagining language is the organizing principle for two opposing positions: diversity-as-a-wonderful-garden and diversity-as-polluting-and-dangerous. These positions, typified as "liberal" and "conservative," are assumed to represent the spectrum of possible understandings of language. They do not: neither is based on an ethnographically or historically accurate understanding of what language is. But they do share the same fallacy: that languages are *things* which come in neat packages matching ethnic, racial, regional, or national types of people. In this imaginary, the historical and social processes that make diversity dynamic and complex fade from consideration.

This chapter examines three sets of linguistic situations in the United States: those of African Americans, of Spanish-English bilinguals, and of Native Americans. The central questions are: how did these linguistic situations come into being, and what kind of sense does it make to contrast them with a white middle-class "standard"? The popular imaginary, whether "liberal" or "conservative," assumes a fundamental polarity between unmarked (the normative, general case) and marked (special cases, non-normative), whether the marked cases are problems to be solved (diversity as pollution) or objects to be appreciated as exotic and colorful (pun intended – diversity as a garden). Either way, the existence of an unmarked standard is taken for granted as *a collection of words, phrases, "rules," and to some extent sounds.*

For most Americans, such perceptions of language have become common-sense (natural, taken for granted) and, for many, heavily ideologized (through explicit articulation of ideas and positions).[1] Any U.S. resident with access to electronic or print media has heard years' worth of arguments for or against an English Language Amendment, federal funding of bilingual education and, more recently, educational recognition of Ebonics. These dichotomies continually reify language and at the same time reinforce the *moral* position that gives these "debates" such teeth. People cannot leave them alone: they feel compelled to take and defend positions because these are not debates about language so much as they are about being "American." Hence the moral edge.

This chapter is a response to the pervasiveness of these cultural attitudes and discourses. There is a large literature on U.S. linguistic diversity – diversity here meaning "a range of formal systems, situations and practices" and not "different kinds of people speaking different kinds of language." The three areas I focus on are too often reduced to types of people, as if Spanish-English bilinguals or African Americans or Native Americans are three essential types that naturally contrast with the white norm, and that's why they talk the way they do. This is not the case. What brought about linguistic variation is not the *type of person* but the historical and social dynamics that led to the development of certain forms and practices, and that also led to the isolation and naming of a group as if they were a natural set. Furthermore, there is no single clear-cut linguistic thing called *Standard English*. Books of usage define what it is not, not what it is. Nor has any linguist ever defined it. It exists as a powerful cultural idea in the same way *whiteness* exists: in contrast to a system of marked people, situations, and practices.

So there are two distinct issues here: on the one hand, how linguistic diversity (or variation) works and how it came into being; on the other hand, how public discourses formulate and politicize linguistic situations. Anderson (1991) goes a long way to explain how centuries of print capitalism have set up the terms by which nations could imagine themselves as fundamentally homogeneous through use of a common *published* language variety, so that insofar as there is a standard, it exists in print (and not in speech). Anderson does not acknowledge the centrality of racial polarization to national and linguistic definition, yet the establishment of colonial power has heavily involved the lamination, the layering together, of race, region, language, and economics that contrast colonized people and colonizing nation.

One thing Anderson does make clear, however, is the way in which a language, as it represents a nation, is imagined as a set of forms, of words and rules: dictionaries and grammar were key nation-making literature in 19th-century Europe. This imagining of language as a set of *correct* words and rules is central to the U.S. linguistic imaginary, and takes for granted that the defining function of language is reference or, as most public media call it, *communication*.[2] As some decades of work in language and culture have shown, reference cannot be autonomous, as it takes place in situated social action in which other linguistic functions operate.[3] This approach makes it possible for investigators to analyze culture in action. The social functions of language build and clarify the terms of human relations, the personas which people construct and project as they interact, and the meanings attributed to the actions and conditions of social life. Not only is discourse, public or private, a culture-making process, it is also the locus of the construction, re-creation, and emergence of selves as social actors. Among cultural meanings made and remade in discourse are those ascribed to language itself, such as the construction of English in influential public discourses. Media and legislative controversies over assigning some measure of public status to languages or language varieties other than "standard English" (the kind referable to usage handbooks oriented toward a written standard) are about U.S. cultural conceptions of English, of language in general, and of associated concepts like *communication*. In important ways, constructions of English are about whiteness and middle class-ness.

Named groups within a society are also discursive constructions: particular historical and social circumstances have brought about their naming. *Hispanic* or *Latino* became essentialized as a category of person as several conditions converged over time: increased immigration from Spanish-speaking countries to working-class U.S. jobs; identification of those immigrants, especially Mexican and Puerto Rican, as non-white; lamination of racial and linguistic "inferiority"; their shared experience of exclusion from good jobs, schools, neighborhoods, and representation; growing political consolidation; identification of political and social consciousness with the Spanish language; new census categories and their institutional deployment. As this partial account suggests, the emergence of a named group depends on particulars. But having emerged as a group in U.S. society, the named group takes on sociopolitical status as a bounded, reified thing. Hence, for example, the growing circulation of *Hispanic Magazine*. Students defining themselves as *Latino/a* tell me that after a couple of years in a college environment, they do start to think in terms of a generic "Latino culture," though they did not before college. For Latino/a students who speak or identify with Spanish, the association of language, culture, and type of person has become internalized as quite real in a relatively short time. A named group can thus become a social fact through institutional discourses.

In short, diversity as part of the contemporary U.S. imaginary is quite different from diversity as a linguistic concept. The following discussion shows the complex, historically grounded basis of linguistic diversity among African Americans, Spanish-English bilinguals, and American Indians.

African American Language Issues

The linguistic literature on African American linguistic form and practice points up some especially important – and fraught – issues in sociolinguistics: What features define a language variety? How does performance figure into definition of the genre? Who are the most "genuine" speakers? Indeed, is the central issue the features or the speakers? These questions impinge on consideration of any language variety identified with a sharply defined persona. The construction of person through discourse involves the creation of shared meaning, and also the tendency to act and interpret in certain ways based in large part on shared circumstances. Where a population has long shared, or has had forced on it, constrained social conditions, it is particularly likely to develop strong connections between form (how it talks), practice (what it does with it), and identity (how it sees itself), especially when all these things are stereotyped by a larger world that largely excludes it from its social venues. Under these circumstances, those who (usually through class mobility) move away from that world's social focus toward the practices of the larger world may be seen as culturally suspect within the group and approved outside it.[4]

The study of African American language began with the study of form. The first systematic work was done by Lorenzo Dow Turner (1949) on "African survivals"[5] in Gullah, spoken in the coastal area around the border of South Carolina and Georgia. Turner collected most of his data as lists of words that he used to compare meaning and grammatical function of Gullah with West African source languages. Turner's work was an important point of departure in understanding the role of slave creoles in forming the varieties of English now spoken by African Americans, and in seeing it as a coherent variety of English and not merely a congeries of deviant forms and mispronunciations. Expanding this line of approach, William Labov (1974) and his associates massively studied the formal properties and narrative structures of teenage black boys in the Harlem neighborhood of Manhattan. In these and subsequent formal studies (e.g. Wolfram 1969; Dillard 1972; Baugh 1983), we see extensive analyses of regular variable patterns in the phonology and grammar of what Labov called BEV (black English Vernacular), now called AAVE (African American Vernacular English).

For example, AAVE speakers are likely to delete the /t/ or /k/ at the end of a word if it is preceded by /s/, as in *desk* (coming out /dɛs/) or *mist* (coming out /mɪs/). However, if the final /t/ actually indicates the past tense marker -*ed*, this is much less likely to happen: AAVE speakers know, at the level of what Chomsky would call *competence*, that a grammatical formation is involved. Thus, they are much more likely to delete /-t/ at the end of *mist* than of *missed*: the words are phonologically identical but grammatically different, so that, as sociolinguists would put it, speakers' behavior is constrained by grammatical function. Grammatical constraints also govern use of copula *is*, which simply indicates equivalence. AAVE speakers might delete *is* in grammatical situations where English-speakers in general might abbreviate *is* to 's – but not elsewhere. For example: *he's* going or *he* going; *she's* smart or *she* smart. In these grammatical contexts, *is* indicates equivalence and is really semantically redundant. Several languages, Hebrew for example, have no copular *is*. AAVE also has grammatical structures that do not exist elsewhere in English, such as the word *be* used as an aspect marker. *Be* indicates actions that are habitual or customary: he *be* doing that for almost a year; we *be* going there every Tuesday.

Narrative structures also have consistent AAVE patterns. Labov and his associates found that boys in their preteens or early teens used complex narrative forms that indicated group coherence. Boys whom Labov (borrowing from his young informants) termed *lames*, non-participants in peer groups, showed much less use of these narrative devices. In studies like these, Labov and the first generation of sociolinguists were able to rebut the claims of some psychologists and educators that African Americans in general were less intelligent, or that their economic disadvantage resulted not simply in setback in school (which it certainly did) but in a cognitive linguistic deprivation (of which there is no evidence). I might add that the same arguments were made at the same time about working-class bilingual children.

The impact of these contributions has been circumscribed to a degree by assumptions about AAVE as culture-defining. Labov's study treats inner-city teenage boys as its defining speakers, in explicit contrast with the less vernacular *lames* and, as Marcyliena Morgan (1994a:328ff) points out, in implicit contrast with all other African Americans (women, adults, middle-class). The linguistic/cultural romanticism of Labov's early work has consequently shaped much defining work on performance genres, so that young male speech activities came to be seen as the defining practices of black culture (see, for example, Abrahams 1976 or Kochman 1981), while the contributions made by Claudia Mitchell-Kernan's (1971) work on signifying was overshadowed until Henry Gates (1988) picked it up in his own work (Morgan 1994a:335). Morgan also argues that the ironic verbal play called *signifying* takes various forms that play out an African American cultural theme of indirectness; this general principle is lost when signifying is epitomized as boys playing the dozens.

We get a clearer sense of how complex linguistic diversity comes about by looking in depth and long-term at socialization, as Shirley Brice Heath (1983) and Marjorie Harness Goodwin (1990) have done. Heath spent a decade or so in black and white working-class communities in the Carolina Piedmont region, in schools and among families with young children. She found, for example, that while black and white children both learned early about stories and story-telling, stories take on quite different meanings: for white children, stories are imbued with literalness and cause-and-effect linearity; for black children, the point to stories is their imaginative and artistic effect. Heath also shows how these contrastive uses of stories are continuous with the way adult relations work, but may pose problems for both black and white working-class children in school, in contrast to middle-class children. Goodwin extensively examines the way arguments work among young working-class African American girls in Philadelphia. Goodwin shows how girls interdependently work out notions of information, truth, and authority, and their sense of themselves as female and black. These studies examine language as social action in ways that go beyond the formalism of much of the sociolinguistic literature: they link form to function in ways that make quite clear the interdependent nexus of the variety itself, the meaning and development of relationships, and the growth of intertwined indentities: age, gender, race, region, class.

Such studies show that a language variety comes to mean what it does, not merely because a person bears a certain label, black or any other, but because of the way that identity operates in specific situations. This also means that one might grow up black and not learn to use language in these ways or even to use AAVE much at all. Does that make one less black? And what of the fact that African Americans sensitive to markers of class mobility do become sensitive to what the forms of AAVE mean to the mostly white middle class. This issue is skirted by most studies of black language issues, as Marcyliena Morgan (1994b) shows in her examination of the complex responses of parents to the 1977 Ann Arbor legal ruling that AAVE be recognized by the School District as a viable language of its students. There is no easy way to specify a bounded community of AAVE speakers, particularly since there is a great deal of variability (not everyone has the same degree, or combinations, of patterning) and a great many speakers codeswitch between what they speak with family, friends, and familiars and what they speak in a middle-class white-dominated school or workplace. This is exacerbated by the problem of defining any contrastive "white speech community." Many works, for convenience's sake, contrast AAVE and AE ("American English") as if there were a generic white standard, but most white Americans do not speak some generic AE. They speak a range of class, regional, and ethnic variants, particularly if discourse and performance style are included. After many decades of research on how African Americans speak, our categories of speakers remain simplistically black-as-marked and white-as-unmarked/normative, which has always been the basis of race ideology in the United States.

Bilingualism in the United States: Ethnographic Cases

Many of the same problems underlie analyses of bilingualism, though, interestingly, not the first (and still among the best) major work on U.S. bilingualism, Haugen's (1969 [1953]) study of Norwegian in the Midwest. Drawing on extensive field recordings done in the 1930s–1940s, and on his own native expertise, Haugen took little for granted ethnographically or theoretically. He specified where people came from in Norway, what their original dialects were like, the contexts they encountered in their personal and commercial lives (many were farmers), what Norwegian language institutions they sustained, from whom they learned Norwegian and English, their borrowing and codeswitching. What emerges from his study is not an essentialized group ("the Norwegians") but a living population in transition. He repeatedly makes the point that the bilingualism experienced by these families was no simple juxtaposition of "English" and "Norwegian": using names of languages as reference points does not allow analysts to assume they are discrete entities.

The bulk of work done on bilingualism in the United States has been on Spanish and English, mostly published as articles or overviews with relatively few full-length ethnographies. Much attention has been focused on formal characteristics such as phonological and grammatical variability, and syntactic constraints on codeswitching. But as with the formal work on AAVE, this raises the issue of how language forms themselves may be linked to identity. This question is pointless without long-term and/or in-depth accounts of linguistic socialization.

Zentella (1997) provides a long-term, close-up, and finely textured study of New York working-class Puerto Rican Spanish-English bilingualism that, again, allows us to see the ongoing synergy of age, gender, class, location, race, language, generation, and place of origin. Instead of overgeneralizing "language" and "identity," she raises specific questions about particular roles and contexts, and particular dimensions of language use. Take a young mother two or three generations removed from Puerto Rico. She is part of a women's network in which verb categories – tense, mood, and aspect – carry particular pragmatic weight. Her capacity to deploy, for example, the Spanish subjunctive is limited compared to, say, her mother's. She deploys what verb categories she can in Spanish but the discourse resources she has at her disposal are somewhat limited. This does not take her out of the network but it does mark a point of attenuation in the range of discourse strategies through which she might develop her cultural persona. It indicates a cultural shift in that being a Puerto Rican woman in New York plays out differently in 2000 compared to 1980, 1960, or 1940. Does this make each succeeding generation "less Puerto Rican"? Does that question really mean anything?

I raise this because the attenuation of grammatical elements of Spanish, especially verb systems, among succeeding generations of bilinguals has become a thorny issue among sociolinguists. Klein (1980), Silva-Corvalán (1994), and Zentella (1997) present clear evidence of shifts; Pousada and Poplack (1979) and Torres (1997) argue the opposite. For some analysts, recognizing the existence of such shifts is tantamount to saying that bilinguals are "losing their culture." The problem here is this amorphous and somewhat essentialized notion of culture. If specific roles in specific networks have been customarily enacted by deploying specific grammatical-discursive strategies, and if people in succeeding generations have less capacity to do so, then yes, something goes away. The only way it is not going to go away is to preserve those discourse conditions. Are those discursive conditions an essential element of culture? Does "preserving culture" mean treating the structures of everyday life as museum objects? Is this even possible? I leave these as open questions because I believe they have no easy answers.

Equating linguistic forms with "culture" masks pragmatic[6] dimensions of bilingual experience. The informative literature on the pragmatics of codeswitching includes, in addition to Zentella's work, studies by Gumperz and Hernández-Chávez (1978), Garcia (1981), Huerta-Macías (1981), Valdés (1981), Lavandera (1981), and others. Cumulatively, these works connect the functional deployment of English and Spanish to the everyday playing out of identity in specific times, places, and roles. Americo Paredes' (1977) critique of the Texas–Mexican "border" ethnography done by hyperliteral Anglo investigators in the 1950s raises a critical and often overlooked aspect of cultural pragmatics: the uses of irony. The playful and satiric turn in everyday language is at least as culture-forming as the use of Spanish itself. I found in my work among working-class Puerto Rican New Yorkers (Urciuoli 1996) that spirited teasing and playfulness is central to family interaction, in Spanish, English, or both, and thus central to the development of a cultural self.

Another critical dimension of cultural formation is class, how people's lives are shaped relative to labor markets and resources, how they came to be where they are and live as they do. The Centro de Estudios Puertorriqueños study (Language Policy Task Force 1982) is located in the working-class networks of a block of East Harlem, as is that of Zentella, in much the same site. The Centro study makes the point that assumptions about "normal" language are about print-oriented, discrete, testable entities, and that bilingual and codeswitching competences are embedded in generational roles and life-cycle structures. Community values toward language revolve around respect and accommodation, making home and family the crucial locus for Spanish. These values are turned invisible by the normative structures shaping the external limits of people's lives, as Walsh (1991) shows in her study of bilingual education in the Boston public schools. My New York ethnography contrasts bilinguals' experiences of Spanish and English in the safe linguistic sphere of neighborhood, home, and family with the risky sphere of middle-class authority (work) and public bureaucracy (schools, public agencies), which bilinguals typify as "white." Correctness and acceptability issues arise in the risky environments, where Spanish has no public place and where their English is seen as marked.

One could combine and compare Haugen's *Norwegian Language in America* with Zentella's *Growing Up Bilingual* as a teaching module to examine the complexity of bilingualism as a lived process. Each is an extensive treatment of a bilingual situation with which the author had native expertise: Norwegian families on towns and farms in Wisconsin and Iowa during the 1930s and 1940s; Puerto Rican families in Manhattan's East Harlem in the 1970s and 1980s. Each is contextualized historically and economically, and based on long-term research. Neither treats the languages involved as undifferentiated wholes with simple boundaries; both locate the particular variants spoken by the people in their studies. Most of all, both highlight borrowing and codeswitching as processes emerging from the conditions of discourse. Haugen coined the term *linguistic ecology* for this kind of treatment; Zentella describes her approach as *anthropolitical* in that it treats language as a set of practices equally sociocultural and political. One could easily select relevant portions to provoke discussion and raise questions. For example: How did the authors set up their data collection and relate collection methods to the goals of their studies? Under what conditions did these communities form, and how can one find traces of those conditions in people's linguistic behavior? How are economic structures reflected in language? How did the conditions of community formation affect the ways in which its residents learned English? How did "official" situations of English use contrast with the ways people used it with friends and family? How did people transmit their native language, and how did that attenuate with succeeding generations? What roles were played by community institutions, and were those the same for both groups? What sorts of linguistic prejudice did each community face? How and why do both authors treat borrowing and codeswitching as normal linguistic processes?

American Indian Language Issues

Public perceptions of American Indian languages are marked by much the same dichotomy as Spanish-English bilingualism and AAVE. The diversity-as-a-garden position tends to romanticize the language of each group, to see them as folkloric and to equate them with "real" culture; this is especially the case with Native American languages. The diversity-as-pollution position was more vocal in the past than now on Indian languages, but the position then was about the same as that currently expressed on AAVE (more recently called *Ebonics* in the press) and any bilingualism, particularly Spanish-English: disruptive, invasive, a barrier to communication. In all three cases, the romanticized essentialism turns up in some academic work as well.

Since the work of Sapir and Whorf, studies of Native American languages have been seen as the classic locus of the language/culture intersection. While that intersection has often been egregiously romanticized and Whorf's and Sapir's ideas about linguistic relativity often have been badly represented and explained, their basic point is not hard to grasp: grammatical structures set up certain options and limits for classifying and labeling relations and concepts, most strikingly when least tangibly, as with notions of time or causation. For example: time has no built-in shape, so the only shape it can have is that built into it through a coding system such as language's verb system (tense or aspect), or adverbs, or nouns. Concrete representations of time in clocks and calendars flow out of that grammatical coding. Facile and uninformed interpretation of these ideas seems to accompany the reified and essentialized conflation of "language" and "culture." In fact, the grammatical principle is only one point of the intersection of language and culture; one must also consider the pragmatics of community participation and the construction of person through discourse. "Culture" is no simple, bounded thing but a process through which people make sense of the world, organizing their sense-making around their core symbols. The result may or may not correspond with what Westerners classify as discrete ethnic identities that ideally map onto nation. But cultural construction does seem to be about defining contrasts and clarifying what makes an "us."

This principle is especially evident in studies of codeswitching and performance, as Keith Basso and Paul Kroskrity show. Basso's work on Arizona Western Apache (1979, 1990) highlights just these points, as he details the workings of the communicative actions through which Apache continually remake themselves: the naming of place, the use of silence, the moral metaphor, the satiric portraiture of whites. Basso locates these actions in relationships and connects semantic and grammatical structure to pragmatic function, and cultural classifications of person, nature, and moral value. Kroskrity's (1993) study of Arizona Tewa compares Tewa-Hopi and Tewa-English codeswitching. When Tewa switch to Hopi, they tend to do so in taken-for-granted ways, because Hopi are part of their social scene. So Hopi can figure into Tewa performance in, say, ceremonial songs, showing that Tewa see their identity in complex ways, sharing much with Hopi. Switching to English, however, does establish sharp borders. It is far more marked, highlighting the white person as intruder, much like the Apache described by Basso.

As with AAVE and Spanish-English bilingualism, the ways in which Native American linguistic practices have become marked have been exaggrated by school policies and procedures. The boarding schools of earlier decades prohibited the use of native languages as disruptive and dangerous, a linguistic ideology echoed in the logic of the English-only movement, though the latter cannot have the same degree of impact on people's lives. Such linguistic ideologies fetishize English almost as a talisman against disorder. But as William Leap's (1993) study of Indian English shows, English can and does pick up formal and pragmatic properties that turn it into a distinct variety suitable for in-group use.[7] Leap shows that what marks English as Anglo (that is, non-Indian) is not only its formal structure per se but the imposition of discourse rules of official and bureaucratic settings; he contrasts these with the in-group uses of Indian English that developed over time, starting with boarding school students. Susan Philips' (1983) Warm Springs Reservation (Oregon) ethnography focuses on the interactive structures in which formal varieties are used. She shows children learning to interact in ways that make cultural sense to them. These cooperative participant structures are an integral part of the communicative events that define Warm Springs society but do not work in white schools, to the disadvantage of Indian children.

An especially underappreciated form of language is Sign, which linguists have only acknowledged as language in recent decades. Brenda Farnell's (1995) study of Plains Sign Talk contextualizes it historically and socioculturally. She shows how Sign Talk can locate the signer in time and space and can provide a cultural orientation that Assiniboine (let alone English) does not provide. She also argues that sign and speech form a continuous semiotic repertoire, but because Sign has, until recently, been dismissed as "just gesture," this dimension of communication has been ignored.

Useful parallels can be drawn between black–white and Indian–white socialization issues, by comparing Philips' *The Invisible Culture* with Heath's *Ways with Words*. Both works describe structures of communicative socialization in home and classroom. Heath's study, which is quite long, contains a great deal more transcription and description of specific interactions than Philips'. Both deal with the socialization of children who are non-white and "below" middle-class. Both deal with the construction of identity in the structures and processes of discourse, and with the ways in which culture-specific notions of person are part of that identity. The following questions might be raised. What participant structures (to use Philips' term) emerge from each ethnographic situation? How does each author link children's participation structures to their respective societies' notions of culturally appropriate personhood? In what ways are the structures of interaction that come naturally to these children seen as "deviant" or at least disvalued by the schools? Why is it necessary (as Heath shows) to link formal knowledge of language to these participant structures? (One could use language examples from Leap to supplement Philips.) How do children learn to "know" things in ways that contrast with what middle-class white people might take for granted as "knowing," or "facts," or "truth." How do these different ideas of knowledge or truth connect to other values in people's lives?

Mapping Race onto Language

Thus far, we have seen a sociolinguistic overview of these three linguistic situations. We should also consider how they came into being, what they have in common, how they came to be foregrounded against the unmarked "standard," and why Americans conceptualize the standard as they do.

There is insufficient room here to review in depth the geneses of these situations but they share a critical feature. Each resulted from a massive appropriation and displacement of resources and people, which became the source of racialization and, in turn, of linguistic markedness for each group. The displacement of African Americans through slavery, and of American Indians through land appropriation is more obviously catastrophic than the displacement of Mexicans, Puerto Ricans, and other Latin American people through labor migration. The point often missed regarding Latin American labor exploitation is that it followed from relations with the United States so exploitative that even if not explicitly colonial (as with Puerto Rico), they were virtually so (as with Mexico and Central America). Colonization, appropriation of labor and resources, and displacement of people have been the matrix of racial formation throughout U.S. history and, in turn, of linguistic markedness.[8]

The essentializing of these three situations turns on the elision of history. What gets typified as "their culture" is in part a historical effect but the role played by displacement and exclusion is romanticized as a *personal* story or elided entirely. The "diversity-as-a-garden" approach gives lip service to exclusion, but focuses on representations of types of people and their experience. The structural, if it appears at all, becomes the stage setting instead of the analytic focus. The "diversity-as-pollution" approach elides history because it works from the ideological perspective that whatever happened before one's lifetime should not count: people need to get over it and pull themselves up by their bootstraps. Either way, the focus is on the *individual* as if that one little unit were the ultimate reality. Moreover, both take for granted their own class privilege, which is in part how both take for granted the idea of an unmarked standard English.

The construction, ideologizing, and fetishizing of the print standard is characteristic of most modern nation states, but the U.S. situation does have its own particular cultural resonances. Michael Silverstein (1987) describes the ideology underlying the U.S. English "monoglot standard" as the assumed existence of an ideal English that any American should be able to achieve, given sufficient initiative and willingness to be educated. It can also be commodified, as indicated by the brisk business in "accent reduction" courses. This construction of language operates within a political economy of language (see Gal 1989; Irvine 1989). The political element is played out (among other ways) as opposition to bilingual education and as support for Official English legislation. Foreign languages, especially Spanish, in public spheres are characterized as invasive, part of an agenda, usually a "Hispanic agenda." Linguistic purity is equated with clear communication, free of "impurities" like "accents" or "bad grammar" (implicit signs of race/class inferiority). Individuals should be able to control such impediments to clarity in their quest for progress and class mobility through education. Model communicators are nearly all business or political "leaders," to use an educational buzz word.

These linguistic visions of American English, espoused by public voices as obvious, natural, and commonsense (and hegemonic in Williams', 1977, sense of internalized power relations), assume that this ideal American individual is motivated by self-improvement and possesses full self-control. Institutionalized race and class relations fade from accountability. Rosina Lippi-Green (1997) examines key institutions through which English standardization is naturalized and maintained: in education, news media, films, courts, and the workplace. She details the actions through which specific dimensions of correctness are formulated, mapped onto region, class, race, and accent, and compared to the ideologized print standard. She also covers timely issues of AAVE and Hawaiian Creole English.

In effect, race has been remapped from biology onto language in key ways: in the idea of inherently superior or inferior varieties; in the way that intellectual traits are "naturally" attributed to those varieties; in the way that, for example, Spanish is seen as "invasive." All these elements had a place in the biologized construction of race. What is different about their relocation in language is that, supposedly, people can and should control their language (whereas no one was expected to control biological race). If people cede control over language, it is considered acceptable for them to take the economic consequences, as in the case described by Lippi-Green of the Hawaiian Creole English accented weathercaster who lost his accent discrimination suit against a Hawaiian radio station.

The mapping of race onto language also drives the English Language Amendment (ELA) movement. Race ideology emphasized the importance of compartmentalization, lest the inferior contaminate the superior. The same ideology appears in what Zentella (1988) describes as the zero-sum logic of ELA supporters: that English is necessarily undermined by the public recognition of any other language.[9] The ironic reverse of this purism is laid out by Jane Hill (1993). Hill examines mock-Spanish used by restaurateurs, greeting-card manufacturers, and developers (particularly in the Southwest) and points out a much-overlooked inversion. While many Anglos habitually criticize what they see as the inadequate or "broken" English of people whose first language is Spanish, it is quite acceptable for Anglos to market bits of Spanish with little regard for grammatical coherence in street or development names ("Rancho Vista") or humorous tags on greeting cards (the dog in the Santa Claus hat bearing the caption "Fleas Navidad") or in menu items or on television ("No problemo"). Bits of Spanish are tossed together, or with English, as if they were junk jewelry from a garage sale, regardless of such niceties as adjective–noun agreement. They are decoration meant for an audience of other Anglos – the same Anglos who might wax indignant over a Mexican-accented speaker codeswitching Spanish and English in public. No other language in the United States is currently accorded quite this same treatment. Linguistic purism is about keeping English safe from Spanish, not vice versa. There is an implicit, naturalized conflation of language and person, of assumptions about "the kind of person" who speaks that language. This long-standing characteristic of racialized joking effectively recreates hierarchic terms, while hiding behind the rubric: "It's only meant to be funny."

Conclusion

Language variation on the ground may be examined as a set of formal features, but its anthropological salience lies in the ways in which difference in form or discourse structure figure into interpretation and identity. That relationship is not a simple matter of form and culture trait; it is an ongoing process of meaning-making. Nor does the result add up to a static mosaic in which linguistic type matches culture matches person. There are no simple boundaries.

Boundary-making and the creation of linguistic mosaics are, however, central to the U.S. ideology that there is one, single standard English. This ideology is deeply persistent because it is not only about language, it is equally about race, class, nation, and person.

NOTES

1 *Linguistic ideology* here refers broadly to cultural belief systems about language: how language is, how it works, what it should be. Woolard and Schieffelin (1994) offer a thorough overview of anthropological approaches to this complex notion.
2 Judging from print and television, the idea of communication as the transmission of information is central to the U.S. linguistic imaginary.
3 The classic statement is by Hymes (1974), after Jakobson (1960); see also Gumperz (1982), Silverstein (1976), and many more.
4 I draw here on Bourdieu's (1991) notions of habitus and field, and on notions of primary and secondary socialization, including linguistic socialization, developed by Berger and Luckmann (1967).
5 The "African survival" was a notion developed by the anthropologist Melville Herskovits, with whom Turner studied.
6 Pragmatics refers to the social use of language: the social interpretation of what people say, the rules for appropriate use, the effect a usage has on a situation.
7 Zentella (1997) and Urciuoli (1996) make the same point about the English of Puerto Rican bilinguals in New York.
8 Urciuoli (1996), chapters 1 and 2, reviews this literature.
9 See also Woolard (1989) for an outline of the rhetorical processes constituting the English-only debate; Adams and Brink (1990) for a further selection of analytic essays; and Crawford (1992) for a survey of ELA-related selections from historical, media and political sources.

REFERENCES CITED

Abrahams, Roger
   1976 *Talking Black*. Rowley, MA: Newbury House.
Adams K. L., and D. T. Brink, eds.
   1990 *Perspectives on Official English: The Campaign for English as the Official Language in the USA*. Berlin: Mouton de Gruyter.
Anderson, Benedict
   1991 *Imagined Communities*. London: Verso.
Basso, Keith
   1979 *Portraits of the Whiteman*. New York: Cambridge University Press.
   1990 *Western Apache Language and Culture: Essays in Linguistic Anthropology*. Tucson: University of Arizona Press.
Baugh, John
   1983 *Black Street Speech: Its History, Structure and Survival*. Austin: University of Texas Press.
Berger, Peter, and Thomas Luckmann
   1967 *The Social Construction of Reality*. Garden City, NY: Doubleday.
Bourdieu, Pierre
   1991 *Language and Symbolic Power*. Cambridge, MA: Harvard University Press.

Crawford, James
1992   *Language Loyalties: A Source Book on the Official English Controversy.*
Chicago: University of Chicago Press.
Dillard, J. L.
1972   *Black English.* New York: Random House.
Duran, Richard, ed.
1981   *Latino Language and Communicative Behavior.* Norwood, NJ: Ablex.
Farnell, Brenda
1995   *Do You See What I Mean? Plains Indian Sign Talk and the Embodiment of
Action.* Austin: University of Texas Press.
Gal, Susan
1989   Language   and   Political   Economy.   *Annual   Review   of   Anthropology*
18:345–367.
Garcia, Maryellen
1981   Interaction at a Mexican-American Family Gathering. In Duran, pp. 195–216.
Gates, Henry L.
1988   *The Signifying Monkey: A Theory of African-American Literary Criticism.*
Oxford: Oxford University Press.
Goodwin, Marjorie Harness
1990   *He-Said-She-Said: Talk as Social Organization among Black Children.* Bloom-
ington: Indiana University Press.
Gumperz, John
1982   *Discourse Strategies.* Cambridge, UK: Cambridge University Press.
Gumperz, John, and Eduardo Hernández-Chávez
1978   Bilingualism, Bidialectalism and Classroom Interaction. In *A Pluralistic
Nation.* Margaret Lourie and Nancy Faires Conklin, eds. Pp. 275–293. Rowley,
MA: Newbury House.
Haugen, Einar
1969 [1953]   *The Norwegian Language in America.* Bloomington: Indiana Univer-
sity Press.
Heath, Shirley Brice
1983   *Ways with Words.* Cambridge, UK: Cambridge University Press.
Hill, Jane
1993   Hasta La Vista, Baby: Anglo Spanish in the American Southwest. *Critique of
Anthropology* 13(2):145–176.
Huerta-Macías, Ana
1981   Code-Switching: All in the Family. In Duran, pp. 153–168.
Hymes, Dell
1974   *Foundations in Sociolinguistics.* Philadelphia: University of Pennsylvania Press.
Irvine, Judith
1989   When Talk Isn't Cheap: Language and Political Economy. *American Ethnologist* 16:248–267.
Jakobson, Roman
1960   Linguistics and Poetics. In *Style in Language.* Thomas Sebeok, ed. Pp.
350–377. Cambridge, MA: MIT Press.
Klein, Flora
1980   A Quantitative Study of Syntactic and Pragmatic Indications of Change in
the Spanish of Bilinguals in the U.S. In *Locating Language in Time and Space.*
W. Labov, ed. Pp. 69–82. New York: Academic Press.
Kochman, Thomas
1981   *Black and White Styles in Conflict.* Chicago: University of Chicago Press.

Kroskrity, Paul
  1993   *Language, History and Identity: Ethnolinguistic Studies of the Arizona Tewa.*
  Tucson: University of Arizona Press.
Labov, William
  1974   *Language in the Inner City.* Philadelphia: University of Pennsylvania Press.
Language Policy Task Force, Center for Puerto Rican Studies
  1982   Intergenerational Perspectives on Bilingualism: From Community to Class-
  room. Investigators: John Attinasi, Pedro Pedraza, Shana Poplack, Alicia Pousada.
  CPR. Hunter College, City University of New York.
Lavandera, Beatriz
  1981   Lo Quebramos but Only in Performance. *In* Duran, pp. 49–66.
Leap, Willlam
  1993   *American Indian English.* Salt Lake City: University of Utah Press.
Lippi-Green, Rosina
  1997   *English with an Accent: Language, Ideology and Discrimination in the United
  States.* London: Routledge.
Mitchell-Kernan, Claudia
  1971   Language Behavior in a Black Urban Community. Monograph No. 2 of the
  Language Behavior Research Laboratory. Berkeley: University of California.
Morgan, Marcyliena
  1994a   Theories and Politics in African American English. *Annual Review of Anthro-
  pology* 23:325–345.
  1994b   The African-American Speech Community: Reality and Sociolinguists.
  In *Language and the Social Construction of Identity in Creole Situations.*
  Marcyliena Morgan, ed. Pp. 121–150. Los Angeles: Center for Afro-American
  Studies, UCLA.
Paredes, Americo
  1977   On Ethnographic Work among Minority Groups: A Folklorist's Perspective.
  New Scholar 6:1–32.
Philips, Susan U.
  1983   *The Invisible Culture: Communication in Classroom and Community on the
  Warm Springs Indian Reservation.* New York: Longman.
Pousada, Alicia, and Shana Poplack
  1979   No Case for Convergence: The Puerto Rican Spanish Verb System in a
  Language Contact Situation. Working Paper No. 5. New York: Center for Puerto
  Rican Studies Language Policy Task Force, Hunter College, City University of New
  York.
Silva-Corvalán, Carmen
  1994   *Language Contact and Change: Spanish in Los Angeles.* Oxford: Oxford Uni-
  versity Press.
Silverstein, Michael
  1976   Shifters, Linguistic Categories and Cultural Description. In *Meaning in
  Anthropology.* Keith Basso and Henry Selby, eds. Pp. 11–55. Albuquerque: Uni-
  versity of New Mexico Press.
  1987   Monoglot "Standard" in America. Working Papers and Proceedings of the
  Center for Psychosocial Studies No. 13. Chicago: Center for Psychosocial Studies.
Torres, Lourdes
  1997   *Puerto Rican Discourse: A Sociolinguistic Study.* Hillside, NJ: Lawrence
  Erlbaum.
Turner, Lorenzo Dow
  1949   *Africanism in the Gullah Dialect.* Chicago: University of Chicago Press.

Urciuoli, Bonnie
    1996   *Exposing Prejudice: Puerto Rican Experiences of Language, Race and Class.*
    Boulder, CO: Westview Press.
Valdés, Guadalupe
    1981   Codeswitching as Deliberate Verbal Strategy. In Duran, pp. 95–108.
Walsh, Catherine
    1991   *Pedagogy and the Struggle for Voice: Issues of Language, Power and School-ing for Puerto Ricans.* New York: Bergin and Garvey.
Williams, Raymond
    1977   *Marxism and Literature.* Oxford: Oxford University Press.
Wolfram, Walt
    1969   *A Sociolinguistic Description of Detroit Negro Speech.* Washington, DC:
    Center for Applied Linguistics.
Woolard, Kathryn
    1989   Sentences in the Language Prison: The Rhetorical Structuring of an American
    Language Policy Debate. *American Ethnologist* 16:268–278.
Woolard, Kathryn, and Bambi B. Schieffelin
    1994   Language Ideology. *Annual Review of Anthropology* 23:55–82.
Zentella, Ana Celia
    1988   Language Politics in the U.S.A.: The English-Only Movement. In *Literature,
    Language and Politics.* B. J. Craige, ed. Pp. 39–53. Athens: University of Georgia
    Press.
    1997   *Growing up Bilingual.* Oxford and New York: Blackwell.

13

Labor Struggles: Gender, Ethnicity, and the New Migration

June Nash

Cultural diversity has been a corollary of migration and conquest throughout human history. From the time when Herodotus wrote the history of the Greco-Persian wars (late fifth ceutury B.C.E.) to the European expansion into the Western Hemisphere in the 15th century, cultural diversity brought about by wars and migrations was structured in racial and ethnic hierarchies that ensured dominance by the conquerors. By studying the movements of populations in the migrant labor streams, we can grasp the multitudinous ways in which ethnic, racial, and gendered groups entered into and transformed society as workers found their niche in the organization of production.

I shall address the major changes in migration streams in the United States, briefly reviewing the work settings that migrants confronted during the 19th and 20th centuries. Contrasts in the ways in which a diverse labor force accommodates to changes in the organization of production provide the key to ideological premises of racism, sexism, and ethnic prejudice. These enter into managerial control strategies as well as workers' attempts to limit competition in the labor pool. In the labor conflicts that emerge in work sites, the new migrants introduce the major transformations in the work process as they attempt to overcome their disadvantages as discriminated-against members of the workforce. The resources that migrants bring with them provide the basis for creative responses to a changing industrial scene. Reacting to the new forms of labor organization, manager/owners devised technological innovations to regain their control over the work process.

This chapter includes two case studies drawn from ethnographic fieldwork. The first is based on the study of a declining industrial city in New England where migration streams in the 19th and early 20th centuries provided the basis first for the textile industry, and then for the electrical manufacturing industry. Industry-wide unions supplanted the craft unions developed by earlier streams of migrants from western Europe and Great Britain. These were developed in the struggles of the new immigrants from eastern Europe and southern Italy who arrived in the late 19th and early 20th centuries. The second case study is based on thc post–World War II migrations of Latinos as they were trying to defend their position in the underground shops and service sector of New York City. In the Latino centers developed by religious and civic groups, they were learning their rights as workers at the same time as they were expanding the role of trade unions in organizing a sector of labor that most unions ignored.

Migration Waves

Migrations into the Western Hemisphere were often promoted by policies of ethnic, class, and religious "cleansing" in the home sites. The Spaniards forced Jews and Moors out of Spain, with some of them finding their way to the Americas. Disinherited sons in families whose property was organized by primogeniture, or sons born out of wedlock, often provided leadership in the conquest of New Spain and the American colonies. Religious minorities, convicts, indentured servants, and the poor made up the bulk of English migration. African migration forced by the slave trade, and Asian contract laborers increased the available workforce when indigenous populations either withdrew into "retreat zones" or were decimated by diseases introduced by the colonizers.

This diversity in populations migrating to the Western Hemisphere created the basis for a pluricultural colonial society where the newcomers collided with indigenous populations. When they could not be subordinated to European rule, the conquerors often decimated their numbers with genocidal and ethnocidal policies. During the colonial period in New Spain, miscegenation intensified social stratification with an ethnic layering superimposed on class and wealth layering. Cultural practices reinforced ever-finer distinctions among ethnic groups as colonial society recognized racial mixtures up to octoroons (Mörner 1967) and imposed legal restrictions on the mating and occupational practices of each segregated group. In the British colonies migrations tended to displace indigenous populations, pushing them ever farther west. Following independence from Great Britain, treaties established the boundaries of autonomous Indian nations that were constantly trespassed as settlers moved westward. The process of "pacification" culminated in genocidal confrontations following the American Civil War. Though fewer formal restrictions on the marriage and occupational opportunities of distinct populations were imposed in the new nations of the hemisphere after independence, race, ethnicity, and gender continue to constrict custom and practice in work and society.

The east-to-west movement propelled by earlier migrations from the 15th to the 19th centuries was overtaken and soon exceeded by a south-to-north movement in the 20th century. Differential wages promoted migrations from the south to the United States seasonally and for longer durations as laborers found employment in agroindustry, services, and factories. Since the 1960s migration flows increased as a result of repressive governments, sometimes put in place by the United States government.

In this chapter, I will discuss the cultural diversity promoted by three migratory waves that responded to changing labor needs in the United States economy following Independence. The first wave of migrants to arrive after Independence in the late 18th and early 19th centuries reflected the ethnic makeup of the colonizers, with English and Germans predominating. They found easy access to land and professions in an expansive agricultural economy. With the influx of poorer refugees from Ireland and Germany, driven from rural areas by the potato blight in the mid-19th century, migrants faced greater restrictions on their mobility. A second wave of almost 3 million immigrants that arrived between 1880 and 1895 included new streams of East Europeans and Italians, along with a continuation of migrants from Great Britain, Germany, and the Scandinavian countries (Montgomery 1987, 1993). Forced out of rural communities in their countries of origin, they were recruited into work on the railroads, in the mines, and in the burgeoning factories. By the early decades of the 20th century, a south-to-north movement began to overtake and, by mid-century, to exceed the east–west movement. In this current migration wave Mexican labor responds to the needs of agribusiness in the Southwest and the steel mills of the Midwest, while Caribbeans enter through the eastern circuits to work in southern agriculture and the urban sweatshops of northern cities. Their presence in the United States results from the restructuring of the world economy in relation to the flexible accumulation of capital after the 1960s (Lamphere 1992, 1994). Women migrate independently as well as in family units, and they find easier entry into underground employment as domestics and assembly line operators than men. These migrants from the Caribbean, Mexico, and South America are providing the energy for a revitalized labor union that responds to minority and women workers.

I shall argue that in each of these moments in the economic transformations of the economy, the new migrant labor force provided the energy for redirecting labor organization. The first wave organized craft unions that responded to small shops with a segmented labor force. When the second great wave of migrants, classified principally as laborers, arrived in the latter part of the 19th century, the consolidation of large factories with an advanced division of labor mitigated worker control over production. This immigrant labor force turned to the International Workers of the World (IWW) that was the precursor of industry-wide organization with nation-wide unions, uniting a wide diversity of labor. The third wave of migrants is now organizing sectors of the work force that were ignored or denigrated by the industrial labor unions formed in the 1930s. These are the agricultural workers, service and clerical workers, as well as employees of small marginalized firms, that include higher proportions of the recent migrants.

My argument will be based on cultural histories and ethnographic studies that show how these culturally distinct streams enter into and revitalize labor organization in ways that were critical for the emergent class structures in the United States. I will also rely on my own fieldwork in a declining industrial city of New England during the 1980s (Nash 1989) and in New York City's garment and retail trade in the 1990s (Nash 1998) to support conjectures regarding ethnic, racial, and gender differences in mobilizing collective action.

Unions and the Structuring of Corporate Industries

The Irish and German farmers and artisans who arrived in the early 19th century soon found a place in mainstream society. Liberal suffrage policies granted to the immigrants enabled them to use their voting power (Montgomery 1993).

The mutual benefit associations these early migrants formed in the first half of the century enabled their leaders, who shared the middle-class goals of established citizens, to develop them into banking, building and loan, and insurance enterprises. Handlin (1959:19) found the correlate of this direction to be antithetical to the organization of unions. Farmers driven from these same countries by the potato famine of the mid-19th century followed them. Lacking the skills and resources of their predecessors, their ethnic sodalities were defensive measures to evade mounting attacks on them as "lazy vagabonds" and to protect their position against new migrants in the mines and lumber mills to which they gravitated (Montgomery 1993:21ff). The Irish were stigmatized both as an impoverished underclass and as a religious minority. They became the prizefighters, loggers, and miners, and when they entered business they became the restaurateurs and pub owners serving the needs of their compatriots.

Manufacturing enterprises thrived after 1870, quadrupling in the next half century in New York City. Labor recruiters added new sources of migration to the continuing streams of migrants from the British Isles and Germany. These were chiefly rural peasants from Scandinavia, East European Jews, and Italians, Greeks, Romanians, and Poles. These workers, recruited directly from rural areas by labor agents at the turn of the century, found an uneasy place in New England factories. Lacking skills and trades, they moved into urban textile and garment industries as unskilled or semiskilled hands (Handlin 1959:23–24). Diversity was particularly marked in the gateway city of New York which had, according to the editor of *Building the City*, "the largest and most varied agglomeration of mankind" (cited in Handlin 1959:38). David Montgomery (1993:174) captures the dynamism of this new labor force:

> So great were the roles of the newcomers as laborers in mills and factories, as hewers and haulers in mines, as diggers of tunnels and layers of tracks, as stitchers in the burgeoning clothing industry, and as operatives in the expanding textile mills that supplied that industry's cloth, as meat cutters and sausage packers – as toilers in both the most modern and the most archaic production settings – that they produced nothing less than an ethnic recomposition of the American working class. After 1900, the customs, ideas, and institutions so carefully cultivated by American workers during the previous forty years remained the possessions of only part of the working class, and a relatively privileged part at that. Symbolically, the term "American worker" came to refer to those who shared that heritage, regardless of the fact that many of them and most of their parents had been born in Germany, Ireland, or England.

These ethnically distinct and socially marginalized workers were excluded from the narrow craft unionism structured by the preceding generations. Montgomery (1987:71) quotes a skilled Pittsburgh worker: "These fellows have no pride. They are not ruled by custom. When the foreman demands it, they will throw down a saw and a hammer and take up a wheelbarrow." Classified as unskilled labor, the new workers tended to organize through the International Workers of the World, a union that did not set restrictions based on ethnicity or skill. The designation of "International" stood for the diverse national origins of the membership, not for a union with branches throughout the world. The marginalization they experienced led to a greater militancy in the strikes and confrontations that occurred with such frequency in the late 19th century and the early decades of the 20th century.

Paralleling these militant labor organizations in the frontiers of labor mobilization – in the mining camps, railroad construction sites, and factories that employed unskilled labor – were ethnic associations that played a defensive rather than an assimilative role. In the New England towns where they worked in textile factories and in the gateway cities where they congregated in crowded tenements, they developed what Handlin (1959:39) called "fully functioning ethnic communities." These became the incubators for organizing self-help groups and political parties supporting clientelist interests. Some sought escape from "wage slavery" in buying land or a fishing boat, or opening a restaurant.

August Sartorius von Waltershausen, a German labor analyst who studied the workers' movement in the United States from 1879 to 1895 (Montgomery and van der Linden 1998), provides us with one of the best accounts of the way unions dealt with the diversity of nationalities. They formed mixed unions covering all nationalities when the trade involved few workers. When the number of workers was significant, they had general unions with distinct national sections governed by a central committee. In a few rare cases they formed separate unions based on nationality. Migration west to the available lands and jobs on farms and in mines minimized the conflict that would have developed if what von Waltershausen called a "Marxist reserve army of labour" had forced down wages (Montgomery and van der Linden 1998:75).

Culturally distinct styles of organization prevailed, with German mutual aid and collective strategies characterizing trades where they predominated, as opposed to the more individualistic strategies of the English. Since each ethnic group tended to have its own spheres of economic activity, they did not compete (Montgomery and van der Linden 1998:72). The English-speakers showed a "tendency toward mystery mongering" expressed in the Freemasons, Odd Fellows, Red Men, and Molly Maguires (Montgomery and van der Linden 1998:99). But secrecy was a part of survival, and even the Knights of Labor were forced to defend themselves with this tactic. Founded in Philadelphia in 1869, the Knights of Labor sought inclusion of all members of the working class, organizing geographically rather than in terms of ethnicity. This quintessentially American labor organization espoused the assimilative ideals of the nation.

With the rapidly consolidating manufacturing, banking, and insurance institutions in the late 1880s, leaders in the ethnic sodalities could no longer find entry into enterprises that provided opportunities for immigrants at the beginning of the nineteenth century. Instead, they often turned to organizing labor unions in the industries in which their ethnic groups counted as a majority. Jewish workers provided the basis for the garment industry's principal unions: the International Ladies Garment Workers Union (ILGWU) and the United Garment Workers (UGW) (Blumenberg and Ong 1994). By 1909 the United Garment Workers was able to organize a strike of 20,000 workers, 15,000 of whom were women (Bonacich et al., eds. 1994). Italian workers provided the leadership of unions in industries in which they predominated in the garment, leather, and construction industries.

The unions consolidated under the American Federation of Labor (AFL), such as the United Textile Workers (UTW) led by John Golden, did little to organize the newcomers. Induced by labor recruiters to seek their fortunes in the mills of New England, rural recruits from Poland, Portugal, Lithuania, Syria, Armenia, France, Greece, Turkey, Russia, Italy, Ireland, Canada, and Germany found low-wage jobs without security or a future. Activists who rose from the ranks to consolidate the massive strike of 1912 in the Lawrence textile mills turned to the more radical unions that represented the unskilled laborers of the mines and railroads. The left-wing labor militants they called in were themselves sons of immigrants who were still on the outskirts of organized labor. These included Joe Ettor of the International Workers of the World, Bill Haywood of the United Mine Workers, Elizabeth Gurley Flynn, and Arturo Giovannitti, a poet and writer. Leaders who rose from the rank and file, such as Annie Welzen-bach, who urged skilled workers like herself to support the strike, Angelo Rocco who called upon national leaders, and Annie LoPizza who was killed while leading a group of women in a march, revealed the diversity of the rank and file they represented.

This early precursor of industrial labor action demonstrated the capacity of workers to organize beyond ethnic and craft lines of distinction. The violence carried out by federal and state troops against workers who joined the strike indicated the recognition on the part of owners of the mills, and the State that supported them, of the new threat posed by class unity. Church and opinion leaders generally condoned the terrorist actions of the managers since the strikers were categorized as aliens.

World War I was a catalyst to labor organization, in part through regulations imposed by government agencies and in part because of the growing prepon-derance of a mass labor force, no longer divided by the skills that once led to internal differentiation. The War Labor Board's insistence on shop committee elections of council representatives outside of the shop broke the paternalistic – and sometimes terrorist, as in the case of the Lawrence millowners – controls exerted by management. These regulations, designed to stabilize labor relations during the war mobilization, became the basis for some of the New Deal reforms during Roosevelt's turbulent presidency. What is often called the "Fordist" labor regime is a product of labor struggles that were incorporated in the labor reforms of the 1930s (Nash 1995).[1]

Cultural identities and communal commitments of the migrants defined both the divisions and collective bases for action in the struggles in which migrants found a place in the new settings. The structural position migrants occupy in their own transitory path, being outside the norms and past commitments of the established workforce, provides a critical basis for their actions. But the experience of being outside the mainstream is not predictive as to what direc-tions these actions will take: it can cultivate both transformative actions to change the structures of discrimination, or it can seek accommodation by finding a place within structures of inequality. Complicating the analysis is the variability within each ethnic group of the experience of individuals, even of members of the same family, conditioned by gender, age, and class (di Leonardo 1984). Furthermore, the definitions of racial and ethnic categories are also changing, just as are the political categories of enemy alien or preferred candidate for affirmative action.

Louise Lamphere's (1987) study of the working daughters and working mothers of New England factories shows that women's commitments to working-class struggles at the beginuing of the 20th century were more often expressed in informal resistance rather than leadership in unions. The working daughters of the early 19th century joined men in the militant strike activities, but their potential for militancy, Lamphere notes, was minimized because of the limitations in trade-union strategy in the textile, garment, and assembly industries in which they predominated. It was not until the industry-wide organization of unions that workers' organization became a permanent negotiating force representing workers' interests. This required a restructuring of government as well as industry to overcome managerial tactics of blacklisting activists and subverting solidarity movements with "replacement workers." The right to organize was not backed by law until 1934, when unions were legalized with laws backed by a National Labor Relations Board.

The appeal to commonality in class organizations was gradually adopted by mainstream labor organizations from the more radical IWW as a counter to ethnic divisiveness played upon by capital interests. Class consciousness, as David Montgomery (1987:2) tells us, was more than the unmediated product of daily life experience. It was also a project engaging working-class activists with individuals from other social strata fostered by the workers' struggles in the workplace as well as in their publications, reading circles, recreational settings, and cooperative stores. This carefully crafted identification as "the working masses" was abetted by managerial tactics debasing the work process, with factory "hands" treated as a mindless and easily replaceable workforce.

Identity politics tends to oppose the insights gained from recognition of individuals' personal goals in entering into political action, against the constitutive conditions of class as relations of production (Laclau and Mouffe 1985). Postmodern analysts who focus on the individual are now unraveling the century-old project of constructing class as a category of unity and struggle. Without doubt it is important to recognize the actor as subject in social movements, but the awareness of subjective identity emerges in conflict that develops between classes, as Touraine (1977:303-313) emphasizes. Subjective identity based on gender, ethnicity, race, and age tends to confirm class consciousness, providing the nexus by which we judge the credibility of people and their commitment to common goals. I shall tell this story through the case of the ethnically diversified labor force in the General Electric Company in Pittsfield, Massachusetts.

Case 1: Ethnic Diversity and Industry-Wide Trade Unions in Pittsfield

Capital-intensive industrialization in the late 19th century stimulated the growth of cities like Pittsfield that incubated the earlier tanning and textile mills (Nash 1989). In the 1890s, Italians, Poles, and Greeks increased ethnic variety in textile mills that had employed English, Germans, French Canadians, and Irish. Each wave built a new church where they could meet, marry, and bury their own; even though the Irish had already built St. Joseph's church, the Italian and Polish Catholic workers felt a need for their own ethnically defined places of worship.

A historian of the Irish Catholic church, Katherine F. Mullany (1924:vii), gives us a sense of why this was a priority. Speaking of the newly arrived Italians she says: "We all remember them flocking into town with their household belongings draped upon their backs, and all their other earthly goods in the roped black boxes carried in their hands; a nomad race, despised and suspected." Her observations on the Polish population were more temperate; she found them, "a sturdy race, vigorous, energetic, thrifty, and generous in support of the church," but they too were "inclined to disputes owing to centuries of fighting blood that runs in their veins." Catholic and Protestant parishes were split ethnically, and each group sought to build their own church. The membership of this was determined on patriarchal premises; an Italian woman of my acquaintance was expelled from the congregation when she married an Irishman (Nash 1989:46–47).

As the textile mills relocated to the South in the post–Civil War decades, the few remaining mills employed a predominantly female workforce as male workers were drawn into the Stanley Electrical Company and other companies formed in the last quarter of the 19th century. When the General Electric Company bought out the Stanley Electrical Company in 1903 there were 1,700 workers. Few immigrants of any nationality other than English, Irish, and Germans were regularly employed in the General Electric Company (GE) until World War I. The French, Poles, Germans, Jews, Armenians, Greeks, Lithuanians, and African Americans who were drawn to Pittsfield to work in the textile mills, or in the construction gangs, and in service jobs or trucking supplies for the company store, found employment for the first time in the GE plant during World War I, when the workforce increased from 5,300 in April of 1916 to 7,500 in December of that year. Assembly jobs that supposedly required little skill or training were segmented as "women's work," and ethnic segmentation prevailed throughout the plant. Because of the racism related to Italian immigrants, they were not hired inside the General Electric Company, although they were permitted entry inside the plant gates to sell vegetables and fruits that they cultivated to the workers on payday. "They didn't call it discrimination then," a second-generation Italian worker told me about his experience trying to get a job in GE in the 1930s, "It was known as, well, you were too old, or you didn't comb your hair straight, or you weren't Irish. But when a construction gang went in to do a job in the GE, the contractor made sure he hired all Italians." Left outside the gates of GE, Italians turned their skills learned as itinerant workers into businesses, forming construction companies, restaurants, and grocery stores.

In the early decades of the 20th century, the older migrant population, now with second and third generations in the labor force, organized in craft unions, some of which belonged to the AFL. Many of the foremen and better-paid machinists and toolmakers belonged to the Masonic Lodges, a Protestant fraternal order that promoted hiring of its own members and discouraged the employment of new ethnic migrants. Even as the plant became more diverse, most of the foremen were chosen from among English, Irish, or German production workers until the high demand for labor exceeded the concern with ethnic origins during World War II. Except for a brief interlude during World War I when blacks and other "foreigners" were brought in as strikebreakers, no blacks or Latinos worked in General Electric until World War II. Even up to the closing of its doors on production work in 1986, GE never counted more than 5 percent blacks and Hispanics in its workforce, and ethnic segmentation within the plant prevailed.

The most militant union activists were found in the textile companies in Pittsfield and nearby cities during the early decades of the 20th century. Textile workers counted in their ranks recent immigrants from eastern European countries along with Italians and Catholic Irish. It was they, not the second-generation German, Irish, and English labor force in the General Electrical Company, who set off the strikes in 1916 inspired by increases in the cost of living. General Electric workers walked out later that same year, calling for similar gains to the 5 percent wage increases gained by the textile workers. The small increment in their wages that General Electric Workers enjoyed over that paid in the textile mills, and their sense that they were the elite of the working classes, minimized their sense of class solidarity.

These textile mill workers, most of whom lived in ethnic neighborhoods, became leaders in the union movement during the 1930s. The few who were able to get a job in GE drew upon their cohesiveness as a group that enabled them to "speak up to management" during the years when GE was sending out "goon squads" to confront labor militants. Furthermore, they were not locked in to the craft hierarchies that subverted plant-wide organizing tactics. This had become the agenda of the CIO union when organizing the plant in the 1930s. Despite their growing support among production workers who did not belong to a craft union, GE workers did not gain a contract with management until 1941 when the imperative need for labor for the "war effort" forced the company to make some concessions.

In the century of industrialization from the mid-19th century to World War II, Americanization signified losing the distinctions among ethnic groups drawn to the United States by the promise of employment in industry. Factory owners played upon cultural and racial difference as a means of controlling the workforce. By branding foreigners as anarchists and terrorists, even executing key people said to embody the subversion they portended, the dominant class tried to defuse the potential of a labor force with an international outlook. The trial and eventual execution of Sacco and Vanzetti served as a warning to many ethnic workers of what they could expect if they persisted in their culturally and ideologically distinct way of life.

Reacting to the divisiveness promoted in the workplace, the more radical labor unions sought unity by promoting an image of the labor force as undifferentiated members of "the masses". This became the name of a socialist journal dedicated to the proposition that all cultural differences were merged in the solidarity of the united working class. When industrial unions adopted the strategy of denying cultural distinctions in the interest of class unity, equality was translated into sameness. Uniformity did not prevail because of internal controls operated by the employees themselves. Skill hierarchies replaced ethnicity in a segmented labor force. The unions never recognized gender equality as an issue, masked as it was by "protective" measures based on assumptions about female frailty that restricted women to lower-paid jobs. Yet skill rankings rarely reflected the performance levels required in jobs segmented as female, and few women rose above the R14 ratings in the job hierarchy that included 25 ranks, even when their jobs required high levels of skill. Ethnic differences also prevailed because of internal divisions promoting unstated ethnic priorities.

It was not until after World War II, when the Italian and Polish men who had been the last hired at the General Electric Pittsfield plant returned as veterans, that the company began to upgrade them into the preferred machinist and testing jobs formerly filled by German and English Americans. Women, who could not claim the rewards of victory for their war work, were urged to withdraw and give their jobs as welders and engineers back to the veterans, and many returned to the assembly work considered unskilled. It was not until the Equal Employment Opportunity Act was passed in the 1970s, and the General Electric Company became concerned about compliance with government defense contracts, that women were able to break into the higher skill and professional categories. Black professionals were also hired during the Reagan years of cost-plus defense contracts.

The Pittsfield case illustrates the way in which diversity in the workplace responded to both managerial and labor initiatives. Italians and Poles, who were the latest arrivals from Europe and who experienced the most intense discrimination in the workforce, became the instigators of an industry-wide labor movement that found expression in the Congress of Industrial Organization (CIO). The denial of difference in the interest of the solidarity of classes became a labor technique to evade the divisiveness promoted in the workplace. Trade unions organized as industry-wide unions relied on bureaucratic procedures based on seniority for hiring and layoffs as well as promotions to ensure equality. The war itself proved to be an integrating force, and the ranks of returning veterans were accepted as "patriots" in ways that neutralized ethnic differences. Race remained a dividing ground set by the town and the labor unions that had always opposed the influx of racial minorities. Italians moved from being a racial to an ethnic minority only after World War II.

During the brief period from the legalization of the unions during Roosevelt's presidency until the buildup of the "cold war" in the 1950s, the hegemonic accord between labor and management known as "Fordism" was created. The anti-communist drive within the unions and the depoliticizing of workers' organizations during the 1940s and 1950s split the unions and left the workers defenseless against the corporate move overseas in the 1970s. Rising wages in the two decades after the war, still pegged to productivity increases because of wartime contract agreements, promoted consumerism. Labor conflicts were no longer staked on the moral grounds defined by the Lawrence workers in 1913. They involved daily squabbles over grievances regarding bureaucratic rules rather than the class struggle. Ethnicity itself was commoditized in "ethnic fairs" that promoted foods, dances, and clothing identified with groups that, in their daily lifestyle, were indistinguishable.

Flexible capitalism and the Latino entry

In the restructuring of industry following World War II, marginal industries that had survived the movement to "right to work" states in the South of the United States, as well as construction and service jobs began to attract migrants from south of the border, particularly from the Caribbean. Flexible production and the relocation of production to offshore sites drew on a predominantly female labor force of industrial workers at the same time as subsistence cultivators were pushed off the land in the countries to the South, causing hundreds of thousands of people to migrate within and outside their countries of origin (Hamilton and Chinchilla 1996). Lamphere's studies of the restructuring that took place after 1965 find two notable trends in migration: (1) because of changes in the quotas, there was a large increase in Asian and Latin American immigration, and (2) this was coupled with a shift from predominant peasant or working-class immigrants to middle- and even upper-class professionals (Lamphere 1992:7).

The burden of the dislocation brought about by migration is borne almost unassisted by households. In the mutual support groups that link together households in the country of origin with those in the country of residence in order to meet the needs of childcare, and caring for sick or aged members of their families, women migrants are forming transnational networks.[2] These networks, responding to the dislocation brought about by flexible accumulation, provide an expanded basis for union organization. Gender distinctions are both enhanced and critiqued by migrants as they experience the unsettling of their lives by migration. The privatized concerns of social reproduction are moving into these public arenas as migrant women challenge the premises formulated in patriarchal societies both in their country of origin and in that to which they migrate.[3] As women are forced into wage work to support their families, practices of wife abuse, genital mutilation, male control over sexuality, and reproductive rights and control over children are challenged.

Households are the sites in which the values of the cultures of origin are contested. These values often spill over into subsidiary organizations that provide resources for mediating the conflicts. Migrant women often seek support in mutual support groups in which they share their concerns. Trade unions, human rights groups and other non-governmental organizations (NGOs) are beginning to draw on the understandings cultivated by women in these groups. Multilateral approaches to class action bypass confrontational approaches cultivated in earlier union action as broader community action draws the employed and unemployed, the documented and undocumented, workers into action networks. The appeals for equality and an end to subordination are more often made to human rights in the wider community than workers' rights defined on the job.

I shall then draw on anthropological studies of community-based workers' organizations and on a study I carried out with students at the City University of New York. This involved us in observations of, participation in, and interviews with members of community organizations, Latino centers, and trade unions in New York City[4] as we tried to assess how some the new migrants are organizing.

Neoliberal attacks on social reproduction

Neoliberal policies in Latin American countries encourage migration by reducing wages to levels that can barely sustain a single male worker at the same time as social subsidies are eliminated. Concurrent with these developments in the periphery, nation states throughout the world have become increasingly punitive in their treatment of migrants. The United States' attempt to gain control over its borders with the 1986 law granting amnesty for undocumented migrants provoked new flows of migrants who arrived during a stagnant economy. This had two contradictory consequences. The provision requiring that employers check the work authorization papers of prospective employees gave them a tool to hold undocumented workers in an underground economy. Countering this, Chinese and Latino neighborhood centers sprang up in many urban communities, and even trade unions began to see a new venue for organizing, assisting migrants to legalize their entry (Gonzalez Behar 1997:6).

The large increase in migrants led to a backlash and the passage of the extremely restrictive 1996 Immigration Reform and Immigrant Responsibility Act. This Act rules that spouses, parents, and children of a legal migrant who are living in the United States without documentation must leave the country until they can get alien registration cards, allowing them to become legal residents (*New York Times*, September 25, 1997: A1, B5). The catch 22 is that they will be barred from reentry for three years if they have resided illegally for 180 consecutive days, and for ten years if here for a year or more. Women were net losers, since they had a harder time establishing a "paper trail" (Gonzalez Behar 1997). The law also requires that each person who sponsors a relative to come to the United States has to earn 25 percent over what is considered the poverty-level income, or $16,225 for a family of three, and they must sign a document swearing financial support until the new immigrant is a citizen. These provisions effectively end the family preference, which was the keystone of immigration policies in the past.

This legislation comes during a period of resurgence in anti–"illegal alien" sentiment brought about by their rise in numbers over the decade (Chavez 1997:67; Ocasio 1995). Claiming that immigrants pose a threat to national security, sovereignty, and control of the territory, California state representatives targeted the sites of reproduction, especially women and children in the reproduction of immigrant families. This is marked in Proposition 187, passed in California with the support of 59 percent of the constituency (Chavez 1997). This law deprives legal as well as undocumented workers of education, medical attention, and other social benefits taken for granted for all residents in advanced industrial states. The denial of services to family members in effect rejects the possibility of incorporating migrants as citizens into the wider society.[5] At the same time, since it does not target the production arena nor criminalize employers who hire undocumented migrants (Chavez 1997:71), it evokes the Bracero Program of 1965 that contracted workers for limited periods of time and without families, but neglects the security provided to workers under that law.

By targeting for elimination programs that address the social welfare of migrants in the sites of social reproduction – education, medical attention, and retirement pensions – the U.S. government is ruling out the chance of incorporation in the American Dream. Yet the anti-immigrant sentiment has stimulated unity among Latinos, erasing the division between native-born, mostly English-speaking Chicanos and immigrant, Spanish-speaking Mexicans, since it affects all Latinos (Martinez 1995:30). This is precisely the setting in which Latino centers, community organizations of civil society, and a revitalized labor movement are trying to find solutions to the problems aggravated by declining public support. I will explore these settings in the final section of this chapter.

Case 2: Labor Organization of the Citarella Fish Store

Latino populations represent one of the fastest-growing ethnic sectors in the United States. Both because of higher reproductive rates and further migration, they are expected to become 15 percent of the population in 2000 and 35 percent in 2030. They are beginning to gain representation in local as well as national governing positions. Their entry into policy-making groups will have a profound effect on the structuring of U.S. society.

In coping with the changes in their life circumstances, migrant women are moving some of the privatized events of social reproduction into public arenas, thereby expanding the scope of the political. This has been true of migrant women's participation in the United States in their own institutions such as "mothers' clubs" in settlement houses and ethnic women's organizations. Throughout the 20th century, these settings prepared them for their struggles to gain control over their political and personal lives (Seler 1994:9). Kinship and ethnicity are cognitive frameworks for relating migrants to their new homes, whether it is the internal migrations of rural people to towns or transnational movements.

The spread of independent, immigrant-led, community-based labor organizations, or "workers' centers" grew in the 1980s when huge numbers of Latino immigrants were forced into exile by U.S. military-backed interventions in Central America and the Caribbean. These new leaders have the political sophisticated eradicated in union ranks during the McCarthy period in the United States. The kind of outreach work needed in organizing a culturally distinct group in the context of racist right-to-work communities of the South requires politically conscious activists. The cynicism and disengagement of North American workers born and brought up in the United States militates against the devoted commitment required in the current organization drives. Latino organizers, who are often the targets of racial as well as ethnic discrimination, are often better able to see the essential link between civil rights and workers' rights.[6] Their transnational connections with members of their communities of origin are helping to overcome the provincialism of trade unions in the United States.

Immigrant centers proliferated in the 1980s during a time of growing hostility to immigrants as the scapegoats for economic decline and unemployment.[7] I discovered one of these in Manhattan through a leaflet distributed by women supporting three Hispanic workers fired by an upscale fish store on the Upper West Side. The Centro Latino shared facilities with the Chinese Staff and Workers Association, a grassroots labor organization based in Chinatown that developed in reaction to the increasingly abusive labor conditions in the early 1980s (Chen 1993:138). The failure of the AFL/CIO unions to address the abysmal conditions of Chinese garment workers prompted the organization of this alternative labor organization. In order to address the specific needs of Latino workers from Mexico, El Salvador, Ecuador, Puerto Rico, Honduras, and Argentina, they formed their own organization in 1992. By mid-1995 they had a radio station, a newspaper, and then they began a period of enormous growth with many public events. Among their activities are meetings of Chicanos, Mayas, and Chabetes with the Federal Department of Labor about the influx of Mexican migrants. They organize protests in front of restaurants and shops where workers have been unfairly treated. In their first protest, about four restaurant workers who had been dismissed unfairly, Monica, the director of the Latino Center, said: "On this occasion, we broke out of *clandestinidad* (hiding)!" Regaining wages that are withheld by employers, who count on the fear of undocumented workers to carry charges against them, is a major issue for immigrants.[8] On October 12, 1996, they staged a march to Washington, D.C., followed by discussions in churches about the rights of workers.

The Centro works with coalitions of the church, trade unions, and consulates of various countries. They go to the consulates to discuss workers' grievances with construction work, and they bring these issues to TV channels 41 and 47 as well as the newspaper *El Diario*. Money comes from foundations such as Programa de Nuevos Ciudadanos, Caridad, and La Iglesia Presbiteriana. Since some churches are reluctant to donate money because some of their members are the bosses, the Centro must also rely on membership pledges of five dollars a month. Those who recover wages with their help contribute 10 percent.

The primary goal of the centers is to educate migrants in their rights as citizens and workers. Discussion leaders engage the students in issues that relate directly to their job and community problems. In the class we attended, about 20 male and female students learned the articles of the National Law on Labor Relations, and routines to follow with the "Migra" – Immigration and Naturalization Service – through drills and role taking. What does an undocumented worker do when the Migra enters the workplace? Run for cover? Refuse to answer any questions? Ask to see the credentials of the agent? Students are urged to report violations of their rights to the National Labor Relations Board, and are supplied with the address and telephone number. Cartoon illustrations with Spanish captions accompany the chalkboard exercises.

It is in these contexts that migrants are now expanding the forms of organization within working-class movements that depart from conventional labor tactics. As we will see below in the recent increases in recruitment into trade unions, these new tactics adopted by both men and women in the trade unions are overcoming the apparent impossibility of gaining representation for an unskilled (in the formal sense of that term) and vulnerable cohort of migrant workers.

Community support for the new immigrants

A new dimension of the transnational interaction of migrants in homeland and receiving countries emerges as organized sectors of the host countries perceive the need to engage in support networks for the migrants. Latino centers are increasingly working together with community organizations. The alliance of U.S. citizens with the Latino community centers provides important resources in direct access to legislators at the state and national level. In addition, the liberal and progressive leaders of community groups often provide free professional services to the immigrant organization.

Our first encounter with this dense web of activists came about when we accompanied the Centro organizers to a hearing held by the Workers' Rights Board, an organization formed by the New York Jobs with Justice Coalition and composed of community leaders, elected officials, and clergy. A coalition of Upper West Side community activists had supported the pickets in an eight-month boycott called by the United Food and Commercial Workers Union against the Citarella Fish Market for firing three workers who had attempted to gain a collective bargaining unit in the shop. Democratic state senators and assemblymen, union representatives, community and neighbor coalitions, and the Citarella workers and their supporters citywide attended the meeting. About 100 people were packed in the Presbyterian Church hall when we joined them at 7:30 p.m.

Mr. Engler, a Gray Panther community leader of the Upper West Side, embodied the new unity among newcomers and the old liberal community. Thanking the three workers who had joined the picket lines for giving the community inspiration, he asked: "Where do we go from here?" He went on to say: "Workers are working twelve to fourteen hours a day, and are not able to enjoy their families. We need community monitoring of shops like Citarella." Later in our interview with him in his Central Park West apartment, hung with posters from earlier community struggles, he told us of his many community involvements, from the 1930s when he was involved in support for the Spanish Republic to current concerns of the aged.

The split labor force at Citarella's reveals the divisions among workers on ethnic and cultural lines. The "upstairs" crew consists of countermen who speak English, were born in the United States, are documented, and are paid well. The meat manager Charlie Gagliardo is a child of Italian parents who were strong union members, but he feels that Citarella's workers don't need a union (Wax 1997). The checkout cashiers are young Hispanic women who rarely interact with customers as they scan and pack the food. The "downstairs" crew consists of packers, working in crowded and, some community observers claimed, unsanitary conditions. All would be included in the vote on union representation for the company. When three of the downstairs crew were fired, the owner, with the advice of his lawyer, prepared for the vote by firing twelve undocumented workers and rehiring a dozen new faces. This created unease and dissension. The divisions within this company are found throughout the service industry that has become the target for union organization. In restaurants it is the "front room" vs. the "back room" workforce, with the monolingual immigrants invisible in the rearguard action.

The Citarella boycott gained some recognition of the depth of the problem in the community. It has also revealed the generation rifts among workers and within the wider community. This is the problem unions are facing in their renewed organizational efforts described below. The alliance of unions with community activists, state representatives, and a wide array of NGOs such as Jobs with Justice, anti-sweatshop activists, and legal aid societies brought about a limited victory in reinstating the workers laid off for attempting to organize a trade union.

Revitalization of trade union organization

In a political climate in which immigrants are experiencing the backlash of resurgent nationalist identity that emphasizes homogeneity and rejection of the foreign-born, there is a revitalization of trade-union organization that attempts to cut through the contradictions that are "disuniting America." The criminalization of the presence of undocumented workers has, throughout the 1970s and 1980s, allowed employers to gain control over an underclass of workers and evade unionization (Bustamente 1985:187–188). Immigrants have become the scapegoat in structural adjustment programs that limit state welfare and pit interests competing for limited funds against each other. At the same time, immigration officials undercut the validity of the laws by permitting labor contracting in violation of restrictions (Bustamente 1985:187). The contradiction between assuring labor rights only to legal immigrants and citizens, and harboring thousands of illegal immigrants who cannot claim even minimal rights such as back pay, punitive damages, and workmen's compensation for on-the-job injuries, was only recently addressed by the Equal Employment Opportunities Commission. On October 26, 1999, officials announced that the commission would not tolerate discrimination on the job of undocumented workers (*New York Times*, October 26, 1999: A1, A19).

In overcoming the contradictions rife in labor relations, unions are turning to familiar organizational forms based on community and working-class organizations (Zamora 1993:8). This is particularly marked by the presence of women in trade union organizations, who draw on their skills in networking. The unprecedented election of a Latina woman, Linda Chavez-Thompson, as the new executive vice president of the AFL/CIO, indicates the drive to represent and incorporate workers who have never been organized (NACLA Report on the Americas 1996). Latino rank and file workers in the garment industry are rebuilding unions in Texas, Florida, and Chicago, according to Hector Figueroa (1996:19), and demolition crews and dry-wallers, janitors, and hotel workers are making inroads in New York City's "unorganizable" immigrants (Delgado 1993; Figueroa 1996:24).

Among the strategies promoted by Latino labor organizers is the boycott. During the 1970s, Dolores Huerta and César Chaves took advantage of the exclusion of farm laborers from the Taft Hartley Act to organize the Union of Farm Workers (UFW). In 1984 the UFW initiated a boycott of grapes, appealing to consumers with information on the cancer-causing effects of chemicals used in food production (Guerin-Gonzalez 1994:137). Workers in lettuce and tomato farms also used this strategy (Valle 1994:150). Coming at a time of rising consciousness of environmentally deleterious consequences on health of pesticides and chemical fertilizers, consumers throughout the United States responded to the appeal to ban chemicals in food production.

Delgado (1993) demonstrates the potential for organizing among migrant workers in a California mattress factory. He found that this depends more on the organizational capacities, forms of labor control, and market forces and legal environment that the workers confront than on their status as undocumented or legal migrants. A principal element reinforcing the solidarity of Latinos from several countries of Latin America was the network of companions and strong family and friendship offering the striking workers alternative employment and resources to tide them over (Delgado 1993:14). These requisites for workers confronting management in marginal, competitive firms are more frequently found among Latina migrants. The boycott was one of the most effective strategies in the strike called by workers in the Camagua mattress factory studied by Delgado (1993). This was especially marked in white affluent areas where store managers came to a settlement before the striking workers even mobilized a picket line because "they didn't want a group of 'dirty Mexicans' to picket in front of their stores" (Delgado 1993:52). Mexican women workers in Camagua also responded positively to the organizer's establishment of a daycare center in the middle of the garment center supported by the employers and the unions (Delgado 1993:10l). The success of the strike was due to the fact that, according to Delgado (1993:103), "the union succeeded in making the issue more than simply a labor dispute drawing in community activists, including clergy, concerned with the rights of immigrants and Latinos."

Labor organizers throughout the country are also learning to avoid sharp confrontational approaches used by labor unions in the past. May Ying Chen (1993:141–142) found that such tactics created polarization and negative feelings by both workers and bosses towards the union in Korean-owned garment shops in New York, targeted in an ILGWU drive. Many Korean garment workers were housewives from middle-class families in Korea, and they did not readily identify with the "working class." The notion of strikes and conflict in the workplace is embarrassing to them.

Cultural sensitivity in the workplace is the new slogan of the revamped unions. This new slogan comes from trade union workers who have kinship connections with working-class communities prior to World War II. In the course of our research with the Citarella workers, we spoke with Nick Unger, an organizer for UNITE (United Needle Industries and Textile Employees), the AFL/CIO. He grew up in Bedford Stuyvesant when Puerto Ricans arrived in the 1950s. As he led us past the conference rooms where women organizers were hardly distinguishable from the rank and file members – an extraordinary makeover in a union that had been characterized by white Jewish males in a predominantly female-based union – Unger commented: "Our union hall is like a day-care center." He swiftly outlined the trends that had weakened the unions since 1965. "There was a current – you didn't have to create it to be more or less carried along – that started with the Immigration Act of 1965. There was a huge shift in migrants in the garment industry that went from black to white to Puerto Ricans to no-holds barred in a short time. With the collapse in the garment industry, there was unstable entry and disappearance of port of entry occupations: immigration with no base to hook migrants into. Where there is no political or cultural leadership and no organized working class, there is no thread. All is polymorphous and perverse; people are drawn in and pushed out. The push-pull form of immigration destroyed the basis for incorporating immigrants."

The workers organized by UNITE AFL/CIO represented a politically diverse group as well. Dominicans had arrived in the United States with splits between the left wing and Communists. None of them wanted to join a union because their minds were still set on returning to the Dominican Republic. Organizing a Bronx furniture factory, for example, seems inconsequential when one has the goal of changing the government of a country. But they had the dynamic of consciousness of power; they brought that with them.

The unions are beginning to respond to changes in the industry and workforce with new initiatives. Among these responses is that of addressing the shift in power from producer to distributor. For example, the AFL/CIO has targeted retail chains to drop contracts with sweatshops. Instead of a moral appeal, they address the self-interest of managers, concerned with image, who do not want picketers announcing that they are selling sweatshop products. They are also targeting consumers, concerned with their own health, when union members campaign about the unhealthy conditions when they work in chemically contaminated fields. Outside the shop, unions are working in educational and cultural programs for developing a broad awareness of workers for their rights as citizens as well as workers.

Conclusions

Migration in the late 19th and 20th centuries used to be considered the beginning of an assimilation process that tended to obliterate cultural distinctions treated as an obstacle to progress (Lamphere 1992:16). Assimilation was so much a part of the hegemonic accord that labor organizations embraced it to the same degree as employers and the gatekeepers of society did. The appeal to class unity was a way of bypassing ethnic loyalties felt to be counterproductive to labor union organization.

The new migrants, especially those that arrived after 1965, face a different labor market and find their way into it by a variety of paths that diverge from practices in the early part of the 20th century. Flexible production schedules demand a multiplicity of adaptations, and homogeneity is not enjoined by employers or union organizers. The most innovative programs are developed outside the usual trade-union channels in centers sponsored by churches, human rights groups, and foundations concerned with social problems. Because they provide settings outside the workplace and often in ethnically distinct neighborhoods, these centers, often directed by leaders drawn from the same ethnic group, can develop the basic adjustment programs for the particular group. Unions are beginning to adopt programs initiated in these centers that respond to a broad array of family, community, and international problems faced by migrants.

Inequality based on gender and ethnic hierarchies is transformed in the migration process. Entering on the lower rung of the occupational scale, both men and women migrants confront discrimination, but they experience it in distinct ways. The earlier wave of migrations in the 19th and early 20th centuries resolved the dilemmas faced by a severely discriminated-against female labor force by seeking a "family wage" agreement in the workplace. In the present wave of migrations, social reproduction in global labor markets is becoming transformed. The "myth of the male breadwinner" is unmasked, as women become chief breadwinners in many households (Safa 1996). They develop transnational networks from New York, or Los Angeles, or Chicago to the Caribbean, or the Philippines, or other low-wage countries as they strive to maintain households. In this transnational commoditized domestic sphere, men lose their priority as provisioners at the same time as they lose ground in employment. As women become domestics in the homes of United States professional women, or enter marginal factories operating underground or on the edges of the fashion centers, they are beginning to politicize their concerns as housewives and workers.

In these multilateral approaches to community organizing and union building, women's participation breaks down the distinction between production and reproduction, merging the focus and strategies of each domain. Women are, in the process, translating their disadvantages into political issues through which they are gaining a changed status in their households and jobs. As yet they have just begun to relate to the United Nations covenants on human rights for immigrants and for women. Central to these is the assertion of the right to family integrity denied in the current immigration regulations. Just as their presence is transforming the workplace, so it is transforming the community and trade-union organizations.

The new labor struggles take place in a variety of settings, the least of which is the production site. The very nature of the new sites of employment for most migrants is either underground, transitory, illegal, or a combination of these traits that make it difficult to enforce labor regulations. As a result, the new union actions turn to retail outlets and consumers themselves to impose boycotts that force recognition of labor demands for wages, healthy work conditions, or a product free of pollutants that affect the consumer as much as the worker.

The new awakening in the labor movement is because of immigrants – women and men – who often instigate unionization in a workforce considered unorganizable. The internationalization of the membership of trade unions has opened up a space to challenge internal hierarchies within the migrant group at the same time as revitalized trade unions challenge the hierarchical ordering of ethnic and class relations. Issues of social reproduction are taking a central place as a leadership that reflects the new workforce takes charge.

NOTES

1   I have argued that Fordism, as a cover term for hegemonic accord, was a misnomer. Fordist measures were unilaterally accorded to workers in the Ford plant to overcome their resistance to the assembly line early in the 20th century. Ford maintained a competitive advantage in the labor market with higher wages and better conditions than those that prevailed in the industry. The hegemonic accord was a product of labor struggles in the 1930s that resulted in the regulatory processes defining the social contract between labor and management, until it was dismantled in the 1970s (Nash 1995).

2   I use the term transnational as defined by Schiller et al. (1992): those social fields that immigrants build linking together their country of origin and their country of relocation.

3   I use the term patriarchal in the restricted sense of a system of balanced responsibilities in which men carry the responsibility of protecting and provisioning familial dependants and women provide non-compensated services. The excesses in exploitation of such services without reciprocation, which are often conflated with patriarchy, I refer to as male dominance (Nash 1988).

4   Support for the research was provided by the National Science Foundation fieldwork experience for graduate students. Among the student interns were Maria Gutierrez, Tiffany Francisco, Patty Kelly, and Maria Hart.

5   Chris Goldman (1987) includes appendix 4, Convention No. 143, in her study "Human Rights and the Migratory Labour System" (Human Rights Project No. 3, Monograph Institute of South African Studies, National University of Lesotho). The convention repeatedly enjoins member nations to make provisions for the accommodation of families, defined as spouse and dependants, of migratory workers.

6   This fits the profile of Yanira Merino, a Salvadoran forced into exile who fell into the hands of death squad activists when she arrived in Los Angeles (NACLA 1996).

7   Jennifer Gordon (1995) organized one of these independent workers' centers in a Latino community on Long Island called the Workplace Project. This addressed problems faced by immigrant workers that were ignored by government agencies and unions. The undocumented workers in the service sector attracted to the Project were, for the most part, non-unionized. They lacked health benefits and other regulations required by law but rarely enforced in the underground shops or the self-employment settings in which they worked. Working "off the books," they cannot even address the violations they experience in the workplace. Unions were reluctant to represent workers with questionable immigrant status or those in workplaces with too few workers to make it worth their while. Providing legal aid, education in workers' rights, and translation in labor disputes, the centers promoted the process of gaining citizenship in immigrant communities. As she indicates, many of the services merely reproduce the system rather than transforming the labor relations they address.

8   Failure on the part of the employer to pay wages is one of the most common complaints of workers. Of the 72 cases filed with the Wage and Hour Division of the State Labor Department in recent years, only two resulted in back payments, and both were only partial, according to Jennifer Gordon of the Workplace Project, a Hempstead-based advocacy group (*Daily News*, February 16, 1996). Minimum wage laws are consistently broken in sweatshops that violate sanitary and safety conditions, as well as forcing overtime work without additional compensation. New York State Commissioner of Labor John F. Hudacs estimated that of the 6,000 garment industry employers in the state, 2 to 3 thousand are illegal sweatshops (Feitelberg 1994). Senator Franz S. Leichter, a liberal Democratic state senator whom we interviewed, estimates two to three times that number, commenting in his memorandum supporting an increase in damages and civil penalties that there were at least 5,000 in 1992 according to the New York State Labor Board, compared to 200 in 1970 and 3,000 in 1980. Laws are ignored, in part because of light fines, and in part because of failure to enforce them.

REFERENCES CITED

Blumenberg, Evelyn, and Paul Ong
  1994   Labor Squeeze and Ethnic/Racial Recomposition in the U.S. Apparel Industry. In Bonacich et al., eds., pp. 309–327.
Bonacich, Edna, Lucie Cheng, Norma Chinchilla, Nora Hamilton, and Paul Ong
  1994a   Introduction. In Bonacich et al., eds., pp. 3–20.
  1994b   The Garment Industry, National Development and Labor Organizing. In Bonacich et al., eds., pp. 365–373.
Bonacich, Edna, Lucie Cheng, Norma Chinchilla, Nora Hamilton, and Paul Ong, eds.
  1994   Global Production: The Apparel Industry in Pacific Rim. Philadelphia: Temple University Press.
Bourgois, Philipe
  1995   In Search of Respect: Selling Crack in El Barrio. Cambridge, UK: Cambridge University Press.
Bustamente, Jorge
  1985   Mexican Migration to the United States: De Facto Rules. In Mexico and the United States: Studies in Economic Interaction. Peggy B. Musgrave, ed. Pp. 185–206. Boulder, CO: Westview Press.
Chavez, Leo R.
  1997   Immigrant Reform and Nativism: The Nationalist Response to the Transnationalist Challenge. In Immigrants Out! The New Nativism and the Anti Immigrant Impulse in the United States. Juan F. Perrea, ed. Pp. 61–77. New York: New York University Press.
Chen, May Ying
  1993   Reaching for their Rights. In Union Voices. Glenn Adler and Doris Suarez, eds. Pp. 133–150. Albany: SUNY Press.
Delgado, Hector I.
  1993   New Immigrants, Old Unions: Organizing Undocumented Workers in Los Angeles. Philadelphia: Temple University Press.
Feitelberg, Rosemary
  1994   Need for Sweatshop Law Stressed at N.Y. State Hearing. Women's Wear Daily, June 7.
Figueroa, Hector
  1996   The Growing Force of Latino Labor. NACLA Report on the Americas 30(3):19–24.
Goldman, Chris
  1987   Human Rights and the Migratory Labour System. Human Rights Project no. 3, Monograph Institute of South African Studies. National University of Lesotho.
Gonzalez Behar, Susan
  1997   The Amnesty Aftermath: Current Policy Issues Stemming from the Legalization Program of the 1986 Immigration Reform and Control Act. International Migration Review 31(1):5–27.
Gordon, Jennifer
  1995   We Make the Road by Walking: Immigrant Workers, the Workplace Project, and the Struggle for Social Change. Harvard Civil Rights–Civil Liberties Law Review 30(2):407–451.

Guerin-Gonzalez, Camile
1994 *Mexican Workers and American Dreams: Immigration, Repatriation, and California Farm Labor, 1900–1939.* New Brunswick, NJ: Rutgers University Press.
Hamilton, Nora, and Norma S. Chinchilla
1996 Global Economic Restructuring and International Migration: Some Observations Based on the Mexican and California Experience. *International Migration Quarterly* 3(4):195–231.
Handlin, Oscar
1959 *The Newcomers: Negroes and Puerto Ricans in a Changing Metropolis.* Cambridge, MA: Harvard University Press.
Harris, Nigel
1995 *The New Untouchables: Immigration and the New World Worker.* London: I. B. Tauris.
Laclau, Ernesto, and Chantal Mouffe
1985 *Hegemony and Socialist Strategy: Towards a Radical Democratic Politics.* London: Verso.
Lamphere, Louise
1987 *From Working Daughters to Working Mothers: Immigrant Women in a New England Industrial Community.* Ithaca, NY: Cornell University Press.
1992 *Structuring Diversity: Ethnographic Perspectives on the New Immigration.* Chicago: University of Chicago Press.
1994 Introduction. In *Newcomers in the Workplace: Immigrants and the Restructuring of the United States Economy.* Louise Lamphere, Alex Stepick, and Guillermo Grenier, eds. Pp. 1–21. Philadelphia: Temple University Press.
di Leonardo, Micaela
1984 *The Varieties of Ethnic Experience; Kinship, Class and Gender among California Italian-Americans.* Ithaca, NY: Cornell University Press.
Martinez, Ruben
1995 Fighting 187: The Different Opposition Strategies. *NACLA Report on Immigration* 29(3):29–32.
Mörner, Magnus
1967 *Race Mixture in the History of Latin America.* Boston: Little, Brown.
Montgomery, David
1987 *The Fall of the House of Labor: The Workplace, the State, and American Labor Activism.* Cambridge, UK: Cambridge University Press
1993 *Citizen Worker: The Experience of Workers in the United States with Democracy and the Free Market during the 19th Century.* Cambridge, UK: Cambridge University Press.
Montgomery, David, and Marcel van der Linden
1998 *August Sartorius von Waltershausen: The Workers' Movement in the United States, 1879–1885.* Cambridge, UK: Cambridge University Press.
Mullany, Katherine
1924 *Catholic Pittsfield*, vol. 2. Pittsfield, MA: Pittsfield Eagle.
NACLA Report on the Americas
1996 On the Line: Latinos on Labor's Cutting Edge. 30(3).
Nash, June
1988 Cultural Parameters of Sexism and Racism in the International Division of Labor. In *Racism, Sexism, and the World System: Studies in the Political Economy of the World System.* Joan Smith et al., eds. Pp. 11–38. Westport, CT: Greenwood Press.

1989 *From Tank Town to High Tech: The Clash of Community and Industrial Cycles*. Albany: SUNY Press.

1995 Post-Industrialism, Post-Fordism, and the Crisis in World Capitalism. In *Meanings of Work: Considerations for the Twenty-First Century*. Fred Gamst, ed. Pp. 189–211. Albany: SUNY Press.

1998 Women and Migration. Paper read at the April 1998 Meeting organized by the SUNY Albany Center for Latin American Studies.

Ocasio, Linda
1995 The Year of the Immigrant as Scapegoat. *NACLA Report on the Americas* 29(3):14–28.

Safa, Helen I.
1986 Female Employment in the Puerto Rican Working Class. In *Women and Change in Latin America*. June Nash and Helen Safa, eds. Pp. 84–106. South Hadley, MA: Bergin and Garvey.

1996 *The Myth of the Male Breadwinner*. Boulder, CO: Westview Press.

n.d. Female Headed Households in the Caribbean: Sign of Pathology or Alternative Form of Family Organization. Unpublished MS. University of Florida, Gainesville, Florida.

Sanjek, Roger
1998 *The Future of Us All: Race and Neighborhood Politics in New York City*. Ithaca, NY: Cornell University Press.

Schiller, Nina Glick, Linda Basch, and Christine Blanc-Szanton
1992 Toward a Transnational Perspective on Migration: Race, Class, Ethnicity, and Nationalism Reconsidered. *Annals of the New York Accademy of Sciences* 645.

Seler, Maxine Schwartz, ed.
1994 *Immigrant Women*. Albany: SUNY Press.

Susser, Ida
1982 *Norman Street: Poverty and Politics in an Urban Neighborhood*. New York: Oxford University Press.

Touraine, Alain
1977 *The Self-Production of Society*. Chicago: University of Chicago Press.

Valle, Isabel
1994 *Fields of Toil: A Migrant Family's Journey*. Pullman: Washington State University Press.

Wax, Emily
1997 Talk of the Town. *Manhattan Spirit*, March 7:12–13.

Zamora, Emilio
1993 *The World of the Mexican Worker in Texas*. College Station: Texas A and M University Press.

Zavella, Patricia
1987 *Women, Work, and Family in the Chicano Community*. Ithaca, NY: Cornell University Press.

14

Poverty and Homelessness in U.S. Cities

Ida Susser

This chapter focuses on analyses of the creation of culture among the poor populations in the United States whose lives have been structured by the global
economy and its changing construction of labor, space, time, and identity. It
examines the generation of poverty, and questions of gender, race, political
mobilization, and resistance. It attempts to understand the implications of the
emerging global economy for the poor who reside at its center.

Homeless populations in the United States are not large in terms of the
general census findings (Burt 1992). However, they are one of the few highly
visible and public signs of the poverty of millions of Americans. In this sense,
they have emerged as a symbol of the new poverty in the United States (Mitchell
1992). Since the 1980s, the gap between the wealthy and the poor has been
increasing in the United States (Jones and Susser 1993). Political concern for
housing the homeless, or at least removing them from the streets and subways,
stems from the need to make the increasing inequality, to which the majority of
the residents are subject, invisible, individual, and private (Smith 1996). For this
reason, studies of the homeless in the United States are studies of the way
poverty is represented as well as the way in which the poor are treated and the
way they live their lives.

Recent concerns about the "underclass" must be viewed in the same context.
While, since the term was introduced into U.S. political discourse, the "underclass" has constituted only about 10 percent of the poor population of the
United States (Corcoran et al. 1985), literature about the underclass, by sociologists, psychologists, political scientists, educators, social workers, and health
providers constitutes by far the largest proportion of research about poverty in
America in the 1990s (Katz 1993). Once again, this group may be more visible,
more subject to public scrutiny. Almost by definition, members of the "underclass" find themselves in direct conflict with public institutions, either through
substance abuse, the criminal justice system, mental institutions, foster care,
vagrancy and homelessness, or, at the very least, the need for public assistance
(Susser 1998). Other poor people who manage to avoid interaction with public
institutions have in fact been classified as the "deserving" poor and are not
counted in discussions of the underclass. This distinction between the deserving
and the undeserving poor is not new and can be traced back several hundred

years (Vincent 1993). In social science we can find its roots in familiar categories such as the "hardscrabble" or "hardliving" poor whose lives are contrasted with those who appear to be able to maintain middle-class norms more successfully (Jones 1993). Such disparaging contrasts were criticized by ethnographies of the late 1960s and early 1970s which demonstrated the situational basis for many of the characteristics described as "hardliving" norms (Liebow 1967; Stack 1974; Leacock 1971; Mullings 1997).

In terms of poverty in the global economy and its place in current theories of advanced capitalism, we can identify two opposing conceptualizations of the poor in the postmodern world, or the new world "disorder." On the one hand, there are those who view the poor as irrelevant to the global economy. Not only are the poor invisible, but their labor is no longer viewed as necessary. From this perspective, deindustrialization in the core countries is a reflection of a decreasing need for manual workers worldwide. This presages a reduction of the needed workforce to fewer, more highly educated people who will be involved in the new informational technology. Low-skilled service workers will still be necessary but not in the numbers of the previously industrialized workforce. The exportation of industry to poorer countries represents not only a search for cheaper labor, but also an overall reduction in the central importance of that labor within world capitalism (Castells 1997). Thus, from this theoretical perspective, policies pursued in the United States and elsewhere which involve cutbacks in government funding for social services, health, and education result from an abandonment of populations whose labor and health are no longer necessary to production in the global economy.

From an alternative perspective, labor in industrial production is still as crucial and central from a global point of view. However, what we are experiencing in terms of the exportation of production from the center to the less media-visible periphery and the development of the informational service economy is an all-out assault on working-class populations. From this point of view, the departure of industry from the strongly unionized welfare states that constituted the core of modern capitalism represents the ongoing search for cheaper, weaker, unorganized labor associated with less regulated state intervention. It is one more step in the battle for control of production and the extraction of profit (Harvey 1990). The shift to the hiring of women workers as well as the creation of a post-Fordist workforce, unevenly in the United States and parts of Europe, can be incorporated into this argument.

While the first view implies that many workers are no longer needed and that massive populations of poverty are a drain on and a threat to nation states and the world economy, the second perspective incorporates the definition of the poor as a massive pool of labor serving to depress all workers' wages. They remain available to be integrated into the workforce and then discarded in relation to the needs of the global economy.

In order to assess the adequacy of these two perspectives, we need to consider what in fact constitutes a labor force at different historical periods with different effects on inequality, poverty, and social welfare. Nation states, employers, and working-class movements define the categories of people available to work differently over time. As social programs and regulations shift, so too do those people who can be viewed as labor. For certain historical periods in the United States women, children, and the aged have been defined out of the workforce. At other junctures they have been recruited to fill employment needs. Such changes can be perceived in the history of protective legislation and the conflicting and historically fluid approaches of feminists, unions, and the state to such regulation (Abramovitz 1988; Milkman 1987; Brodkin 1998). Massive social upheaval by people demanding work and security for the aged during the Great Depression led to the introduction of mandatory retirement through the Social Security Act of 1934 (Olson 1982). The abolition of mandatory retirement in the 1990s and current incentives for early retirement illuminate the ways in which broader political issues interact with the characterization of a reserve labor force.

Changing patterns of prisons, military recruitment strategies, societal handling of the mentally ill and definitions of mental illness, institutional labor, slavery, indentured servitude, and racial discrimination are other areas where the availability of labor and its cost are periodically redefined (Dehavenon 1993; Estroff 1981; J. Jones 1992; Piven and Cloward 1971). As scholars have begun to recognize, there may be more than one form of capitalism, or capitalism may be manifested in a variety of different institutional contexts (Blim 1996). Cultural definitions of available labor are historically produced by nation states, political conflict, and social movements. Alternatively, constructions of legitimate dependency and community responsibility, institutionalized in state regulation, entitlements, and cultural expectations of age, gender, and other social identities, protect certain members of the population from accepting the lowest wages.

From the perspective outlined above, we can view the departure of industries from core industrialized countries, not in the problematic ethnocentric terms of deindustrialization, but as an expansion of the industrial labor force. Workers in areas previously restricted to agriculture and the extraction of raw materials have been recategorized as candidates for industrial employment. In particular, such new developments target women as industrial workers. The new women workers represent some of the least protected representatives of international labor. They are frequently subordinated and sometimes assaulted in their own household settings, historically excluded from most forms of paid employment and education, and situated in the poorest regions of the world. This massive expansion in the incorporation of global labor, in addition to the breakdown of household definitions of gendered labor, combined with the increasingly gender-specific patterns of immigration from poorer countries to the core, must be carefully considered before theorists accept arguments based on a lesser need for labor under the informational technology of advanced capitalism (Castells 1997).

Since the early 20th century, the routines of Fordism incorporated the concept of a "fair day's wage." This included the maintenance of a predefined nuclear household of wife and chidren, the reinforcement of specific gendered interactions, and enforcement of segmented hiring patterns that traced and retraced ethnic and racial hierarchies (D. Gordon et al. 1982). Class conflict under Fordism produced unions that fought successfully for adequate wages, job security, occupational safety, health benefits, and seniority policies. However, industrial unions were themselves threaded through with the racial and sexual presuppositions of corporate hegemony, as well as refutations of such ideology (Kessler-Harris 1982; D. Gordon et al. 1982; see Chapter 25, this volume). Now we find flexible accumulation accompanied by a growing informal economy, enfeebled unions, less security for most workers including middle-income professionals (Harvey 1990), the shrinking of the welfare state, and escalating poverty (Mingione 1996). Under these conditions the hegemonic construction of the white male worker that was encoded as part of the charter of industrial unions has collapsed. Unions were weakened through their own failure to incorporate different visions of race, gender, and the poor of the developed and under-developed worlds into the voices of class conflict (Anglin 1993; Gerstle and Frazier 1989). The definition of who could work was changed by the exportation of industry, and the labor force was expanded to include women and members of poor third-world nations. As a result, unions centered in the urban heartland of capitalism and based on the gendering and racial discrimination of Fordism were unequipped to fight against the destruction of their standard of living. This is the context in which poverty becomes central to workers in core countries as well as the periphery in the 21st century.

Theoretical Approaches to Reinvention of the Social Order

What concepts have social researchers and, more specifically, anthropologists offered in this context? Within the metropoles we have ethnographic studies of deindustrialization and the shift to a service economy (Pappas 1989; Nash 1989; Susser 1982). Some of the most graphic and penetrating studies of the new poverty are to be found in anthropological research concerning health and disease in the United States (Balshem 1991; Pappas et al. 1993; Singer 1994). Among third-world workers, we find studies of the new industries, placed, as they frequently are, in marginal environments, outside the regulatory control of specific nation states and thus avoiding established patterns of class conflict and state compromise (Benaria and Roldan 1987; Fernandez-Kelly 1981; Susser 1985). Studies of transnationalism and migration both locally and transcontinentally, as well as the postmodern emphasis on shifting populations and travel, connect these two parallel examinations of poverty.

This review focuses specifically on ethnographic research concerning such areas as the reorganization of labor and the creation of a new poverty, the construction of space and time for the new poor in relation to the global economy, and new forms of shifting and movement. The review outlines research which suggests the reshaping and remaking of divisions of race and gender and the implications of these new formulations for the analysis of violence. Finally, this chapter considers the ways in which ethnographers have represented the voices of the poor in the contemporary context. Recent research has promoted and stimulated a reexamination of the role of the ethnographer and his or her differentiation from those studied under currently shifting postmodern conditions both within anthropology and within the global economy, which are, as many have noted, directly related.

Labor Shifts in the New Global Economy

The significance of low-paid employment and U.S. deindustrialization in the creation of poverty and homelessness is well established (Bluestone and Harrison 1982; Wilson 1987). Such a perspective is frequently stated at the beginning and end of ethnographies about homelessness and urban poverty. However, since participant observation, conducted over the period of one to several years captures only immediate processes, it tends also to contribute to the reification of the instant in terms of identities and categories that occupy the space and time of the fieldwork. Poor people appear poor rather than unemployed or underemployed. Homeless people appear homeless rather than displaced. Even when the departure of industry can be documented and the rise in real estate costs traced, ethnographers seldom capture the before and after effects.

Two recent ethnographies document what might be termed the making of poverty in the United States. These are *From Tank Town to High Tech* (Nash 1989) and *The Magic City* (Pappas 1989). Both of them describe the reduction of "stable" working-class households to poverty through the departure of industry.

Poor communities are also being created among migrants without access to capital. New Asian immigrants, similar to Haitians, Mexicans, and others are being recruited to fill the low-paid employment created by the new global economy (see Chapters 13 and 15, this volume). Some researchers argue that such immigrant workers maintain nuclear families, avoid public assistance, and generally support themselves more effectively than resident minority poor. However, anthropological research demonstrates that many immigrants are denied benefits on the state and federal level and appear to conform to the "Protestant ethic" of work without handouts because they are afraid to request assistance and do not have many entitlements. Women who are single heads of households may claim that they have husbands supporting them because such connections may be necessary to legalize their immigration status (Zavella 1996a, 1996b). Thus, ethnographic research on household structure does not corroborate arguments concerning the superior cultural adaptation of the new immigrant groups in contrast to the resident minority poor, but rather suggests that many poor immigrants are denied access to desperately needed social, health, and financial assistance that is partially available to the resident population.

The shift to the hiring of women service workers is another area addressed by recent ethnographic research. *Caring by the Hour* documents the experiences of poor black women workers in a North Carolina city (Sacks 1988). Sacks documents the breadth of their work requirements, the limited options for promotion, and the participation of such previously excluded groups in political mobilization. Ethnographies of the new low-paid service workers portray a workforce with reduced control, fewer benefits, and less security than is found in ethnographies of U.S. labor from the 1950s through the 1970s. However, they belie earlier theories that women, because of the dual work day and their household responsibilities, would be unable or unwilling to mobilize around work concerns (Anglin 1993; Bookman and Morgen 1988; Susser 1998).

The core of the new U.S. workforce has become the low-paid worker, outside the unions, living in the "postmodern" family, or alone and subordinated also by gender, minority, and immigrant status. The potential of these groups for unionization or political mobilization constitutes one of the central questions in determining the directions of the new global economy.

Poverty and the Construction of Space in the New Global Economy

Global changes have not only affected the workplace but also the construction of space in the global economy. Real estate decisions, housing discrimination, gentrification, and urban development policies structure the visibility of poverty and the experiences of the poor (Marcuse 1985; Smith 1996; Susser 1982). Poor neighborhoods reflect mortgage restrictions and a losing battle for scarce public services, such as schools, road repair, and health care. The spatial construction of poverty is manifest in the division of communities through the destruction of housing for the building of expressways, the bypassing of public transportation, and the creation of suburban zoning regulations and enclosed shopping malls to separate the middle-income purchasers from the poor (Davis 1990; Low 1996).

The shifts in the global economy also have been accompanied by the destruction of public space amid the construction of contested commercial/private space such as malls, landmarks, markets, and recreational centers epitomized by the much-analyzed Disneyland/World phenomena. All of these semi-public environments marginalize the poor and represent areas of contestation over the resegregation of social interaction by class and income (Sharff 1997).

Urban renewal policies followed by gentrification have isolated the poor in enclosed and practically invisible communities. Such invisible and relatively powerless communities concomitantly became the site of last resort for methadone clinics, housing for the mentally ill, as well as industrial waste disposal plants partially as a consequence of the well-known phenomenon of Not In My Back Yard (NIMBY). The separation of the poor was slower to take place in minority communities, but may be currently in process as minority members of the middle class find ways to enter the better-off suburbs and city neighborhoods (Wacquant 1994; Wilson 1987).

Homeless people in the United States are significant not for their numbers but because they represent the incursions of increasing impoverishment into public space – particularly space occupied or desired by middle-income and even wealthy people (Lovell 1994). Homeless people find their way into railroad stations, public parks, and public transportation. In New York City, people have set up covered shelters right outside the United Nations. In Los Angeles, homeless people congregate on the beaches of Venice, California. Unlike in Martin Luther King's time, when the Poor People's March built a shantytown outside the white House, the homeless people in central tourist spots in Washington DC, New York City, and San Francisco are not making a coherent political statement. They are not constructing their shelters to make a political point. Since the 1990s, people live permanently in such structures and the political point emerges from their visible need.

Cyberspace is yet another area from which the poor have been generally excluded (Smith 1996; Hakken and Andrews 1993; Castells 1996). As informational technology links the household into the wider net of the corporation, those without households or money for computers drop below the threshold of societal communications. However, the overall impact of these changes has yet to be evaluated as poor people have adapted new technologies to their own purposes. Artists have captured the irony of homeless people in cyberspace in the creation of the Poliscar, a vehicle for a homeless person to park on the street and live in, equipped with information technology (Smith 1996).

Time Out and Out of Time in the New Global Economy of Poverty

People's experience of time has changed in the new global economy. The categorization of time under capitalism was first raised by E. P. Thompson (1969) in his classic paper on 17th-century England. Since Thompson and others relate the defining of time precisely to emerging industrial employment, the changing forms of employment under post-Fordism might be expected to change the concepts and usage of time for new century (Castells 1996; Harvey 1990).

As many analysts have pointed out, concepts and uses of time have become social markers in a class-stratified society. Oscar Lewis (1966), in his culture of poverty description, discussed present orientation and other researchers have used similar markers in their definitions of the underclass (Anderson 1989). Such discussions also come up frequently in the AIDS prevention literature where homeless people's evaluation of how long they have to live may be realistically shorter and may reduce people's commitment to efforts at HIV prevention through safer sex and clean needles (Susser and Gonzalez 1992). Similarly, time is the ultimate issue in debates about teenage pregnancy and class-based fertility patterns (Stein 1985).

Researchers have addressed this issue in terms of poverty and homelessness, arguing that time created for and by homeless people takes on different meanings than time for the rest of the population. Poor people must keep institutional time requirements, but when they arrive must wait, in a daily restatement of the unequal power relationship between the poor and service providers. The bureaucracy can be late, but the person dependent upon it is required to come on time and be patient (Urciuoli 1992; Susser 1982; Lazarus 1990). Since poor women serve as the mediators between their households and institutional services, their experience of waiting and unequal control over time may be much greater than men's. In addition, since women are frequently responsible for the transport and needs of children and the organization of reciprocal kin networks based on the needs of many people with conflicting time requirements, they become less able to meet the time schedules of institutions whether these be employers, schools, or the welfare office.

For the homeless, time is not usually determined by a regular work schedule. However, it is clearly constricted and defined by institutional events (Lovell 1992; Gounis 1992). A reversal of time occurs among homeless people who are dependent on institutionalized work schedules for food and shelter. Many of the services that are open to and sustain homeless people are staffed by employees who only work the 9–5 shift on weekdays. On weekends, food and shelter become much more problematic and homeless people frequently find themselves alone, cold and hungry, waiting for weekdays to restart their social life. A similar reversal takes place between night and day. Public places, lobbies, and hallways are used in the daytime by those with homes, as they go to work or enter various commercial establishments. At night, homeless people repopulate coveted niches in the deserted central city in their search for shelter and safety. In another reversal, "seizing the moment" becomes more important for homeless people than maintaining reliable routines (Lovell 1992). When work and money do not come routinely with employment and paychecks, people must be continually ready to react to each random or unscheduled opportunity as it arises. Other groups, such as entertainers and probably most freelance consultants, if not academics, are subject to some of this same kind of pressure to respond to immediate opportunities, in the fear that others may not arise. As the downsizing of corporations continues, professionals may be forced further into non-routine and unscheduled responses to time. For homeless people, unpredictable opportunities (such as they are) are most of what is available. In responding to immediate options, institutional providers see poor people as unreliable and without concepts of time. As is so often the case, the social creation of behavior among the poor is treated as evidence of individual unworthiness.

People who are homeless reconfigure both time and space as they negotiate survival. Once again, in their lack of conformity to the times and routines established by work under capitalism, their very existence represents visible resistance to hegemonic values, whether or not political statements are voiced by the homeless themselves.

Thus the new urban poverty carries with it time hierarchies, time resistance, and time restatement as part of the re-creation of class and inequality under global capitalism.

Re-creating Gender in the Context of the Poverty and Homelessness of the New Global Economy

Poverty and homelessness are clearly gendered (Passaro 1996; L. Gordon 1994; Susser 1998). However, once again we must be cautious of static and reified conceptions. Gender among poor people in the 1990s United States has been an area of open battle, violence and conflict, and sometimes of fatalities. Both men and women have restated, re-created, and resisted the stereotypic portraits of earlier periods.

Since employment, public assistance, social security, and credit differentiate experiences by gender, being poor and being homeless have never been the same for men and women (Abramovitz 1988). But entitlements, employment, and institutional constraints have also altered dramatically since the 1970s. The last two decades of the century have witnessed a crucial period of change and struggle in the definitions of gender by the state, in the expectations between men and women and the structuring of households.

Clearly poor men and poor women share poverty and the responsibilities for households and the next generation. In this sense, they may find common ground and common interest in relation to employment and state policies. However, even in these areas their opportunities and losses are not alike as women may benefit from housing programs while men may have more access to job training. Relations between men and women are important determinants of the experiences of poverty and homelessness. Men and women battle and are battered in struggles over household structure and control of children and resources or they may simply abandon the field. We have to analyze the conflicts that run from the state through the household and the intensifying of those conflicts in the 1990s.

It is no longer sufficient, if it ever was, to talk of male or female domination or subordination among poor people in the United States. A review of gender issues of the 1990s shows arenas of power for men contradicted by other arenas of power or access to resources for women. The complexity of the interactions, rather than equalizing relations between men and women, leads in many cases to escalating conflict.

The Feminization of Poverty or the Disappearance of Men?

In the mid-1980s problems began to be formulated in terms of the "feminization of poverty" (Sidel 1992). As single-headed households were becoming more common, the fact that working women earned less than men who might previously have supported the household, combined with the failure of many men to actually pay child support, resulted in a majority of households below the poverty line which were headed by women. Concomitantly, there was an increase in the proportion of children being reared in poverty.

Along with the recognition of the feminization of poverty came a focus on the problem of violence against women. A leading and rising cause of injury for women between 15 and 45 was violence from their male partners. Ethnographies of the 1980s and 1990s document violence and fear which need to be analyzed more systematically in terms of the changing experiences of men and women and changing expectations of gender (Bourgois 1995; Merry 1994; Sharff 1997).

By the 1990s, the discussion about the feminization of poverty had reversed itself and concern began to center around the exclusion and disappearance of poor men (Dehavenon 1993). The rapidly increasing incarceration rates for poor and minority men as well as the growing disease and homicide rates contributed to this formulation. Figures suggested that while men battered and brutalized women, they killed one another. In addition it became clear that poor men were excluded from public assistance funds, were less likely to find employment, and less likely to finish school than poor and minority women.

Although the gendering of poverty was evident, the lives of poor men and women were so interconnected that the experience of each bore directly on the other. As more men were excluded from employment and public assistance or disappeared through incarceration or death, more women became responsible for poor households (Jencks 1994). In the light of these points of strain domestic violence between men and women became a growing issue. Thus in spite of the clarity of analyses that dealt with the experiences of men and women separately, only an analysis that portrays the integral interdependencies of the two interlocking/conflicting gender hierarchies in terms of class and poverty serves to elucidate the parameters of the new poverty and the violence it generates.

As noted above, it is not enough in the context of the new poverty to speak of one gender hierarchy. Eligibility for public assistance, housing subsidies, and low-paid service employment often favor women over men (Passaro 1996). While men have lost some of the advantages that used to accrue from access to better-paid industrial employment, they may still have access to more forms of income in manufacturing and the informal economy as well as the illegal drug world and more freedom from the costs, responsibilities, and possibly entrapment of child care (Lamphere et al. 1993). Just as with concepts of time and space, concepts of gender have to be reworked to fit the circumstances of the new poverty within different sectors of the global economy.

Homelessness, too, is experienced differently according to gender (Dehavenon 1993; Passaro 1996; Susser 1991, 1993). Women lucky enough to keep their children from foster care are more likely to be assigned private rooms and services available in a rundown hotel. Men and women without children or separated from them, find themselves assigned to large sex-segregated shelters. As a result, homeless women without children are likely to be the most brutalized group of all. They are subject to the miseries, deprivations, and dangers of homelessness and, above and beyond this, to assault by men in similar situations.

Even children experience poverty differently by gender. Jagna Sharff (1997) in her research on the Lower East Side of Manhattan, developed an early analysis of gendered poverty in discussing the experience of poor Latino children. She suggests that poor boys find themselves recruited into the illegal and frequently fatally attractive world of the drug trade in order to fulfill expectations of providing income for an extremely needy household. In other words, from a young age, as fathers may disappear through the forces discussed above, boys in poor households are expected to try to live up to the male role of provider. Poor girls, Sharff argues, are more likely to be kept home busy with domestic tasks and channeled into schooling. They are less likely to be drawn into the competitive and dangerous territory of drug dealing. While this research, unlike Terry Williams' (1989) research, was conducted in the period of heroin rather than crack/cocaine, both ethnographies suggest clear gendered divisions in the production and trading economy of illegal substances. Women may use the drugs, but do not as readily profit from them and for this reason, are also less likely to be victims of homicide in the battles over control of trade.

Sharff's formulations were originally stated in terms of child-rearing patterns and reinforcements for gender differentiation within poor households which reflected limited options available in the wider society. When viewed in terms of systematic channeling through both pressures on poor families and societal expectations and opportunities for boys and girls, her analysis opens a wide and challenging set of questions and theoretical debate, also supported by research concerning the gendering of childhood experience in homeless shelters, that demands further research.

As Castells (1997) has pointed out, the restructuring of gender in the global economy is one of the central features of the informational society. However, gender is being rewritten differently according to class within this new society and these are the concepts we need to rethink. A more textured analysis of variations in opportunities by gender and their impact on the construction of households and the rearing of children would appear to be the next challenge confronting analysis of poverty in the United States.

Identity, Race, Class, and Gender

The political economy of poverty of the 1980s focused on class, race, and gender. Similarly, within cultural studies race and gender were characterized as significant identities. However, in an examination of the literature of urban poverty and homelessness, we find somewhat separate traditions of analysis for gender and for race. We find parallel historical analyses of employment segregation, as in views of the segmented labor force of Fordism. Both women and minorities were excluded from the higher-paying, unionized jobs that carried seniority, security, and benefits. However, the impact of such exclusions on households and class experience were very different by gender and by race. Women were not excluded from housing or from being able to provide a future for their children until the proliferation of single-headed families and the so-called feminization of poverty. Only an analysis that ignores identity, community, household, and social movements beyond the workplace, and in fact ignores the gendering of social life, can view race and gender as parallel identity processes operating in similar ways within a class-based society. While they are not parallel processes or similar hierarchies, race and gender interact within a class system and the existence of both complex hierarchies in combination has contributed to the maintenance of inequalities.

Race

There is the issue of race (Gregory and Sanjek 1994; Harrison 1995); there is the gendering of race, and then there is the issue of a racial and gendered system in relation to class dynamics (Mullings 1997). All of these issues bear directly on analyses of the urban poverty and homelessness of the 1990s.

In terms of race, analyses of the underclass, of homelessness and of urban poverty document the disproportion of people of color who find themselves in these populations. However, in terms of numbers, as has often been mentioned but rarely remembered, most poor people in the United States are not people of color. Nevertheless, as with the homeless, race has become a visible and politically useful metaphor for the new poverty.

Many studies of poverty simply identify the racial composition or racial identity of the people studied and move from there to the circumstances of poverty or homelessness with little attention to the impact of color on the experience (other than perhaps to refer to the history of racial discrimination in the United

States). One might consider those researchers to be utilizing race as a shorthand classification for probable history or opportunities.

Other studies of poverty focus on the racial hostilities in poor neighborhoods and the experiences of racial discrimination of certain populations. While such studies do not illuminate the concept and experience of race they begin to focus attention on the cross-cutting issues of race and poverty in a more dynamic, analytic way.

Mercer Sullivan's (1990) work compares the experiences of teenage criminals in three neighborhoods. He documents the intersecting forces of neighborhood segregation, social networks, racial discrimination in employment, and the structure of the drug economy to explain why young white men find their way out of adolescent criminal behavior while minority adolescents find themselves trapped and defined by the records of their youth.

Gregory and Sanjek's (1994) edited collection on race is a recent effort to confront and "historicize" the concept of race in western capitalism. They provide a political economy of identity by including articles on Jews, Egyptians, and other groups associated with contested racial categories. Other researchers have focused on the significance of the gendering of poverty and race (Mullings 1997).

Perhaps conceptualization of the interplay of poverty, gender, and race can be advanced through a more detailed examination of four ethnographies that address poverty among men and women in different contexts: Philippe Bourgois' (1995) recent research among young men in East Harlem, New York City; Jay MacLeod's (1987) research among working-class teenagers; Elijah Anderson's (1990) perspective on young men in a northeastern city; and Jagna Sharff's (1997) analysis of women's and men's lives on the Lower East Side of New York City.

These ethnographies together force us to confront central questions concerning the ethnographic enterprise among the poor of U.S. urban cities. It is difficult to document the misery of the poor in the contemporary United States without falling either into the problem of romanticizing or minimizing the devastation or of painting such distress, victimization, and brutalization that the description becomes fuel for political assaults upon the poor themselves. Sharff's (1997) description of young men dealing and dying in the drug trade on the Lower East Side of Manhattan in the 1970s and Bourgois' (1995) descriptions of the sale of crack in El Barrio (East Harlem in Northern Manhattan) in the 1990s are similarly graphic and disturbing. Such works might be assailed for presenting the worst and neglecting positive portraits of hardworking or politically active people in the same neighborhoods. On the other hand, the struggle to portray people involved in the most condemned activities of our society in human and comprehensible ways must also be recognized as one of the strengths of the anthropological method.

Each of these ethnographies rewrites gender such that simplistic stereotypes of feminity or masculinity disintegrate in the light of their research. Bourgois describes one woman who shoots her partner and then becomes a crack dealer with power largely because, just as with the men, people believe that she will take action if double-crossed. She does not have to fear violence, because, like a man, she has established that she can fight back. This adoption of the "macho role" and its reflection also in her relationship with her new partner can be viewed as a reversal of gender expectations. This woman does not represent most women in El Barrio. However, her experience dramatically demonstrates the situational nature of gender roles as well as illuminating through contradiction a material basis for the continuity and power of machismo. Such realistic, conflicted portraits are answers to the questions of why participant observation?, why ethnography?, and what does anthropology have to offer? In the face of constant reflexive doubt about our abilities to consider "the Other" and fundamental questions concerning the hierarchy of anthropological authority, such fieldwork demonstrates the importance of continuing to struggle with the method itself.

Sharff (1997) outlines women adopting stereotypic roles as they go out dancing, dressed in sophisticated middle-class styles with the explicit intention of hypergamy. Once again, the manipulation of gender roles as situational strategy emerges from descriptions of women's struggle to support households, rear children, and survive in poverty in the urban United States. Nowhere in these ethnographies do we find the stereotypic portrait of the modest Latina woman, trapped by traditional values, and unable to change to confront the dangers of poverty and mortality facing herself and her kin. In fact we find, in some, descriptions of women empowered by organizing in their neighborhoods, fighting for more services or simply to maintain what they have.

Anderson (1990) also talks about young men and women and the expectations and behavior of youth in poverty. Anderson, however, talks in generalities. While he provides direct quotes, his work does not fit the methodological and ethnographic model of much anthropological research. Each event is not followed to its logical conclusion and the people discussed do not emerge as individuals, followed through their life experiences. Such an approach leaves room to doubt its generalizations. Many perceptions from outsiders, such as older residents, are quoted as substantiation for generalizations about cause and effect. Generalizations such as the following exemplify weakness:

> Children who become deeply engaged in the drug culture often come from homes where they have relatively little adult attention, little moral training, and limited family encouragement to strive for a life much different from the one they are living. . . . Often such teenagers lack interest in school, and in time they may drop out in favor of spending time with their street-oriented peers. (Anderson 1990:91–92)

This contrasts dramatically with descriptions of the humiliation and misery of school experiences such as those of MacLeod (1987) which provide a less pat explanation for the same phenomenon. This is one of the striking differences in contemporary studies of anthropology and sociology. Bourgois, Sharff, and MacLeod are careful to describe individuals, follow situations, trace events, the unacknowledged effect of the Manchester school of anthropology, creating a body of literature and thick description clearly measured by anthropological standards. As a sociologist, Anderson adapts the method of participant observation, but follows no such disciplinary tenets. He generalizes and quotes without describing in their full context and varied interconnections the people and events from which his evaluations are derived.

In spite of methodological differences, Anderson identifies some reversal of gender roles, where young women, he suggests, look for young men in order to become pregnant and then leave them and set up independent households on the public assistance check. He quotes some men as saying such "new" women are "just out to use you" (Anderson 1990:126), a direct reversal of current terminology, which refers to men using women as sex objects. The young women trapped by their middle-class dreams, described by Anderson, are similar to those described by Ruth Sidel (1990) and support Delmos Jones' (1993) emphasis on achievement aspirations among the poor. Anderson argues that public assistance payments allow women to support men and that men become "prostitutes" under such conditions. This is rather a dramatic and disparaging claim, although suggesting the kind of role reversals that other researchers also document. Generalizations combined with the lack of context or discussion of resistance and agency allow Anderson's research to fuel discussions which blame the victim or emphasize the individual problems of the poor without sufficient attention to the structural constraints of unemployment and racism within which people create their lives.

Jay MacLeod (1987) uses the concept of habitus to conceptualize the social reproduction of race and class. This approach differs from concepts of the culture of poverty or the underclass, fostered by Anderson and others, because it allows for variation, agency, and resistance. In terms of issues of social reproduction, MacLeod (1987:139) argues that class is not enough because "the way in which individuals and groups respond to structures of domination is open-ended." In discussing the lives of two friendship sets of teenage boys, one black and one white, MacLeod (1987:140) argues: "although social class is of primary importance, there are intermediate factors at work that, as constitutive of the habitus, shape the subjective responses of the two groups of boys and produce quite different expectations and actions." Is the concept of habitus necessary? Does it mean more or less than socialization, social context, or environment? MacLeod discusses the complex interaction between hegemonic ideas of gender (differentiated by class, although he does not discuss this), structural unemployment, and individual and family history. This he calls habitus. Whatever the label, such conceptualizations allow for more flexibility and difference than a simple class analysis. They avoid the laying of blame on families that is implied in theories of the underclass and culture of poverty, without neglecting the accumulation of social or cultural capital, or lack thereof, which children acquire from family experiences.

In discussing unemployed white teenage youth, MacLeod (1987) emphasizes the significance of gender in providing the macho image that allows young boys to build respect among their own group and to validate violence and marginality in terms of that societal standard. Once again, poverty cannot be understood apart from gender. The image of "mother" is one area in which young girls can find validation no matter how they fare at school or in the job market. Thus, gender once again frames the options also defined by poverty and race.

In response to similar conditions of school failure and unemployment, young men can opt for validation in the macho image while young girls can see motherhood as a route to success.

Political controversy surrounds ethnographies of poverty, race, and gender because of the implications of the research for the possibilities of social change. Not only do ideologies of family and gender vary by class, they are also associated with different forms of political mobilization. They reflect varying conceptualizations of inequality, race, nationalism, sexual orientation, and resistance. For example, Leith Mullings (1997) notes that for African Americans an integrationist approach to race relations in the United States incorporates the ideologies of middle-class nuclear families (although since this is contested among men and women of the U.S. middle class, we must wonder which concept of gender roles in the nuclear family may be adopted). Nationalist or Afrocentric mobilization against racial discrimination involves an idealization of past traditions which invokes the complementarity of male and female roles and reinforces a male/female gender hierarchy. A transformative or revolutionary approach seeks to change society and the basis for class inequality as well as that of race and gender and attempts to combat gender hierarchies along with discrimination by race (Mullings 1997). The representation of gender in ethnography cannot be seen apart from the political impact of such analysis and is clearly contested terrain.

Thus the transformation of gender and its interaction with the historically changing construction of poverty and race, shifting gender hierarchies, and escalating gender conflict have been marked features of the global economy in the 1990s.

Collapsing Time and Space: Relocating Populations and Shifting Identities among the Poor and Homeless in the New Global Economy

In line with the growth of the global economy, not only resident minorities are poor but also migrant populations. Members of many new immigrant groups are poor and live in the inner cities, entering the inner-city schools and facing the structures of unemployment (see Chapters 13 and 15, this volume).

Studies of U.S. poverty, such as Carol Stack's (1996) *Call to Home*, discuss return migration among African Americans. Other studies describe children being sent back to Puerto Rico for discipline and other reasons (Sharff 1997). Many discussions of international migration focus on similar phenomena. Studies of the homeless also portray a constantly shifting population, as people move across streets, shelters, cities, mental institutions, detoxification centers, and jails and are then relocated in apartments in new neighborhoods (Susser 1998). In connecting the experiences of poor immigrants with discussion of urban poverty issues, we can begin to capture the complex and conflicted movement of the poor and the working class associated with the integration of the global economy.

Movement, across nations, between nations, and through urban areas, as depicted in the homeless literature, must be incorporated into views of the "postmodern" poor and working class. This is true whether one perceives such movement and flexibility according to the flexible economy and the associated flexible bodies (Martin 1996), the informational society, or whether one accepts the prevailing paradigm of an unstructured, unexplainable, constantly shifting postmodern world.

The Voids of the Poor and the Creation of Culture in the New Global Economy

Discussions of the culture of the poor have been controversial since the culture of poverty debates of the 1960s. However, ethnographies of the U.S. urban poor echo with the voices of suffering and defeat as well as with defiance, resistance and agency. As Setha Low (1996) has noted, neighborhood residents still rally to religious festivals and local parades. Women and men still mobilize to protect or demand homes, work and services for themselves and their children (D. Jones 1993; Susser 1988; Sacks 1988; Bookman and Morgen 1988). Nevertheless, a consistency emerges in the experiences described and the struggles of poverty in the 1990s. Women's voices describe the miseries of raising children in poverty, with little help and many problems. Children report on their own brutalizing experiences at home, in school, and on the streets. Men describe their efforts to work and go straight and the losses of respect and future which underlie their turn to street life. Whether the ethnographer is Anderson, Bourgois, Sharff, MacLeod, or Stack, many of the experiences and the descriptions cry out in similar ways. The ethnographers' differences surface in the focus on agency and community resistance (Stack 1996), self-destructive resistance (MacLeod 1987; Bourgois 1995), and survival (Sharff 1997), versus misery and defeat (Anderson 1990). None can glorify, clean up, understate, or prettify the miseries of poverty in the United States. No ethnography leaves any doubt as to the depths of suffering occurring daily in U.S. inner cities. The differences lie only in the causes emphasized and the humanity presented in the descriptions of the poor residents.

Reflections and Mirrors in Ethnography in the New Global Economy

As Carol Stack (1996) writes in a discussion of feminist ethnography, "we are accountable for the consequences of our writing, fully cognizant that the story we construct is our own." Ethnographers of poverty of the 1990s have written consciously from a reexamination of their own histories and their own interactions with the people whom they describe. Stack, in contrasting her writing experiences of the 1970s with those of the 1990s, claims a sense of liberation. No longer constrained to locate logical sequences and objective reports, she finds herself able to identify the contradictions in daily life and to enter her discussions from a variety of perspectives.

June Nash (1995) discusses the hesitancy of anthropologists of the current era to conduct fieldwork and thus almost inevitably objectify informants. Other ethnographers begin to reconsider the construction of their own white and female identities. Patricia Zavella (1994) discusses the difficulties of being partly of one group and partly of others and always in a hierarchical relation with informants. As a Latina, she finds herself in a group, but as a middle-class academic, she is not of that group. She also talks about the cross-cutting identities of sexual orientation and the way in which this structures her Latina, feminist, middle-class discourse.

However, as ethnographers grapple with the issues of reflexivity and the incorporation of voices, the hierarchies of "otherness," and the imposition and creation of identities of color, gender, nation, and foreignness, certain messages emerge clearly from the research. Current research has yielded visions both of the ongoing assault on the lives of the poor and working-class in U.S. society and also of the resilience and humanity of those hidden from view by the progressive invisibility generated by the new global economy. With all the imperfections of representation, the voices which emerge from these works need desperately to be heard. Perhaps they can be heard more fully and in all their contradictions when the anthropologist is constructing herself or himself in the same text. However, with the increasing assault upon the living standards and employment security of working people, in which academics are also included, the fear of dominating "the Other" may not be as salient as many believe. The question which Kim Hopper (1991), Kostas Gounis (1995), Carol Stack (1996), Merrill Singer (1994), and others rightfully ask is not: can we describe the lives of the poor? but, how can we fight against the misery we see created?

REFERENCES CITED

Abramovitz, M.
  1988   *Regulating the Women*. Boston: South End Press.
Anderson, E.
  1989   Sex Codes and Family Life among Poor Inner City Youths. *Annals of the American Academy of Political Science* 501:59–78.
  1990   *Street Wise: Race, Class and Change in an Urban Community*. Chicago: University of Chicago Press.
Anglin, M.
  1993   Engendering the Struggle: Women's Labor and Traditions of Resistance in Rural Southern Appalachia. *Anthropological Quarterly* 65(3):105–116.
Balshem, M.
  1991   Cancer Control and Causality: Talking about Cancer in a Working Class Community. *American Ethnologist* 18(1):152–173.
Benaria, L., and M. Roldan
  1987   *The Crossroads of Class and Gender*. Chicago: University of Chicago Press.
Blim, M.
  1996   Cultures and the Problems of Capitalisms. *Critique of Anthropology* 16(1):79–93.
Bluestone, D., and B. Harrison
  1982   *The Deindustrialization of America*. New York: Basic Books.
Bookman, A., and S. Morgen
  1988   *Women and the Politics of Empowerment*. Philadelphia: Temple University Press.

Bourgois, P.
  1995   *In Search of Respect: Selling Crack in El Barrio.* Cambridge, UK: Cambridge University Press.
Brodkin, K.
  1998   *How Jews Became White Folks and What That Says about Race in America.* New Brunswick, NJ: Rutgers University Press.
Burt, M. R.
  1992   *Over the Edge: The Growth of Homelessness in the 80's.* New York: Russell Sage Foundation.
Castells, M.
  1996   The Net and the Self: Working Notes for a Critical Theory of the Informational Society. *Critique of Anthropology* 16(1):9–38.
  1997   *The Network Society.* Oxford: Blackwell.
Corcoran, M. G., J. Duncan, G. Gurin, and P. Gurin
  1985   Myth and Reality: The Causes and Persistence of Poverty. *Journal of Policy Analysis and Management* 4(4):516–536.
Davis, M.
  1990   *City of Quartz: Excavating the Future in Los Angeles.* New York: Verso.
Dehavenon, A.
  1993   Where Did All the Men Go? An Etic Model for the Cross-Cultural Study of the Causes of Matrifocality. In *Where Did All the Men Go? Female-Headed Households Cross-Culturally.* J. Mencher and A. Okongwu, eds. Pp. 53–69. Boulder, CO: Westview Press.
  1995   *Out in the Cold: The Social Exclusion of New York City's Homeless Families in 1995.* The Action Research Project on Hunger, Homelessness, and Family Health, New York.
Estroff, S.
  1981   *Making It Crazy.* Berkeley: University of California Press.
Fainstein, S.
  1994   *City Builders.* Oxford: Blackwell.
Fernandez-Kelly, P.
  1981   *For We Are Sold, Me and My People.* Albany: SUNY Press.
Gerstle, G., and S. Frazier
  1989   *The Rise and Fall of the New Deal Order.* Princeton, NJ: Princeton University Press.
Gordon, D., R. Edwards, and M. Reich
  1982   *Segmented Work, Divided Workers.* Cambridge, UK: Cambridge University Press.
Gordon, L.
  1994   *Pitied but not Entitled.* New York: Free Press.
Gounis, K.
  1992   Temporality and the Domestication of Homelessness. In *The Politics of Time.* H. Rutz, ed. Pp. 127–149. Ethnological Society Monograph Series, 4. Washington, DC: American Anthropological Association.
  1995   Urban Marginality and Ethnographic Practice: Ethical Dilemmas and Political Implications. *City and Society, Annual Review.*
Gregory, S., and R. Sanjek, eds.
  1994   *Race.* New Brunswick, NJ: Rutgers University Press.
Hakken, D., with B. Andrews
  1993   *Computing Myths, Class Realities.* Boulder, CO: Westview Press.

Harrison, Faye
  1995   The Persistent Power of "Race" in the Cultural and Political Economy of
    Racism. *Annual Review of Anthropology* 24:47–74.
Harvey, D.
  1990   *The Condition of Postmodernity.* Oxford: Blackwell.
Hopper, K.
  1991   Research for What? Lessons from the Study of Homelessness. *Bulletin of the
    American Academy of Arts and Sciences* 44:13–31.
Jencks, C.
  1994   *The Homeless.* Cambridge, MA: Harvard University Press.
Jones, D.
  1993   The Culture of Achievement among the Poor: The Case of Mothers and
    Children in a Headstart Program. *Critique of Anthropology* 13(3):247–267.
Jones, D., and I. Susser, eds.
  1993   The Widening Gap between Rich and Poor. *Critique of Anthropology* 13(3).
Jones, J.
  1992   *The Dispossessed: America's Underclasses from the Civil War to the Present.*
    New York: Basic Books.
Katz, M. B.
  1993   *The "Underclass" Debate: Views from History.* Princeton, NJ: Princeton Uni-
    versity Press.
Kessler-Harris, A.
  1982   *Out to Work.* New York: Oxford University Press.
Lamphere, L., P. Zavella, and F. Gonzalez, with P. Evans
  1993   *Sunbelt Working Mothers.* Ithaca, NY: Cornell University Press.
Lazarus, E.
  1990   Falling through the Cracks: Contradictions and Barriers to Care in a Prenatal
    Clinic. *Medical Anthropology* 12:269–287.
Leacock, E. B.
  1971   *The Culture of Poverty: A Critique.* New York: Simon and Schuster.
Lewis, O.
  1966   The Culture of Poverty. *Scientific American* 215:19–25.
Liebow, E.
  1967   Tally's Corner. Boston: Little, Brown.
Lovell, A.
  1992   Seizing the Moment: Power, Contingency, and Temporality in Street Life. In
    Rutz, pp. 86–107.
  1994   The Dispersed City: Homelessness, Mental Illness, and Urban Space. *Le Cour-
    rier du CNRS* 81:170–172.
Low, S.
  1996   A Response to Castells: An Anthropology of the City. *Critique of Anthropol-
    ogy* 16(1):57–62.
MacLeod, J.
  1987   *Ain't No Making It: Leveled Aspirations in a Low-Income Neighborhood.*
    Boulder, CO: Westview Press.
Marcuse, P.
  1985   Gentrification, Abandonment and Displacement: Connections, Causes and
    Policy Responses in New York City. *Journal of Urban and Contemporary Law*
    28:193–240.
Martin, E.
  1996   The Society of Flows and the Flows of Culture: Reading Castells in the

Light of Cultural Accounts of the Body, Health and Complex Systems. *Critique of Anthropology* 16(1):49–56.

Merry, S.
  1994   Gender Violence and Legally Engendered Selves. *Identities* 2(1–2):49–73.

Milkman, R.
  1987   *Gender at Work.* Urbana: University of Illinois Press.

Mingione, E.
  1995   *Urban Poverty and the Underclass: A Reader.* Oxford: Blackwell.

Mitchell, D.
  1992   Iconography and Locational Conflict from the Underside: Free Speech, People's Park, and the Politics of Homelessness in Berkeley, California. *Political Geography* 11(2):152–169.

Mullings, L.
  1997   *On Our Own Terms.* New York: Routledge.

Nash, J.
  1989   *From Tank Town to High Tech.* Albany: SUNY Press.
  1995   The Anthropology of Stranger and Native. *Annals of the New York Academy of Sciences* 749:205–216.

Olson, L.
  1982   *The Political Economy of Aging.* New York: Columbia University Press.

Pappas, G.
  1989   *The Magic City.* Ithaca, NY: Cornell University Press.

Pappas, G., S. Queen, W. Hadden, and G. Fisher
  1993   The Increasing Disparity of Mortality between Socioeconomic Groups in the United States: 1960–1986. *New England Journal of Medicine* 329(2):103–109.

Passaro, J.
  1996   *Men on the Street, Women in their Place: Homelessness, Race and "Family Values."* New York: Routledge.

Piven, F., and R. Cloward
  1971   *Regulating the Poor.* New York: Vintage.

Rutz, H., ed.
  1992   *The Politics of Time.* American Ethnological Society Monograph No. 4. Washington, DC: American Anthropological Association.

Sacks, K.
  1988   *Caring by the Hour.* Urbana: University of Illinois Press.

Sharff, Jagna
  1997   *King Kong on Fourth Street.* Boulder, CO: Westview Press.

Sidel, R.
  1990   *On Her Own: Growing Up in the Shadow of the American Dream.* New York: Viking.
  1992   *Women and Children Last.* New York: Basic Books.

Singer, M.
  1994   AIDS and the Health Crisis of the U.S. Urban Poor: The Perspective of Critical Medical Anthropology. *Social Sciences and Medicine* 39(7):931–948.

Smith, N.
  1996   *The New Urban Frontier: Gentrification and the Revanchist City.* London: Routledge.

Stack, C.
  1974   *All Our Kin.* New York: Harper and Row.
  1996   *Call to Home: African Americans Reclaim the Rural South.* New York: Basic Books.

Stein, Z.
1985   A Woman's Age. *American Journal of Epidemiology* 121:327–342.
Sullivan, M.
1990   *Getting Paid*. Ithaca, NY: Cornell University Press.
Susser, I.
1982   *Norman Street: Poverty and Politics in an Urban Neighborhood*. New York: Oxford University Press.
1985   Union Carbide and the Community Surrounding It: The Case of a Community in Puerto Rico. *International Journal of Health Services* 15(4):561–583.
1988   Working Class Women, Social Protest and Changing Ideologies. In *Women and the Politics of Empowerment*. A. Bookman and S. Morgen, eds. Philadelphia: Temple University Press.
1991   The Separation of Mothers and Children. In *The Dual City*. J. Mollenkopf and M. Castells, eds. Pp. 207–225. New York: Russell Sage Foundation.
1993   Creating Family Forms: The Exclusion of Men and Teenage Boys from Families in the New York City Shelter System, 1987–91. *Critique of Anthropology* 13(3):267–285.
1998   Inequality, Violence and Gender Relations in a Global City: New York, 1986–96. *Identities* 5(2):219–247.
Susser, I., and M. Gonzalez
1992   Sex, Drugs and Videotape: The Prevention of AIDS in a New York City Shelter for Homeless Men. *Medical Anthropology* 14:307–322.
Thompson, E. P.
1969   Time, Work-Discipline and Industrial Capitalism. *Past and Present* 38:56–97.
Urciuoli, B.
1992   Time, Talk and Class: New York Puerto Ricans as Temporal and Linguistic Others. In Rutz, pp. 108–126.
Vincent, J.
1993   Framing the Underclass. *Critique of Anthropology* 13(3):215–231.
Wacquant, L.
1994   The New Urban Color Line: The State and Fate of the Ghetto in Postfordist America. In *Social Theory and the Politics of Identity*. C. Calhoun, ed. Pp. 231–276. Oxford: Blackwell.
Williams, Terry
1989   *The Cocaine Kids: The Inside Story of a Teenage Drug Ring*. Reading, MA: Addison-Wesley.
Wilson, W.
1987   *The Truly Disadvantaged*. Chicago: University of Chicago Press.
Zavella, P.
1994   Reflections on Diversity among Chicanos. In Gregory and Sanjek, pp. 199–212.
1996a   The Tables Are Turned: Immigration, Poverty, and Social Conflict in California Communities. In *The New Nativism*. J. Perea, ed. New York: New York University Press.
1996b   Living on the Edge: Everyday Lives of Poor Chicano/Mexicano Families. In *Mapping Multiculturalism?* A. Gordon and C. Newfield, eds. Minneapolis: University of Minnesota Press.

15

Ethnic Enclaves and Cultural Diversity

Kenneth J. Guest and Peter Kwong

Since the publication of Portes and Bach's *Latin Journey: Cuban and Mexican Immigrants in the United States* in 1985, the concept of the ethnic enclave has caught the imagination of the scholarly community. As immigration to the United States has increased in recent years, scholars have begun to apply the theory of ethnic enclaves to their own studies of immigrant communities. Beyond the academy the term has been applied to address almost any form of immigrant ethnic concentration whether or not it fits within the original formulation. In the political arena, as debates intensify over the merits of affirmative action programs for colored minorities, the concept of ethnic enclaves has introduced an alternative way to examine the incorporation of new U.S. immigrants – who are mainly from Asia and Latin America. And in an era of increasing ethnic identity and pride, Portes and Bach's assertion of ethnic cohesion in the ethnic enclave is extremely appealing to a wide audience. Although their empirical data are narrowly based on a unique Cuban immigrant community in Miami, their notion of ethnic enclaves has provided a powerful theoretical framework for reconceptualizing existing ways of looking at: (1) class, mobility, and incorporation issues within immigrant communities, and (2) ethnic, race, and immigrant relations in the United States.

This chapter aims to review the fundamental concepts of Portes and Bach's original research in the Cuban immigrant community in Miami, to examine how the theory of ethnic enclaves has been applied to other U.S. ethnic concentrations, and to critique both its theoretical formulation and its application by drawing upon research conducted in New York's Chinatown. Finally we explore the possibility that the popularity of Portes and Bach's study may have as much to do with the political climate of our time as with the merits of their research.

Ethnic Enclave: Defining the Concept

In *Latin Journey* Portes and Bach record a case study of a new ethnic formation in the Cuban community in Miami, a formation they call an "ethnic enclave." The history of Miami, since the 1950s, is a history of successive waves of immigration and the resulting impact on Miami politics, culture, and economics. The 1959 Cuban Revolution brought entire groups of privileged

Cubans to Miami, fleeing the collectivization and nationalization under way in Castro's Cuba. A later wave of poorer refugees arrived in the 1980 Mariel boatlift (Portes and Stepick 1993; Card 1990; Portes and Manning 1986).

Portes and Bach argue that the success of Miami's Cuban immigrants derives from the successful establishment of an ethnic enclave. Portes' notion of an ethnic enclave dates from his earlier work and focuses on the advantages available to communities of immigrants who utilize human cultural capital (Wilson and Portes 1980; Portes 1981). Portes originally defines the enclave as containing immigrant groups which concentrate in a distinct spatial location and organize a variety of enterprises serving their own ethnic market and/or the general population. Their basic characteristic is that a significant proportion of the immigrant labor force works in enterprises owned by other immigrants (Portes and Bach 1981:291).

In further developing the concept in *Latin Journey*, Portes and Bach (1985:203) argue that the two most essential and influential characteristics of enclaves are: (1) the presence of immigrants with sufficient capital, either brought from abroad or accumulated in the United States, to create new opportunities for economic growth; and (2) an extensive division of labor.

Portes and Bach suggest that this formulation usually occurs through two successive waves of immigration of the same group. First an entrepreneurial class is successfully transplanted from home to receiving country. This class grows. Its economic activities expand and diversify. When the second wave of immigrants arrives the entrepreneurial class can offer them opportunities virtually unavailable to immigrants entering other labor market sectors.

Most scholars have long accepted the concept of "dual labor markets." In this formulation the primary labor market operates in the monopolistic industries where workers' jobs are highly paid and secure. The secondary market is lodged largely in small competitive businesses, where jobs are low-paid and insecure. Most immigrants and colored minorities tend to fall into the second option.

Portes and Bach's articulation of the ethnic enclave points to a possible third alternative. The enclave's economic structure, they argue, enables immigrants to achieve upward social mobility. Using culturally based social networks, language, common history, and traditions, immigrants are able to find better-paying jobs, more promotion opportunity, and greater ability to use education and skills in the ethnic enclave than they are in the "dead-end jobs" of the secondary labor market of the dominant economic structures.

Despite low wages in the enclave, workers stay in subordinate jobs in order to take advantage of "paths of mobility unavailable in the outside" (Portes and Bach 1985:204). In Portes and Bach's scenario, as immigrant firms expand, so do openings for co-ethnics at the supervisory and managerial level as well as opportunities for ownership and self-employment. In this model the prosperity of the community is built on close-knit family and kinship networks, where both enclave entrepreneurs and workers are bound by and benefit from ethnic solidarity – mutual obligations, trust, and loyalty – which constitutes a form of social capital absent beyond the enclave boundaries. Portes and Bach portray the Cuban enclave as a favorable alternative to the secondary labor market for new immigrants.

A New Immigrant Narrative

Urban ethnic neighborhoods are not new. European immigrants came to service America's first great industrial expansion after the Civil War. They were recruited to work in large industrial complexes in concentrated urban areas, and they worked alongside native-born Americans. The immigrant ghettos they initially settled were transitional way stations, necessary only until they adjusted to the new society and learned English. The pressures of economic survival invariably forced them to move on – to whatever work was available. Eventually, they found homes outside the ghetto, learned English, and integrated into American society (Sowell 1981).

In presenting the ethnic enclave Portes and Bach are offering a very different immigrant narrative than those of the past. Instead of seeing immigrant concentrations as a place of transition – a place to move away from in order to get better jobs and opportunities – they are suggesting a new and extremely optimistic possibility for the incorporation of new immigrants into the U.S. economy. Cubans in the Miami enclave have jobs in the enclave itself. These jobs, suggest Portes and Bach, are in fact better-paying jobs than those available outside in the secondary labor market. And because they are within the Cuban enclave, lack of English language skills is not a barrier to employment. Moreover, they suggest, within the Cuban enclave there is a shared ethnic spirit of solidarity between workers and employers – a sense of helping each other to help themselves. Cuban employers are able to retain motivated workers who are willing to work hard in order to have the opportunity to learn the trade themselves and advance within the firm as foremen and supervisors. Eventually they hope to utilize ethnic connections within the enclave to open up their own business and become self-employed. In this narrative Cubans can move from the status of humble immigrants without skills or capital to achieve self-employment and ownership inside the enclave, and accomplish this within one generation.

The notion of the ethnic enclave turns the traditional "human resources" argument upside down. Human resource theory suggests that new immigrants must start from the bottom and move up the ladder of mobility. It takes time to learn English well enough to get a better job. It takes even longer to learn the skills to be a better-paid worker. Immigrants must leave their enclave to find work because within immigrant communities there are few businesses well-off enough to provide immigrants with jobs. This narrative was prevalent among earlier European immigrants. An Italian immigrant stayed in New York's Little Italy neighborhood just long enough to learn a few words of English in order to get a job in a Brooklyn factory. For a better job he would have to improve his English and acquire additional skills to go elsewhere to work, perhaps in Detroit's automobile industry. This Italian immigrant's mobility would most likely be limited to moving from unskilled to highly skilled union jobs. Dreams of ownership and self-employment would most likely be deferred and realized through the ambition of his offspring. The ethnic enclave as described by Portes and Bach suggests the possibility of an entirely new narrative for today's new immigrants and provides a framework for reconceptualizing notions of class, mobility, and assimilation within immigrant communities. Today's immigrants can find jobs within the enclave. They can learn skills and receive on-the-job training in the enclave. They may even be able to move up the ladder to self-employment without ever leaving the enclave. If true, this is indeed a new trajectory (*see also* Bailey and Waldinger 1991).

Applications of the Ethnic Enclave Model

The concept of the ethnic enclave is hard to generalize, as even Portes and Bach (1985:38) admit. In describing the Cuban enclave, they lay out several defining characteristics. The ethnic enclave is not an ethnic neighborhood. It is primarily focused on ethnic economic activity. The enclave has an entrepreneurial class possessing the capital necessary for the establishment of ethnic businesses. It also has a diversity of employment arising from the growth of ethnic businesses, which in turn offers opportunities for upward mobility both to supervisory and management positions and even to ownership and self-employment.

These are very difficult conditions to fulfill. First, immigrants with professional and entrepreneurial skills, especially those with individual capital, have a larger degree of mobility in the mainstream American economy. They are often not willing to be stranded in an immigrant enclave to work and perhaps live alongside the poor and unskilled. Second, to maintain the diversity of job opportunities that will allow participants in the ethnic enclave to achieve ownership and self-employment, firms cannot grow too large. In small communities, monopolies in any particular sector would severely inhibit options for ownership and self-employment. Yet this scenario – in which immigrants with capital and entrepreneurial skills start businesses large enough to hire workers but not too large to monopolize the enclave – seems extremely rare.

Perhaps there are very few immigrant communities which would satisfy the criteria. In *Latin Journey*, Portes and Bach detail only two other examples, the Japanese and Jewish immigrant communities arriving in the United States during the 1890–1914 period. Both were noted for their tightly knit communities that were not exclusively residential.

They were instead economic enclaves, areas where a substantial proportion of immigrants were engaged in business activities and where a still larger proportion worked in firms owned by other immigrants. For the entrepreneurially inclined, networks based on ethnic solidarity had clear economic potential. The community was (1) a source of labor, which could be made to work at lower wages; (2) a controlled market; and (3) a source of capital, through rotating credit associations and similar institutions (Portes and Bach 1985:38).

Using these parameters, can the ethnic enclave model detailed by Portes and Bach in the Cuban community in Miami be generalized to other immigrant communities? A number of scholars have tested the applicability of the ethnic enclave formulation. Their studies have produced mixed results.

Gilbertson and Gurak (1993) apply the concept of the ethnic enclave to the labor market experiences of Dominican and Colombian men in New York City utilizing data from a survey conducted in 1981. They do not find the positive returns suggested by Portes and Bach. Concerned that previous research on the enclave has focused too narrowly on wages, Gilbertson and Gurak expand their study to compare primary, secondary, and enclave workers not only on wages but also on opportunities for skill acquisition and access to non-monetary fringe benefits. Unlike the findings in Miami, Gilbertson and Gurak's analysis reveals no significant differences in opportunities for skill acquisition or earnings return between enclave and secondary market workers. In fact they argue that in receipt of health insurance and retirement benefits, increasingly expensive items in today's economy, Dominican and Colombian men in the enclave are disadvantaged compared with secondary sector workers. "Our findings are not harmonious with the hypothesis that the enclave economy is a protected sector of the U.S. economy" (Gilbertson and Gurak 1993:218).

In a separate analysis of the same data, Gilbertson (1993) examines Dominican and Colombian women's enclave labor in New York City. Her analysis shows that women working in Hispanic-owned firms do not receive advantages in earnings returns to human capital when compared to women in other labor market sectors. She concludes that ethnic ties do not produce positive advantages for women workers and that ethnic enclave employment, in fact, is highly exploitative of women. Finally Gilbertson suggests that the successes of certain sectors within the ethnic enclave rely heavily upon the marginal position of immigrant women.

In attempting to apply Portes and Bach's concept of the ethnic enclave to the Dominican and Colombian experience in New York City, Gilbertson and Gurak encounter a problem of definition and methodology. They cite Portes and Bach's definition of an enclave as "firms of any size which are owned and managed by members of an identifiable cultural or national minority." As a result their study encompasses firms in a large decentralized area including much of upper Manhattan and all of Queens. Is this really an ethnic enclave? Furthermore, their survey structure identified respondents working for any Hispanic, whereas an enclave is ideally defined in terms of working for someone of the same country of origin. Respondents may have been working in a business with a Hispanic manager but with a non-Hispanic owner. These complications in definition and methodology exemplify the difficulty in applying the ethnic enclave model beyond the Cuban experience in Miami.

Min Zhou and John Logan (1989), later expanded in Zhou (1992), attempt to apply the ethnic enclave concept to New York's Chinatown. They define and analyze the enclave in three ways, examining place of residence, place of work, and industrial classification. They conduct a separate analysis of the labor market situation of immigrant women. Yet even in a study conducted in New York's Chinatown with its many similarities to Miami and conducted by a student of Portes, the findings produce mixed results. Zhou and Logan suggest that for Chinese immigrant men, labor market experience, education, and English language ability, or human capital, do have positive effects on wage earnings within the enclave. However, they find that "human capital returns for men are not greater within the enclave than outside" (1989:819).

Zhou and Logan's analysis of women's experiences within the enclave further weakens the ethnic enclave hypothesis. Despite the increased importance of women in the Chinatown enclave economy, both as consumers and workers (primarily in the garment industry), Zhou and Logan found that the key predictors of women's earnings were hours logged and occupation, not human capital. They found a total absence of human capital effects and no measurable earnings returns on previous human capital. Why? Zhou and Logan identify certain status-based obstacles for women working within the enclave, including occupational segregation by gender, women forced to play triple roles as mother, wife, and worker, and jobs requiring higher education consistently reserved for men. They conclude that Chinese cultural notions of male supremacy reinforce gender discrimination in the enclave. The authors suggest that further research must be conducted to determine "to what degree the positive functions of the enclave for men are derived from the subordinate position of women" (Zhou and Logan 1989:818).

Though the quantitative findings for the success of the Chinese ethnic enclave are mixed in the 1989 study, in her book *Chinatown: The Socioeconomic Potential of an Urban Enclave* (1992) Min Zhou relies heavily on cultural explanations to make the case for the positive returns of participating in the enclave economy. Following Portes and Bach's notion of ethnic solidarity, Zhou (1992:14) argues that in Chinatown the "economic behavior of enclave participants is not purely self interested, nor is it based on strict calculation in dollars." The enclave benefits entrepreneurs who receive profits in large part from the low-wage labor, but in return also incur obligations to the workers. The enclave benefits the workers, who while "willingly exploited" are given opportunities for training in occupational skills which may improve future employment. Chinese immigrant laborers are willing to work for substandard wages, a fact Zhou attributes directly to three factors: a Chinese cultural work ethic, a positive comparison to poorer wages in China, and a willingness to make sacrifices in the short term in order to derive benefits in the future. In the case of Chinese women in the enclave, Zhou argues "their behavior must be understood in the context of Chinese culture which gives priority not to individual achievement but to the welfare of the family and the community as a whole." Zhou concludes that what women lose for themselves becomes a significant contribution to the family. Unfortunately her argument is weakened by the mixed results of her own research, noted earlier.

Other studies of U.S. Chinatowns have challenged Portes and Bach's view of the ethnic enclave as a protected sector for immigrant workers with ethnic solidarity enabling positive wage returns on human capital and opportunities for upward mobility. Sanders and Nee (1987), examining census data for San Francisco's Chinatown and Miami's Cuban enclave, have compared the wage levels of those working in the enclaves with those in the secondary labor market and concluded that in fact employment in the ethnic enclaves pays immigrant workers less than employment in the non-ethnic labor market. While acknowledging that the ethnic enclave confers certain advantages upon ethnic entrepreneurs Sanders and Nee assign these advantages to ethnic entrepreneurs' ability within the enclave to exploit workers, and to draw on ethnic solidarity and notions of mutual obligation to enforce and maintain sweatshop conditions, including low wages and closure to union organizing. Sanders and Nee question the empirical evidence for the claims of ethnic solidarity at work in the ethnic enclave. They suggest that patterns of exchange between bosses and workers will need to receive further detailed analysis before positive effects of ethnic solidarity upon the socioeconomic mobility of immigrant workers can be verified.

Like Sanders and Nee, Don Mar's research in San Francisco's Chinatown (1991) reveals that, contrary to Portes and Bach's positive findings, workers in the Chinese ethnic enclave have "lower wages, higher turnover and less promotional opportunities than workers in other labor market segments" (1991:17). While Mar notes the positive advantage of the enclave providing higher employment levels than the secondary market and serving as a haven for ethnics during U.S. economic downturns, he suggests that enclaves are not a source of increased mobility or a locale for developing ethnic entrepreneurs. To become an entrepreneur, argues Mar, the immigrant requires capital. This is usually accumulated prior to arrival in the United States or through family networks, not as a result of employment in the ethnic enclave. Mar criticizes Portes and Bach's assertion that earnings in the ethnic economy are tied to human capital by suggesting that immigrants with high levels of human capital endowments would be those most likely also to possess high levels of capital accumulation leading to self-employment in the United States. Mar also suggests levels of mobility to self-employment may not be so high when the significant flow of immigrants out of self-employment back into wage labor is taken into account.

Grenier's research in Miami points to a problem in Portes and Bach's research itself. Grenier claims that in their calculations they have underestimated the percentage of workers in their population samples (Grenier, 1992:137–138, 154). Moreover, he claims that contrary to the image Portes and Bach portray of a middle-class Cuban enclave awash in ethnic solidarity, most participants are not successful entrepreneurs. Rather, they are working-class people, with working-class interests, who are active in the labor movement.

Wilson and Martin (1982) use census data and inferred input–output differentials to compare the Cuban and black enclave economies in Miami and attempt "to explain the success of the few prosperous ethnic business communities in contrast to the marginality of other minority business communities." They posit that enclaves achieve relative advantage based on their internal economic structure. Successful enclaves like the Cuban one attain a high level of internal vertical and horizontal integration, reproducing crucial economic features of the central "majority" economy, yet with a great degree of autonomy from that economy. Less successful enclaves, like the black enclave in Miami fail to achieve the same levels of vertical and horizontal interdependencies and instead appear to be merely an extension of the periphery economy.

How did this difference in economic structure develop? Here Wilson and Martin return to historical, cultural, and sociological factors to seek explanation. In particular they point to the unique location of the Spanish-speaking business population in the Cuban enclave during a time of increasing global trade, transportation, and communication with Latin America and the Caribbean. They also cite greater entrepreneurial experience among Cuban immigrants and greater access to capital. The black community, Wilson and

Martin note, lacks investment capital and an exploitable labor force. Most black labor is exported to white businesses and many highly trained blacks – potential entrepreneurs – prefer working with government agencies. Wilson and Martin conclude that the conditions for the success of the Cuban enclave are unique and are not present in the black community.

We believe that comparing the Cuban and the black enclaves is an extremely problematic and potentially dangerous application. In so doing Wilson and Martin take a framework designed for understanding immigrant experience in the United States and apply it to an established U.S. ethnic community. Blacks are not new immigrants. And as Wilson and Martin state, none of the prerequisites Portes and Bach establish for a successful ethnic enclave exist in the black community in Miami. Perhaps most importantly, blacks do not play the same role in the deindustrialized and restructured U.S. economy that new immigrants play. Seeking increased profits, American businesses have decentralized industrial production and relocated production sites to areas with the least governmental regulation, the lowest labor costs, the weakest labor organizations, and the most vulnerable workers. In many cases this has meant shifting production offshore to the Caribbean, Central America, and the Pacific Rim. In other cases it has meant locating production sites in U.S. immigrant communities. New immigrants fill this labor market, not poor blacks or poor whites. The danger of this application, which Wilson and Martin avoid, is in establishing a comparison between two ethnic communities which on the surface may have many similarities yet differ significantly in historical and social context.

It is our opinion that in evaluating the scholarly debates on the issue, the validity of Portes and Bach's claims proves to be elusive. In part this has to do with the problem of defining the parameters of ethnic enclaves and the difficulties in establishing a fixed list of quantitative data to use for comparative purposes. In part, we conclude, this stems from the fact that much of their observed reality involved political factors which they have underrated and which are impossible to verify relying purely on quantitative economic data. While we agree that the ethnic enclave phenomenon exists in some immigrant communities, we seriously disagree with many of the positive attributes assigned to it, particularly claims of increased upward mobility and ethnic solidarity.

New York Chinatown: A Case Study

The experience of the Miami Cuban immigrant enclave appears to be an extremely rare occurrence. In examining New York's Chinatown in light of the ethnic enclave concept, however, we believe we have found a solid case for comparison. A number of key similarities will allow comparison and evaluation of Portes and Bach's claims. First, Chinatown too is an intensely concentrated ethnic phenomenon with a multi-class composition of largely non-English-speaking new immigrants. And while Chinatown has existed for nearly a century, in the early 1970s it took on many of the ethnic enclave attributes, as Asian "refugee capitalists" immigrating to New York to avoid political instability were later joined by thousands of working-class refugees affected by China's Cultural Revolution coming through Hong Kong. Thus Portes and

Bach's two fundamental characteristics of an enclave, namely an entrepreneurial business class with capital to invest and diversity in the labor market, were
achieved in Chinatown during the course of the 1970s and continued to build
in the 1980s and 1990s as additional capital came from Hong Kong and new
workers came from mainland China, particularly undocumented workers from
Fujian Province (Kwong 1997). But do Portes and Bach's claims of ethnic
solidarity leading to greater return on human capital and increased upward
mobility within the enclave hold up in the Chinatown case?

Our research in New York's Chinatown, drawing upon many years of extensive participatory observation and hundreds of in-depth inteviews, suggests a
very different conclusion from Portes and Bach's claims about ethnic enclaves.
In particular, our study documents that within the Chinese immigrant community, while ethnic support and mutual assistance exist, those who have wealth,
education, and who immigrated earlier have accelerated their capital accumulation and established a dominant position in the community by exploiting less
fortunate co-ethnic newcomers. This process has reached a new extreme with
the recent influx of illegal immigrants from mainland China. Our analysis
suggests that the economic dynamics of the ethnic enclave give rise to a particular strategy for accumulation, not a cultural proclivity for mutual aid. Furthermore, we argue that "ethnic solidarity" has increasingly been manufactured by
the economic elite within the Chinese community to gain better control over
their co-ethnic employees.

As stated earlier, urban ethnic neighborhoods are not new in the United
States. At the turn of the 20th century they served as transitional orientation
points where newly arrived European immigrants adjusted to their new environment before moving into mainstream American society (Sowell 1981). From
the beginning, however, Chinatowns were different. The Chinese Labor Exclusion Act of 1882 barred immigration of Chinese workers into the United States.
Anti-Chinese violence, blatant discrimination, and legislated housing restrictions
forced those Chinese already in America into segregated neighborhoods. The
exclusion of Chinese workers from jobs in the mainstream American labor
market for almost a century further maintained the segregation (Kwong 1979).

With the passage of the 1964 Civil Rights Act, Chinatowns and other newer
ethnic immigrant neighborhoods across the nation no longer owed their existence to legally sanctioned racial exclusion. One could therefore expect that they
would finally play the role of transitional neighborhoods, like the old European
ghettos. Instead, many of these new districts, like the Cuban community in
Miami and New York's Chinatown, have developed viable economic structures
providing new immigrants with jobs right in the midst of their own ethnic immigrant communities.

Until 1965, most U.S. Chinatowns were largely bachelor societies whose
residents engaged in low paying self-employed trades. Families and wives of
residents, taking advantage of liberalized immigration policies, began to
arrive under the "family unification" provision of the 1965 Immigration and
Nationality Act. This influx added a substantial number of women to the labor
force, which the garment industry quickly incorporated by subcontracting
work to Chinatown garment factory operators. For the garment industry

the Chinese situation was ideal. Not only had it solved its labor force problem but garment manufacturers could leave factory management to Chinese contractors, who handled the language problem, worked out wage scales, and even dealt with the union. By the early 1980s, there were already 400 garment factories in New York's Chinatown, employing 20,000 workers.

The rise of the garment industry in the immigrant Chinese community stimulated the growth of Chinese restaurants and other service trades, leading to a local economic boom and providing new job opportunities. These in turn attracted more Chinese immigrant workers and more Hong Kong investment. With additional labor and capital, Chinatown's economy expanded both vertically and horizontally, adding more restaurants and service businesses while diversifying into wholesale food distribution, restaurant equipment, and the construction trades. This rapid growth also spawned new satellite Chinese communities in New York City's other boroughs. By the early 1980s Chinese ethnic enclaves had become thriving, predominantly working-class economic entities inhabited by non-English-speaking immigrants (Kwong 1987).

The Fuzhounese

Since the 1980s New York's Chinatown has received a large and persistent influx of illegal immigrants from mainland China (Kwong 1996; Kwong 1997a). Most of them are from the rural outskirts of the city of Fuzhou in the southeastern province of Fujian. In comparison to estimates of all illegal immigrants currently in the United States (conservatively 5 million: and over 60 percent are Mexicans and Central Americans), the number of Fuzhounese is comparatively small, approximately 200,000. But the Fuzhounese situation is unique. Many of them are victims of a large-scale and sophisticated international human smuggling network. After arrival, they may work for years under what amounts to indentured servitude to pay off large "transportation" debts, now more than $50,000 per person. Smugglers, called "snakeheads," enforce compliance in both work and repayment with constant threats of torture, rape, and kidnapping. Employers brutally exploit these vulnerable undocumented workers while brazenly violating American labor laws.

The original Chinatown in Lower Manhattan and the newer enclave in Sunset Park in Brooklyn (established since the late 1980s) are very attractive to the arriving immigrants. There they are able to locate jobs quickly after landing in the United States without ever having to learn English. Chinese employers can count on the service of this cheap labor supply, because these immigrant workers (without English and professional skills) have problems finding jobs in the open, but competitive, low-wage secondary labor markets outside of Chinatown.

While it is easy for a new immigrant to settle within the Chinese enclave initially, our study calls into question the long-term benefits. Regarding language acquisition, for example, once settled there, immigrants are not likely to learn English, since it is unnecessary in the daily activities and social interactions in the enclave. This is not to say that the immigrants lack desire to learn the language. Several different versions of *English Made Easy* audio cassette tapes are available in Chinese bookstores, as are bilingual microcomputers. Thousands of Chinese immigrants attend English language classes offered weekly by dozens of non-profit groups including unions, churches, and social service organizations in the community. But spending two hours in a language class on Sunday, without a chance to converse and practice until a week later, produces meager results. It is common to meet Chinatown residents who, having lived in the United States for more than 25 years, are not able to communicate in simple English. This language barrier, combined with a shortage of jobs outside the enclave, limits the possibilities for Chinese immigrants to escape the ethnic immigrant community. They remain trapped and vulnerable to the power of Chinese employers.

Futhermore, our study suggests that the very existence of ethnic enclaves like Chinatown inhibits new immigrants from seeking other options. The possibilities available to undocumented workers recently arrived from Fuzhou are the most limited. This can be extremely advantageous to Chinese employers. Ethnic workers with little or no access to the primary or secondary labor markets, especially undocumented workers, are more vulnerable to labor exploitation. In this context it may be in the employers' interest to promote an ideology of ethnic solidarity to reinforce Chinese dependency on the ethnic enclaves.

We are all Chinese: manufacturing ethnic solidarity

From the moment Chinese immigrants arrive, they rely on ethnic networks to survive. The newcomers rely on their relatives or friends to get them housing and jobs. They need them also for the very practical purpose of learning how to do the work. With many working 12 hours a day, often for well below minimum wage, no one except a close friend or a relative would take time to teach a newcomer how to sew, how to set tables, or how to drive nails.

The owners in our study prefer not to get involved in the recruitment and training process. Instead, they allow long-time employees to recruit workers through ethnic and kinship networks. From the employer's perspective this helps screen out undesirable candidates. It also immediately places newcomers into a system of social obligations. The friend performs a *ren-qing* (personal favor) by means of *guanxi* (connections) to get the newcomer a job. The newcomer then owes a *ren-qing* not only to the friend but more importantly, to the employer. The job could have gone to any one of many applicants. But the employer has shown his good-heartedness by helping a fellow Chinese, often a fellow villager, and perhaps even taking the risk of hiring an illegal. The newcomer is expected to return these favors when he or she is in a position to do so. This begins by being a compliant, hard worker. Respectful and loyal behavior, in return, ensures special consideration in individual job assignment, work load, wages, and benefits. Thus Chinese cultural notions of *ren-qing* transform a typical labor/capital class relationship into an association based on personal favor and obligation.

Employers effectively manipulate ideas of ethnic solidarity to inspire worker loyalty. For instance, they may attempt to create work environments that are culturally familiar by disregarding fundamental American rules. Mothers are allowed to leave work at four in the afternoon to pick up their children at school and bring them back to the factory. If the family is in financial distress, which all debt-paying illegals are, the owners may "help out" by hiring their children to work in the factory or allowing them to bring consignments home, even though such practices violate U.S. labor laws. Lonely old ladies with little to do are allowed to work as thread cutters on completed garments. Older men wash dishes for a few dollars so they can feel useful and have others to talk with during the day. Our analysis reveals that employers' generosity toward employees and solidarity with their co-ethnics in effect mask a system of co-ethnic exploitation (Kwong 1997b).

Employers' political power

In addition to their economic control over the enclave, Kwong's earlier studies (1987, 1997a) indicate that Chinatown employers also dominate all social organizations within the Chinese community through a system which has evolved over more than a century. When Chinese in the United States were forced into segregated communities in the 1880s the political structure that emerged as the self-policing force of these communities was transplanted from the rural regions of China. In fact, it closely followed the pattern of local, unofficial civic organization that sprang up during the Qing dynasty. Since Chinese communities in America remained in relative isolation until the 1960s, the imported structure had a long time to develop and solidify. It is still operative today, despite the profound changes of recent years.

Early Chinese immigrants, the vast majority of whom were male, tended to live communally, sharing apartments to save money. This arrangement evolved into a formal collective called a *fong*, which literally means a "room." Members of a *fong* developed a close relationship and great loyalty to one another.

Several *fongs* made up of people from the same village formed a village association; several *fongs* composed of people of the same surname formed family or surname associations. A village association might raise funds for famine relief or for the building of schools and hospitals in their particular home village. But the associations also carried out joint functions and lent support to each other. Successful collective action led to the creation of even larger organizations. *Huiguan* (meeting halls) were composed of several family and village association groups together. While the *huiguan* continued to carry out mutual aid and charity functions, they were more commercially oriented than the *fongs* or associations. They arbitrated disputes among members and served as credit and employment agencies. They also ensured their members' obligations in business transactions with others.

The associations were originally formed to defend their members against a hostile American society and to provide order within the community. But an internal hierarchy soon developed. Association members who owned shops and restaurants commanded the respect of other members, who depended on them for jobs. Those who received jobs and favors became obligated, forming patron/client relationships. The patrons thus became association leaders in addition to owning businesses. The resulting hierarchy that developed within the Chinese community was based entirely on wealth. And wealthy Chinatown shopowners and merchants were able to use the associations to maintain social and political control of the community (Kuo 1977).

Our most recent research suggests that Chinatown's class-based political structure remains fundamentally unchanged. Local power continues to be concentrated in the hands of factory owners, merchants, and landlords, who utilize their official positions in the associations to achieve personal political goals. When association leaders gather, they effectively make up an informal government, though one solely representing the interests of the Chinatown elite. Kinship, village ties, trade, and fraternities may cut vertically across the Chinatown community, superseding class lines. The political structure, however, does not. Political power is concentrated exclusively in the hands of the wealthy.

An examination of political relationships with outside government and non-government entities reveals the way the nearly hegemonic control of power in Chinatown is reinforced. The merchant elite are recognized as the "community leaders" by those beyond the enclave who have no idea how to penetrate this isolated community, and often little interest in trying. In recent cases, whenever the mayor's office, a federal government official, or law enforcement authorities seek to reach out to the Chinese community, they do so through the Chinatown elite. Control over access to political networks beyond Chinatown completes the elite's monopoly of the political, economic, and social structure of Chinatown.

Aspects of a successful enclave?

In some instances positive aspects which Portes and Bach identify in the Miami enclave have been experienced in New York's Chinatown. At least in the 1970s at the beginning of the mass Chinese migration, entrepreneurs found substantial opportunities in the restaurant and garment trades. At that formative stage, workers had some potential for moving into management and ownership positions. Our study points out, however, that this "wild-west frontier" environment disappeared quickly as more and more immigrants poured in from Hong Kong and mainland China. Employers took advantage of the surplus labor by offering increasingly lower rewards to their co-ethnic employees. Workers who could not learn enough English remained constrained within the enclave, unable to exit into the mainstream American labor markets. Standards continued to deteriorate as the waves of undocumented Fuzhounese immigrants entered the competition for jobs in the 1980s and 1990s. The potential for upward mobility within the enclave economy reported by Portes and Bach in Little Havana, quickly ended in New York's Chinatown.

Conclusion

Portes and Bach are correct in identifying the importance of the ethnic enclave phenomenon, especially in situations in which new immigrants, mostly from Asia and Latin America, tend not to disperse but reside and work in ethnically concentrated locations. Unlike the ghettos of earlier European immigrant communities, today ethnic enclaves exist which are not transitional. They have capital flowing in to employ new immigrants and they have a multi-class character. Though we disagree with many of the implications of Portes and Bach's study, we believe their introduction of the concept of "ethnic enclave" has made an important contribution by intensifying the debate regarding new forms of immigrant incorporation and related socioeconomic, political, and racial issues.

The concept of the ethnic enclave, however, is not easily generalizable. The specific phenomenon of "Little Havana" in Miami described by Portes and Bach involves an ethnically concentrated, multi-class, and more or less self-sufficient community. This is highly unusual. In most instances of immigrant enclaves today, immigrant workers still reside in ghettos as a transitional place until they locate better jobs in the secondary or primary economy. Entrepreneurs and professionals tend to seek mobility in mainstream society, not in the enclave. For the different classes of Cuban immigrants – elites, small entrepreneurs, middle-class professionals, and working people – to remain together in one enclave in Miami is rare. Given their particular political and immigration history it may even be unique. If so, the characteristics and attributes Portes and Bach ascribe to the ethnic enclave concept may also be unique to Miami. This possibility must be considered.

Our Chinatown study certainly does not support their positive claims for the role of the enclave in the immigrant incorporation process, despite examining a phenomenon perhaps closest to Portes and Bach's Cuban ethnic enclave. Nor do other studies we have reviewed. Claims that workers in the enclaves receive higher pay than those in the secondary labor market and claims of greater opportunity for upward mobility to "self-ownership" are particularly difficult to corroborate.

Key problems exist in Portes and Bach's research data itself, as noted earlier (Grenier 1992). Further problems emerge from their methodology. Their conception of the ethnic enclave – a complex group of people moving and changing into different roles over time – is too broadly conceived. To confirm their observations quantitatively requires an agreement on specific parameters of the study. Whose incomes are to be counted? Must all those considered in the study reside in the enclave? How do you correctly account for mobility over time? How do you compare the conditions inside the enclave to those in the general labor markets? Which part of the general labor market should be used in the comparison? It seems that part of the difficulty of confirming Portes and Bach's claims is that we are comparing apples and oranges. This problem confronts all studies inspired by their ethnic enclave conception.

Ultimately, we believe that Portes and Bach's analysis significantly overestimates the strength of ethnic solidarity and underestimates the existence of co-ethnic exploitation. Furthermore, Portes and Bach consistently underestimate the political power relationships within the enclaves. Ethnic employers do use their political power inside these isolated ethnic communities to their advantage. Our fieldwork in the Chinese community presents a clear example of this. Despite significant scholarly debate on the issue and numerous attempts to apply the concept of the ethnic enclave beyond the Miami case study, the evidence in support of the general applicability of the ethnic enclave model remains inconclusive.

The ethnic enclave and cultural diversity

Reservations and criticisms of their optimistic claims notwithstanding, Portes and Bach's theory of ethnic enclaves is extremely popular. Why? In the final analysis, we suggest the popularity of their study may have more to do with the political climate of our time than the applicability of their research findings. Their claims of ethnic solidarity and ethnic self-reliance are appealing to those new immigrant groups attempting to carve a niche for themselves in the American landscape and who want to distance themselves from what they see as the failures of the traditional colored minorities. In this new narrative, immigrants can count on ethnic solidarity and mutual assistance to succeed without help from the mainstream society. They can develop their own systems of upward mobility in the American economy. And they can accomplish this without "forced assimilation" – without sacrificing their language, culture, and ethnic community.

Claims of ethnic solidarity and ethnic self-reliance have also captured the imagination of those who are frustrated by the lack of economic progress in the ghettos of American communities. If new immigrants can achieve economic success in this manner, why not the African American community? If the ethnic enclave model works, it provides an alternative for evaluating the status of traditional U.S. minorities, especially the African American community, and the lack of progress by the civil rights movement in achieving economic parity. By implication, the success of the immigrant ethnic enclave suggests that African Americans lack a sense of "ethnic solidarity" and "work ethic" as compared to new immigrants. Moreover, if the virtues of the ethnic enclave prove true, and colored immigrants can achieve upward mobility, then African American charges of racism leveled against the U.S. economic system would be undermined.

Here we must be wary of how ideas of ethnic solidarity, designed to further the analysis of immigrant groups in America, may play into other ideological discourses and political agendas. Do the successes of some ethnic groups based on patterns of ethnic solidarity suggest a cultural superiority over other ethnic groups? We argue that the answer must be no. Instead, there are other historical, political, and economic dynamics at work, as suggested in the work of Wilson and Martin (1982). It is important to remember that by and large new immigrants are likely to be better off economically than the most depressed parts of the American population. Today's immigrants, like immigrants of previous generations, tend to be the more personally restless and ambitious elements from their homeland. Additionally, as a result of U.S. immigration preferences, today's immigrants tend to have much stronger family ties, an advantage they have over both blacks and whites in our society. And finally, immigrants from Asia and Latin America, while facing discrimination in the United States as colored minorities, have not suffered the consequences of the intense hostility built up and enacted between blacks and whites through the history of slavery and segregation.

How does the notion of ethnic enclaves engage the discourse about cultural diversity in U.S. society? Portes and Bach attempt to provide insights into a new form of immigrant incorporation into the U.S. economy at a time when immigration is becoming increasingly prominent in academic, policy, and popular discourse. Yet the purported successes and potential of the ethnic enclave may actually provide a misleading framework for exploring and understanding issues of diversity in U.S. society, especially as they play out between traditional racial/ethnic groups and new immigrant communities. Furthermore, the notion of ethnic solidarity may also obscure the complexities, conflicts, diversity, and contradictions within individual immigrant communities.

REFERENCES CITED

Bailey, Thomas, and Roger Waldinger
  1991   Primary, Secondary and Enclave Labor Markets: A Training System Approach. *American Sociological Review* 56:432–445.
Card, David
  1990   The Impact of the Mariel Boatlift on the Miami Labor Market. *Industrial and Labor Relations Review* 43:245–258.
Gilbertson, Greta A.
  1993   Women's Labor and Enclave Employment: The Case of Dominican and Colombian Women in New York City. *International Migration Review* 29:657–670.
Gilbertson, Greta A., and Douglas T. Gurak
  1993   Broadening the Enclave Debate: The Labor Market Experiences of Dominican and Colombian Men in New York City. *Sociological Forum* 8:205–220.
Grenier, Guillermo J.
  1990   Ethnic Solidarity and the Cuban-American Labor Movement in Dade County. *Cuban Studies* 20:29–48.
Kuo, Chia-ling
  1977   *Social and Political Change in New York's Chinatown.* New York: Praeger.
Kwong, Peter
  1979   *Chinatown, New York: Labour and Politics, 1930–1950.* New York: Monthly Review Press.
  1987 [1996]   *The New Chinatown.* New York: Hill and Wang.
  1997a   *Forbidden Workers: Illegal Chinese Immigrants and Chinese Labor.* New York: New Press.
  1997b   Manufacturing Ethnicity. *Critique of Anthropology* 17(4):365–387.
  1997c   The Overseas Chinese Miracle. *Asian American Policy Review* 7:73–87.
Mar, Don
  1991   Another Look at the Enclave Economy Thesis: Chinese Immigrants in the Ethnic Labor Market. *Amerasia Journal* 17(3):5–21.
Portes, Alejandro
  1981   Modes of Structural Incorporation and Present Theories of Immigration. In *Global Trends in Migration.* Mary M. Kritz, Charles B. Keely, and Sylvano M. Tomasi, eds. Pp. 279–297. Staten Island, NY: CMS Press.
Portes, Alejandro, and Robert L. Bach
  1985   *Latin Journey: Cuban and Mexican Immigrants in the U.S.* Berkeley: University of California Press.
Portes, Alejandro, and L. Jensen
  1989   The Enclave and the Entrants: Patterns of Ethnic Enterprise in Miami Before and After Mariel. *American Sociological Review* 54:929–949.
Portes, Alejandro, and Robert D. Manning
  1986   The Immigrant Enclave Theory and Empirical Examples. In *Competitive Ethnic Relations.* Susan Olzak and Joane Nagel, eds. Pp. 47–68. Orlando, FL: Academic Press.

Portes, Alejandro, and Alex Stepick
   1993   *City on the Edge: The Transformation of Miami.* Berkeley: University of California Press.
Sanders, J. M., and V. Nee
   1987   Limits of Ethnic Solidarity in the Enclave Economy. *American Sociological Review* 52:745–773.
Sowell, Thomas
   1981   *Ethnic America: A History.* New York: Basic Books.
Wilson, Kenneth L., and W. Allen Martin
   1982   Ethnic Enclaves: A Comparison of the Cuban and Black Economies in Miami. *American Journal of Sociology* 88:135–160.
Wilson, Kenneth L., and Alejandro Portes
   1980   Immigrant Enclaves: An Analysis of the Labor Market Experiences of Cubans in Miami. *American Journal of Sociology* 86:295–319.
Zhou, Min
   1992   *Chinatown: The Socioeconomic Potential of an Urban Enclave.* Philadelphia: Temple University Press.
Zhou, Min, and John R. Logan
   1989   Returns on Human Capital in Ethnic Enclaves: New York City's Chinatown. *American Sociological Review* 54: 809–820.

16

Perspectives on U.S. Kinship

A. Lynn Bolles

Kinship and marriage have been central to anthropology since the days of Lewis Henry Morgan (1974[1877]), whose work on Iroquois social organization set the parameters of study. Kinship and marriage patterns foster cooperation and group loyalty, and are deemed fundamental to human social organization (Spradley and McCurdy 1994:197). Over the years anthropologists developed a complex categorization system of kinship terminology that classified principles of mating and birth. These principles involved how to reproduce members of the next generation (marriage), where they should live (residence rules), how to establish links between generations (descent), and how to pass on positions in society (succession) or material goods (inheritance) (Shultz and Lavender 1987:180). Following the dictates of the discipline, most of the research on kinship and marriage carried out by U.S. anthropologists took place among "tribes." Kinship in anthropological discourse resided with those whose life experiences were deemed as strange or alien; the traditional simple society centered around face-to-face, interpersonal interactions.

Most studies of U.S. kinship, usually carried out by sociologists, dwelled on the simplicity of the general rules of descent or on the local aberrant behavioral systems that appear among the "exotic within," such as Native Americans, and those deemed a problem, such as African Americans, and immigrant groups. All of those exceptions to the "American" (Euro-Protestant) middle-class nuclear family system were designated as abnormal. At best, other "exotic" U.S. systems were viewed as unassimilated kinship patterns retarded by their unique histories and in-group approved modes of behavior. Patricia Zavella's (1987:12) review of Chicano family studies notes that "values conducive to success in American society – achievement, independence and deferred gratification – [were] supposedly absent in the Mexican-American family." Further, changes toward acquiring American "egalitarian" values and norms would come only with acculturation. There were anthropologists working in the urban United States whose research countered the dominant nuclear family/acculturation/ assimilation model in their studies with "problem" people (e.g. Stack 1972; Valentine 1978; Gwaltney 1981; Susser 1982). Each of these ethnographic accounts focused on kin-based systems of cooperation, obligation, loyalty, reciprocity, marriage, residence rules, descent, succession, and inheritance.

However, since these studies were on "the problem" population, black and working-class families in poverty, they were not incorporated into the larger comparative kinship and marriage sector of the discipline. Even though the research represented certain segments of black America, a plus on the "exotic" side, the population was not intriguing enough in complexity compared to kinship and marriage located in the "so-called" Third World.

At this time, kinship itself was on the wane as a popular subject in anthropology. According to David Schneider (1995:193), a combination of factors contributed to the decline, including the abandonment of structural functionalism as a theoretical tool in many quarters. But more importantly, the main concern in anthropology was: "there were no more interesting questions left. . . . Who cares. . . . Who needs it (kinship)?" But later on, as Schneider explains, the problems changed and "with the shifting of problems, kinship phoenix-like rose from its ashes."

New studies of kinship and family, armed with new sets of problems, frame questions that call for formulating new theories and reexamining old ones. The rethinking of family and kinship came in three important junctures: feminist challenges, family as politics, and family as class ideology.

Feminist challenges came very early in the 1970s as women and men who used gender as an analytic category looked to classic ethnography and began critiquing the old as they charted the new. In the now classic volumes, *Women, Culture and Society*, and *Towards an Anthropology of Women*, authors spoke of public versus private domains, and how each was gendered in very specific ways based on history, politics, the economy, and the household division of labor. Bronislaw Malinowski was the first social scientist to examine what was meant by the term "family": was the family truly a universal, natural human institution? (Collier et al. 1982:25). Speaking of U.S. family systems, Collier, Rosaldo, and Yanagisako (1982:35) argue that despite varied relationships that are a result of complex motivations, U.S. society idealizes relations with the family as nurturing while casting relationships outside the family – particularly in the sphere of work and business – as just the opposite. Therefore, rethinking the family required understanding of the ideological construct that fulfills basic needs, and a refined set of analyses that contextualizes these needs within historical processes. The "ideal family" was not lost, as right-wing critics implied, but rethinking about the family demanded that contemporary theoretical models had to incorporate the power of dominant ideologies more than ever before.

Leith Mullings (1997:72) comments that the United States at the end of the 20th century provides us with "the clearest demonstrations that 'family' is the prism through which ideological battles are waged." Conservative ideologies seek to dominate our conceptualizations of what the family is and its relationship to society. The genius of the right, Mullings states, is the ability to conflate the very real decline in community resulting from the processes of global capitalism with the transformation of the structure and function of the household. The deterioration of community and civility has a trickle-down effect in the decreases in employment rates/earning power, the decline in income of families, and the reduction of social services. Together these factors contribute to downward trends in standards of living, and "create a context for fragmentation of households and community, in which people indeed turn against and fear each other." The cult of the traditional family, like the cult of true womanhood, as Mullings maintains, functions to reproduce, exacerbate, and reinforce class and race differences and aggressively reframes and redefines old and new concepts of "otherness."

The dogmatism of the cult of the traditional family led Rayna Rapp (1982) to examine families and households in terms of their relationship to the economic system, and their access to resources of the society. Kinship studies now include differing social relations to resources of society, and look at how individual members and kin-groups consume produce and reproduce themselves as they cope with the process of downsizing and deskilling of the workforce within an expanding and profit-soaring economy. Across gender, race, ethnicity, religion, sexuality, physical ability, and other differences, families and households are located within a class position situated in a material base. As Ida Susser (1996, 1999) shows in her review of poverty in the United States, the contradictions of gender inequality within the family, in "the cult of the traditional family" and the like, are based on lived material experiences.

U.S. kinship may appear to U.S. popular culture as a simple symbolic representation of biology, but in fact those kin practices house systems of inequality and hierarchy (Yanagisako and Collier 1987). Inequitable positions of women within kin groups and in society at large are ideologically naturalized. The social construction of female inequality is deemed as "God given" and natural, in the same fashion that males hold power in societies where gender is hierarchically maintained (Yanagisako and Delany 1995).

Diverse U.S. Kinship

Kinship and family relations still remain at the center of much of the idealized rhetoric and public policy of contemporary life. While one group laments the loss of "family values" and the vanishing isolated nuclear family, another set of people at a Gay Pride parade sport T-shirts that proclaim "Love Makes a Family." To press the point further, let us not forget that "It takes a Whole Village to Raise a Child," whether voiced by African migrants in Chicago, by an after-school program in Los Angeles, or by a First Lady.

In the following four sections, a select number of case studies demonstrate the diversity of kin systems and family organizations in the United States. Although common interest often replaces kinship as an elementary factor in the larger social organization of U.S. society, kin relationships still serve as a principal frame of reference in contemporary life. People need kin relations in order to survive difficult conditions, to provide for dependants and to have access to the basics of subsistence – food, shelter, and clothing. In the most advanced technological society, people move back to the basics in order to move forward toward the next century.

Immigration

Global restructuring has altered the nature and organization of the economies of the developing world. Lone individuals as well as families migrate to former colonial "mother" countries, to the United States and to other prosperous nations such as Germany, Canada, and Australia. In the process, immigrants forge and sustain multistranded social relations that link together their societies of origin and settlement. They are "people with feet in two societies." Nonetheless, new immigrants must adjust to new, socially alien environments to fulfill their mission.

Between Two Islands, a study of migration from the Dominican Republic to New York City, discusses how two patterns of domestic organization evolved into a third form as a result of immigration. Besides the single-mate mode, where authority resides with the senior male, or in the multiple-mate unit where women maintain authority, the novel third form, produced in the United States is a relatively egalitarian division of labor and evenly distributes authority between partners. Sherri Grasmuck and Patricia Pessar's (1991) ethnographic work showed a profound change in budgetary allocations, particularly in terms of who had control of funds. Of the 55 households under study, few follow a patriarchal pattern of budgetary control and many more pool their income. Income pooling in nuclear households brings women advantages that were unavailable to them in the Dominican Republic. Responsibility for basic subsistence costs was distributed among family members regardless of gender, thereby reducing the contrast between "essential" male contributions and "supplementary" female inputs. In addition, men participated in domestic tasks generally associated with women's work in the Dominican Republic. More than ever before, men through their own experiences better appreciated the skills that women brought to these activities. In response to the question, "Who is the head of the household?" a woman replied:

> We are both the heads. If both husband and wife are earning salaries, then they should rule equally in the household. In the Dominican Republic it is always the husband who gives the orders in the household. But here, when the two are working, the women feels herself the equal of the man in ruling the home. (Grasmuck and Pessar 1991:151)

As migration follows the movements of capital, migrants follow possible employment from location to location. Sometimes families have to separate from one another once again in their new locations. In her study on immigrant networks among Afro-Trinidadians in Los Angeles, Christine Ho examines transcontinental kin networks in North America. Ho's (1991:107–110) findings show that all maintain ties with kin in other cities of North America, such as New York, Washington, DC, Houston, Miami, Montreal, Toronto, Calgary, and Vancouver. Almost half the group have links with two generations of kin, mostly consisting of the sibling generation and the generations of their siblings' children, or else cousins and their children. Despite wide dispersion across the

North American continent, kin keep in touch with one another, often maintaining intense relationships across thousands of miles.

> I keep in touch with my family in New York. I talk to my mother about every other day or so. . . . I think we could have had a house [by now] if it wasn't for these phone bills. (Ho 1991:108)

Of course letter writing continues to be an important form of communication, but included in the correspondence are transcontinental remittances. A Trinidadian, who has done well in Los Angeles, sends money to his mother in Miami on a regular basis. Child support is included here too. A 16-year-old daughter from a teenage romance in Trinidad receives funds in Toronto from her father living in Los Angeles.

The effort to maintain a national cultural presence through ethnic solidarity shifts as children born or raised in the United States are forced to consider how to proceed with their own lives. Are they a "hyphen" people, for example, West Indian-Americans, or Cuban-Americans, or are they blacks and Latinos? Given the national ideology of race, non-white migrants tend to be designated by their race, then by their ethnicity, then by their class. This factors in decisions among immigrants to maintain family links and transnational connections.

Work

In the contemporary United States, earning a living depends on access to resources, such as education, and class position, and dealings with inequitable situations involving racism, sexism, and other differences, such as religion and sexual preference. Kinship studies must consider these differing social relations of work life as they illustrate how individual members and kin-groups consume, produce and reproduce themselves in relation to the economic system. The following examples show how family members aid each other in acquiring the basics of subsistence, finding jobs, resisting management in anti-worker settings, and generally assisting in household survival.

The position of Haitians in Miami is predicated on low-skilled, race-based employment practices. Here, as Alex Stepick and Guillermo Grenier (1994:186) assert, "Blacks are confined to the back of the house and even there an appreciable number of them are Haitian immigrants." The authors (1994:188) recount the story of how Charlie and family became the reserve pool of labor for a seafood restaurant. Charlie is a Haitian who has been working at the seafood restaurant since 1980. His brother-in-law has worked there for more than ten years and his brother for six years. Another brother-in-law, another brother, and a nephew all worked there at some time during the 1980s. Management considered all of them, especially Charlie, excellent employees. Charlie is a hard worker who keeps to himself and does not bother anyone. He never talks back to the boss. Indeed, he seemingly never talks to anyone while working. He just minds his business, paying attention to his work, nothing more. After more than five years of Charlie's exemplary work, the kitchen manager asked, "Charlie, you think your madam would like to work here in the pantry?"

The following day, Charlie's wife Lucy took the bus to the restaurant where the manager, according to Lucy, told her: "Lucy, how about you work today and fill application tomorrow?" Soon after that, the manager asked: "Charlie, do you have any sons old enough to start work?" One son, Vernet, then started working there. Vernet proved to be like his father, resilient and compliant. Other sons followed – Edmond, Sam, and finally Patrick.

David Griffith's *Jones's Minimal* (1993) presents another study of low-wage labor in the U.S. South. How did industrial work, with its lack of opportunity for advancement, no benefits, and poor working conditions, affect workers and their kin?

"Shucking Shellfish, Picking Crab," a chapter in *Jones's Minimal*, examines seasonal employment in the seafood processing industry in coastal North Carolina. Not only do workers hold multiple jobs to offset the variance of this seasonal industry, but they are recruited and their position maintained in these plants, by kinship and informal social ties. Employers utilize current workers' networks of friends and kin to locate and draw new workers into the plants. According to Griffith (1993:125), it is common for mothers to recruit daughters, for aunts to recruit nieces, and for grandmothers to recruit grand-daughters. The data show a labor force pulled in many directions, yet continually drawn back to the low wages and unpleasant working conditions of seafood processing. Similar forces are documented in Mary Anglin's (1999) ethnographic research among mica factory workers in Appalachia.

In her study of the transformation of the female labor force in a New England factory town, Louise Lamphere (1987) looks at the relationships between women, their work, and family life. She followed successive waves of women laborers entering the factory through historical records and fieldwork study with the contemporary working population. Each group of women, across immigrant status and ethnicity, faced similar problems of employment, and childcare, and used kin networks and family relations as resources. Finding jobs, and solving housing problems were sometimes arranged by family already in New England or the United States. In certain instances, networks of friends acted like kin in lieu of family. For example, the recent Colombian immigrant workers relied on friends and employer recruitment efforts rather than kin in helping them find jobs, housing, and childcare (Lamphere 1987:242).

Continuing research on family and work found plural networks to be important strategies used by women workers in Sunbelt industries in the 1980s. Here, the workers are working-class native Hispanos and Anglos, who showed similarities in the way they constructed their work and living situations. Both plural networks were female-centered and combined extended family, primary relatives, and a number of friends. Migration from one town in New Mexico to another, or from other states to New Mexico, in search of employment, was aided by a large number of kin, who might have been left behind, but who were supportive in the move (Lamphere et al. 1993).

Most Mi'kmaqs, a Native American group, have some extended family member keeping the home fires burning while they are away (Prins 1996). Social bonding beyond one's community is crucial to Mi'kmaq survival. Migratory work habits demand that Mi'kmaqs rely on fellow tribespeople in other regions to open up their homes if job opportunities are located there. As a woman quipped: "We count the seasons and jobs more than by years. . . . I get all mixed up about dates of things because I moved so darn many times in my life. . . . Thinking about it makes me dizzy" (1996:192).

Janet Benson (1994) studied Vietnamese and Laotian families as they adapt to, exploit, or resist management control over their production in the meat packing industry in Kansas. Families and households provide much of the "social safety net" when workers are fired or become disabled. Vietnamese and Laotian families and households respond to other working conditions based on their own cultural strategies. For instance, individuals and families try to identify friends or relatives on location with whom they can live, before moving there. This scheme helps defray housing costs until newcomers are able to look after themselves.

One of the major problems faced by families and kin who rely on low-wage employment is how inadequate the money is to satisfy the minimum subsistence needs of contemporary life. Since the 1930s Great Depression, the U.S. government offers programs for families and households whose fortunes fall below the levels provided by low-wage work. From the beginning, funds from public assistance programs were not enough for families and households to meet their daily needs. Thirty years later, anthropologist Carol Stack (1972) used the term "survival strategies" as a shorthand for the combination of ways in which poor people find the means for their subsistence, which also includes the use of public assistance as a financial resource.

These same strategies were the basis for research conducted in the 1990s. The question still remains: How do poor single mothers survive? Kathryn Edin and Laura Lein in *Making Ends Meet* (1997) studied a sample of African American, Euro-American and Mexican American women who were on public assistance. In addition to their "welfare checks," the authors identified three main sources – family members, boyfriends, and children's fathers – whom poor mothers relied on for cash, services, and access to other resources. Many of the children's fathers were listed as absent from the home, although one-quarter of them "stayed" in the household at least occasionally. Boyfriends were critical as they became de facto fathers too in these scenarios. As one woman told the interviewers concerning her boyfriend (Edin and Lein 1997:158): "My new boyfriend Bill, he helps. He lives in now. He works odd jobs around the neighborhood. He gives me as much as I was making cleaning motel rooms. . . . Bill is like a father to my children." However, as Jagna Sharff (1998) documents for families on the Lower East Side of New York City, in a poor neighborhood undermined by rising real estate prices, even such survival strategies begin to falter and, as others have shown, such dependence on men for support does not come without conflict (Susser 1998).

In a contemporary U.S. context, the means of survival include access to a wide variety of resources – food, housing, clothing, education, strategic networks – all based on relative levels of income generation. Since the majority of the population depends on wages and being employed by others, the job market and employment opportunities are critical components for understanding the structures of family and kin. Familial relations vary in numerous ways dependent on class, race, ethnicity, and gender. Clearly, the contributions of men as husbands, children's fathers, and boyfriends are significant to women across class. Family and kin help in finding jobs, provide services to one another, aid in work-related situations, and fulfill roles as stop-gap measures when economic systems fail, or when the inequality in a marriage becomes a reason for female quests for autonomy.

Lesbian and gay kinship

Ellen Lewin (1996:9) remarks that unraveling the meaning of "Lesbian in American cultures" requires a perspective that acknowledges how identity is perceived and experienced by real women, and how it intersects with other sources of identity and belonging. Becoming a member of one group often means abandoning, being rejected, or redefining membership in a former location. Nowhere is this complex of belonging more vivid than in family and kin connections of lesbians and gays. By entering a new group, lesbians and gays often must go through a sense of abandonment, if their family rejects their homosexuality.

Part of the "coming-out" story addresses this process of establishing a personal identity as lesbian or gay. Finding a home in lesbian and gay communities creates a new sense of being, but the old group allegiances based on culture, religion, race, and other differences might still have a role in their lives. Therefore, lesbians and gays understand how they are connected to the world, by community building and belonging that has to do with the construction of a new way of viewing family and kinship. They create family and kinship that may or may not be based on biological ties, but are based on affinity and solidarity. Lesbians and gays are making a way for themselves. Enduring bonds of kinship account for a broad spectrum of people described as "those who are always there for you," a select group upon whom an individual could rely on, regardless of context or crisis (Weston 1995:88). Sometimes, biological kin who maintain their relations with the gay members of their families are a part of this chosen family. In this case, chosen families can incorporate biological kin, heterosexual and gay friends, lovers, and children. Gay kinship ideologies, Kath Weston states (1995:93), recognize all too well the fragility of "blood" ties and celebrate friendships (chosen people) as an enduring bond that assumes the status of kinship. Chosen kin are expected, to "be there" for one another through ongoing, reciprocal exchanges of material and emotional support. The authenticity of chosen kin is not formed in an ideological vacuum, but in a context of social struggle and in real lived experiences, as the following instance illustrates. Bruce Edelman needs to lay a carpet in his home. To do this home repair, he called on his kin to help him with the task. He placed a ten-minute phone call which initiated a chain of communications that crisscrossed the city. The following weekend, seven of his closest relatives converged on his home with hammers in hand. Bruce contributed pizza, beer, soft drinks, and all the necessary materials. To the accompaniment of music from the boom box that followed Bruce wherever he went, this improvised work crew installed the entire carpet in a day.

Recognizing Ourselves (Lewin 1998) is an ethnography on marriage and kinship among lesbians and gays. The popularity of rituals of commitment is contested within the lesbian and gay communities and seen by some as mimicking heterosexual, patriarchal practices. Such rituals are also opposed by many religious and political institutions and in some instances are even considered illegal. Nonetheless, commitment celebrations are a part of life in lesbian and gay communities.

Ellen Lewin (1998) argues that wedding rituals have a profound impact on the way lesbians and gays view themselves and on the way others view them. Lesbian and gay weddings involve multiple levels of communication between and across lines of sexual orientation; they allow, or even demand, the images of lesbian and gay lives to be wrenched from the cliches of "lifestyle." These rituals provide classic examples of the overlapping and indeterminate nature of both cultural performance and tools of socialization. Furthermore, such weddings also mark how families are formed and patterns of kinship are established.

The ensuing illustration of marriage and kinship among lesbians and gays begins with a year-long courtship of "Steve and Tom Rosenthal-Baker." They were married in a Saturday night ceremony in June, 1993. Tom explained why he always wanted to find a life partner and to settle in a permanent, committed relationship (Lewin 1998:112):

> That's always been my dream. To find somebody who you can just tell that it's going to be a fairy tale. I basically wanted . . . what my parents had. And I didn't separate the fact that here is a man and a woman. I just saw the relationship . . . I felt that if I was going to marry somebody, another man, it would either be in a church, in a synagogue, or it would be in my backyard [with] just us saying " 'til death do us part."

Tom converted to Judaism for himself and for their wedding. He said:

> We were really making a big commitment to each other and it wouldn't be a Jewish commitment until I was Jewish as well. . . . I wanted to make sure that I was wearing tallith [the Jewish prayer shawl, worn by men after their bar mitzvah] before we went down the aisle.

Murial and Carol's process of creating their ceremony helped them as a couple, but it also meant negotiating with family members as to who would or would not attend their ritual. Murial's two sons agreed to attend, but would not let their wives or children be exposed to them as a lesbian couple. On the morning of the ceremony, Murial's daughter, accompanied by her teenage daughter, arrived early to give the couple "something old, something new, something borrowed, something blue." She told Carol, "You're now part of our family."

Neither Carol's mother or her stepfather approved of or attended the ceremony. Carol's former fourth grade teacher and her husband came as her surrogate parents. The group that came together for the ritual was diverse, including a number of children, which pleased both Murial and Carol. Lewin reminds us (1998:121) that "lesbian and gay weddings, more than heterosexual ones, are occasions that mark the collapse or the unreliability of family ties more than their resiliency, leaving resentment and sorrow that may persist long after the ceremonies themselves have passed into memory."

Lesbians and gays are creating kinship and family not only through biological ties, but through ties of affinity and solidarity – the family you choose, those who will be there for you. All of the social behaviors of kin are in full operation too. Family helps you fix your house, and the reciprocity is embedded in the relationship. Weddings solidify personal relationships by expressing in public the deep emotional feelings couples have toward each other. Weddings also involve kin. Lesbian and gay couples must deal not only with their new in-laws, and family, but they also must struggle with issues of rejection of their homosexual marital union.

The chosen family, "those who are always there for you," is about creating family without genealogy, and establishing social bonds that are indeed thicker than blood or water.

Assisted reproductive technology

Other ways of creating kinship and family also have been addressed by anthropologists. In response to the use of new reproductive technologies (in vitro fertilization, surrogate motherhood) much of the anthropological literature about family looks at beliefs of procreation and the invasion of technology in personal life. Domestic and international adoption, adoptee rights, the overused foster care system, and the like have received less notice in the literature. Christine Ward Gailey's work on adoption focuses on the impact of race, class, and gender in adoption proceedings, and how adoption agencies shore up the social hierarchy with their own social engineering. All of the new and old technologies have been used more by middle- and upper-middle-class couples, as they are the ones who can afford these options. Such efforts often use traditional ideologies about who belongs to establish kin ties.

Helena Ragoné (1994) studied surrogate motherhood, and the issues surrounding this new approach. The advent of gestational surrogacy, and surrogate motherhood, not only separates reproduction from sexual intercourse, it also separates motherhood from pregnancy, and alters the biological underpinnings of popular notions of kinship.

Women who are surrogates have been quick to dismiss the idea that remuneration for the pregnancy was an instrumental venture separate from family ideals. The surrogacy was viewed as a part-time job that allowed the woman, especially if she was a mother, to stay at home with her own children. The majority of the funds received from the surrogacy were spent on family needs and projects, as almost a reward for sharing their lives with others. One woman proclaimed (Ragoné 1997:114) that the whole process was "a gift of love."

An obstacle for the father is that a woman not his wife would be the "mother" of his child. A primary strategy employed by both couples was to de-emphasize the husband's role, to downplay the significance of his biological link to the child and to focus on the bond that develops between the wife (considered an adoptive mother) and the surrogate mother. As a surrogate mother noted (Ragoné 1997:121): "Parents are the ones who raise the child. I got that from my parents, who adopted children. My siblings were curious and my parents gave them the information they had and they never wanted to track down their biological parents. I don't think of the baby as mine; it is the parents, the ones who raise the child, that are important."

Donor insemination (DI) poses similar problems to those experienced by the surrogate arrangement. Ragoné (1997:114) states that DI places the husband, who is not the child's biological father, in the same structural position as surrogacy places the wife. In the final analysis, it might be difficult to understand what motivates infertile couples to test the limits of the popular understanding of the family, but what unites both groups is their quest for a child – someone else to carry on the traditions.

These new sets of technologies are creating new kinds of families, but often using traditional ideologies in different ways. Surrogacy is a way of maintaining the nuclear family. The two mothers – one surrogate, the other the social mother – deal with each other by underplaying their roles in the birth process. Surrogate mothers and male sperm donors are chosen by prospective parents through a variety of biological reasoning, beyond health issues. The contradictions of birthing, mothering, and paternity are tempered by notions of continuing biological links and the gift of new life.

Conclusion: Like the Phoenix, Kinship Rose from Its Ashes

The family as we know it is not dead. As the host of ethnographic examples above illustrated, not only are families and rules of kinship alive and well, they are fast-forwarding towards the 21st century.

In setting out some of the new theoretical works concerning kinship, there is a determined effort among anthropologists not to make universal statements, but to develop arguments that center on the structures of contemporary society. Kinship is class-based. Notions of kin do have material conditions predicated on access to society's resources. Poor kin have kin and rely on them in the here and now, and do not look for inheritance.

Numerous examples document the way kin are used by people in their everyday experiences. Addressing four different topics, the discussion looked at how people's family and kin ties influenced how they viewed the world, why they seized certain opportunities, and how particular familial modes of behavior made a difference in the quality of life for all. Various new immigrant groups in the United States use the opportunities of the new locale to benefit the old, including family left behind. Enclave social institutions, clannishness, and remittances all center around family networks and kin ties here in the United States and in the homeland of immigrant groups.

Insuring a livelihood means finding employment, or access to resources that provide kin and family, food, shelter, and clothing. Families need to be provided for, and family members help facilitate the job hunt, or provisions in between jobs. Who works, and in what kinds of jobs, are dependent on class, race, gender, and educational level. Kin ties help workers to manage the variability of low-skilled work for members of the working class.

Needless to say, all of these happenings involving kin and family take place in locations called communities. Sometimes these locales are synonymous with the groups of people who live there, and the patterns of social behavior expressed. Kinship becomes the idiom of the community and vice versa. In other kinds of communities, the needs of families shape how other members come to each other's aid by creating facilities for family survival against the ravages of crack cocaine addiction, and the AIDS epidemic. Community members turn to each other in efforts at political self-help, using both neighborhood kin connections and the language of family terminology as a unifying force (Gregory 1998; Williams 1997; Sharff 1998; Susser 1982).

Turning to other ways of creating lines of communication across differences, the lesbian and gay rights movements have made it possible for members of those communities to chart their own course within the multiple fabrics of contemporary U.S. society. Understanding relations between homosexual and heterosexual people are issues of kinship and family. In creating family and kinship that may or may not be based on biological ties, but ones of affinity and solidarity, lesbians and gays choose their family connections. Inclusion in these families crosses a gamut of relations, but the critical elements are those of alliance and togetherness. Marriage and commitment rituals bring all of these familial complexities to the forefront. As a public display of deep emotions, couples must face friends who in fact reject lesbianism or homosexuality as a way of being.

Finally, when technology makes it possible for couples (usually heterosexual) having reproductive difficulties, to have children, it is the sociocultural meanings of biology that come into play. Surrogate motherhood and donor insemination require both sets of women and men to reconfigure their notions of genealogy, procreation, and parenting. This also means that family ideologies are transformed in one sense, but not in another.

Thus, as the fashioning of a multicultural and diverse anthropology, the discipline brings to the study of kinship, family, and marriage an understanding of patterns of human behavior, close social ties, affinity and other relationships in contemporary life. This is how anthropology must construct a more inclusive understanding of what U.S. kinship systems look like.

REFERENCES CITED

Anglin, M.
  1999 The Hills of Carolina: Workings of Power and the Articulation of Dissent. University of Kentucky, unpublished MS.

Benson, Janet E.
  1994 The Effects of Packinghouse Work on Southeast Asian Refugee Families. In Lamphere, Stepick, et al. Pp. 99–128.
Collier, Jane, Michelle Rosaldo, and Sylvia Yanagisako
  1982 Is There a Family? In *Rethinking the Family*. B. Thorne and M. Yalom, eds. Pp. 25–39. New York: Longman.
Edin, Kathryn, and Laura Lein
  1997 *Making Ends Meet*. New York: Russell Sage Foundation.
Grasmuck, Sherri, and Patricia Pessar
  1991 *Between Two Islands*. Berkeley: University of California Press.
Gregory, Steven
  1998 *Black Corona*. Princeton, NJ: Princeton University Press.
Griffith, David
  1993 *Jones's Minimal*. Albany: SUNY Press.
Gwaltney, John L.
  1981 *Drylongso*. New York: Random House.
Ho, Christine
  1991 *Salt-Water Trinnies*. New York: AMS Press.
Lamphere, Louise
  1987 *From Working Daughters to Working Mothers*. Ithaca, NY: Cornell University Press.
Lamphere, Louise, Helena Ragoné, and Patricia Zavella, eds.
  1997 *Situated Lives*. New York: Routledge.
Lamphere, Louise, Alex Stepick, and Guillermo Grenier, eds.
  1994 *Newcomers in the Workplace*. Philadelphia: Temple University Press.
Lamphere, Louise, Patricia Zavella, Felipe Gonzales, with Peter Evans
  1993 *Sunbelt Working Mothers*. Ithaca, NY: Cornell University Press.
Lewin, Ellen
  1996 *Inventing Lesbian Cultures in America*. Boston: Beacon Press.
  1998 *Recognizing Ourselves*. New York: Columbia University Press.
Morgan, Lewis Henry
  1974[1877] *Ancient Society*. Gloucester, MA: Peter Smith.
Mullings, Leith
  1997 *On Our Own Terms*. New York: Routledge.
Prins, Harald E. L.
  1996 *The Mi'kmaq*. New York: Harcourt Brace.
Ragoné, Helena
  1994 *Surrogate Motherhood*. Boulder, CO: Westview Press.
  1997 Chasing the Blood Tie. In Lamphere, Ragoné, et al., pp. 110–27.
Rapp, Rayna
  1982 Family and Class in Contemporary America. In *Rethinking the Family*. B. Thorne and M. Yalom, eds. Pp. 168–188. New York: Longman.
Schneider, David M.
  1995 *Schneider on Schneider*. Durham, NC: Duke University Press.
Sharff, Jagna
  1998 *King Kong on Fourth Street*. Boulder, CO: Westview Press.
Shultz, Emily A., and Robert H. Lavender
  1987 *Cultural Anthropology*. St. Paul, MN: West Publishing.
Spradley, James, and David McCurdy
  1994 *Conforming Conflict*. 8th edition. New York: HarperCollins.
Stack, Carol B.
  1972 *All Our Kin*. New York: Harper and Row.

Stepick, Alex
   1998   *Pride against Prejudice: Haitians in the United States*. Boston: Allyn and Bacon.
Stepick, Alex, and Guillermo Grenier
   1994   The View from the Back of the House. In Lamphere, Stepick, et al., pp. 181–196.
Susser, Ida
   1982   *Norman Street: Poverty and Politics in an Urban Neighborhood*. New York: Oxford University Press.
   1996   The Construction of Poverty and Homelessness in U.S. Cities. *Annual Review of Anthropology* 25:411–435.
   1998   Inequality, Violence and Gender Relations in a Global City: New York, 1986–96. Identities 5(2):219–247.
   1999   Creating Family Forms: The Exclusion of Men and Teenage Boys from Families in the New York City Shelter Systems, 1987–91. In *Theorizing the City*. Setha Low, ed. Pp. 67–83. New Brunswick, NJ: Rutgers University Press.
Valentine, Betty Lou
   1978   *Hustling and Other Hard Work in the Ghetto*. New York: Free Press.
Weston, Kath
   1995   Forever Is a Long Time. In *Naturalizing Power*. S. Yanagisako and C. Delany, eds. Pp. 87–110. New York: Routledge.
Williams, Brett
   1997   Reinventing the South. In Lamphere, Ragoné, et al., pp. 175–191.
Yanagisako, Sylvia, and Carol Delany
   1995   Naturalizing Power. In *Naturalizing Power*. S. Yanagisako and C. Delany, eds. Pp. 1–25. New York: Routledge.
Yanagisako, Sylvia, and Jane F. Collier
   1987   Toward a Unified Analysis of Gender and Kinship. In *Gender and Kinship*. J. F. Collier and S. J. Yanagisako, eds. Pp. 14–50. Stanford: Stanford University Press.
Zavella, Patricia
   1987   *Women's Work and Chicano Families*. Ithaca, NY: Cornell University Press.

17

Ethnicity and Psychocultural Models

Michael Winkelman

Ethnicity, culturally based identity, is a principal issue in contemporary intergroup relations. Anthropology's theoretical contributions to the study of ethnicity have foundations in psychological anthropology and its predecessor "culture and personality." These approaches show culture, self, and personality to constitute conceptually distinct but necessarily interrelated phenomena at the foundations of ethnicity. Ethnicity involves personal social identity constructed from the integration of cultural and broader social influences into self-concept and personhood. The basis of ethnicity is in the interaction of the inclusive social other as self and the social other as "not-self." The multiple influences upon ethnic identity require systematic models to elucidate both within-group commonalities and variation. Ethnographic and autobiographic approaches illustrate considerable intragroup and situational variation in ethnic identity. The limitations of simplistic models of cultural identity are superseded by the range of factors addressed in the psychocultural model (Whiting and Whiting 1975); the evolutionary model of population psychology (LeVine 1982[1973]); indigenous psychologies (Heelas and Lock 1981; Morris 1994; Kim and Berry 1993); the "primary message systems" (Hall 1959, 1966, 1976, 1984) or social interaction rules; and social role theory or "positionalist" approaches (Bock 1988). These are integrated in a meaning-centered psychocultural open systems approach which identifies the primary contexts within which both psychocultural commonalities and intracultural diversity are produced, and provides a framework for both micro- and macro-level contexts which channel development of biopsychosocial potentials and create identity.

This systematic, culturally based framework for analysis of intra- and intergroup cultural diversity provided by the psychocultural and population psychology models incorporates materialist systems approaches (infrastructure, structure, and superstructure) and concerns with human psychobiological dispositions within frameworks which recognize situational factors and emic perspectives in the construction of identity. These a priori open systems models are supplemented with emic views exemplified in the positionalist and indigenous psychology approaches which provide cultural content and meaning. These different perspectives are integrated within a model which includes: culturally specific socialization of biological structures; historical and environmental influences; primary and secondary socialization contexts; work effects on social-ization; social statuses and associated roles; cultural values and ideals; and pro-jective and expressive systems' representation of psychocultural dynamics in indigenous psychologies. Ethnic identity involves culturally specific knowledge, perceptions, and beliefs about "personhood" or personality, illustrated by emic perspectives found in expressive culture and indigenous psychologies represen-tations of the person and collective identity.

Culture and Personality: Foundations of Anthropological Contributions to Ethnicity

Cultural diversity involves the relationship of identity, behavior, and personal-ity to culture and others – long-standing theoretical and research issues in culture and personality studies and later in psychological anthropology (Bock 1988; LeVine 1982[1973], 1974; Bourguignon 1976). This recognizes the nec-essary interdependence and interaction of human psychology (representing psy-chobiological potentials of the species for organizing behavior) and culture (the collective influences which provide the support necessary for the development of personality). The integration of psychobiological, sociocultural, and other transdisciplinary understandings of the aspects of human nature that provide the basis for culture is the core concern of psychological anthropology (Su á rez-Orozco 1994). While psychological explanations can be reductionist, psychobiological capabilities – perception, memory, emotions, and symbolic processes – are necessary for culture, require a sociocultural framework for development, and reciprocally sustain and create that framework (Heelas 1981). These psychological potentials are structured through the influences of culture, and can be used to understand ethnicity and cultural diversity.

Ethnicity emerges from the intersection of two major foci of research by psy-chological anthropologists: the characteristics of the individual and collective characteristics of culture. Ethnicity is derived from the relationship between psy-chology and culture – that is, how the identities of individuals relate to the char-acteristics of the groups with respect to which they construct their identities. Ethnicity is based in the interaction of self with both internal cultural and exter-nal social influences, the interaction at microsocial level of the individual and their primary familial and community relations with the macrosocial institu-tions of the broader society.

Culture and personality studies were concerned with cultural personality con-figurations, basic personality structures, modal personality, and national char-acter (Bock 1988; Bourguignon 1976; Barnouw 1979; LeVine 1982[1973]). These approaches assumed that all members of a culture shared the same psy-chocultural dynamics because of their common formative experiences. Their inaccurate, oversimplified characterizations of the psychocultural profile were superseded by models which acknowledged that societies and cultures are inter-nally diverse rather than homogeneous, and recognized that explanations of psy-chocultural dynamics require explication of variable identities, personality types, and social roles among group members. While culture creates common-alities in personality and identity, all cultures produce internal variation – for example, men's and women's roles, generational and occupational differences, and so on. Different positions (statuses) require a model of culture and identity relations which recognizes internal variation, and differentiates stereotypes or "essentialist" views from normative cultural characterizations. Intracultural variation is captured in the "distributive models of culture" expounded by Schwartz (1978) and Rodseth (1998; Tedlock and Mannheim 1995). Rodseth (1998:55) suggests culture be viewed as "a semantic population of meanings . . . which may or may not be orderly, coherent, or stable," and which are manifested variously in the conceptions and expressions of different individuals.

Ethnicity: Self and Identity in Cross-Cultural Perspective

The standard conceptual categories of the term "race," referring to presumed biologically distinct populations, is of little use in elucidating human differences, because race is based on untenable assumptions about biology. Ethnicity has become an alternative conceptual framework to race, one which is directly linked to cultural rather than biological factors. While ethnic categories are also problematic, they constitute a crucial aspect of collective identity in the modern world. Ethnic categories are social constructions rather than natural entities; they have differentiated internal structures rather than homogeneous ones. This in-group heterogeneity undermines efforts to identify cultural psychodynamics on the basis of categorical ethnic group membership. Keefe (1989) points out that the bases of ethnicity are variously culture, nationhood, descent, political convenience, social necessity, discrimination, or even ascription by other groups. This reflects the multidimensional nature of ethnicity and the importance of social context in shaping what is important about it. Consequently, the dynamics underlying the construction of ethnic identity vary considerably.

The basis of ethnicity lies in the relationships of the collective dimensions of identity derived from the individual's cultural background in contrast to broader societal relations. The linguistic root of "ethnic" illustrates these two social dimension of ethnicity: the collective other-common identity ("we ourselves"), and the social other-not self ("foreign people or nation"; American Heritage Dictionary, 1981:1538–1539). The roots of term reflect its use as a means of designating an identity based upon a cultural group in contrast to others in the society who belong to a different group and with whom the members of the first group have important relations. The necessary foci for construction of ethnicity are: (1) the self as social being; (2) the self with reference to the inclusive other (culture); and (3) the self in contrastive reference to "others" encountered in broader social relations. Cross-cutting uses of ethnicity is an identity in relationship to the inclusive "other" and the excluded "other."

Ethnic groups are socially recognized groups with salient differences with respect to other groups in society. This distinctiveness may be based on many factors – for example, geographical isolation, in-group marriage, a distinctive cultural heritage or national background, a specific language, common values and beliefs including religion, specific social roles and behavioral patterns, or other sources of a common identity derived from occupation, gender, and sexual identity. Ethnic groups are fundamental reference groups, the social category from which one acquires personal characteristics, social and psychological attachments, definitions of self, and a sense of common membership or group belonging. This sense of belonging to the same group (peoplehood) may be fictive rather than actual. Actual characteristics may be less important to ethnicity than people's perceptions and the meanings associated with the groups with which they identify. The sense of ethnic identity is not just a function of one's cultural behaviors and sense of self-identity; it is also a function of the constraints and attributions derived from others in society.

Ethnic categorization may be imposed by external groups upon diverse groups of people who share no sense of inclusive commonality or actual common cultural heritage. Ethnic identity plays an important role in relations between people, because that membership shapes how individuals relate to one another and plays an important role in the differentiation of in-group from out-groups. The greater the differences between an ethnic group and the dominant groups in society, the more likely it is that ethnic identity will be at the focus of conflict between the groups and identity within the group. Such differences tend to strengthen the boundaries between the groups and the ethnic group identity.

The construction of ethnicity

Keefe (1989) suggests three principal approaches to studying the construction of ethnicity: processual, perceptual, and empirical. Processual approaches view ethnicity as a consequence of social negotiation, a dynamic concept which emerges in interaction between groups. Perceptual approaches examine the meanings groups attribute to themselves and others and how these meanings affect interactions. Empirical approaches are concerned with the measurement of traits and patterns which characterize and distinguish ethnic groups. Understanding ethnicity requires addressing the processes of interaction, the perceptions of groups, and their actual characteristics, as well as the social processes involved in their constructions. While some aspects of ethnic identity are derived passively from exposure to one's family and cultural group, identity is primarily created in interaction with others. Ethnic identity requires contrastive experiences with "not self" to reveal one's own characteristics. The role of intergroup relations in construction of ethnicity may make actual cultural characteristics less important than the other's perceptions. The negotiated and constructed nature of ethnicity is exemplified in "symbolic ethnicity," strong ethnic identity with little cultural background. The contextual factors which shape the salience of ethnic identity, the individual's involvement with their group, and the role of that ethnic group label in the broader society mean the importance of ethnicity varies among group members. Ethnicity is "the interweaving of cultural threads from different arenas . . . a matter of finding a voice or style that does not violate one's several components of identity . . . a pluralistic, multidimensional, or multifaceted concept of self as a crucible for a wider social ethos of pluralism" (Fischer 1986:230, 196). Autobiographies illustrate this multidimensional representation of the ethnic self which emerges "id-like," as a form of implicit knowledge about one's essential being experienced as an influence originating and operating from outside of one's self (Fischer 1986). Ethnicity is not strictly a function of group processes and support, socialization and assimilation, but motivated by individually and collectively felt needs to "to renew self and ethnic group" (Fischer 1986:197). Contact with the culturally different ?other? forces an awareness of characteristics of one's own ethnicity, providing a point of reference for assessing self. This role of the social "other not self" in ethnic identity is illustrated by Phinney's (1991) discussion of minority status and the powerful impacts of societal prejudice and discrimination. She suggests this produces a duality within the personality, a dynamic of irreconcilable aspects of one's self, a "twoness" which reflects the influences of both one's own culture and the broader society. This relationship of ethnicity to both one's own culture and the broader society, is illustrated in ethnic identity development sequences.

Ethnic Identity Development Sequences and Influences

Phinney (1996:923) emphasizes that

> ethnic identity can be conceptualized as a process: Individuals progress from an early stage in which one's ethnicity is taken for granted, on the basis of attitudes and opinions of others or of society; through a period of exploration onto the meaning and implications of one's group membership; to an achieved ethnic identity which is not necessarily a static end point of development; individuals are likely to reexamine their ethnicity throughout their lives and thus may re-experience earlier developmental stages.

This may be superseded in the development of bicultural and multicultural identities (Bandlamudi 1994; Winkelman 1999). Exposure to multiple cultural and social matrices produces a range of understandings of cultural influences, their implications for self, and of the relationship between culture and self. Bandlamudi (1994) proposes the development of five qualitatively distinct conceptual categories of identity, which proceed from a global undifferentiated state to increasing differentiation and hierarchical integration. They are: non-relational subjectivism/objectivism; relational-unilateral; relational-bilateral; multilayered/multifaceted; and dialogical/dialectical. Research on ethnic identity development among ethnic minorities in counseling (Thomas 1971; Cross 1971), dominant culture counselors undergoing cross-cultural training (Helms 1985; Ponterotto 1988), and individuals undergoing adaptation to cross-cultural contact (Bandlamudi 1994) reveals similarities in the basic processes by which identity changes as a consequence of exposure to multiple cultural contexts.

Non-relational self

The non-relational self is not aware of self and its relation to culture. The "self is either completely differentiated from the rest of society or totally submerged in it" (Bandlamudi 1994:468), and people are typically viewed as being either all the same or all different. The non-relational self is characterized in terms of personal likes, dislikes, interests, or family, but not in terms of ethnicity, nationality, language, or other groups. It involves an ethnocentric, limited cultural awareness with a naive "color blindness," manifested in the belief in the sameness of people from all cultures. This is exemplified in a "pre-contact" stage among European Americans, with a limited awareness of other groups and little understanding of the nature of ethnic and cultural differences, including one's own culture. For minorities, this stage of conformity, acceptance, and psychological captivity involves a weak or negative ethnic identity and preference for dominant cultural values. This may be followed by a stage of exposure or contact and dissonance or disintegration, with cultural confusion and conflict with conformity to the prejudices and discriminatory practices of the dominant culture.

Relational-unilateral self

Relational-unilateral individuals define their self in terms of a group identity and collective orientation; while capable of relating to various groups, they are not capable of articulating the nature of the differences nor explaining how the cultural factors affect thought or behavior. Cultural differences are conceptualized in terms of the contrasting differences between cultures. This relational-unilateral view focuses upon ceremonial and ritualized aspects of culture and uses "essentialist" concepts, addressing outward behavior, not the influences of culture upon thought processes.

Relational-bilateral self

Relational-bilateral individuals reason about their behavior, find causes for cultural rules, and assess them in terms of their usefulness. Culture is understood as a given – a rule-governed entity and an authority regarding proper conduct, norms, and values which individuals process and internalize to guide their actions. The individual understands cultural rules in relationship to their own and to the dominant culture. This produces a divided sense of identity between dominant and minority ethnic culture which requires a constant adjustment to different contexts, leading individuals to feel as if they were "putting on an act" and having a "split personality." This alienation is typified in the cultural hybrid described in Everett Stonequist's (1961[1937]) *The Marginal Man* who vacillates between two cultural identities and sets of norms and beliefs. Neither culture is thoroughly internalized by the individual, who cannot accommodate to their contradictory demands or find comfort in the identity and social relations provided by either of them. For minority culture members, this may lead to resistance and ethnic encapsulation, voluntary separatism, ethnic ethnocentrism, and pride in group identity developed in a challenge to the dominant culture. For members of the dominant culture, this may result in either a defensive reintegration, with outgroup avoidance and hostility, and withdrawal into dominant culture encapsulation; or a zealot/paternalism stage concerned with compensation for and protection of minorities and accepting responsibility for helping repressed groups and remedying past wrongs and current injustices.

Multilayered/multifaceted self

Multilayered/multifaceted individuals recognize the self as derived from complex processes in the relations between cultures, "open units, constantly engaging in a dialogue" (Bandlamudi 1994:477). Intergroup differences are assessed in terms of the underlying thought processes and of their sources and relevance in specific contexts. They are aware of the social sources of meaning, the cultural processes that construct self and other, and that "consciousness is formed through social interaction" (Bandlamudi 1994:478). Aware of cultural influences, they also strive to reject certain influences and norms. There is nonetheless a strong sense of identification with both specific ethnic identity and broader societal identity without a feeling of a divided self. The multilayered self seeks out diversity and enjoys and appreciates it. This has been classically exemplified in what are called mediators and middlemen. These individuals have effectively integrated both cultures into their personal identity through a true integration of two different cultural selves, or through a compartmentalization of their lives.

Dialogical/dialectical self

Dialogical/dialectical individuals experience a breakdown of the division of self and culture; they recognize that the self is located in a specific sociohistorical context which produces one's psyche. The dialogical/dialectical self is characterized by beliefs that one can transcend those influences (Bandlamudi 1994:481). This autonomous identity understands cross-cultural differences in identity and has a securely incorporated self-fulfilled cultural identity, with cross-cultural learning a part of personal growth. The individual is aware of "historicity," the influences of the cultural matrix and the interconnectedness with others; consequently, the self is viewed as a relational being, a consequence of influences from the economic, social, political, and ideological realms of culture. The self and the social are recognized as creating each other in a dialectical process; consequently, the self is seen as in a state of constant evolution.

Some models of ethnic identity development propose that these achievements may be followed by biculturalism and multiculturalism, where one is capable of effective functioning in two or more cultures (Banks 1987). This does not necessarily abandon ethnic identity, but encompasses it within a broader perspective. Gardiner et al. (1998) suggest a modification to unilineal models of ethnic identity development. They propose a developmental sequence moving from cultural dependence towards a cultural independence based upon cross-cultural experiences. Their novel suggestion is a subsequent stage of multicultural interdependence in which sharing of new cultural experiences with one's own cultural group produces changes in one's setting. This can produce changes in the attitudes of members of one's own culture, as well as reinforce one's original cultural identity.

The Multidimensionality of Identity

Phinney (1996) points out that ethnicity is a multidimensional construct with variable impacts upon the psychology of the members of the group. Since members vary along a number of dimensions – social, interpersonal, emotional, and cognitive relations to their cultural matrix – the concept of ethnicity must be "unpacked," and the specific variables associated with it explained. The ability of people with similar cultural backgrounds and social contexts to create divergent identities points to the necessity of differentiating the cultural and social matrices which produce them. The need to recognize multiple selves for articulating the structure and content of ethnicity is illustrated in Fischer's (1986) analysis of black autobiographies which show multiple egos and identities or alternative selves constructed in explicit contrast to dominant ideologies. Variation in the use of ethnic labels by the same person as a function of context illustrates that broader societal influences on the self are negotiable – a consequence of both the individual's desire to associate with specific shared group memberships and ability to resist dominant labels and attributions.

Fischer (1986) emphasizes the necessity of the cross-cultural comparative approach which reveals the unique nature of specific cultures, as well as their differences in relation to other groups. Far more effective are cultural models which exemplify major dimensions of difference in behavior and organization. As Phinney (1996:920) points out, it is essential to identify the ethnic group's specific cultural characteristics and to "unpack" culture in order to "explain cross-cultural differences in terms of specific antecedent variables." Assessment of ethnic identity is not possible with ethnic categories or reference to traditional norms and cultural patterns alone. It also requires assessment along a number of dimensions of acculturation and in terms of strength of identification with or commitment to group identity, norms, and values, and the experiences associated with minority status. Assessment of ethnicity includes personal association with broader societal relations and experiences associated with minority status – such as prejudice, discrimination, and sense of powerlessness. This points to the necessity of representing both cultural influences and those of the broader societal systems. "[E]thnicity is a process of inter-reference between two or more cultural traditions" (Fischer 1986:201).

Ethnicity is a social identity derived from the ways in which different social group memberships affect the individual's self-concept, where membership in one group contrasts with the others. Identity involves the totality of self-concepts one has in relationship to reference groups, with the presence of multiple reference groups producing multiple aspects to identity. Hecht (1993) provides a four-dimensional view of identity: communal, social (relational), role (enacted), and individual. The communal level of identity is that provided by a group of people bound together by ethnicity or culture, providing a self-referent in selected aspects of collective life, a cultural past, and a sense of membership in an in-group. The role (enactment) identity is created in social interaction and through social roles and social rituals in relationships between people in the cultural community. These aspects of identity derive from communicative process involving the exchange of messages between people to express their ideal social identities about their characteristics and relationships. The relationship aspects of identity are those which are constructed in the process of social interaction which define people's identities in terms of their relationships with others with whom they are bound in role sets. The individual (personal) frame of identity includes self-cognitions, a self-concept or self-image, and feelings about self, all influenced by the other levels of identity. The different aspects of identity reflect different ways in which people's views of their identity are expressed.

The idea that culture reflects subjective experiences, expressive forms, and the manifestations of human consciousness – that it is a root metaphor for understanding organizational identity – requires the integration of multiple symbolic perspectives and entails more complex models which can embody the contradictory realities produced by our multiple images of our selves (Winkelman 1998, 1999). It is necessary to combine native cultural systems with comparative and critical perspectives (Schwartzman 1993). These organizational theory developments of identity suggest that open systems models of organization and their mechanical and organic modeling be supplemented with cultural models focused on the creation of meaning. This pays attention to cultural behavior at the micro-level of interpersonal interaction and its meaning to participants.

Psychocultural Open Systems Models and Evolutionary Population Psychology

Beatrice and John Whiting's (1975) psychocultural model provides an integrated systems approach for examining the diverse structural, socialization, and ideological influences upon the development of identity and social self. The psychocultural model, combined with the evolutionary model of population psychology, provides a broad framework for examining the components of cultural systems and their effects on identity. The Whitings' psychocultural model focuses on history, environment, the maintenance (cultural) system, the child-rearing environment, innate needs, learned behaviors, and projective systems. LeVine (1982[1973]) proposes that cultures create four distinct aspects of adaptation for the individual's personality: environmental; primary parental socialization; secondary socialization; and group adaptations to population norms.

Psychocultural and population psychology models illustrate the myriad influences that must be considered to appreciate the cultural influences upon personality and identity. Culture-behavior-identity dynamics can be partially described within psychocultural open systems perspectives which incorporate the materialist systems approaches (infrastructure, structure, and superstructure) with emic perspectives on personality and meaning. This "open" psychocultural systems approach recognizes the need to incorporate change, conflict, and opposition; the cultural (emic) symbolic perspectives; the structural organization of the culture; and the relationships to external structural conditions (e.g. economic, political, etc.) which bind together different cultural and ethnic groups. This open systems framework can incorporate additional dimensions of cultural influence and intergroup relations which form individual identity in relation to others. The diverse nature of inputs to the model, as well as the variation at every level of the model, provide a basis for assessing both intercultural and intracultural variation (Winkelman 1998, 1999).

Variation among members of the same culture in terms of their socialization experiences may derive from internal variation in family histories and

Table 1 Expanded psychocultural open-systems model for research on self, personality, and identity

History	Environment
Traditions and beliefs	Ecosystem relations and adaptations
Intergroup relations	Migrations and borrowings
Maintenance system/cultural and social system	
Production	Domestic economy
Subsistence and work patterns	Family organization
Means of production	Kinship patterns
Division of labor	Community organization
Reproduction	Political economy
Population size	Political systems
Fertility patterns	Social structure and stratification
	Law and social control
Primary learning environment	
Settings occupied	
Caretaker relations and teachers	
Tasks assigned	
Mother's work	
Socialization of biological needs	Learned
Needs, drives and capacities	Behavioral styles
Emotions and attachment	Skills and abilities
Sex and family roles	Value priorities
Secondary social drives	Conflicts and defenses
Secondary socialization	
Stages of life-cycle development	
Social roles	
Initiation and adult transition	
Mesosystems, exosystems, and macrosystem relations	
Individual adult	
Material and social organization of behavior	
Social roles	
Population ideals and norms	
Projective/expressive systems	
Religious beliefs and practices	Ritual and ceremony
Art and recreation	Games and play
Deviance, crime and suicide rates	"Culture-bound syndromes"
Indigenous psychology	

structures, economic opportunities, secondary socialization experiences, adult models, and so on. While the psychocultural models suggest a linear causal process, the relationship of culture to behavior and identity is much more complex. Potentially any aspect of the system can directly impact socialization and development patterns at another part of the system because of systemic interaction and integration in cultural systems. The relationships of components of the psychocultural model to the processes of socialization are integrated with the evolutionary model of population psychology of LeVine (1982[1973]) as a tool for assessing identity (see Table 1).

Population Psychology: The Socialization of Biology

LeVine (1982[1973]) analyzes processes of socialization relating culture and personality from a Darwinian perspective that incorporates both biological and social dimensions. These processes involve four primary dimensions of adaptation: environmental adaptation; deliberate primary socialization; secondary socialization practices and goals; and the aggregate characteristics of populations, ideal and real. These involve, respectively: adaptation of the child-rearing practices to ecological pressures; deliberate aspects of the socialization process; secondary adaptations of the personality to the roles, attitudes, and behaviors required for adults; and the adaptation of the aggregate personality characteristics of the population.

This perspective provides a framework for addressing the development of ethnic identity in culturally specific adaptations to human universals. The psychocultural dynamics addressing biosocially based needs, structures, and behaviors provides insights into the culturally patterned ways of manifesting human nature through: human needs and drives; sex roles and family structures; emotions and reactions; life-span developmental stages; daily activity rhythms; cognitive modes and their applications; conceptualization and management of illness, particularly sick roles and "culture bound syndromes"; and deviant behavior and models of heroes.

Needs and drives

Identity, personality, self, and cultural psychodynamics are revealed in the structuring of basic needs and the socialization of primary and secondary drives. Universal biosocially based features such as attachment, sex, sex roles, and emotions provide important vantage points for examining the role of cultural processes in the construction of ethnic identity. More significant aspects of cultural identity are found in the secondary and derived needs.

Gender and family identities

A universal aspect of psychocultural dynamics is differentiation of male and female behaviors. While there is a biological basis for male and female distinctions, culture provides the most important patterning of differences in identity. Understanding culturally normative patterns, as well as their variation within a cultural group, is a fundamental aspect of psychocultural dynamics and identity. Basic male–female roles are also culturally structured in spousal and parental behavior and parent–child and sibling relations which are realized in culturally specific ways reflecting a particular culture's psychosocial dynamics and identity. Cross-sex gender identity also provides an important aspect of self and identity in some cultures, expanding dimensions of intra-cultural variation.

Life-cycle development and stages

The life cycle provides a number of perspectives on socialization processes and the ideals and behaviors instilled. How cultures respond to universal processes

(e.g. birth, first menses, puberty, adult transition, marriage, menopause) provides a perspective on culturally significant features of identity and cultural
motivations, interpretations, and influences. Life-cycle development stages
reflect culturally specific conceptualizations about development which provide
important perspectives on valued aspects of identity, social expectations, and
culturally specific aspects of the personality.

Emotions

Emotions are an important focus of psychocultural socialization, because they
include biologically based potentials always shaped by the psychocultural
dynamics. The universality of facial expression of emotions (Ekman and Friesen
1969, 1986; Izard 1977; Ekman 1972) indicates a biologically based affective
dynamics, but cultural norms about acceptable and unacceptable displays illustrate normative and ideal cultural values for personality and cultural psychology. In spite of biological bases for emotions, culture influences what evokes
them, how they are expressed, and their meaning and significance to group
members. Emotions are a central issue in what Levy (1983) characterizes as a
universal tension between the private and public aspects of the self (person) and
their selective expression in social behavior. Emotions provide information
about cultural personality and psychology, particularly normative and ideal
cultural values.

Organizational behavior

Cultures require the regularization of social behavior and interactions, producing culture–behavior relationships illustrating ethnicity. Cultural psychologies
are illustrated in specific expectations for social behavior: institutional goals;
the normative institutional rules and sanctions for role performance; situational
norms for managing institutional and motivational pressures; patterns of behavior in social situations; personality dispositions; success in attaining institutional
goals; experienced satisfactions and frustrations of the population; and behavior disorders and deviant behavior (LeVine 1982[1973]:226).

Microlevel dynamics: social interaction rules

Anthropologists studying organizations recognized that psychological and social
needs and motivations – the informal culture – were the most important factors
determining actual behavior and relationships. Hall's (1959, 1966, 1976, 1984)
work on the spatial dynamics of interpersonal relations (proxemics) and non-
verbal communication exemplifies the importance of emic perspectives of this
informal culture. He proposed a model to organize and classify data which illustrates fundamental "bio-basic" aspects of "infra-cultural activities," represented
in "primary message systems." Whiting and Whiting (1975) have proposed 12
categories of behavior for cross-cultural comparison. These systems provide
major categories for assessing differences in human activity; but as Bock (1988)
points out, these categories of behavioral description are derived from the

Table 2 Social interaction rules

Language codes and dialects	Non-verbal or contextual communication
Paralinguistic cues	Meta-linguistic messages
Communication (direct/indirect)	Relational styles (technical/personal)
Interpersonal interaction	Appearances
Greetings	Formality of relations
Family roles	Sex roles
Respect	Personal relations
Presentation of self (face)	Self-disclosure
Emotional communication	Proxemics
Kinesics	Facial expressions
Eye contact	Gestures and signs
Body posture	Time orientation
Learning styles	Authority styles and relations
Decision-making processes	Persuasion and argument styles
Negotiation approaches	Conflict management
Power distance	Work values and attitudes

ordinary use of English, which introduces unassessed cultural biases. Both etic and emic perspectives on the social patterns of behavior provide illustrations of externally manifested aspects of ethnicity in the culture's normative styles of behaving, relating, communication, socializing, reasoning, managing and negotiating, and so on. These social interaction rules, behavioral patterns which characterize the microlevel social interaction patterns and norms of everyday behavior, underlie cultural competence. They include: paralinguistic conventions; kinesics and proxemics; behavioral communication, including gestures, gaze, and postures; emotional communication; interpersonal disclosure and self presentation; and patterns of social reasoning (see Table 2). Social interaction rules include both consciously known rules (e.g. how to greet people), and unconscious rules (e.g. proxemics, lengths of pauses in conversations). Effective functioning in a social group requires manifesting a wide range of arbitrary behaviors and styles which conform to cultural expectations; this competency provides a statement about group membership and identity. These behaviors constitute salient aspects of observable intergroup differences which provide the basis for maintaining group solidarity and boundaries.

The Psychocultural Model

The Whitings' (1975) psychocultural model explicitly considers environmental, historical, material, social, and ideological influences on development. The environment and its resources have many influences on development. Child-care practices are part of adaptation to ecological pressures. Cultural history provides models for parents and children. The maintenance or cultural system focuses upon the infrastructure for production and the political economy. These influences of the domestic economy and family and kinship structures are primary determinants of the child's learning environment, which transmit and instill cultural influences in development. Secondary socialization (e.g. schools, military, peers, work, initiation, etc.) may involve distinct influences in the secondary adaptations of self to normative roles, and broader social relations producing the adult personality. This personality both reflects and projects its influences and dynamics in the projective and expressive systems such as religion, mythology, cosmology, or ritual art.

Family, kinship, and primary socialization

Family influences upon identity are the most fundamental of all cultural influences since family is the most important primary group in all societies. Although family is universal, its specific roles, and influences are quite variable. Family provides the primary context for development of social roles, gender, personal identity, emotional expression, learning styles, and behavioral patterns. But family structures, roles, and influences vary widely, with intercultural variation in families' positions (e.g. the statuses of mother, father, or eldest son) and associated role expectations, intergenerational relations, and the nature and function of kinship networks. Some functions of kinship systems relevant to identity include care and socialization of children and social reference group.

The organization of work and identity

Principal aspects of the Whitings' maintenance system and learning environment are explicitly work-related: subsistence patterns, means of production, the division of labor, task assignment, and mothers' work patterns. The fundamental work behaviors and organization provide characterizations of desired social behavior and ideals for primary role identification. The universal aspects of work (Applebaum 1987) can be used as a structure for assessing specific aspects of the workplace socialization for social behaviors and values. The work-related approach emphasizes social structural influences on personality development, and the psychological characteristics of social classes. The importance of subcultural class psychologies is indicated by a broad range of findings which show class differences in parenting styles and other characteristics, such as achievement motivation, that reveal differential psychodynamics of their subcultures.

Psychocultural aspects of expressive culture

Expressive culture (e.g. art, performance drama, myth, ritual, stories, proverbs, poetry, music, ballads, myths, legends, and oral traditions) provides information on cultural psychology and identity. It reveals ethnicity through expressions of group sentiments and psychodynamics, particularly emotions. It reflects social relations with the supernatural, itself a projection of society. It abstracts the unconscious representations of the culture, providing insight into psychocultural patterns and identities. Religion is an important source of expressive culture, indigenous psychology and the cultural conceptualization of the person through its models for humans, values, and behavior, and in providing meaning to the world. Representations of humans in supernatural systems provide symbolic depictions of the social domain, societal forces, and interpersonal conflicts, as well as projective systems which reflect and model personality and self. Religions can provide global perspectives on psychocultural dynamics, indigenous psychology, and identity since they embody ideals for individual behavior and linkages of individual to group (Bond 1988; Heelas and Lock 1981; Morris 1994).

Indigenous psychologies

Western cultural-bound conceptualizations limit our ability to accurately represent the psychodynamics of people from other cultures, including the nature of their identity. A primary problem is the assumption that the psychological structures and processes known from studies in Western cultures are the same as those of people in other cultures. Other cultures' conceptions of person, self, emotion, motivation, and other aspects of humans are represented in indigenous conceptions of psychological structures and processes. Person and self are symbolic representations, and key to cultural psychology and the conceptualization of identity. Emic approaches based upon cultural representations and conceptualizations of human beings are found in ideological and expressive sources embodying an indigenous cultural psychology (Bond 1988; Heelas and Lock 1981; Kim and Berry 1993; Morris 1994).

Indigenous psychology and cultural psychosocial dynamics are represented in the cultural superstructure – ideology, mythology, folklore, religious systems, cosmology, and other aspects of expressive culture. These projective systems represent cultural conceptualizations of internal structures of persons and the forces which motivate behaviors, constituting ideals for the individual. They present personality, including: how humans and social groups are represented; social behavior and expressive manifestations; and the emotional associations with beliefs and experiences. Indigenous psychologies contrast with Western psychologies in being concerned with a much broader range of conceptions of consciousness, agency, and the self's relationship to the world.

> Indigenous psychologies . . . are the cultural views, theories, conjectures, classifications, assumptions and metaphors – together with notions embedded in social institutions – which bear on psychological topics. These psychologies are statements about the nature of the person and his relation to the world. They contain advice and injunctions about the way that people should act, should feel and how they can find happiness and success in life.   (Heelas 1981:3)

Explaining indigenous psychology requires knowledge of the culture's frames of reference for understanding behavior, emotions, and self.

Indigenous psychologies are necessary for human beings for several reasons (Heelas 1981; Lock 1981a, 1981b). They fulfill interrelated functions, including: sustaining the inner self; adjusting the self in relationship to the sociocultural; and enabling operation of the sociocultural institutions. They provide the action schemas which organize individual and collective social life and the creation of sociocultural institutions. In their focuses upon inner self, emotions, states of consciousness, will, memories, soul, and agency, indigenous psychologies provide a system of meaning to delineate what is human nature and to link the individual to the sociocultural order, producing ethnic identity.

Personality and Self

There are biopsychological structures that provide the basis for individual and collective behavioral patterns which permit participation in culture. The biological structures which enable cultural behavior include personality, self, social roles, identity, emotions, and mind. These biological capacities are culturally developed and constructed, creating culturally specific (indigenous) psychologies and psychocultural dynamics. Wierzbicka (1993) suggests lexical universals escape the artifacts of any one language and provide a bias-free framework for developing cross-cultural psychologies through cross-cultural linguistic evidence indicating underlying universal structures. All languages contain a word referring to "person" and the concept "I," as well as a range of other concepts – thinking, knowing, doing, saying, wanting, and feeling. "Person" and "I" refer to two principal foci for understanding humans' psychobiological nature. These reflect what is referred to as the personality and the self, representing biologically based and socially mediated aspects which all humans develop through the processes of socialization. The use of personality as a universal for analysis of ethnicity is justified on the basis of the lexical universal for person, combined with the universals for activities of the person which constitute basic aspects of personality (e.g. thinking, feeling, wanting, knowing, etc.). Human symbolic and cultural capacities mediated through these human features of "personality" and "self" provide a framework for describing cross-cultural differences in identity.

Personality and self are used and defined in different ways in psychology and the social sciences. It is necessary to distinguish between personality and self (Spiro 1993). They involve, respectively, the cultural conceptualizations of the nature of the person and the social characteristics of a person acquired by virtue of occupying certain roles or positions. Personality refers to the overall organization and systemic properties of persons which generate behavior, while self is how the individual is presented and identified in specific social interactions. These conceptualizations provide a context within which to explore the interaction of biology, socialization, and culture in the formation of the similarities and differences among members of a culture and their differences with respect to people of other cultures. Ethnicity derives from the role of culture in shaping the stable patterns of personality and self.

Personality refers to the overall organization and dynamics of humans' capabilities – perception, attitudes, beliefs, values, dispositions, drives, thoughts, and so on, embodied in consistent patterns of behavior. It involves the totality of processes mediating between external environment and the individual's behavioral responses, including cognitions. These internal mediating processes include: symbolization, cognition, emotions, memory, and learning, which enable humans to interface with the external world, both physical and social, with their internal symbolic maps of that world and their position within it.

The diversity of perspectives and conceptual frameworks for describing personality reflects the fact that these capabilities are too complex to be exhaustively described within any single model, particularly when we examine personality cross-culturally. But anthropological perspectives provide frameworks for the cross-cultural conceptualization of personality. The personality has been viewed as a "projective system" reflecting underlying psychocultural dynamics, and characterized with a "pluralistic" multimethod approach with both emic and etic perspectives. These multiple perspectives can approach a more complete view of the manifestations of personality in culture.

Since these internal processes are not available to direct observation, they must be inferred from other forms of information – experiences, behavior, and expressive modalities. Schwartz (1978) suggests four basic constructs must be considered in conceptualizing personality: (1) self-reflexive constructs; (2) behavioral constructs developed in close association with significant others during socialization; (3) general affective and cognitive structures underlying ways of constructing experience; and (4) general constructs representing knowledge, beliefs, norms, and expectations. These constitute concepts of what it is like to be a person. Heelas (1981) points out that human beings require some concept of what it is to be human. To function as a human being requires that we have a psychological structuralization, which is provided by culturally derived concepts providing a sense of one's characteristics and identity as a person. These cultural conceptions of the nature of persons constitute an indigenous psychology or "folk psychology" which is vital to understanding ethnicity and the relations of culture and personality.

The social self refers to interrelated aspects of humans in social relations. It includes the individual as social actor and the socially presented aspects of their person; the person's ideal social self-presentation, based upon the internalization of social standards and socially acceptable role behaviors; the person's sense of social identity and personal continuity; and the individual's reflexivity, their self-perception, and cognitions about themselves in social interaction. These capabilities are based in and dependent upon the operation of personality.

Self and culture are interdependent. Self is a product of culture, which constitutes and nurtures the self, and culture is a product of a community of selves and depends upon the self for its transmission and acquisition (Lock 1981a). This involves a self-awareness of one's own behavior and its appraisal with respect to social standards. Self-awareness is necessary for the performance of multiple roles, and requires the ability to treat one's self as an object. This self-awareness necessary for social life is a product of sociocultural processes, seeing oneself from the perspective of others within a symbolically and culturally constituted behavioral environment (Lock 1981a). The nature of that culturally construed self plays a fundamental role in shaping the personal self (Heelas 1981) and provides the basis for identity.

Cultural characterizations of identity provided by ideal population personality traits are differentiated by perspectives identifying the situational (context) and positional (social position, status, or role) determinants of behaviors, self and identity illustrated in "role theory" approaches, and social structural influences on personality and social behavior (see Bock 1988 for a review of this "social structure and personality" or "positionalist" approach based on the ideas of George Herbert Mead). Role theory has developed around phenomena which are basic features of social life in all societies and cultures. Self involves socially constituted identities developed in the context of social relations with others and the meanings they ascribe to us. Biddle (1986) suggests that core concepts are: *social positions* (status) – parts to be played, the positions allocated by society; *roles* – normative expectations about characteristic behaviors of people in certain positions; and *expectations* – scripts for behavior, including norms as to what people should do, beliefs regarding whether or not people will fulfill them, and their preferences or attitudes. Related concepts are role taking (adopting a certain social position and associated behaviors) and the relationship of roles to self-concept, emotions, and role stress. The concepts of social status or role (a position) and role behavior (activities and responsibilities associated with the position) provide a conceptual framework for examining cross-cultural differences in psychosocial dynamics and identity, and patterns of within-culture variation.

Functionalist perspectives recognize that not all people conform to ideal expectations and may experience role conflict, role ambiguity, and role overload. Structural approaches have emphasized the stable social organizations created through social positions and how they direct people in certain patterns of behavior in interaction with others in the social structure. Consensual expectations associated with social positions are augmented by understanding cognitive and affective processes linking social roles to actual behavior and self. Symbolic interactionist approaches have emphasized the improvisational, volitional, and undetermined aspects of behavior, within societal constraints. Symbolic interaction perspectives reveal mechanisms for variation in roles by people of the same status through individual options and creative adaptations to the evolving social dynamic relating culture of origin to other societal groups. These social roles represent aspects of self and overall personality dynamics and personal identity. The range of social statuses present in a culture illustrates varying normative identifications of self in society.

Ethnic identity derives from common roles and behavior expectations of culturally defined social positions. Social positions and idealized roles are models for behavior. Multiple shifting positions across contexts in cultural life produce intracultural diversity in social self and identity. Intracultural diversity is articulated in social class analysis and assessment of occupational positions which further differentiate social roles and styles. Class psychologies, the conditions of material production, and the organization of work are articulated by "positionalist" approaches, which include other criteria – for example, ethnicity, sex, age, occupation, differential socialization – as a means of illustrating primary role identification and identity (Bock 1988).

Conclusions

Advantages of the psychocultural model for representing historical and contemporary group psychologies derive from its open-system approach and in the resolution of conceptual, theoretical, and methodological problems in relating psychology and culture. As Kim and Berry (1993) emphasize with respect to indigenous psychologies, understanding the manifestations of ethnicity requires a multidisciplinary perspective within a cultural framework that gives coherence and reveals meaningful patterns. A meaning-centered, psychocultural open-systems model provides the basis for such a complex characterization of the dynamics of identity. Multiple aspects of identity can be examined in terms of the cultural and social systems, focusing on historical identifications, external environments, work organization, child-rearing environments, secondary socialization, intergroup relations, and ideological and expressive materials like projective systems. These characterizations can represent diversity and commonality in behavioral dynamics, intragroup behavior, intergroup relations, and the cultural self-images constructed in cultural ideology and indigenous psychology.

The psychocultural model provides mechanisms that explain the processes through which both cultural patterns and internal diversity are produced. The diverse nature of inputs to the model and variable options provide a basis for intracultural variation. Psychocultural differences are manifested in variation in occupational specialization and economic resources; family structures, composition, and dynamics; different primary and secondary socialization experiences; different adult models; and various linguistic, communication, educational, religious, and other ideological factors.

The psychocultural models provided here are points of departure to be complemented by a contextualization through the emic perspectives. The social structure and personality approach provides tools for constructing culturally specific forms of behavior, social self, and personal and group identity. Statuses (positions) and the associated responsibilities reveal how social behavior is organized within a culture and a sense of self is inculcated, providing the linkages of the individual to sociocultural institutions, and permitting social conditions to illustrate group psychology. Psychocultural dynamics are further represented in expressive culture and indigenous psychologies revealing emic perspectives.

REFERENCES CITED

Applebaum, H.
    1987   Universal Aspects of Work. In *Perspectives in Cultural Anthropology*. H. Applebaum, ed. Pp. 386–410. Albany: SUNY Press.
Bandlamudi, L.
    1994   Dialogics of Understanding Self/Culture. *Ethos* 22:160–193.
Banks, J.
    1987   *Teaching Strategies for Ethnic Studies*. Boston, MA: Allyn and Bacon.
Barnouw, V.
    1979   *Culture and Personality*. Homewood, IL: Dorsey Press.
Biddle, B.
    1986   Recent Developments in Role Theory. *Annual Review of Sociology* 12:67–92.
Bock, Phillip
    1988   *Rethinking Psychological Anthropology*. New York: W. H. Freeman.
Bond, Michael, ed.
    1988   *The Cross-Cultural Challenge to Social Psychology*. Newbury Park, CA: Sage.

Bourguignon, Erika
   1976   *Psychological Anthropology*. New York: Holt, Rinehart, and Winston.
Cross, W.
   1971   The Negro–Black Conversion Experience: Toward a Psychology of Black
   Liberation. *Black World* 20:13–27.
Ekman, P.
   1972   Universals and Cultural Differences in Facial Expressions of Emotion.
   In *Nebraska Symposium on Motivation, 1971*. J. Cold, ed. Pp. 207–283. Lincoln:
   University of Nebraska Press.
Ekman, P., and W. V. Friesen
   1969   The Repertoire of Nonverbal Behavior: Categories, Origins, Usage, and
   Coding. *Semiotica* 1:49–98.
   1986   A New Pan Cultural Expression of Emotion. *Motivation and Emotion*
   10:159–168.
Fischer, Michael M. J.
   1986   Ethnicity and the Post-Modern Arts of Memory. In *Writing Culture*.
   James Clifford and George E. Marcus, eds. Pp. 194–233. Berkeley: University of
   California Press.
Gardiner, H., J. Mutter, and C. Kosmitzki
   1998   *Lives across Cultures: Cross-Cultural Human Development*. Boston, MA:
   Allyn and Bacon.
Hall, Edward
   1959   *The Silent Language*. Garden City, NY: Anchor Press/Doubleday.
   1966   *The Hidden Dimension*. Garden City, NY: Anchor Press/Doubleday.
   1976   *Beyond Culture*. Garden City, NY: Anchor Press/Doubleday.
   1984   *The Dance of Life*. Garden City, NY: Anchor Press/Doubleday.
Harris, Marvin
   1987   Theoretical Principles of Cultural Materialism. In *Perspectives in Cultural
   Anthropology*. H. Applebaum, ed. Pp. 301–306. Albany: SUNY Press.
Hecht, M.
   1993   2002 – A Research Odyssey: Towards the Development of a Communication
   Theory of Identity. *Communication Monographs* 60(1):76–82.
Heelas, Paul
   1981   Introduction: Indigenous Psychologies. In Heelas and Lock, pp. 3–18.
Heelas, Paul, and Andrew Lock
   1981   *Indigenous Psychologies*. London: Academic Press.
Helms, J.
   1985   Towards a Theoretical Explanation of the Effects of Race upon Counseling.
   The Counseling Psychologist 12:153–165.
Izard, C. E.
   1977   *Human Emotions*. New York: Plenum.
Keefe, S.
   1989   *Negotiating Ethnicity*. NAPA Bulletin 8. Washington, DC: American Anthropological Association.
Kim, U., and J. Berry
   1993   *Indigenous Psychologies*. Newbury Park, CA: Sage.
LeVine, R.
   1982[1973]   *Culture, Behavior and Personality*. Chicago: Aldine.
   1974   *Culture and Personality*. New York: Aldine.
Levy, Robert I.
   1983   Introduction: Self and Emotion. *Ethos* 11(3):128–134.

Lock, Andrew
1981a   Universals in Human Conception. In Heelas and Lock, pp. 19–36.
1981b   Indigenous Psychology and Human Nature: A Psychological Perspective. In Heelas and Lock, pp. 183–204.
Morris, Brian
1994   *Anthropology of the Self*. London: Pluto Press.
Phinney, Jean
1991   Ethnic Identity and Self-Esteem: A Review and Integration. *Hispanic Journal of Behavioral Sciences* 13(2):193–208.
1996   When We Talk about American Ethnic Groups, What Do We Mean? *American Psychologist* 51(9):918–927.
Ponterotto, Joseph
1988   Racial Consciousness Development among White Counselor Trainees: A Stage Model. *Journal of Multicultural Counseling and Development* 16:146–156.
Rodseth, L.
1998   Distributive Models of Culture. *American Anthropologist* 100(1):55–69.
Schwartz, T.
1978   Where Is the Culture? Personality as the Distributive Locus of Culture. In *The Making of Psychological Anthropology*. George D. Spindler, ed. Pp. 419–441. Berkeley: University of California Press.
Schwartzman, Helen
1993   *Ethnography in Organizations*. Newbury Park, CA: Sage.
Spiro, Melford E.
1993   Is the Western Concept of Self "Peculiar" within the Context of World Cultures. *Ethos* 21(2):107–153.
Stonequist, Edward
1961[1937]   *The Marginal Man: A Study in Personality and Culture Conflict*. New York: Russell and Russell.
Suárez-Orozco, M.
1994   Remaking Psychological Anthropology. In *The Making of Psychological Anthropology* II. M. Suárez-Orozco, and G. and L. Spindler, eds. Pp. 8–59. Fort Worth, TX: Harcourt Brace.
Tedlock, D., and B. Mannheim, eds.
1995   *The Dialogic Emergence of Culture*. Urbana: University of Illinois Press.
Thomas, C.
1971   *Boys No More*. Beverly Hills, CA: Glencoe Press.
Whiting, Beatrice, and John Whiting
1975   *Children of Six Cultures: A Psycho-Cultural Analysis*. Cambridge, MA: Harvard University Press.
Wierzbicka, A.
1993   A Conceptual Basis for Cultural Psychology. *Ethos* 21(2):205–231.
Winkelman, M.
1998   *Ethnic Relations in the U.S.: A Sociohistorical Cultural Systems Approach*. Dubuque, IO: Eddie Bowers.
1999   *Ethnic Sensitivity in Social Work*. Dubuque, IO: Eddie Bowers.

18

Aging in the United States: Diversity as a Late-Life Concern

Maria D. Vesperi

A Biocultural View of Aging

Human aging reveals the intersection of biology and powerful, culturally constructed categories. While all people age, what it means to grow old is determined by values and institutions. Anthropologists who study aging recognize that expectations based on kinship, class, and access to social and economic networks are as significant as biological factors in determining the older person's experience. At the same time, the biological status of older people cannot be viewed apart from material and social conditions.

One might say that research on aging yields a view through the wrong end of a telescope. Condensed around the older person is a full range of beliefs and practices that can be deconstructed to reveal how social institutions operate in relation to concepts of health, personhood, and community. This system, in turn, interacts with elements of the larger political economy in a cultural process whereby local communities work, as Sahlins (1994:413) puts it, to "integrate their experience of the world system in something that is logically and ontologically more inclusive: their own system of the world."

The U.S. Experience

Cross-cultural examples demonstrate that a shared worldview can make the associations among age, health, and social connectedness quite straightforward; explanations of biological and social phenomena are mutually reinforcing. The historically and culturally layered experience of growing old in the United States seems bewilderingly tangled in comparison. Here, the elderly must contend not only with the weakly articulated yet fiercely dominant structural realities of "American" culture and its place in the world economic system, but also with cultural legacies from around the world. The variety of life circumstances among older people points to underlying and often contradictory constructions of class, gender, and racialized identities.

Beginning with the case of recent immigrants, it is easy to see how conflicting expectations about age can cause confusion. For example, Barbara Yee (1997:295) writes: "Many middle-aged Southeast Asians are surprised to find that they are not considered elderly by American society." This can be viewed superficially as a profound but direct challenge of acculturation, of realigning one's beliefs about chronological, biological, and social time. Beneath lies a much more intractable problem: the contested status of generalized categories such as "middle-aged," "Asian," and "immigrant worker" within U.S. culture itself. Paradoxically, these labels have both indexed and masked structural inequalities that cannot be adequately addressed at the individual level. As Sokolovsky cautions in his discussion of ethnicity and aging: "In the United States the cultural dimension of ethnicity must also be understood within the framework of a class system which has created minority groups" (1997a:257). One obstacle has been the traditional unit of analysis, as Mullings (1987:4) explains: "Given the focus on ethnic boundaries and the use of the community studies model . . . it is not surprising that the inextricable link between class and ethnicity was not adequately drawn."

Yee provides evidence that many older Southeast Asian immigrants adapt readily to the notion that they are considered to be of working age, particularly in a society that touts equal opportunity for all. But what can they make of the institutionalized racism, sexism, and ageism that may prevent them from earning a living wage in the U.S. economy? Yee (1997:300) found that "age bias against older men and women coupled with poor English skills created the situation in which few elders found gainful employment outside the home."

Research within the United Sates often highlights diversity in the oldest generation. However, it would be an essentializing theoretical and methodological error to focus on salient differences among groups of elders outside the context of their shared experiences as residents of the United States. With the exception of the Amish (Brubaker and Michael 1987) and a few other intentional or indigenous communities, reified statements about "the African American elderly," "older Mexican Americans," or "Chinese American elders" are no less tautological and stereotypical than generalizations about "black youth" or "generation X." Such labels signify social distancing and point to operant structural inequalities which must be closely examined. The lives of many older people present great disparities between the experience of the self and unexamined cultural constructions about what it means to be old (Vesperi 1998a). Using points of contrast between generalized beliefs about "the elderly" and the lives of older people in well-articulated settings, the anthropological study of aging can provide a critical context for appreciating diversity in its fluid, everchanging, historical context.

Just as the human content of the category "aged" shifts with each generation, a diachronic perspective reveals that beliefs and practices related to old age are far from static. Hareven (1995:13) argues eloquently for "a knowledge of the larger processes of change that have affected the timing of life course transitions, family patterns, and generational relations." Given the relatively short – if eventful – history of the United States, one can situate any number of cultural constructions about the aged in their evolving social and economic settings. For example, it is commonly said that older people enjoyed more "veneration" or "respect" in the preindustrial past than in the postindustrial present. However, it is difficult to appreciate such terms historically because "respect" in its contemporary usage is often conflated with positive feelings. Embedded in the message to respect one's elders is the idea that one should feel good about them; conversely, to withhold respect in the absence of positive feelings is seen as an action of the authentic self.

Giddens (1991:187) highlights this association in his discussion of the pure relationship, "a social relation which can be terminated at will, and is only sustained in so far as it generates sufficient psychic returns for each individual." He links this to the concept of "radical doubt," an ironic effect of modern adherence to the principle that "no matter how cherished, and apparently well established, a given scientific tenet may be, it is open to revision – or might have to be discarded altogether – in the light of new ideas or findings" (Giddens 1991:21). Thus, all beliefs and actions are viewed as choices. In the absence of structural sanctions, sustaining a social relationship demands a level of trust that leaves each person uniquely vulnerable to being judged unworthy of the other's commitment.

"We just sold my mother-in-law's house," a middle-aged man commented to me. "That means she has to stay in the nursing home. She can't come back and bother us anymore!" He spoke of this newly severed contact without remorse, as a triumph of the authentic self over structural obligations.

In *Growing Old in America*, David Fischer makes useful distinctions concerning respect and veneration as structural terms. He begins by stating that old age was indeed respected during colonial times, "perhaps in part because it was comparatively rare" (Fischer 1978:29). He explains: "Veneration was an emotion of great austerity, closer to awe than to affection. It had nothing to do with love. A man could be venerated without being loved – without even being liked very much" (1978:30). Fischer notes that veneration, as distinct from generalized respect, should be analyzed within the context of Puritan religion.

> The Calvinist doctrine of limited atonement – the idea that Jesus had not died for all men – presented a truly formidable problem. How could the choice be known? The doctrine of Election posed the same dilemma. How could one recognize the Elect? One indicator was old age. In early America, as in many other societies, survival to a great age was sufficiently uncommon to seem unnatural or even supernatural. (Fischer 1978:34)

The association of material and spiritual worthiness so axiomatic of Puritan cosmology found social structural support in the consolidation of wealth among elderly white men. According to Fischer (1978:58):

> The powers and privileges of old age were firmly anchored in the society. Wherever we turn we find it – in the arrangement of the meetinghouse, in patterns of officeholding and landholding, in family organization – in fact, the exaltation of age was a central part of a *system* of age relationships, a set of interlocking parts. (emphasis in original)

Not surprisingly, the single, elderly man who was poor lacked respect, and "the legal records of the colonies contain many instances of poor widows who were 'warned out' and forced to wander from one town to another" (Fischer 1978:63).

If advanced age placed white men at the political-economic apex of colonial society, the opposite was true for enslaved Africans. In *Labor of Love, Labor of Sorrow*, Jacqueline Jones (1985:40) points out that over half of the enslaved population from 1830 to 1860 was younger than 20 while only 10 percent was older than 50, an age regarded as elderly. Both Jones and Fischer note that plantation owners considered older slaves a liability; responses to this perception ranged from work reassignment to reductions in rations and housing. Fischer (1978:64) cites testimony that "planters tried to sell off their aged workers, or even to free them before they became a burden upon the plantation. When that expedient failed . . . an old slave was often turned loose to fend for himself, without food, without clothing, without shelter."

Within the enslaved community, however, elders were highly regarded for their skills and knowledge – in sharp and conscious opposition to their treatment by whites. Older women used their skills to better the lives of their families and as a form of resistance. According to Jones (1985:41): "The honored place held by elderly women in the quarters serves as a useful example of the ways in which the slaves constructed their own social hierarchy (based on individuals' skills and values to the community), in opposition to the master's exclusive concern for the productive capacity of his 'hands.'" Jones (1985:40) notes as well that older women who practiced medicine, dream interpretation, and conjuring "served as a tangible link with the African past." Following Michael Fischer's (1986:196) description of the construction of ethnic identity as an effort to forge an ethical model for future social relations, the enslaved Africans' focus on elders and their knowledge emerges as an early model for appreciating the dialectical nature of cultural diversity in the United States.

Ideological links between longevity and the relative worth of the individual are equally evident today, presenting a complex picture. While it is often said that the United States promotes a "youth culture" which values appearance and the appearance of health over life experience, the notion that the advertising industry has simply promoted youth at the expense of the aged is much too facile. The number of children who lack access to health care, the striking proportion who are overweight and unfit, the high percentage lost to violence, and the prevalence of cigarette smoking and other commodified behaviors that hasten biological aging make it difficult to argue that the health status of children is categorically privileged.

At the same time, wellness has become the mantra of the middle-aged middle class (Vesperi 1998b). One could argue that the equation is no longer youth/power but health/power. The economically powerful increasingly script their privilege on their bodies; they are marked as "responsible" adults who "manage" their health as competently as they manage their investment portfolios. Access to advanced medical care and expensive corporate wellness plans confers the power to override the aging process, enabling a mediation of

biological and social selves that could be said to mirror the Calvinist association between material and spiritual worthiness.

Jacquelyn Zita (1997:107) portrays the body as a "bio-cultural" text in her
discussion of menopause in social, political, and economic context:

> individuals and populations maintain and continuously produce the social,
> political, economic, and sexual relations of production and reproduction. . . .
> What is produced and reproduced . . . is social power and bodies infused with it
> or its lack; the aggregates of all these bodies crystallize into the macro-level rela-
> tions of race, gender, class, and other significant social divisions of domination
> and subordination.

In contrast to well-managed, middle-class bodies are the so-called irresponsible poor, who "spend" their health; their populations are identified by high
rates of heart disease and other conditions traditionally associated with the
aging process. "Ethnic lifestyles" and "ethnic foods" are often targeted in
popular discussions of health and aging, while the baseline presence of under-
nourishment and malnourishment among the U.S. poor remains structurally
normalized and rarely addressed as a society-wide concern. Anthropologists
who study aging are acutely aware that a powerful older person is one who
commands social and economic resources. Faced with a disparity between
"well" and "unwell" populations, these researchers will look immediately to
the presence of structural disparities. As with studies of infant mortality, close
attention to factors that shorten the life expectancies of marginalized groups
reveals the totalizing impact of structured social inequality on health and welfare
(Harrison 1994; American Medical Association 1990; R. Gibson 1986). Even
"universal" entitlements are less equally distributed among populations with
significantly lower life expectancies. During the 1980s, for instance, when fiscal
conservatives proposed raising the threshold for collecting Social Security benefits to age 67, the Congressional black Caucus was quick to remind them that
the predicted lifespan for African American men was only 66.

Kinship, Diversity, Aging

In the 1970s, the average nursing home resident was a white, childless female.
Situating these women's lives in historical and economic context, it is evident
that many delayed marriage and childbearing during the Great Depression,
resulting in lower fertility and small kin networks in old age. Today, looking at
women who delay childbearing into their late thirties and forties, it seems clear
that some will have few offspring, if any. What level of social support will they
command in their eighties? How is cultural diversity a factor?

The technological manipulation of fertility provides delayed but significant
new variables in the ever-changing environment of what it means to be old in
the United States. For the first time in the 1960s, women could easily and reli-
ably exert influence over fertility based on life-course expectations, delaying
procreation to pursue education and employment or to conserve household
income by limiting family size. It followed that many middle-class women

sought contraceptives during this era. At the same time, poor women – pressured by the state to limit births but still denied the opportunities afforded middle-class folks who deferred childbearing – sometimes viewed contraceptive technology as a form of genocide. Diverse cultural expectations were also highlighted in the early adoption or avoidance of contraception; the choice was often tied to religious beliefs or kinship structure. Even more basic was a woman's exposure to medical knowledge and her ability to purchase care. With regard to more recent technologies, Lois Gonzalez (1988) has suggested that cultural expectations about kinship held by childless couples are traceable factors in a woman's willingness to pursue aggressive, expensive, and physically challenging fertility treatments.

Colleen Johnson (1995) has argued strongly for a focus on family in understanding cultural diversity and its influence on the lives of older people. Despite the popular perception that intergenerational ties are weakening, most ethnographic studies show that the bulk of reassurance, caregiving, and material support still takes place within the family, whether through long-distance contact or first-hand (Climo 1992). Yet family remains one variable among many. An approach to cultural diversity that focuses too narrowly on kinship will essentialize differences among groups and subsume the highly relevant economic, social, and world-historical conditions that transect group boundaries. Not only will such an approach fall short of providing the guidance needed to address social and economic inequalities that confront so many older people today, it may actually exacerbate the problems. As Sokolovsky (1997b) points out, the stereotyped assumption that certain groups take care of their own generates rhetoric for those who would reduce social welfare programs.

Diversity amid Choice and Constraint

In an era when romantic love and emotional attachment are primary motivations for the formation and maintenance of social ties in the United States, the veneration commanded by aged Puritan males seems as unappealing – and "un-American" – as arranged marriage. Instead, like younger adults, some older people today are empowered to continually reinvent the self, to relocate from their natal communities, and to establish new ties. The concept of family of choice, identified in discussions of gay and lesbian social organization (Weston 1991), has long been promoted by intergenerational activists such as the Gray Panthers and practiced informally by residents of retirement communities (Keith 1977; see also Johnson's 1995 discussion of the opportune family).[1] Postmodern commodification of aging identities is evident in the tireless promotion of lifestyle "choices" provided by age-segregated or age-identified housing, recreation, and venues for physical, emotional, or intellectual development.

Yet, as Weston (1991:110) cautions: " 'Choice' is an individualistic and . . . bourgeois notion that focuses on the subjective power of an 'I' to formulate relationships to people and things, untrammeled by worldly constraints." The fact that few U.S. retirees resemble the sleek models in advertising aimed at older consumers points once again to the complex relations between cultural diversity and structural constraints. Phillipson and Biggs (1998:20) urge researchers to remain mindful of "the structural inequalities that seem to be ignored in post-modern perspectives. . . . In this context, material resources may be crucial in terms of providing opportunities for lifestyle change and flexibility." (See Bradley 1996; Cole 1992.)

Emphasis on the social construction of whiteness in the study of cultural diversity (Harrison 1994, 1998; Hartigan 1997; Page and Thomas 1994; Frankenberg 1993; Morrison 1992) should be particularly helpful in developing critical perspectives on aging in the United States. The ability to reinvent the social persona is not just a matter of money, it is a privilege of those who occupy unmarked social categories. As Faye Harrison (1994:91) so aptly puts it: "Given the burden of U.S. racism, the racialized ethnicity of, for instance, black Americans cannot be erased by the popular force of mere semantic ethnicization." Interestingly, it is only with advanced age that white residents of the United States experience broad, categorical marking based solely on perceived physical differences. Studies of the intersection between the social construction of whiteness and the construction of aging should yield new information about how phenotypical differences influence cultural typologies (Mukhopadhyay and Moses 1997).

Cultural Diversity and Social Discourse

Keeping these issues in mind, it is important to note that older adults who have experienced institutional racism and other forms of marginalization during their working years actively resist additional barriers imposed by the cultural construction of old age. In his analysis of a genre he labels "ethnic autobiographies," Michael Fischer (1986:195–196) found that these writings share "the paradoxical sense that ethnicity is something reinvented and reinterpreted in each generation by each individual," and that a goal of such reinvention is an ethical, future-oriented vision (see Seyhan 1996). He stresses that the genre's relative newness is itself a salient feature: "to be Chinese-American is not the same thing as being Chinese in America. In this sense there is no role model for becoming Chinese-American. It is a matter of finding a voice or style that does not violate one's several components of identity" (Fischer 1986:196).

The range of variables in such an individuated process would resist analysis at the level of cultural systems were it not manifested through texts, films, music, and ritual practices. All are subject to commodification, and hence to a contemporary understanding of how their meanings are disseminated, received, and modified. Hebdige makes excellent use of this material in his discussion of new musical traditions in Great Britain. He notes that ethnic minorities must position themselves in relation to British cultural hegemony, nationalist movements, and postcolonial legacies. In rap, sampling, mixing, and such diverse styles as "militant Celtic" and bhangra music, Hebdige (1994:234) finds "part of an ongoing process of active self-definition." He regards this process as amenable to systematic analysis, and his description of the data suggests a method for collecting it: "Through the patterns of belonging and distancing established in these forms of cultural production, new forms of 'British' identity become available which circulate along with the records themselves in the clubs and cassette players and on the pirate radio stations" (Hebdige 1994:234).

Myerhoff (1978) offered an early model for understanding the dynamic nature of cultural diversity among the diasporic elderly in her study of a Jewish community center in Venice, California. While they shared the experience of immigration from Eastern Europe and all emphasized their Jewish identity, these elders were markedly heterogeneous and sometimes at odds with regard to ritual knowledge, religious belief, and the meaning of their life experiences. In an ongoing dialectical process undertaken through study, conversation, and shared activities, they mined a communal storehouse of memories, ideas, practices, and texts in an effort to shape new ethical and social guidelines that would meet their contemporary experience. Drawing on both Bakhtin and Williams in a perceptive discussion of Myerhoff's work, Kaminsky (1993) provides support for the analysis of cultural performance among the aged as a means of contesting the dominant social discourse. A study of recent Jewish immigrants also suggests that ideology stabilizes individual narratives, and that people ground their identities by carrying on dialogues with their ideological beliefs (Thomas et al. 1996).

From Sartre's mid-century discussion of the dialectical relationship between past and future to what Giddens identifies as a post-traditional concern with "How shall I live?" it is evident that today's older people face unprecedented challenges. Among these is a need to manage the barrage of "social and psychological information about possible ways of life" (Giddens 1991:14), and nowhere is this more evident than in the contemporary United States.

In a Philadelphia-based study of ethnic identity and bereavement among older widowers of Irish, Jewish, and Italian heritage, Luborsky and Rubinstein (1987, 1997) found that men reclaimed elements of their distinctive cultural traditions to help make sense of loss and craft plans for the future. From drinking in clubs and bars to participating in organized religion, behavior patterns which had not been followed since the men were young and single were revisited in an effort to reflect on who they were – and who they might yet become. Giddens (1991:33) would go further in identifying the process of revisiting the past as "part of a reflexive mobilizing of self identity; it is not confined to life's crises, but a general feature of modern social activity in relation to psychic organization."

The active selection of cultural identity markers is also emphasized in Taylor's work on older African Americans in small midwestern towns. Taylor rightly protests the social scientific literature's depiction of African American elders as "vulnerable, at risk of impoverishment and suffering from multiple chronic ailments" at the expense of attention to the positive view of self which is so notable among this group (Taylor 1998; see also Shenk et al. 1998; Peterson 1997; Groger 1995; Vesperi 1998a). Taylor explores the significance of place and its mediating role in situating individual experience over time and in historical context. For instance, some places evoke memories of segregation: "Having survived this period provides another link in understanding the significance of place in one's identity in late life" (Taylor 1998). In Taylor's work and the other research cited here, it is evident that cultural diversity must be appreciated as a life-course concern. Life-course studies view the person as an individual, but one who has been influenced by cohort experiences as considered in historical perspective. Interviews with aged African American women about their experiences under Jim Crow laws by Shenk et al. (1998) provide a good example of how life-course research can contribute to the critical study of the United States.

The following case study speaks to many of the issues and approaches raised thus far, particularly (1) that identity is actively selected from diverse elements; (2) that it encodes ethical, future-oriented goals; and (3) that musical performers position themselves to address complex social concerns by manipulating identity markers.

Case Study

How do you reach people? By telling them the right way to go and telling them about the Lord and telling them the life that you live and tell them how you came up and tell them what you gone through with, and that's it.
                                             ("Diamond Teeth Mary" Smith McClain)

In *Black Pearls: Blues Queens of the 1920s*, Daphne Harrison (1988:66) writes: "The blues singer evokes, matches, and intensifies the 'blue' feeling of the listener in the act of singing the blues. . . . Neither the intent nor the result is escape, but, instead, the artistic expression of reality." In order to be considered successful, then, a blues performer must call out the unique emotional experience of each listener and restate it as part of a larger cultural construction. Drawing upon transcripts from performances by Mary McClain, an African American blues singer who continued to attract culturally diverse audiences well into her nineties, I will examine some of the markers and devices employed by an older narrator to establish an authoritative voice, or, more specifically, to situate the self with regard to an audience as a credible conveyor of reality and/or as truth-teller. No small achievement in the postmodernists' era of "radical doubt," the highly self-conscious use of identity markers to establish credibility sheds light on the dynamic nature of diversity in the contemporary United States.

Gottschalk, Kluckhohn, and Angell (1945) cite age, failing memory, and the actual or intended presence of an audience as cautions in using personal memoirs, which they note "were written late in life, when memory was beginning to fade, thus making the particulars untrustworthy, and very often they were apologia or polemics, thus making gravely suspect their selection, arrangement and emphases of the particulars" (Gottschalk et al. 1945:20). Here memory loss was regarded as a given of physical aging, just as the drive to favorably resituate oneself with regard to the past was seen as a likely – and quite suspect – correlate of social aging.

Since then, anthropologists and others have reassessed the historical contributions of older narrators. First, cross-cultural researchers recognized that many communities rely heavily on the highly developed memory skills of their oldest residents, and that the association of old age with failing memory is not universal. Second, the view of the life course shared by Western researchers shifted from the notion of a generalized senility in old age toward a narrower association of memory loss with individual-specific disorders, such as Alzheimer's disease. Gradually, the aged narrator has come to be regarded as both credible and competent.

> I'm a big, fat woman
> Meat shakin' on my bones
> Every time I shake
> A skinny woman lose her home.
>> ("Walking Blues"; arrangement
>> by "Walking Mary" McClain)

Attention to metaphor is key in any culturally situated discussion of autobiographical narrative. In his portrait of the Moroccan tilemaker, Tuhami, Vincent Crapanzano (1980) warns readers against "the presumption of collapsing the real and the true." The events as Tuhami relates them often lack chronological consistency and focus on extended encounters with demons. Yet Tuhami's stories are thematically consistent, and they metaphorically reflect culturally recognized predispositions and concerns. An interpretation of events need not be technically accurate to be "true" when constructing a culturally recognizable version of the self (see Angrosino 1989; Tierney 1991).

For the accomplished narrator, mastery of literary devices that make reality culturally recognizable can render the issue of biographical "truth" superfluous. Audiences don't sweat the details when they respect the authority gained from a performer's lived experience. Older performers sketch situations which resonate with shared values and contrasting tensions in a diverse society, using metaphor to establish the character and perspective of the story-teller as omniscient.[2]

Diamond Teeth Mary

During the 1930s, 1940s, and 1950s, a West Virginian known sometimes as "Walking Mary" and sometimes as "Diamond Teeth Mary" (for the diamond inlays in her front teeth) was among the brightest lights in the small, mostly rural constellation of traveling medicine shows and all-black variety reviews that toured the South. "I wanted to be just like Mary," remembers Leroy Watts, a former vaudeville performer who met her when he ran away from home at age 16 to become a dancer. "Mary was a star."

Mary retired from show business in 1961 when Dr. Milton Bartok's Bardex Minstrels, the nation's last large, traveling medicine show (Glenn Hinson, personal communication, 1984), folded in Sarasota, Florida. She settled in nearby Bradenton and joined a church, where her vocal accomplishments drew attention. This distinguished Mary from the many blues performers who began as students of gospel music and later moved to the public stage. "I didn't start in show business from the church," she explained in a 1983 interview. "Lot of people say they started there, but . . . I didn't know nothing about no church until 1962."

Mary made her home in a rented, tin-roofed shack on a dirt road; like many other highly talented performers of her generation, a lifetime of artistic dedication had yielded her no financial security or lasting artistic recognition. "I don't live in the best of house," she said. "But I've been there 17 years with a shelter over my head. . . . I ain't paying that $300 to $400 a month rent. I don't have that big an income, and my husband didn't have that big an income . . . so I stayed right there. I married in 1965 and I've been right in that little home, that broke down house what you see, ever since."

Mary began singing in public again when the Smithsonian invited her to appear at Wolftrap in 1980. She was soon performing regularly for overflow crowds at Florida blues clubs and bars. In mid-1982 I became involved with recording Mary on videotape.[3] The original goal was to preserve her riveting performances but the project was quickly expanded to focus on the cultural context of Mary's artistry, on her increasingly controversial presence in the church – where her return to the blues stage was condemned as scandalous – and on her interactions with the various musicians who worked with her. Some were veteran bluesmen whose own songs helped to situate Mary's rural African American experience within a larger context, forming a second narrative voice for much of her autobiographical referencing. Mary also performed with much younger, white musicians; here she shared nuances of phrasing and timing with new apprentices within a living tradition. At age 97 she sang from a wheelchair and her appearances were infrequent, but she continued to attract large, diverse crowds and media coverage until her death in April, 2000.

Mary engaged her audiences with startling directness, alternating songs, stories, pronouncements, and pointed criticism. The following 1984 transcript of a story about her youth, performed in the style of a sermon with little variation from one show to the next, demonstrates how she foregrounded gender, class, and regional identity to establish her presence on stage.

This is the true story of my past life. . . .
I had a broken family. My father left my mother when I was a little bitty girl. Thank you, Jesus. I can remember me and my two brothers; my mother had one piece of bacon, she'd divide it in three parts. And a little hoecake of bread, she'd divide that in three parts. She gave each one of us a piece; while we were eating, she drank a cup of coffee.
I can remember when I didn't have a place to lay my head. I can remember the day I didn't have shoes on my feet. Had no water for three or four days to drink. I ran away from home when I was 13 years old, didn't go back home until I was 28. I was 18 years old before I had a new pair of shoes on my feet. Thank you, Jesus. Slept in box cars. Slept under hay. Slept in empty houses, find the empty houses. Slept where the snow run down my face. Go to the creek and drink muddy water.
For all of that, God brought me thus far. You don't know what it is not to have a mother. You don't know what it is to be a long way from home and nobody to know, and know nobody. But if you want to *be* somebody, you can make *yourself*. You can make something out of yourself if you want to. I'm talking directly to the young people. You don't have to *use dope* or *drink liquor* and all that kind of stuff.

I didn't get a chance to go to school like you young people today. All the chance I ever got was fifth grade in public school. I was raised in the coal mine country. Thank you, Jesus. All my family died back home, in the coal mines. But I grew up better, I made it.

I went to visit her. And she said, "Mary, I'm so glad you came to see me. My children's so cruel to me. They won't give me no food, no water, anything. I'm afraid to ask them for anything."

Lord, I wish you could see the heartbreak they committed on her. *Children*, don't be cruel to your mother. *Love* her. *Cherish* her. Because when you lose your mother, you've lost everything. Your mother sees that you have shoes on your feet, clothes on your back and she tucks the cover under you at nighttime when it's cold. Love your mother, and always be nice to anybody. Speak to people.

I want to thank God for these 81 years because I came up the hard way. This is just the beginning of to tell you how hard I came up, but this is a true story that I am telling you right now. And you know, that's so bad.

This excerpt and the one that follows draw attention to two artistic vehicles used by blues singers to achieve an evocative response. One, as Daphne Harrison has noted, is the process of "matching" in which the performer employs the self as an empathic vehicle. Here the singer refrains from generalities, focusing instead on individual, first-person accounts of experience. As Harrison (1988:67) observes with regard to the cultural stage upon which performances by early female blues singers were set, "the underlying assumption is that content and style are an outgrowth of both the personal and professional experiences of these women."

Initially, then, the audience is admitted to the singer's world as a voyeur; an impression is formed but there is no interaction. What happens next, however, is a rapid, emotionally potent transition from voyeurism to introspection. In the understanding of symbolic process introduced by Langer (1974:71–72), "just as quickly as the concept is symbolized to us, our own imagination dresses it up in a private, personal *conception*, which we can distinguish from the communicable public concept only by a process of abstraction" (emphasis in original). The singer's "blue feeling," so vividly presented, becomes an object of contemplation and ultimately a mirror for the listener's emotional experiences.

The second element of blues performance style emphasizes the *establishment of authoritative voice*, laying claim to listeners' innermost thoughts and experiences directly, through omniscience. This is the realm of the traditional storyteller, the community elder, and the preacher; its fluid boundaries can be continually redrawn to include appropriate aspects of the community's moral code. Again, metaphor is significant. Ethnomusicologist Chris Waterman (1990) traces how metaphor operates to ground social relations, forging correspondences between the musical and social orders.[4]

All blues artists incorporate elements of both matching and authoritative voice, but authoritative voice is primarily, and most effectively, the province of older performers. The older person can successfully manipulate both positive and negative stereotypes about aging in ways that lend credence to his or her pronouncements about the world. On the one hand, age is linked with social wisdom. On the other, the indignities and hardships of old age can be added to the repertoire of experiences that generate the "blue feeling."

Mary often included the following narrative in her performances, building on elements established in "The True Story of My Past Life." In "The Good Boy and the Bad Boy" (1983) she further indexed class, gender and, in this case, age and specific markers of African American identity such as Black Vernacular:

> I want to tell you about the good boy and the bad boy. The good boy, the mother worked so hard. She gave her sons an education. He got to be a teacher. So he became active . . . he became a student of something, a dean of something at the school. So he told his mother, he said, "Mama," he said, "You worked so hard for me and took care of me and you brought me up to where I am today. And when I get me a job and get some money, I'm going to take care of you just like you took care of me."
>
> His mother made her living washing and ironing. Twenty-five cents a day, or 25 cents a load, or on a 25 cent basis – always 25 cents. But anyway, she educated those two children. But one of those boys turned out to be a *junkie*. A dope-head. You all know what I'm talking about. *Some* of you know. You *act* like you don't know, but you *know* what I'm talking about. You know what I'm talking about now, 'cause some of you out there might be a *junkie* yourself. I don't know. So don't start me to no lying; I don't know.
>
> But anyway, the good boy told his mother, said, "I'm going to take care of you." And when she knowed a thing, he got married. So he came to his mother and said, "Mother, I'm married now. And I want you to come and live with me. Take care of my house, my home and everything. You won't have anything to worry about."
>
> Quite natural, a child's going to sweet talk his mother, *especially* a boy. He'll tell mama anything; he don't care what he tell her because she'll believe him. Some soft-hearted mothers will believe anything her child say.
>
> So anyway, he got to be a father of two children. He says, "Mother, I got two children now. And I want you to take care of my children just like you took care of me. Me and my wife has got to work. We got to make ends meet. We got our home to pay for, got our car to pay for, and yep, yep, yep, yep, blah, blah, blah, blah, blah." So anyway, he went to work. So the mother, she took care of the two grands, as he asked her.
>
> So she began to get old and feeble. That's what I'm saying about young people – don't like old people. But that's bad. Never turn your head or never turn your nose up at an old person. Because honey, God will punish you. Respect gray hair, baby, anywhere you see it. Black, white, purple, old gold, green-gray, anybody, you respect them. You understand what I'm saying? Don't walk by anybody. You see an old lady walking by, *help* her across the street. You see an old gentleman on a walking cane, *help* him across the street. If you see him walking somewhere, give him a ride. Your car, the car don't belong to you, it belongs to God. Anything we got that belongs to us, it belongs to God. Now you can believe that. He'll loan it to you for a certain amount of time. And when that time runs out, you'll run out. So don't ignore old people because there has to be somebody. . . . If it hadn't been for old people none of you would be in this world today. It takes somebody older than the other one to get the other one. See what I'm saying? Children, don't look over old people, because whenever you do, God will punish you.

So I'm saying that to say this. This young man, his little girls got to be some size. So his wife, she got disgusted, well, "Honey, I want to talk to you today. I got something to tell you."

He kind of felt what was going on, but he went on and didn't say anything.

She said, "I just got to talk to you." She says, "You know, we got to get rid of your mother. She's getting too *old* to take care of these children. She's not using correct *English*. She's using *dis* and *dat* and all that kind of stuff. And I don't want that to rub off on my children. And you just have to find her somewhere to go."

He didn't say anything, with his little heart busted, broken. He went on for about another week or more, and she went back to him again, she says, "Honey, I don't think you understand what I was quoting you about. I was trying to tell you that you got to *get rid of your mother*. Because she using the wrong English, she done got too old, and her eyesight's bad, and her walk's bad, and so I don't want her messing around with my children."

So he decided to take his mother to a nursing home. He went to her one day, and said, "Mother, I want to talk to you."

She said, "Yes, I know what it's all about." She said, "God done showed it to me a month ago and told me that your wife don't want me in this home. I can feel it because I am one of God's chosen children."

He says, "Mother, I'm gonna take you to the nursing home and you won't have to want for a thing. I'm gonna get you a color TV, everything you want, telephone, everything. You don't have nothing to worry about. Now I'll be there to see you every day."

So she dropped her head and went to humming to herself [here Mary hums the introduction to her following song] and she just got her little bag, packed up her bag, and whatnot.

He said, "Well, Mother, I'm going to give you the last ride in my brand new Cadillac, and I'm gonna let you ride in it first, but don't you worry. *We'll* be to see about you."

So they're going on down the road, she was humming. Just a-humming [here Mary repeats the opening bars of her next song]. He said, "Mother, why you humming like that?"

She said, "I was just wondering, talking to the Heavenly Father. Asking Him why would you turn your back on me when I worked my fingers off to the bone for you. All the skin was off my fingers. I had a skin infection. The doctors thought I was going to lose my fingers trying to bring you up. I brought you up to where you could be on your own, but now, you're throwing me away. You're forgetting about what I done for you when you was a little bitty baby. When I tucked you under the cover. When I seen that you was eating. I saw that you had the proper food. I seen that you had the best of care. Now, you're throwing me away."

"Oh, it's not that. Oh, it's nothing but that you know my wife say blah, blah, blah, blah, blah. You know how women are. You know how women is, and yibbi, yibbi, yibbi, yibbi."

So they started on down the road, and he's gunning his car. So she *looked* back. She looked back and she said, "*Wait! Stop this car right now!* Stop it right now! I believe I see that no good son coming. *That's* my boy."

He jumped out of his car. He said, "Mother, what's the matter? Where are you going? What's wrong?"

She said, "*Your* brother done throwed me out, was carrying me to the nursing home. He said that's where I'll have to live the rest of my life. After all I've done for both of you. Went hungry, bare-footed in the rain to take care of you. Now *he* don't want me and I'm quite sure *you* can't take care of me because you ain't nothing but a *junkie* yourself."

He said, "Mama, I ain't got nothing. I got an old, raggedy shack. *Thank you, Jesus*. I got a can of pork and beans. I got this old, raggedy car, but if you don't mind, Mama, you can come go with me. You can eat these beans out of this can with me. Mama, I'll share because you are my mama. Remember, you are my mother."

He said to his brother, "Why would you take Mother to the rest home when you got a good place for her?"

"Well, Sally Janie don't want her there, blah, blah, blah, blah."

He said, "Well, remember, Mama worked for us. Mother raised us. She gave us an education. Now I know I haven't done right. But you supposed to be *up*right. And you the first one to turn your back on *our* mother. Remember, that's our mother. But I'm gonna take her home with me and we'll eat beans out the can, but she'll never go to no rest home." And this is what she said to him:

[Song: *I'm your mother don't drive me away . . .*]

"The Good Boy and the Bad Boy" established Mary's credibility in two ways. First, she reached directly for the experience of her adult but relatively young audience members. She situated them within the story as children, and, in some cases, as the "bad" character: ". . . some of you out there might be a *junkie* yourself."

A second level of credibility was established as Mary created a narrative that resonated with shared cultural values and tensions. Most basic was the theme of kinship obligation – of mother to children, of grandmother to grandchildren, of grown children to mothers and mothers-in-law. Also stressed was the value of generalized respect – not love – for the elderly. It is no accident that Mary dwelt on this theme, exhorting her audience to "respect gray hair." She had already told the audience her age, and she capitalized upon her elderly status to reinforce her authority as omniscient storyteller: "You understand what I'm saying?" "See what I'm saying?" "So I'm saying that to say this."

Another primary theme is Christian religion. Here Mary employed verbal references to God and Jesus, supplemented by other verbal and non-verbal rhetorical conventions learned in church, to lend credibility and to provide a familiar framework for audience acceptance of her morality play. Mary's hero, the elderly mother, was also imbued with omniscient powers, conferred by God: "I know what it's all about . . . God done showed it to me . . . I can feel it because I am one of God's chosen children."

A basic tension in the story Mary constructed is the situation of the upwardly mobile African American family within the wider context of the U.S. middle class. The mother is identified as a low-paid servant, "always 25 cents," who works her fingers to the bone to provide for her two sons. Mary had already claimed authority in this realm by relating her own childhood memories about her mother's sacrifices. Mary marked and devalued the "good" son's choices at every stage, first by failing to properly identify, and thus distancing, his profession: "He became a student of something, a dean of something at the school."

Then Mary zeroed in on the wife's rejection of her mother-in-law, a conflict of values springing from tension about social-class standing and ethnicity. The issue is symbolically condensed as embarrassment about the older woman's use of Black English: "She's using *dis* and *dat* . . . and I don't want that to rub off on my children." Here Mary also held up for inspection the more generalized notion that prolonged contact with the elderly is polluting to the young and should be avoided. She punctuated the wife's statement by rubbing her arm as if she had brushed up against something unpleasant.

Throughout, Mary stressed how the so-called "good" son consistently chose material acquisition and display over kin-based sharing. In a final insult, he offered his mother the first ride in his new Cadillac, a thin substitute for the extended family ties he has just broken. Ultimately, in a classic moral and structural reversal worthy of Lévi-Strauss, the "bad" boy becomes the "good" boy by demonstrating the value of sharing with kin above all other considerations.

At no point did Mary present the experience of the elderly mother as her own; in fact, her autobiographical introduction identified her most closely with the errant child, who runs away and does not appreciate the mother's sacrifices until later. Mary exhorted, accused, and sometimes berated, highlighting difference at every level. Yet her accumulated understanding of poverty, her introspection over a lifetime and her authoritative interpretation of theological constraints – in short, her status as an elder – allowed her to speak in cultural generalities that resonated with the members of her audience, no matter how diverse.

NOTES

1   Atchley (1993) uses critical theory to provide a brief but well-grounded discussion of retirement, with attention to issues of economic distribution.
2   My association of metaphor with character and perspective for the purpose of analyzing performance is taken from Kenneth Burke. On the subject of reality as presented through metaphor, he writes: "It is customary to think that objective reality is dissolved by such relativity of terms as we get through the shifting of perspectives. . . . But on the contrary, it is by the approach through a variety of perspectives that we establish a character's reality" (Burke 1969:504).
3   In 1983 I obtained a grant from the National Endowment for the Arts Media Preservation program, with matching support from the University of South Florida and in-kind contributions from video technicians and consultants. Collaborators on this project were cinematographer Nik Petrik and Peter B. Gallagher, a writer and musician.
4   Here Waterman (1990:218) follows Turino's 1989 observation that "music . . . is not just socially structured; the social order is, in part, musically structured since musical activity comprises one important public domain in which a world view is made patent in a multileveled and powerful form."

REFERENCES CITED

American Medical Association
    1990   Council on Ethical and Judicial Affairs: Council Report, Black–White Disparities in Health Care. *Journal of the American Medical Association* 263(17):2344–2346.

Angrosino, Michael
  1989   *Documents of Interaction: Biography, Autobiography, and Life History in Social Science Perspective*. University of Florida Monographs No. 74. Gainesville: University of Florida.
Atchley, Robert C.
  1993   Critical Perspectives on Retirement. In *Voices and Visions of Aging*: Toward a Critical Gerontology. Thomas R. Cole, W. Andrew Achenbaum, Patricia L. Jacobi, and Robert Kastenbaum, eds. Pp. 3–19. New York: Springer.
Bradley, H.
  1996   *Fractured Identities*. Oxford: Polity Press.
Brubaker, Timothy H., and Carol M. Michael
  1987   Amish Families in Later Life. In *Ethnic Dimensions of Aging*. Donald E. Gelfand and Charles M. Barresi, eds. Pp. 106–117. New York: Springer.
Burke, Kenneth
  1969   *A Grammar of Motives*. Berkeley: University of California Press.
Climo, Jacob
  1992   *Distant Parents*. New Brunswick, NJ: Rutgers University Press.
Cole, Thomas
  1992   *The Journey of Life*. Cambridge, UK: Cambridge University Press.
Crapanzano, Vincent
  1980   *Tuhami: Portrait of a Moroccan*. Chicago: University of Chicago Press.
Fischer, David Hackett
  1978   *Growing Old in America*. Oxford: Oxford University Press.
Fischer, Michael M. J.
  1986   Ethnicity and the Post-Modern Arts of Memory. In *Writing Culture: The Poetics and Politics of Ethnography*. James Clifford and George F. Marcus, eds. Pp. 194–233. Berkeley: University of California Press.
Frankenburg, Ruth
  1993   *White Women, Race Matters: The Social Construction of Whiteness*. Minneapolis: University of Minnesota Press.
Gibson, Jane W.
  1996   The Social Construction of Whiteness in Shellcracker Haven, Florida. *Human Organization* 55(4):379–388.
Gibson, Rose Campbell
  1986   *Blacks in an Aged Society*. New York: Carnegie Corporation.
Giddens, Anthony
  1991   *Modernity and Self-Identity*. Stanford: Stanford University Press.
Gonzalez, Lois
  1988   The Lived Experience of Infertility: A Phenomenological Study of Infertile Women. Ph.D. dissertation, University of South Florida, Tampa.
Gottschalk, Louis, Clyde Kluckhohn, and Robert Angell
  1945   *The Use of Personal Documents in History, Anthropology and Sociology*. New York: Social Science Research Council Bulletin 53.
Groger, Lisa
  1995   Health Trajectories and Long Term Care Choices: What Stories Told by Informants Can Tell Us. In *The Culture of Long Term Care: Nursing Home Ethnography*. J. Neil Henderson and Maria D. Vesperi, eds. Pp. 55–69. Westport, CT: Bergin and Garvey.
Hareven, Tamara K.
  1995   Historical Perspectives on the Family and Aging. In *Handbook of Aging and the Family*. Rosemary Blieszner and Victoria Hilkevitch Bedford, eds. Pp. 13–31. Westport, CT: Greenwood Press.

Harrison, Daphne Duval
  1988 *Black Pearls: Blues Queens of the 1920s*. New Brunswick, NJ: Rutgers University Press.
Harrison, Faye
  1994 Racial and Gender Inequalities in Health and Health Care. *Medical Anthropology Quarterly* 8(1):90–95.
  1998 Introduction: Expanding the Discourse on Race. *American Anthropologist* 100(3):609–631.
Hartigan, John, Jr.
  1997 Establishing the Fact of Whiteness. *American Anthropologist* 99(3):495–505.
Hebdige, Dick
  1994 After the Masses. In *Culture/Power/History: A Reader in Contemporary Social Theory*. Nicholas B. Dirks, Geoff Eley, and Sherry B. Ortner, eds. Pp. 222–235. Princeton, NJ: Princeton University Press.
Johnson, Colleen L.
  1995 Cultural Diversity in the Late-Life Family. In *Handbook of Aging and the Family*. Rosemary Blieszner and Victoria Hilkevitch Bedford, eds. Pp. 307–333. Westport, CT: Greenwood Press.
Jones, Jacqueline
  1985 *Labor of Love, Labor of Sorrow*. New York: Basic Books.
Kaminsky, Marc
  1993 Definitional Ceremonies: Depoliticizing and Reenchanting the Culture of Aging. In *Voices and Visions of Aging: Toward a Critical Gerontology*. Thomas R. Cole, W. Andrew Achenbaum, Patricia L. Jacobi, and Robert Kastenbaum, eds. Pp. 257–274. New York: Springer.
Keith, Jennie
  1977 *Old People, New Lives: Community Creation in a Retirement Residence*. Chicago: University of Chicago Press.
Langer, Suzanne K.
  1974 *Philosophy in a New Key*. Cambridge, MA: Harvard University Press.
Luborsky, Mark, and Robert Rubinstein
  1987 Ethnicity and Lifetimes: Self-Concepts and Situational Contexts of Ethnic Identity in Late Life. In *Ethnic Dimensions of Aging*. D. Gelfand, and C. Barresi, eds. Pp. 35–50. New York: Springer.
  1997 The Dynamics of Ethnic Identity and Bereavement among Older Widowers. In *The Cultural Context of Aging: Worldwide Perspectives*. Jay Sokolovsky, ed. Pp. 304–315. Westport, CT: Bergin and Garvey.
McClain, Mary
  1983 *The Story of the Good Boy and the Bad Boy*. Recorded at the Florida Folklife Festival, White Springs, FL.
  1984 *The True Story of My Past Life*. Recorded at Morrissound Studios, Tampa, FL.
Morrison, Toni
  1992 *Playing in the Dark: Whiteness and the Literary Imagination*. Cambridge, MA: Harvard University Press.
Mukhopadhyay, Carol C., and Yolanda T. Moses
  1997 Reestablishing "Race" in Anthropological Discourse. *American Anthropologist* 99(3):517–533.
Mullings, Leith
  1987 Introduction: Urban Anthropology and U.S. Cities. In *Cities of the United States*. Leith Mullings, ed. Pp. 1–15. New York: Columbia University Press.

Myerhoff, Barbara
  1978   *Number Our Days.* New York: E. P. Dutton.
Page, Helan, and R. Brooke Thomas
  1994   White Public Space and the Construction of White Privilege in U.S. Health
      Care: Fresh Concepts and a New Model of Analysis. *Medical Anthropology
      Quarterly* 8(1):109–116.
Peterson, Jane W.
  1997   Age of Wisdom: Elderly Black Women in Family and Church. In *The Cultural
      Context of Aging: Worldwide Perspectives.* Jay Sokolovsky, ed. Pp. 276–292.
      Westport, CT: Bergin and Garvey.
Phillipson, Chris
  1998   *Reconstructing Old Age: New Agendas for Social Theory and Social Practice.*
      London: Sage.
Phillipson, Chris, and Simon Biggs
  1998   Modernity and Identity: Themes and Perspectives in the Study of Older Adults.
      Journal of Aging and Identity 3(1):11–23.
Sahlins, Marshall
  1994   Cosmologies of Capitalism: The Trans-Pacific Sector of "The World System."
      In *Culture/Power/History: A Reader in Contemporary Social Theory.* Nicholas
      B. Dirks, Geoff Eley, and Sherry B. Ortner, eds. Pp. 412–455. Princeton, NJ:
      Princeton University Press.
Seyhan, Azade
  1996   Ethnic Selves/Ethnic Signs: Invention of Self, Space, and Genealogy in
      Immigrant Writing. In *Culture/Contexture: Explorations in Anthropology and
      Literary Studies.* E. Valentine Daniel and Jeffrey M. Peck, eds. Pp. 175–194.
      Berkeley: University of California Press.
Shenk, Dena, Beth Croom, and Dorothy Ruiz
  1998   Discussion of African American Women Aging after Jim Crow. In *Voices
      of Experience: Listening to our Elders.* Robert J. F. Elsner, ed. Pp. 95–119.
      University of Georgia Gerontology Center Technical Report UGAGC-98-001.
      Athens, GA.
Sokolovsky, Jay
  1997a The Ethnic Dimension in Aging. In *The Cultural Context of Aging:
      Worldwide Perspectives.* Jay Sokolovsky, ed. Pp. 253–261. Westport, CT: Bergin
      and Garvey.
  1997b Aging, Ethnicity and Family Support. In *The Cultural Context of Aging:
      Worldwide Perspectives.* Jay Sokolovsky, ed. Pp. 263–275. Westport, CT: Bergin
      and Garvey.
Taylor, Sue Ann Perkins
  1998   Place Identification and Positive Realities of Aging. Paper presented at the
      14th International Congress of Anthropological and Ethnological Sciences,
      Williamsburg, VA.
Thomas, L. Eugene, Matvey Sokolovsky, and Richard I. Feinberg
  1996   Ideology, Narrative, and Identity: The Case of Elderly Jewish Immigrants from
      the Former USSR. *Journal of Aging and Identity* 1(1):51–72.
Tierney, Geraldine
  1991   Spoiled Goods: Profiles of Skid Row Women. Ph.D. dissertation, University of
      South Florida, Tampa.
Turino, Thomas
  1989   The Coherence of Social Style and Musical Creation among the Aymara in
      Southern Peru. *Ethnomusicology* 33:1–30.

Vesperi, Maria
    1998a   *City of Green Benches: Growing Old in a New Downtown*. 2nd edition. Ithaca, NY: Cornell University Press.
    1998b   Toward Intragenerational Equity. *Generations* 22(1):92–93.
Waterman, Christopher
    1990   *Juju: A Social History and Ethnography of an African Popular Music*. Chicago: University of Chicago Press.
Weston, Kath
    1991   *Families We Choose: Lesbians, Gays, Kinship*. New York: Columbia University Press.
Yee, Barbara
    1997   The Social and Cultural Context of Adaptive Aging by Southeast Asian Elders. In *The Cultural Context of Aging: Worldwide Perspectives*. Jay Sokolovsky, ed. Pp. 293–300. Westport, CT: Bergin and Garvey.
Zita, Jacquelyn N.
    1997   Heresy in the Female Body: The Rhetorics of Menopause. In *The Other within Us: Feminist Explorations of Women and Aging*. Marilyn Pearsall, ed. Pp. 95–112. Boulder, CO: Westview Press.

19

Sexual Minorities and the New Urban Poverty

Jeff Maskovsky

Paulie (sometimes Paulina)[1] sat across from me at a corner table at the Street Eats Diner, a greasy spoon located in the heart of Philadelphia's downtown gay neighborhood. He lit a cigarette, took a sip of coffee, and began his life story, which he told with much flamboyance and flair, in the style of the jaded drag queen:

> My name is Paulie Robertson. I'm 34 years old. I'm the youngest of seven children. I grew up in North Philadelphia in a fairly nice home, nice parents. Two-parent home until I was about 15. Then, at last, there was just mom and seven children. Went all the way through school. Graduated from school. And decided to start working. Then decided I wanted to hang with the in-crowd because those were the disco days and all that. I was 15 years old. Phony ID and everything. I would just party hard. I would go to Center City and party. I would go to West Philly to the Olympia Ballroom. Wherever the party was that's where I went. To be in with the in-crowd, that included drinking and smoking cigarettes, and smoking reefer, just a total wild, crazy life. So, that was that. Sowing my oats, not knowing whether I wanted men or women. All that good old happy stuff.

In many respects, Paulie's life history resembles that of many lesbians and gay men, particularly gay men and lesbians of color, who have come of age, and come out, in major U.S. cities. Indeed, from Paulie's point of view, coming of age was about the pursuit of sexual freedom, identity and community:

> In the long run, we all find out exactly who we are after a little while. The in-crowd, where I was going back in those days, was where you could just go and let your hair down, and dance with other men and all that other stuff back then. You thought you were hot stuff back then. Didn't need that much money like you do now. And then I got with the transgender community, those girls in dresses. I went from the in-crowd to finding the transgender crowd, and "oh, doll, you'll look good in make-up and hair and a wig and all that." "And smoke some of this

good stuff right here, and it will make you feel good, and you'll be Diana Ross."
It was crazy, but it was fun.

But Paulie's story of personal liberation is also a story of social suffering. Framed through the lens of drug addiction and prostitution, Paulie tells me not only about how he became a part of Philadelphia's gay and transgender communities, but also about his descent into poverty:

> So I thought it was fun. And one thing led to another. You start off with pot. You get tired of smoking pot. Then you want to drink beer. You get tired of beer. Do you want vodka? You get tired of vodka. Then crack came along. So you want to try that too. Back again, trying to be with the in-crowd. And things just got crazier and crazier. At that time, I was working in different restaurants in town, waiting tables or bussing tables. I worked in just about every restaurant, every good restaurant in Center City, from one to another. After you start doing a drug you're scamming this one and scamming that one. You scam enough people, and then you move on to the next place. Then when I started really doing hard drugs, which was crack, then it became a prostitution time, because no matter how many jobs you've had, or how much money you had coming in, if you needed to put on a skirt and go in a corner to make some money, there I was. That led to about eight or nine years . . . doing that. Still working two jobs, still standing on the corner turning tricks, and it was just crazy. Losing jobs and losing apartments. And mother putting you out. And all that good stuff. "Get out. Come back when you get yourself together."

Paulie's life history is but one reminder that lesbians and gay men are not immune to poverty.[2] Indeed, while cities are traditionally described as places of sexual freedom, expression, and community for lesbians and gay men in the United States, the same political-economic developments that have facilitated the growth of these liberated communities have also caused economic deprivation and immiseration affecting a growing number of sexual minorities.

In this chapter I place poor lesbians and gay men like Paulie at the center of analysis. This focus represents a shift from current preoccupations in the field of lesbian/gay studies that privilege consumption-based theories of identity formation and, consequently, elide class-based differences *within* the categories of lesbian and gay. Specifically, I show that consumption practices and commercial contexts are central in the lives of poor sexual minorities, but they operate very differently than for middle-class lesbians and gay men. Poor lesbians and gay men form communities within commercial contexts, but these are communities of workers, not consumers. Conversely, poor lesbians and gay men adopt consumer identities, but they do so in relation to the services of the welfare state, not to an ever-expanding world of retail goods and services. The chapter ends by considering the ironic and even perverse consequences of neoliberal political developments, which include the tempered yet increasingly popular embrace of gay consumer culture, for poor sexual minorities.[3]

Consumption, What's Your Function?

Foundational works by historians, anthropologists, and other scholars have identified the importance of urban-based consumerism to the development of gay and lesbian community and politics (D'Emilio 1983; D'Emilio and Freedman 1988; Duberman et al. 1989). They have shown how sexual minority identities and politics are consolidated and transformed through social relations forged in commercialized leisure sites such as bars, clubs, and theaters (Beemyn 1997; Chauncey 1994; Newton 1993). For instance, Kennedy and Davis (1993) explore how working-class lesbian communities built around the bar culture of the 1940s and 1950s in Buffalo served as a precursor to the lesbian and gay liberation movement. It was in these bars, they argue, that lesbian identity was first consolidated and then transformed into political consciousness. This and related work in the field of lesbian/gay studies focuses on sites of commercial consumption, and for good reason: for most gay men and lesbians, workplaces were, and continue to be, sites of extreme homophobia, heterosexism, and harassment. It is only in locations outside of work, in spaces where gays and lesbians are relatively, but by no means absolutely, free from harassment, that gay and lesbian identity, community, and politics have been forged.

Yet this approach overlooks the important fact that the commercialized sites of lesbian and gay consumption – whether they be bars, theaters, or even street corners – are often workplaces as well.[4] The bars and theaters that have helped to consolidate lesbian and gay communities are sustained by the labor practices of other lesbians and gay men, who typically are of different socioeconomic status than the patrons they serve. In other words, leisure sites are social spaces that are constituted not only through the consumption practices of customers, but also through the labor practices of workers. The failure to attend to labor practices has created an uneven view of lesbian and gay community formation in lesbian/gay studies. It has prevented us from asking the following questions:

1 What role do workers play in the creation of community? How do the relations of exploitation – defined here as relations that pit low-end service workers against owners and consumers in the context of the workplace, and that are structured along class lines, with their race and gender dimensions – shape the politicization of lesbian and gay identity?

2 What happens to lesbians and gay men who cannot get work? How do they form communities and politics?

3 To what extent does the emergence of lesbian and gay consumption-based communities represent a politics of exclusion in which the poor are separated for economic and/or cultural reasons from their more affluent counterparts?

4 What is the relationship of the poor to sexual minority politics?

The remainder of this chapter discusses several examples of sexual minorities living in urban poverty in the United States – examples that have until now been largely excluded from much of the academic literature in lesbian/gay studies.

Sexual Minorities in the New Urban Poverty

The growth of lesbian and gay neighborhoods and commercial zones during the past 35 years must be viewed in connection with wider economic changes affecting cities throughout the United States. Since the 1950s and 1960s, manufacturing plants have left the major mid-Atlantic, northeastern and midwestern cities, first for the Sunbelt and then for other countries. This shift has had two major results. First, the number, quality, wages, and security of low-skill and semi-skilled jobs have decreased nationwide, especially in large urban centers. Second, the high-skill service and financial sector has grown to manage, coordinate, and speed up production processes that have become nationally and globally dispersed to an unprecedented degree as production has been relocated across the globe. As a result, many cities are marked by what Neil Smith (1991) calls "uneven development." In this situation, the service and finance firms cluster in central business districts, sometimes accompanied by gentrified housing for their employees, and by retail outlets that employ low-end service workers; whereas older, formerly industrial neighborhoods are marked by declining social services, decaying housing stocks, and concentrated poverty. Faced with budget deficits, declining bond ratings, declining amounts of federal assistance, and loss of population and businesses, municipal leaders have been forced to pump a disproportionate share of public resources into relatively small, targeted areas in the hopes of jump-starting their local economies. "Uneven development," says Smith (1991:5), "is social inequality blazoned into the geographical landscape, and it is simultaneously the exploitation of that geographical unevenness for certain socially determined ends" – in this case, neoliberal efforts to improve cities' images and, by extension it is hoped, their economic fortunes.

An emerging body of literature locates the development of lesbian and gay communities within the dynamic of uneven development. One strand of the literature argues that gay men – and to a lesser extent lesbians – often take advantage of economic and social opportunities in developing urban areas by becoming urban pioneers and gentrifiers. By participating as urban pioneers, some argue they form residential and commercial enclaves that help to insulate them from many forms of anti-gay discrimination (Bell and Valentine 1995; Castells 1983; Ettorre 1978; Lauria and Knopp 1985; Levine 1979). Others have challenged the putatively progressive, identity-based premise underlying this argument to show how gay and lesbian developers and small business owners place their class interests above the interests of a community based on sexual identity. Knopp (1997), for instance, shows how gay neighborhood development in New Orleans was structured by class interests. Developers, many of whom were gay, sought to make profits by building luxury housing in a gay neighborhood. This strategy of capital accumulation pitted them against middle- and low-income gay residents, with the consequence that the community became more stratified along class lines. Similarly, Weston and Rofel (1997:40) argue for a view of class as "property relations and the division of labor [that] continuously generates class divisions" in their discussion of class struggle between lesbian workers and owners in an auto mechanic shop. These studies explore the class-based contradictions that emerge in the formation of gay and lesbian communities and politics, and they do so by approaching class not exclusively as the outgrowth of consumption practices. Rather, they connect class to sexuality by examining how sexualized identities, communities, and politics are forged in contexts shaped, first and foremost, by the objective political-economic processes that produce class relations. This view of community and politics – forged out of class and its connection to sexuality – serves as the basis in this paper for my discussion of gay and lesbian poverty.[5]

This chapter builds on Knopp's and Weston and Rofel's work to show how the economy and the state (through the provision of social welfare) have become key features in the growth of community and politics for poor lesbians and gay men. I will review several examples that describe the making of poverty for lesbians and gay men, and that highlight the importance of large-scale economic restructuring and the role of welfare state policies in shaping lesbian and gay identities, communities, and politics among the poor (Maskovsky 1999).

Gay Ghetto Service Work and the Construction of Gay Identity

I begin with a description of the work history of Drew, an African American gay man in his fifties. Unlike the migration narratives that are widespread in the literature on community building in lesbian/gay studies, Drew did not come to Philadelphia from a small town in the Midwest. He grew up in a black neighborhood outside the city center that has been hit hard over the last 30 years by the elimination of manufacturing jobs, disastrous urban planning, and the withdrawal of social services (Adams et al. 1991 describe the political-economic developments). Drew left home at 16 in search of "community." He began hanging out on 13th Street, the heart of Philadelphia's main gay neighborhood. Several gay-oriented adult bookshops are located on the street, as is Philadelphia's largest gay bar and disco. Over the years, 13th Street has become a major site of sex work for black gays and transgender men and women. It quickly became Drew's primary site not only of community but of work. Soon after his arrival, Drew started working at a local gay bar as a female impersonator.

Drew was very successful as a professional drag queen, and eventually earned enough money and notoriety to take his show on the road. For 20 years, he toured as a headliner, and helped other young gay men by hiring them to perform with him. Despite his relative fame, however, Drew always had difficulty making ends meet. While the pay was good, expenses associated with being a professional drag queen are quite high. He had to pay the other drag queens out of his own pocket; he also incurred expenses for travel, lodging, and the materials used in making elaborate costumes. Even after 20 years, he still struggled to get by.

Eventually, Drew stopped touring. Audiences, he said, lost interest in drag, and life was too hard on the road. The young men he hired often left the road without warning, and they often stole from him. He returned to Philadelphia and performed infrequently at local gay bars, which, he complains, now prefer go-go boys to drag queens. His connections in the community got him a job as a short order cook at the Street Eats Diner, which is less than two blocks away from where he used to hang out on 13th Street. He now makes about $250 a week, without health or retirement benefits, vacation pay, or sick leave. He has moved into a one-bedroom apartment nearby. Drew now lives on the edge of impoverishment. So long as he can keep his job or another one like it, he will avoid total destitution, but old age with minimal social security payments (since his income was mostly off the record) will probably push him below the poverty line. Despite all this, Drew is still very positive about the gay community. He says:

> I learned to be gay on 13th Street. I brought other young ones from there with me and taught them the business. It was crazy and there was a lot of fighting, but it was just my way of giving them a little fame.

As to his work situation, he adds:

> I am the same as everyone else who comes in here [to the coffee shop] or who watches my shows, except I have a little bit more fame. The only thing that I don't like is that sometimes they don't pay you. They don't know how to run a restaurant or a bar, so they run out of money and you are out of luck.

Drew's story allows us to make a number of important points about sexual minorities in the low end of the labor market. First, his experience accords with what Weston and Rofel (1997:27–30) call "bridging the public and private" in the workplace. For Drew, as for the lesbians who worked at the garage where Weston and Rofel did fieldwork, working in a gay-owned business breaks down the binary opposition between work and leisure by bringing gay identity – so often theorized only in the context of leisure activities in the private sphere – into the public sphere of the workplace. It would be a mistake to conclude that bridging the public and the private is seamless or easy, as Weston and Rofel demonstrate. As Drew's experience confirms, the politics of the gay community masks economic inequalities in the workplace. His attitudes exemplify the uneasy coexistence of gay identity and class. By viewing himself as "just like everyone else," he deploys a universal gay identity; in nearly the same breath, however, he also recounts the relations of class exploitation that differentiate him from the white middle-class employers and clientele he serves.

Drew's story also calls into question the primacy of consumption practices in shaping lesbian and gay identity. His role as a female impersonator and his efforts to train younger gay men as apprentices provides one example of the importance that workers play in the consolidation of lesbian and gay identity in commercial locales. Indeed, it is often the sex workers, bartenders, barbacks, go-go boys, go-go girls, and other performers – usually from different racial groups and class positions than the consumers they serve – who become central figures in gay and lesbian communities and struggles. In Philadelphia's downtown gay community, for instance, every politically involved lesbian and gay man knows Drew. In New York, famously, the drag queens and lesbians and gay men of color who worked at the Stonewall Inn started the riot.

Drew's story also exemplifies how many men and women of color find jobs in the low-wage, low-end service sector of the gay and lesbian economy. This is the result of wider labor market trends that are exploited by gay and lesbian business owners without a second thought as to the effect on equality and solidarity within "the community." Drew's comments suggest that he has experienced a lifetime of exploitation, including the refusal of several employers to pay him for work. In the name of the gay community, employers exercise their entrepreneurial spirit on the backs of their workers, thereby reinforcing race, class, and gender divisions within lesbian and gay communities.

Poverty and Lesbian and Gay Community Formation

But what about lesbians and gay men who, because of constraints on labor markets, spend time outside of the paid workforce? For them, the institutions of social welfare play a determining role in the formation of community. In fact, as we shall see in the following example, publicly funded service programs often form the crucible in which community is formed.

Dawn and Sandi, both African American lesbians, grew up in poor neighborhoods in Newark and Atlantic City, respectively. Hit hard by the economic crises affecting inner cities in the Northeast, Dawn and Sandi experienced family lives characterized by extreme deprivation, violence, and abuse. When Dawn was 15, she was institutionalized for a month and then thrown out of the house after her mother discovered her *in flagrante delicto* with her female babysitter. For her part, Sandi ran away from home when her father, after having initiated her into drug abuse, put pressure on her to return to high school. Both were addicted to street drugs by the time they were in their mid-teens. For decades, they worked in the informal drug economies of Newark, Atlantic City, and Philadelphia.

The quasi-institutionalized setting of publicly funded drug rehabilitation programs inadvertently provides opportunities for sexual minorities like Dawn and Sandi to form community. Dawn moved to Philadelphia to get clean. She entered the New Directions Treatment Center (NDTC), an inpatient detox program, after several other attempts to stay clean had failed. Detox was a harrowing experience for Dawn. One of its advantages, however, was forced segregation between men and women. This situation helped Dawn to get to know other women. She explains,

> For the first couple of days I laid in my own pee. I was a mess. And I had the shakes. I could hardly talk. The thing there was we don't talk to the men only 'til night. Then everyone [the women] get into a community room. And then we had the chance to talk or say what you feel about an individual so that there wouldn't be any trouble. And I didn't mind that part about not speaking to the men. I was real happy that the women could not talk to the men because I was gay and that only left me for them to talk to. And that was real good to me. So that stipulation didn't bother me at all. They [the men] walked on one side of the wall, and we had to walk on the other side of the wall. . . . And in the program I learned who I was. And I learned that I wasn't really a bad person. I just never had a chance to pull it together. And I learned that I was an alcoholic. And I learned that I was also a part

of gambler's anonymous. And, you know, I learned a lot about me. When I left the program I left there with more friends than I had made in my whole life, I mean, real friends.

The race, class, and gender dynamics of this situation are worth mentioning. Inside NDTC, contact between drug users – most of whom are poor black, inner-city residents – is highly regimented and severely constrained. This strategy accords with wider cultural assumptions about the inner-city poor, the so-called underclass, whose (hetero)sexuality is pathologized as one aspect of the "culture of poverty." Indeed, the sexuality of the black poor – often implicitly characterized in poverty studies as "lacking monogamy" or, worse, "hypersexual" – is viewed as a causal factor in preventing their upward mobility (e.g. Wilson 1987; for a critique of this view of "underclass" sexuality, see di Leonardo 1997). It is no surprise, then, that detox programs would segregate their client populations along gender lines.

Dawn's story shows how poor lesbians and gay men can, even under the most dire of circumstances, use the presumption of heterosexuality – based in this case on racialized and gendered categorizations of poverty – to form community within state-based institutions. Furthermore, state-based institutional contexts can also be places where lesbians and gay men actively and openly pursue relationships. In Sandi's case, she spent eight years in prison and agreed to enter rehab as a condition of her parole. She had already arrived at NDTC by the time Dawn entered the program. They met at a lesbian and gay dance sponsored by a recovery group spun off from NDTC. In order to spend more time with Dawn, Sandi volunteered to be Dawn's detox counselor a few weeks later. Thus, it was through the institutional practices associated with recovery – Narcotics Anonymous meetings, recovery dances, peer-based drug counseling – that Dawn and Sandi's intimacy was forged.

Dawn and Sandi eventually became central figures in a gay and lesbian community of poor, black recovering addicts. Their wedding was publicly recognized in a marriage ceremony in a downtown Unitarian church in March 1992. Evidence that the ceremony served as an important symbol of lesbian and gay community for the poor appeared the following month in a locally produced newsletter that is read by many low-income sexual minorities. In a commentary entitled "The Wedding of the Century," one community member wrote:

> The royal court has assembled in the great hall. The women are flawlessly dressed in their finest attire. The men are handsomely modeling two and three piece suits in colors that shame the most brilliant of rainbows. The atmosphere is charged with laughter, joy, and a sense of celebration. The crowd waits anxiously for the arrival of the bride and groom in anticipation of the wedding of the century.
>
> This is not the wedding of English Royalty or the climax of some happily ever after fairy tale, but the wedding of two lesbian women. On March 7, 1992, at 1:00, before family, friends and many well wishers, Dawn Sampson and Sandi Jones affirmed their love for each other. Their vow was to love each other with the seven types of love. The ceremony brought tears to this writer's eyes as the soloists moved the souls of the audience (which sent accolades rising to the rafters). Then we all vowed to support and nurture their union. At that moment I moved

from awestruck spectator to an active participant in the support of not only a marriage but the affirmation of our Gay lifestyle itself. . . .

My sincerest thanks go to Dawn and Sandi for allowing me to be a part of their
celebration of love, and for being a positive example of our gay and lesbian community. The affirmation of self experienced at their wedding was outstanding. In
a world where negative forces and homophobia abound, where racism, oppression, suppression and hatred are the norm (no matter how subtly); It is truly a
blessing to be a part of what binds us together and encourages our triumphant
survival as Gay and Lesbian MEN AND WOMEN.   (Williams 1992:5–6; emphasis in
original)

Elaboration of community building through gay marriage shows that
the poor are in a contradictory relationship to the social norms that seek to
justify and excuse their poverty. On the one hand, Dawn and Sandi's wedding,
while it displaces popular representations of sexual minorities as outside the
normative assumptions about marriage and family, can nonetheless be seen
as a capitulation to the bourgeois values of marriage that are sanctioned by the
very state that oppresses them. This is particularly so since the institutions
of the state serve as major sites in the formation of poor sexual minority
communities, and, hence, are much more implicated, in a pernicious way, in
their community-building practices than in the community-building practices of
their more affluent counterparts. On the other hand, this wedding challenges
the representation of poor blacks as deviant and pathological members of
America's underclass. Indeed, while some may interpret gay marriages like
Dawn and Sandi's as further evidence of pathological familial dysfunction
among the inner-city poor, the overwhelmingly affirmative tone of the article
quoted above refutes the abjectness that is often considered to be the essential
condition of urban poverty. Thus, the uncritical and arguably conservative
embrace of gay marriage functions in this instance to disrupt the "culture of
poverty" argument. It provides an important, albeit contradictory, basis for the
poor who are doubly oppressed by social norms (in the sense that they are not
only asked to conform to them, but their ability to conform to them is then put
under intense scrutiny) to legitimatize themselves in the face of a wide array of
racist and classist cultural valuations that seek to blame them for their own
impoverishment.

Poverty, Sexual Politics, and Sexual Citizenship

It is often said that poor sexual minorities do not participate in lesbian and
gay identity politics and, hence, are not political. However, my research in
Philadelphia suggests that poor lesbians and gay men are indeed political,
but the dynamics of their politicization vary significantly from those of their
middle-class counterparts. Excluded from leisure activities associated with the
arenas of retail-oriented consumption out of which lesbian and gay identity
politics was born, the politicization of poor lesbians and gay men nonetheless
relates to their consumer identities. However, for the poor, these identities are
forged in relation to the services of the welfare state. A case in point is poor
sexual minority participation in AIDS politics. In the following example,

the intersecting history of AIDS politics and poverty provides the context in which it is possible to explore avenues for political mobilization involving poor lesbians and gay men.

In Philadelphia, competition for funding between white-led and black-led AIDS organizations has manifested itself in a political discourse pitting "black providers" against "gay providers." This discourse was framed by the state's model of structuring competing claims to political authenticity and community leadership that required the emphasis of key social markers (e.g. gay, black, Latino, women) in the name of communities affected by HIV. This selective, asymmetrical, and nonsensical emphasis on sexuality vs. race as the central political struggle affecting the provision of life-supporting AIDS services had a number of consequences for HIV-positive people, particularly the poor. The harnessing of social identities conventionally used in political mobilizations to "provider" identities has displaced a class-based discourse and allowed those who identify as "providers" (i.e. the professional staff of AIDS service organizations) to gain prominence in the political field. As a result, HIV-positive people, the vast majority of whom are poor and black, have been forced to adopt the identity of "consumers" of AIDS services in the context of battles over AIDS service provision. While the adoption of this identity tends to mask issues of poverty, deprivation, and political exclusion by treating the receipt of life-supporting health services as a matter of consumer choice, it has nonetheless fostered and sustained key forms of political action among poor PWAs, such as when they demanded an adequate HIV standard of health care as their "consumer" right.

However, this situation has impeded poor sexual minorities from elaborating their demands to the state as sexualized political subjects. In fact, the emergence of consumer identities in the realm of the AIDS services system must be viewed as part of the state's effort to use service provision in combination with neoliberal ideologies of "empowerment" and "consumer choice" to promote self-regulation and to quell dissent among PWAs. One aspect of this strategy of incorporation is that consumerism works to delink gay and lesbian identity from consumer identity by linking it instead with provider identities. This makes poor people into desexualized political subjects in the language of the state. Said differently, the state effectively forces poor lesbians and gay men to sacrifice their sexual identities in order to gain access to the political process as consumers. Similarly, lesbians and gay men who rely on other public services are increasingly being recast in public discussion as consumers, thereby erasing their sexual identities at the same time as consumer-based political constituencies are formed.

Yet despite efforts by the state to desexualize poverty in AIDS politics, many poor people nevertheless continue to see themselves as gay and lesbian political subjects. For instance, many refer to themselves as lesbian and gay activists after having become involved with We The People, Philadelphia's largest coalition of HIV-positive people, and one composed predominantly of low-income people of color who are active and recovering drug addicts. One such activist, Rose Williams, spoke to a group of low-income PWAs who were attending an educational program at a local AIDS organization. She said:

When I was in my addiction I didn't think of anyone but me. Now I think of myself and other people. I made a big change. I am proud of myself from where I've come to where I am today. I'm a lesbian, I am proud to say that. I'm one of the biggest lesbian activists in the city. I fight for us. You figure, you're black, lesbian, poor, got AIDS. They don't care about us, so you got to do it yourself. We have to empower ourselves. A couple of years ago they would have said here lies a dope fiend who would have killed anyone who got in her way. Now I joined We The People, and am an actively involved woman, helping people get food stamps, get medications, get healthcare. We all have a message, I don't know how long I will be here, but while I'm here I got something to do. My higher power has allowed me to be the type of person I am today, to try to help you help yourselves.

It is important to recognize that Rose's political subjectivity is complex. Her politicization as a lesbian is linked to her politicization as a PWA, as a recovering drug user, as a poor person, as an African American, and as a woman. This is but one example of how poor sexual minorities invent overlapping (or, to use the postmodern term, fragmentary) political identities born out of historically contingent and institutionally defined circumstances.

This leads me to make a point here about gay and lesbian citizenship, an aspect of politicization that relates to, but is not wholly subsumed under, organized political activity. Specifically, I want to elaborate on the role of state-based institutions in enabling and constraining gay citizenship in relation to AIDS. The AIDS mobilization effort of the 1980s brought about the establishment of publicly funded social services, provided through organizations formed largely by activists who had fought for their creation. Most of these organizations went through a process of professionalization, where activists developed service provision skills and certification, and developed structures to offer services following increasingly formalized standards. This process of formalization has had a contradictory effect on the promotion of gay citizenship within organizations such as these. Brown (1997) argues that AIDS organizations, formed initially as voluntary organizations located in civil society and then transformed into bureaucratized agencies of service provision, are important sites of gay citizenship because they serve as gay community-centered associations where volunteers come to participate as members of the gay political community. However, he adds, these organizations have also become bureaucratic entities that disempower citizens by treating them as "clients."

As Rose's story suggests, AIDS service organizations have, to a certain extent, became a site in the expression of gay citizenship for the poor. Moreover, in these institutional contexts, the poor, like their middle-class counterparts, face increased pressure to assume formal roles in these organizations as either clients, professional staff, or board members as these organizations receive more public money to provide social services. However, unlike their middle-class counterparts, for whom there exists a wider array of privately controlled institutional locations in which it is possible to pursue gay citizenship, and for whom it is possible to take on a number of professional or voluntary roles within state-funded organizations, the poor have fewer options. They are more reliant on public institutions, and, as these organizations become more bureaucratized, ongoing professional participation and volunteerism by middle-class gay men and lesbians is more likely than it is by the poor. Indeed, a disproportionate share of poor sexual minorities are forced into the disempowering "client" role in many AIDS organizations. This shows that gay citizenship, as it is constituted in state-funded organizations, is a particularly tricky business for the poor since it is determined, first and foremost, along class lines that are structured and reproduced by the state. Still, these organizations tend to serve as important sites of community formation for poor lesbians and gay men, even if they ultimately discourage gay citizenship by promoting clientism, or, rather, consumerism, among the poor.

Towards a Lesbian/Gay Poverty Studies

In this essay, I have attempted to flesh out, albeit briefly and tentatively, the link between political-economic processes and the formation of poor people's sexual-minority identities, communities, and politics. I want to conclude by discussing the consequences of these findings for lesbian and gay studies, a field that is presently led by a queer theoretical vanguard that, while actively engaged in staking out the contours of a so-called "transgressive" political project, remains largely oblivious to the poverty amongst us. In an oft-cited queer theoretical statement on the connection between capitalism and gay identity, Michael Warner (1993:xxxi) writes:

> Gay culture in [its] most visible mode is anything but external to advanced capitalism and to precisely those features of advanced capitalism that many on the left are eager to disavow. Post-Stonewall urban gay men reek of the commodity. We give off the smell of capitalism in rut, and therefore demand of theory a more dialectical view of capitalism than many people have imagined for.

For Warner, this more "dialectical" view involves the elaboration of a politics of queer identity and theory as a challenge to "the regimes of the social" under advanced capitalism. "The social," as Warner understands it, is modernity's pre-eminent site of normalization, a discursive domain in which subjects are constituted as either normal or deviant. More than just defining itself against what has come to be considered "normal" behavior, queer politics and theory challenge the process of normalization itself. In this way, queer identity and theory offer the possibility of unmasking broader assumptions about the economy and the state. Warner (1993:xxvii; emphasis in the original) writes:

> The social realm, in short, is a cultural form, interwoven with the political form of the administrative state and with the normalizing methodologies of modern social knowledge. Can we not hear in the resonances of queer protest an objection to the normalization of behavior in this broad sense, and thus to the cultural phenomenon of societization? If queers, incessantly told to alter their "behavior," can be understood as protesting not just the normal behavior of the social but the *idea* of normal behavior, they will bring skepticism to the methodologies founded on that idea.

As for others for whom queer theory and politics has now become *de rigueur*, Warner envisions the politics of desire as a challenge to the dominant organization of sex and gender, which in turn, translates into a paradigmatic blow against society itself.

But do we all in fact reek of the commodity, and if so, how can the politics of desire release us from commodification as it is variously constituted under the regimes of the social? For Warner and others, gay men and lesbians reek of the commodity because we are implicated in advanced capitalism's rampant consumerism. Fair enough. But positing queer subjectivity as an alternative to gay and lesbian subjectivity is hardly a solution. As Donald Morton (1995) has argued, the queer subject is also a commodified subject, and thus is an inadequate political alternative in and of itself. He writes:

> Under the ideological regime of Queer Theory, the subject is – first, last, and always – the *subject of desire* who takes the form of Warner's "cruising" (commodified/commodifying) subject and Deleuze and Guattari's "desiring machine" and lives for the "intensities" of the moment. The queer subject is utterly distrustful (incapable?) of rational calculations which inevitably "constrain" desire. The queer subject is, in other words, the model "consuming" subject for the regime of late capitalism.

I want to extend Morton's argument by suggesting that the regime of late capitalism requires both rational and irrational "consuming" subjects. For this reason, we must specify how exactly different groups of lesbians and gay men – and other sexual minorities as well – become implicated in the political economic processes of commodification if we are to hope that our academic work may have political purchase. The above examples specify the class (as well as race and gender) dimensions of poor and working-class sexual minority experience. They therefore demonstrate the class- (and race- and gender-) specific nature of our commodified selves. Specifically, I have shown how poor and working lesbians and gay men reek of the commodity, not universally as consumers in a gay marketplace, as Warner's formulation implicitly suggests, but rather as workers who must sell their labor power to gay business owners, or as "consumers" of publicly funded social services.

The implications of this argument for lesbian and gay identity politics and queer politics are significant. It is now time for us to recognize that the liberatory dimension of lesbian and gay identity politics that was operative in decades past has been replaced in the era of neoliberalism by a politics of desire that remains uncritical of the commodification of sexual minority identities. Likewise, while queer identity may be a necessary condition for building progressive political communities, it, too, is not wholly sufficient. Whereas the challenge to normalization that is envisioned in queer theory's politics of desire does move us beyond the minoritizing strategies of lesbian and gay identity politics, it does so through a heady idealism that replaces old political boundaries within sexual minority communities with new ones. Moreover, whether one believes that gay consumer power (represented, for instance, by the Martina Navratilova Visa card or gay-oriented Budweiser ads) will lead to increased tolerance and acceptance, or that the rejection of sex or gender identity under the banner of queer politics represents a radical transgression, both positions (which, tellingly, are not necessarily mutually exclusive) encourage the creation of commercialized sexual minority subcultures. These subcultures – or, in neoliberal parlance, marketing niches – work in their own ways to mask the objective political-economic processes that fragment sexual minority communities along class lines.

This point is particularly salient in the present political context. Recent shifts in health and welfare policy – shifts designed to regulate the poor through surveillance rather than supportive services – are likely to have an increasingly negative effect on the community-building strategies of poor lesbians and gay men. Indeed, as funding for health and social services associated with the welfare state has been withdrawn, voluntary detox programs, recovery programs, subsidized housing, and other supportive social and health services have been scaled back, and public funding has been diverted towards the expansion of the prison industrial complex and the development of welfare-to-work programs. This shift places more poor people in daily contact with institutions that are, for various reasons, sites of overtly coercive state control. Concomitantly, the collective survival strategies of the poor have been undermined by these shifts in social welfare policy, which have worked in tandem with wider economic restructuring to suppress wage levels for low-end workers to near historic lows (Piven 1999). As a consequence, the poor are forced into even more dire social and economic circumstances. This pattern is likely to exacerbate tensions between various groups of poor people, particularly in the context of public institutions, with increased harassment perpetrated against poor and homeless sexual minorities a likely result.

Given this likelihood, it is vital that we make our politics more meaningful for poor and working-class sexual minorities. This requires the reversal of decades-long trends in social theory and politics that have disavowed the importance of class and avoided direct challenges to capitalism itself. We should think seriously about revisiting some of the earliest debates within lesbian/gay studies, debates that occurred in the early years of gay liberation, and that focused on the relationship between sexualized political subjects and socialism. Some may be appalled by this suggestion, viewing it as a giant step backwards. Others will see it as an opportunity to align lesbian/gay studies more closely with the working-class struggles that are once again on the move in the United States and abroad. In the current neoliberal climate, poverty is becoming invisible in both popular and academic treatments of urban life. Those of us in lesbian/gay studies should do our utmost to avoid collaborating with this new regime of disappearance. If we fail to contend with the material basis of poverty, and with the neoliberal ideologies and policies that mask increased inequalities inside and outside sexual minority communities, our work will continue to ignore poverty as an issue which an increasingly large number of sexual minorities have no choice but to face in their everyday lives. But if we meet the challenge of a lesbian/gay poverty studies, our future contains the potential for a historical realignment with the perspectives and needs of a major segment of the population in whose name we carry out our work.

Acknowledgments

This chapter was based on research supported by grants from the National Science Foundation (Grant SBR-9632878) and the Wenner Gren Foundation for Anthropological Research (Grant #6107). A version of it was presented at the session Lavender Language and Space: Multiple Locations, at the 6th Annual Conference on Lavender Languages and Linguistics, Sunday, September 13, 1998, at American University in Washington DC. I wish to thank Jennifer Alvey, Sidney Donnell, Bill Leap, Ellen Lewin, Matt Ruben, and Rudolph Gaudio for helpful comments and feedback on earlier drafts.

This chapter was originally written for inclusion in *Anthropology Comes Out: Lesbians, Gays, Cultures*, Ellen Lewin and William Leap, eds. Urbana: University of Illinois Press, 2001. I wish to thank Ellen, Bill, and the University of Illinois Press for allowing it to be reprinted here.

NOTES

1   All of the names that appear in this chapter are pseudonyms. All place names have been changed as well.

2   A joint report published by the Policy Institute of the National Gay and Lesbian Task Force and the Institute for Gay and Lesbian Strategic Studies, authored by M. V. Lee Badgett (1999), suggests that gay men and lesbians are found across the spectrum of income distribution and may, in fact, earn less than their heterosexual counterparts. One survey discussed in the report found that approximately 20 percent of lesbians and gay men earned less than $15,000 per year (as compared to almost 12 percent of heterosexuals); another found that household income is less than $10,000 for 7 to 8 percent of lesbians and gay men (and approximately 12 percent for heterosexuals).

3   Neoliberalism is commonly characterized as the strategy that promotes the primacy of unhindered market forces as the most effective means toward achieving economic growth and guaranteeing social welfare (Sanchez-Otero 1993; Bourdieu 1999). The valorization of the market is coupled with the vilification of the welfare state to justify a range of public policies that diverted public dollars from spending on social programs and insurance and uses them instead to make direct subsidies to private firms. This reframing of public policies away from universal access and toward market-based models is justified as a necessary step to eliminate dependency among the poor and other marginalized groups. The economic imperatives lurking behind these policies should not be overlooked, however. Mike Davis (1986) has shown that privatization became imperative in the 1970s and 1980s, as the U.S. economy entered what became a long postwar downturn. In this period, the state's intervention is explicitly aimed at sustaining the health and growth of the private sector. Indeed, the devolution of public health and welfare from public institutions to private firms is a form of state intervention and subsidy designed to avoid the impending crisis in capital accumulation. Thus, while a major tenet of neoliberalism is that government regulation hinders competition and prevents the system from reaching its "natural" efficiency, the truth of the matter is that government intervention has been essential in promoting economic growth in a period of declining profits (Davis 1986). In fact, one of the most misunderstood and oft-ignored differences between neoconservatism and neoliberalism is that while the former simplistically (and ironically) rails against government from within the halls of Congress, the latter embraces ideologies of "good" government and "efficient government," acknowledging in code the state's role in promoting

the "free" market. Yet the economic imperatives lurking behind these reform efforts are seldom discussed in policy debates. Instead, debates center around the moral and political imperative to eliminate dependency and the forms of social insurance that encourage it. Neoliberal policy, then, is a form of governance to which the poor and other groups are increasingly subjected, and the rhetoric of "reform," framed historically in the United States in terms of progress, social improvement, and mobility, is used in the present period to mask the material causes of poverty and to justify a range of new policy initiatives that subordinate poor and working people's quality of life concerns to the interest of private enterprise.

4   Neoliberalism is the post-Keynesian model of the social order that champions unhindered market forces as the most effective means towards achieving economic growth and guaranteeing social welfare (Sanchez-Otero 1993; Bourieu 1999). At the economic level, neoliberalism became imperative in the 1970s and 1980s, as the U.S. economy entered what has become a long postwar downturn (Davis 1986). Faced with a profit squeeze, U.S. capital abrogated its "Fordist" contract with labor, down-sized and relocated the manufacturing industry to the low-wage, non-union South and Southwest and overseas, and began a political and ideological assault on civil rights, environmental and other regulations, and Keynesian policies that sought to regulate the economy with public investment.

The federal government has embraced not only the legislative agenda of corporate America but also the ideology and culture of the free market. Increasingly, the government has tried to act like a corporation; it has downsized welfare, public health care, public education and a host of other important social services, and it is threatening to privatize social security and other programs that most people consider to be a public trust. Although these changes finally led to the "restoration of profitability" among U.S. firms in the 1990s, they have also created almost unprecedented social and economic polarization in the U.S. and abroad (Henwood 2000).

Yet the political and economic imperatives lurking behind these reform efforts are seldom discussed in policy debates. Instead, debates center around the moral and political imperative to eliminate dependency and the forms of social insurance that encourage it. Neoliberal policy then is a form of governance to which the poor and other groups are increasingly subjected, and the rhetoric of "reform," framed historically in the U.S. in terms of progress, social improvement and mobility, is used in the present period to mask the material causes of poverty and to justify a range of new policy initiatives that subordinate poor and working people's quality of life concerns to the interest of private enterprise.

Although the reframing of public policies away from universal access towards market-based models is justified as a necessary step to eliminate dependency among the poor and other marginalized groups, the devolution of public health and welfare from public institutions to private firms is a reactive form of state intervention and subsidy designed to overcome the crisis in capital accumulation. Thus, while a major tenet of neoliberalism is that government regulation hinders competition and prevents the system from reaching its "natural" efficiency, the truth of the matter is that government intervention has been essential in restoring profitability. In fact, one of the most misunderstood and oft-ignored differences between neoconservatism and neobliberalism is that while the former simplistically (and ironically) rails against government from within the halls of Congress, the latter embraces ideologies of "good" government and "efficient government," acknowledging in code the state's role in promoting the "free" market.

5   This approach departs not only from the dominant understanding of sexual identity in lesbian/gay studies, but also from the typical treatment of poverty by anthropologists and other scholars and policy makers. Indeed, as economic inequality increases in the United States, old assumptions about the causes of poverty have reemerged and are once again fueling new attacks against the poor by politicians, policy experts, and media pundits.

Underlying popular and political responses to poverty in the last three decades of the century has been the well-known "culture of poverty" thesis. This thesis, originally formulated by Oscar Lewis (1966) and disseminated widely through the Moynihan report (Moynihan 1965), argues that impoverished people's antisocial cultural practices prevent their upward mobility. The "culture of poverty" thesis, although thoroughly critiqued by progressive policy makers and scholars, continues to hold sway, and indeed has been resurrected and promoted most enthusiastically in recent years both in policy circles and among large segments of the American public. A more useful approach treats poverty as a political and economic problem affecting working-class neighborhoods, communities, and workplaces. Building on the work done by social scientists who challenged Oscar Lewis' original formulation, a new generation of scholars are challenging the newest versions of the "culture of poverty" thesis. By using new theoretical approaches that situate different groups' experiences of poverty in dialectical relation to global, national, state, and local political and economic change, and in relation to the interconnected ideologies of race, class, gender, sexuality, and nation, the new poverty studies treat poverty not as a static condition but as a dynamic, historically contingent process (see Susser 1982, 1996; B. Williams 1988, Goode and Maskovsky forthcoming).

REFERENCES CITED

Adams, Carolyn, David Bartelt, David Elesh, Ira Goldstein, Nancy Kleniewski, and William Yancey
  1991 *Philadelphia: Neighborhoods, Divisions and Conflict in a Post-Industrial City.* Philadelphia: Temple University Press.
Badgett, M. V. Lee
  1999 Income Inflation: The Myth of Affluence among Gay, Lesbian, and Bisexual Americans. A Joint Publication of the Policy Institute of the National Gay and Lesbian Task Force and the Institute for Gay and Lesbian Strategic Studies. URL: <http://www.ngltf.org/downloads/income.pdf> (February 6, 2000).
Beemyn, Brett
  1997 A Queer Capital. In *Creating a Place for Ourselves: Lesbian, Gay and Bisexual Community Histories.* Brett Beemyn, ed. Pp. 183–210. New York: Routledge.
Bell, David, and Gill Valentine, eds.
  1995 *Mapping Desire: Geographies of Sexualities.* New York: Routledge.
Bourdieu, Pierre
  1999 *Acts of Resistance against the Tyranny of the Market.* New York: New Press.
Brown, Michael P.
  1997 *Replacing Citizenship: AIDS Activism and Radical Democracy.* New York: Guilford Press.
Castells, Manuel
  1983 *The City and the Grassroots.* Berkeley: University of California Press.
Chauncey, George
  1994 *Gay New York.* Chicago: University of Chicago Press.
Davis, Mike
  1986 *Prisoners of the American Dream.* London: Verso.
D'Emilio, John
  1983 *Sexual Politics, Sexual Communities.* Chicago: University of Chicago Press.
D'Emilio, John, and Estelle B. Freedman
  1988 *Intimate Matters: A History of Sexuality in America.* New York: Harper and Row.

di Leonardo, Micaela
  1997   White Lies, Black Myths. In *The Gender/Sexuality Reader*. R. Lancaster and
    M. di Leonardo, eds. Pp. 53–70. New York: Routledge.
Duberman, Martin B., Martha Vicinus, and George Chauncey, eds.
  1989   *Hidden from History: Reclaiming the Gay and Lesbian Past*. New York: New
    American Library.
Ettorre, E. M.
  1978   Women, Urban Social Movements and the Lesbian Ghetto. *International
    Journal of Urban and Regional Research* 2(3):499–520.
Goode, Judith, and J. Maskovsky, eds.
  forthcoming   *New Poverty Studies: The Ethnography of Policy, Politics and
    Impoverished People in the U.S.* New York: New York University Press.
Henwood, Dong
  2000   Boom for Whom? *Left Business Observer* 93 (February):4, 7.
Kennedy, Elizabeth, and M. Davis
  1993   *Boots of Leather, Slippers of Gold*. New York: Routledge.
Knopp, Lawrence
  1997   Gentrification and Gay Neighborhood Formation in New Orleans: A Case
    Study. In *Homo Economicus*. A. Gluckman, and B. Reed, eds. Pp. 45–64. New
    York: Routledge.
Lauria, Mickey, and Lawrence Knopp
  1985   Towards an Analysis of the Role of Gay Communities in the Urban
    Renaissance. *Urban Geography* 6:152–169.
Levine, Martin P.
  1979   Gay Ghetto. *Journal of Homosexuality* 4(4):363–377.
Lewis, Oscar
  1966   The Culture of Poverty. *Scientific American* 215(4):19–25.
Maskovsky, Jeff
  1999   Fighting for Our Lives: Poverty and AIDS Politics in Neoliberal Philadelphia.
    Ph.D. dissertation in Anthropology, Temple University, Philadelphia.
Morton, Donald
  1995   Queerity and Ludic Sado-Masochism: Compulsory Consumption and the
    Emerging Post-al Queer. In *Post-Ality: Marxism and Postmodernism, A Special
    Issue of Transformation* 1:189–215.
Moynihan, Daniel P.
  1965   *The Negro Family: The Case for National Action*. Washington, DC: U.S.
    Department of Labor.
Newton, Esther
  1979   *Mother Camp*. Chicago: University of Chicago Press.
  1993   *Cherry Grove*. Boston, MA: Beacon Press.
Piven, Frances Fox
  1999   Welfare Reform and the Economic and Cultural Reconstruction of Low Wage
    Labor Markets. *City and Society* (Annual Review), pp. 21–37.
Sanchez-Otero, German
  1993   Neoliberalism and its Discontents. *NACLA Report on the Americas* 26(4):
    18–21.
Shields, Rob, ed.
  1992   *Lifestyle Shopping: The Subject of Consumption*. New York: Routledge.
Smith, Neil
  1991   *Uneven Development: Nature, Capital and the Production of Space*.
    Cambridge, MA: Basil Blackwell.

Susser, Ida
  1982   *Norman Street: Poverty and Politics in an Urban Neighborhood*. New York: Oxford University Press.
  1996   The Construction of Poverty and Homelessness in U.S. Cities. *Annual Review of Anthropology*, 25:411–435.
Warner, Michael
  1993   Introduction. In *Fear of a Queer Planet*. M. Warner, ed. Pp. vii–xxxi. Minneapolis: University of Minnesota Press.
Weston, Kath, and Lisa B. Rofel
  1997   Sexuality, Class and Conflict in a Lesbian Workplace. In *Homo Economicus*. A. Gluckman, and B. Reed, eds. Pp. 25–44. New York: Routledge.
Williams, Brett
  1988   *Upscaling Downtown: Stalled Gentrification in Washington, DC*. Ithaca, NY: Cornell University Press.
Williams, Rodney
  1992   The Wedding of the Century. *Alive and Kicking* 6:5–6.
Wilson, William J.
  1987   *The Truly Disadvantaged: The Inner City, the Underclass and Public Policy*. Chicago: University of Chicago Press.

Part V

Theorizing Diversity

20

Studying U.S. Cultural Diversity: Some Non-Essentializing Perspectives

Douglas Foley and Kirby Moss

The post-1960s critiques of Marxists, feminists, postmodernists, and peoples of color have disrupted the self-assured production of holistic, timeless portraits of cultural diversity. Many anthropologists (Ortner 1984; Marcus and Fischer 1986; Rosaldo 1989; Abu-Lughod 1991; Keesing 1994) have already outlined the general direction of a new anthropology of cultural diversity. We see two major themes in these critiques.

First, anthropologists now study the cultural politics of constructing cultural differences rather than cultural difference itself. Increasingly, cultural anthropologists are interested in how mainstream, dominant society produces stigmatized, inferior cultural others. The other side of that story is how these stigmatized cultural others counter the symbolic violence inflicted upon them by producing their own self-valorizing images. The new studies of cultural difference address questions of power and the interests being served by these stigmatized constructions of cultural others in multicultural societies.

Second, since cultural difference/diversity is no longer treated as a social fact but as a social construction, anthropologists are also deconstructing their own practices of creating cultural others. They now interrogate their interpretative, writing, and representational practices and their primary analytic constructs such as culture, field, text, identity, class, race, and gender. Such personal, reflexive studies of the poetics of producing cultural images explore the extent that anthropological constructs reify and misrepresent cultural differences.

These new studies of the politics and poetics of constructing cultural others rest upon very complex philosophical foundations. The enormous influence of a new interdisciplinary field called cultural studies can neither be overestimated, nor chronicled in a short paper; consequently, we will highlight how key post-Marxist and postmodern ideas from this new field are reshaping the anthropological study of cultural diversity/difference. These categories or perspectives are slippery and ambiguous at best, but if used heuristically, they may help characterize the interpretative trends in post-1960s ethnographic studies of cultural diversity. In reality, however, there are no pure, ideal types of post-Marxist or postmodern ethnographies. Most of the texts to be cited are a complex, hybrid mix of feminist, critical race, queer, and Afrocentric perspectives as well. After presenting key post-Marxist ideas, we will review various ethnographies that utilize that perspective. Those sections will be followed by a similar discussion of postmodern ideas and ethnographies. The chapter concludes with a few suggestions on teaching a class on U.S. cultural diversity from these two general perspectives.

A Post-Marxist Paradigm for Studying U.S. Cultural Diversity

The term "post-Marxism" represents the culmination of extended, complex theoretical debates both within and outside of Marxism. Within Marxism the debate is between pre-1960s orthodox Marxists (McClellan 1979) and their critics, unorthodox "western Marxists" (Klare and Howard 1971), and post-1960s "new left" Marxists (Best and Kellner 1991). Rather than recapitulate the intellectual history of these debates, we will focus on how the post-1960s British New Left (Forgaces 1989) has reconstructed Marxism into what Laclau and Mouffe (1985) call "post-Marxism." The debates at the Birmingham Center for Contemporary Cultural Studies (CCCS) are quite instructive on how the New Left has generally reconstructed Marxism (Storey 1996; Morely and Chen 1996). Their brand of Marxism, sometimes labeled "cultural Marxism," and based on ethnographic studies of everyday cultural and ideological practices, is particularly appealing to American cultural anthropologists (Lave 1992).

The most well-known, influential voice of this new synthesis is the former CCCS director, Jamaican Stuart Hall. Many of his main theoretical writings can be found in a recent volume edited by Morley and Chen (1996). Hall (1996) begins his reconstruction of Marxism by appropriating Louis Althusser's notion of capitalist society as a multiple-leveled and multi-determined social formation. After critiquing Althusser for lapsing into economic determinism, Hall proposes to salvage the social formation construct with Antonio Gramsci's theory of hegemony. By now, most anthropologists are familiar with Gramsci, but to briefly recapitulate his perspective, Gramsci places greater emphasis than orthodox Marxists do on superstructural or cultural institutions and ideological factors. Gone is the causal model of the material base or economic mode of production determining the cultural superstructure of ideas, belief, and consciousness. Gone also is the notion of a unitary capitalist class that rules through a coercive state. Gramsci argues that ruling historical blocs, since their power is never secure, are always faced with the problem of building civic consent. They build consent by controlling what Marx called civil society, the public and private spheres of life shaped by the state and its educative institutions (schools, mass media, church, voluntary associations, and families). A historical ruling bloc's ability to control these cultural institutions, through legal and moral force, creates the political consensus and stability necessary for capital accumulation and expansion. This concept of capitalist society and state has as many implications for the ruled as it does for the rulers. Since ideological hegemony is never secure, there is always the possibility that the working class may create a progressive counter-hegemonic historical bloc through a series of political alliances rooted in a well-developed working-class culture.

What is novel about this formulation is its highly processual notion of structure, state, social classes, and society. The accent is on a constantly shifting consensus that each ruling bloc must create and sustain. Gramsci characterizes the ongoing struggle between historical blocs as a series of "articulations" between the different levels of the social formation and the institutions of civil society. No observer can understand the construction of a hegemonic process without focusing on those key conjunctural moments or "articulations" within a given social formation. In a novel conceptual move Hall gives the Gramscian notion of "articulations" a poststructuralist, linguistic turn. He contends that anyone interested in ideology and hegemony must also study the "articulations" between various popular discourses, for example, nationalism, Catholicism, racism, classism. Such articulations take place in a multitude of everyday discursive practices through a variety of everyday institutional rituals. Studying such "discursive articulations" helps highlight the inherently contradictory, non-unitary nature of "commonsense" or popular world views/ideologies.

This new linguistic turn opens up the classic Marxist paradigm to a multiple dominance perspective that privileges the study of how collective cultural identities are produced. In this new formulation, Marx's original notion of alienation and objectification through wage labor has been broadened to include everyday cultural practices (Foley 1990). From this general perspective, various cultural identity groups produce themselves daily through everyday communicative or expressive cultural practices in various cultural institutions like schools, media, and family. This cultural "self-production" can be as dehumanizing and alienating as capitalist factories and offices. The stigmatizing discourses about inferior "cultural others" that circulate in various cultural institutions can arrest or "steal" people's subjectivity and humanity in much the same way that laboring in commodity-producing factories does. Cultural studies researchers have just begun to document how cultural processes of objectification and "othering" work, and how stigmatized identity groups resist such alienating processes.

Ultimately, the British post-Marxist perspective, although focused more on cultural/ideological processes than on political economy, retains some vital links with a classic Marxist perspective. It retains a notion of social classes in the broader, less deterministic idea of historical blocs. But, as Hall so aptly puts it, this is a "Marxism with no guarantees," a Marxism stripped of its grand, utopian theory of a progressive proletariat and the inevitability of socialism. No historical laws inexorably lead to social order, dominance, growth, or progress. Although no longer very sure about world revolutionary processes, most post-Marxists subscribe to the development of a thoroughly democratic political culture. Laclau and Mouffe (1985) emphasize that once the Old Left has been thoroughly sensitized to multiple forms of cultural objectification and dominance, they will be ready to build a new, more genuinely egalitarian oppositional historical bloc.

To sum up, a politicized, processual, discursive concept of multiple cultural struggles is at the center of most post-Marxist accounts of cultural diversity. Such studies generally call attention to the ways in which "cultural differences" are produced through complex power relations and multiple discourses. What we experience as "natural," inherited cultural differences are the product of complex cultural struggles that vary at given historical junctures and moments. Cultural differences or group traditions are not stable bundles of traits and practices handed down from one generation to the next. Cultural differences are social constructions, the ever-changing product of institutional and discursive articulations between competing historical blocs and/or fragmented identity groups. With this brief characterization of post-Marxist thought, we would like to illustrate how some recent ethnographies, influenced by this perspective, study cultural diversity.

Some Post-Marxist Ethnographies of U.S. Cultural Diversity

Not unexpectedly, scholars from cultural groups who have endured a civil society ruled by white bourgeois males find post-Marxism an attractive paradigm. One can make a strong case that ethnic and feminist scholars have led the way in revitalizing and reshaping the original Marxist paradigm. White male scholars – who have not embraced their class, racial, and gender privilege – are, of course, allies in this conceptual revolution. Perhaps the British ethnographers with close ties to CCCS (Gilroy 1989, 1993; Bauman 1996) have produced the most extensive examples of post-Marxist ethnographies. Gerd Bauman's *Contesting Culture: Discourses of Identity in Multi-Ethnic London* is an ethnography of a suburban district near Heathrow airport. Southall is a multiethnic community of Afro-Caribbeans, Muslim Sikhs, Indian Hindus, and East Africans. Bauman provides a fascinating description of how the local ethnic groups strategically use the dominant society's essentializing, biologizing hegemonic discourses to equate community and culture into a highly reified view of ethnicity. Both mainstream politicians and oppositional ethnic politicians ply these reified notions of their culture to gain civil rights and government largesse. Bauman leaves the reader with the image of individuals within the groups borrowing cultural practices, assuming multiple subject positions, and crossing ethnic boundaries, thus destabilizing the commonsense categories of Asian, African, and Afro-Caribbean.

The other CCCS-related study, Paul Gilroy's *"There Ain't No Black in the Union Jack": The Cultural Politics of Race and Nation*, is an exhaustive account of how national discourses of race, national identity, and class articulate through media, government policy, right-wing political groups, civic education, and discourses on crime and family. In response to images of black rioters, muggers, welfare cheats, and disloyal rebels, the counter-hegemonic discourses of the West Indian immigrant community are traced through various forms of black music, especially reggae and its Rastafarian philosophy. The importance of an emerging African diaspora community is emphasized, and his second book *The Black Atlantic: Modernity and Double Consciousness* develops further the notion of a black diaspora culture with organic black intellectuals articulating a new hybridic, pan-African identity.

Gilroy's work has many affinities with the seminal work of Chicano folklorist Americo Paredes (1958, 1993) on the ballads, music, dance, humor, and various folkloric performances that inspired resistance to objectifying racist, classist, and nationalist discourses. Parades' colleagues (Peña 1985, 1999; Limon 1994; Flores 1995) have deepened this critique of white bourgeois hegemony with more nuanced, detailed ethnographic studies of resistance folklore. The explosion of studies that highlight counter-hegemonic aspects of oral and written expressive cultural forms is too vast to document fully in a short chapter. One can find many earlier cognate studies on African American slavery (Levine 1977), urban folklore (Abrahams 1970), and music (Keil 1970) as well. The same is true of other marginalized American ethnic and gender groups.

Studies of everyday oral expressive forms and folk artists cover some of the same ideological terrain that postcolonial literary scholars (Said 1994; Krupat 1992; Saldivar 1990) studying "resistance literature" cover. Various anthropologists and humanities scholars have also advocated the importance of studying the suppressed voices of ethnics (Fischer 1986) and women (Harlow 1987) through autobiographical novels. Other feminist scholars (Behar and Gordon 1995) and ethnic scholars (Harrison 1991) have pointed out the importance of decolonizing the anthropological discourse and the discourse of science (Haraway 1989; Martin 1987) by highlighting their oppressive, ideological character. In much of this work, post-Marxist concerns with ideological hegemony, organic intellectuals, and resistance are fused with poststructuralist/postmodern concerns over disciplinary canons and institutional practices that "normalize" the minds and bodies of culturally different groups.

A recent AAA volume on *Gender and Anthropology* (Morgen 1989) underscores the important role that feminists are playing in reformulating Marxism. Key socialist feminist theoreticians (Sacks 1989; Susser 1989; Lamphere et al. 1997) are now emphasizing the importance of specific racial and gender experiences in wider community and kinship networks, and unwaged forms of domestic labor. Like post-Marxists, they are trying to expand orthodox Marxist notions of labor exploitation and class resistance through a wider analysis of how women's paid and unpaid work articulates with their racial and gender experiences. Ida Susser's chapter (Morgen 1989) on the anthropology of the United States is particularly instructive on the new trends in poverty and family studies. Susser, like Lamphere et al. (1997), continues to explore classic political-economy topics such as wage labor, labor struggles, migration, state regulation of families, and poverty programs. Such works are also beginning to incorporate more of the post-Marxist emphasis on objectifying identity discourses as sites of exploitation and cultural struggle. Lancaster and di Leonardo (1997) move even further towards a post-Marxist perspective on families and gender. This volume presents ideological critiques on everything from Madonna to allegedly scientific discourse on the body, sexuality, and the family. Such critical cultural studies scramble the conventional, popular notions of gender roles, sexuality, exploitation, and resistance.

It is not possible to review more than a few exemplary works in this vast "poverty studies" literature. For example, di Leonardo's (1986) study of the interplay of class, race, and gender on Italian American families, like Stack's (1974) classic study of African American kinship, speaks from within women's kinship networks. This allows both authors to thoroughly deconstruct the patriarchal, middle-class white constructions of these ethnic groups and their family systems. The important work of Stacy (1990, 1996) and Weston (1991) challenges the bourgeois, heterosexual family ideal by revealing the extraordinary diversity of the "postmodern" American family. Ethnic scholars (Williams 1990) highlight the growing diversity within their kinship systems and challenge popular stereotypes of ethnic gender roles and families.

A related, broader ideological critique in the field of poverty studies centers on the "poverty discourse" of policy makers who regulate a growing "underclass" allegedly trapped in an inferior, morally degenerate "culture-of-poverty" (Katz 1989). This conservative, bourgeois discourse about the poor articulates classist, racist, and sexist discourses into a class position as a stigmatized "class culture." This pernicious poverty discourse about the working class has provoked progressive academics to produce a sustained body of empirical work that dismantles the culture-of-poverty view of the way of life of the poor (Foley 1997). These scholars have produced an impressive array of studies that counter the objectifying poverty discourse about the pathological black family, hard-living poor whites, immoral single female parent households, uncaring, macho Latino males, and so forth.

A particularly good example of a post-Marxist poverty study is Bourgois' (1995) account of street life in a New York neighborhood. In search of a better life, Puerto Rican immigrants from American-owned sugar plantations come to East Harlem, but arrive during a period of "deindustrialization." Their choice is poorly paid, demeaning service sector jobs, or demeaning predatory street culture jobs as crack dealers, thieves, and prostitutes. The study blends post-Marxist and political-economy perspectives, and thus highlights both ideological and macro-economic forces. The depictions of working in the white corporate and schooling scene highlight cultural struggles against the hegemony of white middle-class communicative styles. Bourgois argues that rural, working-class Puerto Ricans simply do not fit into corporate office culture or the public schools, and thus are pushed into a search for self-respect in drugs, mugging, and violent gang rape. Ultimately, he calls for public policies that sustain women against irresponsible, hateful males and remorseless politicians and bureaucrats who spread reckless rhetoric about uncaring crack mothers and immoral welfare cheaters.

Other related work on the street culture of African American males also uses a cultural production perspective (E. Gordon 1997). Such studies highlight the complex mix of traditional, communalistic African American kin- and church-centered cultural practices with the exploitative, entrepreneurial, individualistic logic of street capitalism and hustling. These new hybrid images of "black culture" disrupt easy notions of a black underclass and a dysfunctional culture of poverty. They also take a new look at the ideological hegemony of white liberal academics and policy makers to racialize cultural differences in a way that obscures the underlying hegemony of white superiority.

Perhaps the most interesting ideological critique of white racial hegemony, however, is in legal studies. Legal scholars called "critical race theorists" (Crenshaw et al. 1995) blend Marxist and postmodern theories into a powerful critique that deconstructs the allegedly race-neutral legal civil rights discourse. Like African American cultural studies scholars, these legal scholars have deployed what the postcolonial scholar Gayatri Spivak (1988) calls a "strategic essentialist discourse." They argue against the tendency of whites to position themselves as the rational, fair, neutral center of the racial order, and to construct black culture as inferior. In a counter-hegemonic move, they racialize the social science and law discourses, thus disrupting allegedly neutral, scientific, universalistic discourses about cultural difference.

A related literature on schooling as a cultural reproduction institution also generates many ideological critiques of cultural diversity. This literature is too extensive to review thoroughly, but a few studies (Willis 1981; Foley 1990; MacLeod 1995) will illustrate how educational anthropologists disrupt hegemonic views of ethnicity, class, and gender. Paul Willis, a well-known member of CCCS has written the classic post-Marxist study of youth and schooling. Willis (1981) dismantles a culture-of-poverty view with a positive, self-valorizing image of working-class culture. Foley's (1990) study of Mexicano youth in South Texas covers similar terrain but adds a race/class/gender articulation missing in Willis. The Mexicano community and ethnic reform movement is marked by significant class and gender variation. Sweeping class or racial explanations of political resistance, cultural identity, and school achievement suppress such in-group differences. Moreover, such perspectives will fail to capture how some rebellious Mexicano youth deploy essentializing cultural nationalist discourses and middle-class white discourses. They control their communicative labor, and thus manage their public images for success in capitalist educational labor markets.

MacLeod's (1995) detailed ethnography of two adolescent peer groups highlights the marginality of rebellious white working-class youth and the conformity and achievement of African American youth. In the process, MacLeod turns the commonsense perceptions of whites and blacks on their head. When he returns to the community ten years later, the white youth have sunk into abject despair and the black youth have lost their innocence and optimism about civil rights reforms. Many others, especially feminist scholars (Weis 1990; Eder et al. 1994; Davidson 1996; Fordham 1996), deploy multiple systems of dominance perspectives and attend to complex discursive articulations and identity constructions. Previously passive, low-achieving, essentialized female and minority cultural others are suddenly more assertive and academically successful through everything from subtle deployments of mainstream linguistic practices and impression management to open confrontations.

Recent anthropological critiques of higher education also draw heavily upon post-Marxist ideas (Collins et al. 1999). Wesley Shumar's (1997) *College for Sale* illustrates nicely the incorporation of ideological critiques into a more conventional political-economy critique of higher education. The commodification of everything from curriculum to ethnic faculty tokenism is taken up in detail. Bourdieuan notions of cultural capital, symbolic violence, and academic market places, and Foucauldian notions of surveillance, professional discourses, and intellectuals mark these new post-Marxist critiques of academia. Not all poststructuralist accounts of schooling institutions fit neatly into post-Marxist formulations, however. Devine's (1996) study of the culture of school violence in New York City presents a ringing critique of much post-Marxist educational ethnography as an overly romantic view of these cultural institutions and their heroic student rebels. For Devine the capitalist economic order is creating a culture of violence in urban schools that makes them dehumanized war zones. He emphasizes the destruction of the stable categories of ethnicity, identity, subjectivity, institution, dominant culture, and counterculture.

Finally, post-Marxist studies of cultural production permeate critical media studies (Kellner 1989, 1995) and ethnographic studies of popular culture. Studies of romance novels (Radway 1984), pornography (Williamson 1989), talk shows (Shattuc 1997), fairy tales (Zipes 1997), soap operas (Modleski 1982), and *National Geographic* magazine (Lutz and Collier 1993) explore how ideological hegemonies are consumed, resisted, and inverted. Foley's (1995) ethnographic study of white–Indian relations in a small Iowa community focuses on the articulations between media and academic representations of Indians and local representations. The study illustrates how local storytelling and academic and journalistic studies produce an objectified Indian culture that provokes a sustained, vigorous cultural struggle. Various Mesquaki everyday oral narrative practices counter the local and extralocal white story-telling practices that objectify and stigmatize Indians. Ultimately, a new group of Mesquaki organic intellectuals emerge and produce their own counter-hegemonic literary, historical, and media representations of an Indian cultural other.

The mass media are generally a major terrain of cultural struggles over objectifying images. Although such studies do not always directly document cultural differences and diversity, they often explore how women and minorities are misrepresented. Many of these new studies suggest that minorities and women are anything but passive, dependent consumers. Women cultural consumers often invert the objectifying tendencies of romance novels, soap operas, and pornography in creative, empowering ways. Even talk shows, allegedly sites of bourgeois dominance, can be used to build solidarity networks and to explore various identity constructions critically (Shattuc 1997). Finally, the study of youth subculture's appropriation of mass mediated cultural forms and images is a particularly rich body of literature on counter-hegemonic practices (Griffin 1993).

Postmodern Studies of Cultural Difference and Diversity

The concept of postmodernism was originally used to describe a cultural or intellectual trend that opposed the rigid modernist style in art, architecture, and design (Jameson 1984). However, it has come to be applied to a much wider range of philosophical and social science discourses concerned with the "crisis of modernity" – the end of assumptions, overarching theories, and meta-narratives that have gained prominence since the Enlightenment or the Age of Reason centered in the mid-18th century. The postmodern condition is said to signify a world of ever-multiplying signifying processes, a myriad of images, a dissolution of established categories and identities, and an ever-increasing skepticism toward claims of truth, meaning, and value, all perpetually linked to ideological positions of authority. What, then, is the importance of such fragmentations and contradictions for social science theory?

A catalyst in the rise and influence of the postmodern paradigm is the often referred-to debate between critical theorist Jürgen Habermas and Jean-François Lyotard concerning the significance of reason and rationalization in advanced capitalist society. Lyotard (1984) boldly proclaimed, against the tradition of modernist social theory and its emphasis on foundations of universal criteria of truth, that knowledge generated through the medium of grand or meta-theory had lost its legitimacy as either a critical or emancipatory narrative. Within the modernist paradigm, Lyotard argued that human agency and fluidity of experience had become lost within the confines of positivist, deterministic Marxist concepts. For Lyotard and other postmodern theorists, to continue to believe in the emancipatory potentials of grand theory was to be seduced by the logocentric pretense of the Enlightenment. Lyotard suggested that meta-theory was on the wane and in the process of being displaced by the development of new technologies and specialized discourses that relativized society and rendered meta-theory's normative foundations superfluous, elitist, and, ironically, hegemonic in the Gramscian sense.

Such redeployment of advanced liberal capitalism was leading to what Lyotard (1984:37–38) called the "elimination of the communist alternative and the valorization of the individual enjoyment of goods and services." He contends that the legitimation of knowledge claims can only arise from "their own linguistic practice and communicational interaction" (1984:41). In other words, knowledge is produced and disseminated through discourse and representation. For Lyotard, the postmodern condition was homologous to knowledge or epistemology, which he linked to the ubiquity of power throughout society. Therefore, it was power rather than "truth" or "ideals" that would become the standard of the postmodern era.

The general influence of postmodernism on anthropology remains a seldom-told piece of intellectual history, but postmodern/poststructuralist critiques of anthropology's objectifying master narratives (Fabian 1983; McGrane 1989; Clifford 1988; Said 1979) share some of the same terrain as post-Marxism. Both focus on the discursive regimes of the new social sciences and their objectifying discourses such as "orientalism." Postmodernists have generally been even more skeptical about science, rationality, and metalanguages, than most Marxists are; consequently, postmodernists have initiated a more sustained attack on the positivistic, scientific foundations of ethnographic description. Postmodernists influenced by literary theory have also raised new issues about the production of cultural texts and cultural representations.

The most cited and best-known account of the general confluence of Marxism, feminism, postmodernism, and interpretivism into anthropology's "experimental moment" is Marcus and Fischer's (1986) *Anthropology as Cultural Critique*. They argue that the ethnographer's rhetorical use of a scientific realist narrative style often masked the ideological or theoretical interests of the author. Marcus and Fisher called for a style of ethnography that decenters the authority of "scientific anthropologists" to render detached, objective portraits of whole cultures. Having eschewed grand meta-theories that produce totalizing cultural accounts, postmodern ethnographers strive to evoke a multiplicity of different perspectives and voices. By complicating rather than resolving the issues of the writer's authority and ethnographic holism, these new more fragmented, multivocal ethnographic texts may lead to less monolithic, objectifying portraits of cultural others.

Ironically, the very groups with whom postmodernists hope to ally – marginal scholars of color and feminists – have produced some of the most powerful and insightful criticisms of postmodernism. Some feminist scholars (di Leonardo 1991; Mascia-Lees et al. 1989; Weston 1997) and scholars of color (Harrison 1991; Rosaldo 1989) argue that postmodernism perpetuates entrenched academic standards while reproducing traditional Eurocentric conclusions about non-European cultures. Micaela di Leonardo (1989) in an article titled "Malinowski's Nephews" calls many notions of postmodernism "Eurocentricity or high (elitist) modernism" in a new guise which still ignores insights and contributions of marginalized anthropologists. Renato Rosaldo takes di Leonardo's critique even further by arguing for conscious subjectivity in social science research. He contends that social and cultural analysts can rarely, if ever, become detached and value-free observers. He adds that anthropology, even the relativistic postmodern ethnographer, still struggles to maintain this imperialistic tendency.

Although the postmodern call to give voice to the voiceless is neither new nor always necessary and possible, it has helped legitimate the efforts of marginalized scholars of color (Harrison 1991; E. Gordon 1997) and feminists (Behar and Gordon 1995) to attack conventional academic and anthropological canons and practices. If nothing else, the postmodern discourse may have opened up some ideological space for previously marginalized scholars. Saldivar (1990) suggests that Chicano narratives should be read as critical and ideological takes on the "human experience." It is precisely because such marginal views are different from conventional dominant views that they offer readers nuanced insights that help deconstruct static images of the "Other." Vizenor (1989) makes a similar argument for Native American narratives.

Some Postmodern Ethnographies of U.S. Cultural Diversity

One of the most explicitly postmodern texts we have encountered is Kathleen Stewart's (1996) ethnography of a coal-mining town in West Virginia. Her study is marked by an extended polemic on the need to abandon cultural analysis based on grand master narratives and strong knowledge claims. Rather than presenting a tidy empirical place or subject, her narrative tracks experience where it happens, as it happens. Her study takes readers in and out of the local dialect, sifts through the seeming randomness of the everyday, and tacks restlessly between the conscious and unconscious. Ultimately, Stewart's ethnography disrupts negative popular and scholarly representations of Appalachia and its inhabitants as it portrays the residents heroically reinscribing themselves in time, space, and narrative memory.

Another work guided by a postmodern sensibility is Dorst's (1989) depiction of a Philadelphia suburb as an idealized, timeless theme park, and Gomez-Peña (1996) who, as a "fluid border-crosser," writes a "post-Mexican literary hypertext" (1996:ii) in his search to dispel the myths and barriers of identity borders. Poststructuralist feminists Patti Lather and Cris Smithies (1997) juxtapose the voices of HIV-positive women, factoids, parables about angels, and authorial reflections in a highly unconventional, disruptive, nonlinear narrative. Their text provides one with a dignified, self-valorizing portrait of these women as complex individuals. Relatively few anthropologists writing about U.S. cultural diversity have produced thoroughly postmodern ethnographies, but previous studies are clearly more experimental and evocative in interpretative and narrative style.

Black scholars have also experimented with textual, storytelling practices. Gwaltney (1980) and John Stewart (1989) pursue two unconventional routes into lived experiences of black folk that challenge anthropological methods pertaining to subjects and the writing of ethnography. Gwaltney's research relies on the local black knowledge of "ordinary people." He notes: "My main intent is to be an acceptable vehicle for the transmission of their views" (Gwaltney 1980:ii). The people in the book speak for themselves about themselves and others, analyzing and interpreting their lives and the broader society which so heavily influence their culture. From an anthropological point of view, Gwaltney's research opens the discourse to a marginalized, often-silenced group creating a venue for them to define their own reality. He argues ultimately that despite common assumptions, black men and women are capable of literate self-expression and abstract thought which can and should be incorporated into the broader theoretical realm of academic research.

Stewart (1989) acknowledges that he uses anthropology in a "personal way" in his study of a village in Trinidad. Experimenting with literary theory, he argues that the subjective side of culture may be better captured in ethnographic fiction than in standard ethnographic writing (perhaps inspired by Zora Neale Hurston). Through eight stories in the book, Stewart experiments with culture theory, ethnography, and literature to show why the aesthetic should not be separated from the intellectual; how fact and fiction are often fluid and linked, not separate. Through this method, Stewart's stories succeed, particularly in showing how people interact where multiple cultural heritages are in close contact. At the same time, his text is replete with lessons on innovative fieldwork methods and ethnographic writing style.

Various postmodern-influenced studies (Kondo 1990; O'Nell 1996; Fordham 1996) explore the psychological contradictions of identity construction in greater depth than post-Marxist studies of collective identity struggles generally do. O'Nell shatters popular images of the stoic, taciturn noble savage with her portrait of how one Native American group has adjusted to cultural loss and racist indignities. Signithia Fordham's (1996) recent study of the identity struggles of black adolescents is a good example of a more complex, intimate psychological portrait of cultural diversity. Fordham stresses the double bind of black students who yearn to be successful and attain "an education," while at the same time trying to deflect criticism from their black peers for "acting white." She demonstrates that the educational journey for black students is tenuous and often teetering on the edge of disaster because the price of success is painful cultural liminality.

Another less conventional study of cultural assimilation focuses on the middle class – the group that many consider the foundation of mainstream, assimilationist ideology (Newman 1988). Newman's revealing ethnography presents a portrait of a serene white suburbia whose residents are sliding down the ranks of the social class ladder due to corporate cost-cutting and downsizing. This ethnography shows a vulnerable, fragile, bewildered side of the middle-class managerial lifestyle, and it undermines a number of idealized images of mainstream middle-class white American families as a homogeneous, universal ideal lifestyle.

Other white researchers have begun to interrogate the assumed racial neutrality of the whiteness category. White as a color, a race, a privileged space, an oppressive ideology or hegemony, is hardly a "postmodern" discovery. Non-whites (Harrison 1991; hooks 1991) have witnessed and recorded, to use a term from Sennett and Cobb (1972), its "hidden injuries" for decades. Nevertheless, white scholars influenced by postmodernism have begun to deconstruct this privileged category, as well. Ruth Frankenberg's (1993) ethnography explores how white women view themselves under the privileged social, economic, and cultural canopy of whiteness. She shows how both conservative and liberal whites practice a "race avoidance discourse" and construct themselves as neutral on racial issues. Such a construction allows them to justify and maintain their transcendental privilege, a privilege she argues is based on an ideal present and future, but often void of a present historical reality.

To minimize racial inequities, "whiteness scholars" (Frankenberg 1997; Wray and Newitz 1997) argue that the protected space or category of whiteness has to be "named" and thrust into the arena of social and racial conflict. Some researchers point out that white identities are not allotted exclusively to whites and are commonly appropriated by other racial groups. Winndance-Twine (1997) shows how mixed-race girls who grow up in a "white" suburb attempt to live out a "neutral" mainstream existence. She reveals how the girls come to be stripped of their "white identity" as they grow through puberty on their way to attending college, where they develop a "black consciousness" to shelter them from the rejection of a mainstream culture once believed to be their culture.

Moss (1998) offers a somewhat different perspective on whiteness studies in his cross-cultural work on the negotiation of privilege among poor whites in an urban midwestern city. In critiquing the essentializing nature of whiteness studies, he shows how privilege becomes a contested asset in a decontextualized space of confused racial and social class identities. Seldom do black researchers ethnographically study white culture, and in doing so Moss uncovers many of the nuanced ways poor whites align themselves with positive constructions of whiteness while distancing themselves from common negative constructions of poverty. The influence of postmodernism looms central in Moss's work, however, in a paradoxical way because as he employs postmodern ideas, he critiques postmodernism and whiteness discourse through a Derridean framework of deconstruction.

To elaborate briefly on this point, in exploring ideas of race and class Moss interprets how the method of deconstruction systematically employs the concepts or premises of one idea or dichotomy to undermine the other. The deconstructive idea works to systematically displace conceptual hierarchies (male/female; black/white; lower class/working class/middle class; center/margin). An ethnographic interpreter must work within a conceptual hierarchy or paradigm by producing an exchange of similar properties and, in doing so, displacing and disrupting that very same paradigm. For instance, the first move of a deconstructive analysis is to identify a marginal idea or image, and the second move is to disrupt the assumptive flow of the hierarchy in which this idea or image is contained. For Derrida, the focus is language and an insistence that language always embodies a relationship of power between terms, one being used rather than another possible term in any text. From his perspective, terms in language are used positively (or negatively), effectively banishing those other terms from which they are differentiated. In this logic, language is structured in terms of oppositions, each term depending on and being supported by the other in order to gain or establish meaning. Although such terms interpenetrate each other, they are treated as though they exist in a hierarchical relationship of power with one term dominant over the other. Based on this very simplified interpretation, deconstruction is the means by which Derrida operates on texts – and the world itself can be viewed as a "text."

Moss notes that critics of this method argue that deconstruction is nothing more than a simple inversion project where the bottom term (in text) or category (in the social) is valorized and juxtaposed in place of the esteemed top term, nothing more than a flipping over of politics and ideologies. A good deal of "popular academic" postmodern and post-Marxist interpretation may fall into this very trap, but a thoroughly deconstructive method turns its own critique onto itself. Deconstruction, then, differs from other critical postmodern and post-Marxist perspectives because it turns postmodern arguments (anti-essentialism, anti-metanarratives, hybrid identities, multivocality) in on itself and uses the paradigm to analyze its own foundations and arguments.

What this means in terms of textual practice is a narrative which literally dislocates the people and groups being represented. Moss goes on to argue that a more deconstructive ethnography disrupts the static, dichotomized metatheoretical anthropological locations or conceptual code (working class/middle class; workers/owners; black/white). Such ethnographies portray people and places with ambiguous, fragmented, decentered, destabilized, expanded images. Such ethnographies are also highly "deconstructive" in the sense that they help disrupt our conventional academic and popular notions of cultural identities and differences. Some of the new whiteness studies illustrate nicely the potentially powerful deconstructive logic of a more rigorous postmodernism turned on a dominant group that has historically represented all cultural others.

The postmodern impulse to rework all metaconcepts for inscribing cultural difference such as class, gender, ethnicity, and race ultimately includes the concepts of space, time, and body as well. McDonough (1993) interprets the experience of black Catholics in Savannah, Georgia, and reveals the continuous tensions among discourses that sustain stereotypes. He demonstrates how people become "located" in conceptual spaces like religion, and when they fail to occupy that space, their identity is thrown into question. In a related piece, David Goode (1994) interrogates the way our constructs of the human body bear upon identity questions. Goode's ethnography about two children who are profoundly disabled illustrates how the disabled are easily dismissed as not quite human. Robert Murphy (1987), disabled in mid-life from spinal cord disease, wrote an auto-ethnography about the "process" of disability and the social perception of partial bodies. He weaves an illuminating narrative that challenges "able-bodied" notions of physical mobility, cognitivity, and congruity. In defining himself and other disabled people as "liminal" and "ambiguous," Murphy writes: "The long-term physically impaired are neither sick nor well, neither dead nor fully alive, neither out of society nor wholly in it. They are human beings but their bodies are warped or malfunctioning, leaving their full humanity in doubt. This undefined quality, an existential departure from normality, contributes to the widespread aversion to the disabled" (Murphy 1987:131). Both of these texts on the disabled are marked by a strong personal authorial voice, a non-linear text, giving voice to stigmatized subjects, and a reflexive account of how the ethnographic texts were produced.

To sum up, we have tried to locate various new ethnographies of American cultural difference/diversity on a broad theoretical continuum of post-Marxist and postmodern thought. The limitation of such an intellectual exercise (for writers and readers alike) is that ideas, like cultures (Gupta and Ferguson 1997) are located and then presented through narrow channels of possibility and imagination. Our construction of these two post-paradigms is obviously nothing more than a conceptual device for navigating through a complex, changing anthropological practice. It is doomed to spawn some misrepresentation of its own, but hopefully, it also helps sort through the flood of recent studies on cultural diversity.

A Pedagogical Philosophy for Teaching about Cultural Diversity in America

Given the emphasis on cultural difference as social constructions, we would want a course on American cultural diversity to teach students what Kellner (1995) calls a "critical media literacy." We want students to realize that they live in a media-dominated society that produces a multitude of objectified cultural others. We want them to understand this phenomenon on at least two levels, the institutional and the textual.

On the institutional level, we want students to realize that various educative or cultural institutions of civil society systematically produce objectifying cultural images for various political and economic interests. We want them to be able to understand specific historical articulations and discern whether they live in an era of ideological "backlash" or "romanticizations" of certain cultural groups or nations. We want them to understand the institutional role of anthropology in the production and deconstruction of objectifying images, in general and during historical moments of backlash and romanticization. Finally, and most importantly, we want them to appreciate the cultural struggles of stigmatized others to produce their own self-valorizing cultural images.

On the textual level, we want students to be much more critical about their general consumption of cultural images. We are especially concerned about mainstream middle-class white male students reflecting critically upon their privileged ideological position. But we want all students to be able to read cultural texts more politically, and thus to recognize and deconstruct objectifying discourses about cultural others. We want students to understand how anthropologists and others rhetorically and narratively produce both objectifying and deconstructive texts. We also want them to be able to read and appreciate the counter-hegemonic images and messages in the texts of marginalized cultural others as both aesthetic and political expressions.

A key pedagogical practice for creating such a course is a multitextual approach. A good set of ethnographic cases that deconstruct objectifying cultural images is essential, but academic texts must be supplemented with autobiographical, fictional, cinematic, and popular mass media materials as well. The juxtaposition of scientific, popular, literary, and media representations is essential to disrupt students' naturalized, commonsense understandings of popular cultural images. Using multiple texts is also essential to convey that scientific texts and voices are not necessarily superior to popular texts as reasonable representations or as disruptors of hegemonic discourses and images.

Another key pedagogical practice is to get students to collect and represent the dissenting voices of stigmatized cultural others. This would involve small field projects in collecting oral and life history and written texts by marginalized cultural others. A corollary exercise would be to collect the oral and written texts of groups that are explicitly organized to represent and misrepresent cultural others. Having collected the oral cultural texts of ordinary people, it is important to demonstrate how students' own everyday speech practices are a part of ongoing objectification and de-objectification processes. The point is to bring the previous analysis of "out there" stigmatizing discourses closer to the everyday experience of students. Students need to see that they are both passive consumers of cultural misrepresentations and active producers of such images. Once these issues are personalized, changes in their ideological consciousness may be more likely.

Often, the way students (throughout elementary school into college) learn to perceive themselves and cultural groups unfamiliar to them is through the images they have seen on television or heard in their cultural group. Seldom do they personally experience cultural difference, and the role they play in its construction. For example, students from marginalized identity groups may not be aware of their own complicity in constructing overly positive images about an assumed ideal group at the expense of their own collective and individual identities. Consequently, it is not enough to simply present counter-histories of a group's virtues and triumphs. Nor can identity construction processes be presented in a narrowly contextualized manner. It is important to present the cultural histories of various groups in a less dichotomized context than black vs. white, or gay vs. straight, or native-born vs. immigrant.

In pedagogical terms, one way to open up the context is through discussion and dialogue in which students share viewpoints and work through narrow dichotomous ways of thinking about each other. The days of long-drawn-out, one-way lectures are slowly (and we emphasize slowly) giving way to a multimedia as well as multisituational mode of presenting knowledge and ideas where critical theory and critical practice supplement each other in the classroom. Our point is to adapt such theory into class practice by incorporating multiple contexts of learning (i.e. videos, discussion, personal narratives, student projects) and a more "open discourse dialogue" that allows for cultural vulnerability, liminality, and possibility.

REFERENCES CITED

Abrahams, Roger
    1970   *Deep Down in the Jungle*. Chicago: Aldine Press.
Abu-Lughod, Lila
    1991   Writing against Culture. In *Recapturing Anthropology: Working in the Present*. Richard Fox, ed. Pp. 137–169. Santa Fe, NM: SAR Press.
Bauman, Gerd
    1996   *Contesting Culture: Discourses of Identity in Multi-Ethnic London*. Cambridge, UK: Cambridge University Press.
Behar, Ruth, and Deborah Gordon, eds.
    1995   *Women Writing Culture*. Berkeley: University of California Press.
Best, Steven, and Douglas Kellner
    1991   *Postmodern Theory: Critical Interrogations*. New York: Guilford Press.
Bourgois, Philippe
    1995   *In Search of Respect: Selling Crack in El Barrio*. Cambridge, UK: Cambridge University Press.

Clifford, James
  1988 *The Predicament of Culture: Twentieth Century Ethnography, Literature, and Art*. Cambridge, MA: Harvard University Press.
Clifford, James, and George Marcus, eds.
  1986 *Writing Culture: The Poetics and Politics of Ethnography*. Berkeley: University of California Press.
Collins, James, Fiona Thompson, and John Calagione, eds.
  1999 Culture, Dream and Political Economy: Higher Education and Late Capitalism. Theme issue. *International Journal of Qualitative Studies in Education*.
Crenshaw, Kimberle, Neil Gotanda, Gary Peller, and Kendall Thomas, eds.
  1995 *Critical Race Theory: The Key Writings that Formed the Movement*. New York: New Press.
Davidson, Anne Locke
  1996 *Making and Molding Identity in Schools: Student Narratives on Race, Gender, and Academic Achievement*. Albany: SUNY Press.
Devine, John
  1996 *Maximum Security: The Culture of Violence in Inner-City Schools*. Chicago: University of Chicago Press.
di Leonardo, Micaela
  1986 *The Varieties of Ethnic Experience: Kinship, Class, and Gender among California Italian-Americans*. Ithaca, NY: Cornell University Press.
  1989 Malinowski's Nephews. *The Nation*, March 13:350–351.
di Leonardo, Micaela, ed.
  1991 *Gender at the Crossroads of Knowledge: Feminist Anthropology in the Postmodern Era*. Berkeley: University of California Press.
Dorst, John D.
  1989 *The Written Suburb: An American Site, an Ethnographic Dilemma*. Philadelphia: University of Pennsylvania Press.
Eder, Donna, Catherine C. Evans, and Stephan Parker
  1994 *School Talk: Gender and Adolescent Culture*. New Brunswick, NJ: Rutgers University Press.
Fabian, Johannes
  1983 *Time and the Other: How Anthropology Makes Its Object*. New York: Columbia University Press.
Fischer, Michael
  1986 Ethnicity and the Post-Modern Arts of Memory. In *Writing Culture: The Poetics and Politics of Ethnography*. James Clifford and George Marcus, eds. Pp. 194–233. Berkeley: University of California Press.
Flores, Richard
  1995 *Los Pastores: History and Performance in the Mexican Shepherd's Play of South Texas*. Washington, DC: Smithsonian Institution Press.
Foley, Douglas
  1990 *Learning Capitalist Culture: Deep in the Heart of Tejas*. Philadelphia: University of Pennsylvania Press.
  1995 *The Heartland Chronicles*. Philadelphia: University of Pennsylvania Press.
  1997 *Deficit Models Based on Culture: The Anthropological Protest in the Evolution of Deficit Thinking – Educational Thought and Practice*. Richard Valencia, ed. Pp. 113–121. London: Falmer Press.
Fordham, Signithia
  1996 *Blacked Out: Dilemmas of Race, Identity and Success at Capital High*. Chicago: University of Chicago Press.

Forgaces, David
    1989   Gramsci and Marxism in Britain. *New Left Review* 176:70–88.
Frankenberg, Ruth
    1993   *White Woman, Race Matters: The Social Construction of Whiteness.*
    Minneapolis: University of Minnesota Press.
Frankenberg, Ruth, ed.
    1997   *Displacing Whiteness: Essays in Social and Cultural Criticism.* Durham, NC:
    Duke University Press.
Gilroy, Paul
    1987   *"There Ain't No Black in the Union Jack": The Cultural Politics of Race and
    Nation.* Chicago: University of Chicago Press.
    1993   *The Black Atlantic: Modernity and Double Consciousness.* Cambridge, MA:
    Harvard University Press.
Gomez-Peña, Guillermo
    1996   *The New World Border.* San Francisco: City Lights.
Goode, David
    1994   *A World without Words: The Social Construction of Children Born Deaf and
    Blind.* Philadelphia: Temple University Press.
Gordon, Edmund T.
    1997   The Cultural Politics of Black Masculinity. *Transforming Anthropology*
    6(1–2):36–53.
Gordon, Lewis R., ed.
    1997   *Existence in Black: An Anthology of Black Existential Philosophy.* New York:
    Routledge.
Griffin, Christine
    1993   *Representations of Youth: The Study of Youth and Adolescence in Britain and
    America.* London: Routledge.
Gupta, Akhil, and James Ferguson, eds.
    1997   *Anthropological Locations: Boundaries and Grounds of a Field Science.*
    Berkeley: University of California Press.
Gwaltney, John L.
    1980   *Drylongso: A Self-Portrait of Black America.* New York: Vintage Press.
Hall, Stuart
    1996   New Ethnicities. In Morley and Chen, pp. 441–450.
Haraway, Donna
    1989   *Simians, Cyborgs, and Women: The Reinvention of Nature.* London:
    Routledge.
Harlow, Barbara
    1987   *Resistance Literature.* New York: Methuen.
Harrison, Faye, ed.
    1991   *Decolonizing Anthropology: Moving Further toward an Anthro-
    pology for Liberation.* Washington, DC: American Anthropological
    Association.
hooks, bell
    1991   *Black Looks: Race and Representation.* Boston, MA: South End Press.
Jameson, Frederic
    1984   Postmodernism or the Cultural Logic of Late Capitalism. *New Left Review*
    146:53–92.
Katz, Michael
    1989   *The Undeserving Poor: From the War on Poverty to the War on Welfare.* New
    York: Pantheon Books.

Keesing, Roger
  1994 Theories of Culture Revisited. In *Assessing Cultural Anthropology*. Robert
    Borofsky, ed. Pp. 301–310. New York: McGraw-Hill.
Keil, Charles
  1970 *Blues People*. Chicago: University of Chicago Press.
Kellner, Douglas
  1989 *Television and the Crises of Democracy*. Boulder, CO: Westview Press.
  1995 *Media Culture: Cultural Studies, Identity and Politics between the Modern and
    Postmodern*. London: Routledge.
Klare, Karl, and Dick Howard, eds.
  1971 *The Unknown Dimension: European Marxism since Lenin*. New York: Basic
    Books.
Kondo, Dorrine
  1990 *Crafting Selves: Power, Gender, and Discourses of Identity in a Japanese
    Workplace*. Chicago: University of Chicago Press.
Krupat, Arnold
  1992 *Ethnocriticism: Ethnography, History, Literature*. Berkeley: University of
    California Press.
Laclau, Ernesto, and Chantal Mouffe
  1985 *Hegemony and Socialist Strategy: Towards a Radical Democratic Politics*.
    London: Verso.
Lamphere, Louise, Helena Ragoné, and Patricia Zavella, eds.
  1997 *Situated Lives: Gender and Culture in Everyday Life*. New York: Routledge.
Lancaster, Roger, and Micaela di Leonardo, eds.
  1997 *The Gender Sexuality Reader: Culture, History, Political Economy*. New York:
    Routledge.
Lather, Patti, and Cris Smithies
  1995 *Troubling Angels: Women Living with HIV/AIDS*. Columbus, OH: Greyden
    Press.
  1997 *Troubling the Angels: Women Living with HIV/AIDS*. Boulder, CO: Westview
    Press.
Lave, Jeanne
  1992 Coming of Age in Birmingham: Cultural Studies and Conceptions of Subjec-
    tivity. *Annual Review of Anthropology*. 21:257–282.
Levine, Lawrence
  1977 *Black Culture and Black Consciousness: Afro-American Folk Thought from
    Slavery to Freedom*. Oxford: Oxford University Press.
Limon, José
  1994 *Dancing with the Devil: Society and Cultural Poetics in Mexican-American
    South Texas*. Madison: University of Wisconsin Press.
Lutz, Cathrine, and Jane L. Collier
  1993 *Reading National Geographic*. Chicago: University of Chicago Press.
Lyotard, Jean François
  1984 *The Postmodern Condition: A Report on Knowledge*. Minneapolis: University
    of Minnesota Press.
MacLeod, Jay
  1995 *Ain't No Makin' It: Aspirations and Attainment in a Low-Income Neighbor-
    hood*. 2nd edition. Boulder, CO: Westview Press.
Marcus, George, and Michael Fischer
  1986 *Anthropology as Cultural Critique: An Experimental Moment in the Human
    Sciences*. Chicago: University of Chicago Press.

Martin, Emily
   1987   *The Woman in the Body: A Cultural Analysis of Reproduction*. Boston, MA:
   Beacon Press.
Mascia-Lees, Frances, Patricia Sharpe, and Colleen Ballerino
   1989   The Postmodernist Turn in Anthropology: Cautions from a Feminist Perspec-
   tive. *Signs* 15(1):7–33.
McAdoo, Hariett, ed.
   1988   *The Black Family*. Newbury Park, CA: Sage.
McClellan, David
   1979   *Marxism after Marx: An Introduction*. Boston, MA: Houghton Mifflin.
McDonough, Gary
   1993   *Black and Catholic in Savannah, Georgia*. Knoxville: University of Tennessee
   Press.
McGrane, Bernard
   1989   *Beyond Anthropology: Time and the Other*. New York: Columbia University
   Press.
Modleski, Tania
   1982   *Loving with a Vengeance: Mass-Produced Fantasies for Women*. Hamden, CT:
   Archon Books.
Morely, David, and Kuan-Hsing Chen, eds.
   1996   *Stuart Hall: Critical Dialogues in Cultural Studies*. London: Routledge.
Morgen, Sandra, ed.
   1989   *Gender and Anthropology: Critical Reviews for Research and Teaching*.
   Washington, DC: American Anthropological Association.
Moss, Kirby
   1998   Interrogating Images: Poor Whites and the Paradox of Privilege. Ph.D. disser-
   tation, University of Texas at Austin.
Murphy, Robert F.
   1987   *The Body Silent*. New York: Henry Holt.
Newman, Katherine S.
   1988   *Falling from Grace: The Experience of Downward Mobility in the American
   Middle Class*. New York: Free Press.
O'Nell, Theresa
   1996   *Disciplined Hearts: History, Identity and Depression in an American Indian
   Community*. Berkeley: University of California Press.
Ortner, Sherry
   1984   Theory in Anthropology since the Sixties. *Comparative Studies in Society and
   History* 26:126–166.
Paredes, Americo
   1958   *With Pistol in His Hand: A Border Ballad and Its Hero*. Austin: University of
   Texas Press.
   1993   *Folklore and Culture on the Texas–Mexican Border*. Austin: University of
   Texas Press.
Peña, Manuel
   1985   *The Texas–Mexican Conjunto: History of a Working Class Music*. Austin:
   University of Texas Press.
   1999   *The Mexican American Orquesta*. Austin: University of Texas Press.
Radway, Janice
   1984   *Reading the Romance: Women, Patriarchy, and Popular Literature*. Chapel
   Hill: University of North Carolina Press.

Rosaldo, Renato
1989 *Culture and Truth: The Remaking of Social Analysis*. Boston, MA: Beacon Press.
Ross, Andrew, ed.
1988 *Universal Abandon? The Politics of Postmodernism*. Minneapolis: University of Minneapolis Press.
Sacks, Karen Brodkin
1989 Towards a Unified Theory of Class, Race, and Gender. *American Ethnologist* 16(3):534–550.
Said, Edward
1979 *Orientalism*. New York: Pantheon.
1994 *Culture and Imperialism*. New York: Vintage.
Saldivar, Ramon
1990 *Chicano Narrative: The Dialectics of Difference*. Madison: University of Wisconsin Press.
Sennett, Richard, and Jonathan Cobb
1972 *The Hidden Injuries of Class*. New York: Vintage Books.
Shattuc, Jane
1997 *The Talking Cure: TV Talk Shows and Women*. New York: Routledge.
Shumar, Wesley
1997 *College for Sale: A Critique of the Commodification of Higher Education*. London: Falmer Press.
Spivak, Gayatri
1988 In *Other Worlds: Essays in Cultural Politics*. New York: Methuen.
Stacey, Judy
1990 *Brave New Families: Stories of Domestic Upheaval in Late Twentieth Century America*. New York: Basic Books.
1996 *In the Name of the Family: Rethinking Family Values in the Postmodern Age*. Boston, MA: Beacon Press.
Stack, Carol
1974 *All Our Kin: Strategies of Survival in a Black Community*. New York: Harper and Row.
Stewart, John O.
1989 *Drinkers, Drummers and Decent Folk: Ethnographic Narratives of Village Trinidad*. Albany: SUNY Press.
Stewart, Kathleen
1996 *A Space on the Side of the Road: Cultural Poetics in an "Other" America*. Princeton, NJ: Princeton University Press.
Storey, John, ed.
1996 *What is Cultural Studies? A Reader*. New York: St. Martin's Press.
Susser, Ida
1989 Gender in the Anthropology of the United States. In Morgen, pp. 343–359.
Ulin, Robert
1991 Critical Anthropology Twenty Years Later: Modernism and Postmodernism in Anthropology. *Critique of Anthropology* 11(1):63–89.
Vizenor, Gerald, ed.
1989 *Narrative Chance: Postmodern Discourse on Native American Indian Literatures*. Norman: University of Oklahoma Press.
Weis, Lois
1990 *Working Class without Work: High School Students in a De-industrializing Economy*. New York: Routledge.

Weston, Kath
   1991   *Families We Choose: Lesbians, Gays, Kinship*. New York: Columbia
      University Press.
Weston, Kathy
   1997   The Virtual Anthropologist. In *Anthropological Locations*. Akil Gupta and
      James Ferguson, eds. Pp. 163–184. Berkeley: University of California Press.
Williams, Norma
   1990   *The Mexican American Family: Tradition and Change*. New York: General
      Hall.
Williamson, Judith
   1989   *Hard Core: Power, Pleasure and the Frenzy of the Visible*. Berkeley: Univer-
      sity of California Press.
Willis, Paul
   1981   *Learning to Labor: How Working Class Kids Get Working Class Jobs*. New
      York: Columbia University Press.
Winndance-Twine, France
   1997   Brown-Skinned White Girls: Class, Culture and the Construction of White
      Identity in Suburban Communities. In Frankenberg, pp. 214–243.
Wray, Matt, and Annalee Newitz, eds.
   1997   *White Trash: Race and Class in America*. New York: Routledge.
Zipes, Jack
   1997   *Happily Ever After: Fairy Tales, Children and the Culture Industry*. London:
      Routledge.

21

Diversity in Anthropological Theory

Karen Brodkin

If anthropology is about anything, it is about cultural diversity. Yet anthropology has been at best a marginal player in the discussions of multiculturalism in the United States. Addressing this contradiction in a course about the history of anthropological theory can provide an opportunity to understand how it came about and can suggest ways to make anthropological perspectives a more important part of the current American conversation. How have the discipline's core ideas helped – and hindered – anthropology's participation in contemporary discussions of racial, ethnic, gender, and sexual diversity? Who are the anthropologists excluded from the canon but whose work is important in order to understand this diversity? What can we learn about the discipline's current marginal contributions to today's debates by asking why such anthropologists have been "lost" from the history of the discipline's main lineage? Are there particular moments or issues in the history of anthropology that shed particular light on anthropology's relationship to racial and ethnic diversity in the United States?

Current discussions of cultural diversity in the United States focus on racial and ethnic diversity. But they also deal with their relationship to diversity in gender, class, and sexual orientation. This literature is large, growing exponentially, and spans the disciplines from critical race theory in law to studies of popular and high culture, from literature to history, from science studies to sociology and anthropology. The literature shares a theoretical framework that rests upon several points. (1) An understanding that race, gender, class, and sexual orientation are constructed institutionally and culturally, and that they are changeable. (2) Each of these dimensions of social organization is constructed dichotomously – white and not-white, women and men, and so on. (3) Each is also constituted of the others. That is, there is no such thing, for example, as an ungendered white person; the nature of racial whiteness depends on the gender, class, and sexual orientation of the individual. These points become clear in studies that examine the ethnoracial constructions underlying cultural constructions of national belonging, of being a citizen of the nation state. (4) These ideas and the rules by which social identity is constructed in the United States are part of a larger Western Enlightenment pattern of organization and thought.

Although much of this scholarship comes from outside anthropology, it shares a fundamental mission with anthropology in seeking to understand the cultural patterns and organizational forms which are at the heart of the culture. They try to make visible those things which most natives take for granted, those practices that seem natural and commonsensical to insiders. Although anthropology has a great deal of practice in analyzing non-Western societies, it has only recently begun to take seriously the sociocultural tradition of which it is part. This is why any efforts to discuss cultural diversity in the United States (within or beyond an anthropological theory course) need to be familiar with the multidisciplinary scholarship that seeks to do just that.

The first part of this chapter discusses three major themes in contemporary analyses of diversity in the United States. The second part looks at 19th-century evolutionary theories and Boasian anthropology through that analytic lens.

Three Themes in Multidisciplinary Scholarship on Diversity in the United States

Cultural construction of race/ethnicity, gender, and sexuality

Anthropology's antiracist efforts have focused on showing that race is not a biological category. These discussions are not always well connected with multidisciplinary work that dissects the ways in which American social institutions and cultural practices create race both as phenotypic patterns and systems of social meaning. The latter efforts show how race matters greatly for allocating unequal and often invisible social privileges and how it is used to make forms of exclusion and oppression seem natural and commonsensical, the product of a group's culture, or an individual's actions, rather than outcomes that are institutionally and discursively structured.

There is a great deal of popular and scholarly confusion about the meanings of race and ethnicity. In some popular understandings ethnicity is what whites have, while race is what non-white people have. Others – notably Joan Vincent (1974), Leith Mullings (1984), and Robert Blauner (1991) – argue that race is externally imposed, while ethnicity applies to a cultural identity one embraces, so that people racialized as non-white, or "of color" are likely to be both, racial and ethnic. Building on this insight, I find it useful to conceptually distinguish racial assignment from ethnoracial identity (Brodkin 1999). Thus all Americans are assigned to a race, but not all embrace an ethnoracial identity. Indeed, as Ruth Frankenberg (1993) has found, part of America's racial problem is that white Americans tend not to regard themselves as having a race, but rather see themselves as the color of water, or "normal."

Some anthropologists define ethnicity as partly an inherited category and partly a relationship of opposition to other groups. They argue that what gives ethnicity enduring force is its utility for organizing people to pursue shared socioeconomic interests. Brackette Williams (1989, 1996) has argued that such approaches disregard the ways in which the modern world of nation states shapes ethnicities and makes them matter in terms of economic and social privileges. In this perspective, the difference between race and ethnicity, both of which are nationally constructed categories, recedes. Her view is given force by the current confusion in U.S. census categories, where Americans are asked whether they belong to one of four "races," or one ethnic group (Hispanic). Michael Omi and Howard Winant (1994) have coined the term "racial state" to refer to the ways in which law and public policy make race/ethnicity matter as a basis for unequal treatment in the United States.

Many recent studies of ethnoracial categories in the United States describe the ways both race and ethnicity are fluid and changeable (Gregory and Sanjek 1994). For example, before about 1880 and after World War II, southern and eastern European immigrants and their children were treated as fully white. But between the 1880s and the 1940s, they were not-quite white in that they lacked the freedom of whites to live, go to school, and work where they wanted (Brodkin 1999). The Irish also began their history in the United States as racial non-whites, suffering discrimination and social marginalization, but gained the privileges of racial whiteness at about the time southern and eastern Europeans were losing them (Ignatiev 1995). Likewise, Almaguer (1994) has shown how Mexicans were declared legally white when California became annexed to the United States. However, by the end of the 19th century, the state increasingly treated them as Indians, a racial category denied citizenship, and subjected to forced labor under California vagrancy laws.

Feminist scholars use the term gender to refer to the ways cultures construct womanhood and manhood and to distinguish these from sex as a biological concept. Margaret Mead's *Sex and Temperament* was an early demonstration of three different ways in which cultures constructed maleness and femaleness. Each of the three New Guinea societies Mead described believed that their way was "natural." Feminist anthropologists in the 1970s and early 1980s played a key role in analyzing the organizational and cultural underpinnings of gender diversity and gender relations (Morgen 1989).

The practices of key social institutions in the United States also help construct gender. Scholars across the disciplines have attended to the ways in which constructions of American womanhood have been shaped by public and corporate policies and by the notions of masculine and feminine that undergird them. Central to these have been studies of the ways that work and motherhood have been deployed in defining masculinity and femininity. For example, Alice Kessler-Harris (1990) has shown how early 20th-century minimum wage laws and discussions surrounding them have constructed white women as dependants of white men, the former as mothers and the latter as breadwinners. Others have demonstrated that similar assumptions shaped protective labor legislation and welfare policies (Abramovitz 1988; Gordon 1994; Mink 1995; Boris and Bardaglio 1991; Rose 1995). Other studies highlight the institutional as well as the cultural constructions of what is presented as "natural" or "appropriate" work for women. Thus, in the 19th century, office work was deemed appropriate for men and was the first step up the corporate ladder. Beginning slowly during the Civil War as government clerks, and then in far larger numbers in the 1920s, women entered clerical work, so that since the 1950s, office work has appeared to be the quintessential women's work. The image of "Rosie the Riveter" during World War II is another well-known example of how federal policies briefly made heavy industrial labor (and decent wages) compatible with femininity.

Notions of motherhood as women's "natural" calling have also been culturally constructed and – as Evelyn Nakano Glenn (1994) and many others have shown – been reserved for white women. The policies and practices of child support, welfare, and workfare have consistently distinguished between good and bad women, fit and unfit mothers, with white women (especially widows) deemed worthy of support, and women of color deemed unworthy. They have been forced to work (allegedly to improve their character) and have only conditional rights to raise their children. Nancy Naples (1997) has analyzed recent congressional rhetoric justifying the policies that force mothers into the labor force. Their key tropes, really stereotypes, are that women on welfare are African American, hence unfit for motherhood unless taught responsibility through workfare.

Not only is gender culturally constructed, but so too is sexuality or sexual orientation, as anthropologist Gayle Rubin (1975) first argued theoretically, and Esther Newton (1972) and Elizabeth Kennedy and Madelyn Davis (1993) demonstrated ethnographically. Anthropologists have been central in analyzing the organizational structures within which contemporary lesbians and gay men construct their cultures and identities through marriage, kinship and motherhood (Lewin 1993; Weston 1991), and claims to public cultural space (Kennedy and Davis 1993). Anthropologists and historians have also demonstrated the cultural construction of sexuality by showing its fluidity.

American women and men have constructed their attractions to and behavior with those of the same or the opposite sex in different ways at different times (D'Emilio and Freedman 1988). Historians have documented the ways that homosexual attraction, the notion of a sexual identity, and the construction of gay and lesbian space began to develop in the early decades of the 20th century, and bloomed during World War II. George Chauncey (1995), Allan Berube (1990), and Elizabeth Kennedy and Madelyn Davis (1993) have documented the ways in which men and women created their own notions of homosexual identities and the institutions and changing norms governing those identities. They document historically cultural shifts, first from homosexual behavior to homosexual identity, and then in constructions of who is regarded as homosexual, both within the community and in the wider society. Early constructions of lesbians and gay men included only butches and effeminate men. Femmes were regarded as not quite lesbians, while active/masculine men were regarded and regarded themselves as heterosexual. Scholars have also demonstrated the importance of butch/femme and active/passive roles in the making of gay and lesbian identity and in claiming public recognition and legitimacy. Not until relatively recently has the word homosexual applied to all those attracted to the same sex, regardless of sexual role. That construction has not been static either. Queer studies scholars have come to see gender as performance and have analyzed the many varieties of bisexual, transgender, and transsexual performances of identities and the complex ways in which they interact with constructions of desire as well as the variability and fluidity of individual constructions of sexual desire (Newton 1972; Katz 1990).

Dichotomous constructions of race and gender

Where the current emphasis in studies of sexuality has been to confound dichotomous categories, studies of gender, race, and, to a lesser extent, of class have attempted to understand reasons for the enduring strength of dichotomous constructions. Anthropological studies as well as feminist perspectives have long understood gender as constructed dichotomously. Conventional notions of temperamental complementarity, companionate marriage, and a division of labor give the appearance of naturalness to this culturally constructed maleness and femaleness. Each is constructed as the opposite of the other temperamentally and in social roles.

Although the United States, like most nation states, has always been a multiracial nation with a complex class structure, it has become clear that labor force practices, law, public policy, and everyday social practices have constructed parallel dichotomies for race and class – white and not-white; mental and manual laborers.

As Toni Morrison (1990) argued, the construction of whiteness has depended upon the invention of a blackness that is the negation of the ideal, the evil twin upon whose evil the goodness of whiteness depends. Morrison, and the historians Noel Ignatiev and David Roediger have all demonstrated how European immigrants and workers have claimed whiteness and its attendant privileges of belonging, of Americanness, by inventing and using racist imagery and racist violence to distinguish themselves from black Americans. Such 19th-century practices, of becoming white "on the backs of blacks" as Morrison (1993) put it, are part of a longer historical tradition that Haney Lopez (1996: 27–28) chronicles through court decisions about naturalized citizenship which "constructed the bounds of Whiteness by deciding on a case-by-case basis who was not White." Race in America – no matter how many races there may be in any given period – is a relationship, of black and white or non-white and white, whereby the white pole is defined as the opposite of the invented and inferior non-white pole. Neither races nor ethnicities have been independent and discrete categories. Rather they must be understood as being part of a wider dichotomous relationship.

Mutual construction of race, class, and gender in the U.S. nation state

A third important theme in constructivist studies of diversity is the way that race, class, and gender construct each other. Interest in the relationship of race, class, and gender developed initially from attempts to understand the role of class and racial consciousnesses in social movements since World War II. The great wave of anticolonial and national liberation movements as well as the North American Civil Rights, feminist, and gay liberation movements were animated more by ethnoracial, gender, and sexual consciousnesses than by class identities. Earlier white Marxist class essentialism came to be challenged with racial and gender counter-essentialisms, as activists and scholars argued about which basis of organizational allegiance was most likely to produce an effective democratic movement. Such arguments soon gave way to understandings that people engaged as members of all categories, but in situation-specific ways. The question then became more sophisticated, to understand how different facets of political identities, or consciousnesses, fit together in people's constructions of themselves as social actors, and how these were connected to the hegemonic constructions of race, ethnicity, class, and gender themselves.

Although the impetus came from the ways in which subordinated groups construct themselves as political actors, the bulk of scholarly work has focused on understanding the ways that dominant groups have used race, class, and gender in naturalizing social subordination and cultural hegemony. I have suggested that this can be seen as the "metaorganization" of the American nation (Brodkin 1999). That is, if race, gender, and class are each key forms of organizing the nation's society and culture, then the organization of these organizations – the ways they constitute each other – is the metaorganization of the nation.

One way to understand the metaorganization of this national hegemony is to focus on the racial and gender organization of the American labor force and the policies and discourses that have sustained it. A long tradition of African American scholarship has connected the invention of race, specifically the cultural construction of blackness as subhuman and the civil state of blackness as property, with the immense profit that planters made from the inhuman treatment of Africans (E. Williams 1944; Bennett 1970; Fields 1982, 1990; Smedley 1993). This literature suggests that labor was organized one way when done by free whites, and quite another way on plantations where it was done by African bondsmen and -women. The word servile came to be attached simultaneously to African Americans and to the work they did such that white workers joined planters and legislators early on in policing the separation as a way of maintaining their own freedom and respectability (DuBois 1935; Saxton 1990; Roediger 1991).

Venus Green's study of the Bell System is one useful contemporary case study of the way a large employer continued to reproduce that segregation. Until forced to do so in the 1970s, Bell refused to hire African Americans. When they ultimately did hire them, it was for specific jobs that the company had slotted for deskilling and speed-up. In particular, the job of operator, which had previously been a white women's occupational niche, came to be one for African American women. According to an AT&T vice president in 1969:

> The kind of people we need are going to be in very short supply. . . . Most of our new hires go into entry level jobs which means we must have access to an ample supply of people who will work at comparatively low rates of pay. That means city people more so than suburbanites. That means lots of black people. . . . We need them because we have so many jobs to fill and they will take them.
>
> It is just a plain fact that in today's world telephone company wages are more in line with black expectations – and the tighter the labor market the more this is true. (Green 1995:S120–121)

Green reminds us that there was nothing natural in Bell's decision to structure the operator job this way in the face of white flight. "Instead of raising wages and creating less stressful work environments to attract people of all races, the

Bell System segregated black women into departmental ghettos (operators and low-level clerks) where there was little opportunity for advancement" (Green 1995: 121).

I have suggested (Brodkin 1999) that it is also the case that those who do degraded and driven labor come to be constructed – by economic opportunity structures, political practices, and hegemonic cultural systems – as racially something less than white, and concomitantly, their racial non-whiteness supports reorganization of their work in this fashion. The changing nature of work and the racial assignments of American Jews and Mexican Americans can be used to illustrate this connection.

Jews had been in the United States long before the massive influx of Eastern European Jews toward the end of the 19th century. Although anti-Semitism certainly existed, Jews were nevertheless racially categorized and treated as white in the United States. By the 1890s that began to change as an expanded scientific racism came to reconstruct Europe as composed of superior (Nordic and Teutonic) and inferior (Alpine, Mediterranean, and Semitic) races. The mass of new immigrants were assigned to the latter races. These immigrants, each occupying a particular occupational and local niche, were also the vast majority of America's industrial workers. Jewish women and men both became the backbone of the nation's exploding garment industry, centered in New York.

Jewish immigrants entered an industry that was organized along craft lines. But as Jews came to work in the needle trades, the manufacturers reorganized the work in such a manner as to deskill and industrialize it while vastly increasing the output. Wages and working conditions deteriorated commensurately. Garment making went from an industry marked in part by skilled labor to one solidly dependent upon "unskilled" labor and paying low wages in the form of piecework. This was not because the new workers lacked the skills of earlier ones. Russian Jews entered the United States as a particularly skilled group, not only in sewing, but also as printers, building tradesmen, blacksmiths, and bakers. There were more skilled Jewish immigrants than English, Germans, or Scandinavians.

Manufacturers deskilled and intensified the work despite, and not because of, the skill levels of their workforce. They were able to do this because native-born workers in other trades, especially in the unionized construction and transportation sectors, refused to work with Jews, as well as with others whom they regarded as not white.

The links between race and work are made particularly clear by contrasting the deskilling of labor in the garment industry with the maintenance of construction and transport as both white and skilled. Agreements between employers and unions maintained the organization of these jobs as skilled and autonomous. That such an organization was a privilege of whiteness emerges by contrast with the "servility of labor" that inhered in the deskilled and assembly-line jobs in the garment industry. Ethnoracial segregation in living complemented that at work and reinforced commonsense understandings that Europeans came in different and differently endowed races.

About the same time that industrial work was revolutionized in the East and Midwest, agricultural work was revolutionized along similar lines in the West and Southwest. Here the labor force of the new factories in the fields became predominantly Mexican. When California became a state, it legally categorized Mexicans as white. Racism against working-class Mexicans remained sporadic until the 1880s. This changed with the growth of agribusiness, such that by 1930 Mexicans nationally came to be classified as members of a non-white "Mexican" race, unless the census taker knew the individual to be "white."

An examination of the relationship between a group's racial assignment and its place in the labor force suggests that the core of America's working class, those who have been concentrated in the industries which generate the vast bulk of the nation's wealth in any given period, have been assigned to a non-white race. Agriculture, whether by bondspeople or by free people working under the industrial conditions of agribusiness, has been a preserve of non-whites. The labor force of the U.S. industrial revolution, between the 1880s and the 1930s, was overwhelmingly made up of southern and eastern European immigrants. Indeed, as late as 1920, immigrants and non-European people were the majority of the entire American labor force. By contrast, white, native-born workers were concentrated far from the industrial centers and were in marginal industries such as farming (but not agribusiness), ranching, and timber. This was also the period of U.S. history when those southern and eastern European immigrants were treated as racially other than fully white, and were denied the civil and political privileges of whiteness.

That the U.S. labor force is also structured along lines of gender is no secret. Women have always been clustered in a relatively small number of occupations and at the bottom of the wage and salary hierarchy. However, understanding the racial places of women in the labor force lets us understand how race, gender, and class organizations come together as key parts of a single system of national organization.

Important pioneering work by Evelyn Nakano Glenn (1985) showed that historically women of color, and not-quite white Euro-ancestry women have worked in the waged labor force in greater numbers, often far greater, than their fully white counterparts. Women of color have worked side by side with men, in the fields, in factories, and as live-in domestic workers. Although white women have had to work for wages since colonial times, until the last few decades, they have worked in far fewer numbers. White women entered the workforce in significant numbers only with the rise of sales and clerical work as clean, genteel, and protected white women's niches. About the same time, white women entered professional occupations in specifically "women's professions" of social work, nursing, and teaching.

Alice Kessler-Harris' (1982) important study of women in the U.S. labor force argues that as late as the 1950s a woman worker was understood to be a woman out of place. In a culture that defined women's place as in the home and under the protection of a man, women's participation in the labor force constituted a potential threat to their virtue. Indeed, much of the evidence of non-white women's lack of virtue was deduced from their mingling with men in the "coarse" conditions of the workforce. Sexual harassment was understood as something women asked for, a sign of such women's immorality, which in turn confirmed that presumption.

I have argued (Brodkin 1999) that white women's respectability and racial purity in the workforce have been historically supported by jobs organized in a manner that segregated them into specifically white female clerical, sales, and professional niches. If racial and gender segregation protected white women's virtue, their whiteness was also marked by the organization of their work. Compared to the jobs of women of color and non-white men, white women's jobs had a modicum of the autonomy and freedom from supervision that has historically characterized the jobs of white men.

The racial and gendered organization of the labor force has also been a place that confirms ethnoracial stereotypes of whites as morally superior, as civilized in contrast to everyone else as animal-like or savage. As will be discussed in more detail below, work in cultural studies has shown that a key part of this construction is the notion that non-white women and men are more like each other in temperament and physique than are their white counterparts. Thus for example, Irish, African American, and Polish women and men both have been negatively stereotyped as strong of back and weak of mind, while Chinese and Jewish men have both been represented as effeminate, and, along with their women, as devious and manipulative. In contrast, white womanhood and white manhood have been positively stereotyped as opposite and complementary, with white women as domestic, maternal, and virtuous, and white men as chivalrous family men, protectors and citizens. Gender and racial separation of white women and men, each in their separate and racially white niches, then confirms the naturalness of whiteness and its attributes. Likewise, gender mingling, of other than white men and women, underscores the commonsenseness of the negative stereotypes of their ethnoracial non-whiteness.

The ways that ethnoracial, class, and gender organizations come together into a single system emerges from work dealing with the interplay of race, gender, and nationalism. Their focus has been to analyze the ways that conventional norms and discourses of belonging and political citizenship have worked to create real Americans as white (Morrison 1993; Frankenberg 1993; B. Williams 1996). These studies incorporate the understandings just discussed of whiteness as constituted from protective masculinity and domestic femininity as well as from a range of privileges that include the right to respectable work, families, social respectability, and residential freedom. Real Americans then become constituted as a white artisan and business class of responsible family men and women devoted to domesticity, not unlike the colonial notion of citizen-soldiers and mothers of the nation, the population to which democracy applies. The wider construct of "America," then, is of a white nation. However, as a nation, the United States has always been dependent upon the labor of a diverse but non-white, manual working class to produce the nation's wealth, but has historically constructed this class as alien, dangerous, and unfit for inclusion in the national fabric.

The United States is far from unique in its constructions of national belonging. Many studies elaborate similar themes for other nations, for European colonial society and culture and for postcolonial nations (Gilroy 1991; Medina

1999; Mohanty et al. 1991; Stoler 1989). The emphasis in all these diversity studies has been on questions of cultural stability, how rulers gain the consent of the ruled through categories that everyone uses.

But these are only one kind of question to ask about the cultural constructions of diversity in the United States. Many other questions are still to be investigated. Not least are those that deal with cultural and social change, for example, about the ways in which subjugated and nationally marginalized peoples construct their own identities. Are these similarly dichotomous? What is the relationship of different kinds of constructions to different kinds of activism?

Case I: Unilinear Evolution and Anthropological Theory in Relationship to Enlightenment Thought

Racialized constructions of the nation state have structured Western understandings of colonialism and of cultural diversity among the world's peoples. Thomas Patterson (1997) has recently argued that the concept of civilization is key for comprehending the ways that anthropologists and others in the West have conceptualized this diversity. Civilization has been constructed historically in much the same way that race, class, and gender have been – as a dichotomous relationship with an invented and inferior savagery. Unilinear evolution was the dominant 19th-century framework for analyzing that contrast and one in which anthropology figured prominently. Unilinear evolution was "good to think with" as Geertz might have put it.

All the key figures of mid- to late-19th-century anthropology used unilinear evolution to explain how Euro-American liberal, industrial capitalism evolved from societies that were just then being "discovered" in the process of imperialist expansion. All worked with an implicit contrast between a primitive other and a civilized us. But cultural evolution was understood differently by anthropology's variegated apical ancestors.

Studying Herbert Spencer (1899) and Frederick Engels (1972), two major figures of the 19th century who are not so often included in the core anthropological canon, can help foreground the place of race and gender in 19th-century contrasts of primitive and civilized. Reading them helps connect the diversity of early evolutionary anthropology to contemporary discussions about cultural constructions of race and gender. Reading Spencer and Engels together also helps place the specific contrasts dealt with by anthropology's core ancestors in the larger framework of Enlightenment and modernist thought in ways that reading them alone is not likely to do.

At one level, Spencer and Engels were about as different as two thinkers could be. They both used the same information but developed diametrically opposed portraits of human nature and sociocultural evolution. Their theories came from and undergirded their very different political philosophies, Marxism and social Darwinism. These contrasting worldviews on industrial capitalist culture and society continue to shape popular and scholarly thought today, not least in the areas of racial, ethnic, and gender diversity. Marxism and social Darwinism embed very different visions of the good life, of ideal relationships between women and men, between individuals, and between ethnic groups.

Spencer's story of social evolution chronicled humanity's rise from a condition of savage warfare and brutal treatment of women as the private property of men to a condition of peaceful industrial existence where women were well treated and taken care of by men. Engels described humanity's original condition as primitive communism, marked by egalitarian relations among men and between women and men. His evolutionary trajectory is downhill to class society where most men and all women are exploited and oppressed by a small ruling class, and where women are subordinated to and economically dependent upon men. Where Spencer writes a story of human betterment and progress that celebrates the social order of laissez faire capitalism, Engels' story of decline and degradation critiques that same social order from the perspective of those at the bottom.

For Spencer, competition, the survival of the fittest, whether in the struggle between people and the environment, between societies, or between individuals, shaped the capacities and temperaments of women and men, and of different races. Competition selected for certain biological and psychological traits, and these have had lasting impacts on future social forms. Thus Spencer believed that the different natures of women and men were forged in savage times and have continued to shape gender relations in modern society. Spencer believed that women's physical and mental development have been stunted by their reproductive functions, and that their emotional character has likewise been shaped by reproduction. His portrait of gender relations in "savagery" was one of brutality – women and men were equally brutal – but because women were disadvantaged in size and strength, they became prey, and ultimately property of men, destined to face a life of violence, incest, and rape, as well as a short lifespan after their childbearing years. In order to survive in such a hostile environment women developed character traits of guile, manipulation, flattery, and an attraction to men of power. These traits together with a stunting of intellectual functions and development of nurturance have persisted into civilized times and explained for Spencer why women are not suited to participate in government or the economy, and why men must govern and serve as chivalrous protectors. As Marvin Harris (1968) observed 30 years ago, social Darwinism, with respect to race, class, and gender, is more accurately described as Spencerism. In Spencer one finds the most fully developed argument that the way things are, so must they be for the future of the species.

Engels' rejoinder was that "natural" human relationships in general and gender relationships in particular have been perverted by the rise of private property and by monogamy (which he sees as the ownership of women by men). Engels has less to say about race than Spencer. Instead, what is crucial is the relationship of people to natural resources and ownership of the means of production. Communal ownership supported gender equality in primitive communism and early kinship-based society. Private property, first in livestock cared for by men, gave men economic dominance and allowed them to turn women and many men into economic dependants. For Engels, humans seem to be infinitely plastic in their attributes, shaped only by forms of economic organization. In this view gender has been socially constructed along a continuum from identical and egalitarian to unequal and contrastive.

This evolutionary framework shaped the theories of early feminist anthropology (Morgen 1989). Although the neo-evolution of the 1960s jettisoned Spencerian political baggage, the idea that there was a direction to human cultural evolution in general – from simple to complex, from egalitarian to hierarchical – persisted. Anthropologists continued to interpret the past by reference to the diversity of then-extant societies and sought to understand the forces for movement from one evolutionary stage to the next. Among early feminists, debates centered on whether or not gender-egalitarian societies had ever existed. One stream of feminist thought argued that it did, among some early foraging and horticultural societies, but that the rise of state societies and colonialism brought about inegalitarian gender relations (Reiter 1975). Another stream argued that previously universal ways of organizing culture – women doing the child rearing, and association of women with things natural and men with things cultural – meant that full gender equality never existed, but that equality was possible under current conditions (Rosaldo and Lamphere 1974).

We can step back from the differences between Engels and Spencer to ask what they have in common. This will allow us to connect early evolutionists' concerns with forms of social organization, specifically with the ways class, race, and gender are and should be organized, to the broader stream of modernist thought, and to current analyses of its biases, assumptions, and limitations. From this perspective, Spencer and Engels shared an Enlightenment, Western view of the world. They both believed that human history was a working out of natural law and that the diversity of contemporary non-Western societies provided a window on the past by which one could develop scientific ways of predicting the future. Natural law replaced divine will as a mode of argument for both of them as it did for other 19th-century anthropologists.

Anthropology has continued to engage with this paradigm. Studies of foraging peoples have continued to be loci of covert and overt battles about "natural," "original," and possible class and gender relationships among people. Marvin Harris (1968:249) has argued that much of the early 20th-century history of anthropology was an attempt to refute Engels' view of evolution. Thus, reigning views of hunters and gatherers emphasized private property and patrilinear/patriarchal band society. From a Marxist point of view, Eleanor Leacock (1980, 1985) explicitly challenged these biases in her historical and ethnographic work on egalitarian relations among Naskapi peoples of Labrador and their transformation under the influence of fur trading and missionaries. Some early feminist anthropologists saw gender equality in accounts of foraging peoples by way of arguing that such relationships were "natural," possible, and desirable in the present. Other feminist anthropologists also focused on such groups to show that egalitarian relations had never existed, by way of arguing that patriarchy was deeply ingrained in the human condition and that it would take a great deal to change it. In opposition, Spencerian positions about the naturalness and necessity of hierarchy and patriarchy (separately and together) were also developed by a few anthropologists (Tiger 1969;

Tiger and Fox 1977), and by E. O. Wilson (1975) in establishing the field of sociobiology.

In the last 40 years there have been several waves of social Darwinist racism in popular and scientific literature. In the 1960s, Daniel Moynihan (1965) explained African American poverty as a product of a "deficient" matrifocal culture in much the same way as Edward Banfield (before he became Nixon's urban advisor) explained the poverty of southern Italians as a product of "amoral familism" (Banfield 1958). Theories of cultural deficiency were complemented by renewed theories of biological deficiency. Arthur Jensen, William Shockley, and Richard Herrnstein all advanced well-publicized theories that argued that African Americans were not as intelligent as whites. Herrnstein went further and argued that the racial and class hierarchy of the United States was a product of natural selection, with the richest and most powerful also being the best and the brightest. More recently the idea of biological racial inequality has surfaced again and been given still wider credibility in a climate of political conservatism and heightened monopolization of print and electronic media. Publicity of Charles Murray's and Richard Herrnstein's warmed-over racist interpretations of IQ in *The Bell Curve* (1994) as bold new ideas is one case in point. Notions of cultural inferiority have again become popular, for example, in the ways in which sociologist William J. Wilson's (1980, 1987) notion of a black underclass has been taken up in social science circles as well as been popularized in policy circles. Each of these efforts has had no shortage of critics (see, for example, Ladner 1973; Steinberg 1995; Crenshaw and Morrison 1992).

Anthropology has been peripheral to this debate because until very recently it has largely avoided the issue of race. Anthropological understandings that race is not a valid concept for describing human biological variability could be useful in combating the inevitable outbreaks of biological racist explanations. However, anthropologists' renewed interest has sometimes also carried an unstated assumption that if race is not biological, then it is not "real." This does not address the more prevalent forms of racism, that the cultures of peoples of color are somehow "deficient," in contrast to those of whites. It matters little in terms of outcome whether a racist theory argues that the status quo is natural by reference to genes or by reference to racially transmitted cultures. This means that anthropology needs to critique race as a biological concept and simultaneously attend to the ways in which race is culturally constructed and deployed in the United States. Doing the former without the latter is insufficient in a context where patterns of job, school, and residential segregation, policy, science, and mass media discourse all conspire to make race self-evidently real.

Case 2: Boasian Anthropology and Its Legacy Regarding Race in the United States

In the early decades of the 20th century, Spencerism had much more influence in U.S. scientific circles outside anthropology than it had within it. Universities became important sites for generating the social Darwinist racial theories that naturalized and legitimated prevailing power relations by denigrating and stigmatizing non-European peoples and working-class southern and eastern European immigrants. Racist and social Darwinist theories were key elements in claims by psychology and sociology to be professional fields. Quantifying intelligence through development of an intelligence test helped psychology to rise in status and gain federal support. Likewise, the Chicago school of sociology under Robert Park also contained a kind of anti-immigrant bias (Park and Miller 1921). Social Darwinism also had a strong institutionalized base within early anthropology, particularly at Harvard, the University of Pennsylvania, the Bureau of American Ethnology, and the New York Museum of Natural History and the Bronx Zoo. As Lee Baker and Thomas Patterson (1994), Patterson (1993), and George Stocking (1968) indicate, these institutions were part of an Anglo-Saxon gentleman's tradition of an anthropology centered around a mission to show the inequality of races, the undesirability of immigration, and the progress of white civilization.

Boasian anthropology in the United States began a tradition of anthropological critique and alternatives to this framework. Indeed, it has become commonplace to describe the rise of American anthropology under Franz Boas as a response to the social Darwinism that came to characterize the other nascent social sciences. Boas' adamant anti-evolutionism can be understood as a response to the way the evolutionary theories of his day naturalized the racism of American society. Boasian anthropology positioned itself as perhaps the only openly antiracist social science and allied anthropology solidly with movements against racism (Baker 1994a; Stocking 1968; Hyatt 1990; Boas 1963[1911]; 1948[1912]; Benedict 1934).

Boas was not a lone anthropologist, but is better seen as part of a broader Jewish–African American alliance, which as historians Hasia Diner (1977; see also Frank 1997) and David Levering Lewis (1992) note, was fighting anti-Semitism "by proxy," as Diner put it. Indeed, Boas' emphasis upon the autonomy of culture, language, and race, on cultural relativism and historical particularism needs to be understood as an effort to discredit the social Darwinism of unilinear evolution and to develop an alternative theoretical platform upon which to erect an antiracist science (Boas 1963[1911]).

The Boasian concept of culture and treatment of race became that platform. This was elaborated in three main themes which Boasians pursued to counteract racism and nativism: The first was a discussion of sophisticated kingdoms and cultures of Africa to show what African Americans were capable of before being degraded by slavery, that it was not innate ability that was lacking (Boas 1974[1906]; Herskovits 1958). The second showed that race, language, and culture varied independently, and that each was malleable, that even physical characteristics could change. This was done most forcefully in Boas' *Changes in the Bodily Form of Descendants of Immigrants*, a report for congressional commission (Boas 1948[1912]). The third was treating culture as a non-determinist concept. This was done most clearly in Benedict's (1934) notion of cultures as coherent configurations and world views chosen from the great arc of human possibilities, as an alternative to Spencerian notions of cultures as products of biologically rooted temperaments.

Boasians were not race-avoidant, and they were activist: Boas taught under-graduate courses on race and racism at Columbia; he urged Columbia to adopt a black studies curriculum to teach about African culture and history. He trained anthropologists like Herskovits, Benedict, Klineberg, Hurston, Dunham, Pow-dermaker, and Montagu who dealt with race and racism. He gave public lec-tures in New York City and wrote popular articles. He was involved in the founding conference of, and continued to work with, the National Association for the Advancement of Colored People (NAACP), and to speak out against seg-regation (Baker 1998; Harrison 1992; Hyatt 1990).

But Boas was not a radical, and he was a less than perfect antiracist. As Har-rison (1992) has suggested, he may have worked with DuBois, but he didn't publicize or cite DuBois' work, and as Hyatt (1990) suggests, he had some rather strange ideas about race and intermarriage, and wasn't sure black folks were fully equal to whites. Also, as Lee Baker (1994a, 1998) has argued, Boas really did not understand the political forces that sustained racist thinking. He was naive about dynamics of African American politics: he tried to get funding from Booker T. Washington while allied with W. E. B. DuBois. Moreover, he failed to understand why he was turned down by "the Tuskegee Machine" and why his idea for a museum of African culture was ignored by its patron, Andrew Carnegie. He didn't understand the connection between political economy and racism; for Boas racism was a product of ignorance, and not part of the fabric of U.S. institutions (Baker 1994a; Hyatt 1990; Stocking 1968).

There is an ultimate irony to Boasian anthropology's antiracist legacy. Although it played a major role in undermining the hegemony of biologically based theories of racism, it has also left anthropology in a theoretically weak position to combat the rise of culturally-based racist theories, which are the most widespread form of racist beliefs today. Boasian notions of culture were themselves underdeveloped, tending toward the realm of belief and value, with little attention to the ways in which race is institutionalized in political and eco-nomic relationships. Nor did Boasians do much in the way of analyzing con-temporary American society and culture.

The Boasian attack on racism did not challenge popular notions of nature and nurture, biology and culture as opposed and mutually exclusive. Thus, Boas understood biology, or nature (here race) as something determined by heredity. In contrast, culture, or "nurture" was interpreted as being chosen freely and without structural constraints. The current idea that nature (here race) is socially constructed and can be changed (as a phenotypical phenomenon and as a cat-egory of cultural meaning) by the same culture that constructed it was not part of the Boasian paradigm. Nor was the broader idea that nature and nurture are mutually constituted rather than mutually exclusive.

In a similar vein, Boasian celebrations of cultural diversity were part of a larger cultural relativist mission that offered an alternative to the ethnocentrism of social Darwinism. They worked with an implicitly voluntarist model of culture. Each culture was one choice among many possible along the "great arc" of culture, as Ruth Benedict put it. This "possibilist," or open-ended orienta-tion contrasted with the determinism of unilinear evolutionary thinking. As with a mutually exclusive nature/nurture model, this one had no place for the complexities of structurally constrained choices, whether those choices were constrained by ecology, political economy, or other aspects of an intercultural field. This lack greatly limited the power of Boasian analyses of race and racism.

African American anthropology and the road not taken

However, there were important African American contemporaries and colleagues whose work did all that their white counterparts did not. Not only did Boas ignore their work, but they are still excluded from the anthropological canon. Attention to the work of W. E. B. DuBois, Allison Davis, St. Clair Drake, and Horace Cayton on the political economy and culture of race and class in American society can still provide students in anthropology with a sophisticated perspective on contemporary issues of diversity and discrimination in the United States. *Deep South* (Davis et al. 1941) is an ethnography of race, class, and gender relations in a southern town, and *Black Metropolis* (Drake and Cayton 1962[1945]) is an ethnography of Chicago's African American community. Both works understand race as culturally constructed and very real. They also analyze racism as a social system rather than as aggregated ignorance. They demonstrate the economic and social stakes of white Americans in racism, and show that more than individual enlightenment is needed to change it. Both deal with the relationship of race and class as key to understanding American social structure. *Deep South* analyzes the social system as linked systems of caste and class, brought together around the enforcement of separation between white women and black men. Drake and Cayton also analyze the class diversity within the African American community and show how the racism of the larger American capitalist political economy has been the constraining context within which African Americans created the black metropolis and African American culture. Both discuss the ways in which racism is also a cultural system which manifests itself in stereotypes, symbols/rituals of subordination, and in blackness as master symbol. Emerging clearly in both works, too, is the use of coercion to maintain segregation and racism, and to keep black people subordinated. The models of society and culture these works create are much more robust than those of their white contemporaries. They are holistic in that there are clear links between political economy, institutions, beliefs, and values. They are also complex, recognizing that American society and culture has more than one culture and system of values, and that each of these is also full of contradiction. Drake and Cayton also foreshadow an important current view that African Americans are necessarily bicultural, that they have to learn the master's culture as well as master their own, and that they are thus likely to know white America better than white Americans know black America.

Anthropology's relationship to American racial policy: The Japanese American Internment during World War II

Early in 1942, President Roosevelt signed Executive Order 9066, which uprooted, dispossessed, and dispersed all Japanese and Japanese Americans living on the west coast. Some 120,000 Issei and Nissei were housed for the duration of the war in ten hastily built detention camps in inhospitable and isolated areas of the West. Peter Suzuki's (1980, 1981, 1985, 1986) work provides the fullest documentation of the significant role played by anthropologists in a program of federally employed ethnography in these camps, especially in the Community Analysis Section (CAS) of the War Relocation Authority (WRA), and to a lesser extent in the Japanese American Evacuation and Resettlement Study (JERS) housed at the University of California at Berkeley. Gordon Chang (1993) has documented Phileo Nash's efforts (and their limits) as a media analyst in the Office of War Information to counter media racism against Japanese Americans. The Internment and the anthropologists' role can be studied as part of the larger history of governmental constructions of Asians as permanent aliens. While it is common to discuss the wartime efforts of American anthropologists – especially Ruth Benedict's work on Japanese national character – in history of theory courses, a study of anthropologists' role in the Internment can shed light on the theoretical underpinnings of anthropological work and of the camp ethnographies themselves. It has become commonplace to analyze the work of British functionalists as colonial anthropologists. But a parallel argument can be made for their American contemporaries' work for the WRA and JERS. Reading Peter Suzuki, Yuchi Ichioka (1989), as well as Rosalie Wax's (1957, 1971) candid recollections of her work as a graduate student ethnographer at the Tule Lake internment center allows students to explore these questions in a complex manner.

With hindsight, it is hard to imagine that most Americans including anthropologists, who were aware that Germans and German Americans, Italians and Italian Americans were not locked up as potential traitors, would accept incarceration of Japanese and Japanese Americans. But they did, especially in the West, and apparently across the political spectrum, from the Communist Party to California's then attorney general, Earl Warren, to President Franklin D. Roosevelt. There was resistance from the American Civil Liberties Union, the Quakers, and by mid-1943, from a larger swath of liberal public opinion largely outside the western states (Chang 1993:46–48). Yet World War II was popularly perceived as a "just" war, and anthropologists were eager to contribute their expertise. They accepted the political context within which they worked, and it shaped their work in significant ways.

Many anthropologists who were committed to undoing the racism of U.S. culture seem not to have noticed that they participated in a set of institutionalized racist practices. Some, like Phileo Nash, fought the cultural manifestations of anti-Japanese racism while ignoring the institutionalized racism of the Internment itself. Nash and others spoke out against wartime racist stereotyping, but they did so by portraying Japanese as good Americans willing to assimilate and disperse if allowed to leave the camps on an individual basis. Indeed, they feared that a rise in anti-Japanese racism would work against government policies of resettling internees in the East and Midwest (Chang 1993).

Inability or unwillingness to confront the racism inherent in the institutional framework within which they worked shaped the questions ethnographers framed and the range of possible answers they proposed in three ways. First, given the cultural (as distinct from social structural) bent of American anthropology, national character studies were one way anthropologists sought to understand Japanese culture. At one extreme, Weston LaBarre's (1945) characterization of Japanese culture as compulsive and neurotic was racist. Others, most notably Ruth Benedict's *The Chrysanthemum and the Sword* (1946) were respectful and insightful (Suzuki 1985). Second, Suzuki argues that anthropologists who worked as camp ethnographers for the most part accepted the rightness of the government's mid-war policy switch toward emptying the camps and relocating internees to other parts of the United States. Consequently, they tended to interpret any behavior that worked against the way the policy was to be implemented as resistance to the policy, rather than examining the policy and its implementation. The result was a trend toward blaming-the-victim analyses. Third, although ethnographers, especially those working for the CAS, were not supposed to inform on internees, some did. Most useful here is then graduate student Rosalie Wax's candid confession of how becoming embroiled in factionalism at Tule Lake led to her informing to the FBI on someone who was subsequently stripped of his citizenship and deported to Japan. Ironically, Wax was among the very few anthropologists who were opposed to the Internment. Studying her action helps students to deal with the complexities of fieldwork and political engagement.

Suzuki (1981:40–41) argues that Marvin Opler's work provides a model of what anthropologists could have done. As the CAS analyst at Tule Lake, Opler made the political and social field within which he worked part of his analysis. He criticized the policy of segregating so-called disloyal and loyal internees, and was able to predict the factionalizing and unrest caused by government policy. In addition, by publishing in academic journals "he announced to his colleagues and his readers that, in effect, the culture patterns of these Japanese Americans were worthy of note and respect" (1981:40). However, anthropologists did not deal with the wider field of U.S. politics that produced the Internment in the first place, nor, later, of efforts by internees and the ACLU to seek legal redress and end the incarceration as unconstitutional. Raising these issues through a study of the Internment allows students to grapple with the ways implicit theoretical perspectives shape what anthropologists do and do not see, do and do not study, do and do not do, and despite as well as because of one's intent. Equally important is consciousness and analysis of the political field within which anthropologists work.

Summary

This chapter has examined the ways that anthropology's theoretical legacy has helped and hindered the discipline's participation in dealing with issues of cultural diversity in the United States. I have argued that diversity issues are being most effectively addressed in multidisciplinary conversations that are looking critically at race, ethnicity, and related core concepts of Western Enlightenment culture. Anthropological approaches to diversity often embrace these cultural concepts unconsciously even as they try to challenge racism and its cultural justifications. I reexamined three areas of anthropological theory – theories of cultural evolution, Boasian analyses of race, and anthropologists' involvement in the World War II Internment of Japanese Americans – to show how Enlightenment assumptions in anthropology's established theoretical traditions undercut the discipline's effectiveness in analyzing race, racism, and cultural diversity in today's world.

Acknowledgments

I would like to thank Thomas Patterson and Ida Susser for their helpful comments, and Mary Hardy for help in preparing the bibliography.

REFERENCES CITED

Abramovitz, Mimi
　1988　*Regulating the Lives of Women: Social Welfare Policy from Colonial Times to the Present.* Boston, MA: South End Press.
Almaguer, Tomas
　1994　*Racial Fault Lines: The Historical Origins of White Supremacy in California.* Berkeley: University of California Press.
Baker, Lee D.
　1994a　The Location of Franz Boas within the African-American Struggle. *Critique of Anthropology* 14(2):199–217.
　1994b　Moving the History of Anthropology from the Memorial to the Contextual: The Case of Lewis E. King. Paper presented at the Annual Meetings of the American Ethnological Society, April 13, Santa Monica, CA.
　1998　*From Savage to Negro: Anthropology and the Construction of Race, 1896–1954.* Berkeley: University of California Press.
Baker, Lee D., and Thomas C. Patterson
　1994　Race, Racism, and the History of U.S. Anthropology. *Transforming Anthropology* 5(1–2):1–7.
Banfield, Edward
　1958　*The Moral Basis of a Backward Society.* With the assistance of Laura Fasano Banfield. Glencoe, IL: Free Press.
Benedict, Ruth
　1934　*Patterns of Culture.* New York: Houghton and Mifflin.
　1946　*The Chrysanthemum and the Sword: Patterns of Japanese Culture.* Boston, MA: Houghton and Mifflin.
Bennett, Lerone
　1970　The Making of Black America. *Ebony*, August: 71–77.
Berube, Allan
　1990　*Coming Out under Fire: The History of Gay Men and Women in World War Two.* New York: Free Press.
Blauner, Robert
　1991　Racism, Race, and Ethnicity. Paper for thematic session "Reexamining the Commonly Used Concepts in Race/Ethnic Relations," Annual meetings of the American Association, August.
Boas, Franz
　1974[1906]　The Outlook for the American Negro. In *The Shaping of American Anthropology, 1883–1911: A Franz Boas Reader.* G. W. Stocking, ed. Pp. 310–316. Chicago: University of Chicago Press.

1963[1911]   *The Mind of Primitive Man.* Revised edition. New York: Collier Books.
1948[1912]   Changes in the Bodily Form of Descendants of Immigrants. In *Race, Language and Culture.* Pp. 60–75. New York: Macmillan.
Boris, Eileen, and Peter Winthrop Bardaglio
    1991   Gender, Race, and Class: The Impact of the State on the Family and the Economy, 1790–1945. In *Families and Work.* Naomi Gerstel and Harriet Gross, eds. Pp. 132–151. Philadelphia: Temple University Press.
Brodkin, Karen
    1999   *How Jews Became White Folks and What That Says about Race in America.* New Brunswick, NJ: Rutgers University Press.
Chang, Gordon H.
    1993   "Superman Is about to Visit the Relocation Centers" and the Limits of Wartime Liberalism. *Amerasia Journal Commemorative Issue: Japanese American Internment Fiftieth Anniversary* 19(1):37–60.
Chauncey, George
    1995   Gay New York. New York: Basic Books.
Crenshaw, Kimberle, and Toni Morrison, eds.
    1992   *Race-ing Justice, En-gendering Power: Essays on Anita Hill, Clarence Thomas and the Construction of Social Reality.* New York: Pantheon Books.
Davis, Allison, Burleigh Gardner, and Mary R. Gardner
    1941   *Deep South: A Social Anthropological Study of Caste and Class.* Chicago: University of Chicago Press.
D'Emilio, John, and Estelle B. Freedman
    1988   *Intimate Matters: A Social History of Sexuality in America.* New York: Harper and Row.
Diner, Hasia
    1977   *In the Almost Promised Land: American Jews and Blacks, 1915–1935.* Westport, CT: Greenwood Press.
Drake, St. Clair, and Horace R. Cayton
    1962[1945]   *Black Metropolis: A Study of Negro Life in a Northern City.* New York: Harper and Row.
DuBois, W. E. B.
    1935   *Black Reconstruction in America, 1860–1880.* New York: Harcourt, Brace.
Engels, Frederick
    1972   *The Origin of the Family: Private Property and the State.* E. B. Leacock, ed. New York: International Publishers.
Fields, Barbara Jeanne
    1982   Ideology and Race in American History. In *Region, Race, and Reconstruction: Essays in Honor of C. Vann Woodward.* J. M. Koussar and J. M. Mcpherson, eds. Pp. 143–177. New York: Oxford University Press.
    1990   Slavery, Race and Ideology in the United States of America. *New Left Review* 181:95–118.
Frank, Gelya
    1997   Jews, Multiculturalism and Boasian Anthropology: Ambiguous Whites and the Founding of an Anti-Racist Science. *American Anthropologist* 99(4):731–745.
Frankenberg, Ruth
    1993   *White Women, Race Matters: The Social Construction of Whiteness.* Minneapolis: University of Minnesota Press.
Gilroy, Paul
    1991   *"There Ain't No Black in the Union Jack": The Cultural Politics of Race and Nation.* Chicago: University of Chicago Press.

Glenn, Evelyn Nakano
  1985   Racial Ethnic Women's Labor. *Review of Radical Political Economics*
    17(3):86–108.
  1994   Social Constructions of Mothering: A Thematic Introduction. In *Mothering:*
    Ideology, Experience and Agency. Evelyn Nakano Glenn, Grace Chang, and Linda
    Rennie Forcey, eds. Pp. 1–29. New York: Routledge.
Gordon, Linda
  1994   *Pitied but not Entitled: Single Mothers and the History of Welfare, 1890–1935*.
    New York: Free Press.
Green, Venus
  1995   Race and Technology: African American Women in the Bell System,
    1945–1980. Supplement to *Technology and Culture* 36(2):S101–S143.
Gregory, Steven, and Roger Sanjek, eds.
  1994   *Race*. New Brunswick, NJ: Rutgers University Press.
Haney Lopez, Gerald
  1996   *White by Law: The Legal Construction of Race*. New York: New York Uni-
    versity Press.
Harris, Marvin
  1968   *The Rise of Anthropological Theory*. New York: Columbia University Press.
Harrison, Faye V.
  1992   The DuBoisian Legacy in Anthropology. *Critique of Anthropology* 12(3):
    239–260.
Herskovits, Melville J.
  1958   *The Myth of the Negro Past*. Boston, MA: Beacon Press.
Hyatt, Marshall
  1990   *Franz Boas: Social Activist*. Westport, CT: Greenwood Press.
Ichioka, Yuchi, ed.
  1989   *Views from Within: The Japanese Evacuation and Resettlement Study*.
    Los Angeles: Asian American Studies Center, University of California, Los Angeles.
Ignatiev, Noel
  1995   *How the Irish Became White*. Cambridge, MA: Harvard University Press.
Katz, Jonathan
  1990   The Invention of Heterosexuality. *Socialist Review* 90(1):7–34.
Kennedy, Elizabeth L., and Madelyn Davis
  1993   *Boots of Leather, Slippers of Gold*. New York: Routledge.
Kessler-Harris, Alice
  1982   *Out to Work*. New York: Oxford University Press.
  1990   *A Woman's Wage: Historical Meanings and Social Consequences*. Lexington:
    University Press of Kentucky.
LaBarre, Weston
  1945   Some Observations on Character Structure in the Orient: The Japanese.
    Psychiatry 8:319–342.
Ladner, Joyce
  1973   *The Death of White Sociology*. New York: Random House.
Leacock, Eleanor B.
  1980   Montagnais Women and the Jesuit Program for Colonization. In *Women and*
    Colonialism: Anthropological Perspectives. Mona Etienne and Eleanor Leacock,
    eds. Pp. 25–42. New York: Praeger.
  1985   *Myths of Male Dominance*. New York: Monthly Review Press.
Lewin, Ellen
  1985   By Design: Reproductive Strategies and the Meaning of Motherhood. In *The*

Sexual Politics of Reproduction. H. Homans, ed. Pp. 123–138. London: Gower Press.

1993 *Lesbian Mothers: Accounts of Gender in American Culture.* Ithaca, NY: Cornell University Press.

Lewis, David Levering
1992 Parallels and Divergences: Assimilationist Strategies of Afro-American and Jewish Elites from 1910 to the Early 1930s. In *Bridges and Boundaries: African Americans and American Jews.* J. Salzman, with Adina Back and Gretchen Sorin, eds. Pp. 17–35. New York: George Braziller.

Mead, Margaret
1935 *Sex and Temperament in Three Primitive Societies.* New York: William Morrow.

Medina, Laurie
1999 A Class "Politics of Difference": Ethnic Mobilization among Workers in Belize. *Transforming Anthropology* 7(2):20–34.

Mink, Gwendolyn
1995 *The Wages of Motherhood: Inequality in the Welfare State, 1917–1942.* Ithaca, NY: Cornell University Press.

Mohanty, Chandra Talpade, Ann Russo, and Lourdes Torres, eds.
1991 *Third World Women and the Politics of Feminism.* Bloomington: Indiana University Press.

Morgen, Sandra, ed.
1989 *Gender and Anthropology: Critical Reviews for Research and Teaching.* Washington, DC: American Anthropological Association.

Morrison, Toni
1990 *Playing in the Dark: Whiteness and the Literary Imagination.* New York: Vintage.
1993 On the Backs of Blacks. *Time* 142(21):57.

Moynihan, Daniel P.
1965 *The Negro Family: The Case for National Action.* Washington, DC: U.S. Government Printing Office.

Mullings, Leith
1984 Ethnicity and Stratification in the Urban United States. In *Racism and the Denial of Human Rights: Beyond Ethnicity.* J. Berlowitz and R. S. Edari, eds. Pp. 21–38. Minneapolis, MN: MEP Publications.

Murray, Charles, and Richard J. Herrnstein
1994 *The Bell Curve: Intelligence and Class Structure in American Life.* New York: Free Press.

Naples, Nancy
1997 The "New Consensus" on the Gendered "Social Contract": The 1987–1988 U.S. Congressional Hearings on Welfare Reform. *Signs* 22(4):907–946.

Newton, Esther
1972 *Mother Camp: Female Impersonators in America.* Englewood Cliffs, NJ: Prentice-Hall.

Omi, Michael, and Howard Winant
1994 *Racial Formation in the United States from the 1960s to the 1990s.* New York: Routledge.

Park, Robert E., and Herbert A. Miller
1921 *Old World Traits Transplanted.* New York: Harper and Brothers.

Patterson, Thomas C.
1993 *Archaeology: The Historical Development of Civilization.* 2nd edition. Englewood Cliffs: Prentice Hall.

1995   *Toward a Social History of Archaeology in the United States.* Fort Worth, TX: Harcourt Brace.
1997   *Inventing Western Civilization.* New York: Monthly Review Press.
Reiter, Rayna R., ed.
1975   *Toward an Anthropology of Women.* New York: Monthly Review Press.
Roediger, David
1991   *The Wages of Whiteness: Race and the Making of the American Working Class.* London: Verso.
Rosaldo, Michelle Zimbalist, and Louise Lamphere, eds.
1974   *Woman, Culture, and Society.* Stanford: Stanford University Press.
Rose, Nancy
1995   *Workfare or Fair Work: Women, Welfare and Government Work Programs.* New Brunswick, NJ: Rutgers University Press.
Rubin, Gayle
1975   Traffic in Women: Notes on the "Political Economy" of Sex. In Reiter, ed., pp. 157–210.
Saxton, Alexander
1990   *The Rise and Fall of the White Republic: Class Politics and Mass Culture in Nineteenth Century America.* London: Verso.
Smedley, Audrey
1993   *Race in North America: Origin and Evolution of a Worldview.* Boulder, CO: Westview Press.
Spencer, Herbert
1899   *The Principles of Sociology.* 3rd edition. New York: D. Appleton.
Steinberg, Stephen
1995   *Turning Back: The Retreat from Racial Justice in American Thought and Policy.* Boston, MA: Beacon Press.
Stocking, George W., Jr.
1968   The Scientific Reaction against Cultural Anthropology, 1917–1920. In *Race, Culture and Evolution,* by George W. Stocking, Jr. Pp. 270–307. New York: Free Press.
Stoler, Ann
1989   Making Empire Respectable. *American Ethnologist* 16(4):634–652.
Suzuki, Peter T.
1980   A Retrospective Analysis of a Wartime "National Character" Study. *Dialectical Anthropology* 5:33–46.
1981   Anthropologists in the Wartime Camps for Japanese Americans: A Documentary Study. *Dialectical Anthropology* 6:23–60.
1985   Ruth Benedict, Robert Hashima and *The Chrysanthemum and the Sword. Rikka* 13(1):3–14.
1986   The University of California Japanese Evacuation and Resettlement Study: A Prolegomenon. *Dialectical Anthropology* 10(3–4):189–213.
Tiger, L.
1969   *Men in Groups.* London: Secker and Warburg.
Tiger, L., and R. Fox
1977   *The Imperial Animal.* London: Secker and Warburg.
Vincent, Joan
1974   Brief Communications: The Structuring of Ethnicity. *Human Organization* 33(4):375–379.
Wax, Rosalie
1957   Twelve Years Later: An Analysis of Fieldwork. *American Journal of Sociology* 63(2):133–142.

1971   *Doing Fieldwork: Warnings and Advice*. Chicago: University of Chicago Press.
Weston, Kath
   1991   *Families We Choose: Lesbians, Gays, Kinship*. New York: Columbia University Press.
Williams, Brackette
   1989   A Class Act: Anthropology and the Race to Nation across Ethnic Terrain. *Annual Review of Anthropology* 18:401–444.
   1996   Introduction. In *Women out of Place: The Gender of Agency and the Race of Nationality*. B. F. Williams, ed. Pp. 1–33. New York: Routledge.
Williams, Eric
   1944   *Capitalism and Slavery*. New York: Russell and Russell.
Wilson, E. O.
   1975   *Sociobiology: The New Synthesis*. Cambridge, MA: Harvard University Press.
Wilson, William Julius
   1980   *The Declining Significance of Race: Blacks and Changing Institutions*. Chicago: University of Chicago Press.
   1987   *The Truly Disadvantaged: The Inner City, the Underclass, and Public Policy*. Chicago: University of Chicago Press.

Part VI

Teaching Diversity

22

Building Bridges and Empowerment: Anthropological Contributions to Diversity and Educational Practices

Steven F. Arvizu

Anthropologists live and breathe diversity as they study culture, a major concept inherent to our discipline. If anthropology is what anthropologists do, then using some of our work involving diversity could be helpful to new students of anthropology as well as to educators struggling with the challenges of teaching and learning about diversity.

This introductory chapter, which consists of four segments, presents material on the anthropological contributions to futuristic classroom practices, and explores significant elements of culture and other ideas related to diversity and educational futures. The first segment presents an introduction on social issues and definition of terms; the second offers a historical overview of anthropological contributions to education; the third describes conceptual and methodological contributions to diversity efforts in education by providing some specific examples of the use of life history and other ethnographic fieldwork techniques; and the fourth discusses cross-cultural leadership, the creation of special projects, and the operationalizing of pluralism in educational settings.

Anthropology and Social Issues

There are some obvious examples of anthropologists' involvement in major issues in our society, worth mentioning as an introduction to the idea of our contributing to consideration of diversity and change. Early discussions of evolution and debates on race and intelligence benefited from empirical anthropological research illustrating the principle of within-group differences in intellectual capacity being greater than differences between groups. Early studies of indigenous populations described their language and cultural behavior based on fieldwork and insider (emic) forms of analysis, providing a basic literature for protection of endangered communities and legal advocacy for their land, water, and natural resource rights. Qualitative ethnographic research on educational challenges such as desegregation, bilingual education, new-arrival immigrant integration and gender inequities has enriched the educational discourse for improving pedagogy, updating teacher education and educational practice, building congruence between schools and communities, and understanding different learning and motivational styles among diverse learners. Anthropological studies of delivery systems for health and human services among diverse client populations have been used to minimize conflicts and to improve relevance and effectiveness in the cross-cultural delivery of services.

In more recent decades American anthropologists have used anthropology to "study up," to understand and explain power hierarchies, elites and corporate structures and their impact on those with less power. In addition, as minority group members in our society have become anthropologists, we have seen an interesting development of "insider" research where the "studied" have become the "studiers" challenging previous assumptions, methodologies, and content generated from an outsider's perspective. Similarly, recent critical models of cultural analysis have attempted to deconstruct realities influenced by the background and biases of the researcher and writer. As our society has struggled with diversity, anthropologists have been in the midst of these challenging changes, testing our conceptual tools and methods by applying them to better understand the nature and dynamics of diversity among human beings.

Definitions

For the purposes of this chapter it is important to define such key terms as culture, diversity, anthropology, ethnography, cross-cultural literacy, cross-cultural leadership, and pluralism. They are either so common that they have multiple meanings, or are so specific to an anthropological perspective that they may not be used in traditional educational literature.

Culture is what guides people in their thinking, feeling, and acting, and serves as an emotional road map or plan of action in their struggle for survival. Culture is a state of being – a process rather than a person, place, or thing; a verb rather than a noun. Because of the culture-creating capacity of people through the exercise of free will, and because of the complicated influences of cultural transmission and transformation across generations, cultural change is an ever-present reality for all groups, whether through or without contact with other groups. Culture gives meaning to people's lives and is symbolically represented through language and interaction.

Diversity is a term whose meaning varies with the background, concerns, theoretical framework, and context in which it is discussed. For example, in a political and public policy sense, diversity has been interpreted by former Secretary of Education Lamar Alexander as relating to quotas and affirmative action in the accreditation controversy involving the Middle Atlantic States Accreditation Association (*Chronicle of Higher Education* 1991).[1] An anthropological approach to diversity focuses upon culture and includes a cross-cultural perspective. For the purposes of this chapter, it means recognition of variation among people related to their cultural heritages, racial and ethnic identities, and gender and class experiences. The concept communicates the need to understand universals and differences in the human species, as well as the translation of understanding into behavior respectful of people and their many forms of interaction. Diversity is relevant to a cultural approach to learning in that learning and motivational styles and cross-cultural pedagogical strategies assume attention to diversity in learner populations and pluralistic learning outcomes.

Anthropology, the scientific study of peoples and cultures, is a discipline that explores human diversity on a worldwide basis in historical, contemporary, and futuristic contexts through its major branches, which include archaeology, linguistics, physical anthropology, and cultural anthropology. As anthropology has been applied to the discovery of alternative sources of knowledge and to the explanation of commonalities and differences among cultural groups, such subfields as medical, psychological, political, and educational anthropology have developed. An anthropological approach encompasses attention to culture, a comparative perspective that enables the understanding of particular groups in the context of all human groups, a holistic orientation, the use of cultural relativity to avoid prejudgment of groups, and the use of fieldwork and ethnography methodologies that require long-term contact and cultural description and analysis.

Ethnography is the process of systematic inquiry to discover, describe, and analyze a culture or group of cultures, and is the major method used by anthropologists in conducting fieldwork. Ethnography involves gaining access to and having long-term, continuous contact with people, and using such techniques as participant observation, interviewing, event and network analysis, life history, and projective and other qualitative means for collecting and analyzing data. Ethnography, done through an anthropological approach, centers on the human and interactive element in research with attention to culture, comparative perspective, insider views, and the balance between the independent pursuit of truth and accountability to those studied. Ethnography is a method that distinguishes anthropologists from other behavioral scientists and from most educational researchers (Wolcott 1976).

Cross-cultural literacy (Saravia-Shore and Arvizu 1992) is the use of an anthropological approach to develop diversity and pluralism and to improve our ability to adapt, survive, and relate to one another in a respectful and fulfilling manner. It includes understanding critical issues that involve diverse cultural groups in a holistic context, and encompasses the recognition of cultural differences in learning populations, the integration of new arrivals into our schools and society, and the teaching of American cultural heritage(s). It embraces the development of a cross-cultural perspective among teachers, students, and adults in the home environment, and it enables people to connect and transcend cultures in study and action.

Cross-cultural leadership is leadership characterized by skill, art, and influence in cross-cultural problem solving and pluralistic community building.

Pluralism is the consideration of more than one way of life in the conceptualization and operation of curricula, programs, policies, and institutions of society such as schools, religious, political, and governmental entities. Pluralism is also a concept that organizes reform efforts in education to integrate equity with quality in learning environments (Saravia-Shore and Arvizu 1992).

Historical Overview

From its inception, anthropology has dealt with the description and explanation of cultural similarities and differences through different theoretical schools of inquiry. The historical particularists, under the leadership of Franz Boas, developed the notion of cultural relativity and were meticulous in advocating fieldwork, the learning and describing of each language and culture in the context of its own history and sense of continuity. Many of these investigations involved the study of socialization (teaching/learning of societal knowledge and proficiency) and enculturation (teaching/learning of knowledge and proficiency of a particular cultural community) at work informally within these societies, and some described the various means by which teaching occurred between generations in nonschooling contexts. For example, Whiting and Child (1953) investigated the cultural influences of socialization in cross-cultural childrearing studies, and Margaret Mead (1928, 1935) studied cultural differences in enculturation in American Samoa and other non-Western societies. The culture area and culture and personality theorists studied cultural transmission, borrowing, and diffusion as means of understanding acculturation (culture change) and as typical or modal developmental processes for people within cultural communities and cultural contact situations in the development of personality and identity. Many life histories and autobiographies of American Indian leaders/survivors typify an era (1920–50) commonly referred to as salvage anthropology, where endangered and disappearing cultures were reconstructed and measured through qualitative presentation of the lives of key informants. These later anthropological studies gave great emphasis to understanding the role of schooling as a means of modernizing indigenous populations, as well as a means of understanding missionary and trade influences on the shifts in values and behavior of people. Functional and structural theorists attempted to study small portions of daily life and behaviors to infer the nature of culture and the meaningful relationships among people, for example, the role and function of schools in integrating new arrivals into the United States mainstream. Symbolic anthropologists studied people's interactions in ceremonies and activities analyzing symbols, worlds of objects, and the interpretation of perceptions and meanings.

Educational anthropology is a field of specialization that has evolved over the past 50 years, even though attention to acquisition of language and culture through formal and informal learning has historically been a part of traditional anthropological studies. Educational anthropology grew in popularity and gained attention in academia in the mid-1950s through conferences organized and chaired by Dr. George Spindler of Stanford University. These resulted in several major books explaining the relationship between anthropology and education. Over the next several decades the series Case Studies in Anthropology and Education was published by Holt, Rinehart, and Winston, providing simple ethnographies that addressed cultural transmission and formal and informal learning in different cultures. Several key universities (Stanford, Columbia, Pittsburgh, Florida) concurrently developed doctoral programs in educational anthropology and many others integrated educational anthropology into graduate programs in education.

The development of the Council on Anthropology and Education (CAE), an affiliate organization of the American Anthropology Association (AAA) since the early 1960s, serves as a milestone in the organization of anthropological efforts in education. Anthropologists and educators aggressively created an active committee structure within this organization to apply anthropology to education.

The following summary gives some key examples of development and applications of anthropology to education over several decades and demonstrates the variety of activity among educational anthropologists in the CAE.

The Kamehameha Project in Hawaii serves as a classic example of several decades of applied research being used to impact educational reform. Hawaiian children were studied out of school in home settings to discover learning styles and to engineer culturally relevant classroom lessons. Educational practices derived from this research resulted in improved attendance, engagement in learning, and academic achievement (Gallimore et al. 1974). The Mexican-American Education Project (MAEP) and the Cross-Cultural Resource Center (CCRC) at California State University (CSU), Sacramento, similarly integrated anthropology into teacher training and technical assistance efforts in the western United States and Micronesia. The MAEP was a large multiple-year fellowship program that trained approximately 200 educators on how to use anthropology to improve linkages between schools and the Mexican American community, how to design culturally relevant curricula and programs, and how to change the culture of schools (Arvizu 1974). Jules Henry's (1960) "Cross-Cultural Outline of Education" provides a listing of learning modalities in different cultures around the world, illustrating by comparison how learning approaches in the United States are limited. John Gumperz and Dell Hymes (1964) brought the use of ethnographic methods for the study of languages and communication processes to the attention of sociolinguists and education researchers with their article on "The Ethnography of Communication." Henry Wolcott did several studies on teachers and administrators, including a classic ethnography entitled *The Man in the Principal's Office* (1973). To illustrate the power of ethnographic tools in qualitative cultural studies of schools and communities, John Ogbu's (1974) very influential case study, *The Next Generation*, analyzed the structural problems between schools and minority communities suggesting a social and structural framework for explaining differential achievement among minority students. Douglas Foley's (1977) *From Peones to Politicos* is an ethnography of educational and political change in South Texas that uses qualitative interviews, participant observation, and historical reconstruction to explain insider and outsider views of cultural and power shifts in schools, city government, and regional political structures.

Methodological Contributions to Educational Practice

To understand the future potential of anthropology to impact educational practice, it is important to state briefly its historical role in educational research methodology and its contributions to pedagogy and training.

The contributions of anthropology to educational reform efforts have dealt with language and communication, socialization and social interaction, and cooperation and conflict between and among cultural groups. These contributions have come from a wide variety of theoretical orientations over the 20th century, primarily through the use of the ethnographic method. One particular technique in traditional anthropological studies – life history technique – is just beginning to be used as a research and training tool in education. While anthropology has been used to study schooling, there are also several areas where contributions from anthropological literature have been applied to impact the quality and nature of educational practice. Anthropological literature, for example, has impacted the content of the curriculum in history and the social sciences, and also has influenced the development of ethnopedagogical practices in learning contexts. Moreover, it has been used in staff development and training efforts to improve educational practices among diverse learner populations and to improve parental involvement in education.

Life history in educational anthropology research

In this segment, ethnography is discussed as a method of discovery, as well as in terms of its fieldwork techniques, particularly life history, for didactic and pedagogical application in the development of classroom practices and educational programs. Life history technique is an important tool for understanding educational problems. Even though life history was not used as a research or pedagogical technique in major early works in educational anthropology, it is beginning to be used more frequently in the movement to strengthen qualitative research and evaluation, and in applied education anthropology. In this context, some examples are presented of strategic use of life history technique in school-related areas such as research and evaluation, teacher training, curriculum, staff development, parent participation, and community involvement in schools, together with the development of cross-cultural competencies among counselors and special educators, and in the preparation of mentors from the private sector who work with dropouts.

Strategic uses of life history

For this author, life history has been the most concrete technique for enabling educators to learn about themselves and others culturally. During the past 18 years, he has had many occasions to use life history technique in the conduct of his work as an educational anthropologist. The examples that follow illustrate the value and, in some instances, the strategic use of this particular technique where it is almost uniquely suited for application. Life history also has been used in research and evaluation, in teacher training, in curriculum development, and in the development of cross-cultural understanding and competencies in conflict situations. Life history has proved invaluable in the process both of teaching anthropology and of applying anthropological tools to problem solving in educational settings.

It is common for educational anthropologists to parallel the training of anthropologists in the training of educators. One reason for this is the similarities in the processes of learning a language and a culture different from one's own. Another is the knowledge that learning about others and learning about self are interrelated. In fact, becoming conscious of culture in one's self is important to becoming conscious of culture at work in others. Thus, overcoming ethnocentrism (the belief that one's own culture is superior to others') and the development of a culturally relative perspective are complicated processes that involve self-discovery and the study of others, the use of an insider and an outsider frame of analysis, and an appreciation of multiple cultural realities in the world.

Life history can be used as a starting point to get people to begin introspection and presentation of self in cultural terms, and as a means of getting a diverse group of educators to get to know one another's values and way of life. This author has used life history to show teachers how they can model disclosure of cultural information about self with students. Life history also has been used to show teachers how they can use students, adults, and themselves as relatively low-cost learning resources in the classroom.

At CSU Sacramento, life history was used as a technique in the Mexican-American Education Project (MAEP), in the Cross-Cultural Resource Center, and in a variety of training and educational projects. The MAEP trained approximately 200 educators at the B.A. and M.A. levels in cross-cultural education and the use of anthropological theory and methods to solve educational problems involving minority learners. Life history and fieldwork experience were invaluable to individual development of participants and in the development of cross-cultural competencies. In fact, the live-in experiment was cited repeatedly over a five-year period as one of the most significant learning experiences of the students (Valencia 1972). The MAEP fieldwork experience often used life history and ethnographic journal techniques to develop cultural self-analysis, as well as a cross-cultural perspective among trainees. Many of the graduates of this project became leaders in bilingual/cross-cultural education contexts as project directors, principals and superintendents, teacher trainers, and curriculum developers.

Ethnographic films were also developed to facilitate cross-cultural teacher training. *Demystifying Culture* is a film that introduces conceptual tools for studying culture to non-anthropology audiences. *Dia de los Muertos, Estilo Chicano* gives an insider (emic) view of how and why Chicanos in the Sacramento community celebrate a Mexican holiday, modifying the celebration for their own purposes as a means of community building among different age groups. The film *Kamadipaw: Panapean Feasting* reconstructs and preserves community feasts in Micronesian islands where a community struggles to protect itself from outside influences while also borrowing from the outside to modernize. *Alejandra's Story: Life History Technique* shows how Hispanic parents can be a powerful hidden resource in the education of their children.

Alejandra's life history is collected and told on film in her own words through simple use of strategic interview and life history technique. All of these films are available through the Cross-Cultural Resource Center in Sacramento or through the author at Oxnard College.

In a workshop in Palau (now the Nation of Belau), 75 elders, parents, and educators went through two weeks of training in cross-cultural problem solving. The traditional leaders were very excited about the use of life history technique, about the telling of their stories of the past, about struggles involving competing values, and about developing a relevant curriculum for Palauan students consistent with the goals of their nation and schools. They collected group life histories and, with translation and assistance, developed interesting learning units subsequently integrated into learning materials.

Similar experiences occurred in summer institutes at the University of Guam, in Ponape, the Marshall Islands, and other places when a variety of cultural communities were interested in cultural relevance in their schools. Workshops presented anthropological theory, ethnographic method, and fieldwork techniques in direct application to program development, staff training, curriculum, and evaluation efforts, and to build stronger parental involvement and home–school linkages. In fact, in Hawaii, at the Pacific Leadership Institute at Kamehameha School, life history technique was used as a means of conducting program evaluations, analyzing economic and educational development, increasing parent participation and community involvement, and coordinating staff development among leadership teams from throughout the American Flag Territories among Samoan, Chamoro, Marshalese, Trukese, Ponean, Yapese, and Palauan, and Southeast Asian reference groups.

Through the Cross-Cultural Resource Center, Micronesian, Polynesian, and Native American personnel were trained to develop, direct, and evaluate their own educational programs. Over a ten-year period, between 1975 and 1985, students obtained master's degrees, as well as experience in applied educational anthropology, to mount major efforts in cross-cultural education resulting in the creation of multiple-year projects and in a shift in administrative leadership from outside to inside control. These indigenous graduates became leaders and CEOs for their nation states' educational systems.

More recently, in Bakersfield, California, life history has been used in multiple ways: first, in the training of special-education graduate students to discover sociolinguistic and cultural contexts for working with exceptional learners; second, in preparing graduate students in counseling for the Marriage and Family Counseling Certificate sequence by teaching them cross-cultural values and mores; and third, in the use of life history technique with potential high-school dropouts and private-sector mentors to enable them to learn about one another in cross-cultural mentoring situations. In addition, it has been used to prepare students in service-based learning to work in cross-cultural settings. This program, the Career Beginnings Project, funded by the MacArthur Foundation, also uses Arnold Van Gennep's framework of rites of passage to help students to transcend conceptually the world of family, school, and work in graduating from high school and going on to college. The service-based learning course at CSU Monterey Bay was part of a required learning experience for all students.

The American Humanics project at Oxnard College also uses anthropological techniques.

In this author's research on educational change, comparative life histories of activists are used as a means of explaining the process and cultural dynamics of innovation and problem solving in educational and community settings (Arvizu 1992). The psychocultural adaptation strategies of these individuals and, in particular, their explanation of how they overcame discrimination and became committed to working for educational change would not have been possible without the use of life history technique. Life history was also useful in related research on exemplary bilingual educational programs in Parlier, California, and Milwaukee, Wisconsin, in a comparative study of schools and communities (Arvizu 1992).

Cross-Cultural Leadership

For the purposes of this chapter, cross-cultural leadership is defined as action influencing others to spread cross-cultural understanding, behavior respectful of cultural diversity, and relevant cultural change in environments and organizations. A cross-cultural leader is defined as one who is knowledgeable and comfortable with self, who clearly identifies with a particular cultural community, and who relates well with others from the same and other cultural communities. A cross-cultural leader is also conscious of cultural, sociopolitical, and structural variables and relationships, as well as being proficient in processes of change.

Cross-cultural leadership is a valuable asset to our future because it provides an understanding of cultural change from within and across cultural communities. It also assists in the development of better means of communicating in a world complicated by miscommunication due to people's relative inability to cope with multilingualism, multiculturalism and multiple identity.

Effective cross-cultural leaders seem to evince the courage to disagree with their own ethnic groups, as well as with powerful decision makers within universities and schools, in support of a greater principle. Cross-cultural leaders also work at earning the respect of others by dealing with complex, controversial situations day after day. They exhibit special sensitivities, abilities, and strengths in critical conflict situations and special events. Reputations and past achievement are not enough to sustain long-term leadership. Rather, working through others and continuing to perform effectively seem necessary for sustained leadership. Cross-cultural leaders strategically use support systems that ensure continuity of their efforts, and build "communities-of-interest."

Implications for Future Theory and Classroom Practice

Anthropological concepts can contribute to an important framework for diversity, for understanding the dynamics of the classroom and especially for reform of classroom practices to accommodate diverse learners. Other theories also will develop from the study of practice settings, which means that anthropologists and educational anthropologists, as well as educational researchers, by using anthropological approaches are in a strategic position to explore the qualitative explanation of the "schooling" experience.

Anthropology and ethnographic method, particularly life history technique, can contribute to a better understanding of what occurs in schools and communities, and what works and why. Cross-cultural leadership that evolves from ethnography of successful attempts to deal with communication, integration, and cooperation across cultures probably will become a more visible tool and a competency to impact classroom practices in the future.

Ethnography and ethnographic techniques such as life history technique serve as a major available alternative for researchers and practitioners in studying schools and attempting reforms. As a qualitative method in the science of the study of people, ethnography has already contributed an invaluable understanding both of the social structure of United States society and United States schools, and of the many varied educational contexts at work in a multiple and heterogeneous society. Ogbu's (1974) work in Stockton contributed greatly to the understanding of school failure among minority students in settings where the world outside of school communicates a powerful message of stratification on issues of diversity. In Ogbu's world the smart students figure it out early and drop out of a system that they perceive is not working in their immediate and long-term interests. But he discovered these realities through ethnography, long-term fieldwork, and continuous contact with the people central to the problem. If he had used life history technique with successful and non-successful students, even in an environment structured by lack of opportunity, he might also have uncovered the key to educational reform, a problem with which he and his protégés struggle even today. They can say what is wrong from their theoretical perspective, but they cannot guide the rest of us through the process of how to fix it. A power struggle is implied as underlying Ogbu's structural world of stratification, but he does not deal with identity or power in this power struggle nor in the resolution of related problems.

Ethnography plays an absolutely essential role in the work of the social-context-of-learning theorists; it also helps them discover experimental designs for the improvement of schools. Witness the Kamehameha Project in Hawaii, now past its third decade in experimenting with the study of Hawaiian children at home to create more harmonious learning and pedagogical practices in the non-Hawaiian classroom. The project has gathered a monumental body of data which show that schools can transmit and transform culture if they are smarter about how they communicate, integrate, and cooperate. Life history technique could enhance the evaluation of the project by giving in-depth insider information on the impact of such approaches as those used in the project. In addition, it could have given great insight into the quality of cross-cultural leadership needed to build bridges between the home and school. But here again, these theorists have neglected the role of identity in the behavior of students, teachers, and parents and the power dynamics of educational decision making with regard to language, culture, and school organization.

Ethnography of innovative pedagogy will probably be our most effective means of understanding successful experimentation, and an essential step in the diffusion of innovation to broader audiences, especially through qualitative study of experiments and strategic life histories. New practices have probably already been developed, created by decades of experimentation in Headstart, compensatory education, migrant education, and bilingual education that have not been carefully documented by qualitative methodology or by individually based technologies. Perhaps in the future?

Future practices in education will be greatly impacted by either the presence or absence of cross-cultural leadership, especially in areas of empowerment of historically underrepresented and disenfranchised groups. Without cross-cultural leadership factionalism, separation, and inter-ethnic conflict will increase. With cross-cultural leadership, within-group and between-group cooperation will increase. However, cross-cultural leadership will not develop efficiently without clear sustained support from diverse constituencies, especially from power elites who through enlightened self-interest will see the necessity of cross-cultural leadership for long-term stability of established world systems. In some instances, the empowerment of the underclass will threaten those in power or those motivated by upward mobility, and those threatened will resist such empowerment efforts.

Education and Empowerment

Education is one ideal mechanism for opening opportunity to the "have-nots" in United States society. However, opportunities for low-income and powerless groups are currently affected by such conditions as: fewer resources; personnel quality; overcrowdedness; inadequate curricula, facilities, and equipment; insufficient financial assistance; and the lack of cross-cultural leadership in our educational institutions. In the continued absence of cross-cultural leadership, education will continue to function as a socializing agency for the undereducated, even though it may have a value-added character for some.

Cross-cultural leadership and empowerment are interconnected concepts affecting the quality of life of many communities in our world. Where there is increasing contact, conflict, and change between groups there will inevitably be creative tension and struggle among individuals and groups around vested self-interest. In such situations, sensitive mediators, innovators, and leaders are in high demand and (at least currently) in short supply. Identity and power will be key concepts that impact communication, cooperation, and integration.

The role of educational anthropology and cross-cultural education in the dialogue on diversity will depend upon several important factors. The ability to demonstrate conceptual and programmatic utility to educational problem solving will likely determine the relevance of conceptual and methodological contributions. However, it is in the training and development of personnel that the field will be mostly tested. Successful development of the field will require development of cross-cultural leadership. This will require recruitment and training of the best and brightest from powerless communities, enabling them to work within their own and others' communities. It will also mandate the development of cross-cultural competencies among more of our educators and community leaders. It will require the provision of support to existing professionals at risk for conducting unpopular research and developing new ideas for creative action. Becoming more proactive about cross-cultural leadership among ourselves and among various segments of the educational world will also be needed.

We all face together an uncertain future with constant change and surprise coming from new discoveries, political power shifts, natural disasters, and creative developments. One of our biggest challenges will be our ability to understand one another and to learn to behave in understanding ways. Perhaps anthropology can offer us some of its conceptual tools, and methods and techniques for the study of diversity among people.

Our ability to overcome factionalism and build unity requires greater cross-cultural competence among our educators and leaders. For us to treat those who are culturally different from ourselves with respect we must enable everyone to develop a healthy and wholesome sense of identity. Our effective problem solving for a common future requires us to have a better comparative perspective on our diverse communities, and an increased number of cross-cultural leaders capable of understanding and managing diversity.

Our future in education will require more bridge builders and more tools for bridge building than in the past. Anthropology offers added concepts and methods for understanding and action to create pluralistic learning environments.

NOTES

1   A more detailed explanation of culture as applied to education is provided in a Monograph Series by Arvizu et al. (1977–81) entitled *Demystifying the Concept of Culture*, which includes: no. 1, *Conceptual Tools*; no. 2, *Methodological Tools*; no. 3, *Cultura Chicana*; no. 4, *Anthropological Study of Play and Games*; and no. 5, *Home School Linkages*, available through the Cross-Cultural Resource Center, California State University, Sacramento. In educational anthropology, early research described cultural influences on childrearing and in formal and informal schooling. Later research described the culture of schools in contrast to the cultures of service populations and analyzed sociocultural influences on learning, particularly within diverse linguistic and cultural learner populations. In business contexts, the concept of organizational culture has been used to describe differences in values and in management approaches in order to study productivity and change.

2   Diversity: An accreditation-based definition of diversity is included in the Western Association of Schools and Colleges (WASC) Handbook, under Standard 1B, as integrity and respect for persons that fosters educational diversity (1988). A draft Commission Policy on Diversity also provides multiple meanings for diversity in overlapping institutional efforts that go beyond matters of representation to consider goals, attitudes, and practices; curricular adaptation; pedagogical improvements; giving voice to new arrivals; expansion of scholarship in women's and ethnic studies; and assessment of diversity efforts (Caughlin 1991). Diversity applied to learner populations is also explained in cultural contexts in *Cross-Cultural Literacy: Ethnographies of Communication in Multiethnic Classrooms* (Saravia-Shore and Arvizu 1992) and in *Cultural Diversity in Schools* (DeVillar et al. 1994). Diversity is also related to multiculturalism and activism as exemplified by Christine Sleeter in her book *Multicultural Education as Social Activism* (Sleeter 1996).

3   Marvin Harris's (1968) *The Rise of Anthropological Theory* gives a detailed analysis of the historical developments of particular theoretical schools, along with their methodological characteristics. More recent theories in American anthropology are being developed through ethnographic studies of schools and communities in the tradition of educational anthropology, as can be synthesized through key articles and debates in the *Council on Anthropology and Education Quarterly*.

REFERENCES CITED

Arvizu, S. F.
  1974   One Plus One Equals Three. Master's thesis, Department of Anthropology, Stanford University.
  1988   Cross-Cultural Leadership and Empowerment. Paper presented at the American Anthropology Association Annual Meeting, Phoenix, Arizona.
  1992   Cross-Cultural Leadership. Paper presented at the American Anthropological Association Annual Meeting, San Francisco, California.
  1999   Anthropology in the Next Millennium: A Case Study on Service Learning and Ethnography at California State University, Monterey Bay. James Peacock (ed.), Whither the Academy; Publication of Proceedings; AAA Presidential Symposium.
  1999   *Putting Something Back: Comparative Histories of Chicano Activists*. Austin: University of Texas Press (forthcoming).
Cortes, C.
  1990   Pluribus, Unum, and the American Future. *Today* 15(3):8–10.
DeVillar, R. A., and C. J. Faltis
  1991   *Computers and Cultural Diversity*. Albany: SUNY Press.
DeVillar, R. A., C. S. Faltis, and J. P. Cummins
  1994   *Cultural Diversity in Schools*. Albany: SUNY Press.
Foley, D.
  1977   *From Peones to Politicos*. Austin: University of Texas Press.
Gallimore, R., J. Boggs, and C. Jordan
  1974   *Culture, Behavior and Education: A Study of Hawaiian-Americans*. Beverly Hills, CA: Sage.
Gumperz. J., and D. Hymes
  1964   Ethnography of Communication. *American Anthropologist* 66(6):1–34.
Harris, M.
  1968   *The Rise of Anthropological Theory*. New York: Thomas Y. Crowell.
Henry, J.
  1960   A Cross-Cultural Outline of Education. *Current Anthropology* 1(4):267–305.
Mead, M.
  1928   *Coming of Age in Samoa*. New York: Morrow.
  1935   *Sex and Temperament in Three Primitive Societies*. New York: Morrow.
  1974   *The Next Generation: Ethnography in an Urban Neighborhood*. New York: Academic Press.
Saravia-Shore, M., and S. F. Arvizu
  1992   *Cross-Cultural Literacy: Ethnographies of Communications in Multiethnic Classrooms*. New York: Garland Press.
Sleeter, Christine
  1996   *Multicultural Education as Social Activism*. Albany: SUNY Press.
Spindler, G. D.
  1959   *Transmission of American Culture*. Cambridge, MA: Harvard University Press.

1973   *Burgbach: Urbanization and Identity in a German Village*. New York: Holt, Rinehart, and Winston.

1976   Village or City? Identity, Choice, and Cultural Change. In *Schooling in the Cultural Context*. J. Roberts, and S. Akinsanya, eds. Pp. 114–128. New York: David McKay.

Spindler, G. D., ed.

1955   *Education and Anthropology*. Palo Alto, CA: Stanford University Press.

1963a   *Education and Culture*. New York: Holt, Rinehart, and Winston.

1963b   *The Transmission of American Culture: Education and Culture*. New York: Holt, Rinehart, and Winston.

1970   *Being an Anthropologist: Fieldwork in Eleven Cultures*. New York: Holt, Rinehart, and Winston.

1974   *Education and Cultural Process: Toward an Anthropology of Education*. New York: Holt, Rinehart, and Winston.

Valencia, A.

1972   The Mexican American Education Project: Evaluation Report. Sacramento: California State University.

Whiting, J., and L. Child

1953   *Child Training and Personality: A Cross-Cultural Study*. New Haven, CT: Yale University Press.

Wolcott, H.

1973   *The Man in the Principal's Office: An Ethnography*. New York: Holt, Rinehart, and Winston.

1976   Criteria for an Ethnographic Approach to Research in Schools. In *Schooling in the Cultural Context*. J. Roberts, and S. Akinsanya, eds. Pp. 23–43. New York: David McKay.

23

Teaching Ethnicity and Place in the United States

J. Diego Vigil and Curtis C. Roseman

Ethnicity and place as anthropological and geographical concepts are really intertwined. In studies of ethnicity, we find that race, language, religion, cultural habits, social boundaries, and a number of other factors figure prominently. When place or environment is the focus, human migration, rural to urban transition, size-density-heterogeneity, and various demographic features are examined. While a case can be made for the conceptual distinctiveness of ethnicity and place, invariably one must consider both of them in any analysis. Particularly is this the case if a course is developed to teach students about the ethnic identification process, theirs and others', which requires that they carefully unravel the time, place, and people dimensions (Vigil 1998a, 1998b). As such, the authors propose to summarize how students can learn about themselves and others by combining the tools and techniques of anthropology and geography. This chapter outlines how a "geoethnic family history" (Roseman and Vigil 1997) is constructed by tracing ethnic identification developments with the aid of ethnographic and mapping methods.

The principal aims of the course are: (1) to reflect upon and assess the different meanings and interpretations of ethnicity, comparing and contrasting the interplay between public knowledge (e.g. literature) and private (socially constructed) practice; (2) to examine the nature of ethnic groups and ethnic identity processes, including other related facets such as race, language, religion, class, and gender; (3) to review and integrate geographical perspectives on ethnicity, charting how individuals and families experience place and migration, particularly in the context of the emergence of ethnic neighborhoods and "EthniCities" of diversity; (4) to combine documented, demographic trends with biographical information, to help gauge the shifting tides that American ethnicity has taken in various times and places, with a focus on Los Angeles as a global city; (5) to highlight issues of ethnicity and place with visual aids and methods (ethnographic films and documentaries and mapping exercises) to aid students' appreciation and understanding of other groups; and (6) to involve students in the examination of their own ethnic backgrounds and ethnic identity trajectories by having them chart and develop their own geoethnic family histories and in so doing learn about other students' lives and personal trajectories.

We first provide below an overview of some of the ethnic and geographic concepts that are covered in the course, and then we describe the mechanics of the course and the methods used for collecting geoethnic family histories.

Ethnicity refers to the distinguishing criteria used to describe a group of people who are set apart or who set themselves apart from society at large (Thernstrom 1980). "Minority" groups as well as distinct cultural groups are encompassed by this concept, as are separate factions that exist within indigenous populations. The criteria used to assess the ethnicity of a group are based on a people's historical and geographical origins, cultural characteristics such as language and religion, physical characteristics such as "race," and structural features including economic status, territoriality, and societal or spatial marginalization (DeVos and Romanucci-Ross 1995).

Utilizing an interdisciplinary framework for an assessment of ethnicity and place requires that several conceptual and theoretical points be addressed. Vigil (1998a, 1998b) presents the broadest framework with the 6 Cs Model of Culture Change. In this model, an ethnic group's Class (i.e. socioeconomic or structural status, such as income, occupation, home, neighborhood, prestige, and so on), Culture (world view, relio-philosophy, language, values, and so on), and Color (physiognomic traits and how race and racism, prejudice, discrimination and the like, affect self-image and create superiority or inferiority feelings and relationships) are examined to describe an intact social system. The other elements of this model help us understand how and why a social system is transformed when Contact (meetings of social systems either by design or chance, often motivated and initiated by self-interest and political-economy issues), Conflict (a range of human interactions, from military confrontations to social oppression and religious persecutions), and Change (partial or total revamping of one or both social systems, minor or major transformations to society) create a transition to a new social system. A careful reading of an ethnic group's (or an individual's) historical trajectory over time and place is possible with the 6 Cs model, as for instance, tracing all the different social systems (e.g. Mexican Americans would have Indian, Spanish, Mexican, and Anglo American antecedents). Group and individual variances are accounted for with this broad pen where ethnicity and place are the featured elements.

Moving from a macro analysis of the topic, and looking at more micro, intricate features, DeVos and Romanucci-Ross (1995) have addressed a number of facets of ethnicity in describing ethnic identity. To be sure, there are several overlaps with the 6 Cs model, but DeVos and Romanucci-Ross's approach to unraveling ethnicity (and also the influence of place, in some cases) requires an assessment of several dynamically linked characteristics. First on their list is race, and in fact, the Greek word for race is *ethnos* and the authors consider it crucial to an understanding of ethnicity and the formation of ethnic identity.

As several other authors have suggested, DeVos and Romanucci-Ross maintain that there are personal, internal aspects of race, or more correctly the effects of racism, when a sense of inferiority or negative self-image results. The external, outside world in the case of the dominant societal group shapes racial attitudes and practices and thus creates a countervailing sense of superiority. Experiences of prejudice and discrimination are especially crucial in the context of U.S. society. People of color in the United States are often subjected to racism, both structurally as well as overtly in their everyday interactions (Aguirre and Turner 1995; Brown 1995; Jackson 1987; Van den Berghe 1967).

The authors also stress that, along with race, there are other factors, for example, language, religious or cultural features, status, historical and geographical features, which combine to affect the shaping of an ethnic identity. Depending on the time and place, a subject emphasized by geographers especially (Baker and Billinge 1982; Carter et al. 1993), DeVos and Romanucci-Ross state that one or another, or a combination, of these facets is operable in the lives of individuals or groups. In short, using the metaphor of the kaleidoscope, which has the same objects and colors but aligned differently each time, the salience of each ethnic facet changes for the individual or group. Sometimes, when a large number of people are subjected to harsh treatment or discrimination for one reason or another, for example, racism, religious persecution, or language exclusion, the similarity of the experience (i.e. all kaleidoscopes more or less match) makes for strained ethnic relations and often major conflict (Boucher et al. 1987; Aguirre and Turner 1995). The strength of the DeVos and Romanucci-Ross model is that it considers different facets of ethnicity, allows for an accounting of salience and individual or group variation, and examines the continuities and changes over time.

For an even closer look at ethnicity, Barth's (1969) concept of ethnic boundaries provides a clear framework of the external and internal factors that separate one group from another, and shows how group boundary lines are permeable or impenetrable and allow or invite relations and interactions. For example, when an ethnic group has a history of exclusion or separation from other groups, usually the dominant ones, either because of religion or race, then there is a tendency to withdraw into one's group as a measure of protection or insulation from negative treatment. On the other hand, ethnic boundaries can be less rigid and open to contact and exchange if the past shared experience reflects success and beneficial results with this cultural orientation. Thus ethnic boundaries and processes become a vital part of the enculturation and identity experience of growing up in that ethnic population.

Barth's theory helps locate and aid definition of DeVos and Romanucci-Ross's array of ethnic facets, in some ways assembling and reassembling them according to each ethnic group's experience, and by doing so helps us understand the permeability or impenetrability of their ethnic boundaries.

The resources that have been used to maintain the boundaries of an ethnic community can also be examined from different angles (Eriksen 1993). Among immigrant groups, transnational links with the homeland might be significant. Such connections often affect the rate and direction of educational and religious changes, and also kinship and marriage patterns. The intermarriages that occur and the ethnic and racial hybridization that result are especially significant (Alba 1990; Funderburg 1994; Forbes 1993; D'Innocenzo and Sirefman 1992; Root 1996; Spencer 1997; Spickard 1989; Zack 1995). Variations in physiognomic traits, customs and habits within a population can reveal very interesting and diverse historical backgrounds of intermarriage and ethnic group exchange.

Macro and middle-level micro frameworks of analyses of ethnicity would not be enough without a word on ethnic group contact and interaction on a more personal level (Allen and Turner 1997; Parillo 1994; Boucher et al. 1987; Rex and Mason 1986). Culture contact and change was noted very broadly by Vigil (1998a). However, culture change can include as transformative phenomena, among other things, acculturation (i.e. two cultures meet and change takes place in one or both cultures), assimilation (i.e. total absorption into a dominant culture), syncretism (e.g. certain areas of New Mexico where Indian, Mexican, and Anglo culture have merged), separation (e.g. early Mormons, black Muslims), nativism (i.e. Ghost Dance Movement of Native Americans), minority status, urbanization (i.e. the processes and adaptations of living in a complex society or big city), and modernization (i.e. shifting from a traditional, often peasant, way of life to modern urban culture as defined by industrial capitalism). There is always a need to clarify which aspect of culture change is the focus of the experience and discussion, particularly on the personal, psychological level. Spindler and Spindler (1990) have provided a very facile model that looks at culture change, or in this example, acculturation, over time and how new places and peoples affect one's concept of self. In addition to addressing the usual acculturation features, such as generation, language, values, and so on, the authors creatively introduce the notions of enduring, situated, and endangered selves. The enduring self constitutes the person who was enculturated in an ethnic group in a particular place; it is the core of one's make-up. But contact and exchange, especially through human migration or social mobility, with other groups requires adaptation and adjustment and generates a situated self. The latter can be a relatively smooth adjustment or fraught with many conflicts and ambiguities on a personal level. When this occurs an endangered self emerges because there is strain between the enduring and situated selves. It is this clash which plagues many ethnic groups worldwide, and in its wake produces extreme examples of marginality or ethnic identity confusion. Culture conflict and ambivalence is what it is often referred to, and in large part, this dynamic process creates new ethnic styles and categories. However, this complicated process is parsimoniously understood when enduring, situated, and endangered notions of self are considered in the assessment of ethnic identity – time, place, and people are accounted for.

Within our course, all these different aspects of ethnicity – including language, religion, economic status, intergroup relations, ethnocentrism and racism, and ethnic group maintenance – are reexamined and reinterpreted in terms of their place contexts (Carter et al. 1993). For example, language shift or religious change may go hand-in-hand with transnational macro-migration or even local micro-migration from one neighborhood to another (Castles and Miller 1993; Gmelch 1992). Incidence and intensity of racial discrimination might also change with location.

Two major geographic concepts are significant in an analysis of ethnicity: migration and place. Both individual and family migration processes can be reviewed within the broader context of migration patterns, taking care to assess settlement and place characteristics. Some pertinent questions to be asked include: why, when, and where do individuals and families decide to migrate? Economic reasons, such as greater employment opportunities, generally trigger longer-distance migration, whereas local mobility (between neighborhoods) tends to be reflective of housing needs or household change events such as divorce, death of a spouse, or the need for assistance (Johnson and Roseman 1990; Long 1988; Stack 1996). Life-course transitions can also stimulate migration: going to college, getting a new job, getting married, and so on. International migrants, however, may be responding to much more than the availability of employment opportunities and life-course transitions. Broad economic and geopolitical factors often spark international migrations and affect the rate and direction of their flow (Basch et al. 1994; Chambers 1994; Pedraza and Rumbaut 1996).

Migration can be temporary or permanent when the time element is introduced. Temporary migratory movements include seasonal or cyclical migration processes, such as labor migration. For many Mexican migrant workers, their cyclical movement between Mexico and the United States is often a precursor to subsequent permanent migration of family members to the United States (Moore and Pachon 1985; Vigil 1998a). In some cases, the route of these migratory movements determines the permanent destination choice.

Migration is often channeled in space, connecting particular origin and destination areas. This is the process whereby migrants (especially from rural areas) follow kin or friends along their migratory paths. Those who have already settled into their new location, as cultural brokers, are then able to help the new arrivals find housing and employment. Extended family networks are often strengthened through this process, and "social" capital enhanced, as people travel back and forth between the two locations for vacation or business, or for holiday celebrations, weddings, funerals, and the like (Vigil 1998a).

Migration can also be examined and interpreted through the lens of broad national or international migration trends and patterns. Migration patterns within the United States have included the Dust Bowl migrations of the depression era, the Great Migration of African Americans from the rural South from the World War I period to the 1950s, and the westward movement of people in the post–World War II era (Lemann 1991; Trotter 1991). Another powerful trend, during the past few decades, has been the high rates of suburbanization in many major American cities. In this context, questions need to be addressed as to why some people decided to move to suburbia while others stayed in the city. For some inner-city residents, reasons for not suburbanizing might include: choice, economics, or discrimination (Sibley 1981; Wilson 1988).

Similar analyses are possible for international migration patterns. America is a nation made up of immigrants (Pedraza and Rumbaut 1996). From the first pilgrims to the arrival of Vietnamese refugees in the 1970s, people have been coming to the United States to flee religious and/or political persecution as well as for various economic reasons (Haines 1985; Gmelch 1992; Light and Bonacich 1988; Rutledge 1992). An examination of immigration and refugee policies is relevant in any analysis of international migration trends (although it should be recognized that undocumented immigration is also a route for some). Many second-generation Americans have parents who immigrated after the 1965 revisions of the U.S. Immigration Act. These liberal adjustments opened the doors to large numbers of newcomers from Latin America and Asia, many of whom were trying to escape from political unrest in their home countries (Takaki 1989). Their migration paths often involved hopping between several countries before arriving in the United States (Knoll 1992).

Migration to a new country and culture is a definite accelerator of ethnic identity transformation (Chambers 1994; Rutledge 1992). Moving from one place to another is often accompanied by rapid changes in language, religion, and/or other cultural behaviors. The time and place of subsequent settlement greatly influences the degree and direction of this change as syncretic dynamics (mixing and melding of cultures) vary across locations (Vigil 1998a, 1998b). Problems of racism, xenophobia, or discrimination can also be exacerbated in the new location. In general, different place contexts can be powerful in circumscribing the lives of ethnic group members. Deeply ingrained place-based institutional forces can shape ethnic group development, often perpetuating segregation, discrimination, and marginalization, or encouraging full participation of ethnic groups (Berry and Henderson n.d.; Chisholm and Smith 1990; Wilson 1988).

An important product of the migration, domestic and international, of ethnic groups has been the increase in the diversity of ethnic groups living within the largest metropolitan areas, both within the United States and in other western countries (Allen and Turner 1997; Sibley 1981; Waldinger and Bozorgmehr 1996). The term "EthniCity" has been coined (by Vigil) to refer to those cities having diverse collections of ethnic groups (Roseman et al. 1996). Because many different peoples have come together in these places, EthniCities share both the problems and advantages of ethnic diversity. Problems include widespread uneven political representation, inequities in housing and employment, language instruction difficulties in schools, and interethnic tensions. Advantages might include a wide array of cultural activities, such as festivals and restaurants (Rogers and Vertovec 1995). Even though several ethnic groups may be sharing the same city or metropolitan area, however, they may not be sharing residential space. Significant residential segregation still exists and ethnic enclaves, barrios, and ghettos are still a prominent feature on the residential landscape of major cities (Vigil 1998b; Wilson 1988; Waldinger and Bozorgmehr 1996).

Understanding the ethnic identification process thus requires an examination of multiple forces and sources, some external and outside the control of a group and others internal to the group. How these structural, cultural, historical, and locational forces shape ethnicity and where and how they intersect with gender, social class, race, age, and sexuality are all of relevance in this course (Kendall 1997; Cyrus 1993; Balibar and Wallerstein 1991; McAll 1990; Di Leonardo 1986; Steinberg 1981).

REFERENCES CITED

Aguirre, Adalberto, Jr., and Jonathan H. Turner
  1995   *American Ethnicity: The Dynamics and Consequences of Discrimination.* New York: McGraw-Hill.
Alba, Richard
  1990   *Ethnic Identity: The Transformation of White America.* New Haven, CT: Yale University Press.

Allen, James P., and Eugene J. Turner
1988 *We the People: An Atlas of America's Ethnic Diversity.* New York: Macmillan.
1997 *The Ethnic Quilt: Population Diversity in Southern U.S.A.* Northridge, CA. Center for Geographical Studies, California State University, Northridge.
Baker, Alan R. H., and Mark Billinge, eds.
1982 *Period and Place: Research Methods in Historical Geography.* Cambridge, UK: Cambridge University Press.
Balibar, Etienne, and Immanuel Wallerstein
1991 *Race, Nation, Class: Ambiguous Identities.* London: Verso.
Barth, Frederick, ed.
1969 *Ethnic Groups and Boundaries: The Social Organization of Cultural Difference.* Boston: Little, Brown.
Basch, Linda G., Nina Glick Schiller, and Cristina Szanton Blanc
1994 *Nations Unbound: Transnational Projects, Postcolonial Predicaments, and Deterritorialized Nation-States.* Langhorne, PA: Gordon and Breach.
Berry, Kate, and Martha Henderson, eds.
n.d. *Geographical Identities of Ethnic America: Race, Place, and Space.* Boulder, CO: Westview Press.
Boucher, J., D. Landis, and K. A. Clark, eds.
1987 *Ethnic Conflict.* Newbury Park, CA: Sage.
Brown, Rupert
1995 *Prejudice.* Oxford: Blackwell.
Carter, Erica, James Donald, and Judith Squires, eds.
1993 *Space and Place: Theories of Identity and Location.* London: Lawrence and Wishart.
Castles, Stephen, and Mark J. Miller
1993 *The Age of Migration: International Population Movements in the Modern World.* New York: Guilford Press.
Chambers, Iain
1994 *Migrancy, Culture, Identity.* New York: Routledge.
Chisholm, Michael, and David Smith, eds.
1990 *Shared Space, Divided Space.* Boston: Unwin Hyman.
Cyrus, Virginia, ed.
1993 *Experiencing, Race, Class, and Gender in the United States.* Mountain View, CA: Mayfield.
DeVos, George, and Lola Romanucci-Ross, eds.
1995 *Ethnic Identity: Cultural Continuities and Change.* Thousand Oaks, CA: Altamira Press.
Di Leonardo, Micaela
1986 *The Varieties of Ethnic Experience: Kinship, Class, and Gender among California Italian Americans.* Ithaca, NY: Cornell University Press.
D'Innocenzo, Michael, and Josef P. Sirefman, eds.
1992 *Immigration and Ethnicity: American Society – "Melting Pot" or "Salad Bowl"?* Westport, CT: Greenwood Press.
Eriksen, S. H.
1993 *Ethnicity and Nationalism: Anthropological Perspective.* London: Pluto Press.
Forbes, Jack D.
1993 *Africans and Native Americans: The Language of Race and the Evolution of the Red-Black Peoples.* Urbana: University of Illinois Press.
Funderburg, Lise
1994 *Black, White, Other: Biracial Americans Talk about Race and Identity.* New York: W. Morrow.

Gmelch, George
   1992   *Double Passage: The Lives of Caribbean Migrants Abroad and Back Home.*
   Ann Arbor: University of Michigan Press.
Haines, D. W., ed.
   1985   *Refugees in the United States: A Reference Handbook.* Westport, CT:
   Greenwood Press.
Jackson, Peter, ed.
   1987   *Race and Racism: Essays in Social Geography.* London: Allen and Unwin.
Johnson, James H., Jr., and Curtis C. Roseman
   1990   Increasing Black Outmigration from Los Angeles: The Role of House-
   hold Dynamics and Kinship Systems. *Annals of the American Association of
   Geographers* 80:205–222.
Kendall, H., ed.
   1997   *Race, Class and Gender in a Society: A Text-Reader.* Boston, MA: Allyn and
   Bacon.
Knoll, T.
   1992   *Becoming Americans: Asian Sojourners, Immigrants and Refugees in the
   Western United States.* Portland, OR: Coast to Coast Books.
Lemann, Nicholas
   1991   *Promised Land: The Great Black Migration and How It Changed America.*
   New York: Knopf.
Light, Ivan, and E. Bonacich
   1988   *Immigrant Entrepreneurs: Koreans in Los Angeles, 1965–1982.* Berkeley:
   University of California Press.
Long, Larry
   1988   *Migration and Residential Mobility in the United States.* New York: Russell
   Sage Foundation.
McAll, Christopher
   1990   *Class, Ethnicity, and Social Equality.* Buffalo, NY: McGill–Queen's University
   Press.
Parvallo, Vincent N.
   1994   *Strangers to these Shores: Race and Ethnic Relations in the United States.* New
   York: Macmillan.
Pedraza, Silvia, and Ruben G. Rumbaut, eds.
   1996   *Origins and Destinies: Immigration, Race and Ethnicity in America.* Belmont,
   CA: Wadsworth.
Rex, John, and David Mason, eds.
   1986   *Theories of Race and Ethnic Relations.* New York: Cambridge University
   Press.
Rogers, Alisdair, and Steven Vertovec, eds.
   1995   *The Urban Context: Ethnicity, Social Networks, and Situational Analysis.*
   Oxford: Berg.
Root, Maria P. P., ed.
   1996   *The Multiracial Experience: Racial Borders as the New Frontier.* Thousand
   Oaks, CA: Sage.
Roseman, Curtis C., Hans Dieter Laux, and Gunter Thieme, eds.
   1996   *EthniCity: Geographic Perspectives on Ethnic Change in Modern Cities.*
   Lanham, MD: Rowman and Littlefield.
Roseman, Curtis C., and J. Diego Vigil
   1993   From Broadway to Latinoway: The Reoccupation of a Gringo Landscape.
   Places 8(3):20–29.

1997   Geoethnic Family Histories. In *Teaching American Ethnic Geography*. Lawrence E. Estaville and Carol Rosen, eds. Pp. 119–126. National Council for Geographic Education.

Rutledge, P. J.
1992   *The Vietnamese Experience in America*. Bloomington: Indiana University Press.

Sibley, David
1981   *Outsiders in Urban Societies*. New York: St. Martin's Press.

Spencer, Jon Michael
1997   *The New Colored People: The Mixed-Race Movement in America*. New York: New York University Press.

Spickard, Paul R.
1989   *Mixed Blood: Intermarriage and Ethnic Identity in Twentieth Century America*. Madison: University of Wisconsin Press.

Spindler, George, and Louise Spindler
1990   *The American Cultural Dialogue and Its Transmission*. London: Falmer Press.

Stack, Carol
1996   *Call to Home: African Americans Reclaim the Rural South*. New York: Basic Books.

Steinberg, Stephen
1981   *The Ethnic Myth: Race, Ethnicity, and Class in America*. New York: Atheneum.

Takaki, Ronald
1989   *Strangers from a Different Shore: A History of Asian Americans*. New York: Penguin.

Thernstrom, Stephan
1980   *Harvard Encyclopedia of American Ethnic Groups*. Cambridge, MA: Harvard University Press.

Trotter, Joe William
1991   *The Great Migration in Historical Perspective: New Dimensions of Race, Class, and Gender*. Bloomington: Indiana University Press.

Van den Berghe, Pierre L.
1967   *Race and Racism: A Comparative Perspective*. New York: John Wiley.

Vigil, James Diego
1998a   *From Indians to Chicanos: The Dynamics of Mexican American Culture*. 2nd edition. Prospect Heights, IL: Waveland Press.
1998b   Time, Place, and History in the Formation of Chicano Identity. In *Many Americas: Critical Perspectives on Race, Racism, and Ethnicity*. Gregory Campbell, ed. Dubuque: Kendall Hunt.

Waldinger, Roger, and Mehdi Bozorgmehr, eds.
1996   *Ethnic Los Angeles*. New York: Russell Sage Foundation.

Wilson, William J.
1988   *The Truly Disadvantaged: The Inner City, the Underclass, and Public Policy*. Chicago: University of Chicago Press.

Zack, Naomi, ed.
1995   *American Mixed Race: The Culture of Microdiversity*. Lanham, MD: Rowman and Littlefield.

24

An Archaeological Approach to Teaching U.S. Cultural Diversity

Ruben G. Mendoza

It must be stressed that archaeology as the study of human occupation of the American continent is incompatible with the mission of the schools in the USA.

Material evidence of a non-English, Precolonial past can be permitted only insofar as it appears simple, crude, and a component of nature on the American continent.   (Kehoe 1994:213)

Anthropologists have long held the mandate to explore non-Western peoples and cultures. However, U.S. anthropologists, particularly archaeologists, have largely failed to acknowledge or to engage nationwide educational mandates for the teaching of cultural diversity (Selig 1997; Smithsonian Institution 1994). This fact has led to challenges from within the discipline that anthropology move toward the ethnic and cultural diversification of the academy and its curriculum (Kottak et al. 1997). Recent debates draw directly from arguments that either promote the teaching of cultural diversity within diverse contexts or question the purportedly non-Western or postmodern orientation and condition of cultural diversity and multiculturalism in the academy (Davis 1993; Foster 1997; Mukhopadhyay 1997; Marcus 1997). They bolster views that anthropology has promoted the subordination of the non-Western traditions (Selin 1997; Stone and MacKenzie 1994; Wolf 1982). Anthropology's failure to address the relevance of non-Western or U.S. ethnic minority cultural and scientific traditions is particularly problematic when viewed in terms of the diverse and culturally eclectic subject matter of the discipline (Cheek 1997: Jasanoff et al. 1995; Mendoza 1997a, 1997b, 1997c; Mendoza and Jordan 1997; Mendoza and Wolter 1997; Selig 1997). This chapter examines the seemingly "undocumented heritage" of ethnic "minority" and non-Western scientific traditions in U.S. public schools and universities (Loewen 1995). It provides a case study for the teaching of U.S. cultural diversity through a practice-, project-, and problem-based approach that draws directly on existing resources in archaeology and museum anthropology.

Retrospect, Practice, and Prospect in Applied Contexts

Studies of cultural diversity and the market for multicultural curriculum materials have led anthropologists and other social scientists to examine the role they should play in defining the content and contexts of such research and curriculum development (Schmidt and Patterson 1995; Selig 1997; Smardz 1997; Stone 1997). Anthropologists have only recently begun to address questions of cultural diversity and multiculturalism – that is, gender, race, ethnicity, and class – and its impact on the teaching of anthropology (Kottak et al. 1997). Clearly, archaeologists and physical anthropologists have yet to engage fully those issues raised by the impact of cultural diversity on university curricula and research since the 1970s. This failure promotes the appearance that anthropologists are isolated from the larger body of scholarship in the academy and that their oversight is the product of a political aversion to the questions raised by cultural diversity studies (Loewen 1995; Wajcman 1995).

In order to address the pedagogy of American cultural diversity – particularly as it applies to archaeology and museum anthropology – this paper presents case studies and discussion of the potential contexts within which we may effectively address questions raised by cultural diversity studies and teaching borne of the hyphenated or "dissonant heritage" of the American past (Tunbridge and Ashworth 1996).

Pedagogy and the Y2K Curriculum

Anthropology is being subjected to increasing levels of scrutiny arising from the rapidly changing learning styles and pedagogical paradigms posed by the transformation of teaching and learning in the Information Age (Berge and Collins 1995; Boschmann 1995). Fueled by the expansion of the internet and related online learning communities, information is now available in increasingly diverse formats and instructional contexts. In December 1998, the National Education Association reported that "about one-third of all college courses . . . now use the Internet as part of the syllabus. That's up from about 15 percent in 1996." Given the global charter and mandate of the internet, many universities now strive to prepare students for the challenges of a global and multicultural world of information and experience (Stanley and Ouellett 1998).

For archaeologists, the use of technologies developed outside the discipline, and the project-based and problem-oriented approaches advocated here are not new (Barber 1994; Hester et al. 1997; Rice 1997, 1998). In fact, archaeologists and museum anthropologists often draw upon the technologies and tenets of social anthropology and other disciplines in order to make use of the broader fund of practices and viewpoints available (Trigger 1989; Fagan 1995; Alexander 1996). Similarly, interdisciplinary approaches are not new to archaeologists and museum anthropologists. Interdisciplinary investigations have been conducted by a number of archaeologists including Richard MacNeish (1978) in Mexico and Kent Flannery (1972) and others in Mesoamerica and the Near East. Despite the wealth of information acquired on the scientific and technological contributions of non-Western peoples, we have generally failed to disseminate such information beyond the narrow confines of the academy (Schmidt and Patterson 1995; Trigger 1989). In short, we have not succeeded in diversifying the curriculum.

One reason for the slow response of archaeologists and physical anthropologists in coming to grips with cultural diversity in the curriculum is that we have yet to deal with it in the academy. The discipline is largely dominated by white males. People of color are virtually invisible and women are vastly underrepresented – either in the ranks of the professorate or among recent cohorts of graduate students. This does not reflect the demographic reality of the United States as a whole, or of many of the classrooms in which undergraduate anthropology courses are being taught.[1] As a result, scholarship produced in academic departments and museums perpetuates and expands an all-white, largely male academic and professional culture.

While many archaeologists and physical anthropologists do not consider this disparity to be "their" problem, the reality for the discipline is that this "separate reality" served to fuel the implementation of the Native American Graves Protection and Repatriation Act (NAGPRA). NAGPRA brought to bear a legislative mandate that made archaeologists, physical anthropologists, universities, and museums – that have exploited Native North American and other ethnic cultural remains for "scientific" ends – accountable to the affected descendant communities and tribal peoples. Moreover, the failure of the archaeological and physical anthropological communities to actively facilitate and promote access to – and alternative interpretations of – scientific collections and academic opportunities for native peoples and their descendants, has in turn spawned a "culture of suspicion" toward archaeologists and physical anthropologists on the part of descendant communities and scholars of color. Vine Deloria (1970), Michael Blakey (1987), and Charles Cambridge (1992) have challenged the colonialist, separatist, and racist traditions within U.S. anthropology (Biolsi and Zimmerman 1997).

The long-standing failure of archaeologists and physical anthropologists to engage the challenges of U.S. cultural diversity necessarily raises questions about our ability to contribute in important ways to prevailing dialogues of diversity. How then can we move toward an objective assessment and appraisal of our potential contributions to the teaching of U.S. cultural diversity? And how can we do this in ways that avoid further complicating tendencies to take the scientific contributions of the field and turn them into fodder for reactionary or nationalistic diatribes such as those surrounding Kennewick Man? (see Chapter 3, this volume; Schmidt and Patterson 1995). Recent publications concerned with archaeological approaches to gender and ethnicity tout the conceptual and theoretical while ignoring application and practice.

Archaeology, I believe, has a real, though largely untested, contribution to make to the dialogue on U.S. cultural diversity. Much of this contribution necessarily rests with its project-based and problem-oriented approaches to analysis and interpretation within the framework of non-Western and ethnic "minority" cultural contexts.

The Project-Based Approach

The laboratory and field orientation of archaeology has a decided advantage in the pedagogical arena. This is particularly true for the practice-, project-, problem-, and participant-oriented approaches to learning and teaching now advocated by U.S. educators. Current concerns within archaeology with "presenting archaeology to the public" and with "problems, issues, and decisions . . . [in] the teaching of anthropology" underscore the sense of urgency engendered in making the discipline and its findings relevant to the public, especially in an Information Age when entire learning communities are emerging at an exponential rate within and beyond the academy (Jameson 1997; Kottak et al. 1997).

Archaeologists are increasingly preoccupied with questions about teaching and learning in traditional laboratory and field contexts (Michaels and Fagan 1997; Rice 1997, 1998). Karolyn Smardz (1997:105–113) argues that the key to interpreting the past through archaeology in a multicultural context, like Toronto, necessitates (1) access, (2) comprehension, and (3) relevance. This has been done by providing public programming, media visibility, and multicultural outreach and contextualization. In one instance, the Archaeological Resource Centre has worked to "help immigrant adults feel more comfortable in their new land by showing them artifacts left behind by earlier generations of Italians, or Chinese, or Poles who made their homes in 19th century Toronto." In another context, it "combine[s] French immersion lessons with an introduction to Canadian prehistory by setting up classes where students learn vocabulary while cooking and eating traditional foods of Canada's First Nations communities" (Smardz 1997:105).

While both approaches provide a hands-on experience and orientation to the understanding of the past, neither adequately addresses the demands inherent in dealing with the "dissonant heritage" of the U.S. school curriculum (Tunbridge and Ashworth 1996). For instance, where material culture is concerned, it is clear that like ethnicity, artifacts are fraught with ambiguity and prone to divergent and conflicting traditions of interpretation and valuation (Jones 1997; Schlereth 1996:208–217). In California, where Mexican Americans and Native Americans have divergent, historically rooted views about the contributions of the Spanish colonial presence – and the mission-based colonization of early California – the exhibition of early Mission relics tends to inspire outright pride, or ambivalence, among those of Hispanic Catholic origin; or contempt and anger among those of California Native American and non-Catholic ancestry. It is clear that "such portable symbols of the past, like the permanent artifacts of any landscape, aid in maintaining human continuity" (Schlereth 1996:220) for the groups in question. In effect, artifacts become benchmarks of ethnicity and reify present-day identities that did not necessarily exist in the past.

It is critical that museum artifacts displayed in multicultural contexts pay attention to public history and interpretation through what Schlereth (1996:217–221) calls "people's history" and "above-ground archaeology." According to Schlereth: (a) *History is inquiry*; (b) *History is communal*; and (c) *History is personal*.

Regarding the teaching of cultural diversity through archaeology, Schlereth's recommendations can be reformulated to read

1 *The archaeology of diversity should be inquiry-based* (ever critical, self-evaluative, analytical, interpretative, and problem-oriented);

2 *The archaeology of diversity should be communal* (collectively informed, both individually and institutionally oriented, and the product of inter- and intra-disciplinary research, analysis, and communication that orients the whole enterprise of teaching, researching, and communicating cultural diversity);

3 *The archaeology of diversity should be personal* (a "people's archaeology" serves as a pathway to knowing one's self and one's community; particularly from an interdisciplinary and community action-oriented approach, aspects of which may entail "service learning").[2]

The Problem-Oriented Approach

The problem-oriented approach characteristic of laboratory and field archaeology provides an effective means of tackling questions posed by cultural diversity in the United States. Posing questions that challenge the problem-solving skills of students in the classroom affords opportunities to engage real problems within a context in which the students may "safely" confront preconceptions about cultural diversity, ethnicity, and gender; and do so by way of otherwise non-threatening dialogues and interactions facilitated through the creation of classroom-based learning communities.

In teaching in community colleges and universities, I have noted a tendency for students to react to or resist dialogues that center exclusively on questions of equity and diversity among underrepresented minority groups in contemporary U.S. contexts (Cruz Torres, personal communication, May 1992). Students from dominant U.S. ethnic groups (Anglo or Euro-American) tend to see themselves as "American" rather than as members of particular ethnic groups. They see dialogues pertaining to ethnicity as the subject matter of anthropology; and, as such, not relevant to their own sense of social or cultural identity. Students of color in similar contexts tend to identify with a broad range of ethnic identities and affiliations. Among those of Hispanic ancestry, self-identification is often situational and interchangeable, ranging from Hispanic through Chicano, Mexican, *Californio*, *Manitos*, Mexican American, *Hispano*, Latino, *Cubano*, *Puertorriqueño*, Spanish-surnamed, and Spanish American.

In cultural diversity courses, many instructors place an inordinate emphasis on getting students to express their particular "ethnic" perspectives. This is often a means of seeking ethnic validation for issues and questions centered on the culture of the "Other" – whether that otherness is born of ethnic or gender differences. Thus, the question of cultural diversity becomes unstructured and thereby promotes conflict-ridden interactions on affirmative action, entitlements, civic and moral responsibility, "un-American" activities, entrenched attitudes, biases, and stereotypes. Within such contexts, questions of victimization and blame are necessarily reduced to avoidance, denial, outrage, or outright apathy and polarization. Similarly, when cultural diversity courses are required by administrative mandate, expectations that they include group discussions, reflective journals, and a largely formulaic approach to diversity – irrespective of class size, instructor training, public relations, and FTE-driven requirements to maintain such courses – are unrealistic and prone to generate conflict between faculty members and administrators who support or do not support such teaching and learning.

Where such problems and attitudes are the norm, teaching and learning cultural diversity from the standpoint of archaeology or museum studies provides a relative comfort zone. This may allow the "distance" needed by some students and faculty – who might otherwise react in a defensive or hostile manner – to considerations of ethnicity and gender in a culturally diverse context.

In a word, the project-based, problem-oriented approach characteristic of the laboratory and field aspects of archaeology can be repackaged for classroom-based teaching and learning so as to provide an information-rich, collaborative, project-oriented, cooperative, and student-mediated environment for engaging the subject matter of cultural diversity. The curriculum modules, resources, and learning outcomes outlined in this review are intended to provide a laboratory- and field-based, and problem-oriented approach to issues raised by the study of cultural diversity in archaeology and museum anthropology settings.

Curriculum Resources and Learning Outcomes

Laboratory and field settings described below range from the local museum to the campus library, and the archaeology lab to the "smart" classroom. In each of these settings, the instructor is asked to engage students in authentic research, teaching, and learning (Tinto 1997; van Willigen 1997).

Module 1: The archaeology of museums

Given the challenges of the project-based approach, I will first describe a project developed with existing community resources. According to Schlereth (1996:219): "once we do use museums more extensively, we will quickly realize that the creative process of exhibition – a museum's most fundamental means of communication – is one of the best contexts for exploring the intersection of material culture and its larger constellations of meaning in the American experience." Within such an arena, gender, race, ethnicity, and class are explored in a culturally constructed setting that imparts a community's perception of its history.

In Monterey, California, the composite, ethnically eclectic character of the area's history – derived from an amalgamation of Native American, Spanish colonial, Mexican, Asian American, Euro-American, African American, and recent immigrant heritage and ethnic identity – would seemingly provide a rich laboratory for the study of American cultural diversity. Despite its historical and cultural complexity, local historians and historic preservationists have largely failed to take into account the ethnic diversity and complexity of this portion of California's Central Coast. Examined from the standpoint of documentary history, many of the museums and historic sites of the Central Coast fall far short in their attempts at a representative portrayal of the diverse peoples and cultures of the coast. Stated differently, they reify "a 'history' that clearly demonstrates an insensitivity and a kind of cultural imperialism that places a premium on the recovery of the pasts of European Americans" (Muller 1994:83). Despite the historic preservation of some 35 adobe structures built during the Spanish colonial and Mexican Republic periods of early California history (ca. 1769–1846 C.E.), including *Ranchero*-era structures (ca. 1824–1865 C.E.), and a significant contemporary population of people with Mexican American or Mexican origins in Monterey County, local histories are largely bereft of any mention of the founding Hispanic colonists and Mexican communities of the Central Coast. When historic preservationist Edna Kimbro approached one area politician about the prospects of obtaining government assistance to restore the endangered Andres Castro Adobe, she was told, "We're having problems with our Mexicans, why would we want to preserve their heritage anyway?" As for local museums and historic sites, "caricatures" of Hispanic heritage range from that of historical subordination to that of outright denigration. The "living history" exhibit in Monterey's Colton Hall uses Mexican *sombreros* and *serapes* to portray the former occupants of the first American jail in the city. This is in marked contrast to the views of Chicanos and other Hispanics who know the early history of the Monterey Bay area and see it as the Boston Harbor of the Hispanic tradition in the United States: the veritable fourteenth colony.

Thus, the challenge is one of introducing students to the inherent diversity of those aspects of material culture deemed significant for curation and exhibition. Given that museums and repositories are guided by specific cultural and historical themes and curatorial objectives, the inclusion or exclusion of research-related and private collections in museum acquisitions and exhibitions often serves as a cultural benchmark for what a community values and seeks to preserve of its cultural repertoire and collective perception of other cultures and histories.

James Nason (1987:47–52) provides a useful list of the criteria that curators use to determine the "significance" of particular collections and donated materials. These include:

1 *functional significance*, derived from the specific use made of the specimen by the museum;
2 *inherent significance*, derived from one or more values intrinsic to the specimen;

3   *relational significance*, which derives from a specimen's relationship to some-thing else, particularly to groupings or constellations of specimens or his-torical relationships to specific groups or individuals;

4   *anticipated significance*, which derives from the possibility that some new analytical technique or documentary source may in the future enhance its importance;

5   *political significance*, the "contested" value that might accrue as a result of the political importance of the donor.

When conjoined with the five major types of "museum specimen research" conducted by curatorial personnel: (1) exhibition research, (2) contextual research, (3) typological research, (4) reference research, and (5) symbolic/aes-thetic research; the categorizations of professional practice within museums provide a fertile context for a first-hand examination of representations of eth-nicity and culture. Within the local museum, the contested notion of what con-stitutes an "archaeological culture," ethnicity, or identity as revealed by material culture takes on an aura of authenticity and applied relevance.

Student journals and idealized collections of those museum specimens they view as representative serves to fuel discussion about the epistemology of cul-tural interpretations that currently dominate approaches to the study, interpre-tation, and representation of material culture. The inherent interpretative contradictions, "contested identities," and "dissonant heritage" that constitute the U.S. cultural landscape, and the role of class, ethnicity, race, and gender in structuring that political landscape provide further source materials for students to draw upon and incorporate in their analyses (Scott 1994).

Learning outcomes

The primary objective of the intended learning outcome is to provide students with an authentic field-based teaching and learning context within which to explore the nature of cultural representations and portrayals of U.S. cultural diversity. A second objective is to consider how material culture has been and might be used to provide information about underrepresented groups and their contributions to U.S. society.

Learning pathways

To provide students with a study setting with the potential for critical, self-evaluative, analytical, interpretative, and problem-oriented approaches to the study of U.S. cultural diversity, I begin with visits to local historical settings and examinations of museum representations. By "museum representations" I mean the visual and material cultural representation or "construction" – (as opposed to reconstruction) – of whole cultures by way of museum displays, exhibitions, heritage days, and living history reenactments. In each context, diverse cultures and ethnic groups are portrayed by way of material culture grouped into sup-posedly representative cultural samplings (Nason 1987; Stott 1987). While archaeology continues to grapple with the problems inherent in equating ar-chaeological "cultures" with ethnic groups and boundaries (Jones 1997:106), museums and their curatorial staffs continue to make this equation explicit in public contexts, and therein lies the problem (Nason 1987).[3]

Research and discussion questions

The objective of these excursions is to have students select museums and collections they believe reflect the culture and history of the region under consideration. They are then asked to select a representative sampling of objects and collections they believe accurately or adequately portray a specific cultural group. In other words, do the artifacts and texts used to represent the group adequately and objectively portray the relative place, impact, and historical significance of the culture under study? Concomitantly, students are asked to consider the venue in which the exhibition is housed. Is the exhibit space and design appropriate to the objective representation of the culture portrayed? Does the space allotted serve to magnify or diminish one's sense of the cultural and historical significance of the group represented? Does the particular collection of artifacts included in the exhibit group adequately convey the core characteristics and essential complexity of the group represented? If not, how might the exhibit space and content be modified to represent more appropriately the fundamental characteristics of the culture, gender, or ethnic group under consideration? Finally, how does the museum in question deal with issues and questions of cultural diversity in past societies?

Students can also draw upon and respond to questions regarding the Eurocentric orientation of U.S. cultural representations and "histories" posed by Muller (1994:83), who asked:

> For whom does the recovery of these various pasts have meaning? In whose vernacular are the "stories" of the past distributed? Where are the "products" of the past located, if not in museums and laboratories or on bookshelves? . . . As these pasts remain largely the academic business of "white folks," often white men, in whose image are these pasts being recovered? Who goes back to these culturally created pasts as a reference point? In other words, who is experiencing whose past for whom?

Lab and field exercises

Students, either individually or in teams, select a local heritage center or museum. After a "walk through" of the museum, they select a cultural, ethnic, or gender history or heritage display, exhibition, or living history demonstration area they deem suitable for an archaeological assessment of their chosen culture. They then prepare journal entries that provide a brief technical description of the exhibition space, context, content, and captioned descriptions. They are then asked to identify and describe a minimum of five artifacts from the exhibition area that they believe serve to describe the core features of the culture, gender, or ethnic community in question. Having selected and described the core features, they then are required to provide a theoretical justification for their selections. Using entries from their field journals, students then formulate a list of core features they believe provide an interpretative bridge for describing the group in question. Using the previously mentioned questions as a guide, they present their conclusions for class discussion.

Literature review

Theoretical and methodological issues that both frame and challenge contemporary archaeological and ethnographic approaches to the study and interpretation of material culture and ethnic identity are discussed by Nason (1987), Schlereth (1996:184–203), Jones (1997:106–127), White (1997b), Stott (1987:13–30), Newton (1987:129–153), and Spindler and Spindler (1997). Elizabeth Scott's (1994) *Those of Little Note: Gender, Race, and Class in Historical Archaeology* contains essays concerned with race and gender. She argues (1994:7–8) that the triumvirate of gender, race, and class has only recently come to the fore "as a result primarily of criticism by women of color." She cites Nancy Hewitt's (1992:315–316) assertion that where the said triumvirate is concerned, such a construct "will only be applied to women, blacks, and workers and not to men, whites, and owners . . . [and that it will continue to be assumed that] women have more gender than other groups, that blacks have more race, and that men have more class." As such, the study of gender cannot be examined in the absence of further considerations of race, ethnicity, and class. In addition to works already cited, Alexander (1996), Alderson and Low (1996), Reynolds and Stott (1987), Ardouin (1997), Stone and MacKenzie (1994), and Jameson (1997) review the means by which archaeologists and museum professionals construct culture in public contexts.

Module 2: Science and technology in non-Western contexts

I am often amazed by the extent to which the scientific and technical contributions of U.S. "minority" and non-Western peoples are undermined and maligned in seemingly reliable scholarly sources emanating from the academy (e.g. Froeschner 1992). What constitutes science and the scientific method in the Western tradition is often called "magic" and "superstition" in non-Western traditions. This is particularly true for Native American and Precolonial African scientific traditions and contributions. Recent studies of Native American and African metallurgy and Aztec medicine, health, and nutrition challenge earlier studies that minimize the originality and contributions of these traditions (Selin 1997; Schmidt 1996; Ortiz de Montellano 1990). Nevertheless, many scholars continue to explain away evidence for Native American and African technological innovations. For example, the recent discovery that Andean metalsmiths invented the electrochemical plating of precious metals more than 1,500 years ago has been received with skepticism (Lechtman 1991; Mendoza 1997b). The skeptics argue that the recovery of a number of electrochemically plated objects from diverse cultural and chronological contexts does not demonstrate the existence of a technological tradition. Lechtman, who did much of the original research on this topic, finds it difficult to reconcile current evidence with her belief that Andean technology never rose to the level of a "technological tradition."

Recent publications, such as Helaine Selin's (1997) *Encyclopaedia of the History of Science, Technology, and Medicine in Non-Western Cultures* and Joseph O. Vogel's (1997) *Encyclopedia of Precolonial Africa: Archaeology, History, Languages, Cultures, and Environments*, reveal "invisible traditions" of science, technology, and medicine in Africa, Asia, and the Americas. Ironically, they provide documentary evidence that non-Western scientific traditions were often the source of innovations that were subsequently adopted in the West (Merton 1970; Smith 1972; Gies and Gies 1994; James and Thorpe 1994; Needham 1982; Ronan 1978–95). These and other works provide a basis for refining our understanding and appreciation of non-Western traditions and for reassessing and challenging entrenched views about the lack of originality displayed by the ancestors of non-Western peoples here and abroad.

Learning outcomes

The primary outcome of this learning experience is to explore the contributions of non-Westerners, U.S. minorities, and women in the development of science and technology. Particular emphasis is on those contributions obscured by a Eurocentrism that dominates the history of science and technology literature presented in U.S. schools and colleges.

Learning pathways

In his now classic paper on "Science as a Western Phenomenon," Roshdi Rashed (1997) documents the subordination of Islamic scientific and technical contributions by Western scholars intent on using the history of science to obscure and dismantle the non-Western tradition. He documents Islamic contributions in mathematics, physics, philosophy, literature, and engineering, and points to a number of technology transfers and translations of Greek and Roman philosophers that were adopted during the Renaissance. In Rashed's view, European and American historians have "constructed" a European vision of the history of science and technology that diminishes the significance of Arabic contributions to things European before and after the fall of the Roman Empire. The learning pathway in this module begins with Rashed's account and moves to a consideration and discussion of the ways in which history is written to enhance the role of the dominant culture, that is, the victors, in given times and places.

Research and discussion questions

Drawing on works cited above or in the References Cited below, students are asked to assess the veracity and implications of the assertion that: "Early Western culture relied much on the science of other cultures, but as academia became more Eurocentric, much of the science in non-Western cultures was undervalued or lost" (cf. Mendoza 1998). In other words, how is it that, given the overwhelming body of scientific evidence, the Western tradition has somehow managed to overlook, undervalue, and undermine those non-Western traditions that have a direct bearing on the development of Western science and technology? Do archaeologists and museum anthropologists continue to interpret evidence in publications and other discipline-related media in ways that subordinate and marginalize non-Western scientific and technological traditions? How do they do this? How might experimental archaeology and studies of the "heuristics" of creative thinking help students reassess the value and scope of preindustrial and non-Western technological contributions?

Lab and field exercises

The available literature on the history of non-Western science and technology has grown exponentially since the early 1990s (James and Thorpe 1994). It provides a base from which to engage students in the assessment of non-Western epistemologies and scientific traditions and technologies. Potential lab and field projects could cover a range of topics and experimental procedures (Whittaker 1994; Cotterell and Kamminga 1990; Orton et al. 1993). I have generally drawn on a comparative survey of metallurgical and stone-tool technologies recovered from or identified with New World and African Precolonial contexts.

If a lab or enclosed outdoor projects area is available, the traditional flintknapping (stone-tool) demonstration can be expanded in scope to engage students in considerations of the "heuristics" – mechanics and/or physics – of preindustrial and non-Western technologies at the most basic levels of analysis.

While obsidian and chert may be collected in some parts of the country or purchased in others, a number of inexpensive raw materials ranging from bottle glass to porcelain may also be substituted. Using a large 10×14-foot canvas tarp covered with an inked metric grid based on 20×20-centimeter units and alphanumeric unit designations, I conduct a "flintknapping" exercise in which I prepare a series of stone tools in the presence of my students. After crafting both crude tools and more sophisticated artifacts, I then have the students examine and describe the tools and discuss their potential functions. Wearing gloves and goggles, students work to craft stone tools and provide technical descriptions of the techniques they use to produce such tools. The purpose of the technical description is to engage students in an exercise that requires detailed and selective assessment of the items produced. This then becomes the basis for discussion centered on the criteria and cultural biases inherent in describing and illustrating aspects of "alien" material cultures.

Having completed initial technical descriptions, students are then asked to engage in the random sampling of artifact debris or "debitage" and tools from selected 20×20-centimeter units located on the grid. Having conducted the random sampling of the artifact scatter, students are then asked to quantify and table their data by grid unit. This portion of the exercise is used as one means for delivering the message that the artifacts of the past are only "sampled" from a far larger universe of potentially recoverable or irrecoverable artifacts. As such, students are provided with a firsthand glimpse into the superficial, relative, and potentially "non-representative" character of any and all archaeological collection strategies and cultural assemblages.

Finally, drawing on Robert J. Weber's (1992) *Forks, Phonographs and Hot Air Balloons: A Field Guide to Inventive Thinking*, the students are asked to consider the heuristics – that is, "general principles underlying invention" –

that are inherent in the stone tools they manufactured in this experiment. Using what Weber (1992:15–23) calls an "invention" or "problem-based diary," they are asked to describe and categorize the physical characteristics and composite elements of those stone tools produced during the demonstration and experiment. Given the artifact variability, students are then asked to consider those aspects and principles of "problem-solving" and "inventive thinking" that underlie the respective development of artifact types and their potential functions.

Having begun a problem-based diary originally concerned with the stone-tool exercise, students are then asked to use journals as a means of studying elements or examples of non-Western and U.S. "minority" material cultural traditions (Mendoza and Torres 1994). In the final analysis, this exercise has proven useful in allowing students to engage an experiential, "reflective," and analytical exploration of cultural diversity from the standpoint of diverse forms of material culture and human creation. The ultimate value of this lab exercise is generally put to the greatest test when students are challenged to "invent" new uses for the tools in question – whether by continued modification and experimentation, or by way of the discussion of projected tool functions and their respective heuristic principles.

Literature review

Those works cited above provide the background for exploring non-Western science and technology. For this module, the heuristics of stone-tool production and invention are discussed by Whittaker (1994), Keeley (1980), and Weber (1992). Cotterell and Kamminga (1990) discuss other possible experiments in the mechanics of preindustrial technology that build on various physical principles.

This exercise introduces students to an "experimental archaeology" devoted to the understanding of – and experimentation with – the mechanics and heuristic principles of non-Western technological contributions and scientific traditions. Whether the case study in question centers on Paleoindian stone-tool production, Peruvian pottery or textiles, African iron smelting, or the tools, practices, and contributions of the Mexican American "cowboy" or *vaquero*, this approach ultimately provides an experiential and experimental context within which students can explore the tangible and cumulative byproducts of human endeavors and inventive thinking.

Ultimately, the larger goal of this exercise is to foster an appreciation of the ways in which women, U.S. minorities, and non-Western peoples have contributed quite directly to the larger world of science and technology. In effect, this exercise decentralizes the focus on Europe as the source of all legitimate – ancient and modern – scientific and technological innovation, thought, and practice.

Acknowledgments

I would like to thank Dr. Steven A. Arvizu (Oxnard Community College) for his continued support and encouragement, and Linda and Natalie

Mendoza for seeing to it that the manuscript received one last review prior to submission.

NOTES

1   As of 1996, the California State University system reported that less than 600 of its more than 11,000 full-time faculty were Latina(o), less than 3 percent African American, and far less than 1 percent of Native American heritage. When broken down by disciplines, these percentages vary considerably, and the discipline of anthropology hardly registers in the department by department demographic tallies. When considered in light of the significantly large Latina(o), predominantly Mexican American heritage, population of the state of California, these figures are in stark contrast to the majority of that population now enrolled in the K-12 curriculum (i.e. 50 to 60 percent Latina(o) in many school districts throughout the state of California, and many areas of the U.S. Southwest).

2   Service Learning pedagogy has emerged as a critical area of scholarship and as an experiential paradigm for teaching and learning within diverse contexts. It entails placing students into community service projects. At CSU Monterey Bay, such efforts have received widespread community support, resulting in a sizeable network of internship sites on the California Central Coast. My work at Old Mission San Juan Bautista combines field archaeology with a Museum Education Project that has contributed thousands of hours of student and volunteer talent to the restoration and public interpretation of the Old Mission. Concomitantly, inmates from the Gabilan Conservation Camp at Soledad have provided more than 2,500 hours of community service to the archaeological and museum anthropology projects of the CSU Monterey Bay Institute of Archaeology since 1996. See http://archaeology.monterey.edu.

3   See David Macaulay's (1979) *Motel of the Mysteries* for a humorous, largely irreverent, and outrageous characterization of the problem of interpreting "Other" cultures from archaeological remains.

REFERENCES CITED

Alderson, William T., and Shirley Payne Low
    1996   *Interpretation of Historic Sites*. 2nd edition. Walnut Creek, CA: Altamira Press.
Alexander, Edward P.
    1996   *Museums in Motion: An Introduction to the History and Functions of Museums*. Walnut Creek, CA: Altamira Press.
Ardouin, Claude Daniel, ed.
    1997   *Museums and Archaeology in West Africa*. Washington, DC: Smithsonian Institution Press.
Banks, James A.
    1987   *Teaching Strategies for Ethnic Studies*. 4th edition. Boston: Allyn and Bacon.
Barber, Russell J.
    1994   *Doing Historical Archaeology: Exercises Using Documentary, Oral, and Material Evidence*. Englewood Cliffs, NJ: Prentice Hall.
Barrett, Terry
    1996   *Criticizing Photographs: An Introduction to Understanding Images*. 2nd edition. Mountain View, CA: Mayfield.

Berge, Zane L., and Mauri P. Collins, eds.
  1995 *Computer Mediated Communication and the Online Classroom*, vol. 1. *Overview and Perspectives*. Cresskill: Hampton Press.
Biolsi, Thomas, and Larry J. Zimmerman
  1997 *Indians and Anthropologists: Vine Deloria, Jr., and the Critique of Anthropology*. Tucson: University of Arizona Press.
Blakey, Michael
  1987 Skull Doctors: Intrinsic Social and Political Bias in the History of American Physical Anthropology. *Critique of Anthropology* 7(2):7–35.
Boschmann, Erwin, ed.
  1995 *The Electronic Classroom: A Handbook for Education in the Electronic Environment*. Medford, NJ: Learned Information.
Cambridge, Charles
  1992 Historical Contributions of American Indians. Workshop for Governmental American Indian Heritage Month, Region VIII, U.S. Department of Health and Human Services. June. Denver.
Cheek, Dennis W.
  1997 Anthropology in the Science and Social Studies Curriculum. In Kottak et al., pp. 308–315.
Conkey, Margaret, and Christine Hastorf, eds.
  1990 *The Uses of Style in Archaeology*. New York: Cambridge University Press.
Connah, Graham
  1987 *African Civilizations: Precolonial Cities and States in Tropical Africa: An Archaeological Perspective*. Cambridge, UK: Cambridge University Press.
Cotterell, Brian, and Johan Kamminga
  1990 *Mechanics of Pre-Industrial Technology*. Cambridge, UK: Cambridge University Press.
Davis, Barbara Gross
  1993 *Tools for Teaching*. San Francisco: Jossey-Bass.
Deloria, Vine, Jr.
  1970 *Custer Died for Your Sins*. New York: Avon.
Dorrell, Peter G.
  1994 *Photography in Archaeology and Conservation*. 2nd edition. Cambridge, UK: Cambridge University Press.
Fagan, Brian
  1995 *Time Detectives: How Archaeologists Use Technology to Recapture the Past*. New York: Simon and Schuster.
Flannery, Kent V.
  1972 The Cultural Evolution of Civilizations. *Annual Review of Ecology and Systematics* 3:399–426.
Foster, Michele
  1997 Strategies for Combating Racism in the Classroom. In Kottak et al., pp. 127–132.
Foster, Nelson, and Linda S. Cordell, eds.
  1992 *Chilies to Chocolate: Food the Americas Gave the World*. Tucson: University of Arizona Press.
Fraser, Douglas
  1968 *Village Planning in the Primitive World*. New York: George Braziller.
Froeschner, Elsie H.
  1992 Historical Vignette: Two Examples of Ancient Skull Surgery. *Journal of Neurosurgery* 76:550–552.

Gies, Frances, and Joseph Gies
  1994   *Cathedral, Forge, and Waterwheel: Technology and Invention in the Middle Ages*. New York: HarperPerennial.
Gonzales, Norma, and Cathy Amanti
  1997   Teaching Anthropological Methods to Teachers: The Transformation of Knowledge. In Kottak et al., pp. 353–359.
Hester, Thomas R., Harry J. Shafer, and Kenneth L. Feder
  1997   *Field Methods in Archaeology*. 7th edition. Mountain View, CA: Mayfield.
Hewitt, Nancy A.
  1992   Compounding Differences. *Feminist Studies* 18(2):313–326.
Irby, Beverly J., Karon LeCompte, and Rafael Lara-Alecio
  1997   New Approaches to Collaborative Education: Thought and Action. *NEA Higher Education Journal* 13(1):59–65.
James, Simon
  1997   Drawing Inferences: Visual Reconstructions in Theory and Practice. In Molyneaux, ed., pp. 22–48.
James, Peter, and Nick Thorpe
  1994   *Ancient Inventions*. New York: Ballantine Books.
Jameson, John H., Jr., ed.
  1997   *Presenting Archaeology to the Public: Digging for Truths*. Walnut Creek, CA: Altamira Press.
Jasanoff, Sheila, Gerald E. Markle, James C. Petersen, and Trevor Pinch, eds.
  1995   *Handbook of Science and Technology Studies*. Thousand Oaks, CA: Sage.
Jones, Sian
  1997   *The Archaeology of Ethnicity: Constructing Identities in the Past and Present*. London: Routledge.
Keeley, Lawrence H.
  1980   *Experimental Determination of Stone Tool Uses*. Chicago: University of Chicago Press.
Kehoe, Alice B.
  1994   "In fourteen hundred and ninety-two, Columbus sailed . . .": The Primacy of the National Myth in U.S. Schools. In Stone and MacKenzie, pp. 201–216.
Kottak, Conrad, Jane J. White, Richard H. Furlow, and Patricia C. Rice, eds.
  1997   *The Teaching of Anthropology: Problems, Issues, and Decisions*. Mountain View, CA: Mayfield.
Lechtman, Heather
  1991   The Production of Copper-Arsenic Alloys in the Central Andes: Highland Ores and Coastal Smelters? *Journal of Field Archaeology* 18(1):43–76.
Lechtman, Heather, and Ana Maria Soldi, eds.
  1985   *La Tecnologia en el Mundo Andino, vol. 1: Subsistencia y Mensuracion*. Mexico: Universidad Nacional Autonoma de Mexico.
Linne, S.
  1957   Technical Secrets of the American Indians: The Huxley Memorial Lecture, 1957. *Journal of the Royal Anthropological Institute of Great Britain and Ireland* 37(2):149–164.
Loewen, James W.
  1995   *Lies My Teacher Told Me: Everything Your American History Textbook Got Wrong*. New York: New Press.
Macaulay, David
  1979   *Motel of the Mysteries*. Boston: Houghton Mifflin.

MacNeish, Richard S.
1978   *The Science of Archaeology?* North Scituate, MA: Duxbury Press.
Marcus, George E.
1997   The Postmodern Condition and the Teaching of Anthropology. In Kottak et al., pp. 103–112.
Mendoza, Ruben G.
1997a   City Planning: Maya City Planning. In Selin, pp. 205–208.
1997b   Metallurgy in Meso and North America. In Selin, pp. 730–733.
1997c   Trephination. In Selin, pp. 985–986.
1998   *Review of Encyclopaedia of the History of Science, Technology, and Medicine in Non-Western Cultures,* edited by Helaine Selin. *Anthropology Newsletter* 39(4).
Mendoza, Ruben G., and Gretchen W. Jordan
1997   Road Networks in Ancient Native America. In Selin, pp. 868–872.
Mendoza, Ruben G., and Cruz C. Torres
1994   Hispanic Traditional Technology and Material Culture in the United States. In *Handbook of Hispanic Cultures in the United States: Anthropology.* Thomas Weaver, ed. pp. 59–84. Houston: Arte Publico Press.
Mendoza, Ruben G., and Jay R. Wolter
1997   Medicine in Meso and South America. In Selin, pp. 703–706.
Merton, Robert K.
1970   *Science, Technology and Society in Seventeenth-Century England.* New York: Harper and Row.
Michaels, George H., and Brian M. Fagan
1997   The Past Meets the Future: New Approaches to Teaching Archaeology. In Kottak et al., pp. 239–246.
Molyneaux, Brian L.
1997   Introduction: The Cultural Life of Images. In Molyneaux, ed., pp. 1–10.
Molyneaux, Brian L., ed.
1997   *The Cultural Life of Images: Visual Representation in Archaeology.* London: Routledge.
Moser, Stephanie, and Clive Gamble
1997   Revolutionary Images: The Iconic Vocabulary for Representing Human Antiquity. In Molyneaux, ed., pp. 184–212.
Mukhopadhyay, Carol C.
1997   Using Anthropology to Understand and Overcome Cultural Bias. In Kottak et al., pp. 89–102.
Muller, Nancy Ladd
1994   The House of the Black Burghardts: An Investigation of Race, Gender, and Class at the W. E. B. DuBois Boyhood Homesite. In Scott, pp. 81–94.
Nason, James D.
1987   The Determination of Significance: Curatorial Research and Private Collections. In Reynolds and Stott, pp. 31–67.
National Education Association
1998   "They're Talking on Campus...": About the One-third of all College Courses that Now Use the Internet as Part of the Syllabus. *NEA Advocate* 1(2):1.
Needham, Joseph
1982   *Science in Traditional China.* Cambridge, MA: Harvard University Press.

Newton, Dolores
  1987 What to Do Before the Archaeologist Arrives: Doing Culture History in the Ethnographic Domain. In Reynolds and Stott, pp. 129–153.
Ortiz de Montellano, Bernard R.
  1990 *Aztec Medicine, Health, and Nutrition*. New Brunswick, NJ: Rutgers University Press.
Orton, Clive, Paul Tyers, and Alan Vince
  1993 *Pottery in Archaeology*. Cambridge, UK: Cambridge University Press.
Plog, Stephen, and Fred Plog
  1997 Central Themes in Archaeology. In Kottak et al., pp. 218–222.
Rashed, Roshdi
  1997 Science as a Western Phenomenon. In Selin, pp. 884–890.
Rathje, William, and Cullen Murphy
  1992 *Rubbish: The Archaeology of Garbage*. New York: HarperPerennial.
Reynolds, Barrie, and Margaret A. Stott, eds.
  1987 *Material Anthropology: Contemporary Approaches to Material Culture*. Lanham, MD: University Press of America.
Rice, Patricia C.
  1997 Participant Archaeology. In Kottak et al., pp. 247–253.
  1998 *Doing Archaeology: A Hands-On Laboratory Manual*. Mountain View, CA: Mayfield.
Rodriguez-Sala, Maria Luisa, and Jose Omar Moncada Maya, eds.
  1994 *Enfoques Multidisciplinarios de la Cultura Científico-Tecnologica en Mexico*. Mexico: Universidad Nacional Autonoma de Mexico.
Ronan, Colin A.
  1978–95 *The Shorter Science and Civilization in China; An Abridgement of Joseph Needham's Original Text*, 5 vols. Cambridge, UK: Cambridge University Press.
Schlereth, Thomas J.
  1996 *Artifacts and the American Past*. Walnut Creek, CA: Altamira Press.
Schmidt, Peter R., ed.
  1996 *The Culture and Technology of African Iron Production*. Gainesville: University Press of Florida.
Schmidt, Peter R., and Thomas C. Patterson, eds.
  1995 *Making Alternative Histories: The Practice of Archaeology and History in Non-Western Settings*. Santa Fe: SAR Press.
Scott, Elizabeth M., ed.
  1994 *Those of Little Note: Gender, Race, and Class in Historical Archaeology*. Tucson: University of Arizona Press.
Selig, Ruth
  1997 The Challenge of Exclusion: Anthropology, Teachers, and Schools. In Kottak et al., pp. 299–307.
Selin, Helaine, ed.
  1997 *Encyclopaedia of the History of Science, Technology, and Medicine in Non-Western Cultures*. The Hague: Kluwer Academic.
Shanks, Michael
  1997 Photography and Archaeology. In Molyneaux, ed., pp. 73–107.
Silverberg, Robert
  1968 *Mound Builders of Ancient America: The Archaeology of a Myth*. New York: Greenwich.

Simmons, Marc, and Frank Turley
   1980   *Southwestern Colonial Ironwork: The Spanish Blacksmithing Tradition from Texas to California*. Santa Fe: Museum of New Mexico Press.
Singleton, Theresa A., and Mark D. Bograd
   1995   *The Archaeology of the African Diaspora in the Americas. Guides to the Archaeological Literature of the Immigrant Experience in America*, No. 2. Ann Arbor, MI: Society for Historical Archaeology.
Smardz, Karolyn E.
   1997   The Past through Tomorrow: Interpreting Toronto's Heritage to a Multicultural Public. In Jameson, pp. 101–113.
Smith, Alan G. R.
   1972   *Science and Society in the Sixteenth and Seventeenth Centuries*. History of European Civilization Library, Geoffrey Barraclough, General Editor. London: Harcourt Brace Jovanovich.
Smithsonian Institution
   1994   *Willful Neglect: The Smithsonian Institution and U.S. Latinos*. Washington, DC: Smithsonian Institution.
Spindler, George, and Louise Spindler
   1997   Teaching Culture Using "Culture Cases." In Kottak et al., pp. 77–82.
Stanley, Christine A., and Mathew L. Ouellett
   1998   The Diverse Classroom. *NEA Advocate* 1(2):5–8.
Stone, Peter G.
   1997   Presenting the Past: A Framework for Discussion. In Jameson, pp. 23–34.
Stone, Peter G., and Robert MacKenzie, eds.
   1994   *The Excluded Past: Archaeology in Education*. London: Routledge.
Stott, Margaret A.
   1987   Object, Context and Process: Approaches to Teaching about Material Culture. In Reynolds and Stott, pp. 13–30.
Tinto, Vincent
   1997   Enhancing Learning via Community: Thought and Action. *NEA Higher Education Journal* 13(1):53–58.
Trigger, Bruce G.
   1989   *A History of Archaeological Thought*. New York: Cambridge University Press.
Tunbridge, J. E., and G. J. Ashworth
   1996   *Dissonant Heritage: The Management of the Past as a Resource in Conflict*. Chichester, UK: John Wiley.
van Willigen, John
   1997   Innovative Applied Anthropology Research Practices Should Be Used in the Precollegiate and Undergraduate Classroom. In Kottak et al., pp. 266–272.
Vogel, Joseph O., ed.
   1997   *Encyclopedia of Precolonial Africa: Archaeology, History, Languages, Cultures, and Environments*. Walnut Creek, CA: Altamira Press.
Wajcman, Judy
   1995   Feminist Theories of Technology. In Jasanoff et al., pp. 189–204.
Watson-Verran, Helen, and David Turnbull
   1995   Science and Other Indigenous Knowledge Systems. In Jasanoff et al., pp. 115–139.
Weber, Robert J.
   1992   *Forks, Phonographs and Hot Air Balloons: A Field Guide to Inventive Thinking*. New York: Oxford University Press.

White, Jane J.
  1997a   Teaching about Cultural Diversity. In Kottak et al., pp. 70–76.
  1997b   Using the Construct of Culture to Teach about "The Other." In Kottak et al., pp. 334–341.
Whittaker, John C.
  1994   *Flintknapping: Making and Understanding Stone Tools.* Austin: University of Texas Press.
Willey, Gordon R., and Jeremy A. Sabloff
  1974   *A History of American Archaeology.* San Francisco: W. H. Freeman.
Wolf, Eric R.
  1982   *Europe and the People without History.* Berkeley: University of California Press.

25

Teaching Against Culturalist Essentialism

Judith Goode

Every year I incorporate U.S. cultural diversity in an introductory anthropology class. When I reach this point, I inevitably hear students invoke culturalist racialization as they comment on allegedly immoral behaviors by saying, "*They* can't help it, that's *their* culture." Immutable behavior which was once located in the body ("blood") is now just as firmly fixed in the mind ("culture"). Culture displaces the problematic concept of race but is used in similarly essentialist ways.[1]

With expanding interest in "multiculturalism," cultural anthropologists are often called upon to teach about diversity in general education classes. The pernicious cultural essentialism frequently expressed by our students has been reinforced in public discourse and the academy by the intersection of dominant U.S. discourses of official multiculturalism[2] with a popular view of timeless, bounded "cultures" fixed in individuals through early childrearing. A central goal of anthropology courses which address cultural diversity is to counteract this creeping culturalism.

This chapter will focus on strategies to denaturalize commonsense cultural categories. Such strategies make explicit the ways in which global, national, regional, and local institutions shape the formation, maintenance, and shifts in categories and hierarchies of difference. In doing this, we must replace the view of cultures as primordial with dynamic processes in which power shapes the boundaries within which cultural ideas and practices develop (Barth 1969; Hannerz 1992).

After discussing the contemporary context in which our students have learned to essentialize culture, several case studies will demonstrate the contingent nature of boundaries and hierarchies. These include historic shifts in the extension of whiteness to new populations, the role of the state in generating panethnic movements, the importance of local contexts in creating variations in "ethnic culture," and the effects of contemporary transnationalism.

The Complicity of Anthropology in Culturalism

As Eric Wolf (1982:3–23) has argued, the view of cultures as discrete and stable, like the concept of race, can be traced to the emergence of the discipline within colonial capitalism. Enlightenment beliefs in progress within a context of labor and resource exploitation encouraged the classification and ranking of "ways of life." In the academic division of labor, anthropology took on "the Other" while other disciplines focused on the ancient roots and contemporary forms of Western culture newly imagined as homogeneous. Anthropology's acceptance of this division persists in the way we marginalize studies of Europe and North America today.

Earlier definitions of culture in anthropology emphasized homogeneity and stasis (structural functionalism), geographically bounded systems of traits (culture areas), and automatic cultural reproduction through the internalization of culture (culture and personality, national character). These tendencies were linked to the privileging of closed local spaces in developing fieldwork methods (Gupta and Ferguson 1997), the Freudian moment with its emphasis on internalized early childhood experiences, and most significantly the Boas-Benedict project, which used cultural relativism to counter scientific racism and ethnocentric models of cultural evolution (Wax 1993).[3]

Since the 1970s, anthropology and social theory in general have shifted to viewing cultural boundaries and practices as dynamic. People are no longer seen as determined by "culture" but as producers of shifting meanings and practices within the context of historically contingent power relations.

Yet the essentialized view of culture is still embedded in our teaching. In introductory textbooks, cultures are often portrayed with unproblematized boundaries and described in terms of particular uniform and internally integrated traits. Colonialism, urbanization, and international migration are discussed separately and viewed as events which disturb otherwise stably reproduced traditions. This conceptual framework now undermines our attempts to illuminate the contingency of boundary-making processes and identities, in the United States as well as the rest of the world.

From Race to Culture in U.S. Nation-Building Discourses

Ideas about race and culture are fundamental to all narratives of the nation (Williams 1989; Dominguez 1995). Unlike many European and postcolonial national myths which emphasize common descent and history, the United States, "a nation of immigrants," uses a national narrative which focuses on unifying the culturally different through liberal democracy and presumed equal opportunity. Unity is symbolized by *e pluribus unum* (one out of many). Giving such significance to cultural heritage while denying exclusion and structural inequality encourages culturalist explanations for inequality. Just as 19th-century scientific racism based on biological inheritance produced hierarchies,

20th-century "culturalism," based on cultures as fixed rules, leads to the construction of hierarchies of moral worth (Chock 1995). Moreover, culturalist essentialism by invoking bounded cultures masks possibilities for changing relationships. We need to teach students that boundaries between groups are not natural but are formed and dissolved through historical contingencies which alter identities and relationships.

Understandings of national unity have varied in different historic moments. Current "unity in diversity" describes the nation as a mosaic, tapestry, or salad of different cultures in which the parts retain their integrity as they contribute to a better whole. This contrasts with the earlier prewar models of Anglo-conformity which required the relinquishing of all specific elements of foreign cultural practice through forced Americanization (elimination) or through a "melting pot" in which new elements are melted down and absorbed.

As Steinberg (1981) argues, the "new ethnicity" which generated today's "unity in diversity" pluralism emerged in part to deny the existence of racial inequality. It covered over the overt discussion of racial oppression which characterized the civil rights initiatives of the black, Chicano and red power movements of the 1960s and 1970s.

The celebration of the United States bicentennial in 1976 allowed the state to replace an image of racial conflict with one of unity and provided an opportunity to institutionalize this new ethnic form of pluralism based on national origin. European American groups who immigrated at the turn of the century had formerly been racialized and subjected to the Americanizing project of the state. Now such groups were provided with money for museums, parades, and festivals which encouraged ethnic performances and reified the pluralist mosaic. In becoming culturally hyphenated Americans, they stressed the way groups used traditional cultural heritage as resources to overcome hardship.

The new pluralist master narrative (Chock 1995; Goode and Schneider 1994; Urciuoli 1996) supported an ideology that linked group success and failure to cultural values and reinforced the construction of hierarchies of moral worth. The effects of major historical political-economic processes and increased race and class inequalities are completely masked by such an emphasis.

Yet at the same time, a competing and contradictory understanding of U.S. diversity was becoming encoded in law and political action. The civil rights model of difference which emphasized the history of systematic racial exclusion was made official by the state in 1977 when OMB Directive 15 created official categories of difference to be used for purposes of evaluating civil rights remedies. Five official groups of difference were constructed. Four were ostensibly based on "race" (white, black, American Indian/Alaskan Native and Asian/Pacific Islander) while Hispanic was considered an ethnic category based on language, history, and culture.

These categories ignore vast differences in identities and experience. They also reflect the degree to which European immigrants have become "white," the unmarked default category against which African Americans, Native Americans, Asian Americans and Hispanic Americans are defined as minorities. While designated as racial, such categories were not biological realities but reflected social constructions through state laws, judicial decisions and policies related to the regulation of land and labor (see Chapter 8, this volume). They were often reciprocally accepted as collective identities (Espiritu 1992).

In 1997, the American Anthropological Association suggested that ethnic origin be substituted for official race and ethnic categories to capture the fact that all members of the nation state, with the exception of indigenous peoples, come from somewhere else. However, it would not impute to ethnic origin the fundamental significance in "determining" one's essential identity, social affiliations, beliefs, or behavior in the way that post-1970s popular understandings of race and ethnicity do.

These official categories which conflate biology, culture, and geography have become the official categories of difference ("unity through diversity") utilized by the media, schools, churches, workplaces, and other civil institutions. The concept of multiculturalism reflects an avoidance of talk about race. Culture, seen as a positive term, bears all the weight of talk about difference. Yet, as race is submerged, the two terms are conflated, and culture becomes the polite proxy for race in much discourse (Dominguez 1995).

Student Experiences with Official Multiculturalism

Our students have grown up amongst varying discourses of multiculturalism produced by different institutional interests (Paredes 1996; Paredes and Pohl 1995; Goode 1998; Urciuoli 1996) and come to us with many preconceptions. In mainstream schools (and many public parades and festivals), multiculturalism denies that race and class matter. "Unity in diversity" is celebrated with emphasis on discrete cultures of long-term ethnic and immigrant-becoming-ethnic groups as the fundamental building blocks of the nation. In these celebrations, sanitized, packaged performances of culture at a distance allow other Americans to consume aestheticized commodities like food, music, and dance. These "good" folkloric presentations of culture are silent about the perceived "bad" parts of some heritages: the contested moral arenas relating to stereotyped "family values," work habits, and violence. Such silence leaves racialized images intact. "They can't help it, it's their culture."

University campuses became important sites of action for cultural identity movements in the 1970s and 1980s. Ethnic studies programs were demanded and became spaces in which a generation of community intellectuals formed a collective political consciousness. However, today, many university administrations use multicultural programs for their own purposes: to defuse conflict and to market "multiculturalism" in order to recruit and retain new students. Such programs often return to and promote a naturalized and essentialized view of bounded, objectified cultures which own icons and monolithic historical narratives (Segal and Handler 1995).[4]

One of the most essentializing uses of official multiculturalism permeates professional training in which multiculturalism is seen as a commodified professional skill. Professional authorities construct uniform "traditional" cultural contents for each official category. These are then taught to professionals to enhance patient compliance, market transactions, or conflict resolution on the campus or in the workplace.

Finally, students have been exposed to the marketing of exotic culture as a postmodern leisure commodity, a form of stimulating experience. In this way multiculturalism is used to attract consumers to cities like New Orleans and Miami. These efforts exploit ethnic neighborhoods and create cycles of festivals packaged for the consumption of exoticism.

There are significant differences in cultural systems of meaning and practice in the United States. However, students need to learn that meaningful communities of practice are neither permanent, nor do they conform to standard multicultural categories.

Denaturalizing Categories and Demonstrating Boundary Processes

Cultural boundaries often emerge and shift as groups ally with, oppose, or avoid each other within complex structures of power. Cultural practices shift as boundaries and relationships across boundaries change and groups invert, subvert, or reinterpret ideologies and practices of dominant, competing, and allied groups in relation to their own. Boundaries can become more inclusive, for example, as panethnic movements create alliances between groups who do not share close common descent. Similarly, competition and conflict within populations with common cultural lineage can produce avoidance, opposition, and ultimately new boundaries. As boundaries shift, new cultural forms and practices are invented or reinterpreted. Resistance to assimilation leads to rejection of cultural practices identified with dominant groups.

This chapter focuses on boundary processes rather than individual identity. Yet students also need a framework for understanding their place as individuals in this process. As Zavella (1994) points out in discussing Chicana diversity, we need to understand how categories affect shifting and multiple individual subjectivities. While people first experience life within natal families, they later move through diverse, expanding networks of relationships in differently structured local spaces. As they are exposed to shifting and contingent ideologies of powerful institutions like schools and mass media, or participate in social movements of opposition and resistance, they constantly manipulate their identity, beliefs, and practices.

Extending White Privilege

The ways in which whiteness as a privileged status was extended reveals the significance of population movements, economic shifts, electoral politics and state policy. The two cases below illustrate the extension of whiteness to formerly racialized groups: Irish in the 19th century and Jews after World War II.

Definitions of racial otherness in the United States are contingent on shifting economic and political relationships. Wars of conquest, struggles over land and recruitment, and control of labor influenced the ways in which populations were excluded and racialized. Groups who were conquered such as indigenous populations or residents of annexed Spanish territories (Mexicans and Puerto Ricans) or those exploited economically (slaves and Chinese unskilled labor) were denied suffrage[5] and were excluded from national myths.

At different points in time, the government and the public treated populations differently. For example, Africans, first brought to the United States as free labor were not significantly differentiated from white indentured labor in early settlements (Smedley 1993). Their defined inferiority grew as changes in world market commodity values made slave trading a lucrative capital investment. Exploitation increased as Africans were transformed into chattel slaves and denied personhood and civil rights.

As whiteness became a privileged racial category, many European groups immigrating to the United States were not automatically considered white. The way in which white privilege was extended to the Irish (Roediger 1990; Ignatiev 1995) is a significant example of how major economic transformations and labor force shifts intersected with political events. In this instance, Democratic Party formation within the context of the regional conflict between Northern industrialists and Southern planters helped to shape collective identities and boundaries.

The Irish, denied rights and treated as an inferior group by the British in their homeland, arrived in the United States in the mid-19th century freighted with a racialized identity and victimized by discrimination in jobs and housing. Yet the Irish arrived at a critical moment in the expanding industrial economy and provided an unskilled labor pool different from native-born artisans.

Irish immigrants originally inhabited the bottom of the social hierarchy alongside freed slaves in Northern cities. Both populations worked together in menial jobs and lived in tenement housing. Irish leadership was active in the abolition movement. Yet in the context of the pre – Civil War sectional dispute between Northern industrialists and Southern planters, suffrage gave the Irish both a symbolic advantage as included free citizens and the power that came from the courtship of their vote by potential political patrons. At the same time, free blacks who had been given suffrage within many Northern states were losing the right to vote.[6]

Increasing numbers of Irish citizens who had once supported abolition opposed their Northern Whig bosses who led the abolition movement. Irish laborers were recruited into the Democratic Party and persuaded by Southern planters that freed slaves would take their jobs and that slaves as property received better care from their owners than they did as "wage slaves" to industrialists. As they turned away from their support of abolition, they accepted the "psychological wages"[7] of white privilege which foreclosed the alternative possibility of solidarity with blacks based on shared labor exploitation.

The 20th century provides another example of the extension of whiteness to formerly racialized southern and eastern European immigrants: Italians, Slavic-speaking peoples, and Jews. These populations made up a significant portion of the 1880-to-1920 immigration wave. Their arrival in large numbers during the expansion of industrial capitalism coincided with and exacerbated the developing ideology of scientific racism. Physical characteristics such as head form were used to create hierarchies of racial types which allegedly correlated with aspects of intelligence, behavior, and morality.

Assimilationist policies were carried out by schools and settlement houses. These policies pushed the new populations to become American and discouraged Old World habits, particularly those related to diet and language use.

World War II and the economic expansion and public policies which followed the war changed all this. Descendants of the turn-of-the-century migration wave were whitened as they moved into the suburban middle class. First, the prewar New Deal enabled collective bargaining which provided middle-class wages, benefits, and job security to the working class. The cessation of massive immigration through restrictive quotas in the 1920s diminished the visible threat of foreigners. The war also dissolved the line between excluded foreigner and citizen as the children of immigrants bled for the nation. Finally, the GI bill, a policy response to the fear of mass unemployment, contained educational provisions and related mortgage subsidies for home ownership. Educated veterans were easily absorbed by the demand for educated technical, professional, and managerial workers in the expanded economy. New highway construction coupled with massive federal mortgage subsidies favored new building and opened up suburban development. This loosened the links between the new middle classes and the older urban neighborhoods.

Brodkin (Sacks) (1994, 1998) demonstrates how this process worked for Jews who had been formerly excluded from many residential spaces and professional careers through deed covenants and university quotas. They were extended white privilege in the postwar expansion through the extensive affirmative action programs for veterans. Anti-Semitic racism was severely constrained as Americans became aware of the effects of Nazi racism on Jews in the Holocaust.

As the formerly racialized turn-of-the-century immigrant populations gained access to the professions, new corporate workplaces, and suburban residential spaces, their collective ethnic identities became less salient both inside and outside the boundary. As the boundary softened, everyday cultural practices changed and, for many, ethnically specific practices were situationally limited to simple symbols used at holidays and life cycle events (Waters 1990).

Meanwhile, blacks displaced from the rural South were coming north[8] in large numbers into the declining and discriminatory industrial labor market and the aging housing market in northern cities. Mexican agricultural labor was being imported to the Southwest through the Bracero program in the 1940s and 1950s. Both populations remained racialized and were systematically but informally excluded from public programs which subsidized middle-class status.

Panethnicity and the Role of the State

The state has historically played several different roles in creating and maintaining racialist exclusion (Takaki 1979). As Merry (Chapter 8, this volume) illustrates in the Hawaiian case, while indigenous people and in-migrating unskilled Asian laborers are both marked and excluded, they have generally been defined and treated differently because their encounters with colonial settlers involved different issues: land vs. labor.

Policy and shifting Native American boundaries

Mainland Native Americans have been the subjects of unusually rigid definition and regulation by the state (Pevar 1992:2).[9] They were subject to a set of contradictory policies which at different times produced separatism amongst tribes, encouraged assimilation, or promoted panethnic American Indian consciousness.

As European settlement expanded, state-sponsored pacification and control set official tribal boundaries through the treaty process which granted "sovereignty."[10] In the process of forced settlement on tribal reservations, many settlements brought together several different tribes, creating new collective boundaries (Nagel and Snipp 1995). Pressure by white settlers for land produced the Dawes Act (1887) designed to release reservation land to the open market. Indians were in turn encouraged to leave reservation land for work and education and to assimilate.

As part of the New Deal in the 1930s, the Indian Reorganization Act reasserted the importance of tribal separateness by attempting to create local self-determination and economic development (Spicer 1969). Through individualized charters reflecting past tribal practices, reservations would retain sovereign rights to local jurisdiction over criminal law, land rights, and taxation within their territory (Biolsi 1995b). New Deal social services were to be provided through these newly institutionalized and regulated tribal governments.

One ironic unintended result of this program which reified tribal difference was that it forged a pan–Native American collective identity. Tribal leaders converging on Washington to work on these new initiatives came to see themselves as having shared interests vis-à-vis the state, thus laying the basis for later pan-Indian consciousness (Nagel 1995).

In the postwar 1950s, federal policy again encouraged off-reservation relocation to urban labor markets. These urban areas became important sites for the development of the Red Power movement during the civil rights struggles of the 1960s and 1970s, further strengthening pan-Indian consciousness (Cornell 1988).[11]

In 1978, attenuated tribal identities were revived and reinforced when an official recognition process administered by the BIA's Bureau of Acknowledgment and Recognition extended recognition to formerly unrecognized tribes in response to civil rights land claims by tribes that had never had a treaty relationship to the federal government. Tribes had to prove historical continuity through archival and anthropological evidence.

This formal recognition process worked against growing pan-Indian unity by engendering competition between tribes for recognition and a cleavage between recognized and unrecognized tribes. Recently, rights to authenticate crafts and to operate casinos have exacerbated this split.

Self-identified tribes like the Lumbee, who emerged from fragments of separate bands of Tuscarora could not sufficiently document their histories. Blu (1980) and Sider (1993) see a Lumbee identity and boundary as forged over time in an agricultural region in which the white community severely denigrated former slaves. Lumbee identity was forged to differentiate this fragmented population from blacks. Maintaining a strong collective identity for over a century but lacking required documents, Lumbee are excluded from federal recognition as an "authentic" tribe and denied the federal rights and entitlements which accompany recognition.

The state through its policies is deeply implicated in the structuring of Native American tribal boundaries and identities. Compliance and resistance to these policies has produced, in different times and places, heightened tribal consciousness, heightened pan-Indian consciousness and increased assimilation. Each move had significant consequences for cultural beliefs and practices.

OMB Directive 15 and Panethnicity

The civil rights movements of the 1960s and 1970s and the state response in creating the OMB categories of 1977 accelerated panethnic identity movements. Espiritu (1992) has defined panethnicity as shifts in levels of group consciousness from smaller to larger units, which are not as closely related in culture or descent. When the state seeks to allocate resources or enforce political representation through reifying such categories, these constructions have new saliency for collective boundaries.

Panethnic cultural identity movements accept state categories and attempt to seek political power through them. It produces narratives of common oppression and shared practices and symbols to mark new boundaries. Espiritu (1992) describes the process of Asian panethnicity on the west coast as a response to the application of the official state label – Asian/Pacific Islander – to many populations with very different histories. She chronicles the ways in which commonality in history and culture is rearticulated as the new movement attempts to construct a broad new boundary while leaving room for differences resulting from national origin, class, wave of immigration, and the role of U.S. intervention in the homeland.

Today, the contemporary Asian American movement includes both descendants of 19th-century exploited-labor migrants (Chinese and Japanese) and the very different recent Chinese immigrants from Taiwan and Hong Kong who come with financial and cultural capital. Other Asian migrants came to the United States as the direct or indirect result of U.S. military involvement in their home nations. These include Filipinos whose colonial subordination dates back to the Spanish-American War in 1898, and Koreans and Southeast Asian refugees whose dislocation from their homelands is heavily related to more recent U.S. military activity. South Asians (from India, Pakistan, and Sri Lanka) were an ambiguous population added to the Asian category at the last minute. The ambiguities in their relationship to the pan-Asian movement is discussed in a series of essays in a recent volume, *A Part, and Yet Apart* (1998).

Cultural forms and performances are often used to form collective memories and consciousness as the basis for politicization. Lisa Lowe (1997) has documented the emergence of particular Asian American cultural forms (literature, theater, etc.) and spaces (ethnic studies programs) which have fostered an Asian American consciousness. They recognize an alternative history in which Asian exploited labor was "brought in but kept outside" through exclusionary legislative and judicial acts[12] in the 19th century. Later Asians were culturally constructed as the foreign enemy as the result of 20th-century wars (Japan, Korea, and Southeast Asia). She comments on the way in which contemporary anti-immigrant movements serve to further strengthen the common consciousness of Asian Americans from diverse national and class backgrounds.

Similarly, a collection edited by W. Flores and Benmayor (1997) features case studies showing how Latino cultural forms of expression can create legitimacy for Latinos as respected public persons who can make political claims. For example, one case study looks at how participation in a cultural performance group which evokes collective memories is linked to local political action (R. Flores 1997). Another illustrates how the production of cultural meanings transformed women cannery workers during a strike (W. Flores 1997).

Several studies examine how local intra-Latino economic and power relations respectively strengthened or weakened pan-Latino boundaries. For example, this leads to a reassertion of Mexican vs. Puerto Rican identity at certain times within the movement in Chicago (Padilla 1985), where the Mexican community is older and larger.

In these situations groups select, modify, and invent new shared symbols to serve as boundary markers of the new collective space. Often symbols originate with one group but become accepted by the collective. In Philadelphia the Colombian national day in July was for some time celebrated together by a coalition of non-Puerto Rican populations in order to counter Puerto Rican dominance of autumn Latino celebrations, their seniority and their numerical strength (Goode and Schneider 1994). In a similar way in San Francisco, Cinco de Mayo (Mexican Independence Day) was also celebrated by a pan-Latino coalition. Sommers (1991) compares several San Francisco Cinco de Mayo festivals which try to maintain both a national "inner" boundary and a panethnic "outer" boundary within the marked Latino space of the Mission District business strip. Under certain conditions this effort succeeded while in other circumstances it failed.

African panethnicity is also complex and contradictory. The relationship between African Americans and transnational migrants of African descent from the Caribbean and Africa has been negatively affected by U.S. structural racism. There is a growing interest in studying the ways in which pan-African diasporan cultural forms are produced as critique and resistance (Gilroy 1995). At the same time Basch et al. (1994) discuss the ways in which avoiding U.S. practices of racialization plays a role in the use of strong national origin identities by Caribbean peoples and Africans who avoid panethnicity in their desire to avoid racialization as American blacks. Portes and Stepick (1993: 176–202) illustrate this for Haitians vis-à-vis American blacks in Miami. In this way, transnational identities limit panethnic collective consciousness.

The strategic use of panethnic cultural essentialism involves searching for cultural and historical similarities using categories established by state power. Such movements are important political mobilization strategies, but can succumb to the trap of cultural essentialism accompanied by assertions of moral and cultural superiority. This limits the capacity to see common class interests across ethnic boundaries.

Immigrants Become Ethnics: The Importance of Place and Time

In 1965 U.S. immigration laws changed, creating a large-scale wave of immigration made up of large numbers of non-European peoples. Our students have grown up in this changing world and many are immigrants themselves. The long-term journey from immigrant to ethnic can take many different intergenerational turns.[13]

As Nina Glick Schiller (1977) wrote several decades ago, ethnic groups are made not born. In order to understand this process, one needs to examine both the homeland experiences and the nature of the places in which immigrants settle. Cultural reproduction and boundary maintenance in a particular settlement area is significantly shaped by the workings of labor and housing markets, by state and institutional policies relating to education and language, and by the scale of the immigrant wave, the opportunity structure in the host community, and the local racial hierarchy (Lamphere 1992).

Place and Italian American boundaries

The case of Italian immigration is a good example of the way different settings influence the nature of long-term processes. A comparison between the historic formation of Italian ethnicity in two regions of the United States demonstrates that neither Italian American "culture" or collective consciousness is natural, stable, or homogeneous.

Italian settlement was bicoastal. The largest concentrations were in the industrial Northeast but there was also an Italian presence on the west coast, especially in California.[14] Italians came to the United States with little or no Italian national consciousness. The Italian nation state was a new, contested idea and major regional distinctions overshadowed unity.

Italian immigration to the Northeast was predominantly from the more feudal south of Italy and occurred during the massive 1880–1920 wave pushed by a massive southern Italian economic crisis. On the other hand, Italian immigrants to California came from northern Italy before this mass migration. This spatial and temporal difference produced significant cultural differences between the two settlements. On both coasts, the migration stream included people from different provinces who did not at first view themselves as sharing cultural practices. For example, regional status differences became exaggerated in Philadelphia. For two generations, intermarriage between those from Sicily, Calabria, and the Abruzzi was strongly discouraged.

The receiving context was also different for northern Californians and Philadelphians. This led to differences in the ways in which Italians fitted into the racial hierarchy and were clustered or dispersed in space. Northern Italians arrived in California in the 1860s and 1870s at the time of the Gold Rush. They entered extractive economies of fishing, mining, and agriculture, thereby avoiding the exploitative sectors of menial work for which Mexican and Asian labor was being recruited. In the extractive sectors, they developed the small-scale family enterprises. Their settlement pattern was dispersed rather than in tightly clustered enclaves. Compared to exploited Mexican and Chinese labor immigrants who bore the brunt of racial ideology (DiLeonardo 1984) they were not significantly racialized.

In Philadelphia, Italian immigrants, along with Slavic and Jewish immigrants arriving in large numbers at the same time, were racialized by dominant institutions. The three groups entered unskilled industrial jobs while sharing tenement space clustered in South Philadelphia. Yet each group was stereotyped differently by social workers (Juliani 1978) and social scientists (DiLeonardo 1986:19–20). Italians were described as inclined to criminal behavior and unable to extend moral obligation beyond their own families. Their diet was seen as primitive, heavy, and unhealthy. Ironically, today, the fish, vegetable, and olive oil complex of the Mediterranean diet is extolled as light and nutritious as it ascends to the aestheticized world of high cuisine.

Initial racialization is exemplified by the experience of one group of immigrants who were recruited to an industrializing town outside Philadelphia. Stonemasons and their families, recruited from Calabria in the early 20th century, were brought to build industrial sites, public institutions, and elite housing. The immigrants were segregated across the railroad tracks. Occupationally they were forbidden to work in the factories and limited to heavy construction and other menial work (Goode, Curtis, et al. 1984).

Today, in both California and Philadelphia, in the wake of postwar "whitening" and middle-class ascendance, many Italian Americans have been absorbed into corporate jobs and suburban spaces. They are situational ethnics whose ethnic consciousness is limited to special occasions and major life events.

Yet, in both California and Philadelphia, there are many Italians who are still involved in small businesses and local politics in which extended family cooperation and interfamily solidarity is key. For them, the many reinterpreted cultural practices of Italian ethnicity are still salient in everyday life. The following description of difference in three social spaces in Philadelphia illustrates the importance of local experience in the formation of ethnic boundaries, cultural practices, and identities.

Many of the formerly racialized stonemason migrants from Calabria have remained in the same town, now a service center for surrounding suburban housing developments. As they moved across the tracks to middle-class housing, their former housing became occupied by African Americans. They have also moved into positions of control in the local business strip, the local real estate market, and local municipal politics. This local power has been reinforced by preferred Italian American endogamy and an array of strong formal associations and informal clubs which maintain an ethnic boundary. Some children who marry non-Italians move away, but a large number with their outsider spouses and newly formed households remain incorporated. Within the boundary, significant but reinterpreted cultural practices are strongly maintained through everyday domestic practices, life-cycle celebrations, and an annual patron saint's fiesta (Goode, Curtis, et al. 1984).

South Philadelphia, just south of Philadelphia's metropolitan downtown district, is social space marked as "Italian" by most Philadelphians. The large open area "Italian Market" which takes up many square blocks is one significant marker of this space although its vendors and customers are increasingly

Vietnamese. Ironically, this area was never demographically dominated by people of Italian origin. Initially, this was the antebellum residential space shared by Irish and black residents described by Ignatiev (1995). During the turn-of-the-century immigration wave, it served as the initial settlement for southern and eastern Europeans. Italian immigrants who initially emphasized their regional identities, over time took on a pan-Italian ethnicity. Local institutions which promoted this sense of pan-Italian community were the nationality parishes with mass in Italian, related parochial schools, and the market. The market was a place for daily interaction, a distribution point for Italian greens produced in Italian-owned truck farms of southern New Jersey, as well as imported cheeses and olive oil and locally produced bread, sausages, dried fruit, and herbs, etc.[15]

With the postwar extension of whiteness to the descendants of the mass immigrant wave, marriage between white Catholics from any national background became common in this space (Dubin 1996). Nonetheless, many intermarried households retained a strong Italian American self-identification.[16] There were local advantages to Italian American identity and symbolic capital in practicing reinterpreted Italian culture. These were key to belonging to the local community and gaining access to networks of support and opportunity. Italians had dominated local ward politics for generations. A large number of people held patronage jobs. Italian institutions were dominant in the area. In contrast, the institutions for eastern Europeans, for example, were located in a distant neighborhood.[17] After World War II, many families entered professional and managerial jobs and moved to the suburbs. Others remained in local owner-occupied housing and were embedded in common workplaces and networks of work and exchange.

A study of Italian American households in both the suburban town and South Philadelphia in the late 1970s found that both everyday and celebratory food practices symbolically marked households as "hyphenated" Italian Americans. Food patterning was shared across households, even those with mixed national origins. Mothers-in-law taught their non-Italian daughters-in-law how to keep an Italian home. If the woman was Italian, she maintained the cuisine of her family, recognizing that Italian cooking and the rhythm of eating events had symbolic value for many neighborhood young men.

Yet the food system found in the 1970s was very different from that found among the immigrant generation. Contrasts between cultural food practices in a study done in the 1930s, and those of the 1970s demonstrate that the pattern of meals and celebrations had shifted from one which reproduced Old World practices to the creation of a truly hyphenated food system to parallel a growing hyphenated American identity.

Italians initially used food to recall the homeland and to mark Italianness in contrast to their established neighbors who were pejoratively described as having food with no taste or texture such as white bread and mayonnaise.

Today, an elaborate pattern of alternating Italian and Anglo types of meals throughout the week is maintained. This involves the systematic alternation of Italian meal formats called "gravy" meals (pasta dishes with spicy, slow-cooked tomato-based sauces) with "American" meals rigidly structured around segregated meat, starch, and boiled vegetable components of English origin. Celebratory meals also represent a hyphenated identity as equal parts of Italian and Anglo content are presented through elaborate buffets or sequences of courses (Goode, Curtis, et al. 1984; Goode, Theophano, et al. 1984).

Included in these practices are significant inter-household food exchanges which cement the political and economic bonds across local households identified as Italian American. In these social spaces, unlike the households of situational ethnics, women who increasingly work outside the home continue to practice an elaborate pattern of everyday food preparation, celebratory events, and exchange. The study of these two communities as well as DiLeonardo's work in California reveals the importance of women in producing and reproducing ethnic practices.

In a third neighborhood which is today the most diverse in the city, new immigrants from Asia, the Caribbean, and Latin America share space with established descendants of turn-of-the-century immigrants. Here there had never been concentrated Italian settlement, nationality parishes, or Italian-oriented small businesses such as those found in the other two sites. Everyone knew of some descendants of Italian immigrants, but they were not self- or publicly identified as Italian American. The systematic patterning of meals and celebrations was missing.

When multicultural festivals came to this increasingly diverse neighborhood in the 1980s, people were pressured to accept single ethnic identities. In response, families joked about their hybrid nationalities. In fact, at one church's diversity festival, all the Euro-American (or white) women rejected the priest's attempt to organize food by nation of origin, tearing down the national flags and uniting their tables under one American flag. While several of the women were Italian or married to Italians, there was no Italian food. This was predominantly American: cold roast meats, and mayonnaise-dressed salads with a few generic central/eastern European items like sausages and sauerkraut included. Over several decades, these women of the parish had developed this way of diminishing nationality markers in parish food events. As they resisted nationality labels in the festival, they asserted their seniority as Americans ("whites") over their new neighbors. Italian identity was submerged.

Different waves, different "cultures"

Cases in which immigrants from the same nation state arrive in different immigrant waves point out the fallacy of ascribing fixed, timeless "cultures" to nations of origin. Two interesting comparisons are between the Poles of the turn-of-the-century immigrant wave and the post-Solidarity refugee wave, and the late-19th-century wave of Chinese labor migration in contrast to the current wave (Chen 1992; Kwong 1998).

Polish-origin peoples have been studied in Philadelphia (Goode and Schneider 1994) and Chicago (Erdmans 1995). In both cities, the historic moment of immigration produced entirely different experience and practice. The earlier wave consisted of largely peasant agrarian workers who moved into industrial and mining work. Over many generations, they created the symbols and practices of Polonia (the community of Poles in America) with such food symbols as kielbasa and pierogies and such musical forms as the polka. Their Catholicism was based on community parish life where everyone contributes to maintain and reproduce the parish.

In contrast, contemporary refugees[18] are university professionals (intelligentsia) and skilled artisans who have lived urban cosmopolitan lives. They have also experienced socialism and the Solidarity movement and see the church as a site for political action and social service.

This leads to differences in class position as well as cultural ideas and practices. Nevertheless, in Philadelphia, new Poles were settled by state-sponsored refugee agencies in the dominant Polish American space based on assumptions that they shared culture. New Poles value cosmopolitan, urban lifestyles and the high culture of Chopin and Polish writers and artists. Polish Americans see Polish culture in their special foods and dances which they proudly locate in a timeless agrarian peasant past. Such differences engendered conflict over defining Polish culture in the displays for the new Polish museum in Philadelphia. Such differences also create class resentment and an emerging boundary as ideas about the role of the church and parochial education clash. New Poles often leave the neighborhood when they can afford to, thereby negating the U.S. pluralist discourse that constructs both Polish refugees and Polish Americans as part of a homogeneous culture.

Contrasting Chinese waves involve similar differences in class backgrounds and historical experience. In the 19th century Chinese were recruited to the United States for a brief period for menial labor. In 1882 they were restricted from further entry. Those who had settled were excluded from citizenship and encouraged to return home. Today, Chinese immigration from Hong Kong, Taiwan, and the People's Republic of China has resumed since the immigration reforms in 1965. Chen (1992) describes the differences between the community formations of the 19th century and today. The current wave includes both those with significant capital (Horton 1995) and poor workers recruited to work for them in an enclave economy (Kwong 1998).

Transnationalism

While earlier Polish and Chinese refugees were part of a turn-of-the-century transnational labor migration to expanding industrial and plantation economies seeking cheap labor, today's immigrants are part of a broader process of postindustrial economic restructuring.

The mobility of people, capital, information, goods, and services today has facilitated permanent, durable, and intense transnational ties. The U.S. master narrative of one-way migration to freedom and opportunity reinforced ignorance of the substantial degree of return migration and remittances for earlier waves of immigrants. Nonetheless, early 20th-century European immigrants were restricted in contact with their homeland by world wars and the cold war. Today, the extraordinary degree to which people participate in the life of their nation of origin has given rise to the term *transnationalism*, which denotes the double nature of the fields of social, political, and economic activity in which today's immigrants live and the dual nature of their subjectivities.

The creation of new immigrant wealth in the United States has played a major role in the nation-building projects of many of the sending nation states (Basch et al. 1994). This includes funding economic projects in the homeland and participating in politics. Immigrants located in the multinational finance capital sector of the global economy alternate between U.S. or homeland interests.

These structural relationships in turn have an effect on the ways in which those residing in the United States define, value, and act on the possibility of U.S. citizenship (Chavez 1988; Hagen 1994; Ong 1996; Goode 1998). For today's transnational immigrants who remain embedded in more than one state and move back and forth between them, "becoming American" is interpreted in a different way than it is in the master immigrant narrative. This has an effect on both boundaries and cultural practices.

Future Possibilities Depend on Contingencies

What are the future possibilities for diversity? To what extent and under what conditions will we continue to see white privilege extended to some populations and a continued exclusion of others? To what extent and under what conditions will panethnic movements among racialized groups succeed in creating strong coalitions based on official categories? To what extent and under what conditions will national cultural heritages continue to be evoked and affect boundaries and cultural practices? To what extent and under what global circumstances will transnational community boundaries continue to create dual identities and allegiances? Answers to these questions depend on the contingent workings of economic and political power at the local, regional, and national level which change the status quo as well as the way in which people organize responsive social movements.[19]

Class ascendance can contribute to "whitening" as we saw in the case of descendants of turn-of-the-century immigrants. Aihwa Ong (1996) and Goode (1998) discuss the circumstances in which economic power partially whitens Asian immigrant capitalists, allowing them access to some privileged occupations and residential spaces while other Asians continue to be negatively racialized.

An overemphasis on racial and ethnic categories masks commonalities in class position and exploitation. Biolsi (1995a) in an analysis of Lakota Sioux tribal law suits has argued that the legal context of reservation rights has limited political space to issues of protecting Indian sovereignty. This emphasis masks commonalities in class constraints and limitations vis-à-vis the poor white farmers on allotment (reservation) land. This has created racial hostility between the two populations, thereby precluding any class-based political alliances just as the extension of white privilege ruptured the potential alliance between the Irish and freed Blacks in the 19th century. Yet in other circumstances, local cross-racial class-based movements have had some success (Sanjek 1994: 121; Goode and Schneider 1994:254–260).

NOTES

1   Most Americans are not aware that the belief in clearly bounded racial groups among *Homo sapiens* has been scientifically discredited. This is because discomfort with the concept of race leads to avoidance of its use in texts and classrooms leaving the assumptions about "natural" racial boundaries intact (Mukhophadhyay and Moses 1997). Materials that deal with these issues can be found elsewhere in this volume. Visweswaran (1998) comments that Boas, by leaving the race concept whole and placing it in the domain of science (as opposed to denying its reality) played a significant role in legitimating race as a concept.

2   "Official multiculturalism" permits limited areas of difference in aestheticized cultural practices. It is very different from multiculturalism as a critical movement that concentrates on alternative history. However, the critical movement can also be co-opted and transformed into simplifying and homogenizing cultures.

3   Boas' major intervention to separate race from culture was developed to combat biological racialist thinking. Yet culture soon became closely linked with the growing importance of psychoanalytic theories of personality. For many of Boas' students, enculturation through early childhood socialization often veered toward the fixed, natural, and essentialized definition which appears in studies of national character and Lewis' culture of poverty.

4   This kind of understanding of "culture" also ignores the way in which marginalized people actually use forms of expressive popular culture as a way of asserting resistance and collective autonomy (Lipsitz 1990; Gilroy 1993) which will be discussed further below.

5   For example, the Chinese Exclusion Act of 1882 prohibited the naturalization of Chinese, and former slaves were granted suffrage through the Fifteenth Amendment after the Civil War. In 1914, the Jones Act awarded a contradictory set of citizen's rights to Puerto Ricans, under U.S. control after the 1898 war with Spain.

6   For example, in Pennsylvania, a contested new state constitutional revision limited voting to whites in 1847.

7   Roediger borrows this concept from the work of W. E. B. DuBois.

8   While the East and Midwest industrial centers were important in this Great Migration, poor white southerners also migrated to midwestern cities during this period.

9   Native Americans are the only group today subjected by the state to using biological measurements (blood quantums) in establishing group membership. Blood quantums and degrees of "racial" belonging were applied earlier to African Americans but this gave way to the "one drop" rule which regarded anyone with one drop of Black blood as Black.

10 "Sovereignty" in the traditional sense was undermined by later court decisions which interpreted the Commerce Clause of Article I of the U.S. Constitution as giving the legislature increasingly broad powers to regulate commerce with "Indian Tribes" (Frickey 1990) and created a theory of "guardianship" with a federal right to regulate Indian affairs.

11 Armstrong (1998) has demonstrated that the powwow circuit in which Native American craftsmen and performers travel in an annual cycle of events is a contemporary site for developing a continuing panethnic movement.

12 Asian immigrants were not allowed to become citizens until 1953.

13 Many cases illustrate that ideal cultural practices which are declining in their places of origin can be reinterpreted and intensified in the United States in the face of immigrant uncertainties and perceived dangers. This can lead to increased boundary protection, control of children's social relations, arranged endogamous marriage, etc.

14 Family-owned Italian restaurants are ubiquitous in cities in the Northeast and northern California. These enterprises emerged in the "Little Italys" within these cities in the 1920s and are absent elsewhere.

15   In a short time, regional cuisines were amalgamated into a supra-regional, made-in-America pattern of everyday recipes and meals. Regional specialties, especially baked goods, were retained for calendrical events such as Christmas cookies.

16   One inter-household network of 30 households included 12 non-Italian spouse, and all households followed Italian American food and holiday practices.

17   The reverse process occurs in Port Richmond, the locus of Polish institutions. Here families of mixed heritage claim Polish identity and take on Polish American cultural practices to gain access to the nationality parish school and other local organizations.

18   Two small additional populations of postwar Polish immigrants include Displaced Persons (DPs) and those coming in the brief period of lifted restrictions in 1968.

19   Roger Sanjek (1994) also discusses similar competing future scenarios which include racial categories competing for political advantage (panethnicity); developing unity between all peoples of color against white privilege; and the emergence of a new, more complex set of mixed categories which recognizes the reality of intermarriage.

REFERENCES CITED

Armstrong, Travis
   1998   Symbolic Power and Legal Property in Federal American Indian Tribal Identity: A Law and Anthropology Approach to the Right to Represent "Indianness" at Native Panethnic Powwows. M.A. thesis, Temple University.
Barth, Frederic, ed.
   1969   *Ethnic Groups and Boundaries*. Boston: Little, Brown.
Basch, Linda, Nina Glick-Schiller, and Cristina Szanton Blanc
   1994   *Nations Unbound*. Langhorne, PA: Gordon and Breach.
Benedict, Ruth
   1934   *Patterns of Culture*. New York: Houghton Mifflin.
Biolsi, Thomas
   1995a   Bringing the Law Back In. *Current Anthropology* 36:545–571.
   1995b   The Birth of the Reservation: Making the Modern Individual among the Lakota. *American Ethnologist* 22:28–53.
Blu, Karen
   1980   *The Lumbee Problem: The Making of an American Indian People*. Cambridge, UK: Cambridge University Press.
Brodkin, Karen
   1998   *How Jews Became White Folks and What That Says about Race in America*. New Brunswick, NJ: Rutgers University Press.
Chavez, Leo
   1988   Settlers and Sojourners: The Case of Mexicans in the United States. *Human Organization* 47:95–108.
Chen, Hsiang-Shui
   1992   *Chinatown No More: Taiwan Immigrants in Contemporary New York*. Ithaca, NY: Cornell University Press.
Chock, Phyllis
   1995   Culturalism: Pluralism, Culture and Race in the Harvard Encyclopedia of American Ethnic Groups. *Identities* 1(4):301–324.
Cornell, Steven
   1988   *The Return of the Native: American Indian Political Resurgence*. New York: Oxford University Press.

DiLeonardo, Micaela
  1984   *The Varieties of Ethnic Experience*. Ithaca, NY: Cornell University Press.
Dominguez, Virginia, ed.
  1995   (Multi-)Culturalisms and the Baggage of "Race." *Identities* 1(4):297–426.
Dubin, Murray
  1996   *South Philadelphia*. Philadelphia: Temple University Press.
Erdmans, Mary
  1995   Immigrants and Ethnics: Conflict and Identity in Polish Chicago. *Sociological Quarterly* 36:175–195.
Espiritu, Yen Le
  1992   *Asian American Panethnicity: Bridging Institutions and Identity*. Philadelphia: Temple University Press.
Flores, Richard
  1997   Aesthetic Process and Cultural Citizenship: The Membering of a Social Body in San Antonio. In Flores and Benmayor, pp. 124–151.
Flores, William
  1997   Mujeres en Huelga: Cultural Citizenship and Gender Empowerment in a Cannery Strike. In Flores and Benmayor, pp. 210–254.
Flores, William V., and Rena Benmayor, eds.
  1997   *Latino Cultural Citizenship: Claiming Identity, Space and Rights*. Boston: Beacon Press.
Frickey, Phillip
  1990   Congressional Intent, Practical Responsibility and the Dynamic Nature of Federal Indian Law. *California Law Review* 78:1137.
Gilroy, Paul
  1993   *The Black Atlantic*. Cambridge, MA: Harvard University Press.
Glazer, Nathan
  1964   *Beyond the Melting Pot: The Negroes, Puerto Ricans, Jews, Italians and Irish of New York City*. Cambridge, MA: MIT Press.
Glick Schiller, Nina
  1977   Ethnic Groups Are Made not Born. In *Ethnic Encounters: Identities and Contexts*. George Hicks and Philip Leis, eds. Pp. 23–35. North Scituate, MA: Duxbury Press.
Goode, Judith
  1998   The Contingent Construction of Local Identities: Koreans and Puerto Ricans in Philadelphia. *Identities* 5:33–64.
Goode, Judith, Karen Curtis, and Janet Theophano
  1984   Meal Formats, Meal Cycles, and Menu Negotiation in the Maintenance of an Italian-American Community. In *Food and the Social Order*. Mary Douglas, ed. Pp 143–218. New York: Russell Sage Foundation.
Goode, Judith, and Jo Anne Schneider
  1994   *Reshaping Ethnic and Racial Relations in Philadelphia: Immigrants in a Divided City*. Philadelphia: Temple University Press.
Goode, Judith, Jo Anne Schneider, and Suzanne Blanc
  1992   Transcending Boundaries and Closing Ranks: How Schools Shape Social Relations. In Lamphere, pp. 173–213.
Goode, Judith, Janet Theophano, and Karen Curtis
  1984   A Framework for the Analysis of Continuity and Change in Shared Sociocultural Rules for Food Use: The Italian-American Pattern. In *Ethnic and Regional Foodways of the United States: The Performance of Group Identity*. Linda Keller and Kay Musesell, eds. Pp. 66–88. Knoxville: University of Tennessee Press.

Gordon, Milton
    1964   *Assimilation in American Life.* New York: Oxford University Press.
Gregory, Steven, and Roger Sanjek, eds.
    1994   *Race.* New Brunswick, NJ: Rutgers University Press.
Gupta, Akhil, and James Ferguson, eds.
    1997   *Anthropological Locations.* Berkeley: University of California Press.
Hagen, Jacqueline
    1994   *Deciding to Be Legal: Maya Community in Houston.* Philadelphia: Temple
    University Press.
Hannerz, Ulf
    1992   *Cultural Complexity.* New York: Columbia University Press.
Horton, John
    1995   *The Politics of Diversity: Race, Class and Identity in Monterey Park Califor-
    nia.* Philadelphia: Temple University Press.
Ignatiev, Noel
    1995   *How the Irish Became White.* New York: Routledge.
Juliani, Richard
    1978   The Settlement House and the Italian Family. In *The Italian Immigrant Woman
    in North America.* B. Caroli, R. Harney, and L. Tomasi, eds. Pp. 103–123. Toronto:
    Multicultural History Society of Ontario.
Kwong, Peter
    1998   *Forbidden Workers: Illegal Chinese Immigrants and American Labor.* New
    York: New Press.
Lamphere, Louise, ed.
    1992   *Structuring Diversity.* Chicago: University of Chicago Press.
Lipsitz, George
    1990   "How Does It Feel when You've Got No Food?" The Past as Present in Popular
    Music. In *For Fun and Profit.* Richard Butsch, ed. Pp. 195–214. Philadelphia:
    Temple University Press.
Lowe, Lisa
    1997   *Immigrant Acts.* Durham, NC: Duke University Press.
Mukhopadhyay, Carol, and Yolanda T. Moses
    1997   Reestablishing "Race" in Anthropological Discourse. *American Anthropolo-
    gist* 99:517–533.
Nagel, Joane
    1995   American Indian Ethnic Renewal: Politics and the Resurgence of Identity.
    American Sociological Review 60:947–965.
Nagel, Joane, and Matthew Snipp
    1995   Ethnic Reorganization: American Indian Social, Economic, Political and
    Cultural Strategies for Survival. *Ethnic and Racial Studies* 16:203–234.
Ong, Aihwa
    1996   Cultural Citizenship as Subject-Making. *Current Anthropology* 37:737–
    762.
Padilla, Felix
    1985   *Latino Ethnic Consciousness: The Case of Mexican-Americans and Puerto
    Ricans in Chicago.* Notre Dame, IN: Notre Dame University Press.
Paredes, J. Anthony
    1996   Multiculturalism with an Attitude. *Anthropology Newsletter,* May: 56, 54.
Paredes, J. Anthony, and Mary Pohl
    1995   Anthropology and Multiculturalism in a University Curriculum. *Critique of
    Anthropology* 15:193–202.

Pevar, Stephen
    1992   *The Rights of Indians and Tribes: The Basic ACLU Guide to Indian and Tribal Rights.* Carbondale: Southern Illinois University Press.
Portes, Alejandro, and Alex Stepick
    1993   *City on the Edge: The Transformation of Miami.* Berkeley: University of California Press.
Roediger, David
    1990   *The Wages of Whiteness: Race and the Making of the American Working Class.* London: Verso.
Sacks, Karen
    1994   How Did Jews Become White Folks? In Gregory and Sanjek, pp.78–102.
Sanjek, Roger
    1994   Intermarriage and the Future of Races in the United States. In Gregory and Sanjek, pp. 103–130.
Segal, Daniel, and Richard Handler
    1995   U.S. Multiculturalism and the Concept of Culture. *Identities* 1(4):391–408.
Shankar, Lavina Dhingra and Rajini Srikanth eds.
    1998   *A Part, and Yet Apart: South Asians in Asian America.* Philadelphia: Temple University Press.
Sider, Gerald
    1993   *Lumbee Indian Histories: Race, Ethnicity and Indian Identity in the Southern United States.* Cambridge, UK: Cambridge University Press.
Smedley, Audrey
    1993   *Race in North America.* Boulder, CO: Westview Press.
Sommers, Laurie
    1991   Inventing Latinoismo: The Creation of "Hispanic" Panethnicity in the United States. *Journal of American Folklore* 104:30–60.
Sowell, Thomas
    1996   *Migrations and Cultures: A World View.* New York: Basic Books.
Spicer, Edward
    1969   *A Short History of the Indians in the United States.* New York: Van Nostrand.
Steinberg, Stephen
    1981   *The Ethnic Myth: Race, Ethnicity and Class in America.* New York: Atheneum.
Takaki, Ronald
    1979   *Iron Cages: Race and Culture in Nineteenth Century America.* New York: Alfred A. Knopf.
Urciuoli, Bonnie
    1996   *Exposing Prejudice: Puerto Rican Experiences of Language, Race, and Class.* Boulder, CO: Westview Press.
Visweswaran, Kamala
    1998   Race and the Culture of Anthropology. *American Anthropologist* 100:70–83.
Waters, Mary
    1990   *Ethnic Options: Choosing Identities in America.* Berkeley: University of California Press.
Wax, Murray
    1993   How Culture Misdirects Multiculturalism. *Anthropology and Education Quarterly* 24(2):99–115.
Williams, Brackette
    1989   A Class Act: Anthropology and the Race to Nation across Ethnic Terrain. *Annual Review of Anthropology* 18:401–444.

Wolf, Eric
    1982   *Europe and the People without History.* Berkeley: University of California
    Press.
    1994   Perilous Ideas: Race, Culture, People. *Current Anthropology* 35(1):1–12.
Zavella, Patricia
    1994   Reflections on Diversity among Chicanas. In Gregory and Sanjek, pp.
    199–212.

APPENDIX: TEACHING STRATEGIES

Why is this important?

We have all had experiences teaching this material and know the terrain is full
of minefields. Nonetheless, we must get students to explore and understand the
structures and processes that shaped our discourses of difference and to understand that there are and always were other possibilities. This should be an
important thrust in teaching U.S. diversity.

Strategies for overcoming resistance to these new ideas focus on using local
situations and personal experience in classroom debates and discussions as well
as on essays and projects. This enables teachers to engage students by using their
own environment and experience and tailoring the message to the particular
student population at your institution.

In the classroom

(1)   Problems with imposed categories: Collect and distribute a set of the forms
requiring self-identification that students are likely to fill out, including those
used by the university for admissions, financial aid, employment, etc.,
by the government (census surveys, etc.), and the private sector (employment
applications, loan applications). Compare the forms in terms of their similarity and differences in the use of social categories. Discuss how different
qualities are emphasized for different reasons. Collect several forms from
other regions with different racial hierarchies for comparative purposes. Have
students fill out the forms and then discuss their thought processes as they did
this. Have them describe the contradictions between the forms and their own
self-identities.

(2)   Have the class read Ong (1996), Goode (1998), Urciuoli (1996), and
Sanjek (1994). Have a discussion about several future scenarios for hardening,
softening, and realigning group boundaries and the political and economic conditions that would support them.

Out-of-class assignment

Often it is difficult for students to discuss these issues in class, but it is effective
to have them write about their own experience and try to move them to where
they can analyze this experience through the new frameworks of the class. Using
peer evaluation of written work also extends the discussion. Students should be

given a choice in assignments so that they are not forced to work on an issue which they really resist.

(1) Critiquing multicultural programs. Use local and on-campus events and programs. Have students locate sites and spaces in the university or larger community such as multicultural events and multicultural training. Using participant observation, interviews, and documents, have students critically evaluate the degree to which these programs reinforce culturalist essentialism.

(2) Transnationalism. Have students interview both new immigrants and descendants of turn-of-the-century mass migration, asking questions about the ways in which the student's family visits, maintains communication, social ties, economic exchanges, and interest/participation in the politics of the homeland. Have them write an essay about similarities and differences in the salience of the homeland in each case. Are connections instrumental links or more imagined/nostalgic. Tie these differences to historical processes.

(3) Panethnicity. Have students explore the degree to which the categories Asian, African American, Latino/Hispanic, and Native American are used to organize curriculum and student life at the university. Who established these structures? To what degree do all potential students in the category participate? What markers (icons, performances, historical events) are used to symbolize collective identity?

(4) Contextual variation. Have students analyze the differences in the racial and ethnic hierarchies of different contexts in their lives such as the university, the workplace, the personal world of family and friends. Have them keep diaries which record observations and conversations in which the "cultures" of others are compared in terms of behavioral and moral superiority or inferiority. In what way are these differences described as essential and immutable? In which setting does the student feel most comfortable or uncomfortable? (Note: Have students do an early essay about this and reanalyze their experiences towards the end of the semester.)

Afterword: Understanding U.S. Diversity – Where Do We Go From Here?

Louise Lamphere

The major message of this collection is that diversity in the United States is culturally and social constructed. This insight informs not only anthropological research on diversity and multiculturalism, but our teaching as well. Anthropology is a discipline particularly well situated to make this point whether in articles and books or in the classroom, primarily because we approach diversity from so many different angles. The four fields within anthropology – biological anthropology, archaeology, linguistics and cultural anthropology – each utilize different kinds of data to argue for construction, making the case especially strong. In addition, anthropologists are able to demonstrate the importance of social construction both historically (through archaeology and documentary evidence) and in the contemporary period (through ethnographic observation and other kinds of qualitative material). Finally, we are able to examine the processes of social and cultural construction from the point of view of individual lives and from the point of view of social groups. Indeed, these essays demonstrate that there is not only a rich tradition of writing within anthropology about the United States and diversity, but over the past twenty years there has been an explosion of new studies.

One of the products of cultural construction is the creation of bounded categories – those of race, ethnic group, class, and gender, as well the categories of culture itself. Thus ethnic or racial groups are seen as bounded entities, each one having a "culture." Eric Wolf has warned us against this "pool hall" notion of culture, where cultures are seen as discrete and stable, bounded and unchanging, where "the entities spin off each other like so many hard and round billiard balls" (1982:6). Judith Goode (in Chapter 25) reminds us that this view of culture is still presented in many of our introductory textbooks and undermines our attempts to illuminate issues of diversity when we are teaching in our classrooms. It is all to easy for students to say, "*They* can't help it, it's *their* culture." This definition of culture only supports a vision of racial and ethnic groups as homogeneous, with all members exhibiting a set of stereotypical characteristics.

Karen Brodkin (Chapter 21) emphasizes another by-product of social and cultural construction: the creation of dichotomous categories of race and gender and to some extent class. Female is constructed in relationship to male, black in relationship to white. The male and white categories are often "invisible" as a universalistic standard against which the female, black, or minority "other" is imagined and defined.

The task, therefore, both in our research and in our teaching, is not only to show that construction takes place but to teach a more complex notion of culture and to "deconstruct" these dichotomous categories. We need to illuminate the shifting, ambiguous, and processual nature of relationships and the lack of homogeneity within so-called ethnic, racial, gender or class populations. Furthermore, our dichotomous categories of race, class, and gender are actually mutually constituted. They construct each other. As Brodkin points out, "There is no such thing as an ungendered white person. The nature of racial whiteness depends on the gender, class and sexual orientation of the individual" (see Chapter 21 of this volume).

The essays in this collection provide a number of suggestions as to how we can both demonstrate the constructed nature of diversity and how we can help our readers and students understand the more complex processes that underlie these constructed categories. They can help us undermine the "naturalness" of these categories that gives them so much power in our social relationships and our own discourse.

Some essays, by reviewing a part of our own disciplinary history or the emergence of a subdiscipline, give important details on the nature of construction, particularly the importance of race as a constructed category. Analyzing the continued salience of race in the contemporary period, Lee Baker (in Chapter 7) reminds us that the U.S. is not a "color-blind society" and that the debate around IQ (which argues that intelligence and race are correlated), the attack on affirmative action, and recent Supreme Court decisions that are dismantling the gains of the Civil Rights movement all indicate that race is very much alive as a social category. This has certainly been true in anthropology, as well. Alan Goodman (Chapter 3) catalogs the history of race in biological anthropology and its decline after World War II among many biological anthropologists, yet racial categories persist in forensic anthropology and in the "racing" of bones. He makes the argument that biology and culture are intertwined in important ways and that ideas about racial differences have consequences – for example, in the way skeletal finds such as Kennewick Man are interpreted and the way in which race is currently used in studies of health and disease. Cheryl Mwaria and Merrill Singer in their articles (Chapters 5 and 6) examine the history of medical anthropology and its connection to racialist thinking. More recent approaches such as medical ecology and critical medical anthropology often work to deconstruct oversimplified connections between populations and disease patterns (such as the association of Haitians with the AIDS epidemic through various "bizarre" cultural practices). Both articles give us examples of where environmental factors and culture impact health as much as biology and show how racial/ethnic categorization of populations shapes the way disease or health is treated.

Other essays make use of historical, documentary. and archaeological data to show how categories get made and unmade over time. Thomas Patterson shows us how class in the U.S.A. was constructed and reconstructed over a two-hundred year period (see Chapter 9) while Sally Merry examines the construction of ethnic relations in Hawaii over a similar time span (Chapter 8). Elizabeth Scott gives examples of archaeological sites at South Carolina Plantations where racial and class inequalities are captured in the built environment, where ceramic vessels give clues to gender patterns, and where other objects shed light on healing and religious practices (see Chapter 10). Other historical archaeology sites contain data on gender inequality or the ways in which gender intersects with class, race, and ethnicity. June Nash presents a historical case study of Pittsfield, Massachusetts, which examines the economic and political forces that shaped the migration of Irish, Italian and Polish immigrants to the city in the early twentieth century (Chapter 13). She is particularly adept at illustrating the role that General Electric played in excluding some ethnic workers and documenting the ways in which worker militancy and ethnic participation in the GE workforce changed over time, as the company hired more Italian, Poles and Lithuanians, and eventually "ethnicity" became more the stuff of "ethnic fairs" rather than every-day identity.

Finally, several essays suggest pedagogical techniques for helping students to discover the nature of construction in the classroom and during a semester course. Ruben Mendoza (in Chapter 24) outlines a "problem-based approach" for studying the past that includes analysis of museum artefacts (and the deconstruction of ideal-typical displays of cultural groups) and the investigation of non-Western science and technology (for example, the mechanics or physics of stone tool production). The museum project helps students see that a display often "idealizes" or typifies a culture without examining diversity, while the non-Western technology project helps a student rethink how the study of the material past might be represented in a less typo-logical way. Diego Vigil and Curtis Roseman suggest a course on "Ethnicity and Place" (combining anthropology and geography) which involves collecting "geoethnic family trees" connecting family genealogy with space. The course also relies heavily on visual materials including maps and film reviews (see Chapter 23).

Judith Goode suggests a number of techniques to introduce students to the problems of imposed ethnic and racial categories (Chapter 25). She asks students to fill out different forms requiring them to check boxes coding their ethnic and racial affiliation and then asks the students to critique the forms in relation to their own sense of family history and identity. They participate in and evaluate multi-cultural events on campus with an aim to understanding what extent these events reinforce cultural essentialism. The students also interview new immigrants and descendants of turn-of the-century migrants to find out how members of both populations maintain communication and social ties with their homeland. Finally,

Douglas Foley and Kirby Moss (Chapter 20) propose a pedagogical philosophy for teaching diversity in the U.S. They want students to be much more critical of their general consumption of cultural images. They suggest two videos, *Papua New Guinea: Anthropology on Trial* and *The American Experience: In the White Man's Image*. The former shows how anthropologists construct group identity and offers a critique of the discipline, while the latter tells the story of how the U.S. has tried to assimilate Native Americans through education (a process of identity construction) but these attempts have been met with resistance, rejection and in some cases cultural genocide.

Where Do We Go From Here?

In the next decade, the study of diversity in the U.S. needs to expand in new directions to explore the impact of globalization on diversity in our economy, society, and culture. Four important processes related to the globalization of capital are shaping diversity, both in terms of the structure of our population and the cultural meanings surrounding identities and differences. First, transnational corporations are increasingly establishing fragmented and dispersed production processes which in turn require workers to be more mobile. In other words, components are being manufactured in different parts of the world and assembled and marketed elsewhere, while women and men are being forced into an international wage labor force where workers must migrate away from their cultures of origin, often at great cost to their families and their personal lives.

We need a better sense of the changing workplaces where these new immigrants are being incorporated along side already established minorities. Outsourcing and subcontracting has not only affected high-tech software engineers (many from foreign countries), but also large numbers of new immigrants in the burgeoning service economy. Landscapers, motel cleaners, busboys, and domestic workers are often working for "labor ready" firms or employers who have very small labor forces, making their everyday work experience very isolating. These work stituations are much different from the large factories and shop floors common during most of the twentieth century and this has important implications for workers' rights, benefits, and pay.

We already are beginning to think of immigrants as transnational migrants (Ong 1999; Smith and Guarnizo 1998; Baker-Cristales 1999), but we need more careful studies about the way one's location in the political economy shapes these trajectories. Wealthy Hong Kong immigrants can well afford to live on two continents and bring their children up in two different worlds, but working-class Mexican, Salvadoran, and Guatemalan immigrants may also continue to participate in two nations, sending remittances, visiting for important religious occasions, and obtaining U.S. citizenship in order to facilitate regular travel to the homeland they still consider their nation.

Given these global labor flows, it seems unlikely that our constructed categories of white, black, Asian-American, Latino and Native American can continue to contain such heterogeneity, as already indicated by the 2000 census forms that allow subjects to choose more than one "race." Even the notion of "race" rather than ethnicity is being challenged as a category. We need to pay more attention to the ways in which hybridity, biracial identity, and mixed cultural heritage are being dealt with and sometimes validated – perspectives being explored in the recent work of Winddance Twine (1996, 2000) and Brenda Manuelito (2000).

Second, and closely related to this globalization of production are new forms of technology, particularly those connected with high-tech electronics – for example, computerization, communication via the internet or satellite television, and the modernized factory based on automation and robotic technology which contribute to this globalization process. While anthropologists were especially active in studying maquiladoras and factories in import-processing zones, we have been less interested in the impact of these new products on our diverse population at home. We hear about the "digital divide" in the newspapers, but we are not doing enough to document and study its impact in the school, the workplace, and the home on African-American, Latino, and Native American young people. Most upper-middle-class professionals spend hours using cell phones, the internet and fax machines, while most Navajo families do not even have telephones. There is a deep gender divide here, too, as young boys spend more time at computers than young girls, something that may hold for minority youth where boys spend hours with video games and minority girls may be as reluctant to take computer classes at school as their white counterparts.

Third, the rapid development of biotechnology has also reshaped the global market. Examples include reproductive medicine and assisted reproductive technologies (in vitro fertilization, sonograms, ultrasound, amniocentesis, and new forms of birth control), genetics (the Human Genome Project, genetic testing, and gene slicing), and medical approaches to disease (organ donation, AIDS research, and the tracking of deadly viruses). Anthropologists have already produced an important literature on assisted reproductive technologies and some studies have focused on issues of race and class (e.g., Rapp 1999; Ragone 1999, 2000). As genetic testing and the discovery of more genetic connections to disease expands, critical medical anthropologists will need to continue to study how underlying assumptions about race, gender, and sexual orientation shape medical research, treatment possibilities, and access to care.

Finally, the breakthrough in electronic technology has made possible the increased globalization of media through worldwide computer networks, satellite television circuits, and fiber optic connections. The conglomeration of media industries further contributes to the U.S.'s hegemony in the circulation of film, music, and television, including the creation of media icons. Visual and media anthropologists have been studying the impact of television on local cultures and the efforts of indigenous groups to start to control their own media resources (radio stations, local TV programing, and video). This is an area that should not be left only to cultural studies, as anthropologists can contribute much through field studies and intensive interviews that would give us a sense of how diverse populations deal with the new global media "on the ground."

Globalization will impact not only on the ways in which we continue to conduct research on diversity, but also the research tools we will use. For example, the new technologies associated with the Human Genome project and other genetic research will undoubtedly shape the techniques biological and medical anthropologists will use to examine human evolution and contemporary disease patterns. Breakthroughs in technology will provide new ways to analyze archaeological data. The World Wide Web has already made it possible for anthropologists to carry on "field work" with subjects in between field trips or when a country becomes inaccessible because of armed conflict. The internet also makes the connection with colleagues in other parts of the U.S. much easier and can encourage more collaborative relationships with our subjects, consultants, and interviewees.

Some of the papers in this volume have already begun to touch on issues of diversity and the impact of globalization in the U.S. For example, Ida Susser situates her analysis of poverty in the U.S. in the context of labor shifts in the New Global Economy (see Chapter 14). Likewise June Nash discusses the advent of flexible capitalism that paralled increased Latino immigration to the U.S., placing Latino women workers at the heart of a newly feminized work site. More of these kinds of connections need to underlie our research on diversity in the coming years.

In the next decade, anthropologists need to be much more active in translating our research into contexts where we can have an impact on public policy and in bringing our perspectives on diversity into the K-12 and community college classroom. The American Anthropological Association has begun two initiatives in this direction. First, the AAA Public Policy Committee is focusing on five policy issues in order to bring anthropological knowledge to the fore in the discussion of critical social issues. Two of these topics focus squarely on diversity. The first, "Social and Cultural Aspects of Health," concerns the kind of critical attention to the categories of race, ethnicity, gender, and class that is apparent in the articles by Cheryl Mawria and Merrill Singer in this volume. Recent anthropological research also highlights the disparities in health and the higher incidence of disease among minority populations. Finally, anthropologists have documented the ways the health care practitioners often make assumptions about ethnic group compliance based on stereotypical views. The second, "Culture and Diversity in Education," will highlight research in schools which examines how well our schools are serving immigrants and domestic ethnic minorities. Anthropological research on bilingual education and language learning will also be showcased. The committee is constructing networks of experts in each of these areas and helping them to forge strategies for bringing anthropological research on these issues into national policy debates around diversity, health, and education.

The second initiative involves developing class-room curricula at the college and K-12 levels that communicate anthropological views on race – that is, that race has been rejected as a valid "scientific" construct but that "culture creates race." This is the position argued in many of the papers in this volume. The aim of the initiative is to synthesize and assemble current thinking on this position and assess potential ways in which it can be communicated. During a development and dissemination phase, anthropologists will work with colleagues in other disciplines to formulate new courses at the college level, new curriculum models for K-12 teachers, and other visual and case material using new media technologies (CD-ROM, web sites, interactive computer-based teaching materials). Conferences and workshops with K-12 practitioners and outreach to colleges that serve minority populations will support the dissemination of these materials.

Diversity in the U.S. will continue to be a defining issue for American culture and society. It will continue to be debated on Capital Hill and in every classroom in America as the population becomes more heterogeneous. This volume has shown that anthropologists have a unique perspective to contribute to these debates and to a complex understanding of racial, ethnic, gender, and class differences. Our continued research will open up new avenues as we contend with the changes that occur in the initial decades of this new millennium.

REFERENCES CITED

Baker-Cristales, Beth
    1999   "El Hermano Lejano": The Transnational Space of Salvadoran Migration to the United States. Ph.D. dissertation, University of New Mexico, Department of Anthropology.
Manuelito, Brenda
    2000   Dissertation on Navajo Intermarriage. University of New Mexico, Department of Anthropology. In progress.
Ong, Aihwa
    1999   *Flexible Citizenship: The Cultural Logics of Transnationality*. Durham: Duke University Press.
Rapp, Rayna
    1999   *Testing Women, Testing the Fetus: The Social Impact of Amniocentesis in America*. New York: Routledge.
Ragone, Helena
    1999   "Incontestable Motivations." In *Reproducing Reproduction*. Sarah Franklin and Helena Ragone, eds. Philadelphia: University of Pennsylvania Press.
    2000   Of Likeness and Difference: How Race is Being Transfigured by Gestational Surrogacy. In *Ideologies and Technologies of Motherhood: Race, Class, Sexuality and Religion*. Helena Ragone and France Winddance Twine, eds. New York: Routledge.
Smith, Michael Peter and Lluis Eduardo Guarniz.
    1998   *Transnationalism from Below*. New Brunswick: Transaction Books.
Twine, France Winddance
    1996   Brown Skinned White Girls: Class, Culture and the Construction of White Identity in Suburban Communities. *Gender, Place, & Culture: A Journal of Feminist Geography* 3:2.

2000   Bearing Blackness in Britain: The Meaning of Racial Difference for White Birth Mothers of African Descent Children. In *Ideologies and Technologies of Motherhood: Race, Class, Sexuality and Religion*. Helena Ragone and France Winddance Twine, eds. New York: Routledge.

Wolf, Eric
1982   *Europe and the People without History*. Berkeley: University of California Press.

Index